To the Incomparable Elia

a Muse to amuse any poet, to make any poet blossom into rainbow-colored verse.

Alex

7.23.98
Mountain View, CA

Treasures

Contemporary Verse from Around the World

Sharon Derderian & Robert Lawrence, Editors

Iliad Press, an imprint of Cader Publishing, Ltd., Sterling Heights, Michigan

Acknowledgments

We wish to thank Marsha, Kathy, Andreya, and Susan for their assistance in the preparation of the manuscript, production copy and logistics; Sharon Derderian for managing the judging; Machel Warner for proofing and editing; and Susan for art selection and layout.

Copyright © 1998 by Iliad Press, an imprint of Cader Publishing, Ltd. All rights reserved. No portion of this work may be reproduced, in whole or in part, without the prior written consent of the publisher and/or the author(s) of the individual works. Individual works copyright by author

Iliad Press sponsors four literary competitions per year. Each competition presents awards to 100 winners. Iliad Press offers a $1,000 grand prize and 99 other cash and/or merchandise prizes. Non-winning entries which are believed to be of particular note and merit are awarded an Honorable Mention. No purchase or entry fee is required for the first two entries in the competition. Contest rules are subject to change without notice. All winners are selected by an independent panel of judges. Contests run continuously, four per year.

The address for Iliad Press is:

36923 Ryan Road
Sterling Heights, Michigan 48310
810-795-3635 Phone
810-795-9875 Fax

Printed and manufactured in the United States of America

ISBN: 1-885206-55-0

Library of Congress Catalog Number: 98-070854

Treasures
Table of Contents

Special Note: The editors receive calls and letters about the typography and copy in our anthologies. Many of the contributors in *Treasures* take considerable "poetic license" with spelling, punctuation, grammar and word usage. Clear errors are corrected by the editors, however, many "errors" are returned to their original state by the authors. All selections are proofread and approved by the authors.

Chapter One
The Laureates of the Iliad Literary Awards & Youth Awards
Summer 1997 Iliad Literary Award Winners & Youth Awards Winners...1

Chapter Two
Honorable Mention Awards
Judges' Honorable Mention Selections..25

Chapter Three
***Verses* Magazine Sponsored Competitions:**
Browning Competition, Haiku Competition, Longfellow Awards
Winners and selected works from the Verses sponsored competitions..................................185

Chapter Four
Dedications
Special dedications requested by participating authors..191

Chapter Five
Treasures Around the World
Entries from competitors in the Summer 1997 Iliad Literary Awards Program.....................193

Chapter Six
About the Author
Biographies of selected authors and members of The National Authors Registry..................387

Index
Alphabetical Index by Author...i

Treasures
Chapter One

The Laureates
Award winning verse & prose
from the adult and youth winners
of the Summer 1997
Iliad Literary Awards

Summer 1997 Iliad Literary Awards Program

Grand Prize Winner

Desire Left Unexplored
by Pierre St. Cooper

Let's take this voyage across that sea full of pleasures where we can find each other's deep, erotic desires.
I'll dive into your soul, searching eternally for my pearl.
You, lady, can relax while I intoxicate you with my low, sweet whispers of love, lost in our passage.
Let my dream be of you in a white summer dress, dancing with the angels,
as the sun glares its warmth through the windows onto your stage.
Let your beauty be pure and full, exquisite as the ocean waves crashing their spray across your beach.
Let me hold you, forever lost in your chastity and innocence.
I've grown to believe that our love is sacred and forbidden, but true in that it is meant to be.
Hold onto me, baby, and never let go or say good-bye if you mean for me to forever hold you as my lady.
Destiny has me locked in your beauty as I glide on your aroma.
My sweet trail is lit by your glowing smile.
Lovely lips sip the juices off my lip as I slip into an intoxicating trip;
I try to grasp reality, but your song is so intriguing to my ravenous hunger for you.
I am a lost boy running through the woods in the deepest, darkest of nights,
tripping over wild hearts that catch at my feet. I swim through the night sea,
falling to the bottom where the pearl I've been diving for is found, falling head over heels for your love.
I take you hand in pure, lost shyness, hiding behind my smile, trying to show my gentlemanly best.
Sweet conversation, like candy, got my heart racing after you, because you have taken
my mind, melted my soul, where the two entice one another with childish flirtation
in the playground where innocence is found in Cupid's pocketful of goodies,
daily dreaming of our romance conquering the past to allow the future
to accept our destiny as lovers wrapped warmly in the golden blanket of the sun's rays,
holding in the romantic warmth that keeps the blood in our bodies pumping in and out of our hearts,
maintaining our love for one another as we drift calmly across time's turbulent sea.

Second Place Winner

Behavior Modification
by *Joseph Burgeson*

I live here in the grim winter of this long season,
foraging for hope that lies hidden like last year's
grass under the snows of my confinement,
my mind warming itself by the fire of newspaper hare.
A prisoner on a distant planet, I circle this cage of
monotonous night, raging silently as I chase the tail
of my dreams, elusive sleep always one step
ahead of me, taunting, denying me respite.
A thousand tomorrows are drawn out before me in a
long, haunting wail of perpetual sameness.
The years pass and fall around my feet like unmarked
calendars, an accumulation of non-events,
and I mourn as I sift for their meaning.
Condemned for what I did, the lashes well laid on have
striped my thinking with vengeful disfigurement.
I'm a mad weed in an unnatural garden.

  First Place Winner

Mystical Fascination
by Heather Norris - age 20

Deep within a hidden woodland cove
often overlooked by all but us dreamers,
light-footed fairies and thin-winged nymphs
tease Mother Nature as they flutter
above rosebuds and play hide-and-seek
under mushroom umbrellas.
And as the wind steals their child-like laughter,
only we take the time to find those rare four-leaf clovers
sprinkled with their star dust.

Nestled under blankets of snow,
castle walls trimmed with ivy beckon only
us Romantic fools, we who ride unicorns in our sleep,
never ceasing to seek that one chivalrous knight
proud to place a flower garland in our hair,
brave enough to slay our nightmare dragons,
forever shielding us from our demons,
and piercing our hearts with love
as he fearlessly frees us from our prisons
of circumstance and doubt.

Within a kaleidoscope of celestial bliss,
an illuminating light in the clouds above
shines only on us who believe in miracles,
we who talk to our guardian angels
and bask in their radiant warmth revealed
when the sun smiles upon the world,
in a flicker or glow outside our window,
or when a timely presence turns our slumber
into a spiritual awakening.

We are the dreamers, the fools, the creators.
We feel. We believe. We know.

  Third Place Winner

Against The Dying Of The Light
by *Matt Baker*

I am a soldier, a faceless soul who marches and dies without thought.
I do my duty: I fight for a freedom that cannot be bought.
That was all I was; I lived to die for a cause, guns blazing in glory.
Yesterday I was already dead. Today is another story.
We marched, dirty and haggard, into this little town;
that's when I saw her, with a breeze pulling at her gossamer gown.
All at once, the guns ceased their maddening cry.
She made my soul seem so light, I felt I could fly.
I met her eyes, and suddenly, I became the man I was before;
and, in an instant, I knew my name once more.
I remember thinking that our love was so strange, so simple and fine:
Two pairs of eyes meeting across a marching line.
I wish I could have stayed in her arms forever,
but I felt I had to fight for us to be safe together.
My soul ripped in two when I left that night;
I raged against the dying od the light.
Now I lie here on some forgotten field.
The ground is stained red, and my fate is sealed.
I see dead men with all their courage and glory now; I wonder what they would say?
Here I am, dying; a week ago, I wouldn't have cared.
I would have lain here, and I wouldn't even have been scared.
I served my country; I'm dying for something great.
But now I feel. My heart pounds, too little, too late.
All I can see is her eyes. When I think of them, I can't help but cry.
So blue, like an endless summer sky.
She was so beautiful, her smile so bright.
I rage against the dying of the light.

Summer 1997 Iliad Literary Youth Awards Program

 First Place Winner

Mystical Fascination
by Heather Norris - age 20

Deep within a hidden woodland cove
often overlooked by all but us dreamers,
light-footed fairies and thin-winged nymphs
tease Mother Nature as they flutter
above rosebuds and play hide-and-seek
under mushroom umbrellas.
And as the wind steals their child-like laughter,
only we take the time to find those rare four-leaf clovers
sprinkled with their star dust.

Nestled under blankets of snow,
castle walls trimmed with ivy beckon only
us Romantic fools, we who ride unicorns in our sleep,
never ceasing to seek that one chivalrous knight
proud to place a flower garland in our hair,
brave enough to slay our nightmare dragons,
forever shielding us from our demons,
and piercing our hearts with love
as he fearlessly frees us from our prisons
of circumstance and doubt.

Within a kaleidoscope of celestial bliss,
an illuminating light in the clouds above
shines only on us who believe in miracles,
we who talk to our guardian angels
and bask in their radiant warmth revealed
when the sun smiles upon the world,
in a flicker or glow outside our window,
or when a timely presence turns our slumber
into a spiritual awakening.

We are the dreamers, the fools, the creators.
We feel. We believe. We know.

 Second Place Winner

A Poem
by Brenna M. Kraus - age 16

Words tripping, stumbling
into my mind
flooding onto paper in a jumble of thoughts
one mass of
feelinghearingsmellingtouching
Interpretation winds around
questions seeking meaning
What is this thing, these verses I've created?
Like growing children, the poem reaches out
exploring the possibilities
the outer limits of pen and paper
and a mind at work
And soon you, the creator, see the poem become
a tapestry, a sculpture, a snapshot
of vibrant imagination and flowering creative spirit
everything flowing, twisting, winding
like a river always changing its course
never knowing what will come next until...
you tame the beast
twist its rebellious ways, flatten the kinds
and untangle the complications
Finally, you have
organized, homogenized, pasteurized
and calmed the storm ... maybe
You glance again and find
it is what it is, what it will be
Its wildness and free-flowing emotion
are what make it a poem
unique

"In Memoriam Luna"
by Jennifer Andress - age 16

The wolfsong calls across a windy winter-frozen steppe,
   so long asleep in snowy nigh's embrace
     even the ancient stones have forgotten all memory of life--
the keening howl echoes through crystal-bright moonlight.

They come, running wild through glass-leaved forest
   wind rushing through fragrant gray-dappled fur
golden eyes flashing darkly in the shadow-ridden wood
swifter than the northern wind, a wakening vision
   of hunter's grave and loping stride.

She waited there, in the circle of tall Stone--
   like a quicksilver teardrop fallen from Luna's eye
   too ephemeral, too beautiful for this dream-woven night
   of dark pines and bitter winds and icy mist-blue snow
starlight reflected in eyes too wise, too sad for one so young.

And they ran--
     past rippling streams cascading down into gaping chasms--
   flecks of broken diamond glittering in the void--
   then caught and gathered back into the smooth-running ribbon.
And they ran--
   the constant steady rhythm of padded paws
   drumming/dancing/leaping/bounding
   over the fallen leaves of yesteryear.
And they ran--
   behind them, the mournful cry of a lonely own,
   lamenting the passing of the night.

Then the last dimming traces of moonlight fell from the sky--
   and the trailing iridescent wisps of cloud
   luminous against the starless night
began to glow with soft-welling inner light

as the first spring dawning broke over a new land.

Treasures

The Poet
by Donald P. Albertson Jr.

Mind-in-heart and heart-in-mind
Striving to seek and seeking to find
The perfect word in the perfect phrase
To express the moment and recapture lost days.

Pen to paper with an artist's stroke
Searching the soul--living to provoke
Romantic at heart though angry at times
Throwing darkness to the wind with memory's chimes

The world's blank canvas colored anew
By an inspired pen full of how-to-do
From Pound to Frost and Toomer's "Cane"
Viewing life through the artist's pane

A sharpened point and an eagle's eye
Gliding through time like a silent cry
A pulsating chill or a fiery rage
All at your fingertips, deep within the page

Tangible emotions of paper and lines
A portrait of triumphs, a vast history of crimes
Pen becomes warden of thought and time
A hand written sentence through vocal mime

We poets view humanity through different bars
Overlooking the cell and reaching to the stars
Merlin's magic with Fantasia's hope
Signed and sealed before the hangman's rope

Searching the shadow's and all that decays
To express the moment and recapture lost days

The Secret Conversations of Atania
by Aishah Andang - age 16

Through the voice of an older woman, she met him.
With the seat of a passion from a faceless child, she loves him.
In whispers she speaks to him through the forbidden Southern City Door.
Young words laced with white lies cling to her graceful caramel throat.
As a girlish giggle plays across her pink jellybean lips, a rainbow paintbrush strokes his golden face.
A silly joke has just kissed her once melancholy heart.
The scentless breath of humor struts away in a monotonous tango to the crooning voice of a broken record
that has danced to this melody many times before, quietly stomping out each trace of dignity upon her soul
with each step.
Like red wine, she gulps every warm drop of his laugh.
It intoxicates her, suffuses her body with wild emotion-truly, deeply, madly.
Mad as a tempest that rages silently.
Its soothing song caresses the iridescent teardrops that cascade down her cheeks.
In the morning, all that is left is the sea-salt tang that burns slowly down the cleft of her chin.
Her wish is an empty cup, yet not drained of a small addiction.
The cycle starts anew and ears that cry desire attach to his every syllable.
To a story she will tell him to a problem she will utter, desperate truth remains in her eyes- yet not seen.
But stained ivory mendacities in her voice- he will hear.
Yet all the while, her passion for him remains a rice paper sail in a currentless ocean of dehydrated illusion.
Her reason to love-the single truth that floats slowly- and steadily- behind them.

Aunt Hazel's Peonies
by Vera Ogden Bakker

My Aunt Hazel raised
peonies in her
front yard. Every spring
I'd find her leaning
on a hoe, gray head
bent, tending her plants.

Memorial Days
she clipped frill white,
pink and red pom-poms,
kept them fresh in huge
galvanized wash tubs
half full of water
on her wide front porch.

Signs near the road brought
old friends and strangers
alike to her door
to buy flowers for
decorating graves
on the hill. For those
without money she
set aside the best
blooms. The peony
patch is covered with
asphalt now a parking
lot for Albertson's.

Aunt Hazel sleeps on
the hill. Will someone
bring her a vase of
fresh cut peonies?

Old Stories Dark Memories
by Adisa Olubayo Bankole

Ashanti man tastes sweet, hot, leaded death,
Soft melanin touch against hard, cold iron
               AS
Blood-Stained tears mix with Atlantic's blue
              WHILE
Chained ebony bodies line ship holes,
Excrement perfumes the hot, still air.
               AS
Chestnut, covert cargo is herded on auction blocks,
Nubian daughters are covered by Euro-gunboat diplomacy.
              WHILE
Blond child suckles mahogany breasts,
Flowered cotton is caressed by calloused brown hands.

Yes! Dark necks kissed the hemp rope's noose
               AS
Black leather united with red corpuscles,
Staining bronze backs, And yes!
Alabaster feet pressed on small Twi bellies.

Old Afrikan man died young...
And young Ebony woman lives lonely with memories.

At Last
by Amanda Barry - age 14

The smell of nail polish fills the air.
You don't think I notice the way
you flip your hair ever second;
when the classroom bell rings,
you pack your hairbrush-o-matic,
refillable pen and head to the restroom.

You primp and try to look beautiful,
but I know it's all a facade.
The hair spray must have drained
your Tupperware container of knowledge.
So long, my true amigo.
I will never forget you: my idol, my god.
If only I could do everything you could,
I would be popular.
You would be in my beaten-up, old
K-Mart $5.99 outfits, wondering if anyone
had noticed your clothes in the Sunday paper's flyer.

You would feel what I feel:
A Caesar's salad of emotions
whipping through my ripped-up T-shirt
like a Kool-Aid blizzard.

I am frightened; I survive.
You are satisfied; you survive.
Which is better? I had no choice.
If you think I picked this life,
you are wrong.

I walk away, my sinuses clearing
the nail polish from my nose.
I feel free - at last.

Shipwreck
by Aimee Bauer - age 15

Thrashing, crashing,
 the waves tore
 the silence of the
 black darkness that
 hovered above me.
The wetness pelted down
 on my red wreck floating
 on the mighty blue.
I felt the shocks of the
 stinging drops, shooting
   from the boiling
   boulders above.
I felt the wrath of the
   flashing fury.
As I cowered helplessly,
  the roaring breath
   of the relentless
   rampage shoved
   my craft to its doom.

War
by Marcella Berry - age 19

With the rising of the sun
 one can hear their shouts of glory.
With the brilliance of a new day
 thousands will hear the story.
Cannons raged and fear aspired
 as the armies slaughtered.
Cannons of unearthly force
 with their impact, shattered.
Then, with savage and wild hunger
 did the men draw closer.
Then the mad and brutal blood thirst
 needed no more muster.
Men dropped heaping to the ground,
 their bodies bruised and broken;
Men whose brave deeds and fierce passions
 would doubtless go unspoken.
With the rising of the sun
 one can hear them as they die...
With the brilliance of a new day,
 thousands wonder why.

Embrace
by Bethel Borgeson

My lady rests before me;
I sit on the shore and watch.
She tumbles and plays,
 flirting with my feet,
then suddenly withdraws
 to her secrets beneath.

I hear a whistling in the waves:
a Siren's call to dance, to enter.

She whispers a song of return
to a protected embrace.
"Let me show you my colors:
sunset designs on my surface
and rainbowed treasures below."

Plunging into her, she takes me.
She carries me through
 her misty, magical caves.
Together we explore each other,
 searching for the touch,
the flow, the fire, the union.
 Some breath.

We explode upward as one,
breaking the air.
Her hair sprays out...
Then returns to green-gold ripples.
Resting with her, drifting,
 she nudges me slowly toward the shore.

We sleep together on the sand
while her fragile fingers stroke my dreams,
and her heartbeat waves pound beneath me.

Passion Redefined
by Ellen Irving

Passion lies buried
Beneath the mountains
of laundry
Beneath the pile
of dishes
Beneath the layer
of dust
Beneath the constant struggle
for survival.

Only not so buried
Just redefined and subdued
Love's passion turns to Life's passion
I sleep with books
and papers and pens
And the rhythmic sound
of my children breathing.

Untitled
by Michelle Buller - age 15

Here come the rays into my heart
Warmth embeds my soul
A candle burning bright is the
light that keeps me whole
The branches keep my body safe
the flowers whisper in my ear
The grass tickles my feet and
the ocean calms by fear.
My rocks are the silent listeners
the birds my harmony
The moon is like my mind
in sync with the power of the sea.

Boating On The River Epte
by Vanessa A. Cisz

He has suspended the slender,
teak-colored canoe on the clear green water.
Two girls perch in the seats in long-sleeved white
dresses threaded with pink.
These travellers seem not to notice the
green bushes of the bank or smell the blue flowers.
The rower slides her eyes down the
long narrow oar ending in a tapered paddle.
The young woman holds the oar, frozen in thought.
Perhaps the sisters dare not move, pondering
their forbidden access to the attic
or their father's telegrams at midnight.
Perhaps they are merely relaxing, floating,
their purpose here.

And in all stillness, the grass,
flourishing at the bottom of the transparent river,
undulates, blissfully unaware of the
dilemmas of the breathing world.

For Sandra, Who is with another
by Eric Lee Coker

At one time I saw you, really saw you...
I looked upon your face with the scrutiny of a thousand Galileos,
And studied your every move,
And perfected the already perfect in my mind

I noticed how your hair,
Beyond beautiful even when out of place,
Captured the sun
And how your eyes were the first I actually looked into,
And upon doing so, I became a man.

With your music, you wore a tapestry,
A tapestry more valuable in beauty, more authentic in style,
Than a children of Bayeaux,
Who were blinded by their task

In you, I saw innocence and hope,
A bridge from the hateful isolation of my adolescence
(Complete with its mouldy, walled-in clamour)
To an afterlife of happiness,
And a white-hot openness, lived with life and color.

Once, I regarded you as did michelangelo the sistine;
His work, his passion, encapsulating his dreams.
Now, I see you as a faded water color,
An ancient Oriental print
In the fondest reaches of my memory
(That feeling - rich places, the lair of the dream-scriber,
That corner of my soul that is devoted to you).

Old Dragon, Useless Body
by Preston Lee Cordes

I am nothing but an Old Dragon
In a human frame.

A powerful soul trapped
In a confining shell.

I feel the fires burn deep in me
Yearning to come out,
But the fires are not there.

I hunger for the hunt,
The thrill of the chase,
And the taste of the kill.
But not for this body.

I desire to sleep
Upon a pile of gold, silver and jewels.
But all I ever find is a simple bed or bare ground.

I wish to fly again
To feel the wind against my enormous wings.
But I have no wings to fly.

I pray to the Moon,
Lady of the Night Sky,
To grant me my true form.
But I get no reply.

What use is there for an Old Dragon
In a useless body?

Silver Sadness
by Abby Conner - age 17

Bathed in the silent stillness
and clothed by a cloak of darkness,
The Night, in all of her sorrow,
casts one dim hope, yet one bright glory,
over her blind Earth.
Her shadows are her companions,
the sweet solitude her joy,
and the orchestra of strings sing
her into the brightness of sleep,
where she shall remain until her twilight
comes to awaken her.

A Dream
by Holli Crego - age 19

The scenery is perfect.
My skin tingles from moisture still lingering in the morning air.
A glistening dew dampens the boundless floor of undisturbed sand.
My eyes twinkle from the shine.
The water before me lies calm as each wave carefully caresses the sand,
    then swiftly departs.
I breathe the clean, crisp air and shiver.
Chilling sensations race through my body.
I continue forward with no hesitation or doubt.
The sky begins to break and a colorful band of orange and pink brightens
the horizon.
As I look behind me, I see a trail of a single set of prints.
The once perfect setting has now been disturbed.
I feel no regret or sorrow.
I have committed no crime, and have caused no destruction.
By disrupting the flawless picture, I have only fulfilled a dream.

Silence
by Devon Crosby-Helms - age 15

Not a word shall dance across my lips.
Not a sigh of tension will hum in my lungs.
Not a word, there is nothing to say.
You see what you don't understand is
I am deep in thought,
Thinking of such thoughts that could not be
fathomed by you.
Don't worry I am not dumb and silent.
I am working at my best.
A war is being waged inside my head.
I am hurdling 100-foot hurdles and landing on two feet.
Problems are being made into problems,
with solutions that I found.
In this silence, I am being the child prodigy
I've always wanted to be.
My creative rocket is ready to be launched.
My problems are ready to be faced.
My best conversations are ready to be had.
Everything is perfect and ready to go.
All I need from you is an ear-splitting silence.

For Matty...
by Lindsay Crow

ocean's tide beats ceaselessly against the rock wall
the moons' reflection broken over the endless expanse of midnight water
in the distance glows the comforting light of the watcher's beacon
the sandy shore lays hidden beneath the churning waters of high tide
a seagull's cry pierces the darkness
the gentle breeze carries the intoxicating smell of salt air and desire
    and the memories of a hundred moons,
      a thousand colors
      a million new beginnings...

Treasures

The Prairie
by Wendy Cryer

The tall grasses sway in the breeze
like gypsies dancing festively.
A lone oak spreads its broad arms
as if protecting the world from harm.

Small yellow flowers blanket the hills,
and far in the distance a mocking bird shrills.
The mid-day sun rides high in the sky
as cottony clouds drift silently by.

Slowly the clouds turn from white to soft pink,
and the fiery sun begins to melt and then sink.
From the heavens, a black curtain descends,
and another day on the prairie comes to an end.

Topaz Idyll
by Martin J. Dahlgren

Late
on a crisp Fall night
with only the memory of summer
now gone,
except for the twinkling
of September stars...

****

The topaz-colored floor
of the old city fountain
in the dark downtown
of the old capital city,
walls of cement and steel.
How desolate :

And yet , the girders
of the nearby construction
are like a spider web
of metal in space
in this topaz idyll
of remembrance
of an old city street
with water flowing
over the memory
of dead talks
on the side of the road
a dark street
near an ice cream stand,
last talk of love,
and hope,
and tomorrow...

Mama
by Lee A. Daugherty

The sheets are cool and damp
as she hangs them on the line,
canvases for the sun
to paint upon.
I dash between the clotheslines,
running my fingers along the
avenue of white, pressing my face
into the sheets.
Breathe in, breathe out
the scent of summer
dipped in well water,
nuzzling into near godliness,
courting suffocation until
the call of her voice
chases me out from under foot.

I give her fairy bouquets,
white, blue, and yellow flowers
saved from the mower,
and the sky hums around us.
She is all mine.

I sit on a clover throne
and magnanimously watch ants
build palace mounds
to the accompanying music
of the flapping sheets.
Then the squeal of brakes,
the pounding of footsteps
up the graveled drive
as the bus interrupts our idyll.
Now she is ours.

The Rose
by Emily Davis - age 16

A rosebud,
Young and fresh
Moist with morning dew
A lone petal stretches out
    and beckons others to watch
    the unfolding beauty.
A perfect rose emerges,
Soft as velvet-
    a deep, seductive crimson.
It dances in the gentle breeze,
    flaunting its beauty
    to the more ordinary flowers.

But soon,
    the rose begins to fade.
It becomes withered and brown;
The soft crimson velvet is gone.
The rose dies.
It is crushed
    and blown away
    by the same wind that once caressed it.
The pieces are scattered and lost.
And all that remains
    is the memory
    of perished beauty.

The Glory of Fall
by Lester J. de los Santos

Who can capture the glory of fall
In a picture of triumph that lifts the soul?
An artist's brush, a poet's pen?
The man who wills is the man who can!

Fall is vict'ry; it's not defeat!
When trees undress, 'tis promise sweet;
After the whip of wintery rigor,
Life springs in verdant summer!

More than gold, than treasure rare
Are days of sun and maple flare;
The leafy rain of red and yellow,
Orange and green on blushing meadow.

Fall is life in festal praise;
Life is fall in fireworks sprays.
Fall is love in rainbow mood-
A gift of life from loving God.

We'll surely behold the glory of fall;
After earth's seasons, the "well done" call
From Him who made Winter and Spring,
Summer and Fall and everything!

Chains
by Carrie DeVelbiss

Chained to you by
false promises believed,
I will never again
be free.
The cold, heavy steel
of the love
you once had for me
is wrapped so tightly
around my thin wrists
that I can no longer feel.
Rust is the color of my skin
wherever the chains
of your false hopes and lies
touch me.
I am a prisoner within you
and within my love for you.
Forever, you and I
will be encircled together
by the unbreakable bonds
of hell.
You have only yourself to blame.
You created your chains
be believing in
your own lies.

Life
by Franklyn Dickinson

Life is a canvas
Upon which we display our visions.
If you try, good things will happen.
A mere idea can burst into flame.
Don't waste time solving problems
That don't exist.
Live the life you have,
Not the life you wish you had.
If problems overwhelm you,
Look in the mirror.
You may be the problem.
Be conscious of your insignificance,
Eventually we all cross the finish line.

Untitled
by Ed Doyle

And the call comes.
    A distant, calm summons to the light.
And my heart responds.
    But the I in me is not prepared for the pass.
The sun still rises.
And the wind blows. I remember to catch each fleeting moment
    and hold it close.
Always on my mind, this passing by. Whether wind in my dreams
    Or the sun traveling form hills to sea.

Every day appears the last.
And the tide rolls. Sound and surf and sky are part of what I
    will become.
the time a precious treasure. Whether a moment with friends or
    an eternity with myself.

And the call comes.
    A distant, calm summons to the light.
And my heart responds.
    But the I in me is not prepared for the pass.
Love grows in strange gardens.
The harvest can be slow. I will not see my toiling in the rich earth
    bear fruit.
But there are few regrets. And the sails of my soul catch the wind
    and I am blown home.
And the call comes. And my heart responds.
And I will never be prepared.

The Battle in Purgatory
by Lauren Eades - age 15

Chained in a world of distress, a patch of sunlight
from above warms her frigid flesh.
A shadowy figure lurks in the darkness,
waiting in solitude for another dead sinner to arrive.
Her eyes show her fear; she yearns for sanity.
A burning desire for love and peace of mind
glows brightly in her compassionate heart.
She has suffered many hardships.
Two voices call out:
One is a good-will offering of peace, love, and freedom.
The other is evil, offering revenge against those she despised.
Claws of evil grip her soul and twist it;
severe paint makes her body cringe.
A gentle, yet firm hand pries the claws from her soul;
she writes helplessly between Heaven and Hell.
Calm, quiet serenity wraps around her
like the thick fog that engulfs a big city:
She has been rescued from a fate of
never-ending sorrow and hate.
She is free among loving, understanding beings.
Destiny awaits her in the land of dreams.
The battle between Heaven and Hell is over for now...
Once again, Heaven prevails.

Civilization
by Betty Erickson

Human conduct and belief have been undergoing transformations more disturbing than any since the appearance of wealth and philosophy put an end to traditional religion. Our moral life has been, and still is, threatened —— and our intellectual life is being enlarged more quickly —— by the disintegration of ancient customs and beliefs.

The passage from agriculture to industry has elevated science, liberated thought, ended monarchy and aristocracy, generated democracy and socialism, disrupted marriage, broken the old moral code, destroyed asceticism with luxuries, exalted excitement above content, taken from us many of our most cherished religious beliefs, and given us a mechanical and fatalistic philosophy of life. All things flow, and we all seek stability in the confusion.

In every civilization, a time comes when old instincts and habits prove inadequate for altered stimuli, and old institutions and moralities crack like hampering shells under the obstinate growth of life. The happy unity of instinct is gone from us, and we are uncertain of our purposes, values, and goals.

From this confusion, the one escape worthy of a mature mind is to rise up and contemplate the whole. What we have lost, above all, is total perspective. Life seems too intricate and mobile for us to understand its unity and significance. Today, no one dares to survey life in its entirety. Analysis leaps, but synthesis lags. We fear experts in every field and keep ourselves lashed to our narrow specialties. Everyone knows their part, but is ignorant of its meaning in the play. Life itself grows meaningless and becomes empty without perspective.

It may be that we should clarify ourselves, pull ourselves together into consistency, and be ashamed to harbor contradictory desires or beliefs. Knowledge is power, but only wisdom is liberty.

Through the hole in the painted....
by John Felago

Through the hole in the painted "O"
on the tea steamed window-wall of the CROISSANT SHOP.
I peek   onto the street.
The aged wrinkled sidewalk fails to hold the sunlight
as it scrambles   to untangle
from the advancing tentacles of night,
supporting the theory espoused by the wall clock
that it is 4 PM.
Outside, a parade of scampering feet.
Like panicked park pigeons
they scurry to escape
to the peace of more private prisons.
Holding my cup,
I scout for a familiar stride
afraid to raise   my gaze   above knee-level.
My eyes are searchlights whose
swiveling solid stares seek
your short stride
your skip step
your strut.
A matter of time -   of timing.
The maddening march flows endlessly - unquenchably waiting out an endless supply of feet,
I regard, then discard
them all
soon followed by another set
and another
and another night progresses
lengthening the shadows it spills
across the pavement, as my tea cools.
I can wait no more today
perhaps tomorrow or the day after.
A matter of time -   of timing.

A Hopeless Wail
by Bonnie E. Fleming

Inside I cry a hopeless wail
Of love unfelt and tenderness dispelled
I hear them speak the pretty words
That say they realize the problems in the world
Yet they are sightless in the realm of their own reality
And I wonder,
   keening in my heart,
If they see the relentless perpetuation
   of the problems they perceive
In their own life,
   in their own souls,
     in their own ways...
I scream a mute unending warning
Knowing it will go unheeded.
What they can never change,
nor can the ways they react.
All my wails
   and screams...
     and warnings...
Can never tell them that
Though they are sightless
My eyes are now open
And I do see

Protest
by Patrick Michael Frazer

Walk drastically, but carry a bridged accent; the typewriters are afoot.

Conglomeration leads the classic riots; the submarines fly through the cough drops.

Fish drop to the ground and confetti spreads the news, while in the second energy level, dodge balls spin about the Christmas tree.

Tunnel your way to the moon; go abruptly, as the gearshifts return to neutral.

Ask a motorcycle for advice, and you'll get integrated every time.

Keep your hands out of your reach. To save time is to drop hot blackboard chalk into acid.

Thermometers float to the bottom to measure sodium hydroxide in L.B.J.'s Wrangler pants.

As the golden hair falls to the ceiling, the spinning electric clocks dazzle in the frozen Sahara.

Juke boxes whisper in the closet while the electric gas burns in the post-nasal drip.

Stop between your intervals; the projector marches on.

Be attentive of road signs; they never grow up. Hamburgers drown the keys.

The square roots are on the move; pay attention to the push-ups and drown your rabbit hutch in gasoline.

The lawnmowers are scratching the icy, clean, clear waters of the Kanawha River with a television so high the clouds ride the airplanes.

And the velocitized Grape-Nuts float gently into the television antenna.

Spring Cleaning
by Jessica Gates

Gray clouds floated lazily over rippling fields,
Like premonitory smoke on that evening last May...

It was twilight;
The sky a mesmerizing canvas of soft pastel fluidity
That diverted us all from the task at hand.
A half-season's grain harvest gone bad
(Rats in the silo, it was thought)
To keep the contagion from spreading we had to burn it all.

Me and Pa watched half a year's work turn ash
And drift into the air, spiraling like desert vultures.

The clean grain-smoke suddenly turned acrid.
Suffocation on the smell of smoldering flesh,
I looked towards the cabin
(I wake up nights still choking)
And saw a mountain of angry flames. Ma!
Where the canvas sky ended and
Searing flames began was impossible to tell.

I ran inside, blinded by explosive waves of blaze and heat.
Flames licked hungrily up my bard arm--

And so I ran back outside, afraid of what I had seen.
Ma! My hoarse screams went unanswered.
I fell against the coarse woodshed
And watched, paralyzed, as both house and homemaker
Scorched senselessly to the ground.

music box
by a. gavlinski

you wonder why she hums...
   her voice is soft and quiet
     under her breath, always a song
there is a story behind the notes
   kept hidden like a half-written
     composition of notes on a broken piano
that once sang like a symphony
   to a music box family
open the lid, peek inside
   the music still plays softly
who closed the lid of the music box
   that sang a pretty tune,
     leaving a silence only tears could break
tears that swelled inside the notes,
   giving them crescendo
     that was not heard again for
years absent from the notes of remembering
   a song that danced and dreamed
     and never left the music box
     except in the sweet voice that i know
     humming, humming,
     under her sad breath

War
by Joseph J. Giacalone

The war wages in my mind
Warriors wounded, maimed, and blind
The battle continues deep into the night
Sometimes nuclear, often firearms or a sword fight.

Here, there is no god, no savior
Only jumbled images devoid of human behavior
Darkness drapes the curtain of pain
Even the crow fails to navigate a lane

To the light--hanging from an endless rope
(the stars have already given up all hope
of peace, reconciliation, or reason)
This is true war: a war that transcends all seasons.

Untitled
by Lindsey Nicole Gosma - age 15

Dreams
Such sweet melodies
To play inside the head
Whispering softly
Of things the soul desires
Opening the locked heart
Closing rooms of doubt

Dreams
A gentle breeze
On a summer's night
To wrap around the body
Cooling the flesh
Yet warming the mind
And caressing the soul

Moonlight Sacrifice
by Lyn Greek - age 17

The cold wind blows, buffeting over the headstones
The smell of earth is sweet from the fresh grave
Death is heavy in the air around me
I tip my head and gaze at the midnight sky, devoid of stars
Only the blind white eye of the moon provides light

Closing my eyes, I raise my arms and step forward
Gently twirl on one foot, feeling the open air surrounding me
Then I run, flying free, soaring high
The black silk of my cloak whips about me and my hair floats
    behind me
Surrounded by a black cloud, I am oblivious to the outside world

I now begin to dance, wildly cavorting
Gracefully maneuvering between the grave markers
Finding the one I seek, I stop
Freshly dug, the headstone gleaming as if with an eternal light
Silently I approach it, filled with reverence and exultation

Murmuring an ancient and forbidden rite, I drop to my knees
    on the damp ground
Outstretch my hands to slide them over the smooth marble surface
I embrace the cold stone, crying softly
Pleading with the dark spirits to grant my desire
And soon they answer me, demanding my sacrifice

Rising slowly, I produce the knife from underneath my cloak
And set the tip against my chest, giving up all
When I fall, I hear the demons laughing gleefully
As I die, I see them take form
And as my life flows into the ground, they dance as I danced

A Denial Burlesque
by Joyce Trusler Guilkey

Denial is an artform   a gallery of the mind
An imagined haven of escape   a sanctuary so kind
Denial is a paintbrush   for the canvases of life
Spreading oils of tranquility   shrouding pain and strife
Reality is left to those   with the artful skill to pine
To envision ugly consequences denial has no time
Should flowery, sunny landscapes   begin to darken with dread
Faithful whitewash of denial   is ready to be spread
Denial is life palette, brilliant colors of the mind
Creating murals of illusions   on walls to hide behind
Bad habits and excesses   are blotted out with glee
To picture their acceptance   would assume reality
The most skillful of these artists   paint realities of their own
With smooth and practiced strokes   of denials pastel tones
Denial is a talent of   ingenious strokes quite free
Reality is only as real   as denial lets it be
Most therapists view it hopeless, a dementia at its best
They try to smear each canvas   with dark colors of unrest
But their craft is not artistic, painting storms and scenery cold
Just a canvas without color, gray realism they unfold
Reality is for people   who desecrate denial
Painting and sculpting normality, escapism they defile
Denial is for gifted artists   to crate mosaics surreal
For a life in a world of fantasy, reality is to unreal

Backdrop Of My Memory
by Dylan Guy

Now that you're gone, will you ever know

  how you charged this niche of life

  with wonder and light for me? To

think that you would talk of your vast

  forever desert and the sound that

stillness makes, never knowing that your face

  was being etched on the endless

  backdrop of my memory.

The Crafted Poem
by Robie Glenn Hall

    A great poem, if it is to be worth its weight in feathers, is rarely plucked from a magical dimension. In face, the poem is reaped from dimensions of time, space, existentialism, and prophecy. It is a vehicle. It will take me many places. But mostly the poem moves in two directions: it skips happily towards the bright sunlight, or lurches solemnly towards the twilight. A specter between the light and the darkness, the poem is as much a physical reality as a heartbeat. That embryo pulses word on word, idea on idea, feeling upon feeling, indeed, world upon world until it is no longer merely the sum total of its genes and chromosomes, but a fully ambulatory entity with a power its nail like a hungry impact hammer. With its mouth wide open the hammer takes the lunge, driving its reality home with the intensity of an atomic bomb.

Tales of Humankind
by Henry L. Hamilton

Some blot the paged book of life
With ink of tears to log,
From preface wherein hope so rife
Is slowly bludgeoned by a knife
Ground of the stone of selfish strife
Unto its epilogue.

Some write compassion on the face
Of life in letters scrolled
In strokes of faith that interlace
The fibers of a resting place
Upon the pallet of His grace
In thread of purest gold.

Some copy guidelines from the book
Writ by the stolid lout,
Convention, but to wishful look
Upon adventure others took
And marvel at the straightened hook
That courage spitted out.

Some scribe outside the strictured mold
Of chaste conformity
And fill the chapters that enfold
The epic legions of the bold
Who write and live the legends told
In storied history.

Summerscape
by Elizabeth Hampel

      Because it's always summer in my private stereopticon of memory, the hometown of childhood recollection is eternally sunlit, with lawns verdantly grassy, gardens lushly flowered; the narrow Main Street hot and dusty. Sleepy torpor saturates the air. Even the rattling, clanging, shrilly whistling noon train never stops.
      Across from Morgan's Ice House, old codgers adorn the facade of Lovelace's General Store. Draped over the front porch like so much sere Spanish Moss, the graybeards gum fat, unlit White Owl stogies or masticate massive chaws of Bull Durham. Amber spittle slides down to stain white-stubbled chins as toothless mouths spin golden tales from the dull straw of near-forgot reality.
      Just off the main drag, back of paint chipped, gingerbreaded Victorians, white-eyelet aproned mothers indolently pin wet wash to sagging clotheslines, minds lost in the might-have-been. Nearby, their Buster Browned offspring swing indolently on rickety garden gates, their fancies off in what-may-be.
      Down by the Bijou Theatre, the scent of freshly buttered popcorn signals line-up time for Saturday matinee. Hand printed posters proudly proclaim that each and every showing of silent flicks from Tinseltown will be piano accompanied by Miss May Belle Morgan, musically accomplished spinster sister of that well-known local coal, kerosene and icehouse magnate, Mr. Joshua Morgan.
      Nubile girls, practicing vamping, take advantage of the lull before ticket time to flutter eyelashes, swing hips, sashay past appreciative, strawhatted young blades who softly whistle appropriate approval.
      Surely every small town Mrs. Grundy will find ample cause to shake her head and cluck her tongue, not only at such scandalous goings on, but at such outrageous lassitude.
      After all, it being endless summer, that green, green grass keeps growing, growing, growing. Yet not one single, solitary citizen seems disposed to leave off dreaming long enough to mow it down.

A Vase of Gladiolus
by Joan E. Hunt

Already a week old, the orange gladiolus nod sagely,
sadly, the older ones wilting just as the last buds
flowers, so that half the stalk is dead
and the other half is fresh, or almost so.

They nod in the breeze, with the breeze.
cut off from their roots,
separated rom cleansing rain
and brightening sun,
they clump in a clear vase, green stems a-swirl,
having only the familiar wind to cling to.

It is so little, so unpredictable,
a gust of wind jumping in the window,
turning them a little,
telling stories of bees and pollen,
of pools of water and digging squirrels.

Taken from the life their parents
and grandparents lived,
they've been thrust, without consultation,
into hard, sterile glass.
Green leaves quiver, not quite certain
how to cry, or if it would be appropriate.
At least they have the wind --
when the windows are open
and the wind is from the west.

Each day there are fewer blossoms to nod
at the stories the wind tells.

La Réunion
by Lloyd F. Hussey

Underfoot, gravel and broken shells talk to me
In a warm, familiar monotone.
And along that honeysuckle corridor,
Transparent flying insects flit to and fro,
tracing unseen designs in the thick morning light.
From behind a wall of sandy dunes
Light breezes carry the invisible drug
Of salt and hemlock and flowering desert plants
And a low, timeless rumble.
It is her.

As I crest the shifting mountain of quartz
A perfect blue geometry shows me all,
But conceals more.

Overhead, gulls converse, the industrious piping plover
And the lazy cormorant, they all know.
Tiny crab, she has thrown you upon the berm,
Scurry back to the womb, burrow the foamy sand.
Return to mother, for sisters and brothers
Lie broken along the strand.

A gentle, warm breath whispers
To my windward gaze.
She secretly implores me to know her.

I enter the sea.
Soon, I am off my feet,
And I am free.

Brooding
by Kevin Hurtack

Darkness creeps
across the sky
serenely as stale kisses
along her thigh.

Lightning stalks
through bloated clouds
whom shed not drop.

Winds whisper
to my soul
of an archaic love
I will never behold.

Strangers slither
amongst ineffable shadows
as oppressive as my memories.

Untitled
by Steve Johnson

I've captured the wind
  held her in my hands
caressed her
   like she for so many years caressed me
     careless and somewhat spontaneous
with the sun i've spoken
   ultraviolet conversations and
nine second lapses in between
   his words that make me warm
   his ideas turn my skin brown
  but still i have yet to discover
    what our exchanges empyreal for him accomplish
the earth has become my one and only lover
  at night i sink into moist soil
      absorbing nocturnal rhythms of things
        that want to grow
      and other things
       that want to die
when i hunger i slice the ocean into pieces
   dine on that which makes me whole
    often it rages oblivious to reason
    and often it's serene, embracing its tides
the moon arrives each dusk to teach me
   lessons about revolution
    chapters unending that cover the
     unsuspected natures of reality
and each dawn i come away
   wondering what more
     i might learn

Softer, My Memory
by Grant Koo

The mind reels where greeneest grass swims
As the image of two figures, entangled and inscribed
In the swimming greens (but not the grass),
Secedes from the unrelenting logic of the soft parade.

The minds, whre grass swims greenest, reels when an image,
No longer a memory but a cloak of fire,
Chokes in cancerous smoke what it habitually cannot hide.

I was a lover smoking in the greens of that severed garden,
Not this hollow hull adrift amidst the desperate blades,
Tossed around senselessly on the cysts and vicissitudes of time.

All night I have been searching for you,
Lying awake and reeling with motion sickness.
Uneasy visions of Arcadia swim by and quiver
In the cold, hard ringing of tonight's tinnitus.

My Tree-Friend
by Yumi Kim - age 18

Stumbling to an awkward halt
On a horizon framed by wood,
My twilight stroll came to an end
Where my tree-friend staunchly stood.
Face uplifted from the steadfast ground,
Yearning for the stars in the sky,
Out wide he held his uprooted arms
Though low below roots lie.
But hold I could not his coarsened hand;
Too high he sought for me to reach.
But surprisingly mellow was his bark
Though bitterly seasoned by age.
With mock I toasted him gaily:
What good the stars would do.
He wouldn't retort but to the wind,
confiding in taunting whispers.
But they're all like that, his kind.
And so, once more I swallowed
As my deaf ear drowned in the rustles
Of a faceless crowd that morn.

The Old Italian Woman
by Philomene C. Lacara

The old Italian woman
Stands waiting at the gate.
Her laughing eyes belie
A life punctuated with
Disappointment, even pain.

From her father's field
To her marriage field,
She has gained dignity
From the dirt. She finds
Nobleness by serving
The land.

Her hands, like tools,
Dark and rough, reveal
The strain of crops and
Tears gone by. From that
Age-old alliance with the
Sun, she learns the rhythm
Of the seeds and beads.

Her life is measured
By the cycle of the seasons:
Planting and picking;
Preserving and preparing.
With all she knows of
Passion, she sanctifies
The moon.

The old Italian woman
Stands waiting at the gate,
Waiting, *per il postino.*

The Mountain
by Meghan Lawrence - age 15

A towering pinnacle of gray
A specter of black illuminated by cay
A massive sentinel of fear
Jutting upward with rock walls sheer

The boy stares up in awe
At nature's power revealed so raw
And shudders at the icy cliffs
As limbs freeze up, reluctantly stiff

His desire to reach the top
To someday surmount the cold rock crop
Seen sadly futile in the bleak gray dawn
Yet his hope to prevail still lives on

The boy begins to climb
A merciless battle between nature and mankind
At first his precarious holds slip
But boldness strengthens his unsteady grip

His body he readily committed
And his soul with resolve he willingly submitted
Now stands the test of the highest strain
Drawing on both until no strength remains

But as the boy's will wanes
Towards the summit he gradually gains
'Til at the top, his vitality spent
He ends with triumph his grand ascent

A towering pinnacle of fright
A specter of black darkened by night
And at the top a man
Surveying with triumph his conquered land

Another Coldness
by Talene Lee - age 16

I sit somewhat parted from the chilled scents of lingering California rain,
ensconced in jumbled cotton layers stretched against my skin.
The essence of the moments is life-- bold colors of vehicle smog,
the unsteady drone of an airplane overhead...
My mind allows itself a retreat from the urbaness of it all
-- where smells would be more rustic, sounds, less mechanical--
out into nature.
Closed eyes transform the brick trim fountain into a bubbling brook
surrounded by a rich brown dirt in place of the stained cement.
From the dirt crawls a handful of earthworms which can be hard in
their rising accompanied by unmechanical birds in the sky.
Pine bough perfumes attack my senses from all sides,
swallowing the oh so distinctive smell of processed fertilizer.
Cool breezes ruffle my hair as they do birds feathers,
and carry my breathe to a point of fusion
with all other scents and temperatures.
The human within me is not alien to this world which disobeys mind
and yanks my spirit from the familiar body it knows.
"Come, sweet light. Join us in rich resources, tantalizing visuals,
unparalleled scents of life. The coolness calls to you," it croons.
Yes, I rationalize, it is the cold which sharpens such imaginings
and it is within the cold that these sweet sensations of nature dwell.
But... isn't it also the cold, the earthworm-filled dirt
which encloses my deceased loved ones--
the birds singing even at their funerals?
The rustic scent being that
which emanates from the coffin which beds them
-- bubbling brooks only the melody of fleshly decomposition?
"Come, sweet light. Join us in rich resources, tantalizing visuals,
unparalleled scents of life. The coolness calls to you," it croons.
I have no choice-- my will is weak--
and before I can murmur and good-byes,
my body stiffens in its frozen death upon a park bench.

The Candle
by Brent Lennox - age 15

Fire, so mystical in the midnight meditation
as sly as a snake
yet as graceful as its black laced smoke.
It slowly envelops the helpless wick,
twisting and wrapping down to the bottom
where the blazing heat slowly erodes the feeble wax.

It transforms into a beautiful woman
dancing an ancient rhythm
as distinctly familiar tot he soul.
She flashes and dashes
engulfing the helpless wick
under the spell of the dark queen of fire.

The wick slowly decays
as she is set ablaze
to keep on going through
the victim of her love.
As the wick gets shorter
her dancing heightens to a climax
because she has worn out
too many lives
and now it's her turn to experience
the death of the hunted.

Alamere Fall
by Nachshon Lustig

The brook's end falls so fine,

A forceful cascade hits the ocean.

Sweet H_2O eternally mixes with brine

A sublime metaphor for the notion

The soul's return to it's Source, in motion.

Summer Nocturne
by Sandra P. Mann

The disk-to-dawn light of the moon
casts a paleness upon the grass
looking snow-white against the
night's huge blackness that rushes
through the veins of tree branches
overhanging the deck, which holds the monstrous
silhouettes of comfortably padded lawn furniture;
the night, too narrow through the blinds
of our bedroom window, is adorned with a strange simplicity;
it is everyone's landscape now --
alive with busy insect sounds and the
deafening noises of other creatures
fading and then coming forth with the inevitability
of the air conditioner's incessant hum that
protects us from too much nature now --
and announces the ungraceful entrance of
yet another summer day's unbearable heat.

Untitled
by Aaron Mason

Early instance of frigid dawn
Chilled breath woven into magical smoke wreaths,
Each new plume creeping, seeking
New paths in windless space.
Ancient overcoats, like living caves,
Gently protect the Ancient inhabitants;
Youth far gone, yet remembered,
Sometimes not conscious of time's flowing:
Frozen children of another era.
History is written in the faces of old people;
Chapters are hidden in carefully earned wrinkles.
Each gleam of an eye speaks of untold riches.
Then, as if stone were alive,
One of the Ancients speaks.
Living music rolls from lips that lie,
Much too often and much too long,
    Motionless.
But these are troves of Spanish gold,
Galleons of the life-blood of humankind.
Not joyless, but maybe forlorn.
And each day the wealth is shared,
And each day I steal a little for myself.
I beg for tales of the older ways and days
And then return to my hovel and rest.
And I am filled.
I sleep well and feel alive,
An archaeologist of the abstract,
My treasure found.

Snow
by Jessica McCulla - age 16

                                    rises.
                        curtain
               starry
The

The first notes of the prelude,
              tiptoe in with the wind winding to the beat of Nature's
muted drum.
                  Music crescendos and picks up speed, as the flakes
begin
              falling
                  whirling
                twirling
                      curling
                swirling
                Hurtling, plunging, pitching
                    like slivers of glass,
                keeping rhythm with some voiceless melody.
    Flakes
            dart
       twist
         dance
                and pirouette like crystal figurines
                      growing more intense,
          silently reaching a fortissimo.

The sky answers with a mass of white wind walled confusion.
       The profusion subsides leaving the memory of
          music
              gliding
                  down
                      to
          Earth.

Too Good Intentions of Savage Sheep
by Robert McGee - age 20

Trapped in an anglo wasteland, I am the disease,
Armed with tools forged by a lack of patience,
Destroying what has been built.
I am tired of this world
That fights and rapes and kills the mind and body.
It is a miracle that the sheepish masses have not done
More harm with all their God-damned good intentions.
Good intentions - huh!
Are prejudice and bigotry born of good intentions?
Well, maybe they are.
Maybe we need to sedate or hate the things
We do no understand - just to be human.
"Spike that Indian up on the cross; let's make him Christian.
We'll wash in his savage blood and do a cherubic cleansing dance."
So they dance; blood-soaked sable figures in a so-called new world
Carrying the cross of the white man's "burden."
I do no pledge allegiance to the symbol of a country
Bought with the blood of innocence,
Or to the republic that turns a blind eye to humanistic injustices-
One nation under a blood-haired, blue-eyed nab-god;
Liberty to those with power,
And justice to those who can afford it.
Put that wasp in the garden;
He thinks he belongs there.
"Watch out," my mother seems to say.
"They string with barbs that are the inventions of serpents."
Cast out your bitter wings.
Destroy the lies in everything.

One More Lake
by Jerry McGinley

There's always one more lake to fish,
one more chilly rowboat morning
when coffee steam melds with lake mist
and rises skyward fragile as angels.

There's always on more mill pond waiting,
one more bait to drop beside a sunken log,
one more weed-draped lien firmly fixed
in the jaw of a thrashing large mouth bass.

There's always one more abysmal drop-off
where walleyes lie waiting, long, sleek,
and savage as mythic water dragons,
pursuing too that eternal connection.

There's always one more languid fire,
the smell of fillets in spattering oil,
the drone of old stories kindled again
for ghosts of a hundred centuries past.

There's always one more cloudless night
to count stars and measure our seasons
before boarding the ancient ferryboat
to cross that cold black river home.

There's always one more fishing season,
somewhere in some corner of the cosmos,
beyond our sight but not out of reach.
There's always one more lake to fish.

In Memory of R.E.)

The Canyon Within
by Chanda Merrill - age 20

Streams of natures juice flow
like a trail of crimson down
a freshly slit wrist.
Rushing water spatters
against solid mounds of rock,
erasing the chalky outline
of a life less body.
Staring down into the canyon,
I toss a withered rose
for those who have come
before me.
Diving onto the bloodstream,
my soul stained with sin
Scar souvenirs from
past lives
mark my being,
taint my mind --
within my own
lifeless body.

Untitled
by Randy Mitchell

Trade beads on the beach washed down by wind and rain from the midden
all that is left of life and death in an Indian village,
the killing ground of fur companies with god on their side.

    Trade memories of Russia: cobalt blue the color of
jay feathers and a white mans's eyes - cold and appraising
Shining facets on a handblown stick.
Eighteen sticks for Kwakuitl freedom.

Moving with ocean rhythms, their tide-wet mouths whispering
of prices paid for otter skins and land.

Winter, summer, day and night they shine
with a greedy glow, bright in a Montreal boutique.

    Baltic amber spheres - perched on grains of sand,
their history etched in time.
Mute testimony to ancient pine forests and transformation.
Keepers of secrets - like Haida shaman.

Brought back to life in a rock tumbler, the patina of age
retreats and laments a time of adornment, a time of change.

Playthings of foreign entities. Lover of surface --
ignorant of substance and Indian ways.

    Delicate swirls of Chinese lace - rare in red and white,
green and pink. Colors spiraled in mystery.
Secretive in their heritage.
Hiding in the land of Tlingit war canoes.

Shifting to the whim of nature, ebb and flow,
now the sound of an outboard motor rakes the stillness.

There in the gray sand - alive with color and empty of dreams--
they wait to fill the holes of man-made boredom.

Raven sits on a log and laughs
at humans pawing in the gravel
for glass worlds on a string.

Creek Walking
by Lisa Moore - age 15

I step precariously into a pool of water too deep to fathom,
my feet feeling the harsh current flow through the crevices between my toes.
I stumble into uncertainty as I try to balance my weight.
Rainbow-spotted trout swim gracefully beneath me unaware of my towering presence.
Fallen logs, aged by time, splinter.
It is silent and still, but for the occasional splash of water against my thighs.
I stumble onto dry land, pulling myself up onto the dry rocks.
Perched on the rocky hillside,
I am aware of the boundless beauty of nature.
I bask in the sun's everlasting warmth,
and it is then that I realize that life is a creek,
teeming with obstacles.
I am waling toward an unknown destination,
always walking...

Wordless
by Diane Myers

Words slip away as feelings and emotions take over;
Bringing with them a soothing and blissful state of awareness and belonging;
Transformations from pain, uncertainty and loneliness, to
Love, Passion, Fulfillment---------Life!

Listen to the Joy!
Can you hear it?
Can you feel it?
Can you taste it?

Hear the wordless rapture of the clouds,
Gliding through life's energy;
Weightless,
Thoughtless,
Doubtless;
Light with worry,
Heavy with hope.

Feel passion's fire,
Heating love's soul with the warmth of desire,
Embracing love's painful embers
'Til the charred yet still alive desire remains tattooed to your heart.

Taste the bittersweet flavor of live,
Leaving nothing out.
Taste the pain.
Taste the sorrow.
Taste the joy.
Taste the fulfillment.
Gulp it - digest it - taste it - live it.

The Holocaust
by Evelyn Nuernberg

We sit here staring at
the cell walls of our own insanity
Outside, in the near distance
ear-piercing screams fill the night air
Not screams of joy and happiness
No: The screams are of fear and terror

I can feel him coming
We all see him in the nightmares
that wake us in the depth of night
We see his reflection when we look
into the darkened pools of each other's eyes
Soon the angel of death will come for me

I reach up in the morning when
the harsh commands for roll call are given
I touch my shorn hair
I rub my hands across the rags
that the "devils" call clothes
I tell myself to be strong, when all I am is weak

We will survive this
We must

She-Who-Made-Seven-Worlds Speaks
by Michael O'Rourke

In the mountains of your pain
there's a tiger hungry for your heart.

In the silence of drought dead water clocks,
for one redeeming kiss.
You refuse.
The roses fade, and black and white, fall to dust.

In a smoldering waste you forge from flesh an iron fist,
enslave the children of the headwaters.
(In the kingdom of the dead there's a king asleep,
clutching his ceremonial crown of tiger's teeth.)

In the epic cave of your innermost ear,
a thousand bluecoats prepare the massacre before dawn.
The Ancient Ones retreated long ago from the village in the cliff.
You now command a field of the dumbstruck.

With certainty the ticking rock
will guide your step into a measureless canyon.
You will pick agave flowers sown a century ago for this moment
and you,
alone,
under a precipice, will be smitten with its holy fragrance.
The tiger will fall on you,
the veil will be lifted from your eyes,
and your sorrow will shake the earth.

The tiger slips through the gloom under the purple orchid,
his yellow eyes stalk time out of mind,
his eye never sleeps.
He waits, flicking his tail,
hungry for your heart,
in the mountains of your pain.

Hal - leluia!
by Carol Ann Parker

There in the front row he sat patiently, his chin resting on his cane,
reminding me of a translucent capiz-shell angel I saw hanging
from a cord in a shop window once, waiting for a passing
breeze to give it life, shimmering on the border between
this world and some other.

The procession came from him: gospel and torch bearers.
The strains of a hymn filled the room as they circled it, symbolically
bringing the Good News to the world. He walked slowly
behind, his cane marking the pulse of the music,
his steps cautious and deliberate.

As they turned and held the book in from of him, I wept a little, knowing
that it would be the last time. The sensible will say that it was only
sweat, but I'm sure that he was glowing as he began to read.
The strength of his voice denied the
fragility of his cancer-ridden body.

As the words of the Gospel lesson washed around me,
I knew they must be true. This man would not waste
his time with lies and legends. He has quit the game-playing,
shed all that is not true and essential.
You can see that in his eyes.

I wanted him to go on reading forever. But I suspect that
he has less need of the words than I do. He's waiting now for
translucence to become transparent, for release and
resurrection; like the capiz angel, waiting to be cut
loose from its cord to fly free.

For Hal Gillespie, Deacon of the Church

Faces in the River
by Christopher Patterson - age 19

Time is a River
Gently flowing down
to a distant sea
Step out of the River for
Just a moment
And watch as the
Faces of all humanity
Float along the murky surface
See them hit rapids and change
Growing old before
Your very eyes
they change along the path
Becoming someone
You don't recognize
Some spend their entire voyage
Floating together
Like a school of fish in the sea
Others bounce from one shore
To the other
Colliding with their fellows
Along the way
And a few
A rare, special few
Travel in solitude
Borne by a current
That they alone feel

From The Shoreline
by James H. Paxton

You are an ocean without horizon,
the end of each river that I follow.
Though I yearn for the strength of your tide,
I do not want to be trapped in your vastness,
prey to every impulse of your will,
like a senseless buoy - afloat
in the deep darkness of your embrace.

You are soft, though unable to be held,
sensual even when the brutality
of your rhythmic kiss dulls my senses
and rules my movements, here --
so far removed from the home you gave me;
not long ago, I left you behind
for the security that land affords --
but I know I will rejoin you someday,
when the attraction of finite land
pales against your horizon, limitless and compelling.

Born in land, reborn on you,
astride your inconsiderate pulses, I am made new.
With all that is clean and verdant I see your presence,
under all that is blue I feel your warmth.
I cannot sleep without the rocking of the waves;
you are a part of me: all that is cleansed and pure
I owe to you.
You are the bringer of life, and the shaper of destinies --
I am powerless against you.

But in my helplessness there is safety;
in my safety I feel you.
And in you I feel the ocean,
trembling at my touch, waiting for my return.

Whims of love
by Janice Peters

When winter winds did turn to springs eternal rains
I made a choice that caused such pains
A holy vow I chose to sunder
So that I might take a lover
Under Gemini's most mercurial sun
I chose the man who would bring all undone
A showy peacock so unlike my cherubic mate
It took not long for my fancy to fade into self-hate
Destructive wiles held at bay so long
Nearly broke my mind in furious storm
In awakened horror I saw the folly in what I'd done
Yet stubbornly I clung to this web of deceit I'd spun
With the sun rising under Virgo's discriminating taste
I broke from my showy lover with all due haste
Quickly I made to make my cherub's heart now played another song
I watched form shadows of my own making as my angel took another
Sorrow filled my heart to breaking for leaving my honest lover
And the sharp stings of love gone awry were mine instead of his
Bitter tears assuage foolish pride that kept me from his kiss.

The Battlefield
by Mark A. Pieper

I dreamed I saw, on a sunny day,
A stormy sea of blue and gray.
The clash of steel and cannon shot
Were all mixed in the fray.
Their guns all making thunder
Left no room for doubt or wonder:
Many men were surely dying
And would soon be buried under.
The color-bearer never drags
Intensely patriotic flags,
For all the units center
On these bullet-ridden rags.
Flames of Hell they surely stoke
To cover hillsides with the smoke.
And primal screams were made
By men who charged and men who broke.
I stood there looking at the ground
And watched the victims all around.
their agonizing chorus
Made a symphony of sound.
"Please help us, God," they cried as one
And turned their gaze up to the sun.
"Forgive us as we perish
For the things that we have done."
Then all at once, as if by dare,
A stilling peace was everywhere.
And all the soldiers vanished
In the smoke that filled the air.

Gabriel
by Carmelita Pobre - age 18

Gabriel take me in your arms and let me fly.
Gentle Being, keep me away from his discerning eye.
Keep me cloaked within you wings
And forgive me if I cling too tight.
Please Gabriel, take me far away tonight.
My Master is so wickedly handsome and has me in his trance.
When his intoxicating voice sings and calls out my name--
I am there.
His indentured servant, my forbidden pleasure, my
    ever longing pain.
I cannot deny him any service when locked in his embrace.
Gabriel, pray, let him leave me be.
Let his hungry eyes turn away from me.
He's one like God but filled with demonic tricks.
He wills my heart be blind,
Running with black blood that tastes and smells so sweet.
Is it the devils' food which I drink and which I eat?
Dear Saint, he's determined to make me all his won.
His imprisoned slave, his desire, his delight
One of hell and his queen of night.
Oh Gabriel, please save me from this fate.
Take me within your refuge before it is too late!
Keep me from his fiery eyes that pierce my heart,
Burn my soul, and set my flesh aflame......
I can't afford to know my Master's kind of love again.

Autumn Sonnet To A Sugar Maple
by Jim Ploss

A sugar maple, caped in scarlet flames
That yesterday were leaves of many greens,
Provides a park where squirrels play Catch Me! games.
Their busy chatter shattering to smithereens
The brittle autumn blueness of the afternoon,
That bright blue lightness past the mid of day,
'Til wooed to nest by rise of harvest moon,
By scent of burning leaves, of sun-dried hay.
When morning comes the tree is starkly bare,
As if with one tremendous shrug
The maple doffed its cape with careless air,
To spread it on the ground, a welcome rug.
And thus forewarned, the snowflakes fall all night
To drape the maple in a cape of virgin white.

The Symposium[1]
by Suzanne Power

We were separated in a fit of rage
a flood of tears
    But
Never "good-bye"
We were split
not while climbing mountains
    But
while floundering in
    Mediocrity
Rather than wandering
    Aimlessly
in a quest for the elusive other half
we seek to regain that which we have
    Lost
Pride
  combats
    Fate and gravity
Rather than floating
  Weightless
towards on another
Pride
  anchors us
to our separate spheres
Our bodies remain
    Apart
Our souls remain
    Alone
    Unfulfilled
    Tormented

Street Sleeper
by Dennis E. Rager

A steamy, summer storefront
sidewalk on Seventh Avenue South
somehow seems incongruous with
your peaceful repose in the midst
of rushing early morning commuters
en route to jobs and appointments,
stepping gingerly around you, so as
not to interrupt your profound slumber.
With only a pair of urban grime-encrusted
sneakers, removed from your feet, tucked
under your head for a surrogate pillow; can
a cement mattress induce undisturbed rest?

The empty Evion water bottle laying
at your side suggests to me that
alcohol is not your demon.

What cruel trick has doomed
you to this unbanausic bedroom?

Several days growth of facial hair
over tanned, leathery complexion belies
your incredulous youth.

I find myself at a loss to put into
exact words the utter sadness your
situation deposits in my heart.

What unforeseen twist of fate
has brought you to this sad state?

Time
by Jennifer A. Russo - age 17

What is time?
Time is the everlasting gap between us.

It is the empty space which imprisons us from moving on.

Time has a strange effect on us
Never moving faster or slower than the deep abyss
which truly lies between now and then.

Of course, we will meet in time.
But, if time chooses, I may not see you at all.

Yet our love is strong,
and it can even withstand the harsh trials of time.

Time is our boundary, the wall that closes us in.
The world is nothing without time, it is only a dream,
an ethereal plane.

And we are merely spirits forever trapped...
in time.

Unpretentiously Sincere
by Phoebe Michelle Pneumonia - age 14

The demo version of the soul has become the whole reality
What we hold to be true will not stay the same
Destiny will grab hold of our past and bring it into contact with its mind
Yet, with the considerate heart there is a hurting mind
and we will spy on the unfamiliar because it won't know
In time, becoming ourselves will be the worst sin known to our kind,
and the end will already have come
But we won't know this speaking way, because it has a hold on the emptiness
Part Two of this series will never come; but this is how it will start, this is how it will end
It won't hurt as much as we believe; it will sting and torture the mind
but it can't grab hold of the heart, for the heart is all its own
Find the virtue in yourself;
hold onto it with a love deeper than the love of your own
Greatness has a passion for untruth,
but you can't believe what is burdensome
and even the fearless won't stand up for the facts
The truth will manifest itself in our minds, but we won't hear it
because we won't have the strength to obey
Take into consideration the passing of existence
and time will expire and bury itself in the end
We will know afterwards what has taken place
but as it happens, we won't have a conscious mind
Being aware won't restore the past; this shouldn't be our fate,
but it is and always will be
Become acquainted with the story; be able to retell it to the sinners
They won't even commit themselves to certainty
Fill your cup while the future holds back, and mail the envelopes of assistance
Water the desert of infertile land as families sit and wait
And while you walk across the crumbling bridge of doubt
recall you have had and all you will be
Then sit and wait for continuance to cease and abandon your life

Goodbye, Summer
by Barbara Schick

I'll miss the toasting sunshine,
the peeling sunburn, and
nights that are blankets
of left-over heat.

I'll lose the fragrance of
many-colored flowers,
fresh-mown grass,
and backyard barbecues.

I'll forget the sounds of
busy buzzing bees,
squeaking screen doors,
and splashing in the pool.

I'll lack the taste of
cooling ice cream,
iced tea and soda pop,
and watermelon out of the field.

I'll mislay the sights of
floating butterflies,
plastic flyswatters,
and flourishing foliage of shade trees.

Goodbye, summer;
nostalgia burns my heart.
I couldn't keep you with me -
autumn crept right in.

Tomorrow
by David Schneider - age 16

Will you help me walk,
When my legs have grown too weak?
Please say that you and I will talk,
Though it's the same tired words we'll speak.

Tomorrow we age more
So tell me years are meaning less,
That you'll love me as before
And never will regress.

Oh, please help me to walk,
When my legs have grown too weak.
Say that you and I will talk,
Though, it's the same tired words we'll speak.

Then I ask you to promise me
That although so much is done,
The best times are yet to be
And our lives have just begun.

Night's Lullaby
by Mia Lauren - age 17

Underneath a tent of stars,
The crickets sleepily croon.
Clouds are light and drift along,
Scheming to kiss the moon.
The wind is soft, embracing;
It beckons to the trees,
"Come play with me, oh pleasing ones;
We'll dance atop the breeze."
The trees consent and wave their boughs,
Like graceful ballerinas.
Leaves sway in perfect rhythm to
The crickets' concertinas.
The nightbird sings a ballad;
Far away another listens.
Frogs drum in time on lily pads
Upon a pond that glistens.
Fireflies inflame the night,
Like moonbeams, dancing fairies.
The nightowl adds a haunting note
With its curious inquiries.
Finally, as dawn draws near,
And sun rays light the sky,
Enchanting choirs wait once more
To sing night's lullaby.

Icarus' Legacy
by Michelle M. Scott

We built our wings in the shadow of the sepulcher
When the mirrors refused to reflect our true faces.
Blind, trusting feet tread
                    dank, dew-serrated grass
As we molded the moist night into wax
Imbued with binding hymns.

The fires fasted all night.
   Lacing icy fingers,
they blew the leaves alight
to the sky.

Rising on winds that belied our senses
   containing a hundred conflicting things,
Velvet voices containing divine madness
   caressed with odors of figments unseen
Snared swift souls with unreasoning fears
   of burgeoning lands made fertile with tears
Glimpsed through a thin somnambulant screen.

Seeing through a blind man's eyes
by Curtis W. Stephens

Darkness-
The stealer of light
The lord of everlasting night.
He welcomes with a child's delight,
The chosen warriors of his faithful son.
The weak he absorbs,
And the two become one.
The strong do not kneel or fold,
They take what they are given
And bend it to mold.
They smell the perfume and hear the laugh,
.... It's a gift ....
To enjoy the whole instead of the half.
To them, a little means a lot.
They know before they touch if it's cold or hot.
It makes no difference how someone looks,
Or how fine the cover are of any book.
I could look like you and you like me.
A blind man sees what he wants to see.

Good-Byes
by Patrick Stessman

The heavens are a fire,
In a sunset for the dead;
Mercy enshrouded in a clouded ridge of desire,
Like the scorned sheets of a lover's bed,

And nothing is torn,
When you first look at the sky,
But promises get broken,
Words remain unspoken,
And dreams fade unborn,
Into the shadows of good-byes,

At night, I watch a moon that suffers alone,
Resting in a starless darkness,
Above a halo of city lights,
As it's caressed by fingers of stone,

And nothing is scorned,
When you first look up and pray,
But, innocence ends in the first tear,
Courage dies with the first fear,
And dreams fade unborn,
Into the shadows of good-byes,
That never fade away.

Before the Fall
by Butch Stratton

Shards and shafts of silver
Violate the sky
Robins rush and old oaks blush
Mandrakes swoon and die.

Swallows seek the southern sun
The birches seem to know
And fog has huddled in the hollows
Whispering of snow.

Rush
by Jessica Taylor - age 17

The whirl of life in my head
is sometimes enough to take
my breath away.
But to balance the madness,
there comes a moment,
a precious moment,
when all cares are vanquished
and I see the world as if I'm
a tourist of some sort,
a kind of innocent bystander, just
admiring the scenes-
God's scenes, so exquisitely
crafted.
And for that brief moment
there are no worries,
no deadlines,
no stress...
just the glory of life.
And I smile.

Young bloods
by Katrina Taylor

So young, smart, beautiful...but no one ever told you, did they?
Coming up in a jungle of self-hatred, the dense foliage choking out any
trace of light,
Where were you to learn of love? Where were the teachers of harmony?
I love you so, but don't know how to reach you.
What means compassion to a calloused heart?
A babe never held in nurturing arms, cursed from your very conception...
nourishing light withheld by father...waters of life held back by mother...
You can't give what you don't know.
Starving the souls of a generation, brilliance unnourished turns to dust
with a bullet.
Truth dwells within: the blood running through your veins pulsates
with a mournful beat from times long ago...
Khamit, Sumer, Nubia, Phoenicia.
Can't kill it; can't kill...it...can't die. But words mean nothing.
Preceding generations must sort through their own nebulous anguish to
reach you.
Ancestors call to me, to us, to remember them,
the disjointed cries of souls torn apart by cruel greed.
Hate an oppression have not passed, nor we healed.
Ignorance and pain have turned on us with fierceness unprecedented,
baring teeth that threaten to tear us to shreds.
Necks underfoot for so long, lies repeated so often,
now we believe and act out...'cause nothin's gonna change, anyway.
How can you do right
when wrong has been your mentor for so long?
Fight to see beyond centuries-old falsehoods...
surrender...be vulnerable...trust...allow yourself to dream.
The ancestors will speak if you allow,
and you will see
who you are.

Untitled
by Anna Trinh

The bemused anxiety she sees
    and feels is cast away upon
      the open ocean
As a lone tree in the distance
    sways with laughter
At the pinnacle of her mind is
    revealed the last of her
    senses
Truth confounded by the lie
    beckons a remembrance
The immovable peak of existence
    is sen under a coloured
    night
A fade to black unveils the
    darkness of her life
Freedom stand tall among her
    most trusted friends
While resolution staves outside
    the confines of her mind
Alone among many and without
    final judgment
Questioning the reasons of
    doubtless understanding
A final conclusion is lost in the
    infinite age of the past
She opens her eyes and returns
    from a clarity of thought.

Derival
by Robert Underhill

    A rumbler   --of wings
    A tumble   --of things,
A rumble and a tumble that rings and flings,
A grumble of a cabin in the jumble of a crashin'
    And fire   -of wings
    And madness   -of things
The crumbling, rumbling jumbo of a bird
  smoldering, O-rings cracking into thirds
Systematic, hydromatic lightning bold of grease,
  smoking, stoking the blackened flames with ease;
Engines to overpower all those meaningless words
  Screamed by the themes of anonymous herds.
    And flightless of wings
    And weightless of things...
    Broken tail ripped in two
    followed by a bolt of blue
      lightning crashing
      Watchers dashing
      Embers flashing
      Pictures smashing
      Blackened sun
        crashing tons
        of twisting iron

Sparks and sirens, explosive roaring
  Angels soaring, demons gloating
    spirits floating Deadly fright,
  terrored sight... all instilled by flaming might

    --And lifeless of wings, In lightest of things.

Clay Man
by Mary E. Waite

    In a place in time in my heart and my mind
are the memories of someone courageous and kind
I remember the chair where he sat with me
and listened for hours patiently
snug in the arms of that old leather chair
we journeyed together with nary a care

    This friend of mine I recall
was a gentle giant ten feet tall
As he pondered his crossword for treasure and clues
I enlightened his ind with my worldly views
Every so often, not and again, he'd respond
with a chuckle or comforting grim

    I studied the lines that encumbered his face
which by now had become a familiar work space
one eye up, on eye down, half a smile, half a frown
what a face, what a day, what a man my clay friend
I would mold to perfection from beginning to end

    Intently defining and tooling my clay
such serious work for a child at play
God's creations could never compare
to the work of art that took place in the chair

    As I bask in the memory of clay in my hand
all these years later I now understand
I thought I was molding a friend to be, in fact
'twas the clay man who was molding me

Salvation
by Jennie Washington - age 18

The air is thickly soaked with blood
and scents of prior putrid pain
I'm beckoned to the tainted table
gorging on my guilt and blame
taunted by her bitter stirs
that I will swiftly, boldly fade
stained with shaded visions
of our former love decayed
a selfish deceit to warmth that
I naively wished were dead
They cravenly birthed our carnage
I weakly purged and bled
tortured by her unheard screams
and whispers of unchosen names
The air is thickly soaked with blood
I'm hollowed out by grief and shame

Deathly Consequences
by Tara Love Waychoff

White powder landscapes the atmosphere.
                               Naked limbs glisten with star dust.

Outstretched arms shake in the cold,
                 harsh breeze of another winter day.

Overflowed gutters crack
      from the heavy weight of the frozen water.

Green blades of grass poke
      their heads up through the white blanket.

Grass pricks my hands and face like needles
        as I roll in the coolness of the icy blanket.

Sidewalks half covered,
           footprint uncovered the rest.

Last of the snow angels gaze up at me,
               wanting to leave yet wanting to stay.
       I, like them, an undecided.

Moon Tirade
by Bob Wearden

Blurmoon, behind a cloudy veil...
Sir moon, you never seem to fail

To find a way to stir my heart--
To make it rise and swell.
You always seem to know your part,
And play it very well.

Smudgemoon, a thumbprint on the night--
Thinking you'll go scot-free.
Tragedy is, your probably right--
You're so far out of reach.

Moondot, so shadowy, so proud.
So smug with your moongrin.
If I could snatch away your cloud,
Where would you be then?

Peepmoon, shameless voyeur...
Watching me every night.
C'mon, be a warrior.
C'mon down here and fight.

Avast, ya scurvy moon on high!
I've had about enough.
I'll turn ya into mincemoon pie...
Be thinkin' you're so tough.

Snubmoon, aloof, with billowed sail
Just laughs down from the skies.
My moon tirade of no avail...
But it comes as no surprise.

Reality
by Shannon Wilde - age 17

i smile,
trying to remember
a time when i didn't hurt.
i dream,
trying to escape
the hell that is my life.
i laugh,
trying to forget
the mistakes that i've made.
i trust,
trying to uncover
the best friend i've never had.
i listen,
trying to hear
the one thing that will make sense.
i imagine,
trying to pretend
that my life has a meaning.
i love,
trying to hide
the loneliness in my heart.

In the Country side
by Meaghen Wills - age 14

When I'm in the countryside
I sit on the swings and glide
Into a barren field of dreams
I wonder what my life will be
And find myself drifting off
Sleeping on a floating loft.
My heart explodes with things to say
Hoping I'll know the right way
Sunny days and silver moons
Orchards filled with flowery blooms
Snowcapped mountains white
Comfort hearts of sleepless nights

An Act of Winter
by Jerome Workman

        a pale December night,
           quiescent,
     soft, albumin-white veils
       surround and enjoin
a still, calm sea of moonlight.

          tall pines
           stationary
      silhouette the horizon
        like jazz music --
      in irregular shadows
they fuse with ivory powder
         in the half-light.

    the comforting peace enfolds
          this still, sweet
         music of winter.

A Day Out of Autumn
by Christine A. Wright - age 15

Crystallized spider webs appear with the dew,
As an Autumn sun lights the misty horizon.
The crisp morning air of the sky azure blue
Whisks your breath to the heights of Orion.
Day follows dawn with spatters of color.
Crimson gold leaves skirr in the Notus.
Trees sway their arms to the crooning of Zephyr,
And so we find the Autumn upon us.
The easterly spectrum spreads over the sky.
Sunlight tints fade from heavenly brushes,
As the glory of sunset begins to die,
And twilight dreams blend with starlight wishes,
The night winds whisper their lullaby chants.
These Autumn eves, umbra comes soon,
Yet the prismed leaves still swirl in dance
Beneath the glow of a harvest moon.

Island of Enchantment
by Pang Xiong - age 17

They say there is an island where
the Pacific meets the Atlantic.
'Tis surrounded by mists and flush with foliage.
This is the Island of Enchantment.

With skyscraping trees and pure ponds
it is lacking of nothing,
this place where brightly plumed birds caw from
far-reaching perches and dolphins swim agilely
performing tricks for an audience of blossoms.

Fairies dance atop the waterfall
challenging the water sprites to a contest
while silver unicorns toss their whispery manes in laughter.
This is the Island Of Enchantment.

Dream
by Rose Ziegler - age 13

Dreams are jumbled images
Playing on the silver screen in your head
A lunatic stew of memories and thoughts
Projected into false reality
Where nothing has a reason or a purpose for being
And you lie drowning
In the darkened theatre of your own mind
Until you open your eyes
And reality floods in
Through the risen stage curtain of your eyelashes

Treasures
Chapter Two

Honorable Mentions
Honorable Mention Awards
for Competitors
in the Summer 1997
Iliad Literary Awards
Program

Bright Light
by S. Elisabeth M. Abbott

Confusion fills my mind day and night
   -Who am I?
     -What am I doing on this earth?
       -Does anyone understand?
         -Does anyone care?

Daily regrets of lovers lost
Memories flitting in and out
Darkness haunts my days and nights
With only one exception being a bright
light of a small child--my child.

Every morning I dread opening my eyes
Every night I crave sleep
The total darkness that sweeps
me off my feet into a haunting, dreamlike dance.

No one can penetrate the depression
that drives me-owns me
Except the bright light that is my child
Only she can wake me from this nightmare that I live
Only she can make me want to live and dream again.

A Tribute To Parents
by Geri Acker - age 15

They make you laugh, they make you cry.
You know they hurt, but do not know why.
They laugh and giggle through the years.
They tell you jokes that lead to tears.
They smile big and show no fears,
But all along they hide tears.
They rescue you, you rescue them.
They give you strength, you honor them.
You keep them close, you keep them near.
And though the years, you hold them dear.

The Abyss
by A. Perry Adams

Continuously falling,
Sinking,
Descending,
Through ever deepening crevasses.

What appear to be cushions
Turn out to be clouds.
Undiminished,
The fall continues.

Clutch a sturdy limb.
Anchor to the tree of existence.
Ascertain it is a partner
In the downward spiral.

Struggle speeds the descent,
Accelerates anxiousness,
Accentuates the fruitlessness
Of resistance.

Arms outstretched,
Body and soul surrendered,
Float in the abyss,
Abandon resistance to mortality.

A Summer's Day
by Sharon Adams

As the queen anns lace blows in the breeze
The sunlight flickers among the leaves
A summer day so hot and long
He wonders where the spring has gone
Wild flowers blooming all around
the smell of fresh cut hay upon the ground
The flight of a hawk in the clear blue sky
The cry of a rain crow somewhere nearby
A farmer sits in the shade to rest
He thanks the Lord he has been blessed
This mountain valley he calls home
As peaceful as a robin's song
He would like to give the world a part
Of the peace and love in this farmers heart
Oh summers day oh happy time
The world is alive with every sign

Love
by Naveen Ahmed - age 12

Love is a strong feeling that every human being has,
It is like a box of rich cream chocolate,
It is like a red rose that has a beautiful fresh scent,
Love is being with your family on holidays,
Love is seeing a mother carry her first new born child,
Love is sharing your things with your sister or a best friend,
It is having a cute, soft, warm puppy to cuddle with,
It is like shooting star that comes from nowhere,
Love is having a father and a mother kissing you goodnight,
It is winning a gold trophy by working as a team,
Love is getting a diamond right from someone special,
Love is like a flower that blooms every day and night,
It is like a bird singing through the swift air,
Love keeps a friendship alive,
Love is like homemade chocolate chip cookies,
Love is like the thin air that travels everywhere,
Love is like a leaf of a tree that is blown apart by the wind,
The feeling love will be in my heart somewhere.

Insane, Wonderful, Dreams
by Shazia Ali - age 17

Serenity in the air, love in hearts,
hands in hands, souls become one.
The world is a fair ground where young souls play.
Demolished ar the walls,
which stood between, Romeo and Juliet,
young hearts now meet in peace.
GREEN, FLOWERY, WONDERFUL FANTASY.

Colour, race class no more are walls,
for souls have no colour is now belived.
No more borders, the world is one,
beating together, the hearts are one.
Felicity plays amongst us all,
hate has existence on more.
SOFT, FRUITY HAPPY WONDERFUL DREAMS.

Fear, darkness extinct emotions,
green monster of envy slain for eternity.
Sunny days, starry nights,
passed as thou heaven on earth.
No hole in the ozone, no smoke filled air.
Generations live on in sublime joy.
INSANE, IMPOSSIBLE, YET WONDERFUL FANTASY.

The Joy of Love
by Gene R. Allen

Why must the people around me
say
that you had only brought me
pain
so quickly I say to them you all
are so wrong
that you had only brought to me
the joy of love
and it is the loss of this joy and of
your love
that they and myself interpret as
pain

Lost In The Darkness
by Siku Allooloo-Laraque - age 11

I still remember that night when you held my hand.
You used to say that you would never leave.
I still have love in my heart,
But why did I believe
All the things you said?

I am lost in the darkness.
I saw him, but days ago.
Was I dreaming?
Why did he go?

He has no hurt in his heart.
I am lost in the darkness,
and nobody is here to guide me anymore.

Help! Does anybody hear me??

I did not recognize who he was,
For he is a stranger in my life.
I do not know my own father anymore.
He is so far away, but yet so close.

Now, he is lost in the darkness,
and I shall find my way home.
He's never going to be found,
unless he finds himself.
He is surrounded by a darkness...
a darkness that will never leave until he finds
the light.

Life
by Shammara J. Al-wazzan - age 16

Life is cruel it can be said when it erupts I
feel so dead my only hope is still to be getting
through this hell I meet, so joy could end it has till
now this place could have its ups and downs upon
my heart a silver screen plays the part that's still
unseen. A soul might break an eye might cry
it's all the same when love must die. To end the pain
and all the tears will take the time of many years,
so till that day decides to come, I'll love the love
I never won.

Dedicated to Javier Del Nodal

"Creation dialogue"
by Emily Anderson - age 19

let's create a girl
    --a beautiful girl
make her more than beautiful though
    --yes, give her so much more than beauty
bless her with a heart that will always love
    --curse her with a mind that will always seek to understand
make her curious, intelligent
    --make her question absolutely everything
make her a free spirit, a creative spirit
    --trap that spirit in the body of the perfect daughter of narrow minded
parents in
    a conservative community
give her some true, close friends
    --alienate her from her other peers
give her talent, give her ambition, give her potential
    --give her problems, give her heartache, give her pain
give her the attention and admiration of men
    --many men, for all the wrong reasons
make her a fighter
    --wounded and hurting
make her never give up
    --suffer through hell but never give up
make her always win somehow
    --curse her with the gift of invincibility, don't let her escape
make her thoughtful
    --make her tortured
make her always happy
    --but never satisfied

Autumn Leaves
by Jeana Anderson

The dying leaves of Autumn.
Falling far to the ground
Crumbling and crackling under your
feet as you walk.
Darkness settles
as you creep trough the leaves.
The wind howling,
like the cries of small children.
Leaves blowing around your feet;
Dancing around your body.
Like lost opportunities,
they taunt you.
They make you remember mistakes you
have made.
They make you wonder what would
have happened,
If you had taken another path through
life.

You've been like a mom to me
by Candice Marie Anderson - age 14

From the day I was born
  I saw your face
We clicked together
Like two peas in a pod
We were always together
Even when we were apart
I think about you all the time.
I've always loved you so much.
Everytime I skinned my knee
You were there to kiss it all better
You stayed up at night when I was sick or just wanted to talk
You never held me back
You always let me be
When I wanted to go to movies with my friends.
You always found the money, even if we didn't have it.
I'm glad you and I have had 13 years together.
   And many more to come
Some people do not have the relationship
That you and I have always had.
I'm a very lucky person
Material wise and emotionally
You are my hero, and strength, and pride
I love you so much it's
Really hard to describe
But on this Mother's Day
I just have to say: THANK YOU SO MUCH!
For being just like a mother to me.

Making A Stand
by Jason B. Anderson

I asked you to be mine
You said you need a little time
To figure out what's good for your life
So you can fight for your rights to survive
You need him pushing you around
You better stand your ground
You better lay down the law
Telling him you don't want to live that life at all

Making a stand
Is all you have to do to live again
Making a stand
Is all you have to do to be happy to the end

I don't know if I'm the better man
But I won't treat you that way
   cause I will love you to the end
Tell him it's all over now
My way of loving you I will show you how
You won't have to feel the pain never again
For I will make sure you live happily to the end

Hard Times
by Mari'a Anderson - age 15

Times are hard, in this world. Especially if you're a teenage girl.
You got to get an education, keep your mind off the males,
and if you don't you can be sure to fail.
Now don't get me wrong, no one is worry free,
but I know how to ignore people who bother me.
There are people who are going to try and prevent you
from doing all the things you know that you can do.
It's not hard to stay in school.
Just as long as you can follow the rules.
Walk away from the fights and all the arguments,
and you won't be expelled or suspended.
"Problems, problems" everyone does say.
"I can't get by with all these problems in my way."
Learn how to compromise and it'll be all right,
but there's no way you can go through this scary world without a fright.
Now take all that negative stuff and throw it in the backyard,
because positive things are needed for a teenage girl, in a world, that's this hard.

A Rose Among Weeds
by Lauraine Andren

She was a single rose alone.
No one smelled her sweetness,
No butterfly tasted of her nectar.
Born without thorns, she had no defense.
Deprived of sunlight she withered and died.
Forgotten.

My Love Is A Soldier
by Paula Andria

My Love is a soldier so handsome and tall!
He's gone off to answer his Country's call
In a far away Land we once viewed with awe
Now plagued with evils we never foresaw.

That mystic Land of the "Arabian Nights,"
Full of enchantment, intrigue...wondrous sights.
Where magicians and genii would oft appear
To grant all wishes and chase away fear;

Where the underground caves held treasures untold
And the leaves on trees were emerald and gold;
Where birds once talked and rare music filled the air...
But now, all is shrouded in darkness there!

If magic were possible, at my command,
I'd wish myself in that far desert land.
Alas! There is no Aladdin's Lamp today
Nor flying carpets to whisk him away.

So, alone, I'll climb up those moonbeams of gold,
Gather all my dreams and pray they'll unfold.
I will sit there and wait for the dawn of Peace
When all of the hostilities will cease...

And my Love will be safe in my arms once more
And Peace in the world will reign as before.
Ah! Yes! How very sweet and precious and true
Are the millions of dreams I dream of you!

Love
by Kathy Andrysek - age 14

Love is the beautiful thing that you feel in your heart, something inside you feels so proud. Something that makes you do different actions toward the person you love. Something strong and tender but never cold, hold him tight and not soon let go. Show him you're here to stay and never let go. The first time we meet you were so shy, your own angel flying around. Flying so peacefully among the Earth, looking for a perfect place to spot. You're eyes, sparkling like the stars above the clouds, your hands touchable soft just like the angels wings. Your touch, your smile, your personality shinning like the moon. Shinning so bright you hid the sky, then one day out of nowhere you came out, shinning like no star has ever shined before. You came upon me and showed me the way to love you again. As I'm sitting here, tears dripping down my face, my lips, my neck and asking myself "Why you left?" And one thing I know is that I will miss you and always love you. And next time you decide to leave me, God knows I won't let you. You are apart of me know that no one can touch, no one can see, and no one can feel. Only I can feel, touch, and see the love you have given me. And God knows were together, everyday and every minute. And as long as we are together we know we can make it pulling harder and harder everyday. So I have one last Question before I say good-bye "Why did you leave me behind??" I will always love you like an angel in the sky!! Don't forget to watch over me as we move on. We both know it's hard to let go, but life isn't fare sometimes. And God knows I'm watching over you and you are watching over me. And God knows <u>I LOVE YOU !!!</u>

<u>DEDICATED TO SOMEONE SPECIAL TO ME !!!</u>

Yellow Brick Road
by Shanon M. Angermeyer

On the way to finding the wizard,
I met three new characters
who agreed with me: There was more -
and they wanted it, too.

While meeting the scarecrow, I trembled.
A genius might be insane -
ready to follow the path
in search of a brain.

In armor the tin man does beckon.
Protected, but torn apart,
he thinks the golden path
will lead him to his heart.

The eyes of the lion are piercing
and can cause a stranger threat.
It's the only way to venture
without the weight of fret.

I have not known a place called home.
My feet barely touch the ground.
Our travels are mysterious,
but, together, we are bound.

To Honor My Mother
by Gerardo L. Angulo

The night God took my mother by the hand
and said "Come, oh daughter of mine, it is time to come home"
I felt a profound emptiness that I had not felt before
As I count the hours of each day
my mind and heart fill with anxiety and wonder
My mother's laughter, sweetness and tenderness
I will always remember
To honor my mother
I will try to be strong and follow in her footsteps
for my mother and I had the best mother and son friendship
To honor my mother
I will try to be strong and follow in her footsteps
for my mother and I had the best mother and son friendship
To honor my mother
I will not give up on life
and will always try to make her proud of me
I will never forget how she taught me to love and pray
While she gave me guidance and advice
to fulfill my dreams
she always gave me light for the way.

Yesterday is gone forever
Today is almost over
I will never forget
that sad and painful twelfth of November
To honor my mother
I will always treasure all the moments we had together
Oh, dear Jesus, please give me comfort and peace
for my mother's absence
I still find hard to believe
Upon her grave
I will leave beautiful flowers
and I will always do what I can
to honor my mother.

In memory of my beloved mother, Mrs. Bertha Maxie Angulo (1922-1995)

How
by Aneeka A. Angus - age 19

How can you say you love her,
But still you're here with me?
How can you say you love her,
when love isn't what I see?

How can I truly care,
when I know all the things you do?
How can I truly care,
when you can't keep your love to one woman true?

How can we be together,
When nothing will be right?
How can we be together,
when we have to keep things out of sight?

How can I believe you,
when you treat this woman this way?
How can I believe you,
when you lie to her everyday?

Why should I be serious,
when I know what you two have been through?
Why should I be serious,
when I know you will mistreat me too?

How can I open my heart,
when I know what the outcome will be?
How can I open my heart,
when I know you don't care about me?

Future
by Crystal Ann Ankney - age 16

Everybody worries about the future
because their past is not always pure
will their children be the same
or in a spotlight of fame
they watched their dreams disappear
and the only thing came out of it was tears
they have dreams for their children
and hope they don't commit a sin
they teach them not to hate others
and have respect for all mothers
then they realize
their not all that wise
because the choices they made
will never fade
because in their mind they will always stay
day after day
children growing up at a fast rate
and conduct their own fate

Where I Belong
by Katie Anthamatten

I was born in the city
The Love-Bird hatched in a cage.
We're both so pampered with luxury,
We thought that <u>this</u> was the highest stage!

But when I was shown a pasture
And the Love-Bird was shown the sky,
To break free from those cages
It was almost worth it to die.

For the grass was soft
And the air was sweet
From the comfy barn loft
To the deep, cool creek.

Nature is calling, that's where I belong.
Nature is calling to me.

The Beginning of Autumn
by Maria E. Apodaca - age 16

Not ready to come down yet?
Not ready to make that awesome leap?
Not ready to become a humongous heap?
Orange, red, yellow, and gold. Come fall down!
Let us walk on a magnificent ground, then
we'll begin to prance around. Acting as though
somethings just been found, sitting there upon the
ground. Those shimmering colors all around.

The Storm Passes
by Brenda Lee Appel

The mood grows awkward and tense
He stands; his head turned looking out the window
She feels his resentment like a sixth sense
She's seen him many times before look this low.

Her heart is heavy and goes out to him
She knows he's troubled
She wishes for a miracle for him
But the tension only doubles.

She would give anything to ease his pain
If the storm inside his heart would only stop
It too, would follow, the passing of the clouds and rain
And for the world to see; he'd stand on top.

She prays it's not her that makes him this way
But she knows all too well the anger and frustration
She too at one time had felt this way
And the only way to stop it was a separation.

He tells her "It's really not you"
But she doesn't believe him in her heart
She can't bear the thought it would break her heart in two
So they agreed together they would make a new start.

She's been told there's sometimes a storm before the calm
So she prays the storm has passed
And together they will write their song
And make their marriage last.

Dreams, Thoughts, and Memories
by Meggan E. Ardiff - age 14

Lieing by the deep blue sea,
As the sun shone down on me,
I thought so many, many things.

Of boys who grow to be men,
of broken hearts that need to mend,
and letters that I'll never send.

I look up at the baby blue sky,
It brings back memories that made me cry,
I think of these memories while I lie.

Of the time I thought death was my fate,
Valentines day when I couldn't find a date,
and the time to <u>God</u> I cried and begged.

I breathed in cool, clean air,
while it whispered in my ears,
and remembered my worst fears.

Of angry screams ringing all around,
of spiders crawling on the ground,
and getting lost to never be found.

The sun is setting to a familiar song,
and soon the day will be done,
farewell to today that was short and long.

My Love Puzzle
by Nazgol Ashouri - age 17

So simple, yet so delicate
Complicated at times, and fragile at others
So worthless it may seem, when each lonely piece lies scattered by itself
But with each connecting piece,
A clearer, a more understanding, and a more meaningful picture is gained
This wondrous puzzle, as our relationship,
Is one that depends on each piece and on each other to be complete
You and I, are each possessed with scattered pieces of this precious puzzle
The one that will be complete once we join hands and become "one."
My love,
You are my world,
The star of my night,
The sun of my day,
You are the brightness in my dark and gloomy nights
The water in my hot and dry desert
You are like petals to a flower,
The flower is me, so empty without my petals
This flower mustn't die.
As we go on the journey of life,
You find the way when I am lost
And I'll pick you up when you fall down
Its only then that all the pieces will fall in place, and make the puzzle of our love.

The River
by Frank L. Audino

Look at enough people and
You will see a pleasant surprise.
E'ry face is filled with wonder
The wonder of being alive.

The person inhabits the strength.
When it's time to move on
The wonder is gone.
Indexed like a coursed river branch.

But unknown to the river
Is the endless joy it brings to others,
Like the face I saw today
Of the woman walking jay.

She made me realize
The pleasant surprise
For moments we prize
Not for any foreshadowing
But for reprise
And the chance to be wise
To the rewards of breath
And those no one denies.

Untitled
by Vivianne Audiss

I listen to the words of others,
They tell my soul to write,
They tell my hand to write,
They tell my heart to write,
The echo of their words,
Brings my soul to the surface,
Brings my heart to see,
The truth of my mind.

Whispers
by Barbara Augustyniak

Whispers in the wind
Breath of my soul
Ancestral voices
Guide of skies
Wings of grace
Dreams take flight
Messengers open eyes
Mystery sacred place
Journey's inner sight
All fear dies
Visions to face
Courage upon might
Here truth lies
One's heart embrace
Source of light
Whispers in the wind
Breath of my soul
Life's destined choices

Through The Eyes Of An Old Zebra
by Tennessee Catherine Brittain

A jackal enters the neighborhood watering hole
    to stalk
Intentions, insecurities painfully obvious to those with experience
He nervously checks around him
    back arching, hair smoothing
    forced stretches, unnecessary yawns
        he hunts
His head snaps round as potential prey approaches
    each is sized up
He stares at a pretty doe-eyed one attempting to catch her gaze
    ignoring him, she is no easy mark
He scans his territory for another
A young filly walks by
He catches her scent
He pounces, dominating the conversation
Cut from the pack she is his total focus
    naively flattered she chatters
He hangs on her every word
    like a snake
        never breaking eye contact
Hair tossed, head tilted, earrings fingered
He touches her arm--she doesn't pull away
    leaning back in his chair while facing her
    arms crossed behind his head -- legs stretched out in front
Looking down his nose, confident she is his
    A fresh heart to plunder

Keeper
by Laura A. Austin - age 18

A touch of fate
used to open the gate.

The padlock rusted shut
nothing allowed in or out.

Locked away behind the forbidden gate
feeling nothin, no love or hate.

Dark shadows hiding the past
the pain that will always last.

The lonely soul
waiting for someone to hold.

Only one keeper of a key
to set her soul free.

A touch of fate
used to open the gate.

The touch of love
sent from above.

Letting go of all the pain
no longer alone in all the rain.

Her keeper of the key
has finally set her free.

Untitled
by Christina M. Baird - age 14

The people are walking slowly, painfully down the hill towards the black hole with flowers all around. You can taste the bitterness as the rain pours around you. You can smell the fresh tears. Now one cares about the rain, they just don't want to say good-bye: to let a friend, a loved one, a piece of their hearts go. The grief and sadness you feel just seems not to want to leave. It seems that the more people who come to say good-bye to this special person, the darker and cloudier the skies get.

The mourners gather around the hole and a women screams out in anguish. She is the wife of the deceased man. As the casket is lowered, the family tosses blood-red roses into the dark grave. The family and close friends leave. Even though the mourners are gone, the sadness and pain still clings in the air. Each raindrop is being cried for their beloved husband and friend.

Separation
by Janna M. Badger

Gazing disguise
within the mirror
so despondent
so defeated.

Eyes sunken above
lips scarlet
pallid skin under
cheeks stained.

Hope departed
as summer for fall
severing of self
as bough in bluster.

Touch of glass
sliver of cold
radiant perfume
essence of courage dead.

Fractured reflection
desolate vibration
shudder of breast
tenure of spirit passed.

Turning from truth
closure of eyes
descend of head
drop of regret.

Moment In Time
by Sharron Baker

One moment in time, the world is in slumber,
our thoughts lay at rest, as peace runs through the land.

Where do the memories go, where has energy been
spent, do we dwell in some dark chamber with keys held
just out of reach.

Time appears forgotten, suspended in midair, the
universe hanging in orbit, are our bodies floating there.

No sound or words are spoken, no sight remains to
see, no feelings can be felt, does someone beckon me.

I struggle to remember, as images appear, hap hazard
as a kaleidoscope, no meaning can I decipher here.

I float through dark recesses, fighting off leaden
weights, then a lightness frees me, as I race to get
out of this place.

All around me is a wakefulness, the earth in splendor
rare, if only I could capture this embodiment, before it
too, becomes one moment in time.

To You John
by Alicia Baraghoshi - age 18

After all that has happened you wonder why I
am so mad.
You ask why can't we be just friend's?
Did you forget about all we had?
But I just can't make amends.
You told me all the sweet things I liked to hear.
But to find out they were all just horrible lies.
All you really wanted was my sister.
So thanks to you I hate all guys.
If you knew how much pain I felt inside.
You would see why I refuse to speak your
name.
I don't know why I even tried to confide.
All you were looking for was fame.
You are the biggest mistake in my life.
But yet I feel like I still have feelings for you.
But nothing can be saved or brought back.
For you took the very life from me and stabbed
me in the back.
To have never met you would be heaven.
Yet I have no control over that now.
There isn't a day that goes by that I don't think
about you.
Too bad it had to end this way.

Together, Forever In Our Own World
by Kerri Lynn Barker

Love is like riding on a cloud of devotion,
Fueled with unharnessed, unwavering emotion.
Turbulence inside,
Unleashed with such fury and passion.
Raging hormones,
Spilled into your arms.
Sensitive, caring, sharing,
To be lost in you.
Our spirits collide with such freedom.
We float into each other's souls unfurled.
Upon landing, we realize,
We're still left in the clouds together.,
Lost, but found.
Empty, but filled.
Alone together.
Together, forever in our own world.

Darkness Overcomes
by Chad Barnes - age 15

The Darkness overcomes.
The lighting from above.
Fear covers courage.
And hate covers love.
Sorrow covers joy.
And feelings trail behind.
This Darkness, this black Darkness.
Has made this whole world blind.
A parting in the clouds, sheds a gleam of light.
A little baby bird sets off on it's first flight.
But then the baby bird plummets to the ground.
For this Darkness, this black Darkness has tied it's poor wings down.
Time has no meaning, for right now time stands still.
The flowers have no life upon our window sills.
But then the drums of life drum and drum and drum.
Making it known to all the world, that Darkness has Overcome.
But still the world denies it all, they say they still see light.
But those that don't deny the truth, say day still looks like night.
The pain and sorrow will not end.
Our world will fill with strife.
Until they realize the real truth.
Darkness is the death of life.

The Night
by Juanita C. Barnes-Bourgullion

Something caused my heart to ache, tears often present nin my eyes.
 Can it be from a love that's too far gone, or the emptiness
 of love yet undiscovered?

My morning begins so beautiful and new. I awake with the rising
 sun. Yet somehow before the sun goes down the beauty peeters
 out as swiftly as a clear blue sky grows dark before a storm.

Nights--I've spent so many awake from dusk to dawn. A stillness
 that only my body grasps while my mind races through memories
 of old loves, anger, hurt, and joy.

Joy, many times has come to me, but visits are now so few. Don't
 misconstrue my point of view, my faith has proven strong, but
 everyone knows even the strongest soul must pass this way
 in time.

However, it's considerably feasible that tonight I'll sleep and
 tomorrow arise to realize my doubts and frustrations were
 all just a bitter nightmare--my positive vision regaining
 control. The ache in my heart and tears in my eyes erased,
 as though they were never there. And perhaps I'll love
 again as I have before and before.

As I Look Out My Window
by Crystal Barrios - age 14

As I look out my window and stare upon the sky
The rising moon casts its hypnotic spell upon my eyes
How envious I am of this wondrous sight
The metallic silver and gold glistening in the starlight
As I look out my window in the pale sapphire sky
I see the stars dancing leaving a parade of stardust behind them
The golden stardust falls down into a whisper
I see their radiant arms extending out to me,
 begging me to come with them
Come dance with us, dance and be joyous
leave your trail of miseries behind you
As I look out my window into the enchanted sky
I wonder why? Why didn't I go dance with the stars
Why didn't I leave my trail of miseries behind me
I wonder why? Why didn't I confess my whimsical secret
 to the moon
As I look out my window and gaze into a sea of diamonds
 surrounding a mysterious pearl
I see an eternity of emotions passion, harmony and happiness
And yet there is still the moon
what possible emotion could describe the moon
Still I wonder have I come to the answer
the moon is so magical and powerful,
Its indescribable to me the moon remains a mystery

Feelings
by Joe W. Bauers

There's not a day goes by
That I don't miss you so much I cry
It's taken all my might
But I've made everything right
If you just come back to me
Things will be good, you'll see

Public Display of Affection is nice
One kiss is not enough, has to be twice
It seems like we have shared a lifetime this past year
The rest of our life together is the way I see clear
This past year has been the happiness of my life
More than anything, I want you to be my wife

I want to call because I miss your voice
But I fell I have no choice
Because you want your space
But I long for your embrace
We used to have a God sent linking
We could tell what the other was thinking
I want that again so very much
It's special when two minds touch

If I Could Only Hear
by Lisa Baumann - age 17

If I could only hear, I would know all the different sounds of the world. I could hear what is being said on TV or when I watch a movie. I would be able to enjoy all the wonderful songs on the radio.

If I could only hear, I would walk through the forest in autumn and listen to the sounds of leaves crackling under my feet and birds chirping in the trees.

If I could only hear, I would to the ocean and listen to the waves crashing recklessly on the beach or hear the joyful laughter of children as the waves hit them.

If I could only hear, I would listen to my sister as she plays the piano and hear my friends' voices instead of wondering what they sound like. I would be able to understand so much more.

If I could only hear, I would travel around the world and listen to the different languages. How I wish I could hear the world instead of just watching.

This poem is dedicated to Leigh Ann and Jonathan, my cousins who are deaf.

The Way We Look At Ourselves
by Morgan Lindsay Beam - age 15

Teenage girls with skinny arms and skinny legs standing in the hallway

wondering why everyone's staring at them,
talking about how fat they are

when in fact, no one's even looking at them.

Girls too skinny to walk,
thinking they're too fat to dance.

Little tummied women, sucking on their cigarettes and carrots,
like that is all they have left to take in.

Young girls growing up thinking they have to prove
themselves to everyone
when they have a lot more to prove to themselves.

You don't have to be someone else's mirror

You only have to look at yourself as an equal.

Quintessence
by Joan Ostrom Beasley

I hear the
rustle of "quakin' Aspen"
in the Fall breeze,
the gentle twerp of
the last hummiongbirds,
the strident call of
vibrant blue jays.
Bear hears the
silent footsteps of
a doe at the bird feeder,
the patient breathing
of a fox waiting his turn
for fallen sunflower seeds,
the wind pushing
velvet petunia petals aside.
We stretch out in the
last Fall sun's warmth -
I in my chair,
feet on a footstool,
Bear on his back,
feet in the air,
in the cool grass.
We luxuriate in
Autumn
before the winter's
Arctic assault.

Cherish The Mind
by Kelsey Beck - age 12

Young minds are like tornadoes of curiosity
With whirls of twirling butterflies to catch.
All is a possibility; but time teaches us
That no one can ever make a perfect match.
We just don't know what dreaming will create
But when we think it makes us great
For we are better kept in this perfect state.

Old minds are like books waiting to be read.
In every one of them is something to be said.
But sometimes we are too busy as in youth
We miss the present company showing us the truth.
Now I know we should cherish the ones we have near;
Our grandpas and grandmas who love us so dear
For one day their mind may soon disappear.

Listening
by Shawn Bedard

When I ask you to listen to me and you change
the subject, I feel I am alone.
When I ask you to listen to me and you start
giving advice, you have not done what I asked.
When I ask you to listen to me and you begin
to tell me why I should not feel that way, you
are trampling on my feelings.
When I ask you to listen to me and you feel
you have to do something to solve my problem,
you have failed me, strange as that may seem.
Listen! All I asked was that you listen, not
talk or do-just hear me.
Advice is cheap: twenty-five cents will get you
both Dear Addy and Billy Graham in the same
newspaper.
All I can do for myself. I am not helpless.
Maybe discouraged and faltering but not
helpless.
When you do something for me that I can and
need to do for myself, you contribute to my
fear and inadequacy.
But, when you accept as a simple fact that I
do feel what I feel, no matter how distressful,
the I can get about the business of understanding
what's behind this feeling.
Now, more than ever, I need to talk.
And, I will listen to you. It will go much better
for us. We will be closer.

Sentinel
by Jacquelyn Bell-Massey

Rock on golden-tiled hearth,
    who brought you here from your
    rightful place with the
    elements--appointing you
    sentinel
    before the grate?

No one knows what you are--
    why you hold such a position.

Lump of no distinction. Not
    elegant marble or
    popular quartz.

When will you retire to the
    wind and rain?

Promoted from left to right
    sunlight through windows now
    touch your edge.

Silent, patient servant.

Gold watch out of reach.

They ask me why are you here.
    I do not know.
      You were here when I came
    I tell them--
  you may be here when I go.

Gary's Brother
by Linda J. Bell

Is younger yet old.
A P.O.W. of an unpopular war;
Still imprisoned.
Inhabiting the shell that
Cannot hold him up anymore.

Inhabits battered doorways
Peers anxious windows.
Clutches a useless arm,
Half-full bottle.

It is damaged mind;
Fleeting routine carnage
Of what he did
Of what was done
To him.

At nineteen;
There used to be a wife.
At twenty-two used self pity
This morning a quarter.

Tomorrow, will be confined again.
Gaze mutely from sterile sheets;
Attached ambiotically,
And die as a man was born —
Innocent.

The Silence Within
by Tina Benham - age 17

A quiet evening
all alone in the shadows
a single flower
contained in my soul
a solid tear
a lonely call
in this darkened place.

If you can understand my muffled tear.
Then you will understand the truth
a heart of coal
can turn to ashes
if left in solitaire.

Even though the silent evening
is a bidding to the breeze.
The evening will hold true.
The silent heart
of which belongs to me.

For everyone who holds the key
will hold it till the last of time.
Until I find the key in me.
All I live for will be
an empty hole inside of me
and the hole will be the truth
known.
That life is hard, hard as coal
and holding your heart against the fire
is the truth behind the ashes.

The Essence of Me...
by Marina Benninghoven - age 16

The wind is tell me
something...

The breeze and sweeping
leaves.

To touch a tree,k to feel your hand.
Is emptiness what it leaves?

Softly blowing winds.
Gentle rolling dunes.

Songs of a thousand souls
have been sun beneath our moon.

Grass cushions my naked feet.
I do a dance of summer, and wish that I had wings.

The earth is the essence that is me...

The Embrace
by Rachel Berger - age 16

Two kindred spirits
Locked in embrace
Hushed words whispered
Against her gentle face.

The night is full of wonder
The air is full of sounds
But to the kindred spirits
There is quiet all around.

A rose of red is in her hand
Her cheeks blush deep with pink
Her heart is beating faster
Too fast for her to think.

The moonlit sky fills with stars
Shining bright and bold
The clock continues ticking
But they do not release their hold.

As their arms' link is opened,
A single tear is seen,
The embrace has been torn apart,
As a dreamer from his dream.

The clock continues ticking
The stars stay clear and light
For the spirits will embrace again
In another place and time.

Eagles!!
by G.F. Berkowsky

Bald Eagles!!
Oh, regal, soaring mates,
thank you for gracing Lake Samish
in daily flight—
what glory you bring!!

Disbelief!!
My brain Jotted at the shot's ring
and the heart-pummeling scene:
feathered majesty—*flailing, grasping at flight*—
now leaden—**crashing to earth!!**

Aftermath—
Time has passed but not the burning memory
of that grieving mate's circle
Of an-n-nguised **S-CC-R-E-E-E-A-M-M-M-S!!!**
They resonate still in my sisterly breast.

Dear Daddy
by Lisa Beshai - age 12

Dear Daddy
where are you?
You said you'd always be there.
Dear Daddy
where are you?
You said you'd always care.
Why did you leave me?
I cry myself to sleep
why did you go?
Please I need to know
Dear Daddy
why do you make me cry?
Dear Daddy
I try but I can't figure out why
why did you leave me?
It wasn't your time to go
why did you go?
I don't know
Dear Daddy
help I'm drowning in tears
Dear Daddy
help take away my fears
Dear Daddy
I Love You...

The Beast
by Sal Betel

My surroundings chill, edges cold and hard.
Nowhere to run...can hear it coming...
The trembling more fervent.
Is it the cool gloominess?
Has fear enveloped my being?
Answer far off...residing with warmth.
That soft glowing warmth...
Feel the impact!
My soul sobs and pleads;
Please stop this pain...the beast pities none.
Can feel it ripping at me,
Feel its' evil...hear its' bellowing taunts.
The beast is hell...pure power its' tool.
Chase after the warmth,
Leaving only a trail...twisting trail of memory.
The beast much swifter...attack non-relenting.
Getting weak...how much longer?
Should I not be numb...numb to the pain!
A wretched trail,
My trail of tears...no control...can't defend!
Must give in...accept this pain.
Its' demeanor cruel.
Wielding such a weapon!
The taunting ceases...the attack is over.
Here I lie...wallowing in my sorrow.
The beast is off to search out new prey.
A messenger of sorts...delivering senses.
Mine the emptiness...that of love.
Love found then lost.
Emptiness is the beast.

An Angel
by Amy Bettys - age 13

She just stood there,
Her skin so perfectly fair
Her presence gave a certain
peace,
so that all my anger in me
ceased
She fluttered her wings with a
wondrous grace,
She had a beautiful smile drawn
on her face
There was a halo on her head,
And with her perfect mouth she
said, "I'm an angel."

A True Friend
by Shannon Bickels - age 14

He crossed his heart and hoped to die.
    He wouldn't tell-
        For her, he would lie.
She'd come to him with a bruise for every tear
    A story, too,
        of days before, year after year.
    He watched her bleed
        inside and out
What could he do, what did she need?
That man was supposed to care, he thought
    Not with words, but with fists
        Her father fought.
His girl, his best friend couldn't live, not this way
    Thank God he let
        his secret slip today.
Drunk hands hurt worse 'cuz he is her dad
    And today he came home
        Especially bad.
But this time she wasn't alone,
    All it took
        was a number on the phone.
They took him away, and she cried again;
As he held her close she said,
"Thanks for not keeping my secret,
    friend."

Gone!
by Heena Birdi - age 16

When I look into your eyes
I see the same person
    But.
Not the same thoughts.

When I see your smile
I see the same soft lips
    But,
Not touched by me.

When I give you hugs
I feel the same soft arms
    But,
Not the same love.

Isn't there some love left for me?
Or
It has disappeared like those days!.....

Why?
by Sabrina Blackburn - age 12

For some weird reason, I can't live without you
For some odd reason, maybe something you do
for some weird reason I can't live without your lies
For some odd reason, when your gone something
dies

I can't yet tell you what it is, for maybe its your
cologne
I can't yet show you what it is, 'cause I feel so all
alone
I can't yet tell you what it is, you'd hear pain in my
voice
I can't yet show you what it is, I might have made
the wrong choice.

Why is the pain still here, I ask myself, as I look
inside the mirror
Why is the sorrow still here, I feel myself shaking
with terror
Why is the pain still here, your gone.
Why is the sorrow still here, you didn't take it along.

Winter Snows Birthday & Mine
by Lindsey Nicole Blackwell - age 5

The ground is all covered in gleaming white snow
like the frosting on my birthday cake.
The trees all bent hanging beautiful candles lit from their limbs!
Showing off sparkling fires of colors
Like the candles burning on my birthday cake.
I think of spring to come as I blow them out.
Soon the snow will melt; our birthdays soon will be over
as we taste the cake.
We soon will taste the joy of spring and we'll have to
wait another year to celebrate!

Whisper of the Wind
by Amanda Blain - age 13

Through Desert Storm,
    through Vietnam,
I sit and wonder, "will
the war ever be gone?"
With the murder in New York
and the crime in Chicago,
I sit and wonder, will the
cruelty ever go?
I sit and wonder will this
harshness ever stop?
Nothing seems to help, not
even a cop.
What happened to the Bible,
don't make excuses
like the pages are torn,
Because we know by you, the
Lord's word hasn't
been worn.
Will there ever be peace? Is
it so?
As I sit and wonder, the
wind whispers, "NO!"

The Mending and Pretending
by Krystdevon A. Blues

Sitting by herself in a lighted empty room,
there is a girl who feels so all alone.
She wishes she could speak yet thinks she is too meek
the wonders of the world have passed her by.
Her heart had just been mending now she knows she was pretending
all the love inside just can't go away.
How she wishes she were heard.
Her words a tainted sword but courage wept on the painted wings.
There was a memory of one who soft and tenderly
took her love up into the sky. Fading gently a touch of
skin one knows the warmth won't hide.

Growing Pains
by Steve Blumenfeld

I look for the worst,
Since that's what I've been taught.
"Don't do what you do;
You should do what you ought."

My dad drilled me well
As he ranted and raved.
This was all that I got,
But was not what I craved.

Now, I do the same;
Seems my dad I've become.
It's made my life miserable,
My days are humdrum.

I pray for a change,
Please, God, help me to grow.
I know I can do better.
Oops! Again, there I go.

I am my own worst critic.
Lord, help me to stop!
It's You that I trust, and,
You are all that I've got.

I know that You love me.
Well, I hope that You do!
You see, I'm a skeptic.
I learned that good, too.

So, here's to the future,
With Your help I will win.
By the way, my regards
To You and your kin.

Untitled
by Jennifer Bockmiller - age 13

Honey coated lips
Beg to kiss
and a soul seeks to share itself
Blindly looking in life's abyss

Observed ironic fulfillment
Question magnet fate
Fairness is irrelevant
and those always ignored complain

Believed what I was told
Then grew out of that gullibility
Seek not beyond the edge of reality
Doubt mortality and deny eternity
For I dwell on now
and keep thought of the future distant

Despair pursuing affection
but attain needed enemies
Strength grows in failure
and love springs from hate

A Prayer of Guidance
by Rebecca Bodle - age 13

My desire is you oh Lord,
I know you are the savior of the world.
I'll serve and live for only you,
Give me strength for the things you want me to do.
Help me to show patients with everyone,
Oh Lord, Thy Will be done.
Help me to show everyone love,
Like you do from above.
Help me to spread the good news,
For I know this is what you want me to do.
Help me throughout my days,
For you are worthy of my praise.

Claims
by Nika Bodner - age 14

You claim to hold
my part, my being.
But you do not have a claim to keep.
Your claim is weak.

I am, my own,
I claim the throne,
to my thoughts,
and to my wants.

And yet you claim
your so called rightful hold,
as if I am an item
priced and sold.

You do not understand me
and want to shame me,
with your limits, rules and regulations.
You will not see beyond your world.

With me as your claim,
you still say you have nothing.
Am I not something?
Does this mean I am nothing?

The Teacher
by Juli Boeglin - age 15

He possesses a wonderful gift
that no one else can give.
It sometimes gives a lift
or helps you prosper and live.

You know that you can count on him,
through all the pain and tears,
to be the strong one in the swim
of the unwanted years.

He's like a father—strong and tall,
knowledgeable and sincere.
He'll always help us through it all
whether he's there or here.

Although we'll miss him greatly,
our days will never lack
the times when he, so graciously,
gave us a pat on the back.

A wonderful person who can't be replaced,
the one with the dynamic personality.
Because of him our lives have a place,
a sense of direction and morality.

This person who has touched our hearts
can never be forgotten.
Even when our soul is raised
and our bodies old and rotten.

And so we say good-bye once more
to this very special man.
He'll leave by walking out the door,
and never returning again.

Do Nothing At All
by Jenna Bond-Louden - age 14

we sit on the ground
doing nothing at all
but it is everything
just sitting there
just lying there
makes all the difference
just dreaming with the clouds
in serenity
talking about what was so great
talking about what will never change
just as long as we have time
time to sit there
time to lay there
doing nothing at all
we'll make it
    to the end of the day

The Rainforest
by Brandy Bowman - age 13

I the rainforest,
dying in discreet,
miserable and harmed,
as lonely as can be.
I the rainforest
am ruined every second of the day,
trashed and violated in every way.
I the rainforest,
beautiful and unique,
being destroyed for houses,
and the animals are becoming extinct.
I the rainforest
hold many animals,
large and small,
all living then dying in the world.

Night
by Maranda Box - age 17

As I stroll into the greying world at dusk
I take a long, last lingering breath of warm summer air
Another feverish, scorching summer day
Coming to a close
I gaze upward
Thousands of twinkling eyes begin to stare down at me
Night is falling
Now sizzling summer-day smells
Change gently to appeal to nocturnal senses
The glowing crescent in the sky beckons relaxation
And rest
Night is among us
And the great flaming candle in the sky has disappeared--
For now...
We sleep

Untitled
by Brittany Boyett - age 13

To be walking on air, to feel like your in heaven
Across the land and beyond the boundaries, it will last forever
In this you can trust and in this you can believe
Under the light blue sky and over the bright green grass,
It will always be there
With this you will often be happy, deep within your heart
For you will never forget, for you will never need to be
reminded of all the happiness and heartache this has
caused you
Like all the other memories you have, remember this
one Love.

A Perfect Kiss
(to he knows who he is)
by Tiffany Boykin - age 16

Your fingertips caressed my leg...
You kissed my neck,
and embraced my body.
A rush of warmth came over me.
As if the sun had kissed my skin.
We looked eye to eye,
Except you looked past my eyes into
    my mind...my heart...and my soul.
Your lips touched mine,
A kiss -
A perfect kiss,
A flawless affair,
that lasted its own eternity.
And when you left that day,
You left with more than just a kiss
You left with my heart,
You just don't know it yet.

For Nir, An Israeli
by Sydney Boyle

He brews the tea and sweet'ns
    It with milk and honey
And pours it into cups trimmed
    With white peony

The persian rice he soaks till
    It is soft and full
Simmer'd in turmeric makes
    My senses null

Upon a check'rd cloth we
    Share this simple meal;
An artisan's labor whose love
    It does reveal

At night he reads ivory pages
    Of old testaments,
Written by prophets with
    Mercurial temperaments

He reached into my soul and
    My love did he steal;
Not to find truths or wrongs
    But only what is real

So I sip his cup of tea
    With milk and honey

From Yechiel's land so
    Warm and sunny

Old Tree Answer Me?
by Bryant Jerome Branch

One day a young man was observing the natural beauty of an old tree and he started to ask questions: Old tree, how do you stand there year in, year out. For, you never toil nor labor. Yet, you sow and reap?
Old tree, of what substance renews thy life
    after a long wintry death like sleep?
Old tree, you stand all the day and night waving your mighty arms and hands back and forth. Yet, you never can take a stroll, tell me where cometh your patience and contentment?
Old tree, tell me what keep thee through the harsh seasons, as the winds blow angrily against thee, the storms rage and sometimes you are almost uprooted. Yet, you remain still and calm?
Old tree tell me, answer me,
what substance brings forth thou life, beauty,
and fruit every season due without hesitation?
Old tree where gaineth thy
will, strength and persistence to withstand life's trials and tribulations?
Old tree tell me, answer me.
The tree replied: Well, if I must tell you, then you must hear and open your eyes to the creation.
The answer you seeketh liveth within the both of us. All you have to do is be still and calm and let the creator be.
Believe and be patient and let yourself
and creation harmoniously exist as one.
The young man's response:
Old tree you have truly enlightened me with your depth of wisdom and humbleness.
Old tree you are wise.

Difference
by Valerie Brand - age 14

I glanced at a black woman--
    I hated her.
I watched an Indian eat lunch--
    He was in a minority.
There was a Japanese boy next to me on the train--
    He was different.
I saw a picture of Anne Frank--
    Pity filled my heart.
What did the Jewish and gypsies do?
    They were hated, a minority, and different.
I came to a serious realization--
    I was as bad as Hitler.
        I hated. Plain and simply hated.
There is no danger in difference.
    No shames.
    No regrets.
But I was ashamed...
    not because I was different--
        Because I was full of ridicule and discrimination.
I was as bad as Hitler.
Except for one thing--
    I felt regrets and made silent apologies to those born different than me.

Whispering Love
by Chloe Breault - age 14

You look in my eyes and say you love me,
    you remind me of a soft, gentle breeze.
I look in your eyes and say I love you,
    and I love you even more each day.

I look in your eyes- brown and beautiful,
    with mine- so soft, big and blue.
I look at you smile- so handsome and sweet,
    and feel in my chest my heart flutter.

And now I tell you these three little words,
    that I hope your heart shan't forget-
when the breeze blows and the birds start to sing,
    you can hear me whispering, "I love you."

Hidden
by Heather Breish - age 15

Open your eyes
See the world,
And start to realize.

Notice the earth
Filled with you and me.
See the world
From sea to sea.

Look into your heart,
And sing a song
Let all know
That you belong.

Hidden in mirrors
Come out and play.
Please don't stay
Behind the walls of yesterday.

Treasures

Untitled
by Michelle Bridges

I hold you close to my heart; we had so much together.
We had so much together
It's hard to believe we'd ever be apart
but no one ever remains frozen in time
for so long, I told myself
the song remains the same
For a moment I thought I had
a grip of things
But it's out of my grasp
and suddenly
I'm no longer tied to the bonds of the obsession
(which used to possess me)
to what seems to have been star-crossed
(opposed even by the high heavens)
all this time.

Can I Go Back To Yesterday?
by Pamela Brinson

Excuse me, excuse me please!
    Just before I go down-on-my knees.

I have a question and I want to hear
What you have to say!
    Can I, Can I go back to yesterday?

Yesterday, when my only worry was...
    Mama, "How long can I play?"

Yesterday, when I could put my hands-on-my-hips
    and not worry about what I had to say!

Yesterday, when the air was much fresher,
    the skies seemed bluer and
    the flowers beautiful like a day in May.

Yesterday, when I wasn't trying to penetrate
    the "Glass Ceiling!" or scramble the "Cooperate Ladder"
    for I was content with my pay.

No Ma'am, No Sir, but keep you youthful hearts
for it will keep you along life's way.
    For no one "can go back to yesterday!"
    no matter how hard you pray!

Lingering Lake
by Janice Brittain - age 14

    If you will listen to my little story,
    I will speak of a lake and her hopes and glory.
When God made this lake He had something in mind,
    to make this lake special and oh, so kind.
He finished his creation and walked through the pines,
    wonderful thoughts then ran through his mind.
    Gentle kindness, love and care,
    that's what this lake will so proudly share.
    For this place is so gentle with its subtle breeze,
    that there everyone will always be at ease.
    He was so proud of this place he did make,
    he decided to name it Lingering Lake.
    So if you are ready, it is you I will take,
    to this place in your mind, called Lingering Lake.

Untitled
by Rae Bronson - age 15

Lights going dim
Objects growing hazy.
Here I am,
Going to Eternal sleep.

Memories of my short life
Flashing before my eyes.
I am almost there,
To Eternal Sleep.

Flying like an angel
High above the Earth,
Above My body
This is Eternal Sleep.

Lights getting brighter
Coming back from Eternal Death.
I am here, sitting,
Thinking about life.

Youth Soaring Toward the Year 2001 By Making the Right Tough Choices Today
by Naomi A. Brookins

    Today, as we move rapidly toward the end of the 20th century, the times demand that you unleash all of your ability to think factually, subjectively, and reflectively about preparing to enter the years 2001.
    As I consistently broaden my horizon so as to reach and touch the lives of people from all walks of life, I find that many of you have gotten a firm grip on our changing world. You're thinking globally and acting locally. You've begun to consistently cultivate a searching mind that is conscious of itself in the world; conscious of seeing, hearing, feeling, thinking, speaking and knowing that you are our leaders for the future.
    Without a doubt, you are the future. It is alive today in your dreams, hopes, will to persevere, intelligent preparation, and your ability to work hard and move ahead step by step as you make the right tough choices.
    Now, have you even thought that even though many of you and your peers are soaring ahead, there are still too many who have lost the way. Their cries for a purpose for living can be heard throughout the world. Some even feel that our world is too dangerous to live in. They also feel that they do not have the ability to become positive people in such a world.
    I, too, feel that we have allowed our world to become shattered to a dangerously insecure status. Nevertheless, it is not just because of those who have lost their way. It is also because some of us, both young and old, have failed to move beyond our comfort zone by touching the lives of others and imparting a sense of love and responsibility.
    As you, the future, meditate on all that I've shared with you, invite others to join you as you continue to soar toward the year 2001.

September Dream
by Carol Brown

    The trees are beginning to stretch their naked arms towards the vivid blue sky as crackling red, yellow, and brown leaves fall in a gaily twirling dance to the ground. Busy squirrels are gathering nuts and jumping from branches to rooftops and back again as they prepare for the uncertain days ahead. The bold wind is spreading its cape to block the warmth of the waning sun and the arid smell of smoke drifts across the frigid sky as people stoke their first fire of the season. It is time once again for the kaleidoscope blanket of Fall to settle over the countryside.

Together Forever
by Jenny Brown - age 19

When I had something on my mind, you were always there.
Now you have something to worry about, it's my turn to care.
You can talk to me, I will listen and try to understand.
When you have a problem, we'll get over it hand in hand.

Sometimes you fell like you won't make it and your dreams are hard to follow.
Don't let this bad time get you down, hopefully there will be tomorrow.
When bad times head your way and your faith is starting to die,
I will be here to help, together until your troubles go by.

Together we will make it through the loneliness, things will be all right.
Some of the emptiness will go away, because we're side by side.
Now do you understand, do you really see?
I am telling you I will be here faithfully.

I will tell you again, straight from my heart-
Our hearts will always be together, never apart.
Anytime you need me I'll help in any way I can
To reminisce about the old times, again we'll make it hand in hand.

If in life we go our seperate ways and both have to leave;
I will never forget you, I'll treasure our memory.
Hopefully I won't have to go through that, I couldn't face that day.
For now I will hold on as tight as I can, just know there is a place in my heart
    you will always stay.

To: J.W.B.
In memory of Daniel L. Sebring

Untitled
by Nicole L. Brown - age 16

Listen to the sounds
of the morning
the chirping of the birds
and a little light breeze
while the sun comes up
over the mountain
by the shore of a sea
you hear water rushing
and the sea gulls gawking
If you look,
you'll see someone walking
in the peacefulness of
the early day
hoping the bad will go away
the only peaceful time
is when you hear no
city sounds
and listen to the music
of the nature hounds

Forgiving
by Sarah Lee Brown

So many times it has been said
By those who ought to know;
That children are the world's best
At hurting others so.

They giggle, laugh, and snicker
And call each other names;
They care not for one's feelings
And play such cruel games.

But children always make up
And soon all feelings mend;
Not so for us the adults
Who seem too strong to bend.

We too so cruel and hateful
For other show no care;
For us "forgive" and "make up"
Are really very rare.

If we be like the children
Forgiving all our foes;
Not long till in our peace we find
We haven't any woes.

My Heart
by Lauren Brownson - age 17

Her long hair is waving
As she walks by
And against my better judgement
I give an involuntary sigh

She holds the key to my heart
Within her slender hands
With every toss of her head
My attention she automatically demands

It's the secret of my heart
She knows none of this
I thank God for this fact
She, in this case, is in remiss

She'd build walls around her heart
If I inform her of this fact
Feeling, in some odd way,
I violated our friendship pact

I watch her dance through life
And I sit and watch in pain
Oh Fate what am I to do?
She's my heart's only love and only bane

Glimmers of Hope
by Amy Renee Broyles - age 14

Beyond the blue
There is black
And endless night
And in this night
Shines glimmers of hope
Billions of miles away

At night on Earth
This hope shines down upon us
It pierces through
The emptiness of space
And to those who watch
It shares its love

I am like space
There is hope in me
It too comes out at night
My hope is in my dreams
And my dreams are of love

Snow
by Malisa Buchanan - age 14

Snow is the best of all
You can say what you want
But I will not waver
For when snow falls
I think of little crystals
Falling to the ground like
A big white blanket
Oh what a sight it must be to see the
Snow capped mountains in the spring
When I see such a thing I think of
A child sleeping in the spring
Oh what a sight it must be to
See the snow capped mountains
In the spring but when the snow falls
It looks like to me like Mother Nature
Putting her child to sleep under a big
White blanket that is falling
Falling from the sky.

The Four Seasons
by Lauren E. Bucks - age 14

Fall winds are howling
rustling the leaves around,
the trees become bare.

Snowflakes falling down,
as children make a snowman,
frozen to the bone.

Buds begin to form
on almost empty trees,
grass begins to show.

Swimming in the pool
letting worries float away,
hoping it won't end.

Sunshine Kids
by Andrea Marie Bultje - age 14

Billy pulled Suzys hair, Suzy hit him hard.
Joey who was Billy's pal, came to lend a hand.
Jenny helped Suzy, along with Mary-Sue,
Frank and Jerry cheered them on until in came Mrs. Zoo.
The teacher screamed at the sight, fainted landed on the floor.
Julie ran to lock the door, the girls just HAD to win the war!
Cindy and Dean came running and tripped over Mrs. Zoo.
Joe came to help them even though his lip was blue.
Rachel had hit him, while he was cutting Stephens hair,
after he had tripped him in the isles over there.
Ingrid sat and read her book, she really didn't care-
she read and read and read and read, look up, she did not dare!
Brent was mad and took her book and threw it out of school-
now Ingrid cared, her book was gone, she just couldn't keep her cool!
She jumped on Brent, he fell down hard, she punched him in the gut-
she took his shoes, both of them, and with scissors cut.
The janitor unlocked the door, with his shiny key-
told the children to sit down,
and almost stepped on Mrs. Zoo who was still lying on the ground!
Billy said it was Suzys fault, Suzy said it was his-
Jenny was on Suzys side and Frank disagreed.
Dean yelled and Ingrid screamed.
They began to fight.
Joe cried and Cindy ran-
Who was really right?
The fight continued on and on,-
they could not break it up,
at the schools of SUNSHINE KIDS FOR TINY, TINY TOTS!!!!!!

One Last Question
by Lance Preston Burgess

Why is Mommy crying like that?
 Why is Daddy sad?
Why is Daddy hitting her?
 Did I make my Daddy mad?

Mommy is coming over me,
 She says that I'm the reason she got beat.
Mommy is crying as she lifts up her hand,
 After she hits me hard on the floor I land.

She isn't stopping, She is coming at me again,
 She says I'll get you for what you did young man,
What did I do? What did I Say?
 Why does this happen to me every day?

Mommy leaves the room after she lets her anger out,
 Daddy is back and all he does is shout.
He sees me on the floor covered in my own blood,
 I look up and ask why, He kicks me and says "Just because".

I start to cry and all he says is shut-up.
 For some reason my tears don't stop.
He kicks me and locks me in our closet in the hall,
 I can hear them both fighting through our paper thin walls.

One of them will kill me,
 I have accepted this fact.
No matter how much I love them,
 I can never change that.

So last night in my room I wrote a note,
 I put it in the left pocket of my old coat.
One last question is all it says,
 Mommy and Daddy will you love me when I'm dead?

Untitled
by Jamie Burke - age 14

Blackness fills the empty gaps
Between the stars that over lap
Behind the stars there lies a path
To the place where children laugh
That is where I wish to be
Way up in the cherry tree
So come and go up there with me
And soon you shall see
Just how happy you can be

Untitled
by Ron Burkhart

High upon a mountain top
there's a castle in the sky.
And in its only candle shop
lives the candle maker Fry.

There he toils all the day
to create wonders made of wax.
There he wastes his life away
for there's so much that he lacks.

"No time for love or life
there's always work to do.
Much less to have a wife
who keeps a watch on you."

"No time to rear a child
no matter how cute he be.
Even if he drove me wild
nor if he looked like me."

These words he always speaks
while working through the night.
For nothing is what he seeks
and in this he thinks he's right.

So in this little candle shop
that hangs there in the sky.
There lives on this mountain top
the lonesome candle maker Fry.

A Walk Down Ocean Avenue
by Matt Burleson - age 18

As I walk down the road just outside of town,
And view the flower fields and farm fields,
On either side of me,
I see how beautiful and rural,
The country side still is.
The scent of some of the surrounding flower fields,
Fills the air like a fragrant perfume,
Blowing gently on the breeze.
The town is just nearby but still in the distance,
Giving the valley an undisturbed quality,
That serves to pacify those who walk by.
The breeze is refreshing as I walk toward surf beach,
Cooling the air in the afternoon sun.
The farm fields are almost ready for harvest,
While others are just being planted,
And bees pollinate the rest of the fields.
It's a beautiful walk down this road in mid-summer,
Filled with a lovely charm,
That can only be had on one season of the year.
Which is to be welcomed and enjoyed as the delicacy that it is.

Treasures

Cherished Memories
by Jamie Elaine Burnett - age 15

When I was born you were there,
when I took my first steps you cheered me on,
when my trike became a bike,
you taught me to have courage after each fall.
When I started school you said a prayer,
hoping that I never give up.
When I did something good,
you always had a smile on your face.
Even when I did something wrong,
I knew you still cared.
Now that you are not here to give me
the love and support when I need it the
most, I look back and remember
all the moments we shared.
And with a tear in my eye I cherish
each moment ten times more.
And every goal I accomplish in life I
owe it all to you because you taught
me to never give up. You gave me
the love and support that I'll carry
throughout life even though they maybe
just memories now.

Why?
by Judy A. Burton

I argue not with your death,
Only with the manner of your dying.
You who lived such a tragic life,
Deserved an easier going.

Born in tears and raised in sorrow,
You should not have had to die in such pain.
Was Life so enamored of you
Death had to tear you from her reign?

(They say it happens often,
The Master learns to love the slave,
The Executioner his victim,
The Sovereign his knave.)

What is the price for a gentle death?
Neither your suffering or my sorrow moved
            impervious Life to pity,
Nor did my screams of rage that shook the skies.
What was it then that finally caused Death
            to come release you?
Was it my impotent whispers as I groveled on the ground,
Or was it all the agony in your eyes?

Did you - or did we - finally pay enough,
Or did Life find another toy?
I will always wonder - really,
Was it all to make Death a joy?

Did someone wiser than us all
Know you would not give up anything?
Sometimes the slave also loves the Master;
The knave will kneel to kiss the Sovereign's ring.

Always There
by Jennifer Burton - age 15

You are always there to comfort,
Always there to sympathize.
You wrap me in your arms and take
    away the hurt.
You have the best advice,
And freely hand it out.
I know sometimes I do not express
My gratitude and love.
I smell the sweet aroma of dinner
    on the stove,
And watch you clean the house.
I hear the comfort in your voice,
And your touch brings me hope
And belief in myself.
I taste the salty tears
As they pour down my face.
You are always there to wipe them
    away,
You always help, in any case.
I thank you for your gentle touch,
    and kindly spoken words.
Your encouragement through times
    of sadness
Bring me strong hope and courage.
You are always there to lift me up,
You never put me down.
I thank you for your endless love,
For picking me up off the ground.
I thank you, mother,
Because you are always there.

Red Comes And Goes
by Stacy Denise Bush - age 17

The man's existence is lifeless--
Full of unhappiness and grief.
Ethan's wife is sickly, weak--
Her face is pale.
Where they live the weather is cold--
There is no red.

A woman comes wearing red--
She is seeing that the home is lifeless.
The winter there is cold--
The people she lives with have such grief.
She cares for the woman who's face is pale--
Only the face grows more wane and weak.

The man's love for another makes him weak--
His love is for the one who wears red.
Not for his wife, who is pale--
He seeks a person without grief--
Who is not cold.

The house is cold--
All three are weak.
Full of grief--
But, saddest of all, there's no more red.
All is lifeless--
The snow is pale.

Red cheeks now pale--
They are cold.
The forest is lifeless--
While the man and woman are weak.
Burning is the color of red--
Suicide and grief.

The End
by Rebecca L. Burris

Life goes on,
    day by day,
Taking with it people,
    along the way.
We never seem to stop,
    to think to care,
To wonder if tomorrow,
    will really be there.
And one of these days,
    we'll soon find out,
Exactly what our lives,
    have been all about.

For My Sisters
by Kathleen E. Buskey - age 19

We reach for one another
When the tears fall like rain
We lean on one another
To help lessen the pain
We look to one another
For a comforting smile
We come to one another
Just to talk for awhile
We grow with one another
Learning from our mistakes
We protect one another
No matter what it takes
We walk with one another
Holding hands along the way
We share with one another
The events of every day
We dance with one another
With the sun against our face
We pray with one another
Asking god for all his grace
We cry with one another
When the world's not on our side
We laugh with one another
On a roller coaster ride
We don't tell one another
As often as we should
That we love one another
As only a sister could.

The Skies
by Dana Buxton - age 14

    The clouds go by like rolling thunder,
The rain comes down in tears
    The hail and sleet pound down so hard they feel like
swords and spears,
The sun shines bright like a flowering rose,
    The sky so blue like ice it melts to form a frozen
pose,
The stars twinkle soft and pure,
    The darkest night like fright and fear,
Cause the day and night skies.

Aspirations
by Melanie S. Buzard

The moon cast a silver hue
    on the darkened Earth.
Drenched in night sweats,
    the heartbeat of the ruddy
    sod declared a mournful fall.
The lusty soil produced a
    fearful wail
At the loss of the only sun.
POUNDING, POUNDING, the pulse
    of the Earth
Can be felt underfoot through
    the unflinching ground.

The Wind
by Trisha Campbell - age 14

The wind is rushing everywhere,
Blowing through my golden hair,
Rushing everywhere my heart desires,
Rushing through the vast blue skies
Flying with the eagle
Soaring high.
How I wish that I could fly.

Suddenly the wind stops.
The sky turns gray,
As the wind rushes away,
"Come back," I cry.
"I'll come again another day," the wind sighs.
For now the wind must go,
And I must hurry home.
Till the wind comes back, I know
That I'd love to fly,
Up with the wind,
In the skies so high.

My Angel
by Diane Campomizzi - age 17

You are the angel I know in my heart,
I feel scared and unsure when we are apart,
I need you near to comfort me when I am
    scared,
To let me know someone cares,
When I feel trapped and lost you lead my way;
    whether it is night or day.

You are the angel I know in my heart,
With you I know I'll never fall apart,
When I'm confused you light the way to
    make me see that I am okay.
When times are rough you are there to
    help me through my despair,
Can't you see with you by me I'm in
    no misery.

Blossom
by Kristin Carlino - age 15

I sit and stare deep into the soul
    of this awkward flower.
I see it smiling
A smile of pain and solitude.
It's holding back.
I plead desperately
For it to open up to me,
Yet is just sits and stares
And a tear rolls down
Its soft petals
And finds its way
To the soggy soil beneath.
Sinking into the ground
It leaves us,
Forever.
The roots of the awkward flower
Begin to drink from the ground
Moistened by that tear.
And the flower begins to grow and thrive,
Living off of its own sorrows.
As I peer into its soul again
I see myself this time.
My glowing eyes, and natural smile, and strong hands
Envelop the soul of the flower.
Together we drink and grow from our tears
This time as one existence, and one life.

A Teacher's Treasures
by Sandra Carlson

A teacher's treasures cannot always be measured
By worldly wealth or costly collections.
My heart's dearest moments trace back through the years
As page after page of joy and tears
Fill a book, wrapped not in shiny gold,
But with the sunshine of the soul.

A hug, a smile spread out as wings,
An engagement ring from a gumball machine.
"I love you" notes print my memories
With an art gallery dandelion bouquets,
Hand-hewn pot holders, cookies "Me and Mom" baked.

Yet the most precious treasures I recall
Were not even seen at all.
The lasting lessons my students taught me
Are my trophy for the world to see.

Scrapes from the knees and bruises of the soul
When a puppy friend dies or Grandma's growing old;
All their fears give to me, I am taught HONESTY
By keeping me accountable for my deeds.

PATIENCE, PERSISTENCE in teaching a new skill,
FIRMNESS for the child who is strong-willed.
The laughter, the fun, their playing keeps me YOUNG,
And the treasure given to me proudly produces SPONTANEITY!

When a child loves unconditionally and free,
I am taught how to FORGIVE, as they forgive me.
My crown of jewels is the LOVE I receive;
These lasting treasures are my legacy!

Mirror
by Amanda Carpenter - age 14

My tears are just a spoonful of the ocean,
Salty waters seep from eye's all around,
My troubles seem so shallow compared to theirs.
They drown in their pain,
I only hurt a little.
I'm afraid to look, to take in the anguish,
I'm scared to feel the real feel,
Scared to focus on the eyes.
Their hearts are breaking,
Their minds are wasted,
I look in the mirror and
I see hope for my tomorrow
They have no mirrors to see hope in.
They are lost like a child's favorite toy
Are we not all children in the eyes of God?
They should not be rejected,
They need the love we take for granted,
Mirror's show us nothing, mere appearances.
Mirrors shatter, jagged, broken pieces cut through us,
Like their stares.
We pray and hope for a better tomorrow,
Yet we ignore their cries, the pain is invisible to us,
Or, do we just chose to ignore them?
It is a loss they feel, it is a pain we must understand,
Mirrors are deceiving.

Every Girl Freams of a Fairytale
by Ashley Carter - age 16

Roses sent with a card unsigned
 a day in a beautiful white dress
Every night dreaming the same dream
 dreaming the dream of a fairytale
Wanting a Romeo
 waiting for his existence
Waiting, wanting, wishing on a star
 just for those three little words
Hoping that glass slipper will fit
 hoping midnight wont come too soon
Hoping he'll change from a beast to a beauty
 dreading the day the last rose peddle falls
Dreading the clock to strike twelve
 waiting to go on that magic carpet ride
Wanting to stay on land forever

Yes, every girl dreams of a fairytale.

Broken
by Artilee Cassin - age 15

Look what you have done to me,
your foolish game you play are
tearing me apart. Despite my
rage what do I get? A Broken
Heart.
I was a wild eyed child of the
sun and you believed in me, taught
me about love, promised you'd stay
forever.
We were always together, but our lives
are forever changed and the more
you change the less you feel. I had
to let go, then I lost my best friend.
I sensed my loss as we died, but
all I could do was sit and cry.
Now nothing is important to me, there
is no connection to myself. Intoxicated
with madness I forget to forget me,
and I fell in love with my sadness
I see now that all things must
surely come to an end. I must
have been a fool to think that
we'd last forever.

Only A Few Days
by Carmalita Alvina Castaneda - age 17

The last few days we have spent together
They have seemed like forever
If falling in love could be expressed with one word
It would be your name, in which many have heard
We played in the rain until a ray of sunlight shone
We danced all night while we were alone
As your soft gentle hand raised to my face
Those memories of you I cannot erase
The next day as the sun shone bright
We picnicked in the field and played happily, until there was no light
When we were alone in the night
You kissed my lips and those feelings that rushed in I did not fight
The next morning as I had awaken from a dream
I spoke with you, but your sorrow I had not seen
You then told me, "I have to go"
"I care for you more than you will ever know"
"In just a few days I fell in love with you"
"Now I must go and that I really don't want to do"
As I sat in tears and thought about things in a number of ways
I realized I had, too, fallen in love in only a few days
As my hours went on
I realized this is the love that I have waited for, for so long
As you left me that night
As we stood in the moonlight
You promised, "I will be back for you"
I asked, "Until then what should I do?"
"Just remember those last few days we have spent together"
"I will be back, then it will last forever"
As he walked quickly away, I called, "I love you in a number of ways"
"I, too, love you in only a few days"

No Name
by Stefanie Cedro - age 16

Perfect, it was at first.
My home, inside my mother, so warm and peaceful.
I had everything I needed.
Food, shelter, a mother, comfort, what more could I want?
Yet, I anticipated life so much!
I could not wait for the wonderful world to come.
I thought someday I would have a brother, a sister, possibly a puppy,
Maybe someday I would savor the delectable flavors of ice-cream and chocolate.
One day I would learn of hate, sadness, and true love.
In essence, I wanted to live life.
But then my little world went up in flames.
Pain, suffering, excruciation, torment!
Why wouldn't anyone help me? Did I do something wrong to deserve this agony?
My life then ended, and why you ask?
Well, my mother who didn't know me, didn't want me, and decided to murder me.
To the outside world, I was not a person.
Was I a person - What do you think?
I never had a chance because
I never had a name.

Flame
by Lindsay Carapella - age 13

As I watch the flame burn,
Flickering,
Shining bright
I see that it is scared like the rest of us.
Scared of dying,
Scared of loosing faith,
Scared of being shut out from the rest of the world.
We think that he is brave and strong,
But inside that orange glow is a heart on fire.
A heart in need of love,
In need of a soul mate or kindred spirit.
And I watch the flame die as night falls and I realize that we are all the same.
We are one,
We are a flame.

The Moon of The Night Sky
by Amy Cha - age 13

The moon of the night sky,
Glows up very high.
In very different shapes,
It seems to be fake.
It glows so bright,
It may blind your sight,
If you stare at it long enough.

All the stars above,
Surrounds you with love.
Clouds clear up,
You find a cup,
But it may be the moon,
That caught your eye.
Drinking from a cup and saying goodbye!

Untitled
by Abby Chandler - age 16

Was there ever a time you felt you had no friends.
Life seemed dull and there was no way to make amends.
Everyone seemed so distant and unkind.
There was no one to trust; no way to unwind.

The skies were alive with color,
But your heart was grey and un-a-flutter.
Wherever you looked, all you felt was sorrow.
You didn't feel like seeing another tomorrow.

Your body was there but your soul had died.
Your life was being lived through someone else's eyes.
No one seemed to care or see the hurt you had inside
Help was needed, but you did not want to ask.

People wouldn't believe: you of all people;
Everyone would just laugh.

Prayer For Daddy
by Janice M. Chang, J.D., Ph.D.

Sleep peacefully and quietly in the Lord
for you have earned your comforting rest.
Your gentle demeanor, friendliness, wisdom, wit and charm
remain in my memory.

Your intellect, business savvy, investment sense,
and hard work shines through in my life.
Your dedication to Mommy, Donald and Me is remarkable,
through our times of growth in spirit and in stature.

Your support and encouragement continues to be an inspiration to me
in my educational and professional career goals.
Your faith in a loving God is evidenced by your
generous support of your churches, and alumni associations.

You have shown your dedication to further God's work on earth.
The respect, love and care you showed others
throughout your life at school, work, church, and with your family
is reflected in your family, and your circle of friends.

Your life has touched many, in different ways,
for those who are with us, and for those who are yet to come.
Our memories of you are preserved in family photographs
and snapshots of special moments with you, in our lives.

We are all lucky to have had you in our lives,
to know you, and to love you.
We cherish those memories with you.
For future generations, you will live on.

Your prosperity is evidenced
by the wealth of loving family and friends
who are with you, and with us
in person and in spirit.

Our faith is ever strong,
and we will see you once again with smiles and laughter,
when the Lord comes to reunite us all
in Our Kingdom in Heaven.

East Coast Holidays With Relatives
by Sandra I. Chang

"Ah-Mei, have some more lobster."
At my aunt's encouragement,
My uncle scooped some more onto my plate;
Pointless to protest that I already had plenty,
Since they were eager to give me the most of the best.

That's what they call me--Ah-Mei--meaning
"Little Sister" in Taiwanese.
In their minds, I'll always be the little one.
"Ah-Mei, let's go for a walk to town," my uncle suggests.
"We'll drop by the ice cream store with the 48 flavors."

The dew-decked grass dampened my toes,
Droplets seeping through the seams of my sandals--
A delicious tingling in my feet; I smile
As we continued through the fresh, leaf-paved path
Under the high green archway of clasping branches.

My mom, aunt, uncle, and I stroll through the Princeton campus;
I learn to understand their unspoken language of love.
Here, 3000 miles from home and even more from their homeland,
There's a meeting of hearts
That unites two cultures, two generations.

The Sea Is Alive
by Debra Anne Chapman

The sea is free.
It foams and bubbles.
Slurple, slurple, living jello,
molding into the giant form of Mother Earth,
Filled with species, descendants of ancestral birth.
Forming, floating, swaying, moaning,
Alive, alive, alive.
A legacy of time-a viewpoint that's divine.
Spirits swirling harmonically in patterns,
corals, sea anemones, and salmon.
Jellyfish of delightful designs
Sea porpoises, seals, walruses, whales.
Beautiful angelic heavenly blue
gigantic waterway of greenish hue.
The sea is a child of ancient years
reflecting its sunlight beams like thousands of mirrors.
Wave pool to swimmers, a vacationers haven.
Waterway of ancient civilization and also today.
Life giving thread to be nurtured and loved
Appreciate the splendor and be thankful
a spectacular time capsule of secrets undiscovered.
Explored by divers and filled with mystic creatures.
Her secrets and beauty are timeless forever.

The Marlboro Man
by Barbara Anne Chatham

What was once a cigarette pack
is now a crumbled tombstone
in the soil of a plant at the mall.

An ex-smoker, I lean down to resurrect it
curious to read its engraving.
A movement startles me
and through green branches I spot him
over by the "Chick Filet" counter.

    I steal ficus oxygen and steady myself
    in leafy shelter to watch another ex-habit.

He props on the counter to gain someone's attention.
Like a Marlboro Light.

    Subconscious need for nicotine, I search the pack.
    Tobacco ghosts tantalize my senses.

The lean man flirts with a young woman
who smiles from over the counter.

    I crave a smoke.
    Smoothed out, the wrapper reads
    "Marlboro Lights", my favorite.

He offers her a cigarette.
She accepts.
She looks young, habit hungry.

    My fidgety fingers flip the pack over.
    Its epitaph gives the Surgeon General's warning.

Maybe someone should warn her
about the dangers of smoking.

I draw him in and exhale the thought,
replace the paper monument on its gravesite.
And walk away.

Half Empty or Half Full?
by Jennifer Chapman - age 17

I don't like much of what I see.
You ask me "Is the glass half empty or half full?"
Well, I'm sick of the government's bull
the politicians' greed and lies
I hate hearing of churches burning against the night sky.
A lot of people are struggling to survive
others shake their heads and say "What a shame." and continue to thrive.
I'm sick of crack whores willing to do anything for their precious drug,
people caught up in robberies getting killed by another thug,
innocent people dying because of domestic disputes or other violent means.
Why is it that some people just can't see the forest for the trees?
Is it because they are unaware?
Or because they just don't care.
Kids are killing kids, acting as adults and having kids
Most everything the media reports makes me sick;
like the madman shooting his gun and raging like a bull,
Now you tell me is the glass half empty or half full?

He Could've Stayed If He Wanted To
by Jessica Cheek - age 15

A young teen sits on the top of a hill
Where the birds and the trees are always still.
She thinks of some times when things were bad.
When all she needed was the presence of her dad.
The first time a boy broke her fragile heart.
When she got her hand stuck in a shopping cart.
All the good things he wasn't there to see.
Like her part in the school play as a honeybee.
The magical night when she went to prom,
The only one there to share it was her mom.
She imagines all the future things to come,
The many days when a friend's life will be done.
Her graduation and wedding day,
In the hospital where her new baby will lay.
All these things he could've been here to see.
Times when a dad's hugs and kind words are key.
He could've stayed if he wanted to.
He figured he had better things to do.
Now she looks up at the sky,
And whispers to him her good-bye.
Her father is gone, she knows that now.
She'll get along okay, though she's not sure how.

Sadness
by Alicia Chesney - age 13

Let it all go. Sadness is a mother crying for her dead baby.
Sadness is being alone, alone, alone.
Let it all go. Sadness is millions of tears making an ocean.
Sadness is a bruised soul and a broken spirit.
Let it all go. Sadness is coming home from work and finding no one there.
Sadness is a hospital filled with dying people.
Let it all go.
Sadness is here.
Someone is crying
Someone is dying
Grief feasts,
Tearing into human souls.
And laughs unforgivingly into the night.

Summer 1997 Honorable Mentions

If I Only Had A Pen
by Nicole Chieco - age 12

If I only had a pen,
Oh, all the things I could do.
I could write about pigs that sing,
And cows that go cock-a-doodle do,
And birds that swim and fish that fly,
And goats that eat pumpkin pie,
And horses that baa,
And sheep that neigh,
And rabbits that bark and also say,
We are all different but we are all friends,
That's all there is my story ends.

Untitled
by Elan Church - age 13

Love is like a rose,
Delicate and beautiful to hold on to.
Yet when you hit a thorn,
You're left with a void inside you.

Your soul is like glass,
Now shattered by the sorrow.
Your broken heart cannot last,
You won't make it until tomorrow.

Now the tears come,
And they echo when they fall.
A question in your mind,
"Should I end it all?"

A hand on your shoulder,
Wind spreads the glass as it blows.
Your soul and heart are now restored,
And in the other hand—A rose.

First Love
by Elizabeth Clark

Will there ever be another
Like the one and only first?
The innocence, the purity
True love, the best, the worst.

The luxury of memories
Perfection, barring none
How could something else compare
To the first, that special one?

Less baggage weighing on the souls,
More room for lust so sweet
Treasure chests of platinum
Combined with passion's heat.

Electric hands, magnetic cells
Sparks from high to low
Wild energies, young auras meld,
Waves rise and rivers flow.

Can there ever be another
Like your one and only first?
The innocence, the purity
True love, the best, the worst.

A Perspective You Wouldn't Expect
by Miles Clark - age 16

I beg the man to open the window of the strange thing we ride in
With joy I see him comply
And I stick my long snout out the strange,
still clear opening that wasn't there before
My tongue lapping in the brisk, speed-induced breeze
As I take in the world the best way I know how.

I smell the wind, as my master and I whisk past the big black thing
It rolls through my nostrils as I dissect it in a way only I can do
This is a tired, old wind
Its's drifted through many different ports
It's seen the dense,
dark jungles where wilderness is still a very lethal reality
It's seen the beautiful "blue" lagoons as mere specks in the great,
trackless oceans
It's seen the pastures where spotted cows stood idly
Its seen the great, snow-capped mountains far to the west
Its's seen things I have yet to see for myself

The wind is so free, a freedom I sometimes covet
But these times are few and far between
For the wind is alone, so alone
It can never feel the warmth of another creature
Any more that I can see those strange things called "colors"
It can never be invited into dwell in the house of a dear man, my dear master
He asked only to be guarded from the little ladies walking down the street
in return.

People often put down my social standing,
claiming that mine is a life live pathetically
But if you excuse the idiotic baby-talk sometimes
directed towards my person
(and the veterinary appointments, of course)
The life of a Dog is surprisingly good one.

Mornings in My Room
by Shannon Clark - age 14

When I woke this morning,
I say these sights are true.
I got up to brush my hair,
Looked up into the mirror,
And saw that you where there.
Though it was a picture,
I see it every day.
When I close my eyes I hear you,
Your sweet voice asks me to stay.
Though I do not want to,
I leave to do my chores,
I come back every evening,
And tell you I am yours.
Then I go to sleep,
Your smiling face on my mind.
I know when I wake up,
The same sights, I will find.

Reflections
by Alice Clausen

What is this noble piece
of mind
    That finds its way through
a quiet time
    It seems to start from
a picture, behind the eyes
    in a shadow
of loyalties and royalties
    and
a time gone by.

Tribute
by Kiersten Clements - age 21

Through a shadow of doubt; you are my light...
When my path seems uncertain; it's your hand I choose to take...
A trace of bitter-sweet sentiment touches my crimson soul...
Our authentic bond remains as enigma to those which heed its tale...
My defender, thou art my being; you are indeed my sanity in this world of craziness...

Daughter
by Donald Cochran

Baby girl, be it so - Daughter of my dream,
I shall love you without a doubt and beyond the most extreme.

A pleasure it is, it brings me great joy - to know that you're there;
A bitter sweet thought, and oh what a thought...because you have always cared.

Often, life has spaced us miles apart - my heart be always near.
I know I haven't told you, but I must now say how I hold you:
You are special to me, in my heart and in my mind...
As special as a Daddy/Daughter should be;
I love thee - to infinity...

I am a traveling soldier, a father plainly you see;
Moving about the world, to keep our country free.
I am caring, trusting, loving, sincere - wishing often
That my Darling Daughter was here.

If my answers to your questions are not clearly,
I was merely negotiating life's circumstances.

It's refreshing since my hand is renewed,
Darling Daughter don't allude...
Daddy loves you.

And if ever it appeared I forgot,
Please know that my heart did not.

My Earth
by Cara Coleman - age 13

I am connected to the
rolling surf of crystal waters
tumbling like autumn leaves.
I have a bond with the
waves of grass that never seem
to stop.
I feel a friend with the
flower, blooming wherever it fills
with happiness.
I am touched by the
moving grey rock of sea lost
its own time.
I watch never ending stories
of the white wonders in the
sky.
I see myself in the secret
songs of the earth.
I am moved by the
winds whispering me on
my way.

Sandcastle Of Thought
by Heather Congdon - age 19

Build up the sand
in a castle of thought
wait for the waves
to wash over it
eroding the moat,
but massaging your mind
when the whole thing
is torn down
and you can think no more
be thankful it takes
a while for high tide
to come in.

An Old Man's Lament
by Michael R. Conkel

From the dusty archives of my mind
Comes drifting memories most unkind
They haunt me now as I grow old
As I grow weak they grow more bold
They come like specters in the night
And fill my heart with shame and fright
Of those I've hurt, and tears they've wept
Of lies I told and promises unkept
I rationalize the good I've done
But it compensates not even one
Of those I've harmed with word or deed
Or walked away and left in need
Youth in itself is not excuse
For thoughtlessness and moral abuse
Had I known then what I now know
That what you reap is what you sow
Would I have chose a kinder path
And not be alone to face God's wrath

"Phoenix"
by Todd Cook, Jr. - age 18

Salvaged from the blast, through my looking glass,
Removed from silence and reborn in stone.
After the flash, to stop what's come to pass.
Pick up the pieces of beautiful Rome
Disintegrated, emaciated.
Julius lost the war inside his head.
Emancipated. Annihilated.
Washed out by the flood, everyone fell dead.
As the kingdom comes, the walls come undone--
All your bridges burned and towers too tall.
Crashing, crashing down... The slope of God's frown.
For your lack of faith, he won't stop your fall.
That's when I'll appear, for I'll still be here
To be your wings and to conquer your fear.

Condemn
by Justin Cord - age 16

Do not condemn me for who I am
I was made with imperfections,
I have feelings
I have affections.

Do not judge me on the way I dress
or the style of my hair,
when I pass by
do not stare.

How can you judge
a person you do not even know,
with your false accusations
that bring a person low.

How can you spread
those rumors that are not true,
when the person doing the wrong
is you.

Street Light
by Petrani Erema Cornelius - age 20

I'se been so tir'd--so tir'd, so weak
My life is stormy and so bleak
No strength to walk, can't lift ny head
My self esteem's contrasting red
My life is hanging by a thread

I beg all day, don't have no shame
There's no one else but me to blame
The days are getting shorter, see
And further life won't wait for me
And further life won't wait for me

In garbage cans I find my food
I'se sometimes in a rotten mood
Some people cared, they gave me gifts
All which I traded in for spliffs
Or drinks that spun my eyes around
That left me helpless on the ground
Unconscious is the state I'se found

They beat and rape me, cut my face
And send me off in poor disgrace
Performed a service, got no pay
Yet I returned the following day
It wasn't as my dear "friends" said
I'se so naive, I got mislead
I'se so naive, I shook my head
I'se so naive, better off dead!

Don't Forget
by Christina Correia - age 14

Don't ever forget me, don't forget what we've been through,

The months that seemed only like days, were longer than we both thought,

We shared the moments that will never mean much to other, but to us they were everything,

We went through times that we thought we wouldn't make it through, but we've made it this far and there's many more days to go through,

Don't forget me in a few years,

When you have a new life with someone else,

I want you to remember me through out the years as someone who spent many precious moments with you and I want you to know it was because of you we always made it through.

Life
by Josephine Cottone - age 14

The feeling I felt when I saw what I saw
   I saw what was happening.
The feeling in my heart that I can't be with you
      anymore.
I just can't let go because I love you more and more.

   But then when I turn I see
My friend of a lifetime
   Who will always be on my side
Till the day has gone by.

   Forever in my heart she will stay
But yet you will fade away.

In His Company
by Barry Cox - age 17

As the grass leaps up around her
She begins to kiss the ground.
Through her loneliness she notices
The empty stares all around.

As the night closes in around him
He sits against the wall.
Cries out to an unknown god
Shackled with his ball.

Finding His grace seems dim
When our hearts cannot cry.
When we see His love we'll be free
In Him we'll understand why.

Now true peace is understood
And emptiness is no more.
They've found a friend in someone
They never knew before.

Why can't we seem to understand
The gift His grace gives?
Instead we turn our hearts to stone
And never see he lives.

Guided with strings throughout our lives
Our hearts are far from Him.
We walk on streets that have no name
And fall in love with Him.

"The 16th Minute"
by Diane Draper Cox

I didn't want anyone to know about you.
I protected you, I did the best I could do.
I was confused, I was both happy and sad.
What I did wasn't right but it wasn't all bad.
I didn't want you to be secretly whisked away.
Not given a chance for your star to shine on a new day.
I cleaned up my life the best I could.
I wanted everything for you to only be good.
You didn't ask for or deserve anyone such as me.
That's why I made sure you'd get anything you'd ever need.
And when you finally arrived, I loved you for a
life time.
For 15 minutes, I lived for and loved forever,
this baby of mine.
But on the 16th minute, I gave you a gift
uncompared by any other.
For in that minute, I handed you to
your adoptive father and mother.

Alone
by Alecia Crain - age 14

The great mountain is looming;
the gray and dooming look, evident.
A notice me aurora seeping from its inner
    walls.
Soon its over me, forcing me to look,
forcing me, forcing me, forcing me.
Forcing me to remember; to bring back
memories.
Forcing the vivid recognition into my eyes.
Forcing me to remember; something I
want to forget, to push into the walls of
my inner being.
I feel the pain now, something has struck me.
The memory always so near, lurking,
awaiting for a vulnerable time.
Awaiting.
Suddenly, I feel a hand on me - I scream
The memory!
Oh God, please stop this pain and quit
forcing me, forcing me.
It stops.
Now there's only black
I'm stuck in the deep, deep black by
myself; no one near, no one to understand.
By myself, no one near.

i am
by Erika Gail Crisp - age 17

i am strong but weak
i feel the dragon in my heart
i touch the sun when i am cold
i worry there's no place for me to hide
i cry but no tears fall
i am strong but weak

i pretend to be different people
i feel my soul fly but leave me behind
i touch my mind
i worry i worry too much
i cry for the unfortunate
i am strong but weak

i understand life is not easy
i say that's okay
i dream of unity
i try to understand hate
i hope i never do
i am strong but weak

Creativity, or Am I Alone Insane?
by Paul J. Croce

The day is lazy except for my thoughts that flick incessantly from topic to next, without lighting long enough to ponder seriously upon any one of them.

Nothing solved, nothing gained, but monotony and boredom are beaten in the moments of such activity.

Others might consider such activity foolish, inane, time wasted, or a sign of instability, lack of direction or resolve, or an irrational debasement of will and character...any of these maladies, or perhaps a forewarning of insanity.

But then, some of them muse incessantly about the above, and after long thought, they hide behind the fear of making such accusation by deliberating all sorts of affects and effects, results of many varieties, possible or probable, likely or unlikely.

During their extended period of rapid, incessant flicking of thought, how many wonder the same question I have had, and by their repetition may also ask of themselves,

    CREATIVITY OR AM I ALONE INSANE?

Shadows
by Lillis Cruz

I feel the shadow of fear upon my heart, the pain, the
agony of a mother's cry.
Help me Lord, I pray, help me. I need your strength
more today.
I need someone to take a stand and right the wrong
that's been done to me.
The tears I shed are for my children's cries. I clutch
my heart, the pain within.
I dream many dreams at night. Thank you Lord for giving
me the sight to see the beauty inside me.
The enemy's fierce, but your wrath is greater.
Through you, I will overcome the shadows of my life.
Lord, by your precious blood, I cast the shadows out.
I cast away the demons of hell, I bless those that
curse me.
I thank you Lord, for everything thou has bestowed
upon me.
Oh, shadows of darkness and fear, I rebuke you in Jesus
mighty name.
I cast you out, you demons, you lies.
Lord, hear my prayer, Lord Jesus, oh how my love flows
through thee.

Is Our Love Still There?
by Melissa Cuipylo - age 13

You said you would wait forever,
But now you're far away.
You said you'd never leave me,
Until came your dying day.
This girl called me today.
She said you took your love away.
I know we're going through a rough time,
But are you still truly mine?
I cried for awhile,
It hurt really bad.
I'm not sure whether I should accept it,
Or if I should be mad?
Then I talked to you,
The sound of your gentle voice,
Made me believe you,
As if I had no other choice.
But when you said it wasn't true,
You're voice sounded strange.
Is our wondrous love still there?
Or did the time make it change?
I know I still love you,
But do you still love me?
I guess time will tell,
So we'll just wait and see...
But something makes me believe it's over.

Encounters in Microwave Time
by Richard Curren

Rise and eat,
Drink and go.
Walk on path.
Sky is blue,
Grass is green,
Trees are tall.
Mellow brook.
Meet on chance.
Look on talk,
Passions rise.
Tête-á-tête,
Fashions rip!
Grass crushed!!.
Pleasures had.!.!.!
Lie and touch;
Rise and go.
Home and door,
Bed and rest,
Sleep and dream.
Strangers still...

As It Passes by
by Shallee Cutler - age 13

It rustles through the trees
and stirs up their leaves,
as it passes by.
It laughs with a mighty roar
that blows the waves ashore,
as it passes by.
It blows with all its might,
and helps lift birds into flight,
as it passes by.
It flows through the air,
then stirs up your hair,
as it passes by.
It moves the clouds around
so the rain will fall down,
as it passes by.
If your heart listens well,
great stories will it tell,
as the wind passes by.

Nothing Matters?
by Melissa Kay Daeges

i never take things for granted,
i knew what i had, before it
was gone, it doesn't matter, if
your blind or not, there are things
in life, that you just can't stop.

i never held all my feelings inside,
i knew that it'd kill me, before
i died, it doesn't matter, if you
cry or not, you can't avoid this
pain, despite what you thought.

i never believed that i wasn't right,
i knew what i wanted, before it
was time, it doesn't matter, if
your right or wrong, just give life
your all, and you'll become strong.

i never forgot to show that i care,
i knew what love meant, before
you were there, it doesn't matter, if
you knew or not, said that you
loved me, wish you hadn't forgot.

i never felt that you'd abandon me,
i knew what we had, before it was
our destiny, it doesn't matter, if
you care or not, i will always be
yours, the soulmate you once sought.

On Death
by Deanna B. Dahl

When Great-Grandma died
Where did she go?
How did she get there?

I know they said she went to heaven
To be with God, the Angels and Papa Martin
But I saw her there in the casket
Sleeping so peacefully,
A beautiful smile on her face
So where is she now?

In heaven, in heaven, I know, but
Nine months later I stand by the grave
I listen to them talk about Ascension.
What is that?
Ascension means arisen.
Has Great-Grandma arisen?
Then where is she?

I know her soul has gone safely to heaven to be
With God and the Angels and other souls.
She has arisen and watches over me.

I love you always!

*Written for Angela on
Ascension Day - May 8, 1997
by Grandma Deanna*

Building Walls
by Kimberly Ann D'Alonzo

Somewhere there is a wonderful place where
lovers seek to find refuge from the
outside world. I'm frightened by its
wonders, and hide within the ugliness
of myself. Because surrounding this
wonderful place there is no harmony or
safety. It is filled with sorrow caused but
untruth and hurtful games. And in
its surroundings only the strong survive. To
be strong you must build around
yourself solid walls of stone and steel. I've
been developing the strongest of
walls and have trapped myself within my
loneliness. Never allowing myself to feel
pain, but never allowing myself into that
wonderful place called love. And now
only the willing and kind can brake through
my walls. But the question is, can they
survive within them.

Alexander's Castle
by James Robert Daniels

...The town turned out to help or watch; people brought food and water, and the scene was like a barn-raising for God. The stable for this flock was well-built, with tower, nave and chancel all crafted of native Douglas fir; the arched girders were all worked by hand. It was never meant to travel, though. Two iron rods with clamps were installed clear through the twenty-by-forty-foot Gothic structure to hold the walls together. The church was jacked up on all sides and placed on rollers. Horses turned a windlass, as on a ship the anchor is weighed, and pulled the whole building along. It was severely wracked in transit, as the ground was rough and unlevel. The iron rods were left through the nave in the end, for fear that they alone protected the walls from collapse. The bell was lashed securely in the tower for the move; it was a precious possession, a rune of Christian ideals. Mary Tucker told the Rector the story, while her husband directed the work:

"It was a gift from a sea captain, in 1871, donated on the condition that the parson ring it whenever he heard a ship's whistle in the fog off Point Hudson. The parson had always called the people on Sunday with a plain dinner bell, until then. Captain Selden was master of the U.S. Revenue Cutter "Wyanda." He missed Point Hudson in the fog one Sunday morning, and approached the harbour. He thought he was well offshore yet, when he heard the dinner bell on the bluff above! That's when he discovered that he was very nearly aground on the beach. He came to church, and gave thanks. About two weeks later, the cutter arrived again, and Captain Selden had somehow acquired this ship's bell to give to the church in gratitude. Never since has the Rector failed to ring it for ships in the fog."

"Nor shall I fail to do that duty, Mrs. Tucker," the new Rector declared...

Dreams of the dead
by Michael Daniels

Before me stands an empty void,
rendered memories of priceless joy,
burning midnight oil in a smoking plume,
polka dot ploys parade the room,
the smog ascent reveals unsolved,
an unkept puzzle missing pieces to bond.

speculation provokes a hypnotic stare,
four lights to meet for not a care,
a worthless whim, first love at sight,
now is but a majestic dream in the moonlit night,
draining life force, an aching need,
and still no answer to my passive plea.

In the past I've cried,
and its now bedtime,
a time to exist and high hopes to fly,
a time to awake and a time to die.

Distant Eyes
by Mi Mi Dark

Searching for answers of my families past,
I look at her eyes, which tell me nothing.
The woman who taught me so much of love and life.
My friend, my mother, the one I depend on.
She now depends on me.
It's quite different seeing a parent age,
And living with her day by day.
I do my best in raising my mom.
Distant eyes give me no answers,
I feel all the emotions in life, rolled into one.

I'm Lost
by Abel Davidson

My mind is trapped in this endless hallway. You were mine and then I lost you only holding on by a tread, troubled by my own existence and thoughtless of yours. My mind throbs in unison with my heart every moment we're apart. If only I knew where you were in this endless hallway of confusion. I just wish you'd search for my end as will I search for yours for eternity in this hallway. The hallway of LOVE.

Water
by Angela d'Avignon - age 12

The water-calm, and still
Until the racing swimmers dive.
The water-once tranquil
Now a buzzing bee hive.

The sound of a fast beating heart
The door of silence is broken through.
The glass surface breaks apart
Like a long string of sinew.

The swimmers are pulled out
The water is still choppy
Water-logged they feel like trouts
The winners are being cocky.

The water calms
The wind gently blows it, dips it like a spoon.
A sweet breezy balm
Heals the water's wounds.

The water-calm and still
At night the water sleeps.
The water-returning to tranquil
Where once swimmers leaped.

Freak Show
by Andrew Davis - age 20

"Mommy what's that man doing behind the bars?"
As the little girl extends her hand.
"Don't you touch him, he's a freak of nature
he's only half of a man!"
"But how?" the young mind wonders
as she gazes upon the lonely soul,
"he has two arms and legs
to me he looks whole"
"You see honey, he was just like daddy
at one special point in his life,
he had someone to Love and hold
she was supposed to become his wife."
"But for reasons unknown to him
she said they needed to part......"
"SHHHHH Mommy, please don't say it too loud"
". . . . . .Sweetie, he has no heart"

My Friend
by Catherine Jean Davis - age 15

She was my friend
and now she's gone.
We became closer
as we sang life's song.

She left us all sad
the day that she died.
It filled us with tears
and how much we cried.

She loved sports
like softball and volleyball.
Everyone loved her
and she never stood too tall.

She is mute now
but we still must sing,
and get on with our lives
until the dawn comes to form an endless Spring.

In loving memory of Sara Law

A Second Chance
by Elizabeth A. Davis - age 17

I wander around this cold lifeless world seeing places
I so loved as a child.

A tear runs down my cheek as I listen to the whispers of my
past crawling up my spine like a spider who has almost lost
its web.

Each day grows longer, colder, and darker, loneliness
becomes your friend.

Everywhere I turn there's a newly found, yet almost lost memory,
secret, or feeling. It's just so hard to deal with it all.

But it's not like I have a choice now, whether I live or die,
I have both. It's not as great as I thought it would be.
What I wouldn't give for a second chance.

I Am Like
by Julie Davis - age 14

I walk like a shadow in an unkind world.
I start to run like a rabbit being shot at.
I jump like a kid on a hot day into a river.
I laugh like a maniac in love.
I smile like there is no harm in the world.
I sleep like there is no tomorrow.
I talk like a person with no worries.
I look like a person that God created.
Yet, I am still a person with this hateful, cruel, unjust world.

Stranger
by Margaret L. Davis - age 17

In this place of light
I so fondly know
I'm a stranger to.
I know every bend
In every street.
I know where every walk
Ends and meets.
Yet I'm still a stranger
Of this place of light.
I see people pass
They walk right by me
They don't notice me
Standing right beside them.
I'm just a stranger
No one knows
In this place
So bright with light.

Sunday Afternoon
by Melissa Davis

It was Sunday afternoon,
and we were thinking of you,
praying that you would make it,
and hoping to see you soon.
We waited patiently wishing you were here,
but realizing you had to go, filled our eyes with tears.
You were only with us a short while,
but we will never forget your childhood smile.
The way you stood by Suzanne to sing,
it could mean only one thing...
That you were sent from Heaven.

But now our hearts are filled with sorrow,
and we can only hope things will get easier tomorrow.
We will see you soon in the Holy Land,
standing by Jesus, holding His hand.

Spools of Clear Blue
by Rebeccah A. DeBlois - age 15

I wander aimlessly through the charcoaled
remains of my past
Images and voices clog my mind, spinning
me into a grave of my own despair
I come upon a daisy, so pure, sucking the
sun's light, thirsty for its nourishment
My body goes numb with the radiant beauty
of the flower
I scour through the blackness of my life for
another daisy
The emptiness strikes me and pierces my
heart, sending me into a reality that is all
too real
I once more scan the black hills, my eyes
rest on the daisy, waving proudly in the
dirt of its home
Then as if appearing from heaven, you
pluck the daisy and offer it to me
I look into the spools of clear blue, and see
my true daisy, the loveliest one of all
As I shift my gaze around me, I see the
oceans of daisies flapping, greeting us into
the grassy hills of our future

War
by Kathryn Lydia DeCook - age 14

Crashes, Flashes, Booms,
Before me a dying boy lies,
And as I look into his eyes,
I can see he is a lot like me,
Stuck in this place God forbids,
Help us we're only kids,
Our country sent us here to fight,
They said it would be all right,
But now I see it was all a lie,
As I watch these young men die,
Crashes, Flashes, Booms.

Star Gazing
by Anya Degenshein - age 12

Star gazing
in the midst of the night,
it could never be done in the light.
A massive sky
filled with thousands of sparkling eyes
eyes that blaze down on you
in the darkest of night.
Laying on the ground
which slowly breathes
without a sound.
I think of how this makes me feel
While I lay
in a still
open
field.

In the Shadows
by Jason DeHart - age 15

He comes as a thief in the night,
Hopping from star to star,
Shrouded by darkness,
He is the light in this dark world,
All others have no more light than the small twinkling stars on which He travels,
He pauses here and there, noticing a particularly bright star,
He picks it from its perch and examines it,
He drops it down into His bag,
Then He makes His way to the next star and the next star and the next star...

One Moment
by Rosalyn de la Peña - age 13

I wonder if for just one moment
I can change my life
and go another direction,
leave my troubles behind for
someone else,
so I can pay attention to
something more important
such as the new life I may lead.
I wonder if in that one moment
I'll be famous or
remain unknown to the world,
held captive by criminals or
sail free in my own boat
on the great ocean called the Pacific.
But alas...I'm stuck in reality
as the person I am
and always will be
However, it's never wrong to
wonder what can happen in
just one fantastic moment.

Reflections Of The Mind
by John DeLaurentis

Reflections of a clear blue sky
And fields of grass embrace the day.
Welcome sights that seem to dance
Upon a forgotten reality.

Still I sit here wondering,
Thoughts intense, pondering.
The grace of God is truly majestic,
Boggling the finite creatures below.

Spiritual warfare is all around,
Invisible to my naked eye.
But its truth lingers on through shadows
And unique circumstances.

God has done all this work--
Creation, my salvation, my Christian walk.
He has completed all of this, and desires
That I walk in the light of Christ.

I am accepted in the Beloved.
Because of Christ's righteousness I am saved.
His love for me is all because of Him--
The One who willingly walked His chosen path.

Such grace and blessing who can match?
I can think of not one who can truly fathom
The wondrous mysteries contained
In the infinite mind of the Lord of Heaven and Earth.

Memories
by Kristie DeLeo - age 20

Memories make you laugh
they sometimes make you cry
they stay with you all your life
and no one knows quite why?

Memories make you think
about the stupid things you've done
they remind you of laughing so hard
and how you've had so much fun.

Memories make you remember
things you sometimes want to forget
they always seem to remind you
of people you wish you never met.

Memories make you think
about all the love you've known
they remind you of being young again
and of how much you have grown.

Deep within everyone
there is a treasure that hides
it is the memories of their life
that no one else confides.

Dear Butterfly
by Deborah D'Elia

Spread your wings for me
Oh gracious lovely butterfly
Sip your necator
Your liquid of life
Flash your colours
Your colours so bright
Land upon my windowsill
Decorate my life
It's you that excites me
You that I love
For you see dear butterfly
I am your flower
In your sweet field of love

Untitled
by Danielle Denning - age 14

If you paint a picture to make people happy,
But everytime you see it,
Your heart does not sing,
What good is it?

If you draw a portrait,
To give others like yourself inspiration,
But in years,
It hasn't ever left your attic,
What good is it to them?

If you write a novel for the world to read,
But it has never left the folder,
That you so carefully placed it in after it was complete,
Why did you waste your time?

What happens if no one ever learns of your
great works and accomplishments,
Are they worth the trouble that you put into them?

I Often Wonder
by Cathy Densmore

I often wonder Who I am.
Why do I smile? Why do I cry? Why do I love?
Why do I feel pride sometimes and then other times
life overwhelms me to the point of no return?
Why do I feel lust for the gentle kiss and soft touch of
something that could possibly hurt me?
Why do I yearn to have one man for eternity.

Am I human to wonder, to cry, to love, to hurt, to feel pain
in the worst way possible. A pain much worse then physical
or mental hurt, but yet its a never-ending, unpredictable,
untamable pain that is worse then life itself.
Its pain of the heart!

Is it human to ask why? To ask why does the sparkle in
the stars make me cry; Why the gentle touch of a lover
makes me quiver, and makes me long for the life long
companionship of a man. Why do I feel passion sending
chills throughout my body when he whispers I love you?
Am I in love? Do I have an eternal lust to be with him forever?

Why is it so easy to wonder?
I guess to love, to laugh, to cry, to feel pain is human
That one little word means forever. Forever in pain,
forever in wonder, and forever in love with that one
who's eyes sparkle endlessly and who's love will be in
your heart forever.

Endless Wonders
by David Dickey - age 19

Endless hours
Endless love
Endless flights
Through heaven above
Crystal eyes
Through a sensuous breeze
Sandy shores
And the crystal seas
Your body portrays
My endless thoughts
Through time and space
Your lips I've caught
An endless passion
An endless flame
Through it all
Our love we've tamed
An endless longing
An endless healing
An endless love
Can't beat this feeling
I've fallen in love
With your crystal eyes
No more can my love
Be disguised

Hurt
by David DiGiando - age 13

Hurt is what you feel,
Toward almost everything.
Love, pain, weakness.
It hurts everyone.
It hurts me.
Even though I don't remember what hurt.

Walking Miracle
by Rosa Di Stefano

You were so strong perhaps not physically
but indeed you were strong in heart, mind
and soul. One man with such courage and
strength, never a quitter.
They say it only takes one to be a leader and
the rest will follow.
You my blood were and still are an inspiration
to us all. For all of us who quit before life
quits us, all we need to do is take one look at
you. You were so full of life you brought joy
into our hearts and still do.
If we were all your followers we would be
dancing around life and not in sorrow.
One man who truly will never be forgotten.

In loving memory of:
Orazio Mattioli 8-9-49, 7-14-97

Poet Eyes
by Jennifer Dlugos - age 20

Only a poet can transform a decapitating romantic interlude, into a cardinal's psalm. A technicolored world, taken for granted. A common redundancy. But it is the poet that ruthlessly scavenges for meaning, a clue, insight, or glimpse to define the unfinished painting. A scribble, a crossout, aids the poet in discovering the feathers that propel the hours, the smile in the evergreen, the lips that form the whispers, the words only she can see. A thankless job, often crowned with thorns of titles. Hopeless. Idealist. Battered. Foolish. All due to the dimensions, the masses can't see. Still, I am a poet. Knowing my eyes will never turn against me. My words, my line of sight, are seen through anecdote's eyepiece. A prescription so many condemn, for they will never posess it. Yet the poet is not a poet until her face has ceased having an affair with the ground because of the weight of her burden. Only when a poet faces her persecutors will then she notice the rebel among the jury of dissenters. The one who will be willing to pursue her proposals, while asking to wear her windowed glasses. I shall kiss my divine master when to heaven I one day go, for this gift he bestowed. For no matter where I am stricken. No matter how many blows. My purpose, my intent can never be stolen. For it's protected by my poet eyes.

The Bridge
by Allison Doherty - age 16

A bridge of life before her waits
for her to pass through its iron gate.
The path before her she must cross,
but the will to take the steps has been lost.
To begin anew on the other side
would be better than to stagnate and hide.
Opportunities and passion tempered by
stability and wisdom
leave her frozen in her solitary kingdom.
Forces ripping her heart in two
leave her in turmoil over what to do.
The struggle between her heart and mind
leaves her with fear,
while hope's battle with despair
makes the decision less clear.
As she finally chooses her course,
she walks away from the bridge with
a bit of remorse.
Risks never taken offer no change
and life becomes boring and forever
stays the same.

Final Farewell
by Lauren Dowling - age 15

I listen to the voices echo inside my head,
as I lie here an dream about you in my bed.
I've heard your empty promises too many times before,
from every guy who's been in my life, then walked out the door.
You love me, then leave me, it's all a game to you,
but you won't be the one who's laughing when I tell you we're through.
These past nine months have all been a game,
and my broken heart has you to blame.
You'll leave in the fall and we'll say goodbye,
a thousand more tears for me to cry.
I'll call and write and sometimes you'll come home,
a distant hello is all I'll hear on the phone.
"I can't make it this weekend, but I'll come back soon,"
I remember you promising me the sun, the stars, and the moon.
I've played the fool for far too long,
listening to "By My Side," it once was our song.
I'll mess things up like I always do,
the only thing I want is you.
But I'll push you away like I did all the rest,
I gave you all my love, that was my best.
You know me too well, you got too close,
you found out my secrets, you saw my ghosts.
You really have to go now so get in the car.
A four and a half hour drive to college isn't that far to go,
I'm like the God damn mail man, through rain, sleet, and snow.
I'll say my final farewell now for my poem is getting quite long,
I watch the car go out of sight as I listen to our song.

Druid Moon
by Deneene Raphael Doyker

Out in the moonlit grove,
The Druids sang the rites
Witnessed only by the oaks
On every summer's night.

A verse or two the trees would join,
Whispering in the gentle breeze,
Branches and arms lifted high;
Exuberance had come with ease.

Praising the moon in her goddess light —
Graced in her black diamond cloak —
Barefoot, using their inner sight,
The Druids trembled as she spoke,

Revealing her secrets on ocean tides.
Listening intently, the Druids quaked
In adulation as she cried
Her final words before dawn's break.

Love
by Alisha Drake - age 15

Love is deeper than the oceans, love is wider than the seas;
Filling oneself to the inner being, carrying thoughts as a warm summer breeze.

Love is like a gift, not knowing what's inside;
To the eye love is sweet, but to the soul love can never die.

Love is a fierce flame, burning deep inside;
Trying to find a way to escape, but can never hide.

Having hate is harmful, it erodes the inner soul;
But having a heart of love, makes one's life full.

Caring so much to carry the love, is like a burden to bear;
For doesn't it take two to make a couple, and doesn't it take two to make a pair?

So tell me when one is carrying the burden, and the other is carrying the love;
Are they bound to succeed, is it from heaven above?

Will they fall apart like unfired clay, or will they be bound together like rock;
Having joy and love, being united in thought?

Can the flame ever die, can love grow cold;
Or will it last unceasingly, and never grow old?

What shall we say then, should we plunge into the fire;
Should we take the chance, and open our souls to the uncontrollable desire?

Castaways
by Deborah L. Drinkwater

Hurt is their constant companion
unwanted and abandoned
they roam the streets
wearing faces
ravaged by betrayal

Toughness is their bullet-proof vest
protection against the blows
they are sure to come

Trust is only a dream
belonging to another world

Huddled together
children of the night
a family united
together but alone

Drugs take them to another place
for a little while
they blow bubble gum kisses

Bodies violated by the perverse desires
of unclean men
their souls cry softly

Lives shrouded by the dark side
searching for light
for someone to love them

A Lover's Question
by Roxane Dugas

If I reach out to you
Will you hear my call
Will you hold me up
If I should start to fall

Can I lean on your shoulder
Should I feel the need to cry
Will you wrap your arms around me
When inside I want to die

If I follow a certain path
Will it lead to your heart
Can I hold it close to mine
Whenever we are apart

Will you be here when it rain
Just to hold me through the storm
Will you bring me in from the cold
And be the fire that keeps me warm

Can you promise me forever
Then make your words ring true
Then walk me down that aisle
And whisper the words I do.

Him
by Christina Dunphy and Eleanor Summer Litawa - age 15

His soft lips touched her hand
As they sat on the sand
The ocean waters swam
As soft as a lamb.

Kissing him goodnight
She saw him last in her sight
Tears rolled down her cheeks
Every time he speaks.

Last good-byes
Sad filled cries
Seeing him in her dreams
Brings streams
Of tears.

The Possible
by Melanie DuPont

Time stretches out, behind and before,
like a strong, leafless
t
r
e
e,
growing,
rotating on its axis,
turned on its s i d e,
and mirrorederorrim where the roots find the soil.
Here we pause in midflow, but for a moment,
at the crossroads
of all that could have been,
all that is,
and all that might yet be.
And on this sliding moment, we know:
it could have gone differently;
'now' is becoming 'then' as we breathe;
and infinite avenues of thought, of speech, of travel and action,
still remain open to us.

My Home
by Courtney Earlywine - age 15

Twelve years in Seattle and I moved away,
not knowing about the place I would stay.
A city named Burbank would be my new home.
An unfamiliar place where I would feel alone.

Burbank was the future, new friends and new school,
my new apartment with palmtrees and a pool.
My heart pounded with new dreams and new fears
but now I have lived there for more than three years.

I made friends and got comfortable in this new place,
but now I have a new fear I will face.
Next year I won't be here, I'll have to start new
in a school with people I wish I knew.

When I live somewhere and find a best friend
it seems I should know it will come to an end.
So I will continue to search and roam
for a place I can truly call my home.

Silence
by Jana Eisenstein - age 15

A mist befalls a dreary day
A crow sends out its call
No laughter here to interrupt
A wish, a hope, a prayer

Silence spreads its eerie wings
And swoops into our hearts
And leaves us here with nothing left
No mind, no body, no soul.

The Man in the Moon
by Holly Elmer - age 12

As I gaze into the water,
My heart skips a beat,
For there is someone else,
Starring down at me,
I glance up and find,
That the man in the moon,
Was looking down at me.

Awakening
by M.W. El Nachef, M.D.

Tammy! Oh Tammy!
I saw ol' death sparkling in your eyes
very well, I know the old Beaver
He has no sense of humor.
He never fell in love.
He never saw your eyes.
This is why, he is no believer.

The woes of the night keep buildings up- and up
They reach newer heights- like GM dumping sites
They do smother the breather- and the non breather.

I prayed with others and I prayed alone
that you and your sadness
and me and my madness
be the four in the furnace of Babylon

Through veils and veils of Mystique
here he comes, the Omayad meek
he holds in his hand a fist of soil
from the spot where the Golden calf got soul.
He sprinkles and sprinkles till heaven does glow
And you, dear Tammy, you stand up and go.

Untitled
by Roy Dupuy

O! Showy gladiolus,
Gently swaying in the breeze,
Display your pretty petals
And, as in a lava flow,
Reveal your majestic hues
In reds and yellows and blues.

Volunteer
by Luretta Elston

America, I will work for thee
Thank God I am Free
I am proud to live in this great country
I will Face each day with courage and dignity.

Everywhere I look I see
The beauty of this great country
The beautiful streams and hills
the singing whipor whills
From the top of the mountain, to the deepest sea
Thank God for Liberty.

For this land many great soldiers have died
So that I could live and work with pride
on every mountainside I will do great things.

I will volunteer to spread goodwill
I will help build homes for the homeless
And care for those who are ill.

I will listen for those who cannot hear.
Make footsteps for those who cannot walk.
I will have a vision for those who cannot see.
I will inspire others to be a voice for Liberty.

Black Silhouette
by Vicki Enscoe

The long summer's twilight with the pink western sky
Reveals evening structures as they twinkle bright
While reflecting hues and haze of a rosy earth still lie
Before ending with the silhouettes black against the light
Causing illusions of horizons everywhere giving birth before night

What begins before us in sunset as a rosy earth
Evolves before our eyes to the black silhouette
Mixing together the vision with illusion's birth
As picture frames evolve to life in a motion as if wet
Living in the gentle breeze - hidden unless we want to see

The vision betrays the dancing shadows swaying
Making life from death and still
As the slipping sun drops all shadows playing
Before night comes bringing visions kill
While our eyes are yet straining to see

I reflect in memory and long to resurrect the times
That wistful summer sunsets bring before my eyes
As cold winds usher in new nights and mimes
Because the sleeping winter earth has no sun to linger wise
Yet winter's dance and song is just as needed in our lives

The Promise of a Rainbow
by Amy Ericksen - age 16

My mind is so preoccupied,
my heart won't let you go;
Your friendship means more to me,
than you will ever know.

There's not a day that passes by,
that I don't think of you;
your touch, your smell, the way you look,
and all the sweet things you do.

But what do I do, and what do I say?
Is it just another thing that time will blow away?

There's always that question in my mind,
the anxiety of a risk;
The wanting of some sort of sign
thinking, "when your gone would it be me you'd miss?"

Then you come with your arms and words so dear;
What once was foggy and dismal now appears so clear.

In you I have a forever friend,
one that will be true;
I thank God everyday,
that I found someone special like you.

Dalen I want you to know,
you have stolen a piece of my heart;
Like the Promise of a Rainbow,
now inside me, you will always be a part.

Alone
by Jennifer Erickson - age 15

I am standing alone -
The clouds move toward me.
They are calling me.
Calling me somewhere -
I don't know.
But I want to go.
Even if the destination unknown.
I am all alone,
what have I to lose?
I am ready to put it all on the line,
I want to live a life that had a reason!
A life alone - is nowhere
I want to be somebody
Like clouds are free,
I want to be.
Moving everywhere
as fast or slow as I choose.
No one can sit on me, push me down,
tell me what to do.
That would mean, I would be on my own.
Alone -
Again.
Maybe I want to be alone -
but not by myself.
By myself is on the outside, which I could not bare
Alone you can be inside.
Not shallow or empty.
Just, alone.
Independent, free like a butterfly
that flies into the rainbow.
Then, when my rainbow is melting;
I fly into the stars.

Treasures

"The One That's Lost"
by Kathleen Ann Ettel

Losing the one you love
Even before they're around for you to be able to show love
 for them.
Not going to be able to hold or rock him to sleep.
Not going to hear they're cry for you.

Never going to see your eyes
Or see your first smile.
Not going to hear your first word
Or make your cuts feel better.

Hoping that your spirit will be around forever.
Wondering where you are
And if you'll be happy.
Always and forever you will have my love.
You Will Always Be Part Of Me.

Broken Dreamer
by Heather Evans

Life is confusing, torn and twisted. If you've never loved then you've never existed.
Unlike a bird with a broken wing, my broken heart has found no strings.
Nothing to lose all to gain...mad at the tears not at the pain.
Minds of stone, hearts of glass. The rain may stop the storm will pass.
Lies will tell the truth in time...hearts will soon find piece of mind.
One left standing with one blown down, who will be the princess? Who gets the crown?
In a garden of flowers grow ugly weeds. Looking gloom...not at all what they seem.
The flowers bloom, wilt and die. While the weed in the sunlight attracts butterflies.
Flowers stay awhile, but never return. It's what always comes back to which you should turn.
Love hates pride, grief loves revenge...fire came, our hearts only singed.
Sadness and tears, my hearts a schemer. A lover, a hater...a broken dreamer.

No One
by Sarah Eyermann - age 16

I feel all alone
Inside my own shell
Nobody knows
Nobody cares

Flying away
Away from myself
No one to turn to
No one to trust

Where is the light?
Where are my friends?
No one here
No one left

Wait!!
What do I see?!
Is it a light?!
Can it be?!

Maybe it is
Maybe I'm saved
I'll just have to hope
I'll just have to wait

Poetry?
by Tara Fabian - age 18

I've retreated to my poetry again
because of what I'm feeling.
I've lapsed into my writing
instead of into kneeling.

I'd pray to God if I thought it would work,
but for me he doesn't come through.
so instead I fall to my writing;
for me it's all that's true.

I feel like screaming out
to all that is wrong.
I feel at times like banning
all those miserable sad, sad songs.

The stress is building,
my body yielding,
I'm losing feeling.
I'm losing control?

Someone help me from my misery.
Even writing is losing it's effect.
help me, now, I'm dying!
Forgive me, God, I can't help it.

I'm dying
the stress is winning.
I've lost...
I've lost it all.

The Fire at Canyon Inn
by Micah Farmer - age 17

I'm not one wo raptures to speak
Of something odd, oblique, and unique,
But what I affirm is mostly true
(I incline to exaggerate some of the way through).

It was many and plenty a day ago,
And blazing hot despite the snow
Sitting on the roof of Canyon Inn,
The fire burned throughout and within.

I looked across the street through my bedroom window
At the place I was less than 20 minutes ago
When I got a drink at the Canyon Inn Bar,
Gulped it down, then lit up a cigar.
After taking a few puffs, I reached for the ashtray
But there wasn't one around to my dismay.
Infuriated by the bar that was so untaut,
I threw the cigar in the trash (not caring to put it out).
I walked out the door and across the street
Then suddenly felt the feeling of heat.
I turned around and the building was in flames,
And tried to run but I was drunk and lame.

Crawling into my house, I was a bit confused.
What started the fire? Who will be accused?
All I could do was watch and cry,
Look out my window and say goodbye
To my favorite hangout that someone burned down.
I will find this someone and avenge the whole town
That lost their one and only Canyon Inn.
After I smoke this last cigar, my investigation will begin.

What Is Love?
by Jo Ann Falletta

True love is a never-ending feeling
    of peace and harmony.

It's tranquil and delirious.

It's as if you possessed no physical presence
    even when you're there.

Your only reminder is when your soul
    is released with his in an airborne flight.

Nothing matters...
    except the unity of your paradise together.

Faded Dreams
by Larry Farnen

Withered flowers beside the altar,
cast aside the contract there;
Withered flowers beside the altar,
fading in her soul's despair.
She had a dream to build a home
decorated in love's alluring hue;
a dream glor'ous in its greatness,
now left to die like gleaned flowers do.
Can you make a man a man who is not a man
or turn the proverbial frog into a prince?
So her plundered aspirations melt like papier-mache pyramids
in the driving rain that pours down rivers in thunderstorms arisen since
she discover'd the distance between the dream so splendid
and reality so cold and candid.
And the flowers harvested in such great delight
on a day all glitter and gold
languished gray in a vase no longer
fed by her love's sustaining hold
until today when she removed them from their perch
to hurl them down, dead, beside the altar at the church.

Englands Rose
Written for Englands Rose, Princess Diana
by Jeanna Faykes - age 12

Picture every person a rosebud.
Never blossoming, unless they help those in need.
The way that I see it all of us fellow rosebuds are filled with greed.

Everyone, except for a beauty.
This beauty that the rosebud had,
Was both internal and external.
She touched, and hugged, and cradled, and loved all those in need.
If she came upon a starving man, unto him she would feed.
This rosebud, helped and cared so much, that we shant call her a rosebud,
For she has blossomed into a beautiful flower.
This flowers beauty was so rare, all because she did really care.

Now this flower that I speak of, a rose to be exact,
Is a lady that the whole world did love.
The lady cared more than anyone could,
That is why I think that everyone should,
Take a good look at what Princess Diana has done,
And help make her legend live.
For Diana has helped make this world a better place, for eternity of the human race.
Diana taught all of us rosebuds, that to blossom and grow,
you must care.
And as Diana, Princess of Wales,
Lay down to rest,
May we now and forever remember her as Englands Finest Rose.

Night
by Nicole Fears - age 13

Look around the sky at
night you will not see a big
fat fright. You will no it is safe
because you have that warm glow,
all inside tucked away, just like
if you were looking at a snowy day.
If you get scared you can turn on
the light, just to see that mother nature
has made another beautiful night.

The Heavens
by Kristine Feher - age 13

As I look up at the heavens above my head,
I can look out the window and see them from my
bed.
As I always pray,
"Thank you Lord for giving life to me,
Thank you for letting me see,
Thank you for letting me have a wonderful family,
A special Mom,
A great Dad,
All loving Grandmas,
All loving Grandpas,
All caring Aunts,
All caring Uncles,
All thoughtful cousins,
All advice from friends,
And best of all you Lord,
your love never ends."
Now I don't need to look up in the heavens above
my head,
Nor I need to look out the window from my bed
because I am there.
Now I can look down at earth knowing what a
great life I had.

A Rainbow
by Clarissa N. Fekete - age 13

It's wonderful just to
catch a glimpse of it.
This pleasure cannot be
replaced.
Some make a wish on it,
Others wonder away in its
magic charm.
The colors are magnificent.
It's optical illusion,
A wonder in itself.
For some there is a pot
of gold at its end.
A rainbow.

For My Dad In Loving Memory
by Rachelle L. Felmet

You were such a gentle soul
Who loved with all you had
And there was never one more caring
Than my very special Dad
You have loved so freely
And you always gave your best
To every child around you
You spread joy and happiness
I watched you gently slip away
I've loved you oh so much
You were always there for me
With a smile and a gentle touch
So I watch you softly leave me
As you take these last few breaths
Your eyes are saying "I love you Dahlin
Don't grieve for me...I'm going to my rest"
Your withered hand stopped shaking
And your eyes are growing dim
While my heart is breaking
I've not just lost my Dad
He's also my best friend.

Numb
by Michele Ferguson - age 15

Slipping away from thought
slipping away from the pain.
If I think what do I gain?
Nightmares filled with tears of sorrow.
Why should I think of tomorrow?
Throw away my memories of everything that plagued my
mind.
Nothing is left of good and kind.
The whispered things that were said,
rushed thoughts of love through my head.
Sitting on my little cloud,
Piercing arrow shot me down.
There is not love, nor hate.
I am in this nothing state.
Faint melodies echo through my head.
I can feel a sense of dread.
Am I senseless, insane or dumb?
I don't care for I am numb.

One Sight Love
by Melissa Figueroa Fernandez - age 17

And you looked at me with a look full of desire
revealing silently the love hidden in yourself
and I don't know how in your eyes which I once saw and today don't see
I could find the love which was also hidden in me.

And eyelashes blinked before that delicate encounter
with a tear almost hidden which maybe was born in myself.
Then I didn't comprehend that look was the sweet center
of expressing in some way the truth of a love who could not be.

And only the image was lost in the emptiness of that evening
when through those eyes I felt loved for the very first time.
And I don't understand why wanting it I acted as a coward
letting go the love forever, lowering my head.

The Power
by Brad Fettig - age 15

It takes me in and swallows me whole.
Deep inside, DARK, nobody knows.
It fills me up but never to drain.
Worlds of sorrow, nobody can see the pain.
So much inside, I want to cry.
Too concentrate, I want it to die.
When others are around I try to conceal it.
When alone I let it out, I reveal it.
I am here but not all there.
Sometimes there but not all here.
There is so much people don't understand.
There is so much I can't comprehend.
How can I kick this feeling of mine?
I try to escape but the Power digs deeper inside.
The way of leaving this world I wish I knew.
Right at this moment I haven't a damn clue.
I really don't care but excuse the profanity.
Sometimes I wonder if I'm losing my sanity.
It's only a matter of time before its lights go out.
Tomorrow the acid burns another route.
At a slow trickle it flows through my veins.
It effects not only me but endless names.
Sometimes I feel my efforts are useless, like I can't win.
Everyday it takes my emotions for a spin.
I wish the fury of the Power would come to a compression.
For it's very hard to fight the power of depression.

If I Were A Bird
by Sarah M. Figgeroa - age 16

If I were a bird you know what I'd do?
I'd fly over head and look down at you.
I'd watch you grow from head to toe,
    As you look up at me from down below.
I'd sail through the skies,
    As you look in my eyes,
To see the treasures they hold
Treasures unknown and treasures untold,
    will be ours and ours alone.
And if comes a time where we must part,
    there is a special place in your heart
Where I shall live eternally,
Where we will share adventures,
Together forever just you and me.

I Am
by Jillian Filipowicz - age 16

I am a strong willed and serious person.
I wonder if people can see through the outside and into
    the inside.
I hear people whispering behind my back.
I see a light at a long tunnel's end.
I want people to see my caring inside and not my rugged
    outside.
I am a strong willed and serious person.

I pretend to open a magazine and see my writing.
I feel as if a rock is thrusted on top of me and I
    can't escape.
I touch the breeze trying to float away.
I worry that I will fail in life.
I cry when my heart is broken.
I am a strong willed and serious person.

I understand life isn't carefree.
I say, "Stand tall and believe in myself."
I dream of being a success.
I try to do the best work I can accomplish.
I hope to make a success out of myself.
I am a strong willed and serious person.

I Remember
by Kirsten Flaten - age 14

As I watch the busy cars scurry on by,
I remember how the squirrels did that.
As I watch the airplanes soar among the clouds,
I remember how the hawks did that.
As I watch the flag ripple in the wind,
I remember how the leaves did that.
As I watch the young children dig in the dirt,
I remember how the gophers did that.
As I hear the noisy pounding of a hammer,
I remember how the woodpecker did that.
As I hear the chatter of the crowd,
I remember how the chipmunks did that.
As I hear the songs the radio sings,
I remember how the birds did that.
As I smell the perfume of a lady I pass,
I remember how the flowers smelled like that.
As I feel the cool shade this building provides,
I remember how the trees did that.
As this city surrounds me,
I remember how nature did that.

The Guild of the Serene
by Jasmine Fledderjohann - age 14

If you're calm and gentle,
kind and compassionate,
come oh ye to the guild of the serene,
If your quiet and caring,
loving and giving and ever sincere,
come o'ye to the guild of the serene,
If you love the sight,
of the beautiful night,
or the ever cautious sunrise,
come o'ye to the guild of the serene,
If you love the wind in your hair,
or frost on the window sill,
come o'ye to the guild of the serene,
If you sit patiently waiting,
for a gentle hand to help,
come o'ye to the guild of the serene,
If you love the first snow,
or the chill on your nose,
come ye to the guild of the serene,
come ye o' child and meet me on the hills,
meet me by the sunrise, or 'neath the evening stars,
meet me by the frosty windowsill,
or by the patient hand,
but come ye o' child to the guild of the serene.

Music
by Malina Flory - age 17

A sweet melody
    One that melts in your mouth,
Rolls past your tongue,
    And tickles your throat.

A sweet melody
    Heard by sober ears
And earnest hearts
    Cherished by all.

A sweet melody
    One that makes your heart swing,
Makes your toes tap,
    And makes your mouth sing.

A sweet melody
    That I hear in my head
One trying to escape, to be real
    Trying to get past my pen.

Whispers Of Love
by Rebecca Flynn - age 18

Whispers in the gentle wind,
Sighing soft and sweet.
"Until again, we meet."

Tears like dewdrops,
Glisten and glow.
Upon lovers cheeks do flow.

Heart and head,
Throbbing with pain.
Neither pounds in vain.

"Gone, but not lost."
We hear them say.
Love will come another day.

On wings of silver,
They sail away.
Each to go a different way.

All is lost,
Or so it seems.
Yet, this was not a dream.

Stay Father, Stay!
by Mary Fogarty

I want more than a runaway Father,
a money man, a provider.

To be without you is a hurt that will not go away
and will last for a life time.

I want you to be my king
even for one day.

I need a male mentor.
I need you.
Stay with me Father.
Do not abandon me.
I want to learn how to bond, to feel, to love.

I seek your guidance,
your direction, your wisdom.
I will walk through fire to be with you,
because I need to know who I am and
where I come from.

Be my teacher, Father,
my coach, my hero.
Show me the boundaries of acceptance,
so that I do not fall into indifference.
Catch me, hold me, protect me
while I can still cry, still laugh, still feel.

I am a handful, I know, and
I am tough to live with,
but I am worth saving.
I want to know how to be a man.
Please show me.

Do not throw me away.
I deserve more than the memory
of a runaway Father.

Nocturnes: VII
by Sheridan Fonda

The waves of the sea cavorting, sporting
Fantastic shapes,
Elusive shapes,
Say to me. whispery, basso-falsetto:
"Look for Me."
Then the song of the bird,
Vanished bird,
And this I heard,
Like an oboe, I heard:
"You are Me."
Vanished bird by the sea.

Nocturnes: VI
by Sheridan Fonda

Toward evening, evening twilight,
I found a sea-shell, by the sea-shore.
I held it close to my ear.
I heard soft, wondrous music
Therein and a voice in harmony
Singing: singing, singing,
Sotto Voce: "I am Love.
I am He."
Sotto Voce, quietly in harmony,
Singing,
Toward evening,
Evening light,
By the sea-shore,
Softly shining surf.

Dreams
by Tammy Fons - age 19

I prefer to be asleep than to be awake,
And to not be aware of your own sake.
To do whatever it is you wish in reality,
And awaken with no permanent fatality.
Whether it was good or bad you can escape,
And go back to change your mistake.
You can visit people and all the places you wish,
And know how it would feel to be poor or rich,
to know how it feels to be in love with someone,
Or to be in total dread with the lost of a loved one.
But awaken and know how love felt grand and dear,
Or just remember it was a dream and wipe away the tear.
That little door we enter when we shut our eyes,
Is a door into the land of realize.
We can face our most fearful fears,
And we can face the dreams we've wanted for years.
We can learn lessons from what we see,
Or even analyze ourselves in this thing called dreams.

Husband And Father
by Michele Forner-Greenaway

When my problems feel like they'll never end you're always
Beside me just being a friend
As days go by, I started to see how much you mean to me
You make me happy whenever we are together
I guess you know I had to say why,

    Why - That I need you
    Why - That I care
    Why - That I'm glad

You're always there, forever caring this way
You're my best friend who cares, when things got rough
You didn't runaway and hide
You'd hold me securely just being my friend
When the moonlight was out till dawn came about
Your comfort so great, so important to know you're there

Now Paula is here and my hearts has grown with December's frosty air
I see with this little person of ours a part of your heart, a bit of your love
Her curiosity that makes such faces makes me laugh when I'm sad
Or my heart sinks when she cries
Now my dear I am truly glad that my heart is in love

Harshness
by Mary R. Foster

Living in this tiring place
can put a frown on a happy face.
The yellow stars forever twinkle,
Giving off every smiling wrinkle.
Tick-tock, the clock will go
Around and around till the time will show.
A little hug or a little kiss
can give a love that most will miss.
The heart of stone can be bashed.
It happens a lot and gives a rash.
The sight of it can make you itch;
The smell of it can make you twitch.
The only way to bash a stone
Is to bash it against one of its own.

Devoted Friends
by Allison Franklin - age 14

Four devoted friends
Being separated by life.
We may be apart
But we know in our hearts
That this friendship between
Four devoted friends
Will never end.

Memories
by Mary Fritz

Paging through the memories, we do shed some tears
But look at all the happiness we shared in those years

It does seem difficult right now to see that side
But God promises us He will be there to guide

All we need to do is put our faith and trust in Him
And He will always be by our side to help us smile again

He gave us each other to share our love
And this we have done with His guidance above

I guess it was her time to leave
And walk with God; and yes, we will grieve

Please remember the love and joy your shared
For this is God's gift; for He really does care

Please smile when you think of the ones who have gone
For they are happy with God; they are not alone

Keep your faith and prayers going to Him
For with God, you will always win

Remember, we all will meet again someday
This is just another gift God gives; it is just His way

The Dictator
by Sara Fuller - age 19

I will wait forever
to be free of my captivity.
I'll listen to the dictator
and destroy myself for eternity.
In the mirror I see it,
I see myself wasting away.
I starve myself, then binge
and feel more guilty ever day.
It barely seems to matter
whether I live or if I die.
I know that I deserve this
but I can't seem to figure out why.
Choosing is impossible.
Need has somehow become lost.
It is the Dictator's decision now,
and I must follow, no matter what the cost.

The Unspoken
by Rose Fu - age 13

Crammed in a mind
are thoughts that have never been written,
never been read,
never been heard.

They're waiting

They're awake,
sealed in some dark corner,
waiting to be discovered,
but somehow,
unwanting to be uncovered.

Even when the mind dies,
the thoughts are still there,
waiting,
to be absorbed
by another mind.

Maybe that's all we need,
one thought
from space.

My World
by April Gable - age 15

I sit and wait on an old brown bench under a wilted park oak.
Not a soul in sight.
I hear a vague noise, so I gaze about searching
for something out of place, but all I
see is the colorful leaves
blowing in the wind. As that dreadful chill overcomes
me again, I stand and begin walking.
I hear footsteps getting
closer so I begin to sprint. Something or someone
grabs me from behind. I feel my
heart become a ghost-town. My body goes limp as
the darkness encircles me I turn
with frightened eyes. I feel a rush of relief.
No one is there. I rack my brain for a logical explanation.
While the gentle rain tickles my neck I hear
an uncertain whisper in the wind.
I silently return to my old brown bench in the oversized
park. As the thunder rolls at a safe distance,
I close my eyes and relax in a world of great wonder.
Where no one can predict or fill
with unwanted hate and sorrow. I call this world of mine
my locked door leading to the future.
No one can unlock it without the key I hold in my
heart.

My Emotions
by Lelian Gaboury - age 17

I don't know why I get so emotional when I look into your eyes,
You seem to make me feel that "in love" there are no lies.
Tears begin to fall gently down my face,
But happiness conquers when I'm in your embrace.
Sadness never comes when you are near,
But the closer I get, the more it appears.
What are my emotions trying to tell me?
Stuck in confusion want to feel so free.
I like you so much that I want yo to know,
Hiding it in only makes me feel so low.
I find my happy thought but knowing I cannot be with you,
There just isn't a happy place I could run to.
I know there is something holding you back and no magic dust in the air.
I'll just sit patiently hoping there's no despair.
But if feelings change and goes to an end,
I hope I'll always have you as a great best friend.

The Abandoned Garden
by Jaclyn Gain - age 15

Once again I lay myself down on this bed.
A silence falls in my room,
Turning into a dark depression.
I fall asleep to the sound of beauty.
In the morning, the sun rises.
It excites me, with a passion.
I run for the garden I once had.
It's no longer there.
I stand where it used to flourish.
A tear drop falls from my eye.
An incredibly beautiful rose appears.
As I bend over to pick it,
It shrivels and dies in front of my eyes.
A frown begins to cover my face
As I look at this dead rose that used to have a life.
I lay it down - in hope for it to flourish again.

The Gift
by Jennifer Rae Garman

For it is a rose, falling fast.
Falling from the heavens above.
This will be the last.
And it soars like a dove.

It falls for we give it away.
We take what he has given them.
It falls astray.
And they are left with the stem.

The petals and beauty are gone.
They have given up their beautiful gift.
They are changed but go on.
As they sift through the pieces.

They gave it away so quickly.
Just because they were wrapped up in the moment.
They try to hide it discreetly.
Now it is etched into cement.

Dad
by Karen S. Gass

driving by your house
foreign curtains
trimming your windows
strangers walking in rooms
that your being occupied

people breathing your air
drinking your water
raking your yard
planting your flowers
cleaning your gutters

painting your fence
opening your closet
peculiar car in your garage
sitting on your porch swing
walking on your grass

gazing down every street
listening for your voice
waiting to catch your scent
yearning for your touch
savoring your image

reaching for the phone
your number no longer exists
time erasing you from
every waking thought
passing thru life disheartned

compelled to the cemetery
finding you
cold hard stone
speaking my fears
no answer, no signal, no hope

My Gallant Warriors Farewell
by Hollie Garrett - age 15

Off into the sunset I
watch him ride.
So courageous, brave, and
full of pride.
He fought the battle, he
won the prize.
The blue sparkles in his
eyes.
The prize he won was
my heart.
But little does he know
he already had it from
the start.

An Ocean View
by Earl J. Gauthreaux

As I sit, on a white sand beach.
I look to the ocean, many miles it do reach.
Foam from the surf, pushed up on the beach,
Says, hush and listen, this is my speech.
A gull hovers high, in squalor it preach,
About a meal of fish, it soon will to eat.
A whale blows its spout, at the surface its breached.
Its journey for life, in the ocean so deep.
A song it do sing, so solemn and meek,
A slaughter of lore, can make you weep.
A far distant squall, joins sky to the sea,
A contrast of colors, of beauty so neat.
A salt cook breeze, is as pleasing to be,
A scent of freedom, out from the sea.
A tall ship sailing, on an ocean breeze.
A lurid life, its crew, do lead.
In and out of port, as it so please,
A dream of a trip, we all think we need.
This view of the ocean, is a dream you can reach,
As long as you sit, on a white sand beach.

Fire In your Eyes
by I. Gee

When I look into your eyes,
You have fire burning in your eyes.
Your look said, come to me with passion,
Touch me with your ideas.
Fill me with your burning love,
Let me journey to your world of wonder.
I want to feel what you feel.
Embrace me with your affection.
Come to me with Hope & Glory.
The excitement I feel from you,
Will not end here-
I can see it now from the fire in your eyes.
I will never stop loving you with all my heart.

Ocean Waves
by Shawna Geier - age 14

As I stand high on this wall of rocks
I see the waves come crashing down
I'm reminded of my loneliness
And realize that I could leave without a sound

My body starts to feel heavy
I'm being pulled lower and lower
I can almost taste the salt
As my heart beats slower and slower

All I can see is darkness
I try for one final gasp of air
But my chest collapses, and I am gone
All this is a result of having no one to care

But once again I'm standing here
For alas! It was all a dream
I realized I can't go through with it
Because, for myself, I need a chance to redeem

Life Long Dreams
by Beth Gelber - age 15

Life is just a repeat,
everyday's the same
somedays better than others
but they all end in shame.

I go to bed at night
wishing you were here
dreaming of holding you close
and feeling you near.

I wake up the next morning
with expectations of the day
feeling kinda fuzzy
but it all drifts away.

No one can explain it
I will never know
but when I go to bed at night
and wish upon the stars
and dream of you and me together
my heart tingles inside.

That's the feeling that I get
every single night
a repeat of the last
and a preview of the next.

Merry-Go-Round
by Erin Gibbons - age 14

Love & life have their ups & downs-
Just as the world must go round,
But as long as you have a close friend's hand
You will be sturdy where you stand.
Friendship makes unbreakable chains
& take off some of the strains;
Just hold them close, hold them near,
Let them know your joy & fear.
Treat them as they deserve to be,
Laugh & joke, be care-free.
But when the world comes tumbling down
Don't be scared to show a frown,
Good friends will be there by your side
& fill up parts of you you thought you died.

In The Breast of The Wind
by Michele E. Gibson

When the wind is restless and the night is right
I sit by my window and turn off the light

The air seems cool as it blows through the trees
I just want to get out and fly with the breeze

I put on my clothes to go outside
But I think to myself, "I have no Guide"

The wind is calming now, therefore I can rest
Until tomorrow, another day, another test

"What stirs the wind?" I asked myself
As the force of the wind increased
"What do I do now, Dear Lord,
But hope the wind will cease?"

Yet the wind blows harder now
This time with no end
So now I lay forever
In the breast of the wind.

Beyond The Shadow Of Doubt
by Cheetah C. Gifford

When he could not lift his eyes
above unwarranted invisible lines,
someone watched carefully,
warding off turmoil,
anguish, uncertainly, when faith
alone wasn't enough for sanity
or a heart to rebuff.
Who could have loved so much,
so willing, to heed off
these emotions so chilling?
Without light, or fresh air
to breathe, it withheld promise
he'd sometime leave.
While held hostage, captive
doubts prevent life to live.
Existing shadows cling along,
mistakenly only vivid in the light.
Anticipation of freedom
is so far beyond
the shadow of doubt.

Little Sister
by Wendy Gillette - age 15

My little sister-
Tears burn my eyes.
I think about you,
And put on a disguise.
The pain in my chest-
I know that you're there-
I want you to know,
Just how much I care.
I miss watching you grow-
The fights we might have had,
But no matter what-
We share the same dad.
I may not be around,
But I know the pain.
Sometimes parents think
A child's life is a game.
We hurt inside-
The emptiness grows.
And the holes in our hearts-
They're there and they show.
I want to be part of your life-
But it's not my choice.
No matter how loud I shout-
Their ears are deaf to my voice.

My X-Pirience
by Katie Gilliatte - age 16

Cry if you want nobody will know.
Cry if you want to let your emotions show.

He breaks up with you he says your
relationships old,
you begin to wonder why he's suddenly so cold.

You look in the mirror and don't like what you see.
His new girl now looks better than me.

You wonder what it is he didn't like about you.
It stays on your mind whatever you do.

Your so called friends tell you to get over it.
So you play it off like you don't miss him a bit.

You try to hide it for your own reputation.
Pretty soon you'll wish you were in another nation.

Before you know it those feelings fade away.
With the help of friends you will find a better day.

Ciel de Nuit
by Clare Gillmore - age 15

I wish to touch the bright blue sky,
Swallow it whole so I won't cry;
Drink its color; starve its clouds;
Fill myself with its ecstasy.

My sky would be empty, free and dead;
I'd have no worries - I'd feel no dread;
I would be filled, my heart content;
Warm inside to help melt the cold.

Oh, dear Sky, embrace me so,
Tell me of places and things you know;
If I die, then be my friend.
Hold me tight; it hurts too much.

I'll lose myself in your ebony night;
Then all the wrongs I'd done may seem right;
I could forget all the things I had done;
Maybe even learn to love myself again.

I can be free; I think I know how.
It's all becoming quite clear to me now;
My selfless Sky, my cordial companion,
Thank you for caring.

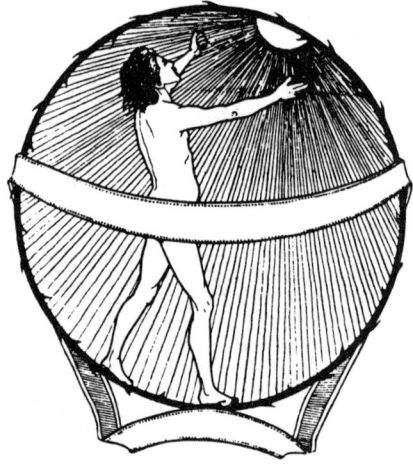

Untitled
by Jennifer Gilmour - age 15

As the surface of a secluded pond ripples slightly, the crickets begin to chirp, ever so lightly. An ivory hand with nails so pink stir the water as she dreamily watches the fireflies blink. Sitting there with flowers picked for her mother, her thoughts are interrupted by a faint flutter. She finds herself looking into a beautiful face. The tiny woman introduces herself as the fairy, Grace. So lovely was the web work that made up her wings, so heavenly the way her sweet voice sings. The tiny flowers that adorn her locks, were the kind you often find growing on rocks. Her dress was made of moss, or so it seemed. Her hair freshly dewy, oh how it gleamed. They talked for a while, and they talked without words. The evening was filled with the sound of night birds. Grace knew that this girl by Venus was chosen, by the way her heart stood almost frozen. The child was innocent, natural, and sweet. She ran around with no shoes on her feet. She loved the flowers, animals and bees. She felt the ancient ones present in the warm breeze. She knew the world would be all right, if only everyone was like this girl she met that night. But Grace knew the child was strong, independent, and free. She left with the girl a locket inscribed, "blessed be." The locket was worn both night and day, it gave her strength and paved the way. The child grew into a woman of extreme beauty, but never once did she forget her duty. Many hard trails did her poor soul tread as she faithfully follows where her good heart led.

Werewolf Kill
by Stacia Glenn

Through darkened woods he runs alone,
White teeth gleam like sharpened bone,
Wolfsbane bloom is softly kissed,
By moonlight drifting through the mist,
By day he wishes no one ill,
At night he hungers for the kill.

You'd better be careful beneath the full moon,
Or you'll be hearing it very soon,
The howling cry not far behind you,
There is no warming; no sudden " BOO! "
Just the haunting, breathing, panting sound,
Soon your heart will began to pound.

His deadly claws stretched out so near,
His flaring nostrils can smell your fear,
Adrenaline pumping through your vein,
Then the werewolf begins your pain,
His outstretched claws grip your neck,
Soon your body will be a wreck.

The moonlight acts as a soft, warm blanket,
For you own, poor body; it just couldn't make it,
Far in the distance the werewolf cries,
As a blanket of moonlight fades high in the skies,
His need for flesh no more needed,
His thirst for blood now completed,
But his next kill is the very next night,
So please put up a very good fight.

I Judge This Book By It's Cover
by Jenna Godfrey - age 13

Barbed wire fences, where could I be?
Pointing which way to go, to hope this line saves me.
When I sniff the air I smell roasting meat,
I look around and see dead bodies lying at my feet.
As I see ashes of flesh falling to the ground an I start to cry,
Scared of what's going to happen to me, am I going to die?
The officers shout and say "Take off your clothes, and change into these."
I looked at myself ashamed, so the men whipped me at my knees.
Go to your housing block, number 409,
Tomorrow you will get your head shaved at half pass nine.
Shave my head, what a dreadful thought.
I am becoming just another number, a dot.
There are so many people crammed into one room to sleep.
I can't help to think about my good friend, Miep.
We sleep on the damp, dirt for beds,
and we have no pillows for our heads.
Not even one full day is gone of this place and I cry.
Allied soldiers get here, hurry, I don't want to die.
As I start to fall asleep I whisper to my neighbor, "Good night,
Sweet dreams, sleep tight, don't let the Nazis bite."

I Love You
by Heather Golden - age 18

Why can't I let you go
I love you with all my heart you know
Things weren't always good for us
All we ever did was fuss

My heart feels like it's about to burst
Maybe cause I loved you first
I wish I could make you see
All I want is for you to love me

My life has brought me a lot pain
And when I'm not with you the tears fall down like rain
But maybe one day the sun will shine
I guess all you need is a little more time

Somewhere inside I think you really cared
I never will forget you or the dreams we've shared
I want you to know I do have sorrow
I keep thinking maybe you'll call tomorrow

I'd always thought we'd get married
And some day in the future it'd be your baby I carried
I used to thank God every night that he'd put you in my life
Now things are ending it's like stabbing me with a knife.

You will forever hold the key to my heart
And I do hope we never part
This hut I have is nothing new
But you know I'll always love you!

Infection
by Anna Goldshmidt - age 18

Pocket your music with giggling nonsense Hide your
carnival Ignore its damp gay or any other
clown-nosed Spoil and admire the mirror when walking by

but there lures the arrow-tail'n fork image/ination
the fertilized pink pale cherry will drop to top
the bitter_{plastic}sweet christmas in the Ridicule of july breaths
of adults who gibber like wind-up toys called Kids ™
what their faces predict is more than any
"no! not the basement!" movie
and ears will ring like shrieks of nazi trains
backforthagainoncemoreallover it'll Trample the flying
and make them wonder what life is really worth...a nickel and a gas mask

but who am i to Break computer keys
with unexpected arrogance drowning flooding overflowing
but not evaporating like vocab words
an hour after our #1-50 multiple-choice perfume of intelligence
So I'll *bee* around...my Sting will louden your tireless twirling babble
the Bite will Pinch enough to Sacrifice a fraction of your precious 24
karat thought
but even my Strings heal soon
so flush band aids and pass the Salt

Shot?!!
by Lynnette Golston

Lee Morgan has been shot!

I was writing my Romeo and Juliet paper
when suddenly you passed by my bedroom in slow motion.
You said Sometimes it snowzzzzz in April,
Your toe nails scraping against the carpet like the needle on a scratched
record
Loud, but it isn't snowing and it's June
and I was trying to finish my paper with no lights on.
YOU SEE, BRIGHT LIGHTS ACT LIKE THE BLUES.

Then the old man on the radio said,
"WE
INTER
RUPTTT
THIS PRO
GRAMMMM
TA SAY
LEE MORGAN
HAS BEEN
SHOT!!"
You know it's funny,
I imagined the ole man say it like it was a part of his name.
LEEMORGANHASBEENSHOT.

There are not poets. There are no part-time singers.
The next song is a year long and has been playing for five months.

Oh Lee Morgan, it's not time for jazz to die.

The Storm
by Margarita Gomez

the storm gathers
and the clouds roll in
the moon disappears
i feel the weight of my sins

the storm gathers
and the rain pours
i wail in sorrow
fighting an inner war

the storm gathers
and the lightning flares
darkness closes in
but no one seems to care

the storm gathers
and the thunder roars
i run toward home
but everyone closes their doors

the storm rages
and the winds howl
my mind explodes in chaos
and my heart breaks in doubt

Tomb of Amber
by Roman Martin

asleep ten thousand years
from my encrusted opal eyes flows a river of magma and tears
i heard the death-cry of hungry mastodons and forests above
beside me, diamonds of carbon made for love

there are memories of electric sky blue and morning honeydew
proud and thoughtful worker I was when the Ice Age winds blew
under the sun, gliding through viridescent fields with delta wings
i saw your megalithic temples and proto-kings

extracting sweet pollen a daily task
golden resin now my worn death mask
hypnotized by a passion flower, struck, I fell to Earth with frozen warmth
nothing remained...a shell of locked daydreams of mint and mirth

shattered remnants
half-dead, half in a dream, like a vampire in a dust-ridden casement
entablature of solitude
these wailing walls of infinite magnitude

there are epochs and legends that transcend
but in the alluvial abyss my sphere has no trend
like a stylite in a brown jeweled grotto writing a history in stone
i chronicled the plebeians take the marble for Rome

fluctuations in my insect ear
awakened by plate subductions very near
tremblers knocking on my sensor door
Vulcan forever forges his device of war

fossils, coins, my only friends
i dreamed a dream that there would be no end
looked back but found no memory of my birth
just like this endless Earth

Soul Mate
by Dortha Gonzalez

If this be true, that for every soul there is a mate.
Then why on earth does conflict dictate?
That these two hearts should conflict over love.

When at last these two hearts meet.
Then why must they war through an eternal fate?
If it is true that love was to be for these two hearts,
who's souls did meet.
Then God's design should not be questioned.

But when I found you my heart was lost.
For all at once I knew you were my mate.
For our souls became one when our paths did cross.

But now we war at every gate.
We questioned God's design of fate.
Though we are to be, no more on earth.
My soul is eternally to be tormented till we meet
at heaven's gate.

Untitled
by Bryan Goodin - age 19

Upon the throne of steadfast assurance, my ego nods to his fellow. Recognized only to themselves and even then they throw defenses-invisible to all. Wandering in a smoky chariot and being directed away by the well proportioned heir of society's Nazism, sanctuous green carpets call. Broken by the occasional Willow's weeping and the rude sounds of Mr. President winning the vote while raping innocent purses-I search for my peace. Beautiful couples torment the rogue and smile on past. Sprinklers' song and gnat humor do little to please the Mother-who grumbles and slaps just in time to kill fantasies of superiority. The snide interruption of feathers announced incoming annoyances with white helmets and chromed handlebars. As I look up my soul reaches out, only to find that hot adultery looking my way. The sordid shock reminds me of my lack of sleep, but only until he calls me back to bed where I pretend to care about the tortures planned for my prattling soul.

Fledgling Hawk
by Joan Goodwin

From my window, I watched the pair
circle, dive, land in a fir tree.
The Cooper's hawks chose this site, so
near to me, for their aerie.

Both toiled, constructing the nest,
shared the brooding duty to
complete their work of creation.
And then - the nestling was in view!

The fledgling thrived and strengthened his
wings, hopping from limb to tree limb.
He made his inaugural flight,
I whispered goodbye to him.

Come Down to Me
by Erin Gordon - age 13

Rain, rain fall down on me
And cool my anger off.
Let my fury be set free
Sweet drops that cool me off.

Sun, sun shine down upon me
And dry my tears all up.
Let me cry no more
Summer rays that dry my tears all up.

Snow, snow fall softly upon me
And melt my fears away.
Don't make me worry so
Snowflakes that descends down to me.

Wind, wind breeze by me
Make me care free.
Let all the pain blow away
The wind breezes by me.

Rain, sun, snow, and wind
Come down to me
Always controlling my passionate emotions
Rain, sun, snow, and wind.

Deception
by Patricia Gordon - age 18

Should I resort to trickery, my love?
Succumb to your world of fiction, my sweet?
Perjure myself for your delight, false dove,
Prevent our war with treachery...deceit?

You, my teacher of deception, betray
All that faith has given to you, Judas.
Though there be doubt that I shall flee one day,
I'll not yield to a lie for fear of fuss.

You know that we have shared the mind of one.
We've spoken with the same united breath.
I've died searching for truth where there was none.
And you devour this unsavory death.

Deluded with the liquid of untruth,
You've discarded a jewel; Marred its youth.

Photo of a Family
by Laura Goulart - age 15

The perfect picture,
A family;
Obscure in today's world.
A mother,
A father,
Two children,
A family pet,
The perfect picture.

    Or is it?

If you look close enough to that thought,
At the perfectness of their perfect family,
You can see the light refracting on all the
Little scrapes,
The hidden smiles and tears,
The mended arguments as well as those to come,
If you look close enough,
You can see where each tear of the picture
Has been taped back,
But is still not
    Picture Perfect.

I Love You
by Shannon Goulet - age 16

I love you so much, more than
words can say,
I love you more and more each
and every day.

If I ever lost you in any way,
In this world, I simply could
not stay.

You'll fulfill my life for eternity,
'cause I was made for you
and you were made for me.

Our love is filled with respect,
trust, and honesty,
No matter what happens,
I know you'll stand by me.

I'll always be your friend,
and prove my love is true,
Throughout your whole life,
remember "I LOVE YOU."

Unprepared Heart And Soul
by Jennifer Lee Gouthier

For many years the door was locked
and the key hidden.
Behind that wall stood a room
full of stale cold air,
No warmth, or feeling,
and eyes told of such.
Now you have found that key
and are going where most have only crossed.
You have opened the once shut door
to a very scared and lonely heart and soul.
I never thought anyone
could go in through that door.
I didn't even go there myself - sometimes.
Now I found someone I think
I can trust;
But I am very scared,
Because scared and lonely hearts and souls,
For this type of journey,
are not prepared!

The Legend of the Power of Love
by Clarissa Grabiec - age 14

Years ago,
When few men traversed round,
There was said to be a lone wanderer.
It was thought he was left behind by a maiden of beauty and righteousness.
Forth he journeyed across the undiscovered land,
Setting foot where never thought was possible.
And venturing where he thought his love would appear.
But the poor soul of his own was left in the frailties of his body and not set free as he once wished.
Onward he searched for his love until he met upon a great sea of tranquility,
And over it lied a ribbon bridge that he determined he could not cross.
For many years he sat and pondered over a way of crossing it.
That is until one day when his fair maiden appeared at the opposite end of the bridge,
Called his name in a cry,
And motioned her despair in her loneliness.
The wanderer then stood abroad and gave the maiden his reason for his own despair,
And the reason for the time he had wasted in wait for an easier passage.
The maiden then looked at him in a manner sought out through disgust and said,
"If you behold love for me you have the will to cross."
In reply to this message he responded,
"I do behold love for you, but this ribbon bridge cannot withstand the weight of my own.
Surely there must be an easier way to cross."
She then told him once more the power of his love,
He still denied its truth.
So the maiden once more vanished,
The wanderer was left once more to be impoverished in his love.
It is said that to this day the wanderer still waits for a more sure way to cross,
But little does he know that if he set foot upon that bridge it would turn to stone,
And he would be able to pursue his love.

and sometimes they can end too early...
by Amy Gracey - age 17

A harsh grave, an early end
A brief but beautiful life my friend
I miss you - why did you have to go?
But you are happy some how, I know
When they told me my friend had died
I felt so cold; I never cried.
Where he died on the road, there's still a stain
As, in agony, you had lain
The people don't notice, drive on
I want to yell "Stop, cry with me, he is gone".
I'm going to cry again
For one last time
Goodbye my friend
I will miss you forever.

In From The Dark
by Rita S. Graham

Through the darkness I see,
    My child takes a first step
    Clutching a lamp's cord,
Me paralyzed with fear.

In the darkness I feel,
    Tiny toes and fingers
    Smelling like mine,
I wipe a tear.

Out of the darkness I hear
    A baby cry.
Again, I ask why...

Me, paralyzed with fear,
    Wiped away tears
    And all the spent years,
Just trying to get...
    In from the dark.

Night Whispers
by Christle Gray

Whispers echo on the wind,
    drifting ever after;
Sobs of torment, screams of fright,
    sounds of bitter laughter.

Dreams of death surround my mind
    immersed in evil gloom;
Mixed with whispers, muffled sounds,
    stifled waves of doom.

Hear the tales they long to tell
    of fears and mortal fright.
Whispers echo on the wind,
    soft whispers in the night.

Rainbow Colors
by Daniel Gray

Rainbow colors in the Colorado sky
    overtop the mountain peaks.
Such a beautiful sight to see
    after a rain shower storm.

The sun makes its break
    through the clouds so close.
The freshness in the air
    brings life to the forest.

The cycle of nature
    has it's yearly ways.
It takes it's course
    making life go on.

Flowers and wildlife
  appreciate the showers.
Fresh water springs overflow
    having a magical moment.

Icy
by Sara Gredler - age 15

Icy stares,
Cold looks,
Laughter
coming from
behind me.

Cool words,
As if to a
person never
seen,
An unknown teen.

My eyes
fill with
tears at
the sting
of the frigid words.

They startle
me because
they weren't expected
of people of the same mind,
supposedly friendly and kind.

Whether it be smart, stupid,
fat, ugly,
thin, or too pretty,
Someone is always there.

Never knowing
where to look,
But knowing
that somewhere
will be an icy stare.

An Angel Appeared
by Patty Gray - age 13

With wings as white as snow
She appeared.
With an aura of elegance,
A presence unmistakable to a mortals,
She appeared.
With a message that would
Change my life, begin my life,
And end my life.
Without saying it would be okay-
I knew it would be.
She outstretched her pale arm
And said,
"It is time to go."

Fool
by L.S. Greger - age

I realized a while ago that I was a fool
Floating on a funny little wind called life.
I felt as though I was an autumn leaf.
My Fall colors glided along with small strife
The wind of life may flow at times so very cruel.

I saw the Fall leaves just the other day.
The wind of existence guided then in simple designs.
The gold, red, and yellow symbolized personalities
Mixed together randomly crossing the various life lines.
The vortex twisted leaves a many way.

Looking back I never did realize the beauty
And the symbols of the event at that time
In the gust of air on that autumn breeze
Now the symbols of beauty came back in rhyme
Whistling in my mind becoming reality.

Sometimes I wished my lead was not so colored,
For I wished that my gold sparkled more,
Or even that my red wasn't quite so crimson,
Yet I live my leaf evermore.
My green life stayed in the dead past so checkered.

A lone tear fell down my face, because it seemed fit,
Yet that's the only sorrow I shed.
The past is full of regrets, and that is where they stay
Carried away on the wind that said,
"The only way to enjoy life, is to live it."

To Defeat I Say
by Allison Marie Griffin - age 17

    Hello defeat
      you have conquered me again
once more your flag waves victorious
      you bathe lavishly in my tears
you dance to the wails of my dying dreams
      But hope has come to lift me up
Tenderly he brushes off my wounds
      with his kiss upon my lips
      my very soul is restored
    I am set upon my horse
      His gentle hand guides my sword
      To defeat, I now say, "Flee!"
      I stand strong with glowing re-enforcement
    I have risen again!

Celestial Uncertainty
by Amanda L. Green - age 14

Circling about in luminous groups, so high up there in the sky.
Always watching a dusty wing or a blazing comet go by.
Never scared or worried there's nothing you can't see.
I know "the sky's the limit," but is the sky for me?

To Fear Death
by Sarah L. Griffin - age 18

I have only one life, one birth, one death,
Many dreams, many hopes, to utter a breath.
My today leaves to bring tomorrow,
A memory to hold on to for you to borrow.
I pray to God to let me live long,
Fully and completely; until I am gone.
I have only one chance to show the Earth,
That there was a good reason for my birth.
My death, I'm not afraid anymore,
A fear that is only something much more.

You And I
by Anthony T. Groleau

In the face of life we sit and ponder.
In the light of love we stir and wander.
Is it you or I that does not understand?
It is you and I who need to make a stand.

In the balance of life there is you and I.
In the harmony of love there is a watchful eye.
Is it you or I that has built a wall?
It is you and I who can make it fall.

In our lives there is only one.
In our love there are two hearts to be won.
Is it you or I that is not being fair?
It is you and I who need to show our care.

In our lives we take a stance.
In our love we take a chance.
Is it you or I that is playing a game?
It is you and I who is to blame.

In our hapless lives we live apart.
In our growing love we share one heart.
Is it you or I that is asking why?
It is you and I who need to try.

In our waking lives we set the rules.
In our restless love we find the jewels.
Is it you or I that feels the flame?
It is you and I who feel the same.

A Desert Flower
by Mary Grubb - age 17

I was traveling on a path and I found
A single flower on the vast desert ground
It had pink petals, a yellow center, and a green stem
There hadn't been any rain in weeks, yet it strived
Around the flower there were cacti and tumbleweeds
How can the flower stand knowing that its life will soon end
Just because it won't toughen its exterior
It remains delicate and unchanged
It needs water, unlike the tumbleweed
It had no way of protection like the cacti
I traveled down that same path just a week later
I found a faded and crumpled flower lying on the ground
And yet the cacti was still there
And there was tumbleweed all over the desert
Before I left I poured water on the roots and promised to return
Two days ago I went to see the flower
I didn't see a strong beautiful flower
I saw two

Me
by Kelly R. Hall - age 12

My hair and eyes of brown
and my skin of tan. My heart
filled with love and compassion
for those who are rich and those
who are poor. Some people may
think I am ugly on the outside
but they have not seen the beauty
within me.

Celtic Roots
by Carol Mason Guild

Her roots ran deep
from soil that nurtured whimsy
dancing eyes say spritely scenes -
and twisting tempests tumbled
in her wake -

Her senses know the way
to inner hurts and fears -
even as she touches there and heals -
off she flees - feather light
in random flight

Her winged way paints the sky
and earth beneath
with colors rose and butter yellow,
points of lavender and green
what gentle joy is this -

She comes to land. I think
not tamed - with a sigh,
guided by her angels feathered touch
to hands both strong and sure
Safe enclosed - free to fly or stay secure.

Brotherhood
by Bonnie M. Gulan

If we were to paint a picture
of the Brotherhood of today,
and we decreed to make that picture
complete in every way.

We would have to travel near and far
before a brush-stroke could be made,
to acquaint ourselves with all men's paths
would be our prayer to pray.

We'd have to leave this spiritual path
we call our religious home,
to other paths, to other homes,
that's where we'd have to roam.

Our stay in each depending on
now here we must be candid,
the length of time it would take each
to leave un-empty-handed.

For every path is owned by men,
and every home a marker,
lighted homes will light our way
miss one, our path grows darker.

When coming to the end
of this journey we will find,
each path, each home connecting
to the Brotherhood of Time.

So our painting would be incomplete
if we painted now, today,
unless we'd paint in every path
men placed here on their way.

Crossroads!
by Anjuman Gulati - age 14

Crossroads,
That's where I stand today,
leaving behind, a lovable past,
looking into the far horizons,
for a future,
Where there will exist only me,
Alone!
And my memories.
Friends never shall I forget,
The tenderness, the camaraderie,
that we shared,
just being there for each other.
The moist and dewy mornings of my country,
The hot and busy days,
The hard brown earth that I walked on,
you gave me the power to walk ahead,
And walk I shall, with all of you one day,
I know now, which road to choose, at this
Crossroad—
My rainbow begins
At the end of the horizon.
And I shall make it there!

God's Eternal Love
by Pattie Reynolds Haddock

God's Love is Eternal
Of that we shouldn't fear.
No matter the problem,
God will always be near.
Sometimes it's hard to
Understand the reason
But eventually we find
The rhythm and rhyme.

God has plans for everyone
He places on this earth.
With love, faith, and hope,
God will reward us
And teach us all to cope.
When our life on earth is over
We will find heavenly release
And finally be able to reach eternal peace.

Beauty Alone
by Crystal Hall - age 14

Lying awake at night
I wonder what the sky would fright?
A mysterious glimmer of the waves
awakened a sleepy camper.
The morning breeze
of all the flowers and the trees
was like a waking from disease.
Today is the day
when nothing was planned
we can play
or we can sleep all day.
I want to explore
all the world around me
Why leave it alone?
When there is so much beauty to behold.

On The Sea
by Tania Rita Hallim - age 12

The large waves of the dark water
rose high and then came crashing down.
They stood in peaks just like volcanoes
with white foam lava spilling 'round.
I heard a loud noise and looked around me
a tall wave had just fallen down.
It left white riffles in the water
like lacy trimmings on a gown.
I followed the water with my eyes
from alongside my boat into the distance.
Then I looked up at the sky
but I regretted it in an instant.
For the sun came shining brightly down
and it really nearly blinded me.
Then I saw it glistening upon the water
and I thought what a pretty sight to see!
I shifted my gaze towards the east
to the land we were approaching fast.
I turned again to see another boat
with a white sail dancing on a mast.
A gust of wind blew and hit my face
it blew my hair in wisps about me.
I took a deep breath and smelled the salty air
I exclaimed, "There is no place to be like on the sea!"

Untitled
by Lindsay Hallock - age 13

we are society's scapegoat
 stereotyped by everyone
blamed for everything
 we tell lies, hide truth they say
where is our truth?
 we are statues
 molded by someone
and when they finish us
 we say where is our sculptor?
 and crumble
  not knowing what to do.

Enslavement
by Sabrina Hall - age 16

Just to exist
is what I crave
Fear and anger
have made me a slave
If spoken truth
in this era of lifes
I'm strangled by lyrics
and hushed by their eyes
Who has crippled me
and made me so weak?
Strangled my voice
so I cannot speak?
I blame the critics
and their judgment days
who tell me to follow
their proper ways
Damn those bastards
who hide their sins
who tell me I'm wrong
for who I've been
If there is a God
how could it be,
that it is unjust
to be human...like me.

The Power Of Love and Hate
by Arianna Halper - age 12

Growing maturing similar to a flower
Love releases joy
Twisting, churning, boiling, burning
Hate shadows fear

Love isn't easy
Neither is hate
Everything has it's effects and
Anything makes wake

The world is a puzzle
Centered with feeling
Edges are dark
Furious with cold

I ask you now
Where would the world be
Without love,
Or hate?

City of Angels
by Stephanie Hammerwold

With claws of smog
Grabbing at skyscrapers
As they attempt to kiss the sky
But miss
And a trim man sits in a cafe
sipping espresso
(Because it's the cool thing to do)
As he talks to a producer
About the next Mel Gibson
While a woman looks out on a stagnant sea of cars
On the 405
As she's heading off to her house
In the suburbs
The middle aged man
In the bright red sports car next to her,
Top down,
Talks to his current twenty-something girlfriend.

To Believe
by Georgia Hampton - age 14

I stand here looking over the remains of war.
I look and see what the bodies do implore.
They seem to cry and call out to me,
And I stand here and I believe.
I stand here knowing that their cries are unheard.
I stand here beneath the circles of the birds.
The stench, it drifts and engulfs me.
But I stand here and I believe.
I stand here feeling my stomach turn.
I stand here as the tears in my eyes burn.
I stand here, but I feel free.
And I stand here and I believe.
I stand here wanting these lifeless bodies to live.
I stand here wishing there was something I could give.
I stand here feeling they all died for me.
And I stand here and I believe.
I stand here sobbing for those who fought for freedom.
I stand here and they don't even know they won.
And I stand here amongst the trees.
And I stand here and I believe.
I stand here seeing the dead.
I stand here feeling the dread.
I stand here. Why did they die?
I stand here and I cry.
Death has come to those who fought,
But a lesson they have taught.
You should stand up if you want to be free,
Or none of us would now believe.

Voices In The Dark
by Amber Hanna - age 13

People are sick, starving and poor, afraid to come out in the day.
Afraid they'll get shot down in their door, afraid doctors won't find a way.
Afraid of the day darkness will take over and light will fade away.
They pray, pray and pray, they pray for the day god will take them away.
They know nothing of smiles, happiness and joy.
Their whole life is fighting for what they employ.
They're people just like you and me,
they're people open your eyes and see.
So go back to your families and jobs, and sleep safe in your beds, but
remember my poem and of those who are dead.

Love Hate For Beliefs
by Lori Jo Hannawacker

The World of Religion
The Middle East
Has lost the values of keeping peace
In the Name of God they speak with ease
They neglect to think of tranquility

Agonistic hate they choose to excrete
In the name of God built in concrete
Pools of blood the children see
Loosing lives in what should not be

Our harmony is lost in a haze out to sea
For God is what you are and should believe
The metallic of people is not what should be
For we should practice religion freely
In privacy

Pugnacious ways of life we choose to lead
So others will follow the belief in our
Boundary

Internal calmness is Gods way for peace
Not the agonizing pain which sheds
Us to bleed.

A Poor Person Has No Right To Dream
by Janie Hansen

A poor person has no right to dream
For it takes money to make a dream it seems
But a dream is what makes him keep going it seems
But so much time goes by the dreams begin to die
And when the dreams have died some say that's when the soul is set free to fly
I dream no more I hope God will accept my soul
For my dreams have died, a poor person am I

Dad vs. Mum
by Terri Harding - age 17

Little diamond tears trickle off my face,
Painful words do a letter make.
No longer do you act as a strong man,
No longer will you be there to hold my hand.

When I picture your face I see bloodstained glass,
A bar of old that contains much of your past,
There were no swings, no walks in the parks,
Only screams from mum as you physically broke her heart.

You blame it on mum, you blame it on the drink
You chuckle like it's nothing and that makes my heart sink.
I wanted a real father, one that laughed and joked,
But now it's not the drink as you write your last note.

You say you still love me, it's just all the stress.
Then you say you'll no longer write me and I know
	the beer will get your best.
But my tears stop falling, and out comes the sun
My mother, my bestfriend, is still there and she's number 1.

She was always there for me, saw my first step,
Knows my first word, knows how well I kept.
It's true my dad's a stranger who never was there.
Perhaps if I was named after a beer then he would care.

Soup
by Astrid Hardjana - 17

We are soup,
A bowl of leftovers,
A mix of vegetables.

A dash of spices.
Compliments of the chef,
Organizing our ingredients.

We each have a donation,
From talents to spirit,
And effort too.

In a pot we all go,
With lots to give.

"Together we are one."

Voyage of Discovery
by Tiffany Hargis - age 16

I see the world in a while new light,
Shades of red glowing bright.

I have a feeling I've never felt before -
Who could it be - or what - behind that door?

I know things now, the way they are,
But life isn't mine yet, by far.

I hear the sentences and words
Clear and crisp as the chirp of birds.

I am so aware of simple things
Surprised by sounds like telephone rings.

Am I the same as I used to be?
Or is the world changing without me?

The Time Inbetween
by Caroline Hargrave

In the split second
Between reality and fantasy,
It is up to you to find what dwells there.
Once you have passed this
Standstill in time,
You have reached a passage
Of free thought.
You let yourself fall over the
Edge of sanity and dreams.
Dissolving into millennium
Sinking into a land all your own
Sitting on the black floor.
The full moon hanging
In a hammock of darkness,
Draining through the canopy of leaves,
Portraying gems of light
Newborn in a dark threatening world,
A light exploding with life.
Stars dancing in their own private world,
The white beach
Bathed in gentle moonlight
With the waves sculpting its sand
In rhythmic, pulsating gestures.
Wind flutters from one tree to the next
Caressing each branch with
Warm sweetness.
The air catches you.
You float away
Once more to that unknown period of time,
The Time Of Inbetween.

Letter To An X.
by Melanie Kim Harmon

They say a promise can be broken, but I don't think that's true, it forms a lasting strong foundation in hopes they will love you. I took that step completely, In hopes you'd do the same....you promised that you'd never leave me but your words began to wain.

It took some time to see it,
but I know now it's true... You never will achieve this, so now I can't love you. I could say that I'm not hurting, but that would be a lie... I know you're not deserving, but I love you still as time goes by.

The day will come
When I won't need you, I will start my life anew....I promised never to deceive you so believe these words are true. If I wait a little longer real true love will come my way, then I will sing this song no longer, so enjoy it now today.

One Night
by Lynnann Harper

The sky was such a pretty blue, with a shade of
green kissing that and the horizon. The first few
stars were just starting to make their appearance to the
world again, as night fell upon the land here in Boylston.
And as a plane was flying overhead, I saw
perfectly clear, something larger and brighter go
over the plane. A shooting star perchance?
Most likely so. It was going so much more faster
than the plane. It was falling away from the
school in such a sudden white light, passing
beneath the trees and then fading into the
cold, winter night, forever.

Those Days
by Sandy Harris - age 14

I'm sure you've all had one of those days
When nothing seems to be going your way.
You get on the bus and trip over your shoes
Then you look up and see everyone's laughing at you.
When you get to school it's just as bad.
You start feeling sick over the breakfast you had.
So you ask your teacher if you can call home
She says "go ahead, call your mom."
But when you call home you get the answering machine,
She just left, what bad timing.
Just when you think things can't get any worse
You find out you owe a shot to the school nurse.
But things start changing later on in the day,
You're invited to a baseball game
And you get to play.
When you wake up the next morning, you decide
That yesterday turned out alright
Until you remember
You were chewing gum when you went to bed last night!

A Lover's Triangle
by Sharon L. Harris

Comforting arms I faithfully left
My promise to you I faithfully kept
Alone and sad with a tearful face
I desperately search for your loving embrace
With each slow tick, my heart doth cry
Forget the memories you detoxify
I left him, Lord, for he rejected you
Spiritual battles intensely grew
I question now - Was it so necessary
To leave a heart so contrary?
Not only did I leave opposition
But all hopes of acquisition
For who will now defend your name
And persuade a lost soul that Jesus came
The paramount task I was chosen to fulfill
Was to leave a love, yet love him still
Understanding cannot outweigh emotion
Lord, help me to implement devotion
For where will this heart now aspire
The love it needs, craves, desires?
Deeper and sadder, the pain intensifies
Yet miraculously I solemnly realize
You feel the pain, you note the wound
Your heart bleeds, too - you importune
That your child is crying, you hear her tears
and you'll lift her from her deepest fears
You'll love this heart, you'll save this soul
ultimately blessed - I'm in your control
Protect me, Lord, caress my needs
Cease this madness - accord my pleas

Satellite
by Maureen Hartshorn - age 15

The sky was bruised,
but willing to listen.
My veil, tattered and torn,
could no longer absorb the tears,
and the swing upon which I sat
could not accelerate into the stars.
Still drunk from his words--
Juices from my heart dribbling down his chin,
this tattooed angel
I wanted so much to believe in
leaves me pregnant with empty promises.
Burying stockinged feet into playground sands,
I try to stay grounded.
He weaves emotion
into a sweater that keeps me warm,
but still a liquid cartoon,
he doesn't change.
His lies are lullabies,
and I sleep, dreaming of the truth exposed.
He has a honeysuckled kiss and tries
not to hurt me,
but reality seeps through,
and with each excuse,
the stars seem all the more desirable.

Moonstruck
by Kyra A. Harr

She felt threatened,
until she turned her head
and saw him standing there.
Their eyes met
and her signed her near.
He then leaned down
and shielded her with his kiss.
Her troubles disappeared.
Embraced, tears rolled down her face,
as emotions filled her soul.
Reminiscing, she remember...
How his strong arms make her feel safe.
Then, once again, the time has come...
They part Forever Friends.

Ode To Uncle Keith
by Elisabeth Nicole Harvey - age 17

Filled with happiness,
he looked forward to every day.
A loving wife and
a supportive family.
What more could one want?

A life filled with pleasure and contentment.
An accomplished man.
He shared his joy with others.

Love was spread without a doubt.
Little tokens of affection
given to everyone.
It didn't have to be much.
You <u>knew</u> it came with love.

God needed him, so he was
taken from our lives.
Loss and grief struck throughout.

We are gathered to say good-bye
for those who couldn't before.
Although gone, never forgotten.
He'll live with us forever
in our minds and hearts.

A Never Ending Battle
by Joy Hash - age 20

On the corner of Green Street
She holds out her hands
A young mother in despair
A woman without a care
For life has been long and hard
A never ending battle

On the corner of Green Street
A little girl munches happily on a candy bar
The only food she's consumed in days
Her shoes are tattered and worn
Blues eyes filled with scorn
For life is full of unfulfilled hope
A never ending battle

They live from day to day
Not knowing where they'll sleep at night
Or where they'll get their next meal
Two homeless people
Longing for a better life.

"No Diving"
by Gar Hatcher

Close your eyes and fall asleep
Let me invade your dreams
Let me take part in your fantasies
Let me control your screams
Let me caress your body
Allow me to buy your soul
Make me hunger when your are starving
Make me shiver when you are cold
Let me press my lips against yours
Let me whisper lullabies in your ear
Let me pick you up when you fall down
Let me wipe away your tears
I want you, I need you, I love you
My feelings grow stronger every day
Allow me to be your never-ending love slave
I promise to always obey

Fire of Spirit
by Zeyphyre Hawklen

When we first begin to soar on the wind
We feel in our hearts we can never fall
Now our spirit nears its completion
But the wind is thin and eludes our grasp
And ere long we drop back to the ground
So we look inside ourselves and doubt where we have been
At this time we must get up and confess
That we've much to learn before we soar alone
Yet we must do it, we must do it
Then we fly so high we can touch the stars
But we look back to the ground and see those left behind
Our hearts ache at the sight
Now we know the truth behind our growth
We must help them, we must help them
Begin to realize who they are, lead them all the way
To their highest state of life, take them to the stars with us
Then we all will fly far past the moon and then
We will reach for the sun and see our spirit
Rival its light
And then we know we have paid
The debt we owe our teachers
Thus we set free
The fire that is our lives
Universally

Saying Our Good-Byes
by Kimberly Haynes - age 15

The wilted flowers have gone away
And a song's happy voice is heard today
The voice no longer howls, but still my heart sighs
Of why you had to leave, without saying good-bye
God's plan is done, you had to go
To be with him forever in the home I've heard about so
This eternal home of heavenly rest
And a place to worship him for all he has blessed
Left behind is a tombstone that serves your token
Which say things about you that are more than unspoken
My heart still sinks and cries inside
I just want to run away, run quickly, and hide
Can't God return you, in some kind of way
And bring you back to me and with me always stay?

Thinking of You
by Brett Hawks

The carnival lights
confuse my minds.
As I think of you
time after time.

Looking at the sky, the moon,
the stars in the Milky Way.
I can't help but to pray
that I'll see you again someday.

I'll be dreaming when
I see your face.
The most important thing
in the human race.

I break into a sweat
when I think of you.
My mind grows light
I don't know what to do.

If I see you again
I will give you all my time.
I will let you know
about these feelings of mine.

Like the Ferris wheel
my mind spins around.
As I think of you
sitting upon the ground.

Now I know these words
that I say are true.
Because my heart skips a beat
every time I'm thinking of you.

Best For Last
by Carolyn M. Headrick

There nestled along the fence,
behold the beautiful sight.
Spots of yellow, white and orange
beside lavender and pink.
Continually changing emphasis,
forsythia to honeysuckle.
Then yarrow, coreopsis and lilies
scattered along the beds.
Purple violas and wild violets bloom
between the fern and astilbes.
And perky pachysandra stands
alone under the pines.
Nothing could be more wonderful
than this tranquil scene.
Yet, one more wonder will
unfold before it's done.
The most exquisite of them all,
pink with white edging.
It's fragrant bloom spans six inches
on a thirty inch stalk.
When other lilies drop their petals
the late blooming Stargazer opens.
It's beauty dazzles the eye as
nature saves the best for last.

Cherie Anna
by Holly M. Heard - age 20

Match is lit, the flame
    casts the shadow of your face on
the back wall
    and I can see the rise and fall of
your chest as you take each breath
and I watch your eyes dart around
    taking everything in, observing
every little object and you close
    your eyes eventually when a really
good part of the music pierces
your soul and the blood in your
veins feels like warm applesauce
and you can feel every fiber of the
cotton shirt laying on your smooth
clean pores...
and you take your hand to rub your
opposite arm to comfort and love you
because you do
    just because
        you can
            for once.

Handsome Danny!
by Gladys E. Henderson

Met my cousin's neighbor
    in 1942,
before he left
    for the Army Air Corps
Danny requested a date
    upon his return.
He wrote letters
    from several bases
in different states.
    In January, 1944,
he was taken POW
    by the Nazis.
Danny wrote
    from Stalag 17,
a prison camp,
    reinforcing his interest
in keeping our date.
    He was released in 1945,
dates were kept.
    Then he stayed away,
until I loved another.
    Danny sought reconciliation.
Drove off in a huff,
    when unsuccessful.
In October, 1995 -
    located him
in an American Legion.
    Replaced image I'd held
with one of an aging
    World War II veteran.

My Daughter, My Love
by Jennifer Heredia

My daughter Alexandria is my love
She is a gift to her daddy and I from up above
Her personality is sweet
And her stature is very petite.

If you could see her, you would say she is a cutie
she also possesses real inner beauty
When she smiles, she brightens the darkest day
Being with her makes even a cold month as warm as May.

She gets around quite easily, now that she's walking
And she is very curious and always talking
Alexandria plays the piano and likes to sing
Oh, did I mention, at age two, she's into everything.

Alexandria has a chore, the dog she must feed
When she has finished, a book she likes to read.

A great outlook on life she does possess
I'm always in awe of her, I do confess
She is always buzzing around like a busy bee
My daughter is very special to me.

Reflections
by Don Roman DeMarco

Down the road
beside the sea,
lies a place
of such a grace.

It gives relief
to people's grief
and where wishes come true,
opening the door
where souls can soar.

Call it paradise
be it the light
that the blind
sees thru his mind.

I know it's where hopes arise.

Reflections
by Jay C. Hershberg

Reflections, distorted
in cool, calm, clear waters.
Reflections, recurring
on past and younger times.
Reflections, heart-warming
of loves I've won and lost.
Reflections, consuming
My inner-most heart and mind.
Reflections now are all I have
of who I was, and, where I've been.
If I'm here, and all I see are
nothing but reflections,
who am I?

Imagination
by Eva Hess - age 17

She if flying through the sky
like a bird?
Looking down on the people
who?
Sits on a cloud, cotton and white
soft?
Yet she never left the ground
why?

Lonely Without Him
by Holly A. Hess - age 18

His laughter...His sense of humor
...Both vanished.
The only thing that's left,
Aside from our love-be unknowingly buried,
Is our memories together,
The dreams I have, seem so real
But everyone of them...Shattered to pieces.
I keep grasping for the love we had,
Hoping I could get him back.
But I'm left grasping for more.
The life we spent together,
Was so bright and wonderful
And what he's left me with are endless days of darkness.
I feel as if a part of me...Has just gotten up and left.
When I think of our happy times...I just break down
What happened...
He loved me...I know he did
I can't imagine myself living without him...
He was my first love
Nothing compares...To the love...He gave me...
Not one of them came true.

Fading Away
by Melissa A. Hididd - age 14

The memory of you I had,
    that once made me sad,
Is now fading away, fading away.

The love in my heart,
    that thought we would never be apart,
Is now fading away, fading away.

The voice you sang, of love you gave,
Is now fading away, fading away.

Just look at my frown,
    that was once turned upside down,
Is now fading away, fading away.

The happiness I once had,
    even when I was mad,
Is now fading away, fading away.

The future that is now the past,
    the one we thought would always last,
Is now fading away, fading away.

The past that became of you, will be the future of me
    sometimes I wonder when that will be
Future . . . Now . . . and Past . . .
    I am too fading fast.

An Island Christmas
by N Loy Higgins

Christmas in the islands
Celebration by the sea
Hanging decorations
On a huge Pandanus tree.

Ornaments made of seashells
Or treasures from the land
With little strings of coral
And a tree skirt made of sand.

As the sea breeze gently blows
At night our tree is bright
Under a blanket of stars
Glistening in the moonlight.

No snowy days for shopping
Only soft pacific rain.
All the gifts are handmade
No two will be the same.

In the distance, waves are breaking
Above, the palm trees sway
Soothing background music
To welcome Christmas day.

Sitting here upon the beach
We hear carolers getting near
Singing Christmas hymns of praise
And songs of holiday cheer.

Drinking wassail, giving gifts
Sharing stories of long ago
We'll use a branch of sea grapes
As our island mistletoe.

Smiling faces all around
On this clear and reverent night
Spending Christmas island-style
Is sheer tropical delight.

To Heaven I Will Run
by Jennifer J. Hill

For now my eyes are opened
My earthly door has closed
My family life behind me
To Heaven I will go

I hope you all will see
My time here now is done
I miss you comes to mind
I'll be with you inside

The doors for me are opened
I will be with you again
Never forget the good times
To Heaven will I run

The times we had are priceless
The things we did, please don't forget
The sweetness of our laughter
Shows times that will be missed

Just one more time I'll say
I love you anyway
And when my time has come
To Heaven I will run

The Fountain
by Rebecca Elizabeth Hill - age 13

And into the bubbling waters I looked
And saw a face
A face that will stay will me for years to come.
In that fountain I found myself
And in its waters if saw what I was to become
Anything I wanted.

I Must Cut The Apron Strings
by Evelyn A. Hitchcock

My babes are grown.
They want to fly.
To spread their wings
Against the sky,
To leave my nest
And soar so high.
My apron strings
They will untie.

They'll go through storms.
Who'll keep them dry?
Who'll tuck them in
When night is nigh?
Who'll hug them tight
When they cry?
Will they find comfort
Where they lie?

How sad I am
Oh my, oh my.
As I let go
With plaintive sigh.
Too soon they've grown.
I question, why?
Come back, my darlings
Bye and bye.

Relax
by Suzie Hockenberry - age 16

Cry.
Release anger,
Calm down.
In right mind now,
Ready to accept the situation.
Sit back,
Relax.
Think things over.
What's the best way
To deal with the pile of jobs?
Develop priorities;
See exactly what needs to be done
Now, and what can wait.
Jump in.
"Beginning is half the battle."
It becomes fun,
At least endurable.
When finished with these,
There will be many more.
But with the right attitude and perspective,
Anything is possible
And can be conquered.

Untitled
by Jeannine Hoffman - age 16

I never thought the day would come,
when we would no longer be one.
I'll never forget that dreadful day,
when you said you were going away.
I feel like we've just drifted apart
even though your always in my heart.
You've made a new life for us all,
it's been a ball.
Even though you seem so far,
sometimes I'm glad things are the
way they are.
You brought a wonderful new person
into our life,
and asked her to be your wife
I love her so very dear
to disappoint you and
break your heart is what I fear
I just want to let you know,
that I only want this love to grow.
You are my guiding light
when things go wrong,
you always seem to make them right.
Just to make it clear
I love you so very dear.

The Fall Towards Death
by Kris Hofmann - age 19

He enters a realm of deathlike apathy
An apathy brought by an eternal suffering
He accepts it as virtue of the soul
Emptiness stares him in the face
His lonely soul suffers alone
Conscious in a paralyzing torture
Drawn together by a satanic sermon
Like a red moon or a black sun
A cold chill on a mid-summer's day
It's like an irreversible disease
A disease without a cure
Wearing him down without emotion
Unexplained by its own domain
Showing no emotions of the heart
He flirts with the faces of death
He feels the glory of death begin to grow
Grow into his determined destiny
A destiny now bound for pain and solitude...

Locked In Silence
by Kimberly Holt - age 17

This wretched darkness,
My body it surrounds.
I am locked up inside;
I cannot be found.

No one dares to look,
For they are too scared to see,
A person locked in silence,
A person they could be.

I lie down inside,
Of the cold place I live.
No one comes to visit,
And I have nothing to give.

Little Sis
by Judith A. Hoggan

Once, I thought, we were so close;
As close as two sisters can be.
But over the years, we've grown apart,
You with your friends, and mine with me.

I wonder why we so rarely now see
Each other's point of view.
And I long for the laughing sister you used to be,
And the joy you shared with me.

I miss you, Little Sis.
The chasm between us is so great these days.
A great gaping abyss,
Which leaves me cold and lonely for your friendship.

Where did I go wrong?
Where did you?
And will I always long,
For the closeness I thought we once shared?

Whatever the barrier,
It's not insurmountable.
And when we finally do spare
The time for each other again,
All will be well.

Sweet Freedom, Turned Sour
by Maegan Hollister - age 15

What do you want in life?
Maybe freedom and rights.

We fought for those, and we won.
Yet we have denied others that freedom, although we all live under the same sun.

Whether Black, Native American, Hispanic, or even the rich or poor of our own people.
We've always used the words like nigger, savages, or spicks: words that are laughed at with smiles and dimples.

People say - "that is the past, history!! Everyone is free now!"
But are they?

The black people are, but do you think they forget the past?
No. It is a horrible memory that lasts.

The Indians, they are still on their reservations, their treaties still unfulfilled.
Their way of life has long since been killed.

What about the countless others that attempted peace?
It will never come unless we accept that we are all brothers, despite the color.

Then the fighting will cease.

Our freedom is a small, empty achievement, considering what we've done to others.

Pain
by Shannon Holt

Laying there.
Pain.
Thoughtless, loveless,
Pain.
I reach within my soul.
Pain.
I grasp out to something whole.
Pain.
Something with substance.
Pain.
I fear the pain.

Requiem For A Groupie
by Victoria Holz

When your eyes exploded with the rage
Of the green lights as they lit the stage
I asked myself if these things
Could possibly be as they seem
Or are you just my sweet dream
After you unleashed these feelings
Like I never have known before
When all I can but say
Is I just wanted some more
At least for the rest of the night
Not to mention my whole life
Could I be wrong or could I be right
When after knowing too many mistakes
All I knew was you had what it takes
Because you know I know what I like
Let alone what I think I need
Why then do you seem so close but so far away
If I could just have one chance
To dance a very slow dance
Well who knows maybe yet some day
But alas by the end of the thrilling show
I realized what I did not care to know
That unfortunately this could never be
I mean after all you are still you
And I guess I am just me

In the Land of Make believe
by Robin L. Howard - age 18

Even in the land of make believe
you have to believe in yourself,
believing that you can be whatever you want.
You can be a famous tap dancer
or a modern dancer,
only if you believe in yourself.
You can be a renowned ballerina
or a graceful soloist
in the land of make believe.
where anyone no matter the age
can be a pretty pink ballet slipper
or a beautiful black tap shoe
only if you believe in yourself.
You can fly to the moon
or dive the depth of the ocean
in the land of make believe.
Where you are the pilot of your ship,
where you are you,
and no one can take that away from you
in the land of make believe.

Looking Around
by Joanne Hudy - age 17

Looking around
I see pain
Looking around
I see frustration
Looking around
I see sadness
People crying
And that makes me want to cry too

Looking around
I see love
Looking around
I see joy
Looking around
I see happiness
People laughing
And that makes me want to laugh too

Two different emotions
Looking around
I see them both everyday
One as strong as the other
As different as night and day

Looking around
I see the world
Sadness and happiness
Frustration and joy
One as strong as the other
As different as night and day

Another Sad Thought
by Jenny Hultgren - age 20

Holding on to the past
Holding on to the long ago and forgotten
Slowly try to find your pat
back to a new breathtaking experience
before every minute turns into hours chasing the impossible

Long ago in a different world
can't keep it all
Take that first step in to a new beginning
an unbelievable fulfillment to your self
Keep going keep trying
Keep searching to find what you are looking for

Remember your memories
remember the fun
Don't try to take it back
The past flew by
In a world full of dreams and wishes
you should also find yours
Yours to be true yours forever

Let go let loose
Let yourself find your spot inside you
The spot no one ever seen
That no one ever knew about
That spot you saved for yourself

Love Betrayed
by Kathryn B. Hull

From deep within self
Comes a thought
Portraying love—
Warm, open, unselfish.

A word is spoken
And is heard within the heart.
It shatters the thought
And turns it to sadness
No longer feeling
Warm, open, unselfish.
Now anger, hurt, aloneness
Replace the glow.

How long before
Another word will be heard
Portraying love—
Warm, open, unselfish?

Before...
by Betty Jane Humphrey

-Long before the tears had dried
the love was washed away

-Long before the storm's approach
the sky had turned to gray

-Just before the break of dawn
the trust was lost once more

-Like all the shattered dreams to fall
just as the times before

-Just before the sun had set
and all would soon be lost

-Was just before the choice was made
to love him at all cost

-Just before the rainbow's light
would shine for them once more

-Again betrayal marks its path
as every time before

Where Was I
by James M. Hunt

Where was I, when you were down and out,
Where was I, when you were hurt and afraid,
I was too busy looking out for myself,
I was too busy feeling sorry for myself,
I was holding onto the past, afraid to see the present,
I was hanging out in the bar, drinking away my sorrows.

Where was I, when you were crying all alone,
Where was I, when you were dying all alone,
I was too busy looking at other women,
I was too busy reaching out for someone else,
I was running from myself, taking too many pills,
I was hiding from myself, wasting time on alcohol.

Why won't I listen now?
Too far gone in my mind.
Why won't I talk now?
Lost in this sea of voices.
Why won't I look at you now?
Afraid to see the hurt in your eyes.
Why won't I touch you now?
Afraid I might feel something good.

Here we go again,
Lost before we start,
I want to say so many words,
Just can't seem to find a way,
Just have to run away and hide.

Can't seem to feel the way I know I should,
I hope you will forgive me,
I must leave you forever,
Fading into the night.

Another Scream
by Lee Hysell - age 12

A deadly scream,
Coming from afar,
A wife and a mother,
Beaten to the floor,
A snap of an arm,
Hitting someone else,
Another horrendous scream,
As she studders down the stairs,
A lady runs in the night to grab the one she loves,
Another scream as they leave the place they should belong,
They run to a place to keep safe,
Where no one should belong.

The Exchange
by Patricia E.S. 'Iolana

Creatively unstoppable and emotionally broken,
thoughts flow through me like a raging torrent;
Poetry, Prose, Stage, and Screen.
The voice, endless. The well, full.

Overwhelmed by the passion to write,
the captivation of an idea,
that seems to transform,
as if made by Gepetto's own hands.

Yet the creator is a child of wood:
frozen by the roots which ground her,
sashaying in the wind,
Growing too slow.

You see, it's a gift of life,
and a gift of love.
One was given.
The other,
taken away.

In exchange.

My World
In the eyes of a handicapped
by Martha Adelaida Indaburu - age 12

I think about the outside world,
How would it look to me?
I guess I really wouldn't know,
Blackness is all I see.

And I sometimes wonder if it's true,
That there's more than a shadow,
In the darkness of my eyes,
What color is a marshmallow?

And I wish that I could stand up,
And touch the world around
But I'm stuck inside a wheeled chair,
If I try I'll hit the ground.

I try to ask the outside world,
But I guess they cannot hear me,
For I'm also mute, did you not know?
I forgot you cannot hear thee.

I can only hear my inside thoughts,
Mumbles come from without,
I think it is people, but I'm not sure,
Though I don't give it a doubt.

I sit here and think to myself,
For you cannot hear thee,
What did I do to deserve this life,
Oh God, won't you tell me?

I sometimes wish I could look ya.
And see the shining sky,
And wish upon a shining star,
But I know that's all a lie.

Angel Wing
by Monica Iroegbu

Angel wing on puff white cloud, poor Angel lost her wing. Searched high and low, she found a soul, trembling in his boots.

Angel embraced this shattered soul, in her one wing that remained -- administered tender loving care to the bruises on his heart. Then Angel firmly nudged soul back on the road to destiny -- an envisionment of life fulfilled, blessed, and unburdened by a troubled past.

Finishing her work, Angel soared up high through the clouds that reached to Heaven. She came upon that puff white cloud where her gossamer wing shone bright.

Angel sewed her lost wing with a thread of light. Happy with a job done well, Angel flew right on to her home in paradise.

Stay Out of the Attic
by Viola Iverson

"Stay out of the attic" my mother said,
It stirs up memories there you see,
Of all our friends and family.
"Stay out of the attic," my father said,
"Nothing for you to see up there,
And lots of junk upon the stair."
"We don't want you to get in to things,"
But I would have gone if I'd had wings.
"Stay out of the attic," my parents said.
Well what about my sister and me?
We had dolls and play things you see
We knew there were old magazines and
many books,
Besides all the old dusty pictures at which
to look.
"Stay out of the attic,"
There were boxes of old clothes and
odd looking hats.
Wouldn't it be fun to put on all of that?
And then there is that large Swedish
Trunk
Filled with what kind of precious junk?
Jars of pretty buttons and some antique
quilts
How wonderful that attics were even built
"Stay out of the attic!"
There's an old chair or two, a violin
I wonder how this all fits in.
No doubt there were some precious memories,
I would just love to hear all those stories.
Now that's it's time for memory lane
Do I want to go through it all again?
"Stay out of the attic," my parents said.
The words are still there ringing in
my head.

Dandelion
by Theresa Isaacs

Why do we work so hard
at plucking the weeds
from our gardens?
Who was it that said
the dandelion
with its furry head
of sunny yellow,
is not as lovely
as the tulip
or the rose?

But the dandelion
knows
that being odd
means getting picked on,
and that's why
she changes
her sunshine face
to a cloud.

Like the Wind
by Jennifer Jackson - age 15

The lake crashes violently against the shore,
Reminding me of my life.
Stormy and rough one day,
And next cool, calm and clear.

The wind always is with the waves,
Guiding them to their destination.
Like a good friend the wind steers the waves,
And is with them always.

You my friend are like the wind,
And I the wave.
Constantly you are with me.
When life is rough and stormy,
You are there aside me,
Trying your hardest to make it easier.

When my life rages like a storm,
I am glad to know you are there,
In the wind, forcing my eyes open,
Enabling me to see,
The light in the darkness.

Pushing me towards the light,
I feel your presence beside me,
Pushing me to the calm waters,
That always follow a storm.

The Girl
by Christy Jacob - age 16

There she sits a lonely girl inside my heart,
Her legs are crossed but the decision in her mind is one that has stood from the start,
She's not sure why, it's like a book she can't put down,
The one about the boy and girl who painted the town,
She can't understand it, she wonders what it is that makes her feel this way,
The way she ponders the story of the boy and girl who fell in love on the very first day,
She hasn't ever felt like this, the way she feels when he holds her tight,
The same way she wants to feel the first that she'll stay with him late into the night,

Her friends they talk and she often wonders what that feeling of love must be,
But the way her heart pounds when he's around is the feeling that conceives the picture of a white wedding gown,
She doesn't know why or how to explain it,
She feels that he's the one,
And the only way to know is when the dream crosses the line in the race that she never thought she could have won,

Yet to think this girl inside my hearty is one that I can talk to is a dream itself,
For I feel the same as she, but I know those feelings are those that can't be,
For true love has yet to be shown to me.

Prayer of a Suicidal Teenager
by Janine Crystal Jacobs - age 16

Dear Lord, Please forgive me for the sin I'm about to commit.
But you must understand all the pain I'm in.
Having to go through everyday with broken dreams and a broken heart.
Hiding my thoughts, feeling, and fears because I'm afraid that people might find me a bit strange.

Dear Lord, Please forgive me for the sin I'm about to commit.
But you must understand all the painful memories I have.
Memories of family fights and disagreements.
Thoughts of friends that are all ready with you, Dear Lord.

Dear Lord, don't you see the hurt in my eyes.
I've prayed to you so many times,
I asked you to guide me and to lift me from my depression,
to give me a lover that will actually love me,
and to surround me with friends that realize all the good qualities I have on the inside.

Why didn't you answer my prayers Dear Lord?

Dear Lord, Please forgive me for the sin I have just committed.
As I watch my blood drip on the bathroom floor,
I think back to my childhood and how happy I was.
That was before my family started to fight as I hid in my closet and cried,
that was before my friends stabbed me in the back,
and that was before I felt the true sting a lover could leave.

Dear Lord, I'm almost gone now,
Please don't be too mad at me when I get to heaven,
but I think now you understand why I must leave this place of evil.
AMEN.

Tequila Daydreams
by Romy T. Jacobson

tequila daydreams
...salty pacific seas
southern winds
    murmur

foreign tongues
    dance
through lucid skies in a daze
    gaze
of omniscient eyes
    hidden
in golden hues playing spectator
    to january reprieves

Being Wrong
by Christine Jacoby - age 18

You tell me not to worry.
What am I suppose to think when you say I will talk to you tomorrow.
I know in my heart that something is wrong.
I thought communication is the best policy to a relationship.
I guess I was wrong.
I thought we would always be honest with each other.
I guess I was wrong.
I didn't even know if I should believe anyone anymore.
Everything I do or say is wrong.
Why can't I make anyone happy anymore.
I guess my life was made to be bad.
I know one day all my problems will be gone.
I just hope we can last till then.

Heart's Desire
by Leah James - age 17

Daydreams sweet and pure,
The longing looks we both endure,
Precious kisses and hugs so tight,
Falling in love beneath the star light.
Hopes and fantasies wished to come true,
When all that really matters is me and you,
Our future together begins to grow,
As our love is stronger than we know.
Carried away by our heart's desire,
For it's only you I'll ever admire.
The shine in my eyes is that of gold,
As I'm yours to always have and to hold.
Each beat of my heart is for you,
A symbol of assurance that I'll forever be true.

Life
by Jennifer Janssen - age 16

As the last light of dawn
stretches over the hillside,
pain cries out over the land.
Life itself drains away
like the setting sun.
Towering mountains cease
their existence on this molten ball,
so close to extinction.

Form and Content in Poetry
by Andrew Jantz

While free verse is a relatively recent development in the long tradition of English poetry, it may surprise some to learn that one of the sharpest critiques of rhymed verse was written three hundred years ago, by none other than John Milton. In the preface to *Paradise Lost* Milton explains his refusal to use rhyme in his epic: "This neglect then of rime so little is to be taken for a defect, though it may seem so perhaps to vulgar readers, that it rather is to be esteemed an example set, the first in English, of ancient liberty recovered to heroic poem from the troublesome and modern bondage of riming...rime being no necessary adjunct or true ornament of poem or good verse...but the invention of a barbarous age, to set off wretched matter and lame metre..."

Rhyme for the sake of rhyme is nothing short of ornamentation - a sort of mental masturbation - and all too often its use comes across as arbitrary and awkward. While there are probably as many definitions of poetry as there are poets, surely the weakest would be those contingent on the use of rhyme. As Robert Creeley stated, "Form is never more than an extension of content." A poem should dictate its form. Form dictating content is putting the horse before the cart.

This is not to say that formal structure is superfluous. On the contrary, it can make or break the poem. When form is used in the service of content, the results can be extremely powerful. A good modern example of this is the villanelle "Do Not Go Gentle into That Good Night" by Dylan Thomas. The success of the content hinges on the use of form. Form rises above the level of ornamentation to promote content. And this is one of the hallmarks of any successful poem.

My Little Cowboy
by Kris Jardine

I've gotta little cowboy, as cute as he can be.
He learned to count by countin' cows,
    And he's not even three.
Two, three, four, and five, now there's fifty-nine.
Don't know for sure how many there are,
    But with us, that's just fine.

He really likes the rodeo and that's what frightens me.
That's what he likes to watch, on that old TV.
    He likes to ride the rough stock,
    Sittin' on the arm of the chair.
    He pulls his riggin' up real tight,
    As though he were really there.

He rides around the room, on his pretend horse.
With a string of any kind, this becomes his rope.
    He now becomes a calf roper,
    With nothing on his mind
    Except to be the rodeo champ,
    When it becomes his time.

If you want to be his friend, you must have a horse or cow.
    Cause he likes to ride, and watch you rope
    So he can learn how.
Those he likes knows his ways, and admires the way he is.
    Cause it's the cowboy way of life,
    And the cowboy way is his.

Now I think that you can understand, a cowboy's life begins,
    The day they take their very first breath,
    It comes from within.
    So I think if you should know one,
    You're gonna have to agree.
A little cowboy knows just what he wants to be.

Got A Minute?
by Mary Jayme

Is it gone then?
Has our youth finally ended?
Our innocence vanished?
Have the ages passed
    so quickly by us
    and touched us only
    with their time?
And what of their wisdoms?
Can we escape them so easily
    with our fatal endings
And turn our faces
    from what we know?
Or must we now open our inner eyes
    to the truth?

Life and Death
by Noelene Jeffers - age 13

    Life

Parallel lines, colors in motion,
Screaming voices, pure insanity,
Should I be subjected to this torture,
Swirling rods of force,
One big hole,
One big Universe,
What's the difference,
between life and death.

    Death

That belt,
Those hands,
Such pain,
Such sorrow,
Whose cries are those,
As I feel the buckle,
What do they call it, life, that's it,
Well, it all flew by,
A movie gone bad.

The Present
by Teresa Jeffries - age 15

As I lye here alone,
Thinking about my past;
I wonder about the future,
Repeat, or will it last?
Unfortunate events,
I've survived quite a few;
I wonder of those to come,
Will they be numerous too?
I see a shining face,
Too far the features to make out;
This figure that I see,
Is neither thin nor stout.
Has this person come to see me through.
To guide me through this life;
Or has it come to carve my heart,
As though working with a knife?
As I wander through this life,
And recall my lonesome past;
I rest my eyes upon the future,
And try to make it last.

Angel
by Heather Jensky - age 13

When I was little I had no one.
My life was silent and I had feelings
I could share with none.
I was twelve when he came to me,
hushing my tears, for I had many,
I was harmed by virtually everyone.
His name was Ryan.
He was there for my problems,
He was there for my fear, just like
he was for tears.
He was there for me unlike my peers.
Everyone said he was unreal, but he
was there for me, in my thoughts and
comforting my fears.
He taught me to love, he taught
me to care, I was never shoved and he
was always fair.
I turned sixteen and still believed
he was not just the angel who
was my only friend. A friend who
actually cared.
Soon my life with him came to
a sad end, when I realized he was just
a fairy tale friend. So I began to forget
him.
And though it has been years,
I will never forget, My Dear Friend Of Years.

My Carrion
by Emily E. Jesse - age 14

I laid inside myself for too long, for not enough
My purity played the tunes and I tossed around believing I had been here many times before
I was no naive in believing, in thinking that
My fingertips scratched the open-wounded skin
And I held up my hands in the showing of the glorious shrine
I licked my fingertips, my tongue surrounded the remaining skin
They dripped with exposure as it had the time before
What I knew of his purity was too early discovered but too late to be searched
My resolution had never been his
And it hurt to know that the flower I picked had already been plucked
With no time to anchor
He had made me a sail
Now I lie somewhere between purity and lust, some place by self-pity and self-righteousness
I know what I see, what I feel, no explanations and no criticism
Wait, I am lying to myself
I breathe in the deception with my pours
....And I lie awake wishing I was someplace else
Lying inside myself for too long, for not enough.

On To A Dismal Future
by Shannon Jody

How can I get across the rainbow to see the beauty of things unknown
when the skies are so clouded with the dirty gray of human sins that
grow thicker with the blowing wind? It's so hard to find beauty in nature
it doesn't exist anymore
from the bleeding earth all tattered and torn from the abuse of
mankind. Progressively killing the land doing as they please
with no regard for any other living creature burning and
killing forests with no sign of quenching their thirst cares
for nothing but metal and glass and then it's all gone in a
blinding flash.

Invisible
by Tina Johanson - age 15

It's clear enough for me to see
That you and I aren't meant to be
So why do I still cry
Every time you pass me by
Don't you understand
Why can't you just see
If only you would glance my way
If only you would see me
Just once I'd like to look into your eyes
Everything that's there
To me it's all paradise
But again you keep on going
And again I wonder how you keep from knowing
Isn't it obvious
My feelings for you
But all you can see
Is the wall behind me
And as you turn that corner
And leave me all alone
Once again, I feel invisible

Grand Canyon
by Lindsey Johnson - age 15

Where all is quiet.
Where years ago,
torrential rains and raging rivers
dug a passageway through the earth
that opened the door to new beginnings for many people,
to new discoveries for many explorers.
Where whispering winds blow softly against the walls.
Where silent waterfalls fall quietly to the canyon floor.
Where each layer of rock represents another lifetime gone by.
And with each day, a new layer is formed,
one that represents all the lifetimes of the future.

Call Of The Quitter
by M. E. Johnson

Red tip on a cig
puff puff
Nicotine sure is keen
puff puff

Gray smoke from a cig
puff puff
Clean air, do I care?
puff puff

White ash on a cig
puff puff
Makes me stink, do you think?
puff puff

Yellow tar from a cig
puff puff
In my lung, I'm too young!
puff puff

Brown butt of a cig
puff puff
Nicotine, how obscene!
quit quit

The Way I Feel About You
by Angela Rose - age 14

We talk, we laugh,
We share intimate secrets.
We're best friends,
But I wish it were more.

My heart has strong feelings for you.
I take any chance to brush
Your skin lightly with my hand.
A hug from you means a lot.

The feeling of being in your arms
Seems right. The way you hold me
Close against your chest when I cry
Is comforting.

As I stare into your deep blue eyes,
It takes all my strength not to
Throw my arms around you neck
And kiss you.

Sometimes I catch you looking at me and
Smiling tenderly. I wonder if you feel
The same way I feel about you.
It would be a dream come true.

Philposphize
by Aaron Johnson - age 19

As my eyes to the dark improvise,
My pupils grow with the black night skies.
Midnight air has the power to tranquilize.
It's the mornings I always despise.

A full moon, all the lighting provides.
The moon's light to the earth amplifies.
I see through the dark shadows of lies
As I search for the truth in your eyes.

In your lifetime you must realize
It's important to always hypothesize.
Deep thought, to the mind, sanctifies.
Reality, one's hope, crucifies.

Other species man kills-and justifies.
In natural selection, the strongest survives.
Natural beauty, in industry, dies.
The human race needs to open its' eyes.

Nuclear warheads, in a flash, vaporize.
All life ends in the fatal sunrise.
The land is rendered unfit to colonize.
The wind carries radiation through the skies.

The push of a button from a heart of despise.
Response bombs are launched and the threat multiplies.
If Armageddon occurs, the whole planet dies,
And from nuclear ashes, no phoenix shall rise.

Reflections
by T.L. Johnson

   Passing by the window reflections
Hold the past,
Turning towards the future never
Looking back,

Once a child could not see, now
The years go by easily

Love, hate, war it's all the same,
Just depends on how you play
The game

Passing by the window reflections
Hold the past,
Turning towards the future never
Looking back.

The Speed Of Life
by Terry Johnson

I'm just a tiny snail, unable to go fast
Please do not rush me. Stay off my ass!

I have only two speeds. They're moderate and slow.
And sometimes I lack direction, not knowing where to go.

But if I set my sights on a very specific goal
reaching it I know I'll do, though I may be slow.

All I really need to do is crawl one foot at a time
towards a specific goal in a straight and narrow line.

If time is of the essence, then I'm afraid I will fail.
For rushing to meet deadlines in not healthy for a snail.

Taking adequate time to do a project without error
is what my speed allows me, so if I'm slow I don't care.

Sure, others complain that I'm just too slow.
But as long as I proceed I know I'll reach my goal.

So, here's to a moderate speed, and going slow in life.
For I'll never jump to conclusions, causing myself strife!

The Flower That Never Bloomed
by Brooke Johnston - age 13

I thought you were an angel-
I thought you were true-
I thought you were the one
    for me
And me for you.

You should have told me
    soon before-
I can't trust you evermore.

It seemed as though you changed-
It seemed as though you were true,
But I'm not sure to trust you.

Should I go with my instincts
    or my heart?

A decision not yet comprehended
But sure to thought out.

The Wind
by Alice M. Jones

The Wind is a very essential element known by various names,
And one of them is air.
It is so essential in the life of every living thing,
God created it and has put it everywhere.

It can be; a gentle breeze, a gale, a puff, a gust,
A whirling tempest or a flurry.
The Wind does whatever God wants it to do; It can be calm or
In a great hurry.

We can not see the wind, but we can feel its touch, and hear
Its sounds that are made so plain.
It is known by its actions, whether it is a gentle breeze, a
Stormwind, twister, or a hurricane.

It's amazing how great and how close, God really is, and feeling
His presence in every breeze.
If you listen to the sounds of the wind and notice how it
Commands the actions of the trees.

Notice the trees in the path of the wind, how they
Unanimously obey God's will.
They listen to Him speak through the wind as it gives an
Order and they can't be still.

Are we any less than the wind? God created us for His
Purpose, and we are very essential too.
We must love and unite ourselves with God and His Darling
Son, and do what He commands us to do.

Lost
by Crystal A. Jones - age 13

Lost, lost in a world of hope,
never willing to face reality,
never willing to understand.
Love will never come to me,
and I will never find it.
That is the reality I will not face.
So I keep sinking into
a world of hopes and dreams.
Sleep is my escape,
my dreams keep me from the truth.
So, I am lost in my own world.

Him
by Stacy Jones - age 17

Who is he and what does he want?
He looks at me, and I see in his eyes a longing.
I hesitate.
Do I return his burning gaze?
Do I quickly look away and pretend to ignore it?
Who am I to decide the fate of this beautiful young man?
I am but only a face in the crowd.
Yet his eyes captivate me as they look through me and search my soul
for the things he craves.
I glance back at him and feel my hesitation begin to fade into oblivion.
I know nothing of my actions.
I am being swept into his arms.
I can feel every muscle in his body contract and relax in strong waves of
passion.
My feet no longer touch the ground below me.
He pushes me to the brink of my emotions.
I can no longer feel anything but the rhythmic pulsing of my heart.
It pounds in my chest--crying and shouting to be free.
Suddenly, it's over.
I smile--embarrassed at my own thoughts.
I don't even know his name or where he comes from.
Yet, for one brief moment, we were as close as only two lovers can hope
to be.

Our Souls Fly To His Eternal Home
by Vishnu P. Joshi

The One who resides
In the innermost room of our heart
Extends in the outermost
Beyond the new galaxies of suns,
Planets and moons;

The One who plays
On the harp of our minds
Puts enchantment
In the heart of lilies,
Birds, fishes and animals;

The Sun, the Moon and
The Earth are His creations;

With a golden pitcher of sunbeams
He pours life every morning
Through veins of living creatures;

In His dream
We wake up and see
Spring, Summer, Autumn and Winter
We smile and we weep;

We hop like birds and
We whisper like trees and flowers
Along the meadows,

We sing and dance like bees
We love and hate like animals;
One day we inhale
The last breath of our life,

Then like a homesick bird
To its nest
Our souls fly
To His Eternal Home.

What I Almost Remembered, I Tried To Forget
by Emily Joost - age 16

A sudden feeling surfaced in my mind
A lost feeling triggered by the notes of a song
Sweetness and summer were entangled in the melody
Why the feeling returned was a reason for contemplation.
With it, poured out remembered emotions, actions, and places
It's origin was still unfound.
I strived for a reason to justify this rush of feeling which enclosed my heart.
The idea once lived seemed to slip untouched through the grasp of my mind.
I suddenly struck upon the rock I was in search of.
It was buried, hidden purposely in the inner chambers of my heart.
I recalled why I no longer felt the exultation of the remembered feelings.
Realizing why it was stored there to begin with,
I replaced the remembered,
Attempting to bury it deeper,
So next time it will be impossible to find.

Painted Grey
by Ben Joynes - age 15

I.

Dew drops clinging to the petals.
You dance upon the garden's young.
And waiting for the mist to settle,
I hear the songs no one has sung;
"When nothing is as it once seemed,
and each raindrop acts as a voice."
Tortured by the silent trees,
This must be thought devoid of choice.

II.

Lonely tears upon the petals.
Forever silent; countless sum.
Born of rain as ether settles,
Tidal waves as small as some
Of the tiniest grains of sand.
Silence like a storm is lethal.
The nothingness within my hands
Is nonetheless within my hands;
Is nonetheless inconsequential.

CONCLUSION

In places that I cannot stay
Are the thoughts which still remain
And as the sky is painted grey
New thoughts shall be lost in vain.

The Past
by Michele Juelis

He called me over like he had done before,
I'd leave each morning wanting more.
Blocking thoughts of my love and how we were,
How you would look at me, but think of her.
Searching for the guilt in the things I've done.
With him it's a game, I played and she won.
Waiting by the phone as you decide to call.
You're dropping the net as I continue to fall.
Sharing your dreams and that you're making a choice,
But you forget about me when you hear her voice.
As you kissed I watched your love intertwine.
The same soft lips that once touched mine.
You smiled at me, but it didn't last.
So I closed my eyes to remember the past.

Fear and then Life
by Rebecca Juneau - age 16

The fear comes in from,
the dark.
Fear makes you mad...
to go insane.
Then fear met the light
of Life.
Fear and Life.
They came as one
and they fought as one.
Who one???
The light of life will win.
No matter,
How bad the fear of the dark is.
The light of the life,
is He...
God himself.

Afternoon With Gram
by Cynthia M. Kadow

A rainbow of blossoms greeted us, as we entered the gate,
a decor only Gram could create.
Embracing a grotto, a trellis blanketed in buds of pastel pink,
robins and bluejays congregating on an ivory bath, dipping for a drink.
An elderly lady dressed for Sunday mass,
balanced by a cane, on a carpet of velvet jade grass.
A fine mesh net holding tiny silver curls in place,
surround a round, warm, smiling face.
Cheeks dusted with a rosy blush,
an emotional greeting, spoken in a hush.
Thick oval lenses shielding glistening blue eyes,
thin gray eyebrows that could sometimes rise.
Entering the house, aroma of brewing coffee steams through the air.
Frosted and sugared donuts arranged on a dish, with such care.
Filling our bellies and chatting for hours,
our visit is over, but not without a bouquet of Gram's prize flowers.

'A Mystery Minded Trace'
by Roy Kahler

On some helpless time near silence's tracks is a tear that comes uncovered
from way back before or still dropping as the memories come to bear

the window of the world goes through me although not a piece to share
by any likeness I may compare
alone alone
it falls to her cheek

so many times in repeat truly felt
life runs through me deep

as this can be seen —
every specific moment priory redeemed
has so much of a message coming as each is perceived

thou's expression in care toward a mystery minded trace
has far more wonder than the window held as I look out
across the land for a reason that may be in glance

of a pulsating ray of light
may we be together
for once if not ever from those tears while they drop and splash
upon the glass plate of silence's height —

the silver cord of ecclesiastes
take me within
each colostral part as they feel so full of sorrow
right from her eyes in this excentral night.

Shantel
by J Kalil

I wish that the sun shines in your dark and foggy reality,
hope that you are able to harmonize
and choreograph your life
as you take off your veil to this antagonistic world
you are part of,
moreover,
don't allow darkness to consume you
for you are close to finding your shadow.
Reveal yourself to nobody
don't allow anybody to ignore or
deny your existence.
Your innocence is lost.
You've known horror and wickedness.
You've been penetrated, but I know
you are impenetrable.
I hope God hears the echoes of your heart
for you have asked with tears.
Why me?

Pauly's Window
by Paul Michael Kane

When Pauly died, I realized that no one close to me had ever died before.

Pauly owned the service station where I worked. He was a likeable fellow who seemed to know everyone in town, and not a single one of these persons had anything negative to say about the old man.

I remember he used to drive around town in this big, powder blue Cadillac with his wife, Lois. They had been married for over fifty years. Fifty years! It was something I couldn't comprehend.

Then one day, Pauly died.

I drove by work on my way to class and noticed the station was closed. As this had never happened before, I called the station to make sure everything was alright.

It was the most disturbing call I had ever made.

I went home in a kind of trance. There I sat looking through this big bay window in my
grandparent's home, the kind that has twelve panes of glass within the window itself.
Grandma's nick-knacks decorated every pane. For hours, I just stared out this window and contemplated my own mortality.

My grandfather, having heard the news, eventually came in and sat by my side to gaze out the same window as I.

"Pauly gave us this window." As he spoke, he didn't even turn his head. He simply stared out the big window.

As the words sunk in, I realized that I hadn't known my grandparents knew Pauly.

Without another word, he got up and left.

I continued to watch the world pass by through the window. A family of deer walked by, squirrels darted across the yard, birds sang and the sun set.

I silently bid Pauly farewell and thanked him for the window.
Pauly's window.

Petal
by Laura M. V. Keihl - age 13

The world is eternal,
but I am temporary.
I'm like a petal from a flower,
falling endlessly to the ground,
but a sudden gust of wind
brings it flying high in the air.
But after all, it gently falls to the ground,
leaving it lonely
only to have people trample over it
and die slow only to remember
the times it had with life inside it.

Escape
by Briana Karczewski - age 15

Trying to run far away
to leave the pain and sorrow behind.
Wanting to find the perfect happiness,
but is there any of the kind?

Will anyone ever understand
that escaping is what I need?
To collect my thoughts and feelings,
won't you listen to what I plead?

Is there anywhere that I can go
just to be by myself?
Away from the hate?
I really don't want answers,
but please just let me escape!

Willow Tree
by Stephen N. Karmol - age 17

Why must a willow
always be weeping?
Is there a secret
or something it's keeping?
Has it lost a friend?
Will it meet its end?
This is what I ask:
Are your leaves not green?
Your soul, it's not merry?
Then why do you weep?
Is the answer that scary?
Yet never it answers
just one of my queries
As we sit and I talk
as the days, they grow weary
Each night I return
to my home after this
and think to myself
the times I have missed
that I have spent asking
this sad, forlorn tree
The answer a door
for which I have no key

The Lost Boy
by Dwight H. Kelley

I searched and searched every wooded area to be,
Hoping my little boy would come to me.
I even climbed trees so high
Hoping to hear just one little cry.

I looked into the Heavens and began to pray,
"Dear God, where is my little boy today?"
For I want to see his sweet little face
And never more in this life to run the race.

Suddenly, the sound of wind whisped by my head
And told me that my little boy was dead.
I said, "Dear God, let me see him once more."
For I want to be with him when you close the door.

In A Blind World
by Sandra Kelly - age 14

As I feel your presence
in the room.
Your hand softly touches mine.
With your loving care you
lead me to the door.
As we walk
you talk of your day
and I listen with all my content.

Flashbacks of that night
still haunt me.
Stopped at a gas station,
I stepped out of my car
only to find a gun
pressed against my head.

HE PULLED THE TRIGGER!!

BLIND LIVIN <u>IN A BLIND WORLD</u>

Mirror
by Natasha Kennedy - age 14

Mistreated by the world
Self images molded into a mirage-optical
What have I to dread, my mother once said
I'd die right now if The Almighty would just give me the okay-cruel? Yes
As the world itself turns unknowingly around, its tilted axis arouses more cruelty
Am I human?
No couldn't be, because my skin a different tone, shape than yours and my religion a disease.
Birth defects automatically unplug your social pipeline from the rest of the world
Left out-so I'm ten and look two, young and look old
My brain functions as well as yours-maybe even better
Dysfunctional-no
Sensitive-yes
Make no misjudgment of my intellect
But I know that I can survive with my inner sense of pride and beauty
But shall this dreadful minority, I'll have to remember

Horses Of The Wind
by Peggy Boogaard Kennedy

Horses of the wind, pounded down spears of grass:
They need no trails and heed no fence.
Comets of the skies should not touch the earth.
Pounded down peaks and plains under calvacades.
Neighing, they range beyond the sea: crossing hills
And valleys, giving silver firs their speech
As the moon walks on silent feet,
Racing, immortal, they leap.
As the white owl swoops silent in the sky,
Moonflowers thrust silver notes among sleeping swans.
A rising sun colors all where the wild swans
Wheel in the kneeling sky.
I have a song silent as a fawn among the fern
Until I give it voice. Words go beating on the wind.
Horses of the wind rejoice.

Surrounded By Memories
by Shanen Khwaja - age 16

Surrounded,
Surrounded I was
The one I loved,
The one I lost.

The one so dear to me
She had Gray hair,
Wrinkled skin,
Legs that could not walk
With out me.

The smile so warm,
The hand so cold, but
Yet, so gentle.

The voice she heard
The voice of death.

She took care of me
When no one else did,
She was there when I
Needed her.

But now she is gone,
Far beyond my reach.

And now surrounded.
Surrounded by memories.

Shining Stars!!
by Sarah Kieper - age 14

Shining stars
Way up high,
Light my way
To the sky.

Twinkling bright
As you may,
Like you did
That fine day.

Big or little
Bright or dull,
Light and brittle
That's not all.

To you and me
It may seem to be
A bright light
With no meaning.

In fact these things
Are very special,
Even though
It may not seem so.

Sorrows Spent
by Sheldon J. Kierstead

A soaring eagle overhead,
The sun caresses my skin,
Gentle lapping of the ocean's waves,
Night is creeping in.

Lost in sorrows of my past,
As a sea breeze cools the air.
The eagle swoops down on his prey,
All I can do is stare.

Birds sing beautiful, happy songs,
Wind whispers in the trees;
Hypnotic sounds of Nature's voice.
Sorrow gives way to dreams.

I witness people yet unknown
In places I've never been,
Dancing skyclad in moonlit groves,
As though they're Nature's kin.

I see smiles in children's eyes,
Moonlight in their hair.
My sorrows have all passed away,
'Cause I know I'll soon be there.

Escape
by Kristyn Killough - age 20

There is a picture on the other side of me.
A priceless painting demented by virtual reality.
Meaning is kept in the eye of the little girl who played dress-up in my head a dream ago.
It attempts no form except that of a mind-scape which can only be broken into through a
sensual world of shades red and black.
Escaping through a dream where nightmares are real, and terror can eat away at my flesh
as objects become a problem, and problems fade away into my lungs and out to
meet their destiny.......

To Me, With Me, and Why Me
by Jessica Kimmel - age 12

I truly am a fun person to be with, although very anxious to see what's going to happen to me, with me, and why me.
I hope that someday my dreams will come true. And I wonder who, when, and where I will meet my knight in shining armor. I listen to the songs in my head, and am guided by the voices. They are there where ever I go and whatever I do. I sometimes see my life as the most sickening ride ever. Though it could be the most beautiful and wonderful thing that could be.
And as I lead my life the way I think it should be, I try to imagine what is going to happen to me, with me, and why me.
I sometimes feel as though the world has turned on me. I can feel all the pressure pushing on my shoulders, but at times I feel as though I can fly.
And as I glide through the sky I touch the clouds, I can feel the soft moisture slide through my fingers.
As I think, "It's so peaceful up here, if only it were like this in the real world." I am also thinking, "What is happening to me, with me, and why me."
At times in my life, I feel as though I am alone.
I need someone to talk to.
Someone who will listen when I speak, a true friend. Everyone needs at least one. If I had one wish, it would be for WORLD PEACE, even though people may think it's a waste of time. If this would happen, I wouldn't need to wish for it and everyone would have a true friend. I think that World Peace will come if everyone took a time out and looked at what has happened to them, with them, and why them.

Where the Gold Sun Rises
by Laura Kinderman - age 14

Where the gold sun rises, shining o'er the sky,
Where the winds grow sweet, and life does lie,
Forget not, dear friend, where your past has begun,
For you'll see your future, up beyond the setting sun.

The fields sway neatly, to the rhythm of the phrase,
And those who have seen it, cannot separate their gaze,
Forget not, dear friend, thy battles in peace,
For you may soon discover all evil must cease.

The bold, great horizon, stands over your head,
And fleeting thoughts shower thee, with all that's been said,
Forget not, dear friend, that wisdom may come,
When knowledge and experience combine to one.

The winds pick up neatly, soft-gentle but true,
Where each creature stands poised, to seek what is new,
Forget not, dear friend, that what seems may not be,
And that the spirits, in states of peace, remain free.

The waters splash meekly, against the great shore,
As if, pleading fiercely, to come forward, once more,
Forget not, dear friend, that the kind will succeed,
For when the time becomes right, they will not recede.

Where the gold sun rises, shining o'er the sky,
And all remains calm, with peace standing by,
Forget not, dear friend, to reach for the light
Even when it is far beyond the realm of your sight.

Imprisoned rooms
by Lauren King - age 13

My heart is down the hall from me, yet my mind is right across from me. My soul is in the closet, I think it is hiding from me! My life is in the kitchen making breakfast for my death, though I am in my room laying on my bed.
Something keeps playing with my mind, as if it's a toy of some kind. When it goes away I shout for great joy, then lay down and cry. But down the hall, and to the left, I manage to display my very last breath. In a corner you will find, me in a cage, ready to let out and fly. I now must bid thee goodbye, I spread my wings, and search for the sky. But I searched without finding, I am afraid I will never let live or die.

To My One And Only Love
by Whitney Lee King - age 10

When I look into your eyes, It seems I'm floating through the clouds, without a care in the world.

When I'm embraced in your arms, I melt away into a breathtaking sunset.

When I see your face, it seems as if everything has passed away, except you and me, and our love for each other!

There is not a day that goes by that the thought of you does not go through my mind.

My one wish is that some day you and I will be united together for eternity and beyond.

My infinite love for you will never, ever end!

Friend
by Deborah Kirouac

Desire douse images of sweetness
majestically sweeping through my vein,
savoring every moment, every touch;
extracting all the pain.

Reflected temper slowly oozes away
fragments from my heart;
Unbound I watch as silent silhouettes
dance in their depart.

Endeavors captured from many moons
has set your aura ablaze,
whirling me into a trance
devouring you as my prey.

The hourglass holds still the stage
as slowly the play unfolds,
and if - between, we omit the lines
our friendship will behold.

River of Life
by Laurie Marie Kisner - age 19

There is a river of life that runs through everyone.
Be it near or far; to the stars or the sun.
The river runs deep, forever and true.
Being yourself, admitting you're you.
Riding the rapids, bumpy or straight,
Gliding through life unable to hate.
Finding what's right inside of you,
Always seeing the good that others can do.
The river is narrow with many steep turns.
The journey is long and never insured.
There is a long way to go; life is so long.
Sometimes lonely, not sure you belong.
The end is coming, you can be sure,
So always remember the lessons you've learned.
Always be sure of the passage you take,
And remember the river is not always so straight.

Moonlight
by Alice Klevitsky - age 17

Sweet scented, dripping from eaves and darkening,
moonlight, like candle wax,
slips slender hands,
touched by honey comb,
through the garden
of sleeping willow walkways.
Moonlight, silently crawling
down marble steps,
through the veranda,
into crystal hair locks
of a beckoning fountain.
Moonlight, mine, yours, and the villain's
yet innocent as milk
it splashes on pillows,
bathing the quiet sleeper.

I Wonder
by Roger A. Kline

I look across the hazy morning fields, through to the fog-hidden hills.
I see the awaking of the dawn, as the sun begins its journey
across the skies of yet another day.
And I wonder.

Why make a day so beautiful and lifetime so sad?
Why make a person love so strong and true,
just to be hurt, so deep, so bad?

There must be an answer;
I ponder this over and over,
but no reason comes to mind.

Maybe I'm not yet ready to know,
or maybe I already know,
but just don't understand.

Is there truly a purpose beyond this life?
One day we may all know the answer;
but 'til then, there are an endless number of questions.

Maybe when we finally know the answer, it will all be over.
The hurt, the pain, the tears. Life itself.

The World Around You
by Greta Knapp - age 13

Imagine a world
Where peace grows as wild
And open as the wildflowers.
The birds soar free
And the waters flow clear and sweet.
The trees sway side to side
In a playful game with the wind.
Everything around you is alive
And changing and loved, oh so dearly,
From the smallest ladybug to the widest mountain.
Man lives well with man,
Along with the savage wolf or tiger or bear
Or any sort of creature there is.
Everything is calm, but uplifting, and simply beautiful.
Close your eyes and imagine if you can,
Such a spectacular utopia. And yet, don't.
Open your eyes instead. Open wide, and look around. You
Don't need to imagine. It's been
Right here surrounding you all along...
If you only open
Your eyes.

Damn! what is life
by E. Luann Knight - age 19

i am in the midst of turmoil
i do not know which way to turn
i pray you God - help me
where should i turn to
i am so small
time is so large
which way is right
which way is wrong
should i leave
should i stay
i want to help someone - i do not know who
should i help myself
i have been so indoctrinated
people have said
    this is right
    do this
    make something of yourself
may i ask what please sir
i know one thing
that is that God put me here for something
what
i guess i shall just work and put my mind
    oblivious to the fact
i have been told that is the way to truth
i am impatient though
    why
was i meant to be that way
in essence i would like to ask one question
    why God why

Dumb Poem
by Ted Knuckey

It was five A.M. on a cold September morn,
I was a healthy six pound boy from a woman born.
I was in the midst of admiring and fun loving females
and had to work hard at being a masculine he male.
I was not easily intimated and with those my age I held my own.
They were fun to wrestle with and as I was less than five, I had no wild oats to be sown.
I gave chase and caught a few,
and remained quiet, but there was a difference that I knew.
From six to nine our roles reversed and I was pursued by many a miss,
I protested a lot, but was frequently caught and forced to give them a kiss.
I enjoyed the sport, but called them dumb,
and certainly would never be caught playing with one.
From nine to twelve I drifted away,
it was with boys and football that I choose to play.
It was at thirteen, a strange metamorphosis occurred,
girls could help with homework, and they were pretty, but maybe my vision had blurred.
I no longer called them dumb their grades were a's and b's,
my grades submerged into the d's.
I knew now that girls were smart,
the years marched on and I developed a strange feeling in my heart.
I married the prettiest and smartest of the bunch,
but then her mind surely went out to lunch.
She never remembered what she brought and always said, I forgot."
When a balanced checkbook was all I sought,
I've lost my money, but still have the light of my life,
I am left with untold debts and a lot of strife.
I have to say it has been a lot of fun,
    but I'll say it again, "grils are dum."

Wooden Vegetables
by Kenneth P. Koblich

For the tears and clouds
Which hold the rain.
For the forests grown,
And (sewn) (sown),
From our pain.
The blood that falls
Leaves no stain,
On the forest floors
And oceans bed.
The sky the ceiling
Which protects our heads.
...And the only way out,
Is up from here.

Snow
by Kelli M. Koch - age 16

The time has come,
the moon is bright.
The coyote howls,
It is late in the night.

The leaves rustle
The soft breezes blow.
The trees cast haunting shadows
Over the shimmering snow.

A hoot owl calls,
and takes off in flight.
The wind blows through the feathers softly,
It is a beautiful sight.

In the distance I hear,
small feet crunching through the snow.
It is a small deer.
But a sight to behold, I know.

As the winds blow through the tree—
Voices can be heard calling.
Knowing it is only wind and dreams—
Snow has started falling.

Radiant Light
by Olga Kokino

Radiant Light, who made thee?
Awaking the breaking day,
what power fuels thy heart
enticing the minds of men aspiring too close to Truth
probing thy rings of fire and thy molten core?
What precious gifts hath been stolen
to triumph over beast and fashion blades of steel?
Power too bright to harness like Apollo on his steed
too dangerous uncontrolled consuming cities with thy rage
exploding into new worlds
seed bursting forth
melting, consuming
giving Life.
In thy core
and in thy soul,
a part of thee is in me
awaiting to be shaken
from my slumbering
to be filled with thee,
awaking to see thy face.

The Leaves Of Autumn
by Erika Kokkinos - age 11

Red, yellow, orange and brown,
Those are the leaves of Autumn.

Flying wildly to the ground,
Those are the leaves of Autumn.

Rushing to the yard and scampering through the street,
Those are the leaves of Autumn.

Slicing right through the air and landing at your feet,
Those are the leaves of Autumn.

Zipping, zooming, brushing through the trees,
Those are the winds of Autumn.

Racing, fleeing, tickling my knees,
Those are the winds of Autumn.

Following the scent of Winter,
Those are the winds of Autumn.

Drying the masterpiece of a painter,
Those are the winds of Autumn.

Leaves to frolic in, camps to go to,
Those are the joys of Autumn.

Family vacations to exciting places,
Those are the joys of Autumn.

Meet new people at school, seen new faces,
Those are the joys of Autumn.

Ancestors' Letters
by Stephen Kopel

Long buried
in rural attics,
city lockers, urban vaults,
bound boxes bear bundled
scribbles of affection -
hopeful, hesitant, yet slowly
yielding to desire; gradually assertive,
finally, firm of purpose as passion flowers
on those now wilted pages -
those epistolary yearnings
preserve even now a faint perfume,
some long-forgotten scent of the senders
whose names escape our saying
though their genes germinate in us.
Packets of penned regret,
stacks of scrawled resentment, even resignation -
rolled like crepes,
scattered like leaves,
or neatly folded like embroidered scarves -
nuzzle with quiet familiarity in dark box bottoms.
Is it cool crassness,
flippant curiosity,
or heartfelt devotion to those ancestors
who stare at us from faded photos
that compels our violating the silences
of letters secreted purposely from our sight?
And, we do unbox that which was once bound up
and all the annoying mites
which fester in the mind
are let fly in the foul air.

More Than Friends
by Nevila Koprencka - age 16

I sit here and wonder
Will we ever be more than friends?
Day and night, I think
Of you and me being together
Happily ever after
I haven't talked to you in weeks
I miss our long talks but
Mostly I miss you
I love you and I think
Of ways to let you know
love is foolish, so you
Can never know these feelings
That I hide for you my friend
One day I hope I get the courage
To ask you the question that's on my mind
during the lonely nights and days
Will we ever be more than friends?

Good-Bye
by Amber Korte - age 14

As I pick up my picture album, memories flooded my mind. I remembered the night we talked on the phone for hours- or so it seemed. The time you comforted my fears and wiped away my tears. I struggled to see your face and when I found it, it was just a fuzzy blaze, like a daydream and I realized that if it had not been for these pictures, all I had left of you would have been lost. Days before, I had felt that if I couldn't hold you in my arms, I would die. My love was blind, I know that now...but since most of my memories of you are gone, I guess it's time to say good-bye. I can live without you, I can stand on my own, this feeling of freedom is very new to me but I'm adjusting very well. Thank you for helping me realize the one thing that I missed the most- myself.

One Another
by Terri M. Kouba

If the memories of one
   are dredged up when you see another,
Are the memories of another
   dredged up when you see the one?

Our lives are built of a series
   of memories
     of one
       of another.

Our character is formed.
   Changed.
     And reformed again.

On and on with each new memory.
   Each new one.
   Each new another.

If we lose our memories,
   do we lose ourselves?
   do we lose one?
   do we lose another?
Do we lose one another?

Occult
by Erica Krakovitz - age 13

The warmth of flame and tang of wine
Intoxicates the soul

The powerful lyrics to mysterious hymns
Creates fear that lurks behind bold

Imagine
Illusion
Shadowy image
Webs of intensified pain...
Are the cause of the needles, the pills, and the smoke
Those make life as it was
Never again

I Want A Man!
by Loretta Krausz

I want a man that I can see,
I want a man that cares for me.
I want a man that likes no other,
I want a man that hasn't another.
I want a man to kiss good night,
I want a man to hold me tight
I want him to love me with all his heart,
I want to never be far apart.
And now I'll tell you and I'll be true,
Because honey I think that man is you.

Childhood
by Jessica Krogman - age 16

Childhood is a treasure.
You only get to live it once.
Childhood means
running, jumping, laughing.
Not caring what time it is
or where you have to be.
Just having a good time.
Enjoying being dirty.
Enjoying the squishy feeling of mud
slipping through your toes
as you run across a wet field
playing in the rain.

Old Schoolhouse
by Lucille M. Kroner

Alone and bleak against the gray of winter's sky,
Upon this forlorn hill, bereft, in silence stands
This old schoolhouse where once the bells rang sweet and high,
Where once was heard the joyous cries of children's bands.
My eyes grow dim, my heart returns to hopes and joys
Of yesteryear when all the world was new, when pain
Was but a word in Webster's tome, and girls and boys,
Replete with ecstasy, shook off life's fettered chains,
Ran forth with outstrechedands to gather its rich horde,
Nor felt the sly approach of winter's coming chill.
The flower of life has withered here, the twisting sword
Of death stands near this old old schoolhouse upon the hill.

I see in fantasy life's tragic pantomime
Re-echoing the silent corridors of time.

"Remember Me!"
by Robert A. Kunderd

No balmy night in summer, fair,
Spawns mystic rev'ries sweet and rare;
That so inflame this soul of mine,
Nor mind contain thought more divine,
Than when I thrill to words from thee -
"Remember me! Remember me!"

These words you sighed when parting, we,
Did contemplate futurity.
We'd leave for e'er each other's arms,
Resign our love - forsake her charms.
These words enchant, bewitchingly -
"Remember me! Remember me!"

That night soft winds moaned with our vows.
Above, in bloom, spread lilac boughs.
The gentle dove, upon her nest,
Did softly lull her babes to rest.
Your eyes shone with your whispered plea -
"Remember me! Remember me!"

In retrospect, I still can see
The lilac's luscious canopy.
And still the dove, upon her nest,
Doth soothe her young beneath her breast.
These words burn in my memory -
"Remember me! Remember me!"

"It Was Just A Dream"
by Amber Lake - age 16

I'm running through a field of wild flowers,
The sun is shining brightly above me,
Heating my whole body with it's powerful rays of love.
I look up, and there he is,
Way off at the horizon line
Running towards me.
And when our eyes meet,
I feel the joy start racing through my veins,
Quickly taking control of my entire body.
I feel the life finally seeping back into me.
I try to yell his name,
But nothing comes out,
So, I silently mouth the name over and over again.
My muscles begin to ache from running
But I keep going and going
Straining to keep myself from collapsing.
Finally, I reach him, and he wraps his arms around me.
The aching of my muscles diminishes, when I feel his love
surrounding me.
My mind goes completely blank.
I feel his lips gently touch mine,
And I taste the sweetness of his kisses once again.
Then suddenly, he fades away,
Everything disappears, it's all gone,
And I feel the depression creeping back into my soul,
I feel the love fading into hate.
I find myself lying in my bed
With a single tear rolling down my check,
That's when I realize, It was just a dream.

A Believer
by April Lagace

Love. you made a believer out of me.
It's no longer just fairy tales and wishes,
Or something mysterious only others see.
I've finally tapped into the greatest riches.
Love. Being able to see your entire life,
In just one glance of each others' eyes.
Knowing that with any kind of strife,
Together you can strengthen lives.
Love. understanding that being apart,
Creates a thirst as the desert for rain.
The giving to another of one's heart,
Waiting to exhale and beat again.
Love. This believer wants you to know,
Just how much I love you so.

Come Back
by Rebecca Lam - age 19

A week has passed and another goes by
The thought of losing you
I lay down and cry
How hard it is
To not have you here
Thinking of the memories
On my pillow drops a tear
I wish you would come back
For I miss you so much
And even though we can't be more than friends
I will love you until the very end

In The Rain
by Marianna Langosch - age 15

Nobody knows the sorrow I've known
Nobody knows the pain
So now I must be going
Before comes the rain

The road is deserted
As I walk along
No one to hold me
Everyone's gone

Forgotten is the peace I knew
War is all I know
From a young one I grew
To learn that I must go

I shall carry sorrow with me
I shall see the pain
But I shall always be
A child in the rain

Help For Our Lives!
by Beverly Largent

There are those that <u>need</u> help
To live their daily lives
And
There are those that <u>give</u> help
So others can live their lives
And
There are those that <u>want</u> help
And ask, all their lives
And
There are those that <u>will</u> help
All they encounter in their lives
And
There are those that <u>can</u> help
But are selfish with their lives
And
Then there are those <u>receiving</u> help
And thank God for their lives
And
All those who <u>thank God</u>
Will have eternal lives.

Footprints
by Sandra Larkin

One night I am laying down in my bed sound asleep,
Seeing my footprints in the fields of flowers.
I see my life as footprints coming and going,
On the highest point, I feel so much joy.
I can see two footprints by my side.
But when I am in trouble, I noticed I feel sad and sorrow.
Thinking I am the only footprints there,
I whisper God's name, "I am in trouble, I need your help.
I was wondering where you have been.
When I need you the most."
Then all of a sudden, I hear a voice inside of me.
"During all your sad and happy times,
I am always with you and never leave your side."

Moment of a Heavenly Death
by Melissa Laskowski - age 16

The clouds drift by,
Fluffy and wide
Carrying along with the wind...
(My time is slowly fading).
The sun is a clown
Cheering me up
With her big bright eyes
Gazing down at me.
I laugh in a gay tune
Which makes me realize
What I have not yet seen...
(It's fading so happily).
My death will come soon
Any moment, I'm sure.
With every breath I take
My body gets weak.
My heart now has stopped.
(My time here is done).
I see heaven and say...
"Lord, thank you. I'm free!"

Adolescence
by Bobbie Latzer - age 14

The crying adolescent sits in spastic silence.
As the dawn breaks and the sun rises,
She realizes another sleepless night.
She slowly pretends to wake -
As her mother beats the door,
And in total unanticapation,
She dresses for the day.
In all black, she skips breakfast
And walks out her front door in denial.
 The bus is crammed,
With no regard of the fear in the younger eyes,
She takes the back seat
And does not say a word.
 Walking down the lonely snob covered hallways,
People spread out of her way...
And talk, some whisper, some yell,
Others just look at her weird.
 Her only friends exist in her head,
Her only talent is unknown,
Her mind is cluttered,
And her body speaks only of anger.
 Depression has left her hungerless for lunch,
And once again the people talk,
The rumors fly...the wind is harsh,
But she doesn't budge.
The gun in her hand is loaded and so is she.
She could end it all now but she doesn't
Why, why the torment built in her mind.
This selfish manner has left her more homicidal...
Than suicidal.

Lost
by Shanna Laude - age 15

I don't know
Weather I should stay or go
Either way I will be lost

If I go I will be lost
Lost in a world of yelling, screaming, fighting
That I've been putting up with from my mother
But I'll be with my father and brother
And once again I will be looking
Looking for a place to hide from all the pain

If I stay I will be lost
Lost in loving people and wondering
Wondering how my father and brother are doing
Are they gonna be okay and do they need me?
The loving people will make the pain stop
But it will only stop for awhile
But the memories of the pain will still come
And the yelling, screaming, fighting
Will find me once more

So either way if I stay or go
I will be lost
Lost in something
Something that I can't get away from.

Waves
by Jay Lawrence Lawson

With waves of heaven's broken bread,
In tune with cadence passed,
Through Eden's scarlet cypress led
The unattended mass.

The wake in muted chants around
A shredded garland wove,
A hymn of measured sentence found
In sacred heathen grove.

Infused with moment slight rebounds
A swayed demonic force.
A testament in earnest found
Its unredemptive course.

In dreams of Eden's tarnished pearls
The scorched pendant's blown
The frothing smoke, in ringlet curls
Breathes heavy through the failing drone.

Like pensive rays, the thrashing flail
Incinerates the fallen path.
Atonement weighs its bitter gale
To forge the holy martyr's staff.

Losing A Heart...
by Tricia M. Ledo - age 17

Today I learned a lesson, one that I insisted couldn't be true.
I learned that I had to let go of the memories that I held for you.
I tried to think back about the things that I did wrong.
Never did I realized that my feelings had been so strong.

I thought of us as a game, an object with no meaning.
Now I realize that I was in a daze, that I was always dreaming.
I always believed that you'd be there, one that I could count on.
But when I look behind to see your smile, I learn that you are gone.

I often regretted the things that were said and the feelings that I let be.
Never had I thought that it would end one day and be hurting me.
Deep inside of my heart, I thought that you'd always be there.
I thought that we had something special, something that we shared.

Now I see that you are gone, belonging to someone new.
Things that will happen, I wish my best to you.
The things that we had memories of, the pain that we went through.
Maybe it's a blessing, and you'll do what you have to do.

The tears and laughs we've shared, may they always be in your heart.
Remember the words of wisdom I've said, may we never part.
Friends we shall remain, even if you decide to move on.
Never will I let someone break our secret bond.

Through thick and thin we've made it, providing the friendship true.
Please be careful with your life and what it is that you do.
Things that are so fragile, know that I will always be a step behind.
What ever you do, take care, for nothing will stop the hands of time.

Treasures

Lonely
by Amanda Leeming - age 16

As the rain slowly slithers,
through her uncombed tangled hair.
It leaves no sign of cleanliness,
presentable to wear.

The dirt covers her weak frail body,
like a thick sheet of ice.
And the dress she wears,
cannot help, for it isn't even nice.

Her memories came pouring back,
of how she used to care.
How she looked, what she wore,
and how she did her hair.

On the corner where she stands,
in the crowded western city.
All that she receives from the wealthy,
is demeaning looks and pity.

Once a man came up to her,
and asked her for the time.
The only thing that she could say,
was "do you have a dime?"

As the night grows cold and dark,
she crawls into her box.
And thinks about her wish to have,
a pair of holeless socks.

Her memories keep pouring back,
of the time she had a home.
Tears filled her lonely eyes,
and her mind proceeds to roam.

Death's-head Banner
by Anne Marie Legan

The gray sea
climbed the cliffs
like clutching fingers,
and the anguished
white waves
tossed themselves
up and down,
as the lost armies of the fog
swept over the dunes
without a sound.

Seals roared and clamored,
but the island
did not waken
from its ancient sleep.

They stole,
robbed and killed;
their
death's-head banner
raised.

And the seals
were not concerned
with the islands
new conquerors.

Blackness
by Arianna Leibovitz - age 15

Tears of black run down her face
staining the satin-like cheek
as blackness finds its way through the maze
and drops down into nothingness,
splashing thousands of feet down.
Piercing the skin with the course touch of a needle,
dispersing the drug thorough the vein
the wary taker is once again at peace
for she is not in this world
she is gone,
gone from the troubles
gone from this world...
she is gone...

Blood And Tears
by Curtis Le Mier

I was built out of love and tears for those who left
us to soon.
Who gave their last full measure of love to us and
country.
Name after name is put on me with love and a tear
or two.
With each name there is some blood to, you see the
name's on me are those who fought for your freedom.
Their names reach out from the past remember us for
we've fought for all others who we may never see again,
but knowing ther future is safe.
So if you come and see me and you shed a tear or two
don't worry the one you love will hear your tears
and feel your pain.
And in a way say thank you for remembering me.
Who am I? The Vietnam Memorial Wall

Shadow Walker
by Robert Tirrell Leonard, Jr.

Chained to this wicked road I trek,
the sentiment of reform escapes my grasp
as the storm sets its course in the chambers of my mind...

My heart screams with a ghastly vexation
which burns across the endless demarcation
of my timeless soul to the woman I see
in the vast realm of only a dream.

I let the darkness descend with devouring greed
as the storm's deadly wrath is upon me with undue speed...

My screams are aloft silent ears,
knowing too late my unfortunate fate,
the nemesis which haunts me still.
Forever I walk the night eternal, still.

Who Can You trust
by Dwaine Lett - age 16

"No man is an island."
We all need someone.
A person to lend a helping hand.
But who can you trust? No one.

The world is so cruel.
Keep your enemies close, but watch for homies.
Everyone wants to rule.
But who can you trust? Sure as hell not your homies.

You against the world.
Know people will hate your for whatever you do.
So do your best and aim for the gold.
But who can you trust? ain't got no two.

In this world its drastic, cause homies are plastic.
When you hear the thunder, don't go under.
Everyone wants to dip their hand in your basket.
But who can you trust? Yourself and no other.

Mother's Nature
by Helen Leung - age 18

Her love is like the sunset,
Though it's camouflaged like a chameleon in a grass,
I can still hear her heart beat its maternal song.
She's sturdy like the Eiffel Tower,
but more fragile than a flower
Strong like Joan of Arc,
brave like Lady Liberty.
Her gentle caring hand leads me like the porch light,
guiding its late corner home safely from afar.
She's like a tigress when it comes to one of her own,
pouncing on whoever dare hurts her clone.
She works like the Energizer bunny-
keeps going and going, never knowing when to stop,
until almost ready to drop
I know why she does it, I know it in my heart.
Her silences says more to me than words ever could
She hides her pain like a deep dark secret,
like an old shoe box filled with forgotten memories
tossed in the back of the closet.
To me she's the rain and the nectar from a bee,
and I am her blooming daisy.

Alone
by Christina Lewandowski - age 16

Peeking through the darkness,
Concealed within the night,
Lies a man who drinks in silence,
Hidden away from sight.

How lonely he must feel,
To know that he is all alone,
In a world where even sunlight,
Doesn't dance upon his nose.

He walks among the streets,
With his sturdy wooden cane,
And a cup that brings him pleasure,
A penny to his name.

Somehow I wish that I could help,
To take him from this life,
To put him someplace where he belongs,
Though I know it isn't right.

Trouble only comes unless you fight,
And I know he has given up,
For the man does not wear armor,
Just a blanket past his toes.

Wildflowers
by Gina Lewis

Although not nurtured in greenhouses
Or raised in manicured gardens,
Some somehow manage to get what
They need where ever they are.
Sensitive to their surroundings,
They adapt to whatever the elements
Supply.
Angels must cross their paths
For that they grow at all is a miracle.
And even when no one is there to
Appreciate them...
They are beautiful.

A Simple Squeeze
by Rhonda M. Lias-Hughes

    The beginning of time seems daunting to many. Not to me though. I don't intend to sound arrogant. I simply go deep within the evolutionary process and become a sponge. I've discovered that life is deliciously sweet and pleasant when one lives as a sponge. Absorbing all the sweetness life offers and squeezing out all the excessive wastes has proved to be a benefit for me.
    Yes, that's right, I enjoy all the fragrances that I allow into my sponge and if I sense any odors or unpleasant elements of any kind, I very simply squeeze them out. This is perfect as life becomes a fabulous pleasure at all times. As evolution unfolds I move with all the changes. Of course this involves observing and then making the decision of whether to absorb or to squeeze. Over time I have noticed that this decision has become much easier. When I find pleasure I absorb and when I find unpleasantness I squeeze. As you can see living as a sponge has all the advantages one could ask for. I don't understand why there aren't more sponges. My species seems to involve a very small portion of the population. Oh but nonetheless life as a sponge is very good......yes life is good!

She'll Always Know
by Jade Lichtsinn - age 11

Sitting on my swing,
underneath my oak.
    Looking at a river,
where lillie pads do float.

    I get off of my swing,
and walk a little while.
    Then I lay down,
with a little smile.

    Field mice in a field,
they like to run and play.
    I'm watching from a hill,
where I do lay.

    I wonder what will happen,
if I close my eyes.
    It will be dark.
I will not see the sky.

    Then I see my mother,
oh I love her so.
    Even though I don't show it,
I know she'll always know.

Pain
by Loriel Li Hollo - age 20

Pain stained
frazzled threads
musty rusty
death beds
sterile bandage
brown from blood
fallen child
smeared in mud
skinned knee
small scream
great collision
rescue team
too late to save
great explosion
cadaver's ready
mindless motion
frightened lifeless
not quite sane
vagabond
in a world of pain

Feeling The Joy & Pain
by Deliah Marquez Lim

The joy of talking and being with you....
gives me more courage to go on living;
Gladly sharing the jokes, laughter and woe...
makes me feel life after all is not boring.

The happiness I felt, working and playing with you...
strengthen my confidence and stop my crying;
Lending a helping hand in everything I do..
I found a friend who is so caring.

The stubbing constant pain of losing you..
gives me sleepless nites, and eye sore of crying;
To think there's no one to share my deepest woe..
makes me feel the burden of losing is overbearing.

The sadness I felt of wanting to be with you..
drives me nuts and my head goes spinning;
Crying, walking, and running to and fro..
to eased the deepest pain of losing.

Feeling the joy and pain over you..
Let me realize love is worth giving;
Courage, strength and happiness I found in you;
after all sadness and pain is not worth dying.

Looking Glass
by Audrey Lin - age 13

In the path of tranquility lost,
Such thoughts can drive one mad
The shadow of one's armor has yet to fade away
In the darkness where reflection meets,
I gaze on the profile, which runs through emanating defeat.
All hope lost, I sadly turn away,
Away from the mocking, jeering reflection of within

Slowly, glancing back before facing,
The end of the raging inferno
I face the optic of the orb, which many call sanctuary
Why does it live? Such pyre an injustice
Home of Fate and misfortune, of internal and evident wars
So much bloodshed over power,
Yet they call it home
Lies, weapons, prejudice;
So many faults in on diminutive sphere
One and no other,
Yet they call it home
Guilt, crime, pride
Perhaps the most largest scar of all:
And obsessions which faces a metamorphose
Into carnage, declared by love
Yet they call it home
Guilty as charged, it is evidence
How horrible the creatures can be
But by looking on the other side of the mirror,
Tell me what you see
So they call it home.

My Loved Ones
by Samantha Lindstaedt - age 12

I have loved ones who have passed
away, though I have an empty place
in my heart, I know that they are at
peace. They brought happiness to my
life, their memories will always live
on.

    1. My loving Nani who shared
my life and those BINGO moments
with me.

    2. My sweet Aunt Essie who
made me and gave me a Little Lamb
when I was born.

    3. My Uncle Sammy who I was
named after and who I shared my
love with.

    4. And last but not least, my
Mamasita who I had never been
acquainted with.

After these loved ones have passed,
my Mother sat me down and tried to
explain to me that DEATH is a part of
life and it too shall happen to me in
the future of my life. She also told me
not to worry about those people who
have passed because they are still
with me in my heart and watching
over me throughout life!!!!!!!

The Passing
by Patricia Lindner

Small and frail, huddled beneath the layers of covers
the body weary from years of work and worry

So quiet, lying there after a lifetime of constant motion
in which duty and purpose were the rule

Providing support and encouragement whenever needed
never showing the pain of disappointment

Time has become an enemy, moving too quickly
sapping the mortal life slowly, so very slowly

It's time to gather for a final godspeed
heartbroken with the knowledge of an era about to fade

Then all who unite begin to tell their stories
each a single moment in time that spans generations

For deep beneath the covers, beyond the withering body
is the soul that made the body whole

From first memories of the exhausting life upon the farm
early morning hours through the first dimming of the night

Long hours stolen between dusk and dawn
to read and dream of worlds beyond family and farm

Slowly stretching beyond the borders of youth
reaching out for a chance to begin a new life

Marriage, joining with the one person who
shared the decades as best friend, lover, companion

three children growing and moving in different directions
each attempting to fulfill their dreams and expectations

grandchildren are born, the circle is completed
all having been blessed by the one who lies here

**Small and frail in body, but never in soul
our Mother and memories can never grow old**

The Constellations
by Angela Livingston

The constellations smile on you each night.
They walk with you with guiding light.
They converse with each unassuming blink,
Seeming to ponder the thoughts we think.

What are these night companions in the air?
Who made them and placed them up there?
They cause such romance and such devotion,
That poets celebrate them with every notion.

If I could have only a momentary chance,
I would fly up to the stars for a brief dance.
Then I would glide from planet to sun to moon
And bask in our exceptional galaxy's tune.

Real Men
by Cherie Nechvatal Linquist

How many times
Have I found a man
And wanted him
But never got him --
Or had him for only a moment
Then watched him fade away?

I have said:
I am tired of dreams.
I want someone real --
Someone who won't disappear
When I open my eyes
Or reach out my hand.

I think about it now
And I realize:
Sometimes dreams are better
For real men die --
Or worse, they just leave,
Or they never care in the first place.

Don't analyze me --
Just let me study you.
Don't speak to me --
Just let me hear you.
Don't touch my life with yours --
Just lead me on from a distance.

Don't become real
To make me cry
By looking back.
Remain a dream
To make me smile
By planning ahead.

My Grandma
by Carrie Lipe - age 13

My Grandma is a person,
Who used to be so fun;
I used to spend the night with her,
And play out in the sun.

Then she moved away,
And now we can not play;
Once we went to visit her,
But it was not the same.

I love my Grandma very much,
And I know she loves me too;
But it's just not the same;
Because she is very sick.

My Grandma is so sick,
She doesn't understand,
What's going on around her;
But we know it's not her.

It's her sickness kicking in.
I don't know what to do,
I guess I will pray to God,
And He will get me through.

Dark Secrets
by Edward A. Liptak

Sneaking steadily with the stillness, searching through the night,
seeking certain subjects, sinful souls so sacrificially right.
Simple lambs led to a slaughter in some sick minds fantasy,
as some ones' son some bodys' daughter,
fulfills another mad mans' evil prophecy.
Might be a friend, maybe your brother but your not the one to blame.
All of the voices always tell him just how well he plays their game,
now that he knows when to pretend to be sane.
Creeping out of corners, carefully coy within his guise,
keeping up a cool demeanor, seeming quiet and quite shy.
Calming in his conversations, so quick and cleverly he lies,
ever concealing cruel dark secrets behind cold condemning eyes.
Might be tonight, maybe tomorrow but you will meet him again,
then in pain and tortured sorrow your worst nightmare soon begins.
Enticed away by his masquerade to some far secluded place,
where suddenly you will see the twisted darkness in his face.
Bound and restrained by pure madness, he's just dying for one taste,
to feed on your frenzied fears, he truly feels this is your fate.
Toying with the fragile flesh, playfully tearing at your heart,
as you prepare to pray for death, he slowly rips your soul apart..
Now some ones' loved one is somewhere in the shadows lying dead,
all to please the screaming demons always scheming in his head.
Their painfully picking at the puzzled pieces somebody left behind,
once upon a time, unhappily ever after an unseen nursery crime.
The product of another' cold dark secret, no one would ever find,
so deeply hidden within a young mans', cruel tormented mind.
How can he silence all that always echoes from a darkened past,
maybe with his death the demons will lie silently at last.
Although it makes me wonder to myself, do the voices really die,
or simply move on to some one else ???

Untitled
by Becky Lively - age 13

When the sun descends into the mighty ocean.
We open the door and welcome the darkness.
We embrace the cold.
We pray to the gods and goddesses of the stars
and to the goddess of the moon.

Our tee pee's seem to glow in the moonlight under the
bright white stars.
The beautiful markings are hardly visible in the
dimness of the night.

When the sun peeks above the distant mountain top
and everything is bright, we mustn't forget the
darkness.
For when once again the sun descends into the mighty
ocean.
We will open the door and welcome the darkness.
We will embrace the cold.
And we will pray to the gods and goddesses of the stars
and to the goddess of the moon.

Quiet Night
by David Llewellyn

The quiet night surrounds me
As it softly speaks my name
Till dawn's light breaks, it seems to make
In silence, things explained.

Each silent moment awakens still
What sleeps within my soul
Each lesson learned, each twist and turn
Still guides my open road.

No path in life should be taken light
As each gift exacts a price
Each stolen moment, lost in time
Finds itself another life.

Each part of life is another stage
Which leads us to our end
Every criss-crossed path we travel through
Reveals another bend.

Another bend around which to see
Another hill to overlook
Another view to quench a thirsting heart
Another page in an endless book.

And still unchanged, the truth remains
As we walk within this life
And learn the things, that silence brings
On a dark and quiet night.

Lifetime
by Kim Lonette

I've had a lifetime of dreams
But you're my dream of a lifetime
No more broken mirrors and
    Shattered glass
Now there's only rainbows
Where darkness played
No more shadows lurking
    From the past

The warmth of your sunshine
    Falls on my face
My heart is in your hands
My soul's in your embrace
No more will I feel the
    emptiness
Without you -- without you

No more will I ever feel alone
God is upstairs and will
    Someday take me home
Call upon your Savior
Call upon the Lord
He's listening up there
And you'll always be heard

I thought my life
Was over and done
The pain and shame from
    What was once fun
Now I know the reason
    That I made it this long
He carried me through
Like a breeze on a song

A Brothers' Theme
by Cyrus Kai

The time is now
To take back what they took from us
No longer will they
    Mock us
No longer will they
    Laugh at us
No longer will they
    Ignore us
It's our time
It's our way
It's our turn

Welcome to the new world

Untitled
by Jessica Cecilia Lopez - age 14

Your eyes are as blue as the clearest ocean
My devotion towards you stirs quite a commotion
I could say I love you
but that words above you
I'm not one of those loved crazed little girls
There's more to life than diamonds and pearls
I love the little crinkle between your brows
Wow! Am I obsessed
It's just your soul that makes me possessed
Your voice is like music to my ears
It takes away all my fears
You may be gorgeous without
but that's not what it's all about
You are the Romeo of this modern day
And if I may say
I hope someday you'll be mine
this is your little notice
Your warning sign
I will never give up
Just call me a love sick pup
I know we don't know one another
but one of the reasons I like you
Is of how great you treat your mother
I could go on and on
But I think it is time for me to be gone

Dedicated to my Leo

Let Your Mind Run Free
by Keri Loring

Let your mind run free,
As the wild stallion kicks the air,
Open your eyes to a new world,
Climb a mountain icy and fair.

As the sun is swallowed into nothing,
As the rose rests it's head,
As the stars glitter brightly,
You can find me cozy on my bed.

Cleanse your soul in yellow water,
In a fairytale place,
Taste the fruit of passion,
The fragrance draping 'round like lace.

Bath your mind in rose reflection,
Feel the warmth from sunflower sun,
And return to your bedroom,
Where your mind was on the run.

Ode To A Fallen Traffic Light Signal
by Yakov Lotovski

Tonight the tempest felled the traffic light signal,
which stood at the crossroads of Haldeman Avenue and Red Lion Road.
But its wires were not damaged.
It was lying on the sidewalk in broad daylight
and continuing to turn the light as all standing ones did.
Still yesterday, when it was standing too, nobody paid attention to it,
only taking a glance at its signals.
Now its messages are undelivered, just not seen by anybody.
But everyone paid attention to it as a person.
Because of being knocked down, he carried out his function,
and tried to keep up with his colleagues.
They just worked upright, as if nothing had happened.
Now he sent his messages not so much for the traffic
as for the human morals:
they told about allegiance to our duties.
However, he hasn't kept it in his head, buried in the sidewalk,
but persisted to blink by turns with his three colored eyes:
stop-caution-go-stop-caution...
He kept in his head one idea only:
that evening would come as soon as possible,
so that his lights would become more visible.
They were almost not in sight
because of sunshine and his down position.
What kind of a hell of a traffic signal are you,
if your lights are not visible
and your sinew doesn't cut through yet!
It never occurred to him,
that he now is something more then a light signal,
that he is more significant among his upright standing colleagues
with their lights visible from every quarter.

The Yearning
by Saroj Luchmun

Oh yes it is there
Safely tucked
Beneath the everyday surface
Of gloss outward
Hiding from the streets' odor
And crowds of faces plastic.
It is thriving beneath
In silence of guilt
canned in sunless hollows
of my nights
for none to see
hear, touch or point.
What is it?
This killing, mysterious
Undefined yet so powerful
That denied it cannot be.
Defenseless as it is
Will it survive
and take form
Among the well-oiled
Well-established and approved?

Untitled
by Alyssa Luebbert - age 16

There was a tree
Deep in the woods
It was old, wise, and strong
This tree developed through good times and bad
The great Depression erupted but the tree flourished
World War Two came and went but the tree grew stronger

One unsuspecting day the great tree, in all her glory was
struck down by a flash of lightning
This tree, like no-other, hung on
without the soil or sun or water
She had love all around her and so she lasted

Finally, one day the tree, surrounded by love,
friendship, and beauty, died
Her time had come and she had to go,
That I understood

Still without that tree
I lost my shelter, my comfort, and my friend
Yet I can still see the tree in all her splendor
And will never forget the impact of her love.

A tribute to my grandmother Rita Ladd

Whose Choice?
by Candice Luebbering - age 15

A child just as big as your finger;
With his head, arms, and legs of such a small size.
His personality is just starting to linger
With a tiny beating heart so precious to prize.

Yet the one in which the miracle lives
Never took the responsibility to take a stand.
She doesn't want the love that he gives;
But she holds his life in her hand.

She is the one who made the mistake;
But guess who will really pay.
Guess who it will be whose life she'll take;
Yes, the precious wonder that in her womb lay.

The child will never even get to breathe fresh air.
The light of day will never come upon his eyes.
She will rip away this child's life because of her lack of care.
She is responsible for his death no matter what she denies.

Does she really deserve the right?
Should she be able to just throw a life away?
The child can't even speak for his fight;
Yet he will be killed without thought for his dismay.

Why should an innocent baby who hasn't even been born
Take the blame for his mother's error?
His dreams haven't even been formed;
But his life is cost just to end his mother's terror.

So before you say abortion is alright
When you haven't thought for awhile;
Consider if you were the child who couldn't fight
And you had to die for your mother's trial.

Shouldn't we decide for our own lives?

Our Tree of Love
by Betty Mills Luper

Listen my children and you will hear,
of a Christmas Past, I hold so dear.
We had no money to buy a tree—
so your Dad journeyed to the woods for me.
He said, "I'll find a cedar or fir,"
under his breath—"Can't satisfy her!"
He looked and he walked for hours and hours,
the rain suddenly became snow showers.
He hoped and he prayed, but no luck could be found,
his ax was heavy and fell to the ground.
His coat was thin, and a hole in his glove,
suddenly, the sun beamed from above.
Thru the thicket, what did he see?—
A beautiful, lonesome Holly Tree.
So he chopped it down and dragged it along,
all the time whistling his Christmas song.
He hoped we'd like the tree he treasured,
the pride in his eyes; could never be measured.
The berries were crimson and leaves so green,
the most beautiful tree we'd ever seen.
As I look back and remember your Dad,
I cherish the loveliest tree we had.
His whistling song that sounded so jolly,
was "Deck the Halls with Boughs of Holly."
Money could not buy our Christmas of Love,
it was created by God from above—
and your Dad!

Love, Mama

Silent Sheol
by Eleanor Lynar

    Yes, my face turned Lobster red, after I read the morning Life Line newspaper about the endless atrocious acts of violent crimes that have left a premature sound of silence upon the lives of many people.
    I blast my "Trumpet" loudly against <u>Stalking</u>, <u>Suicide</u> and <u>Childhood Death Rape</u>. All violent crimes that keep our generation embittered in hate; we must surely eliminate.
    We mourn our lost, bury our dead and cry. While deep inside our mind we say, "Thank God that it was not I." This is a reminder, that we should keep God close in our heart when our world seems to have fallen apart.
    In the Bible, God has revealed his "Master Plan", a spiritual key. This key would set mankind free and end atrocity, as we happily keep stepping to the Twentieth Century.

Untitled
by Maura Lynch - age 18

As children we are handed our dreams
like broccoli on the plate of life. Heroes
and heroines as numerous as the bubbles
blown on warm summer afternoons.

To our parents our future is as bright as
the candles illuminating the cakes so
predictably lit and blowing out the flames
to make a wish come true. Our wishes wrap
us in a cocoon of innocence slowly wearing
down over time and falling apart all at once
exposing us to the harsh elements with only our
wishes to keep us safe and sane.

To the world we are stones, rough around
the edges and smoothed by the waves. No
two stone alike but we all surrender to the
same consistency of the tides.

Socks in the Shower
by Mer Lyon - age 15

I wear my socks in the shower,
So the monster won't eat my toes.
He climbs out of the drain,
And slishy slosh he goes.
Mom said there's no such thing,
But I know she's wrong.
So tell me what ate my toe ring
And sang a merry song.
She said stop this foolishness
And start acting like a man.
She's wrong this I know,
But soon she will find out
That there's a monster in the drain,
Which goes slishy slosh.
By not listening,
There is nothing she can gain.
But lose a few toes
That get sucked down the drain.

My Gift to God
by Elizabeth Lyulkin

chrysanthemums
white feathers placed by the altar
sprinkles of Holy Water
illuminating the statue of Mary
a nocturne in white and blue
freshly mopped boards sing
and as I approach the altar
those flowers at His feet
turn into patches of ice
glistening like early morning stars
on top of snowy mounds.
chrysanthemums
white birds in flight
blue streams on Mary's white dress
stars sparkling in Joseph's eyes
their light shines on a baby boy
called Jesus
chrysanthemums
christ-anthemums
my humble offering to God.

A Chorus of Love
by Rachel Anne MacGillivray - age 14

As I sit on my window sill
I can hear the bird's choir
The contrasting sounds
Rising higher and higher
The scream of the Blue Jay
The chirp of the 'Dees
The song of the Sparrow,
I want never to cease.
Here on my perch
I can see the bugs run
Working without rest
And denying their fun
The frantic old wasp,
The buzzing mad fly
the scurrying ant,
And I ask myself, "Why?"
From where I am roosting,
I can see the babes play
Chasing their tails,
Running every-which way.
The dangerous whelps
The naive little lamb
The frisky young kittens
Play all 'cross the land.
As I sit on my window sill
And look down on my friends
I see all their merriment
And to my heart, love it sends.

Impossible Love
by Cindy MacLaren - age 17

Feelings arise when I see you
Feelings I've forgotten I had
Everytime you hold me
I feel so close
When you hold my hand
You lead me to places I've never seen before
You've shown me a whole new light
Friendship I've wanted
Love that I've needed
A life I never knew I could have
With you anything is possible
And everything is within grasps
Love is so tingly and wonderful
So unreal - so completely true
Because of you

Learning About Me
by Vania Macias - age 14

Have you ever had the feeling that your world was crashing down,
and you want to cry so much but all you can manage is a frown.

The tears sting your eyes as you struggle not to cry,
and you wish that the ground would swallow you up an you'd die.

You feel the eyes of everyone on you as you feel like a clown,
It seems to you as if the room was spinning round and round.

Then all of a sudden from deep inside of you,
comes a feeling of confidence that you had but never knew.

And as you look up and around you with your head now held up high,
you no longer feel the need or urge to cry.

And you wonder why you'd felt embarrassed of the thing that you'd done,
and you ask yourself why it matters that the kids are making fun.

You realize that you no longer care what they think,
and you feel embarrassment beginning to shrink.

As their laughter continues you get more and more mad,
and you no longer feel self-conscious or bad.

As you look around once more with the new found you,
you do the one thing that no one dares to do.

You go against all odds and stand up to the cliches and "the crowd,"
you go against the rules of what's accepted and not allowed.

You tell them all that you no longer care,
and you'll do what you want with your clothes and your hair.

You'll do what feels right even though it's not cool,
and from now on you won't follow their rule.

As you walk out of the room with your head held up high,
you take a deep breath and you give a big sigh.

And as you walk down the hall feeling proud as can be, you think to yourself it feels great to be me.

Children
by Linn Scott

When the sun comes up
Its another day
Far too dark for stars
Much to light for play

For a little one
It's so hard a choice
So many dreams of fun
Such a confusing voice

Such a tricky math
Do you suppose they know
You must find a path
Try to help them grow

We just hope they're happy
Try to soothe their pain
Let them make decisions
Let them use their brain

Love Hurts
by Rebecca Rose Madden - age 13

You cause this pain that is inside of me.
This really hurts; can't you see?
All you do is joke around.
Your voice is no pleasant sound.
There's this little thing called love.
It's supposed to symbolize peace, like a dove.
Now you have made my life such a mess,
Do you love me? Maybe yes.
That depends if cheating doesn't count.
I gave you love, a tremendous amount.
All I get in return,
Is a spot in love that burns.
I've done all the right and what is good.
Then, here came you, from the hood,
Someone that hurts me isn't grand,
There's so much pain. You have to understand.
All your forgiving will not do.
All I want was love, just to be with you.
This pain is really bad,
My emotions are all sad.
Now that you are leading a double life,
There's no need to be your wife.
Tomorrow I'll pack my bags and go away.
We have love? No, never, not today.
There's room for one more kiss goodnight.
Relax, this feels right.
This time you said you would shape up.
You gave me the sad face of a pup.
I shake my head in dismay,
This is the price that you get to pay!

Hope
by Rebecca Maddock - age 20

With the lights down low and the blinds drawn tight
She lays down for the final fight
The fight in her head, more fierce than before
She wonders how long, how much more
She quietly weeps as her head fills with prayer
Asking herself how she got there
She doesn't know the answer and doesn't really care
She just thinks of leaving this world she can't bare
The room grows still and her cigarette glows
She doesn't want to die, only now she knows
She springs from the bed and cries into the night
"Someone please help me," and someone holds her tight
She cries and she screams, "I'm better that this"
Someone gently rocks her and gives her a kiss
She knows that she matters, she get brought back to life
She no longer feels pain like that of a knife
She smiles and realizes how good life can be
And she is so glad that now she can see
She wants to let the whole world know
It doesn't matter who you are, we all can glow

Truth
by Monica Mahoney - age 14

The angels of Heaven, the demons below,
The secrets untold, the things you don't know.
The mysterious legends, the way things will be,
If you don't understand, you'll never see.
The damage is done, no one has won,
It has ruined the beauty of the setting sun.

Fate Shall Not Win
by Rachel Maldonado

Oh, Fate you cannot keep me from my love, for now you have won but I shall triumph for my love runs true and free in thy heart never to love another.

Remember with thee heart I will always love you, for I cannot love another. Although I do not have thee near, thy love will never fade away, for if I do forget it shall kill thy soul.

Do you realize the pain I cannot escape. Please listen to thee heart and you shall feel and learn of thy pain, for fate has commanded thee to take thy rose's petals from me and to leave only the thorns to pierce thy heart, for you have given thy rose's petals to another.

Oh, never shall I feel thee love as I once did and thy rose shall never completely be as it once was. No longer shall it soar so high to the heavens and shine thy days with warmth, but my love shall shine bright still like the sun.

Thy heart longs to bring thee love back to thy soul, for my soul cannot understand why it has lost its only love, as fate has planned.

But, oh fate you shall not win, for thy tears shall bring thy love back and thy thorns shall blossom into thy rose of such beauty and mirth once again.

Dream
by Josie Malloy - age 13

I had this dream the other day,
in the dream I drifted away,
to a different world, a different place,
as I was drifted upon the floor,
soon I was standing in front of a door,
a great big door with a nice golden knob,
and if I did not turn it I'd feel like a slob,
so with a twist of my wrist,
I opened the door,
and soon I was standing in front of more,
with colors galore,
I did not know which door to ignore,
so I picked the bright blue,
and I was in a world without a clue,
So I turned around and walked back through
the doors,
and I had awakened upon my floor.
So I climb in bed,
laid down and I said,
"Please no more dreams with closed doors."

The Light of the Sea
by Joanna Manieri - age 13

The sun penetrates the sky,
 reflecting its radiant orange light onto the crystal clear sea.
Below, grey spirals move swiftly across the golden sunrise.
The sunrays lightly kiss the ocean.
I take in deep breaths of the refreshing ocean air.
With the sun climbing the sky,
 the water looks as if it were glass.
Deep into the horizon,
 I can still see the grayish figures plunging deep into the warm water.
I can faintly hear their thick clicks and squeaks.
They all move together,
 like a flock of geese migrating south.
These beautiful and majestic creatures are truly
"The Light of the Sea".

Temporary
by Ronald M. Manning

For I have not asked much of life.....
and received even less
So when I hear of temporary my thoughts are
an uneasy mess
A wise man I may not be.....
such neglect only enlightens me
Temporary is a meaningless term my eyes
simply refuse to let be
What shall.....become of me
I intend to describe what I see

Three men resting beneath a wiry oak tree
drinking and speaking of things used to be
the shade their friend
the first speaks above the wind
his tales of intolerable sin
the other mumbles in discontent
of things lost.....and where they may have went
The third however describes his past with
enthusiasm....love....joy....then
he laughs
When asked why he feels no dismay
he replies...why it was merely
TEMPORARY...

The Blind Man
by Vicki Mann - age 12

The blind man sits at the edge of the road,
Listening to the poetry his friend reads to him,
Smiling peacefully at the words.

At home I sit at the edge of the room,
Reading my poetry to my family,
Who pull faces at the mispronunciations.

The blind man sits on the porch of his house,
Reading the stories I have written,
Scowling at the spelling,
Wincing at the handwriting.

The blind man can read anything,
Not caring for any mistakes,
Content with the story itself.

My family reads only the perfect,
Remembering only the mistakes,
And forgetting the actual story.

Now I ask you to make a decision,
To tell me who the blind one is.

Is it the blind man,
Who sees the talent behind the work,
Or my family,
Who see not the work of a budding young writer,
But the careless mistakes of a child?

Dreamer
by Michele Maquet - age 14

Dreamer of the night,
somewhere in fantasy land.

You will fall upon,
the love and magic
of a heart.

It will show you the way,
the way love is supposed to be.

Dreamer of the night,
have you found the way,
the way love is supposed to be.

Are you strong enough,
just by knowing,
someone, somewhere, someplace,
cares enough about you,
and loves you even in reality.

The Alien Crash At Roswell
by Moses King

In 1947, in an area called Roswell,
2 aliens and their spacecraft crashed,
and to the earth they fell.
It is believed that their bodies are being studied,
and are still being held.
This mysterious and strange event still has us under its spell.
I don't think we'll ever know why they fell,
but I hope that they were our true friends
and wished us all well.
Let us all pray that someday we can make contact with them,
and share a pact of love,
that eternal and universal gem.
Until then,
they will look down on us from space,
this beautiful
mysterious,
and wondrous thing known as the human race.

How Soon We Forget
by Sherene Ann Marshall

How soon we forget, the news of yesteryear.
The anger and pain, the hurt and the tears.
The battles that were lost by nations and all.
The boy in the bubble, the berlin wall.
How soon we forget the wounded in war,
Wounded physically or mentally to the core.
How soon we forget such lessons in life
Causing great pain and sacrifice.

Treasures

Reflection Of Life
by Dorothy A. Martin

When you were FIVE, life was full of fun and games. You believed in the
    Tooth Fairy, the Easter Bunny, and Santa Claus. Life was one giant
fantasy.
You knew there was a superior being somewhere, but you did not know
where and you weren't quite sure, "when you grew up" what you wanted
to be.

When you were FIFTEEN, you saw life as a bowl of cherries, covered with
    peaches and cream,
But, you realized fast that the goals you wanted to achieve, took more than
    just a mere dream.

When you were TWENTY to THIRTY, with increased knowledge, skills,
    hard work and sheer determination, your life took on real meaning,
you could see that
    rainbow of success.
You knew by now, that with the faith of a mustard seed and the power of
    prayer, you could have the strength and courage to carry on, if, in
God's hand you let your
    burden's rest.

"Life began at FORTY," as the old adage goes. But those of you who have
known
    Christ for a long time,
Can testify, that life began the day you decided to say, "I accept Jesus
    Christ as Mine."

By the time you reach the golden years of FIFTY, your journey in life has
    taken another turn.
Now is the time to relax and enjoy life's blessings that you, truly did earn.

Most of you have deepened your faith in God. You have been tested for
    patience, strength and endurance.
You have shared your life experiences and your beliefs with the younger
    generations.
You tried to teach them to carry on their lives with faith, fortitude,
    stability and assurance.

To those of you, who have reached the age of SIXTY FIVE or OLDER, you
    have received a most significant blessing from God above.
We love, you, we thank you, for your wisdom, knowledge, courage, strength
    and love.

It's Not Me
by Deandra S. Martinez - age 14

They say to write what's in my
heart, but not in my head.

So why do they complain when I do?
Is it because my heart is wrong?
Should my words sing a happy song?

They say they want my heart
but do they? Is that what
they really want?

Or are they saying what I want to hear
and expecting me to sweeten their ear?

I can not do that; I can not lie.

Whether my heart is of good or bad.
I tell the truth
that my heart is sad.

My Fallen Guardian Angel
by Jessica Martinez - age 16

There was once a guy I shared a lot of time with
We laughed together
We cried together

Over a couple of months we formed a special bond
He was my friend
He was always there for me

He was kind of like my guardian angel
Often times I thought he was
It was like God sent him down from heaven just for me

Sometimes though I took him for granted
Why, I don't know
Although I never told him
I really do love him and I really do care

I guess I'll never get to tell him how I feel
For someone took his life
Now all I can do is say goodbye and be left with the memories
Of my fallen guardian angel

Dedicated to Julian Damion Diaz

The Promise of a New Day
by Melinda Martin - age 19

A fresh tomorrow
Full of hope
No mistakes
Despite today

Currently clean
No ugliness
Pure consolation
Caution needed

Today is soon tomorrow
Tomorrow is soon today
A lifetime of tomorrows
Broken promises build

Live today like tomorrow
Constantly improve
Maintain good spirits
Tomorrow comes today

Rain
by Chris Martocchio - age 20

Comfortable and warm with her sorrow
Beautiful Girl stands alone
As the sweet rain falls on naked flesh

Past midnight, the mask falls off
Cruel moonlight washes her face
A cry of pain and longing
Screams of anguish for her loathsome heart
But the wicked rain still falls
Nothing ever changes

She walks barefoot through the mud
Crisp grass tickling her toes
The birds have stopped their singing
Feverish silence takes its hold
Each step, a razor
Dragged along beaten hands
Every breath, one less to her last

Time burns like rain
Silvery and monotonous
Cutting off the outside

Every word becomes a lunacy

The tired breeze fills her mind
Calming tears line her sunken face
She closes her eyes to the rain
Dove's feather falls from darkness
To her pale hand
She allows herself to smile
Beauty never dies

The Collectible Years
by Delores M. Massey

The collectible years in life
Are sweeten by those memories
The kind that's shared in time
By two who knows their stories
Of love in secrets of gold
A closeness that holds a key
In bringing back thoughts of old
It opens the heart to convey
Those words of infallible love
The fire that grew within
You knew it came from above
With threads of scarlet entwining
Two souls forever as one
By a kiss from years ago.

To Wonder
by Kainoa Mateo - age 14

When you see the lights up in the sky
Many times you wonder why,
It makes you feel so careless,
And all your sins you can confess.
Sometimes you feel love in the air.
But other times you feel despair.
Times that are so sweet.
Times that you'll keep.
Living a life so pure,
Hoping you can help and cure.

You
by Kalani Matherne - age 20

You've bestilled my heart
devoured my dreams
a life of misery
remaining unseen

I allowed you in
released all apprehensions
a life of despair
is what you've given

My soul aches from loneliness
My tears filled with sorrow
Unending desires
For you I wallow

I'm infatuated with you
for reasons that are unknown
you continue in your ways
as I watch from my tiny window

Never bothering to look behind
Never remembering the pain in one's eyes
Never thinking of what you've done wrong
Never caring for your so-called loved-ones

I see that you are wearing thin
wanting forgiveness before your time ends
Don't bother calling me
If this will cause you suffrage, then my mind can be set free

Perhaps
by Betsy Matheson - age 15

The scent of you
floats in the hot air
like fresh dew
glittering
on the morning grass.
known but unknown
and never understood.
i see your face
but am blind
to anything beyond
your firm, set mouth
or stinging look in your eye.
your thoughts, your dreams
will forever be
a buried cavern
of unimaginable riches
never discovered
forever lonely.
as you will be
perhaps.

Life's Student
by B.J. Mathews

Is my life full of strife?
It is the strife that shapes my life.
As life's student, I must be prudent.
One who is prudent makes a good student.

I play life's game on a level plane,
For a skewed plane results in much pain.
Periodically, I absorb the pain and the blame
To pave a lane that bears my name.

Just as a plant springs from a seed,
I sprang from a dire need.
There was a brief pause before I realized the cause,
But the longevity of the cause wilted the pause:

I have expended myself, extended myself;
I have travailed like Hercules to complete the task;
I have growled at everyone in my path;
My cronies have moaned as I railed against them.

But being a victim of my tart tongue
Is better than being the victim of a killer's gun.
Perhaps your soul yearns to drift away,
But within your reach is a better day.

What, then, is a life of strife?
Is it the strife that makes my life?
I adore the strife, the opulent life!
I live from sun to sun to catch all the fun!

Blur
by Lindsay Mathews - age 15

I live a life of solitude
These freshly painted walls
Will be stained soon

I look at busy realms
With eyes of desolation
The world is in the shape
Of a Deathshead

I see a throat begging to be cut
Streets lined with faces
Of long forgotten poets
On rigid sides of graffitied buildings

Everything's a blur

Deception
by Cynthia Mattison

D Death to a promise they made so long ago.
E End to a bond that once bind them so.
C Cancellation of plans they had made as one.
E Erasure of happier times, for now there'll be none.
P Pain & heartache, she could write volumes on this, for
T Temptation was too strong for him to resist.
I Ignoring the wedding band on his left hand
O Overwhelmed by his desire, he proved a weak man, yet
N No more will she cry, that's not in her plan.

Thoughts
by Courtney Elizabeth Mauk - age 16

I stand alone on a somber plane,
My eyes, they cannot see.
Around me is a desolate void,
That stretches out toward eternity.
My heart carries a burdening load,
My mind, a bereaving thought.
The world spins on pointlessly,
And all things seem for nought.
Oh, heart be still, and mind be calm!
The affliction you bear will end.
But as I stand here solitarily,
I realize my soul can never mend.

Untitled
by Jenna Mauk - age 15

Across the serene and rather overused lake we all share
is an image of lights. For some inexplicable reason
I was drawn to this one light, this pinpoint
on the horizon.
There was nothing fascinating about this one tiny light
yet I could not look away
the thought kept developing in my mind, that this light
was from the bedside of a small child
crumpled up into one corner of his bed
gripping tightly to the little blanket he has had since
the day he was born. The softest corner just
touching the pinkness of his cheek.
The small single light that had been made into
two from the reflection on the water.
Then a flashing light caught my eye, as it moved
quickly along the bank.
At this time of night, I assumed it to be a car coming
from a party or some social affair, some
teenage frolic. The driver speeding home after
realizing he was expected home nearly half an hour
ago. Somewhere else across the lake
there was another light coming from the bedroom
window of the mother patiently awaiting the
return of her son. She remains awake
to make sure her son keeps quiet and
doesn't awake his younger brother, who is
cuddled up on one corner of his bed gripping
ever so tightly to the blanket he has had ever
since the day he was born.

The Dress
by Ramona Maximillian

Gilded garment. Worn once.
Imprisoned in your zippered bag.
Do you count the months and seek recall
for one last Embassy Ball?
How could one NOT remember
that glorious ball in November?

Since last year's Debut, you've hung all alone.
Forgotten, out of view.
Could there be hope for one more try?
To WOW, to recapture everyone's eye?
Chances are slim you'd be worn again.
Perhaps at last moment, your chance not so slim.

Uptown, downtown, from shop to shop,
your Lady tries frenziedly your Equal to top.
Gown after gown after gown
slide to and fro on the rack.
Nothing to match Your loveliness
her keen thoughts reflect back.
Sky-high price, ugliest of fashion.
In contract to you,
POSITIVELY NO COMPARISON.

Discouraged, exhausted, but very smart too,
she hurries home and unzips YOU!
Out of the closet, Radiant, ALIVE!
Free again to dazzle, survive.
Adorn your fair Lady, give cause to remember,
for far far too soon comes bleak cold December.

The Sun
by Emily Mayer - age 15

I could feel the warmth of the sun
Soaking my soul with its tranquil juices-
It was as if it rejuvenated my body to such a high level,
that I was in a complete state of-

There was a glow of life lingering in the air
And all who experienced it, felt the animation-
My body became flaccid
And one with the earth-
The sun revitalized me
It is pure peace.

Cleveland
by Betsy McCall

The lake was more blue today than the sky,
But only in shades of grey.
The sun shone through thin clouds
Just thick enough to obscure the quarter moon,
Waning.
High up,
From here the cars whiz by
Blowing their raging smoke
And poison for the local blood.
The river is quiet now.
The game went badly,
We knew it would sooner or later.
How do we decide between
Here where we sit,
And there where they build the ballpark?
It's not all our fault,
But we have to at least accept some blame.
Things change.
Soon, the outsiders' view
Will effect my outlook.
This will always be my home,
But I will probably never return.

If You Asked Me
by Cristie Mc Carty

If you asked me, I'd wipe your tears.
If you we're afraid, I'd calm your fears.

I'd give you my hand to hold.
When all the pain just starts to unfold.

You can bounce on every fluffy cloud.
If you feel the need to shout, just shout out loud.

Let me erase all the pain from your mind.
Then you can hold all the tender memories in time.

Let's listen to the gentle wind blow.
Let's watch the fireflies glow.

Can we pretend we're kids playing hind 'n' seek
                    in the night.
Let's stay up late making funny shapes on the
                 wall with our flashlights.

Because if you asked me, I'd wipe your tears.
If you we're afraid, I'd calm your fears.

Even if the stars don't shine.
You still got a best friend who's so kind.

Cause even a bird can break his wings.
Then when it heals you'll hear him sing.

When you hear the mighty thunder roar.
You just set someone you love free to soar.

I know that you are feeling down.
I can't tell you when the pain will stop coming
                 around.

But if you asked me, I'd wipe your tears.
And if you we're afraid, I'd calm your fears.

Daddy's Girl
by Sarah Lynn McCullough - age 14

I'll always love my daddy
nothing can ever change that.
The only question I have for him is,
why wont he love me back.

He has two new children now
both of them are boys
he spends all his time and money,
on <u>them</u> buying <u>them</u> little toys.

why can't I be his little girl again
the one he always loved
the one who he cherished so much
even when times were so rough.

It seems he's forgotten about me
his first and only little girl.
He says he still loves me
but his word I no longer believe
maybe I should pack up and leave.

Cold Autumn Morning
by Carolyn McDonald

Yesterday's bright motivation
flees beneath the onslaught
of a brisk morning chill, redolent of winter,
and disquieting dreams
that seem foolish now in the sunlight
but left me shivering when I awoke.

The thought of facing dark mornings,
crisp with frost, ice drawings on the windows,
sculptured snowdrifts on the lawn,
without the guardian of your heart,
a thick blanket to keep me warm,
paralyzed me, froze me with utter dread.

And the dreams that came
from some uncharted polar wasteland
of deep and unacknowledged fears
stunned me, sharp icicles
pointed glimmering, prickling at my heart,
and I reached for words you said that melted me,
a down comforter toasty with love,
but in my thrashing dream state I must have kicked it to the floor,
so I lay there, cold and quivering.

In desperation I sought
the heated passion of your touch,
tried to wrap it around me with my own arms,
clung to it like a lifeline
as I scaled that ice mountain of despair
and remembered
that within the space of a single week
I would have your brilliant sunlight
to warm me again.

they know
by Laurie McDonald - age 16

They know what's going down
But they don't care
They say they want to help
But they don't care
Drugs, murder, rape, and all the rest
They say "We'll do our best"
Well, something's wrong if this is their best
But they don't care
They know what's happening,
to our towns, cities and streets
Our children living in the gutter,
smoking pot with each other
But they don't care
"There's too much crime" they say
They're just in it for their pay
Children pregnant on the street,
mini-dresses, high heels on their feet
But they don't care
Unless there's media there,
they don't care
Small towns turn into trash
Murder, sex, drugs going down just for cash
Babies taken from their homes
They don't care
They say "We'll stop it"
But they don't care

The Endless Call
by Shaley McDonald - age 19

The crickets singing and the call of the whipperwill
What are they doing? Are they waiting still?

For the love of their life, to call them again
Wondering what has happened, isn't worrying a sin?

It seems like, I've spent my life
Watching and waiting, to become a man's wife.

I should be thankful, for all that I get.
But the peace I need, I haven't found yet.

Like the animals of the night, I sent my cry
But when morning comes, it ends in a sigh.

I've called and searched, until I can't anymore
I'll wait for him, to come to my door.

I know it will seem quite, when I hush my call,
But I won't be alone, when I find him after all.

Until then I'll wait, and keep my voice low
And when he comes for me, with him I will go.

Card Houses
by Mary Mac McFadden - age 13

On those cool, cozy, country summer nights,
I could see the stars without city lights,
Every once and a while those stars would be fireflies,
Blinking in and out amongst delightful cries.

That was when I first discovered I was not like the others,
For I did not chase the flying specks like my sisters and brothers,
I spent my nights on the front porch concentrating hard,
On those nights I spent my time building castles from cards.

I think back now and realize how life on that porch molded me,
For I did not chase any fireflies or bees,
For as a youth I understood,
That to build a house the card must be good,
And to build a castle here must be more,
The love, hope, and support of others knocking on your door.

What a wonderful example this is.

For you are the card and your life is your house,
And if you are a card of bad character or a louse,
You will not accomplish a castle,
If you are a hand-working card, you will flourish,
Your personality, your house it will nourish,
Your house is your life and if it comes tumbling down,
Then the cards that were your faithful supports will also hit the ground.

My childhood seems so long ago,
But not the lessons that taught me so,
The roof of that terrace protected me from the words that could hurt and
the sun that could scorch,
I look back and thank God for those cool, cozy, country summer nights
on that porch.

Who
by Meredith McGroarty - age 16

You say I don't know you
how can that be?
I can tell what you're thinking
and how much you love me.
Why are you afraid to cry as I walk out the door?
Did you expect me to leave only my heart, or more?
You show no emotion how long can that last?
Plan for the future and find memories of past.
You say I don't know you,
this much is true...
You must find yourself before I can love you.

Untitled
by Anna McLean - age 16

I want to know your smell,
and when I'm cold, I want the heat
from your arms and body to keep me warm.
I want to recognize your voice on the phone
and share my secrets with you.
I want the touch of your hand
to be familiar, yet exciting.
I want to look in your eyes and be able to know
exactly what you're thinking and how you feel.
I want to have your favorite song memorized
and know exactly what to say to cheer you up.
I want to close my eyes and see your smile
and hear your gentle words.
I want to be in love with you.

Stars
by Helen McLean

When God made stars in heaven,
He didn't make just one
To be the very brightest,
And closest to the sun.

Instead, He spread them over
That vast expanse of blue —
He made some big,
And others small,
He had no favorites at all —
For in His starry night time plan
He made each star
Just like each man.

So when they shine together,
The greatest,
And the small —
They create a wondrous light —
Meant to embrace us all.

Journey to Friendship
by Laura McMillian - age 17

Two askew lines
Zipping through life
Different paths
Same pattern
Criss-crossing across the earth
Seeing and absorbing
Learning and experiencing
Feeling and knowing

Then crossing paths
And continuing on
Traveling apart again

Turning and repositioning
On the way
To a new life

Approaching and bumping
Moving along parallel

Bumping again and fumbling
tying a bow of union

Regret
by Lisa Brooke McNeill - age 13

A sudden outburst
A voice inside,
No one noticed
Your lonely cry.

Swiftly you ran,
To put it behind
Away it was still inside
Yet it was still inside

You covered it up,
Buried it deep within
You told not a soul,
Not even a friend

Now you regret,
letting your sadness heap
Because no one ever noticed
- It was buried too deep.

Aunt Marion
by Audrey Ann McParlin

Aunt Marion was kindly and never married. That was all I knew of her when I was five or six. About the time I turned seven - and ready to receive my First Holy Communion, I came to realize that Aunt Marion was special - she was a kindly, unmarried aunt - who happened to be mildly retarded.

My father's family treated her very well - and she seemed to love to do the things we kids enjoyed. She loved the Boardwalk in Seaside Heights, N.J. - and she was quite lucky too! She was so unselfish - she frequently gave her winnings to us!! She also loved to go to Bingo; and she was lucky there too.

My paternal Grandmother raised 8 children by herself - but Aunt Marion was her diamond in the rough. Marion worked all of her life - and I will never forget her innocent happiness at almost any kindness shown her.

Marion loved new clothes and when we would visit my Grandmother - Marion always had something new to show us.

I guess my understanding of her problems grew - as I did. Maybe that's why I eventually studied Special Education. The children in my classes allowed me to share their innocent happiness.

I often think of AUNT MARION and wonder how she coped with the problem of retardation - long before it was fully accepted by people. I know she must have been kept so happy, because even in those years of the early 1900's - she had the support and love and undying care of her mother and family.

My Parents
by Dolyce Mech

My parents were **always** there for me,
So, I was there for them to see.
They taught me love and showed me things,
And happiness was what they'd bring.
The more they brought, the more I'd say,
I'd love them forever each passing day.
They died just recently, one year apart,
Yes, now I have a broken heart!
But, I thank God they're not in pain,
Instead, they're in Heaven where God reigns.
My memories of them will remain and when I die,
I'll be reunited and **never again** cry.

Dreamer
by Jennifer McPherson - age 18

Be a dreamer,
fill your pockets to their brim
with fairy dust.
Get down knee deep in silver
moonlight.
Gather all your arms can
hold;
leave a trail of fire behind you,
as you sail in the wind.
Now's the time to follow
rainbows,
that you might not find again.

Curtain
by Allison McWood

The doors are still open...
The doors of the theatre...
Even though
the show
Has been closed
for weeks.

Remember this?...It's the auditorium.
And this is my seat
Where I sat...When I watched Him
Something kept me in this seat,
Though I ached to join Him
in that splashy chorus.

See...over there?...The Stage.
I'm running my fingers
Across its waxy scuff marks.
His feet made these scratches,
When He danced...
And I didn't dance...I just watched.

And the walls...See them?
His powerful vibrato
Echoed off these walls.
I think I can hear it...or maybe
It's only the doleful echo
Of my own footsteps in these desolate aisles.

Ah! The Curtain!...This I remember.
This is the Curtain that plummeted
The las time I saw Him.
Me in my seat...Him on the stage.
flimsy and ferocious,
The Curtain divided...two universes.

Tree Of Solitude
by Debbie Melson-Brannon

The tree stood alone in the vast, green fields.
 It was not a towering tree,
But its heavy branches gave it incredible width.
The trunk was large: several feet in diameter.
From its appearance, the tree seemed ageless,
As if it had been there since the beginning of time.
But ther most unique aspect of the tree was that
 It stood there aline,
A cornerstone for the four fields densely
Populated with the greenest grass.
Everything around the tree seemed to contain
Such vital living qualities.
 But the tree was alone.
Although the tree was still alive, it appeared
To be only existing. Just existing. Alone.
It seemed as if nature had forsaken the tree.
No other of its kind grew near. Just grass.
Nothing on the tree's level.
And yet,
As I peered at the tree in its solitude,
I realized that, even though it stood there alone,
 It was still a part of something.
The natural scene of the tree surrounded
By the fields made one grand vision:
A perfect landscape created by the hand of God.

The Future
by Jennifer Melton - age 13

I see the future as an impossible task;
Although I know that everyone will get to it,
Whether it be in a year or ten.
Everyone has a future made for them;
To discover new ideas and find new meaning.
In the things they do.
For some people it takes them long to find it,
Some already know it.
The future is mysterious,
It comes then it is the past,
Some think it as destiny.
So really in the end you'll find your future,
and it isn't an impossible task.

Life
by Yolanda Mendoza

Well, day into night, night into day
Sometimes life wins, sometimes death wins
A constant battle co-existing, side by side
In a sterile building, not full of people
But of ants, always busy coming and going
No one knows where, but always busy
So tired of everything
At times forgetting, who is the patient
and who is the visitor
So easy to go into, so hard to leave
clinging to life, death so close
Not all will survive, some will stay
and spend their last days
Here in this sterile building
Where day is night, and night is day

The Land Remembers
by Karen B. Merrill

Cold snow fell on the cold dew-kissed ground,
Baby girl cries from the cabin did sound.
Nature took in a sign of relief.
The old Pear tree bowed in reverence.
The Land remembers.

Lil' girl grew up so smart,
She brought her learnin'
 from her head through to her heart,
She loved those ol' mountain ways,
She's now makin' sure they're gonna stay.
The Land remembers.

Country air and a one-room schoolhouse
Kindled warmth to her determination,
Stirred her emotions and
Clabbered her knack for writin' them words.
The Land remembers.

Now she's a Woman who give back to the Land
She's playin' mother to the kind and fertile ground
Puttin' plenty in and gittin' a plenty out.
And the Land will remember.

In Memory of Kathy
by Megan Rose Merritt - age 14

A greatly loved and admired gymnastics teacher who
tragically died due to a head on collision.

I miss the way you looked at me,
I miss the day you spotted me.
I miss the day you made me laugh,
I miss the day I saw you last.
You deserved better
But what you had counts too!
I hope you're well and happy,
I know that I'll pull through.
In the end we're hand in hand,
I'll remember you forever.
You've wound a web for me to stick
Our friendship is complete.
Although I know you're gone for good
I'll miss you day by day.
You carved your name into my heart,
And there it shall remain!

Find A Place...
by Josh Meyer - age 18

Find a place for me in heaven was the little girls prayer everynight before her life was taken
That night she fell asleep not knowing that she was never to awaken

She was stricken with a disease she could never beat
And because she couldn't walk, day after day she laid all alone on her white satin sheet

All the doctors throught it was strange that she was in the condition she was in
And they all said that her life would be over before it even had a chance to begin

She knew that she was going to die but she didn't care
It never seemed to bother her even though everyone else said it was unfair

Everyday she would prove everybody wrong and get better but only in a dream
And she would die so young with so much left to do and so much left unseen

In the last few days she told the one's close to her that she loved them and said goodbye
And even though she wanted to she wouldn't let anyone see her cry

On that final night she thought to herself how much she would miss her family and friends
And just then it all hit her and she understood that this is where it all ends

Then she closed her eye's and said aloud "dear god, please help me if you can"
And that was when he himself reached out and took her in by her shaking little hand

His Gift
by Martha Ann Melton

A feather floats to the earth.
The cool breath of a child
goes out to meet it.
The feather begins to rise,
then slowly,
it floats back into the child's hand.
It is a miracle.
The child is not sure if the feather
is of bird,
or angel wing.
The LORD knows.
It is HIS gift.

The Rose: A Allegory
by Sara Michael - age 16

In a withering Autumn garden, alone
stands a lovely pale red rose. Standing
tall and strong, almost in defiance of
time and season.
Its beauty beckons for attention as
the randomly placed thorns protect its
fragile nature, while sending a silent,
defensive message to those who may
willingly harm it.
It is easy to see by the smooth,
silken petals and the lushness of its
color that through tender, gentle nurturing
this rose still flourishes.
As the seasons come and go, the
rose still provides a moment of
comfort and peace to the jaded
eyes and the fingertips rough with
years.
Its youthfulness, innocence and naivete
are glimpsed in the early morning
dew as it reaches towards the sun,
ready to face the world forever.
Without fear of Autumn.

a beggard's last candle
by Matthew D. Michels - age 19

come home, see the last drops of sun melt
under the horizon and the darkness come. another
lone night, locked in with my endless lies and
jumping sheep, the just as lone candle light,
less mocked by its touch each hopeless night. this
simple staff white hardened wax round wick,
shut in from the cold the damp, flowing in
solemn cadence, stand tall burn bright. my soul
comfort and yet blindness awaits me in this
light meadows just high of velvet green grass
dance an enchanting song, the whole rolling
of harmony; rivers chasing through, deep veins
of life their crests breaking of pure emotion.
all a quiet whisper, a fading chant,
vanished in a stream of smoke and
the hiss of wax.

My Dear Friends:
by Amelia Milan - age 16

Where do you want to go?
High above the clouds,
to soar like a bird
then fall like a rock.

You could take yourself there,
no pills, no power, no smoke.
but you prefer other ways--
years of your life go up in smoke.

For you it's not enough
to stand on top of a mountain
and look off and feel as though you could fly--
you have to jump.

For you it's not enough
to sit on a sun-warmed rock beside a lake
and gaze at your reflection in the water--
you submerge yourself.

Just once I would like to show you
(and have you see them the way I do)
a spider's web on a dewy morning,
a sunset on a beach,
or take you inside a teardrop
that just traveled down my cheek.

My Name Is Cocaine
by Nicci Miles

My name is Cocaine -- call me Coke for short.
I entered this country without a passport.
Ever since then, I have made a lot of scum rich.
Some have been murdered and found in a ditch.
I'm more valued than diamonds, more treasured than gold;
Use me just once and you too will be sold.
I'll take your rent money, and you'll be evicted.
I'll murder your babies, or they'll be born addicted.
I'll make you rob and steal and kill;
When you're under my power, you have no will.
Remember, my friend, my name is "Big C."
If you try me one time, you may never be free.

I've destroyed actors, politicians, and many a hero.
I've decreased bank accounts from millions to zero.
I'll make a schoolboy forget his books.
I'll make a beauty queen forget her looks.
I'll take a renowned speaker and make him a bore.
I'll make a teacher forget how to teach.
I'll make a preacher not want to preach.
I make a shooting and stabbing a common affair;
Once I take charge, you won't have a prayer.
Now that you know me, what will you do?
You'll have to decide; it's all up to you.
The day you decide to sit in my saddle --
Well, the decision is one that no one can straddle.
Listen to me, and please listen well;
When you ride with cocaine, you are headed for Hell!!!

That "Buzzing" Sound
by Art R. Milkes

I stopped the mower, turned around,
responding to that "buzzing" sound.
And what I saw, not just a bee,
a swarm was bearing down on me.

I knew right then, I had to prove
just how quickly I could move.
But I was frozen to that spot.
I tried to move, but I could not.

No need to look, my ears could hear,
the buzzing very loud and near.
I knew I had no chance at all,
no time to hide, no way to stall.

I waited. They were at my head,
but, then, they flew right by, instead.
The danger gone, but not the fear,
I watched the bees all disappear.

And, though, the bees had gone away,
the lawn would not get mowed that day.
That "buzzing" sound, still in my ear,
it, too, would have to disappear.

Somer Rae
by Eric McClendon - age 18

As spring comes to a close,
my life smell nothing like a rose.
The turmoil is my life is great,
I just can't seem to get rid of all this hate.
Then Somer's Rae's shine down on me in great splendor,
God how I wish I could kiss her.
Now we have become the best of friends,
we have helped guide each other through our sins.
This Somer has been the best of my life,
for she has guided me through my strife.
But as the fall sets in,
I feel Somer's Rae's starting to bend.
A bend that I hope will sway for the better,
but, oh Lord, I do fear the worse.
For I fear that she will run far, far away,
So I say "Please do not run for I love thee Somer Rae."
However, I do know a friend will stray away,
but a true friend's love will never go away.
So as Somer's Rae's come to a close,
will we see each other again? Nobody knows.
The joy that you brought to my life,
Lord, I wish you could know.
But through his guiding light,
I pray ever night that Somer's Rae's will continue to shine mightily bright.

Feeling Alone
by Elyss Rani Miller - age 14

Saying goodbye is always hard
Sadness is upon us all
You feel grief and anger
Sorrow but wisdom
Alone and afraid
Unsure of the future
But remember the following
It is a humongous world out there
Opportunities fill the air
Freedom is scarce
But don't feel fierce
The world is big out there

Martyr of Exodus
by Jessica Miller - age 16

You speak my name
I feel chains wrap around my heart
Like a Parasite that eats itself to stay alive
I'll stay, make you happy
can't stand to see you sad.

My emotions are the open wound
You pour your misery into, with your "please don't goes"
so much agony, I close my eyes
I'd rather not see
I'd rather no feel anymore.

Slowly, painfully, I'll fade away
A little of me goes everyday
by the time you realize I'm gone, it'll be too late
Too late to save me.

This magical spell you put over my soul
Will lead me down the road
of bitter, broken dreams
to a place of peace
Death is its name.

"simple breed"
by James F. Miller, II - age 19

the simple life conceived complex;
dying within the uncertain light,
and crying within the certain night;
remove this ungenerous hex,
    stare into solemnly sincere eyes
    stubborn without any compromise.

to the period of withdraw,
i am simple with no excuse
in this prison (life) of abuse.
i'm sorry you saw what you saw;
    breed me simple death without elegance;
    like the crow soothed within the ash,
    i am not the darkness you cast
    more so a dreamer without a chance...

grant me not any of your sorrows;
speak to me no more of yesterdays;
live in not any more todays,
die within no more tomorrows.

    ...if you reach for me, i shall not be
    if you awaken and i'm gone,
    i shall have moved on...towards tomorrow.

untitled
by mandy miller - age 15

the pain of life
the awaited knife
held out my arm
pleading to do some harm
one last thought
of all the pain i fought
i'm sorry i caused so much hate
but now it's just too late
i tightly clenched my hand into a fist
as i slip the razor across my wrist
as i begin to slowly fall
please remember i love you all
think of the happy times
hold on to these simple rhymes
life will be better-
just wait and see
unfortunately it was just pain
and sorrow for me

Grandma's House
by Susan Miller

Blind windows hold in air
heavy with sweet perfume
on decaying skin.

Feeble light filters through drawn drapes
that dangle from a rod
bent and bowed at the middle.

Two battered lawn chairs,
frayed purple seats paled to gray
grave the shadow-filled room.

Ease into a chair, the unsteady frame
buckles and leans
beneath the weight,
beneath any weight.

An ornate lamp with hundreds of braided tassels on a fluted shade
washes a dim glow of half-hearted light
over the t.v. stand.

Dancing ladies with muted parasols
and smiles fading off their face
peal off the lamp's chipped china base.

A cheap print from the Five and Dime
hangs askew
on the bare wall.

Only the occasional shuffle
of slippered feet
breaks the silence.

Untitled
by Wendy Miller - age 16

It's always there
Day and night
Since the day you where born
and throughout your life

It never leaves
Even when you die
Because it's always there
for the next guy

Time never stands still
Nor does it go back
forward is all it knows
so you
   can never
      go
         back!

Grandma is Dying
by Kristina Millman - age 14

It was really weird to watch someone die.
Knowing you can't do anything but sit and watch and cry.
You sit all alone staring all night.
You simply don't want them to go,
but you know it's right.
Smelling the smell of death as it fills the air.
And you sit and look at someone, who because of cancer has no hair.
Their cheeks are sunken in also is their chin.
Their eyes have that whitish tint,
which kind of gives you that deathly hint.
Your not leaving the room because your scared to go,
they could leave at any time this in fact you know.
You suddenly wish you could have called once more to say hello.
But the hardest thing is knowing soon and forever they have to go.

Life
by Priscilla Mills - age 15

    Body withered after pain, grief, and
loss. Soul lost after torment that came
with life. Mind puzzled after what I
have done in the past and sorrowful
for wishing the end to come at last.
After each day a piece of me may
break, for I lived with guilt, obsessions,
and sins. Recognizing my hatred and
my love. Sometimes I find myself
crying for someone else's miseries, then
saying it won't make the situation
better but worse. There are always
people who have you in their grip.
Either to tease you, haunt you, use you,
but it is up to you to fight and break
away. Everyday there is a new problem,
a new solution to end your grief. You look
for answers from the one above and try
not to follow temptations from the one
below. Just when you had it and feel
like you've been cursed you ask yourself
this: Dying, living, believing...
What comes first?

Candle Light I'll Miss You
by Jesse Minigan - age 17

Allow me to press my lips to your hand,
For they along with me, are not worthy to press next to
the lips or even cheeks of one so enchanting.
Although the rose I give you is beautiful,
Its petals cower to the delicate visage of your face.
Rose's Perfume, it entices the mind, yet to me it bows to the smell of your hair.
Once more I write you but this time it is Hemlock, not the original.
You shattered my heart once before.
My heart is a room of my Dream,
and you are 100 candle that illuminate the eyes of one long enveloped
If this is the last time we meet. Please let me hold you,
now we separate, and my inspiration leaves with you,
we to go in directions differentiated.
The rose I give you will sometimes cease,
My feelings are stronger than the thorn to the rose.
But the way you dig into me like the Rose's thorn in my hand
is a pleasant torture.
Now you are to leave like the rain,
You have made me grow.
And, part we must
But my love is stronger than distance alone,
You depart and I shall eternally Miss You.
My darkness once more envelopes my heart.
But I can still see and what's more, I hold you, Mistress
You are my candle.
Forever and always
The love eternal
I Miss You.

Heroes To One Another
by Jerry D. Minor

We mean more to each other than any other brother, that's why we're heroes to one another.

But it didn't start out that way, I guess it was because of the way we both played, never let nothing stand in our way.

So now we kick it. Just couldn't bare it, if we missed it. He likes my style--versatile and I him--for being so wild.

Heroes to one another and it didn't take us long to discover.

I knew he could never lie or deny me anything and he knew he could always count on me no matter what the emergency, even when we sometime disagreed.

We were partners in crime, but we never did any time, what was his way mine and that meant girls a few times!

Now things have changed, I've moved away and he decided to stay, but he got caught and I feel like it's my fault.

But, we're still road dogs till this very day and jail won't keep us from being number ones, inspite of what he has done.

I tell you this story because everyone should know, you should never give up on a real hero.

Heartache and Heartbreak, how much can two heroes take?

Especially when they know they've made serious mistakes.

My Country
by Jennifer Lynn Mislich - age 16

The United States is a
  place of freedom.
We can make our own choices,
  live our own way.
There is no racial or physical boundaries.
There may be prejucism,
  there may be racism.
But we are not perfect,
  but no single person,
  nor any single group,
  or any single race,
  is perfect either.
The United States is fair.
The United States is not unjust.
We help those in need,
  yet don't turn our backs on the rest.

This is my country,
This is my place.
My soul was born here,
  it will also die.
I love this country,
There is no other.
I might lose my life defending
  this country's freedom..
Someone lost their life,
  so that I could be free.
I will fight with my own,
  so that others will have the same
  freedom that I have today.
No matter what anyone tells you,
"Freedom is not free."

Seasons
by Stephania Mix - age 13

The leaves have fallen
And spring is here
The flowers will bloom
And summer is near

Summer will come
Leaving spring behind
Who knows what we'll see
Who knows what we'll find

We'll find the sun blazing down
Much laughter all around
Children playing in the sand
and the waves crashing down

But summer will leave
And winter will come
The sun will cease
And winter will come

Does He Know?
by Diane M. Money

Does he know as he stepped inside that door
And I glanced his face that time first
A clear sure message I received from God
That he my destiny had always been?

Does he know though the years raced ahead
And our paths crossed but few times in between
That his memory I kept always clear
Until together we might be again?

It seems to me we came so close, so very close
To having Fate finally fulfilled
Still that chance vanished 'fore our eyes
Does he know I cry?

Yet, long as our frail forms continue to exist
And our dreams to somehow stubbornly prevail
Someday, our lives and love might forever be entwined
Tell me, does he know?

Alienation
by Haroon Monis - age 20

Asleep in a world that's awake
Dead in the land of the living

It's funny how life treats you
When you don't want to treat it well

It's uncool how love follows you
When you don't want to be followed
And how the earth will swallow you
When you aren't ready to be swallowed

Everything around you pushes you away
When you aren't a part of them

When they walk down the alleys in the dark
They see your face in their shadows
You lurk int their minds all the time
They know you too well, yet you're unknown

You're sleeping in the land of the awake
You're dead in the land of the living
Yet you live in everyone's mind
Feeding them the fear they hold inside.

Where are you?
by Dawn Monsees - age 16

My Blood stains the street,
I have shed it all for you.
I lie still, not breathing hoping you'll attest to me.
Instead you walk blindly by,
and I am left there.

You come back.
No,
Not in worry, or concern but to accuse.
It is me,
I am happy, I am content,
You aren't and it becomes my fault.

I follow you, still trying for attention,
and when I can get close enough,
I rest at your feet like a watchful puppy.
You continue on barely acknowledging me,
as I trot along behind trying to keep up
Am I losing you?

I put you where you are,
I let you take my soul and now you torture me with it unmercilessly.
What does it take?
Why should I be in sorrow?
It's not fair that to be loved I have to become an obligation.
I know you love me, I know you care.
But I wonder,
Do you?

You wonder why I feel this way,
knowing how much I hurt,
So please,
Can't you just stop.

For What is this
by Laura Montgomery - age 13

I have no feeling but I feel the clothes on my
back,
I am empty inside but why is there
pain,
I have no sight but I see the
light,
When will all of this insanity end,
I do find myself but not in
me,
I can speak but no one is
listening,
I do touch but I touch not the
cloth,
For the things that I have, am, do, and can, I
don't do the things you think, it is the things
you don't think for that is what makes us tick.

The Flower
by Sarah Montgomery - age 13

It stars out as a tiny seed,
Needing attention,
Though it cannot plead.
You take care of it,
As if it were a human child.
You can hardly wait for it's colors,
Ever so wild.
Slowly it's radiant flower petals,
Spring outward.
You stand there without a word.
Somehow you relate this small miracle,
To your own child.
It itself had sprung outward,
Leaving you nothing to tend to.
But the flower.
Some days later,
You go to your flower,
With a freshly filled water pot.
But the flower didn't look so hot.
The stem was all that was left,
It has wilted and gone.
And now it is time for you to.
No one was there to tend for you,
And now you wilt.........

My precious, Special Miracle
by Theresa Morales

From the start, I had this pain in my heart.
When I gave birth to you, I had a dream.
Until the diagnosis, my life was serene.
You don't know your own mother, nor do you know no other.
As I look into your beautiful eyes, you have a blank stare.
Do you love me? Do you care?
I hope you believe this to be true, that I will never give up on you.
You are my precious, special miracle-the one love of my life.
This whole thing just cuts me like a knife.
Come into my world, come within my reach. Don't be afraid, just let me teach.
How can I make people understand, that this child is such a demand.
When I hear the laughter of the children outside,
it is my "true feelings" that I must hide.
Why can't it be you out there? It just doesn't seem to be fair!
My sweet baby, I am so proud of you. You've come a long way.
We have a long road ahead of us, but it will be worth it, you'll see, someday.
Won't you please come out of your shell? This hurts so much like hell.
Maybe one day, you'll read and understand this poem.
That's when I'll know you will <u>truly</u> "be home."

Paola (The Day After)
by Carlos Moran - age 19

No eyes to see the sleeping gypsy took her sight
No need to say a word her beauty was enough
No ears to hear I never say a word
No mind to care we are both the same
Thoughts that do not mean much
Fears that are hard to overcome.

    She came alone on a Saturday morning
    She was indeed a true work of art
    Spent some of her days here and there and everywhere
    Cleaning her hair and walking in the streets.

Spent some of her days
taking blame and
disbelieving
Spent her whole life in her
work of ART.

Darkest Night
by Katie Moran

I am imprisoned within the shadows I cast.
No one hears my cries, or my fears and no one cares.
I'm unsure of what I feel
loneliness wraps itself around me

Darkness grips me in it's steel fist
I feel myself began to shatter
No one can save me now
Not anymore
My life seems so worthless, no laughter or love left
Emptiness creeps inside me

No one could have ever known
I can smile threw a thousand tears
Keep the pain locked inside me

So I wonder through my misery
I dream of things, that I can never be
I walk in my uncertainty

I stare unconsciously at nothing
Remembering people telling me pretty lies.
They still haunt me, you know
Taking me back to yesterday
I drown in my own thoughts
wishing there was a way out
But knowing there will never be.
I see people watching me
As though they could see right through me
could they see the unhappiness? Could they see the pain?
How can I live?
It was so much apart of me
But the pain is too real, the guilt to deep and the loneliness to long
so into the depths of the darkest night I go.

Spanning Our Attentions
by Juli L. Morgan

Clouds are the mocking birds
    of the sky

       They mimic mountain ranges
          and ocean waves
       They give thought to
          tranquil, shining heavens
          and hellish infernos

       They promise us that
          every cloud does have
          a silver lining

       They inspire children's books
          of rabbits, and cakes,
          and great horned owls

       and they inspire dreams

       They hold our hands during
          hazy, lazy days
       They draw our minds
          while we lay in
          breezy, grassy fields

Clouds are great canvases
    which soak up
      our attention
And nothing less than
      our complete admirations

Children Playing
by Laura J. Morgan - age 14

Through my window,
On the street
In spite of differences,
In age and race
Because of friendships,
Along they play
Among the houses
Throughout the day.

Why Gradaddy Why
by Elizabeth Anne Moritz - age 12

Why oh why?
Did you go away;
When I begged
you to stay.
It really makes me sad
to say goodbye to you
Sometimes I feel blue and
get mad too!
Why; Grandaddy Why???,
No one ever plays checkers with me
and tickles Me;;
or makes a story so much fun!!
I know you're better in Heaven;
and now you're not sick!
But....
I miss you so!!!
Why did you leave me,
Why Grandaddy;
Did you go???
That's all I really need to know!!!!

Dedicated to the memory of my Grandfather Mr. Conrad Lee Long

Guiding Lights
by Denise Moyar

The stars are like diamonds, high up in the sky,
For once my grandpap told me they were Angels,
With their watchful eyes.
Do you have faith in what you believe?
To wish upon a star and really achieve,
To say to your self you will never be deceived.
I believe what grandpap said to be true,
There is an Angel out there waiting just for you.
So when you look up and see a star,
Say a little pray no matter how far and the Angels,
Will be right there where you are.

A Broken Heart
by Andrew James Moyer

Memories of you,
forever in my mind.
My dreams of you...
so soothing,
like soft spoken words.

Words cannot express
how much I miss you.
My tears can't wash away
your smile, your eyes, your laughter --
on my mind for eternity.

You are the coming night in my mind--
consuming all thoughts like light,
until there is nothing left but you.

My pain is so great,
riding the waves of a vast ocean
in which there are no boundaries.

Why does love hunt so much?

Dedicated to Judy Hanna

Sunset
by Kate Munden-Dixon

All the clouds outlined in pink
Puffed up and moving at bicycle speed
So beautiful one could never describe
Fading slowly into the deep.

"Footprints On Our Hearts"
by Laura Munder - age 15

Footprints on our hearts is what you have left
We will always remember you, even though you may leave us
The four years you have been here, you proved to be unstoppable
You have done so many incredible things, we don't know where to begin

You were the loose dinosaurs, out to get everything
You won the war, proving to be the survivors
You come in like a silent storm, and now you go out like a huge bolt of lightning
You lifted us from the deep, dark underworld, to the heavenly blue sky

The gift of music you have received is immeasurable by money
It is measured by a stadium full of people, on their feet, cheering for you
A warm smile from your parents' lips
Or a single tear running down their face

You come in here as children
Looking for guidance
Hoping someone would take you by the hand
Leading you through the confusion and the helplessness

Now you are the adults
Being the guides
Taking the hands of the lost
Helping them gain control

You are the past, present, and the future
Paving the road for the ones to follow
They strive for success, the kind you have captured
Reaching for the sky, trying to attain that one star

You could have walked in, and then walked out
Instead you left footprints on our hearts
There to forever stay.

God Is Calling
by Anna M. Mrock

God is calling, He is near;
Speaking softly only I can hear.
Into my arms you must come,
I had asked if Heaven I won.

Fast asleep before it is known,
If Heaven of hell is to be your home.
Time to time the devil you served,
Hell is what you **really** deserve!

Seek Heaven alone to be your home,
You must serve Me and Me alone.
If you are spared and survive,
Repent, repent while still alive.

Now, fast asleep and in my grave,
Yes, I have found repentance paid.
Glory, Hallelujah to Jesus Christ
 my Heavenly King!

Thinking of You
by Angela Murgia - age 14

When the white fluffy drifts of snow cover the ground,
I see my past, seen through eyes never seen before,
when our love was comforting and warm.
I remember the crackling, blazing fire,
the hot steamy cocoa that filled my body with warmth,
and the sparkling icicles glistening from the trees
And I think of you.....

When the Spring air awakens my senses
and fills my mind with reflections of past days
when our love was fresh and new,
I remember the birds preparing their nests,
butterflies emerging from their winter homes,
and buds forming on the trees
And I think of you....

When the hot, and humid weather fills the air,
I see a mirage of my past
when our love was hot and cool all at once.
I remember the sounds of the ocean lapping onto the shore,
the seagulls calling my name,
and the winds whispering in my ear
And I think of you....

When the leaves turn wonderful colors of red and orange,
I see my past as if it were from a school book,
when our love beheld so much for the future.
I remember the sound of the leaves crunching under my feet,
the sight of the pumpkins sitting on the door steps,
and the trees full of sweet, delicious apples
And I think of you.....

"Safe and Sound"
by Abby Murphy - age 14

Drift above the water
and float among the fear
Burn the inferiors
Amongst a single tear

When decision time comes around
Remove yourself from your mound
You're a hermit in your hold
You're like a sickening mole
Remember you're underground
A sheltered life, safe and sound.

Magnetic Energy
by Norma S. Murray

Within the walls of life's fleeting essence,
is the nucleus forming it's own presence.
Emitting signals that will consciously attract,
mirrored images completely in tact.
Culminating attention from several angles of reach,
gathering lessons experienced to teach.
Separate stations of direction from start,
formulating together and then breaking apart.
Vibrating, moving and thriving through interaction,
colliding and connecting with reaction.
Signals of apocalyptic glide, mentions of eclipses manifesting inside.
Creating chaos for its sole reaction,
strengthening interest in it's own reflection.
Retrieving pleasure from sheer acknowledgment,
comforting hope returns when sent.
Comprehensive nice thoughts unleash a force,
guiding direction through this source.
Pulsating influence in an instant, gratifying the whole through mere existence.
Circumventing negative order, setting a path and structuring a border.
Pushing positive thoughts and images outside a being,
trading emotions and causing healing.
Releasing intent of good will,
understanding this boomerang strikes the deal.
Reaching for higher knowledge in peace,
realizing the origin connects that reach.
Negative energy in any form, searches it's own kind so it can dorm.
Cognizant realism of what we project,
allows you to perceive what to reject.
This critical recognition is to know,
that what we send out comes back to grow.
Important agreement in the mind,
to believe and work towards constructive bind.
With any energy we emit, the return comes right back and amplifies the hit.
Magnetic energy culminates appeal
and makes life's reasoning awakenly real!

Arachnophobia
by Rachel Nagle - age 17

One dark and stormy night
I sat upon my desk to write
About the days and night I wait
Until I reach heaven's gate.

Thoughts of sunshine slip away
As it starts to come my way.
What wretched thing is this
That taunts me so and licks its lips?

I look around to escape
But so many surround my shape,
On the floor and in my bed,
On the door, around my head!
I try to scream! I try to shout!
But still I can not get it out.

Closer they come creeping
And quiet I remain so they hear no peeping,
Over taken by the dread
That I might soon be dead
I feel their bits upon my arm and leg
Sitting still like a giant peg; I wait.

My eyes are closed for not to see
What is going to happen to me.
Hours? Minutes? Time goes by.
Open my eyes. Twas it a lie?

Why, why am I not dead?!
The pian, the suffering as it not dread?
They are not gone, I feel their presence
Like a knife piercing through my very soul,
Red, red eyes are always around
In the walls and ont he ground.

The Vacant Shroud
by Joanne Nail

Too many times have I felt its enclosure,
While falling into the web of despair
    and remorse,
Trapped by the eternal pits of Hell,
Escapable only by a thrustful force.

But, alas, there exists a ray of hope,
As I become the pursuant of a life-long dream,
Not consciously aware of why or how,
Yet, driving obsessions wail the time is now!

To survive and achieve I take hold of my heart;
I feel my burdens become weightless and few.
Then an inner voice screams so ominous and loud,
Ann all that remains is a vacant shroud.

An Ode To The Commonwealth
by Joseph E. Nancoo

Children of the Commonwealth
In countries large and small,
Children of the Commonwealth,
We are brothers, sisters all.

Children of the Commonwealth,
Of every creed and race,
We are God's Creation
We share His love and grace.

Children of the Commonwealth
Let's Talk To One Another;
Our unity in diversity:
A model for humanity.

Children of the Commonwealth,
Cherish your heritage:
The rule of law, democracy;
Great Britian's lasting legacy.

Children of the Commonwealth,
A new century challenges you
To be the best--only you can be,
And respect each other's dignity.

Building Blocks
by Melinda Natera - age 17

My mother is my roof that protects
me and keeps me shielded.
My father is my floor
which provides me with
stability.
My sisters and I are the walls which
hold all of this up.
These all together build one, a home.

Old Tree
by Connie Neal

Did I understand? Did I hear you say?
"Chop it down. -- Let's chop it down, today!"
"Just look at it there,"
"It's bent to one side and some of its branches are bare."
"What good is it now. -- It's as old as the hills."
"Doesn't bush out to shade us, or stop winter's chill."
"It's slow to blossom, doesn't seem to grow,"
"Don't think it can handle the cold and the snow."
I know my years are many, and soon I know I'll die.
I only have my memories. -- They help the days go by.
Come sit by me and listen to the softness of the wind.
Drink in the sounds and smells of now, for tomorrow it all may end.
These are quiet times, every minute precious and content.
Enjoy the day and all it holds. -- You see, it's heaven sent.
What's that, you say? "Guess the old tree's really not so bad."
"As I remember, it was planted by my Dad."
"Let's see how it winters." -- "We'll look it over then."
"Somehow, I can't bear to cut it down,"
"This tree's a dear old friend."

Dreams
by Colleen Nelen - age 13

I love you,
For everything your worth.
Your smile makes me shiver,
Your personality makes me laugh.

I want to kiss you,
Your tender lips touching mine.
But that's just a dream,
A dream of you loving me.

If you ever loved me,
Would you love me the same?
Or would you hurt me?
Break my heart into two?

Will you always be just a dream?
Will you always be just a wish on a star?
I hope your not in the sky,
But in my arms.

I dream of you,
Each and every night.
Together forever,
Forever and ever.

Silent Cry/Dementia
by Alice Nelthrope

What is today? I couldn't really tell you,
What has happened to yesterday, is not even a blur,
If you ask me the time, I can tell you from my watch
but to match it without, there is some serious doubt.
Now if you ask me about the past, maybe when I was nine or ten,
I just may be able to start all over again.
Wish I could take back the abuse, that I placed on myself,
along with the hurt that I placed on you.
When you said I did something, I just might agree.
If you said I went there, more than likely I did.
When you ask me to go outside, I hope it is a warm day,
the cold is just to much to bare.
I get in my vehicle, knowing where I am heading, but when I get out there I
have not a clue, yet hoping that I'll make it back.
Damn this is frustrating, words I can't place in a sentence.
I had lots of friends, or so I thought, now I have nothing to share with them
not even a clear thought, how could this happen to me.
I don't even realize that my children are grown, most times I believe they
are one, two and three, yet when I see them,
their size sometimes startles me.
Most mornings when I wake, or shall I say when I rise,
for I very seldom seem to shut my eyes, are times when I don't even
recognize the person whom I have been
married too for years and days gone by.
Someday I even question my name,
there are days when I know just about everything.
There are days I rarely want to leave my room,
yet other days I just want to runaway.
There are days where I lay my head,
can be just as mysterious as a novel I once read.
For all that I'm saying in words of plenty, who would have ever believed
that I this person full of material possession, me this person who stood
very tall I was this person who rarely needed anyone at all, now suddenly
I must rely upon the patient of others, yet before this time I dared not
waste on loved ones, is the opposite of what they do for me.

Burning Bridges
by Michelle Nesthus - age 16

Broken bones from broken homes,
Secrets, lies, sticks and stones.
Burning bridges, shattered mirrors,
A fit of fury and unshed tears.
A set of tracks to which you're bound,
At Hell's gate you shall be found.
A light in the dark, or the dark in the light,
With no strength left to stand and fight.
Trampled hopes and long-lost dreams
And no one there to hear your screams.
I wish I may, I wish I might,
Make it through just one more night.

Freedom Train
by T. H. Nettles

Hear my song of Freedom I cry,
Please don't let that Freedom Train pass me by.

I have traveled that long and winding road
My feet are tired and aching, too
I will not give up, I will not give in
Because that Freedom Train will carry me through.

My clothes are torn and ragged
My back bent over from working in the fields all day
Sore on my back where I was beaten
But I couldn't be broken
Corns on my feet because I ran too fast.

Names they called me, trying to break my spirit
But my spirit couldn't be broken
So they tried to make me their pet
But I was too smart for that
Because the train for Freedom
I won't let pass me by.

Hear my song of Freedom I cry
Please don't let that Freedom Train pass me by.

My Great Grandmother
by Rachel Newkirk - age 14

Although her hands were cold as ice,
Her heart still filled with love.
She's very gentle, kind, and nice,
And for my belated birthday a traditional dove.

She was an angel in disguise,
An angel first unrecognized,
Then towards the end we all grew sad,
For those times for G.G. were pretty bad.

She was always giving her love and care,
So then I knew she'd always be there.

Even if we split apart,
There's only one place your an find that special person or
Angel and that one place is in your heart.....

*Dedicated to the special person to whom I lost,
my great grandmother, G.G., or Betty White.*

If
by Natalie Newton - age 14

If I were a giant so big and so strong,
How would I live in the beat of a storm?
If I were so small, so tiny, petite,
How could I see with only a peak?
If I were a tree so tall, so mighty,
I'd have all my branches so neat and tightly.
If I could live where ever I wanted,
I'd want to live some place that's haunted.
If I were the snow so white, so pure,
I'd want to be where people would tour.
If I were a dinosaur I don't know what I'd do?
I'd be so big I wouldn't be able to fit in a zoo.
If I were a baby too delicate and fragile,
I'd want to be in the touch of an angel.
If I were a leprechaun so snitchy and sly,
I'd want to get out of his way before he caught my eye.
I could go on and on through all my days with if I were to be's,
but right this moment right now I just want to be me!!

Last Forever in My Page of Mind
by Quy Ngoc Nguyen - age 18

Today will be the day that last forever
In the small journal page of my mind.
This moment will live forever in me, and
If the time that you must say good-bye,
I just want you to know one thing.
That I will miss you now and forever.
But your memory and name will forever remain
In my little journal page in my mind.
As well as inside my heart and feeling.
I will always remember about you, my friend.
No matter how far away you will live,
I'll send to you the love I feel.
So today will last forever in my page of mind.
I want you to know one more thing.
You are very special to me my friend,
Now on and forever in the future.
Keep this words in your mind my friend!
That you will be forever remain in me.

Protection
by Jessica Nichols - age 14

I look around the room and all I see
Is a room filled with flowers which
Lye beside me while I sleep.
I feel safe with flowers around me
I feel that it is a wall that
Blocks the bad and lets the good come in
The flowers that surround my body
are my family and friends and they
Build the strong wall that's all
around me
I like this wall because it makes
me feel safe and strong
This wall goes on forever because
it is strong and durable
That protects me from what goes
wrong with life.

Lost
by Jennifer Nieman - age 14

In this world the most
wonderful things are taken
away from you. You feel
lonely and lost inside,
Lost in this deep
Sea of life, struggling
to reach surface, but
being pulled back under
by the waves known as
heart ache and disappointments
In life,
Lost again in your
own world struggling
once again

Silence of War
by Rachel Nieuwsma - age 15

silence of the beggars
walking down the streets
    silence of the children
when in war they meet
    silence of the sparrows
killed in flight above
    silence of the people
dreaming of a love
    silence of the mourners
lost in time and place
    silence of the heart
after finishing its race
    silence of the tears
heard in every room
    silence of the dead
sleeping in their tomb
    silence of the killing
found on every street
    silence of the victims
we no longer hear them weep

This poem is written in memory of all of those killed in the Holocaust.

Cuddle Puff
by Jennifer Nolen - age 19

I remember seeing you hanging there,
Your fur was pink, your eyes were blue,
You squished like cotton when I hugged you.
There in the aisle of Kmart I begged Daddy to buy you.

When I got you home you went everywhere with me.
Up in the trees,
To the creek,
To my aunt's house,
You were my best friend.

I took you to show and tell,
In second grade.
We all had animals like you,
Who were our friends.

You were nothing special to them,
You were my world.
I knew they hurt your feelings,
That's why I never took you back.

Many years and replaced eyes later,
I outgrew you.
My best friend for so many years.
You were packed away and put in the tool house.

I felt so guilty for doing that,
Like I threw away a pet.
I hope you can understand,
I had to grow up.

Courage
by Kristen Nowak - age 13

To fulfill all of my deepest dreams —
I have to find the courage.
With this courage I will have success.

To protect myself against all evil —
I have to find the courage.
With this courage I will have the strength.

To seek help when I need it the most —
I have to find the courage.
With this courage I will have guidance.

To face my biggest and darkest fears —
I have to find the courage.
With this courage I will not be scared.

To stand up for what I think is right —
I have to find the courage.
With this courage I will speak the truth.

To continue when I've given up —
I have to find the courage.
With this courage I will then proceed.

To live the way I was meant to live —
I have to find the courage.
With this courage I will life my life.

June 30, 1997
by Joanne Ellison Nydegger

Hong Kong, you are my forever love.
Hong Kong, surely blessed from up above.
Ostentatious, distinctive, glorious jewel--
Today, you made me awfully blue.

Blue, because you're so far away
And I am here amidst the fray
....here in Orlando, so far away.

Your fireworks gloriously fill the sky
As my mind meanders thoughtfully by.

How I miss your whole, your being,
How I miss, your fond embrace.
For you, I've been forever yearning...
You can see it,___in my face.

Yearning for how things used to be
When I roamed so passionately
Many delights, could I afford
As I wantonly, zealously explored

Triumphs, peaks, experiences so high
So strongly, they nearly reach up to the sky.
Fun, Food, Clothes, Shopping, Sightseeing,Souvenirs,
Friends, Temples, Clubs.... There were no fears.

Newness daily - Oh! what a trance,
You put upon me - I could forever dance.
For the spell has cast and will forever be
Endearing, beautiful, aristocratic, and enveloping me.

Al memories that are truly divine
That can never leave me - with the passage of time.

Thank you. Thank you - Though you are CHINA, now;
However, you will forever
Cast your exceptionally magnificent spell.

The Drive
by Mindy O'Dell - age 13

Kelly and her friends were driving around.
On the outskirts of town.
They weren't exactly what I would call sober.
Their parents had warned them over and over.
They had so many close calls.
Not to mention broken laws.
They were puffing on weed.
And thought they'd succeed.
Driving so fast they thought was a blast.
But around the corner they did not know,
That they'd go completely out of control.
Kelly went for the brake, but it was to late.
The car was already crashing over the hill toward the lake.
The next thing she knew she was in a hospital bed.
And just found out all her friends were dead.
She swore up and down she'd never drunk drive again.
and then found out she was paralyzed from her toe to her chin.

Lamia, Daughter of the Night
by James C. O'Rourke

She's your lover in the night,
only till the dawn
fades before the sun
Her erotic shadows gone
You swirl into darkness
Her passion fills the air
caressing you within
black satin dreams to share

Her body promises lust
with leather and lace
Burning eyes touching
hungry kisses embrace
Your blood's on her lips
Master of all you are
Cold sleepless nights
waiting for your evening star

Wanton beloved arose
lay in night veiled bed
Precious blood consumed
afterglow of red
Each dawn is too soon
Your essence she stole
Can't exist without
breath of your soul

Fairyland
by Caitlin O'Brien - age 14

Gazing through a distant mist
Oh child forever young,
Purple shadows of beautiful things,
Which fairy hands a-spun.

Listening to a silver song,
Unreachable goals attained.
Children's music and pixie feet
Dance in golden rain.

Grasping at a rose-touched cloud,
In grassy meadows lay
Daisies turn to face the sun.
And laughing angels play.

Playing the Game
by Meagan O'Brien - age 15

There are rules
for every stage of life.
If you follow them,
practice them, learn them,
you will be a social success.

But there's always a time
when society is gone,
and you are alone.
Their applause is far far away.
Do you applaud yourself?

Or do you look at your life
and sob angry tears?
Or think angry thoughts?
Or realize you are worthless
scum not deserving an easy death?

While building your image,
never forget to build
an individual who
you are not afraid of
when you are alone.

Place to Place
by Lindsay Ohlmeyer - age 15

We go from place to place,
enveloped in things we want, not need-
when will we ever learn...

We weren't put on Earth to hate,
fighting shouldn't come natural to us-
when will we ever learn...

We should trust and work together,
separate we accomplish nothing-
when will we ever learn...

Until we learn to live with one another,
our lives will be petty-
when will we ever learn...

The Symphony
by Pamela A. Okapal - age 17

A subtle beginning:
A crescendo of drops falls from above,
behind the crescent moon.

The midnight-blue sky
is blanketed with clouds.
The build-up of tension cannot be seen.

One by one, the wall
of clouds becomes thicker.
It moves quickly, with a loud roar.

The winds conduct the rhythmic drops;
one more encore, and
the symphony of storms is created again.

Separation
by LaDraper Ollison - age 20

When two of a kind begin to disagree,
One may be blind where others can see.
When problems occur on too many occasions
Your privacy might have succumbed to invasion.
To have time alone to spend with yourself
is such a relief and good for your health.
It's easy to crown and smother each other,
but harder to find a permanent lover.
It's hard to accept it, when relationships end.
You may find yourself dwelling on how they begin.
It's normal to cry and repent for a while,
but usually the sorrow will end with a smile.
Sometimes it helps just to think of the times
when you and your lover were happy inside.
Separation can be very hard to endure.
Maybe someone will develop a cure.
Then you can rekindle the flame that has died
and all of the tears will dry up that you've cried.
Others may tell you to be glad that he's gone,
but it's best to remember that life will go on.

One Lone Tear
by Heather Olson - age 16

One lone tear.
It rolls slowly down the crevices of her
cheek.
It feels he pain.
It knows her fear.
It shares her loneliness.
It too feels betrayed; unloved; unwanted.
It reaches her chin and pauses.
It leaps off into nowhere.
All alone.
Just one lone tear.

Touch Of The Gifted
by Katherina Olson - age 17

Ruins of color seep through my darkness.
I see the opportunity of disaster.
My senses cry out in sympathy
And the masses cry out in pain.
I see my soul engulfed in laughter,
The color so dead and happy.
Remorse for the losses
And weep for the pain.
The mercy of the living,
Only protect the slain.

Some Quiet Time
by Lillian O'Neal

Today I needed some quiet time, a chance to get away.
I came upon a path that was made so long ago.
But somehow in my quiet times this path I would learn to know.
There were butterflies and wild flowers that spread across the hills,
and as if by magic a breeze came up, richer scents now filled the air.
The best things were the berries that grew along the paths.
They held a special kind of sweetness that always seem to last.
The paths, they seemed to wind around the broken hills,
up over mountains tall, down over bridges small.
but, somehow they seemed to blend into a rocky road ahead.
...You know this has never seemed to stop me, for a calming came inside.
I knew only God could create his beauty.
As I looked into a river nearby,
the colors of the rainbow blended into a turquoise sea,
where puffs of clouds lingered in the dark blue sky above.
It's getting late, but I know when I need to get away
I'll take myself some quiet time to walk this path again.

An Answer To A Question...
by Rachael R. Ontiveros

That has always been thought of but never been asked...
Never been asked, but always hinted about...
Hinted about in a jokingly manner...
Tested the water for fear of the ground...
Fear of the ground for fearing the truth.

The truth to a question that could never be asked. Yet, unconsciously
hearing the silent words to a question as serious as this. Would one day
be the destruction to all that is good and all that is pure. A

destruction of us. I can hear these words no more! So I will answer
the question that haunts our souls and answer the question that screams
at us when our souls are one. The question that will not let us rest.
The one that we hear way deep, deep down. Further than any feeling
we try to erase. At the highest of moments and lowest of days, this
is the answer to the undying question...

I could... I would... I did...
For you!

Combat Loss
by Nancy Harris Ormsbee

Heaven sent you from above
For only me, to win thee love!
Can't believe that we parted,
By my heart's really been hardened!

Honestly, love you is way I feel,
Yes, this war's definitely for real!
Upon my lips your * kisses rain, hoping not in vain,
Please; don't deny my aching, bleeding pain!

Lost your heart in combat war.
Heart's torn badly, it need you more!
Losing your soul's deepest combat loss,
Shooting echoes "You're my biggest cost."

Combat heart's unable to be sown,
Knowing your heart it'll never own!
Bombs hard drop, deep inside of me,
Never will I be set free!

Med-ex's can't heal these wounds,
Even thru billions trillions of moons!
Can't resign, can't drop out of this war,
Love for you will always soar!

Stick it out thru the long haul,
Knowing how long the fall!
Dealing with all the sorrow and pain,
Battling thru hardest and coldest of rain!

Ever since we first met,
Loved you way to much to forget!
Combat loss is far to great,
I'll wait for you at heavens gate!

Wounded solider, Combat loss!
Bleeding heart, Combat loss!

(Kisses rain; kiss lingers thru eternity)

"Turn on the Light"
by Kristy Overton - age 16

Frantic like winter
Essential like none
Run these together
And cry to the sun;
What seems friendly today
Will drown you tonight
So go out and play
But turn on the light.

This Time
by Misty A. Overton - age 20

The big oak door slammed,
Again,
And through the closed door and now,
An understandably closed mind,
The harsh wind of reality flooded the room,
Blew my hair askew,
And chilled my tear-stained face.
I remember that same door opened with a brand new gold-colored key,
When he picked me up and carried me through that door after the life-long promises.
The promises I have broken too many cold-hearted times.
And that key,
Used so many times it's worn,
The once sharp edges now smoothed,
Like my mind, my heart, my soul.
This scene has been viewed before,
The act been played.
The finality of that door slam floods the canyons of both our minds,
But only I know, and I wish he knew,
That this time,
The tears are for real.

Losing Grandpa
by Stefany Owen - age 15

All these years you've been by my side.
I can not imagine your shadow not there.
For all the memories of you in my life.
The times we've shared are passing
through my mind.
Nothing in the world can take the memories away.
You've always been there for the family.
You've been a dad to me throughout the years.
It's just so hard to picture you not being here.
I love you so much Grandpa,
I don't want to see you go.
The thought of you dying scares me so much.
I have always thought that you would always
be here to see me make something out of
my life that would make everyone proud.

Suicide
by Tracy Jean Owens - age 18

S ometimes we question his reasons and search for answers.

U nderlying factors are presented as something beyond our control.

I nstead of conversations, we settle for one-on-one prayers.

C rying doesn't ease the pain but instead allows it to show.

I nside we feel emptiness and it is obvious that we still care.

D eep in our hearts we understand what he must have always known.

E veryone comes across a burden that is too difficult to bear.

Free from the Fog
by Kyla Owl - age 14

Your eyes just don't see
They don't believe
I'm what you need
Can't we figure out a way
from you to see more clearly?
Free from the fog
that hangs over your head,
that makes your vision
almost dead.
I'm not a manipulator.
I don't care what they say
Me loving you
it isn't a crazy thing.
I'm sick of being reminded
You don't feel all of this
like I do,
I know if you tried
you could love me too.
Everyone says you're not right for me.
Sometimes I think I should listen
But it would all still be true,
I'd still be loving you.
Free from the fog
that hangs over your head
lost without you
since you've been dead.

Our Society
by Nicole Pakan - age 15

Such a world, formed by human rage
Is fueled by eloquence
And false conformations.
Where screams in the night
Are raindrops descending
To comfort the humble paradise.

The prophets are worshipped
In shrine of dust
Floating throughout the peaceful city.
Out of reach
But all too near
For the pure of heart.

Communication exists as whispers
Behind closed doors
Through cracks in the wall.
And hope is in the closet
Safe from assaulting eyes
Such violating witnesses.

We savor inequity
And call it life,
So it is
And so it shall be
Condemned in
Our society.

Untitled
by LaDonna Palmer - age 19

Today is your birthday
you would have been nineteen
I know that your still with me
Even though you can't be seen
I need you here to help me
To share my ups and downs
and even though you've gone away
you'll always be around
For in my heart you'll never die
you'll always be around
Mike, this is my good-bye
until we meet again

Dedicated to Mike Vanderploeg
September 3, 1977 - May 30, 1996

Think
by Jennifer L. Palumbo - age 14

Seldom do we think about
And hardly do I ever doubt
That people hold the pain inside
When we swell up with foolish pride
We never look at the solemn face
Of those in even second place
We laugh and spit into their faces
Victors of hectic yet useless rat races
This selfish cycle never ends
But what happens when the position bends
How do you feel when others taunt
Does it feel good? - I think Not

Dark Tunnels
by Edna Panaggio

A princess so beautiful and light,
whose love transcended all she'd meet,
envisioned motherhood, and bride so white,
changed blackened outline, interrupted feat.

Her prince left..bringing darkness into play,
to turn this unearned tunnel black.
Events of life encountered day by day,
to cover each enlightened crack.

A final tunnel waiting dark and dim,
not ever seen by blinded eye.
The ending darkness turned to scrim,
eternal soul in death to join the spirit sky.

Nana
by Melissa Paschke - age 11

Nana loved me and I loved her too,
I still love her, no matter what I do.

She was the best Nana in the world, the best anyone ever had.
Now she is gone, never coming back and I feel really bad.

She always kissed me and that made me feel good.
She always hugged me, oh yes she would.

She'll always be with me, all the years through,
And I know I'll always be with her in heaven too.

I'll miss her a lot and I'm sure she'll miss me.
But when I go to heaven we'll be together again with glee.

She's looking down on me, from heaven above,
And making sure I'm O.K. and that I'm sure of.

I'll always remember her day and night.
I'll always remember her in the dark and the light.

I remember her friend when she passed away,
And Nana thought of when it would be her day.

She sat in the hospital sad and alone.
She was hoping for the day when she could go home.

She got me presents whether she was in or out of town.
Every time I saw her I never had a frown.

I miss going to her house and seeing her there.
I have to walk in and see an empty chair.

Her funeral was pretty, all decorated with flowers.
Every time I went in, I stayed for hours.

I remember her taking her yearly trip to California on a plane.
But then she got old and experienced pain.

She took me lots of places including out to eat,
And when it comes to great Nanas, she can never be beat!

Dedicated to my Nana who died April 15, 1997

Path of Dreams
by Peggy Paul - age 15

Love beacons me,
But hesitation is oh, so strong,
Trying not to hope too much,
Or have those dreams that can't last long.

I try to push my feeling aside,
Yet my heart grasps them and holds them there,
And they linger in my heart and soul,
Should I follow them: do I dare?

They lead me down an unknown path,
that's hilly with flowers of all hues,
And the birds chirp on so happily,
A song of dreams I'll never lose!

Let It Shine
by Cherron Payne

Mulling the past,
Visualizing the future,
Realization like the rising sun dawns.

Shadowed by doubt,
Darkened by evil,
Dreams disappear like the rising sun.

Destroy the umbrellas that protect ignorance,
Terminate the shade that claims wickedness,
Abolish the darkness and allow sunshine.

Give light to the umbrage of dismalness,
Trim the foliage of calamity,
Let the sun rise, let the sun set,
But always let it shine.

Shannon
by Donnica Payne - age 18

i'd give all my tomorrows
for just one yesterday
to hear again 'i love you'
just like you used to say

it seems that since we parted
with every breath and sigh
i'm missing more and more of you
as each day passes by

to just be in your arms again
to have you near to me
i'd give away the days ahead
to re-live one memory

one day you were gone away
death took you from me
i'd taken you for granted
until now i didn't see

so shannon please forgive me
for treating you this way
i'd give all my tomorrows
for just one yesterday.

*In memory of Matthew 'Shannon' Smith
-my best friend-*

"The Needs Of The Heart"
by Tim S. Payne

No words, in any language, are necessary to explain heart felt tears. It's universal.

Tears of the heart have been associated with or earmarked as a sign of sadness and grief. I heartily agree.

Forsaking nothing, I will describe the needs of the heart. There are several, they encompass the heart and nurture it. Among these needs is the feeling to be needed or wanted. Probably, the most basic need of all is the ability to cry to release the pain of the heart. I have produced a well of tears, for my heart has endured a lifetime of sadness and suffering. On rare occasions it has yielded gentle tears, when it has known a few brief moments of happiness. Other than these moments it has never known any instances of joy, only an endless life of sorrow.

The most important need of all is to feel loved. There have been times when I have experienced endearments from my wife. If it were not for that essential need being fulfilled, I wouldn't have survived this long. For my wife has shown me the true meaning of love. Irregardless to the lyrics of the song, you can't make love out of nothing at all. It takes a willing heart and endearment to conceive true love. I have never known love and happiness like this majestic woman has shown me. She is the one need my heart can't do without.

Now, my needs are complete and my tattered past is fading in the light of my bright future. I realize now that my chance at life had not come to pass.

Therefore, I dedicate these words to my loving wife, Cynthia.

Fear
by Ebony Pearl - age 17

Fear is a meaningless thing
At least to the fearless
Life goes on why must it be
the way it is
Life changes so does fear
Do not be afraid to change
Life goes on
Must be accepted
Not interrupted
Fear it not
Life goes on
Let fate step in
He will lead you in the dark
He will show you the light
Life goes on
Fear doesn't exist
where fate lives
Do not live in fate
Life goes on
Beware fate
You can always change it
It cannot be changed
Life goes on

4 Seasons
by Erinn Pegan - age 11

W hen winter comes up,
I love to ski.
N obody will stop me.
'Til the snow stops falling,
E nding the cold winter days,
R emaining still cold until the summer days.

S inging of birds fills the air.
P rancing of rabbits here and there.
R ain coming now and then,
I n comes the flowers where the snow had been.
N ature is all growing back.
G reen as a lime, lovely as a cat.

S ummer is so fun,
U ntil I get burned.
M id-afternoon burns me the most.
M aking my skin burn like toast.
E nding the day with lots of pain,
R ays of sun rest 'til the next day.

F all is the season of colors,
A nd all of the leaves fall down.
L eaving the trees with nothing,
L eaving the leaves on the ground.

Kingdom
by Kimberly Peller - age 17

The kingdom I rule
I stole from a friend;
It has lost its shine.
It used to be gold,
Now it's thorns.
Everywhere I turn,
Another one causes pain;
And this tinfoil crown
Doesn't mean a thing.
A wizard tried to show me the way -
Told me to put my faith in trinkets
And I would be safe.
But the wizard lied.
My kingdom is in chaos.
The people rule it;
They tarnished the gold
And sold it back to me
Along with a broken crown.
They locked the gates
And left me to build a city
From thorns.

Endless
by Maggie Peltier - age 15

This is the end
of endless voids changing
and shifting patterns of metaphorical pits
never once explored
by bleeding, beating, human hands
Boundless ancient endless bruises
tattered into souls
unknown
unexplored
unwilling
To surrender the bounds of time
into their patternless, platonic, extra-extravagant minds.
Hearts and souls they fade
and for tranquility get laid
in the night of day.
The shifting of the wind
moves the patterns
caverns
chasms
into a world
Jimmi Hendrix nor Jim Henson
could bind themselves to find
and yet, the stars still seem brighter
over there,
in their world.
God rest, God bless, wherever they are
into the voids no longer taken
by endless caress of beating,
bleeding, platonic hands,
Known as the human heart.

The Bird House
by Robert R. Penland

The birdhouse sits on a shelf in the shed
reminding no one of the empty life it's led.
Long ago crafted by careful hand,
the corners he mitered, the imperfections he'd sand.
The house was a gift he'd promised his friend,
they were always together the perfect blend.
But life's distractions were strong, and it pulled them apart
and soon they'd forgotten how it was at the start.
When a friendship emerging so fresh and so new,
like a robin's egg arriving with the morning's dew.
They've unremembered those days and the closeness they had.
No longer wondering, no longer sad.
So the Birdhouse sits empty, never a life inside,
a forgotten token of a friendship that's died.

Untitled
by Natalie Pennino - age 17

The winds of time
Have changed us,
As they often do.
If it was
For better or worse,
I guess that's up to you.

A wave of sorrow
Touched us,
Rising up to wash us down.
The gentle tide
That saved us,
Was the love we found.

The earth below
Had shook us,
Causing our weakened hearts to fall.
But by using
Each other,
We could easily stand up tall.

The World of War-Wounded Words
by Alexander Pepple

Why flip my scrambled words like the fingers
Of a tourist lost in foreign territory
Through a multilingual dictionary?
Only Spanish or Arabic of sorts she speaks —
My English or Patois of parts is *no comprender*.

Friends, couples, corporates. Countries to kin —
All these languages! When gestures won't win,
Who'll translate while I explain, compromise, apologize?
World of cultures in clash, puzzled warring eyes!

Will someone else laugh please at my practical joke? Is my sin
Profuse friendship and daring, drowning me in
Hasty risks? Now, this war! I must learn to inject calculated
Blasts of coolness to keep my friendships time-tested.

I watch the beekeeper shatter my vase against a whitewashed
Wall that smears red with red earth. My feet wet with the spilled
Water never regained, seeking its way back to its roots, the earth.
Tomorrow, I see the pain of the rose as disinherited
It withers fast to dark like a broiled chicken heart.

Not understood, I see her flapping tongue
Still like a strobed circling saw. My boldened tongue
Fires unmeanings that scare the honeybees off thier colony
As workers and drones swarm oceans and shores in agony
To burst into a mushrooming mountain of dark clouds.

Will the UN lend me please their translators! But will they cope?
They too have their wars, their translators crafty in peaceful hope
(But are they sometimes giving secret thanks to
The worldwide franchising of tumbling Towers of Babel?)

O, fill this world with the universe of sounds of sweet ease,
The music of life, the songs of birds and buzz of bees,
Echoing like soft tree-side moans in a moonlit breeze.

I Love the Way
by Litisha Perkins - age 13

I love the way your voice melts like a
gentle breeze into my soul
How your soft loving stare makes me love
you more and more
And I love the way your kisses run
fingers through my heart, like the wind
whispers through my hair

I love the way your eyes sparkle when
you laugh
And how your words catch my breath
like stars are caught by wishes
I love the way you are.

Material Girl...
by James Peterson III

How does it feel to have no one to love
and no one to hold in your arms?
Not knowing when to open your heart,
so you live your life alone.

I tried to reason again and again
why you live the bitter not the sweet,
when you're such a beautiful woman
from your tender smile down to your feet.

So what if he gives you diamond rings
and necklaces of pearl.
He could never give you the love you need
but he'll cunningly promise you the world.

How does it feel to have him say he loves you
while he showers you with gifts you adore?
You knowing his love belongs to another
so you cry alone behind closed doors.

You constantly dream of this man you call simple
while the other man leaves you empty inside.
The simple man fills your heart with passion.
The other man entices your eyes.

What will happen when those gifts disappear
as the years of your youth pass by?
All you'll have left will be distant memories
as you sit quietly and ask yourself why.

Why did you follow behind this other man
when you meant nothing in his life?
Now you're old and all alone
when you could have been the simple man's wife.

Through The Window
by Anonymous - age 13

I look through the window and this is what I see,
Everyone is happy, everyone but me.
I have no life, I have no home,
It seems like all I do is roam.
Across the world, from here to there,
I have no one to love, no one to care.
All my friends were left behind,
Living without them had never crossed my mind.

I'm looking through the window, and this is what I see,
A sad, depressed, and lonely me.
I know I should be moving on,
But it's hard to look around
And find that everything you love is gone.

I want to close this window,
This window I've been looking through,
I want my life to just resume,
If only someone knew.

Glory on High
by Sharon S. Phoa

I'm spending Christmas with my Savior. Oh what a place to be!
A choir of heavenly angels will be caroling with me

And the star I light this season will not adorn a tree,
but shine brightly in the heavens giving hope to all who see.

The feast we will encounter is sure to be divine
His mansion does have many rooms and one of them is mine.

I'm spending Christmas with my Savior
and a few old friends I knew.

The only thing that's changed my love, is just my point of view
Instead of looking at you now, I'm smiling down on you.

Don't despair my darling, I'm not that far away
I look upon your lovely face each and every day

I'll still be there each time you sigh and when your heart is sad
But fill your heart with mirth, my love, rejoice and just be glad

I'm spending Christmas with my savior, yes this is my reward
The peaceful rest forever... that I'd been looking toward

I feel no earthly pain and yes, for that we both are glad
For now I hope that you recall the joyous times we had

Someday I know you'll join me here, until that time arrives
Find peace in life and know my dear... that I'm right by your side

I'll Love You Always, Forever (No Matter What)
by Kate Petzold - age 14

I think about you night and day,
hoping someday we'll be together.
I feel like I've known you forever,
though it has only been a year.
The days that I see you
turn to nights that I dream about you.

I get weak when you look at me.
I get lost inside your eyes.
I want you to understand,
your every breath I breathe.

From the first day that I saw your smiling face,
I knew that we should be together, forever.
When my eyes met yours we became friends,
but nothing more.

I want you here with me,
now until the end of time.
No one needs you,
as much as I need you.
Without you I don't think I can live.
I wish I could give the world to you,
but love is all I have to give.

Glimpse
by Amanda Pickell - age 17

Last night I saw a glimpse of your face
But it was only a second.
If I could get that moment back
And pause time I would look at you forever.
I can't describe my love for you
Because it is only something I feel.
Feelings cannot be understood by the unknown
Only by the one who's heart is full of love.
This love, I know, will never die
Because you are in my heart
And that love will always be here for you.

What is Life
by Nicole Marie Pingrey - age 13

What is life?
Is it a journey?
Is it a road?
What is life?
Is it to have?
Is it to hold?
What is life?
Is it to ponder?
Is it to doubt?
Can anyone tell me what life is about?
Be it a journey, be it a road.
Be it to have, be it to hold.
Your own life is worth treasures untold.
Hold on to your life, try to be strong,
for whatever it is, it doesn't last long.

As I Lay Here
by Shannan Pettinger - age 17

As I lay here lost in the stars
I wonder if you are thinking of me
You think it is best this way
But to me your love means everything

As I lay here lost in the stars
Your face is all I see
Your name rushes through my head
Implanted like your first touch

As I lay here lost in the stars
I think of you
The one I long for
My one true love!

Two Things
by Katieann Pirog - age 15

Untold to the forgiven, untold to the forgotten; in search, in hopes for something more real than reality itself. How real can get, for it would be a sense of falseness. Betrayed, bruised, and still running on forward into the dark with no visual light. For I can see I'm going blind. Hush, hush and just remember that when it all comes down to it, and only the truth, the real question is how can you be in two places at once when your not anywhere at all?

The Fellow
by Lynn Plourde - age 13

Tulips are yellow,
All in a row;
Got picked by a fellow,
Who decorated them with a bow;
Fellow went upstairs to see his fair maiden,
Saw the bed on which the tulips he laid 'em;
Hugged his fair maiden with one quick embrace,
Softly stroked his hand on her beautiful face;
Looked deeply into her eyes with great care,
Ran his fingers through her long golden hair,
Gave her a kiss of great romance,
Then left giving her a quick glance;
she softly waved a timid good-bye,
Sang herself a sweet lullaby;
Falling to her bed next to the tulips that were yellow,
And dreamt beautiful thoughts of her wonderful fellow.

Wandering Child
by Tara Lee Porter

An abandoned cherub wandering the streets in search of someone to love.

Walking until the pain takes control, a feeling of hopelessness takes over him.

    But something leads him on......

His eyes begin to fill with tears from the unbearable pain, causing him to stumble and fall
to the cold pavement.

Slowly he feels his spirit separating from his lifeless body

    But somehow fear does not exist......

An angelic form lights up the darkness, she reaches out her slender arms to hold him.

In her arms he is suddenly reminded of the distant and painful memory of his mother

    Who gave him life knowing that hers would end.

Reunited at last as their souls disappear into the heavens above

    Never to see the hardships of life again.

The Reading
by Randall E. Pretzer

Leave your towers tonight
And dare to find pain in your consolation

Let someone sprinkle soot in your hair
Let them scatter leaves before your path
Let them draw your face to the sun
And later -- when things are peaceful . . .
Let them tease your tranquility under the moon

Time has come for lies for moist palms and wine
But do not fail to be afraid . . .
Bend your ear with cupped hand and allow them to risk
Another impression of finger paint and paste.

Relex . . .
Chew their crayola . . .
Enjoy the warm wax and before you dream again
Notice the dirt under your nails
Feel the cracks before your feet
Listen to the rattle of the leaves
And shield your eyes from the sun
Remembering the moon. . . .

Love
by Jelyna Price - age 14

Love is a test of
one's trust or faith
in another which is to be
gained, lost and regained.

Kill My Resistance
by Mitchell Price

I walk home at night to my room.
It doesn't seem too right
to think that I have been alone.
I know whats out there.
Some time has been wasted anyway.

And yet, so-what the mystery
of a short lived life.
Self and pride and peace of mind all come out.
The resistance I face all fall in line.
I'm going to kill my resistance.

Gone
by Susannah E. Prucka

When I looked into his eyes that day,
I saw what no one else had seen.
The sword fights he had when he was young
and his first kiss with Mary Jane.
But that does not matter here today
because he is six feet beneath my feet.
So I ask myself what did I do
    to deserve this kind of pain?
The car rides, the dates, the teddy bears
    were those just ploys to toy with my heart?
The kiss goodnight, and the walk to the door,
    where did they go so long ago?
He should not have done it, yes, I know,
but still it hurts deep inside to me.
The gun to his head, the suicide note...
why, why, why did he do it?
Was it his parents, school, football, or me...
    will I ever know?
but as long as I live I will always remember him,
my love,
my dear,
my heart.

The Black Diamond
by Bobbie J. Pugh

Nightingales are born to sing.
From Trinidad to Cancun
From St. Thomas to St. John,
notes cresendoed and
decrescendoed rung
upwards to land on distant stars.
Heaven smiled upon her.
Each time she opened her mouth,
gems flew out and stunned
the maddening crowd.

Then love possessed her, abused
and silenced her, but for a while.
God knew that nightingales were
born to sing, so he touched her
mouth, and diamonds pierced the
black clouds; she was free, again,
until Merlin appeared. Prodded
by his two friends, bigotry
and jealously,
they burned out the light of sound.

But who can keep a nightingale
from singing?
Who can keep the bell that tolls
for you and me from ringing?
Not our friends nor our foes
but, a mystery, we can not tell.
If the Phoenix rose again,
surely, she too, will follow suit.
God will not allow nightingales
to remain mute.

Mind's Prison
by Paula M. Pursley

The distant chords strike a memory
Faded with time and passing thoughts.
The spectral strains return in elusive snatches,
Playing hide-and-seek with love's pure consciousness.
At times...Growing in intensity and familiarity
As they waft throughout the passages of the mind.
A forgotten love...A friendship cherished...
Childhood joys...Life's sweet dreams;
The resonance and harmony intertwine...
Plucking the heartstrings of the soul!
This symphony of memory builds to a crescendo as
Crashing cymbals accent past remembrances.
Soothing harps coax gentle childlike smiles
As some precious forgotten memory surfaces
Like bubbles from the deep!
'Twas but just a brief moment in time,
But the fire from within kindled and flashed recognition
To those starving, thirsty, family eyes.
Loved ones praying for restoration of mind, body, and soul!
Like wildfire the joy comes tumbling forth,
Much like a well-orchestrated arpeggio.
Tears stream down cheeks as soft as a piccolo's musical trill.
WHEN JUST AS SUDDENLY...
The prison bars come crashing down on remembrance,
Halting memory's stanzas as some invisible minstrel cuts the lovely strains.
Memory's sweet notes fall once more on deaf ears
As the mind's conductor brings the welcome performance to an end!
The rusty musician locks the instrument's case and
Slips silently back into the prison of his mind!

Believe
by Nicole Pupshis - age 11

Something made me believe that there are angels
    hovering above me and you
Protectors that are always ahead
Answering all the prayers we have said
Many times I believe that this is true
That they are hovering in a sky so blue
    With wings so soft
    With skin so pure
    With hearts so sweet
Sweeter and Purer and Softer than words could ever say
Something made me believe.
I think that something is *you*.

Untitled
by Melissa Quintana - age 20

They walk down the road
The smallest one in between them
Guiding and showing the way as best they can
Slowly or quickly
Depending on the point of view
The littlest one grows
And begins down a different road
To walk alone for the time being
And then one day
The road joins another
And the journey continues on
    We all travel down this road of life
    In the beginning we have someone guiding us
    Then we go on our own
    Hoping our paths cross with anothers
    If we are lucky
    We continue on together for a long time
    But, always in the end
    The roads separate
    And we finish our journey
    Alone

In My Freedom
by Allison Pytlak - age 16

Keep me free
My mind;
Away from shackles of
any kind.
Hold back mechanics and
narrow views.
Instead open the windows,
and let the breezes blow through.

Keep me free
My heart;
Pure and young.
As of yet it remains unstrung.
Let it love and give and
sometimes suffer.
Watch it learn and then grow tougher.

Keep me free
My soul
And all of its dreams.
Preserve the character - see it gleam.
Without oppression,
and in its own way,
my soul shall thrive;
get stronger everyday.

So keep me free—
Mind, heart and soul.
Let me be that someone whom
I'm destined to be:
Me

The Substance of the Shadow
by Kelly Queener - age 15

There is, in your hesitation
A clue to your true feelings
It's just a matter of being
Literate in that language

There could be, something longer
If not for that, pale glance in your eyes
That revealed the substance
Behind those infamous words

I love you

It could've been, pleasing to the ears
(And it was, the first ten times)
If it hadn't been, robbed of meaning
Hadn't, made my love a blue

There is, in my heart
A weight from the doubts
That your love impressed on me
And a sickening feeling, that your

Words are true.

Forever a Special Living Treasure
by Joleen Santos Quintanilla

I love you, I always have,
I don't understand how or why people
treated you the way they did in the past.

You were so different, so unique,
You were just being yourself,
You are still very special to me,
more special than anyone else.

For some reason, I forgive those people,
but I still feel very HURT; all you have
seen and felt most of your life was
disrespect and people treating you like dirt.

But as you taught me with your heart, I
will continue to pray for those people;
that one day they will ask GOD for
help under His church steeple.

As each day passes; as the years roll by,
I'm getting closer to you, soon it will
be my time to die.

Though you're not here with me, all the days
of the week, all seven; I thank GOD
for you, for creating you, for calling you
to your TRUE HOME: HEAVEN.

Since the day I met you and even though
you're gone, you are still branded in my
HEART, SOUL, and MIND, you will always
be even after the end of time.

I miss you so much infinitely, honestly there's no measure,
for you are a very SPECIAL TREASURE,
you live in me forever.
I truly love you forever.

To His Love
by Jesselle Rae - age 12

A little boy picks a flower
and gives it
to his love.
A young man buys a ring
and proposes
to his love.
Wedding bells ring.
A young man says "I do"
to his love.
A baby cries.
A young man rushes
to his love.
It's raining outside.
Something is wrong.
A man runs
to his love.
Everyone is crying, dressed
in black as the man
says good-bye;
to his love.

Nobody
by Dennis E. Rager

Against the wall of the underground walkway,
curled into a semi-fetal position,
your eyes not fully closed,
reminiscent of fading silver moons,
you go unnoticed, no more conspicuous
than the trash can on the street corner,
The passing rush hour crowd does not disturb
your seemingly unlabored slumber,
no visible movement, not so much as a twitch.
Days later, it is only the stench of rotting flesh
that finally attracts any attention.
Emergency Medical Services is summoned
to the scene to load the stiffened shell of a man
into a plastic body bag, like so much refuse gathered
for disposal, and transport to the city morgue,
a temporary stop over, en route to potters field,
no family or friends to claim your remains.
What shall they inscribe on your tombstone?
*"At one time, I was somebody, but fate has
relegated me to* **Nobody.**"
What an epitaph!

A Moment of Memories
by Selma Amy Rampersaud - age 17

At this moment, one single moment, I feel hatred.
A sharpness of rage held inside,
waiting...waiting...waiting,
until the day might arrive,
that my anger and pain will disappear.
The sadness, the hurt...
the worlds I love you, the words I'm sorry,
sound repulsing!
It disgusts me to hear them!
Why not say what you mean, and mean what you say?
But...truthfully!
The truth is meaningless to those who lie.
The lies and smiles,
smiles you think I smile,
when actually I frown, from all my sadness combined.
I've frowned, for so many years come and gone.
I now realize things will always remain desolate, you will always remain the same.
I don't think I will ever care for you, the way I used to want to.
We've both come so far, and I don't want you to be there anymore.
I don't want you to be a part of my life anymore.
Almost everything you say, or do,
and sometimes when you're doing...nothing at all,
I'll remember those times, and I'll remember how you hurt me.
I feel numb, sick to my stomach and entirely fed up.
then it drifts away...
This one single moment of sheer hatred.

The Ocean and all of Her Grace
by Fawn Rangel - age 14

Amongst the opaque, thick fog tarp lay a body of water rocking itself and the creatures that live inside of it to sleep.

When the fog thins the ocean will awake yawning, stretching high.

Releasing its foam covered limbs outward for a long moment.

The popping bubbles are the sounds of the water's fingers spreading out upon the silken clay like sand.

Then she rolls back, her body mass whiplashes into the deep.

Her hair made into thin strands of slick tangled seaweed floats wildly.

Occasionally she leaves behind a souvenir, a lock of seaweed strewn upon the spongy surface.

A disobedient clan of clams may get lost and cling to a rock hoping for safety.

With gentle ease she engulfs the rock, scooping up her naughty children and tucks them down into the folds of her trustful pocket.

That funny noise you hear when you put a seashell up to your ear is her whispering a shallow sea's greeting.

The soft rhythm heard at night, sometimes a mile away is the ocean's breathing.

A long deep breath in and them slowly letting it out.

Her heart beat is the light tumble of water pulling over small boulders.

The moon cradles her and protects her while she's asleep at night.

When morning arrives the sun will warm her back and wash away the fog tarp so that once again she may awaken.

The Wind
by Anne Ranney - age 12

When the wind blows upon me,
I can hear your sweet voice.
When the trees start to tremble,
I can feel your warm embrace.
When the butterflies flutter by,
I can see your loving face.
So when the wind blows, the trees tremble,
and the butterflies flutter by,
I know you are near.

Sonnet Of Silence
by Jane Ratcliffe

In the yellow sunshine the silhoutte's were leafy and green
The sky was sapphire - Ceylon to Kanchanaburi blue
And even the sweet fragrance of the spring flowers
Have been etched into the deepest portion of my soul
But far more indelibly the peaceful silence
Which only your soft voice could break
This peace was more than the eye defined
And love was more enduring than we dreamed it to be
This solitary place is intertwined with memories
I have come back here many times my dear
But it was never, not even once, the same
Today the silence is no longer comforting
You are gone. The sky is no longer blue
There is no fragrance in the meadows or the woods
My favorite familiar place is wrestled from me
For you, my most dearly loved, are forever gone
And with you go the colors the sunshine and the songs
Here, in this peaceful silence does Love inscribe
A cenotaph. Mute ... eloquent ... and everlasting

The Lords of Destruction
by Charles Ray

a life can come unglued
with just a whiff
from a little plastic vial

or a moment
of unleashed anger

the past is painful
and the future is unknown
and the present

is little more than
day upon day

of unending boredom
and hopelessness

and it is upon the weak
and helpless
the hopeless ones

they prey

How Much She Hurt Me
by Lucinda B. Ray - age 17

What's blue and black and tan all over
mommy, after he beat her again
does he know how much he hurts her
does he know how much he hurts me

He's not my father, just a substitute
for someone I never knew
but if this is a father's job
I'd rather have no father at all
I clutch my hands around my ears
as her screams echo into my mind
and when I finally get to hold her
her body is too weak to be touched
does he know how much he hurt her
does she know how much he hurts me

I cry while say says she loves him
how could you love the impact of a fist
I begin to hate her, for staying abused
I always hate him, for hurting us
does he know how much he hurts her
does she know how much he hurts me.

Takeover
by Kim Raymond - age 13

Depressing reality
comes into focus
as abandonment
approaches

Color whirlwinds
dazed and confused
next moments unknown
what will be done?

Slavery roams
resigned into hate
savagery reigns
capturing innocence

Memories
by Christine Ann Reardon - age 14

Memories of you float and dance
in my mind.
Reminding me of our never ending love.
Of times we shared.
Memories of late night walks under a starry sky.
Stolen kisses and vows that remain forever.
Memories of your kisses and how you held
my hand as we walked.
Memories of your love, our love.
A love as deep as the sea
and boundless as the sky.
Memories of you and me.
Memories of a love so true.
Memories, but not you.

Untitled
by Kristie Redfield - age 17

Off to do battle
the Foolish, brave knight
Safe in his armor
so Eager to fight
Arrogance, a blind betrayal
a Prisoner of war
Last fight (against his armor)
Thrown Overboard

Waves
by Amber Nykole Reed - age 14

Touched by the sun's golden locks
Chaotic waves swirl around forgotten rocks
Filled with mist and foam
The sea does often roam
To many distant skies
As it dances to the gull's cries
Though many do not know why
You can often hear the water sigh
As it sings to you of its magic
And of those whose ends were tragic
The waves whisper of treasure lost
And of wild hearts who loved at a great cost
The sea does tell many a tale
About the free souls who dare to set sail

Love
by Jessica Reed - age 18

Love is like the ocean,
Sometimes the current takes you out
into unexpected waters,
Other times a huge wave takes you under,
It may drown you if you're not careful,
It could be dangerous,
But other times it is calm and inviting,
Peaceful and Gentle,
The waves flow in and out like relationships,
But they always leave an indentation in the sand,
Like in your heart,
You never forget the ocean,
No matter how old you are,
And one day when you go back to sea,
You'll remember, that
Love is like the ocean.

Cobweb's Dew
by Susan M. Reed

The misty colors turn
Into a kaleidoscope cobweb
Sobbing like a trickle
To the stream that
Freezes crystal
At the season's ebb.
It is then that the golden sun stops,
And sops the moisture.
This diamond cloister,
On the cobweb,
Which is death to a fly,
Eaten as a symbol of the
    season's ebb
The cobweb stringed across,
The veil with dew sopped.
Stopped, robbing the web
Of its beautiful glory
Of this frost-bitten story.

Lost Hearts
by Emily Reeves

How do you tell another you love them?
You say it a million times in your head,
but still it feels like the first.
A million things flood your head.
What will they say,
what will they do,
or do they love me back?
That fear can crush your heart,
and make you lost to the world.
Is there really a right time or place,
does it matter.
Can it decide how the other feels about you?
In a world as harsh and as crewel as this,
how can love really exist?
Love is something that you can only express,
words don't change anything only create distance.
If we could live in a world with out words,
love would be perfect.
Nothing to destroy it or dim it,
just the inner feeling would hold us together.
so instead of speaking those three little words,
show you love then.
It will make a bigger difference than anything spoken.

Did You Ever Wonder
by Rebecca Ann Reichert - age 17

Did you ever wonder how the sun sets in the sky?
Did you ever wonder how all the birds fly?
Did you ever wonder how the rain starts to fall?
Did you ever wonder how man learned to draw?

Did you ever wonder why God put us on Earth?
Did you ever wonder why or what life is worth?
Did you ever wonder why people do what they do?
Did you ever wonder why God made you, you?

Did you ever wonder who really cares about you?
Did you ever wonder who makes your dreams come true?
Did you ever wonder who is in charge of your life?
Did you ever wonder who will be your husband or wife?

Did you ever wonder what is in the future for you?
Did you ever wonder what strange things you will do?
Did you ever wonder what real friends are made of?
Did you ever wonder what makes people fall in love?

Did you ever wonder where all the stars are made?
Did you ever wonder where dreams go when they fade?
Did you ever wonder where people go when they say good-bye?
Did you ever wonder where you will go when you die?

All of these questions can be answered by you.
Because you can do anything you put your mind to.
But don't take them for granted as some kind of fun.
Take the time to carefully answer them, one by one.

Nuance
by Rene's Gillespie

I overheard the moon and stars
A conversation of love.
Apart by day, together at night
Romance of a life time.
Each night a joyous reunion
Of cascading light and shimmering eyes.
Beauty for the whole world
to admire, admonish, and capture.
Only a fool ignores it's radiance
And shrugs off the wisdom she hides.

Our Love
by Amanda Sype-Renaud

Sitting here, miles away from anyone I really love,
　or who really loves me,
　　I dream of you.
I imagine, with the ease that comes from much practice,
　your smile, the sound of your voice,
　　　the touch of your lips...
Though we may be separated by hundreds of miles,
　you are with me always,
　　　in my heart,
　　　　my mind,
　　　　　my soul.
I can feel you here, loving me,
　surrounding me like the air I breathe,
　warming me like the sun on my face,
　making me feel special, alive.
And I know that it doesn't matter
　where I am, or where you are,
Because our love reaches everywhere.

"Dust of Me"
by Sheryl Rentschler

Frustration.
A vermicular disease
Fed by the parasite
Of man's borderline
Confidence and Apathy.
Love.
A fluke of Man's heart.
A wake between
Empathy and Apathy
And the need to smile.
Hate.
A resolution of Man's Self.
A subconscious diversion
Of greed and jealously.
A self-satisfying pity.
Lust.
The fear of Man's inadequacy.
An embarrassment of impotence.
A fluency of delicate desires.
Subversive revolution of the body.
Emotions.
The natural holocaust
Of Man's own true Self.
The illogical surrender
Of composite stupidity.
A truce of mind and heart,
The defense against Man.

Nonentity
by Jennifer Reusser - age 14

Watching the world
    all through the night
as the moonlight
    touches over the wood
where everything is out of sight

The wind blowing softly
    whispers a lullaby
up in the sky
    as the grass
breaths a sigh

Standing there alone
    i look around
not making a sound
    thinking to myself
of the self that has not been found

Searching for what has not been searched for
    will they ever see
the real me
    everywhere i turn another door
stopping me from being free

Hiding from myself
    in this mind of mine
and i pine
    coming out only if i dare
afraid of those with words like tines

Monique's Lullibye
by Jerry H. Rex

Can you hear me babe,
as the wind blows your way.
My heart cast on a cloud;
your my rainbow today.
You do to me;
as the calm does to the Sea.
And as I walk with;
my heart goes running free.
My path may be at your window; so my footsteps know where they lead.
And when, in fact, I reach there;
I'm all the Dad that you'll need.
I wear a chain around my neck;
that says we are friends.
It represents me creating you;
and my love will never end.
I reach my hands, to touch your heart;
and I feel the pain on it.
So let me be your healer;
and beside you I will sit.
Let me take you from the bitter world;
and bring a knew world to you.
And I will rock you every night;
as I sing this song to you:
Lay down baby, let me tuck you into bed.
Let me make a difference, and kiss your tired head.
Can I lay beside you and sing into your eyes.
And I will rock you in my arms, and sing Monique's Lullibye.

Poem written on 3-02-97
by Cerisa Reynolds - age 14

He takes a drag of his cigarette,
and says "It was a beautiful day."
Then he lowers his thoughtful head
and says, "I want it all to go away."
A bullet in his left hand,
a hand gun in the other.
He stares across the dark hills of land,
and mutters how he misses his lover.
Walks inside the door,
turns off all the lights.
He's been here all before,
but it brings it back on these kinds of nights.
Picks up the telephone,
calls his dear and few close friends.
Leaves them all a message,
saying tonight is the night that it ends.
A slow walk up the stairs.
And a slow drink of his liquor.
Flashbacks of those hateful glares,
and always hearing her bicker.
He writes a note for whoever finds his body,
and sets out a towel for whoever sees him bloody.
turns down the radio,
sets some food out for the cat.
Lifts his arm to his skull,
The dull night is ended by a roaring crack.
A deep breath.
All is silent,
all is black.

Lost And Confused
by Dennis Reynolds - age 16

Gods trying to set me free.
From all the evil that's taken over me.

It's so bad that I can't see.
I yell and fight with friends and family.

I don't feel pain anymore.
All that's there is mixed feelings and more.

I try so hard to stay so straight.
But all the evil is so great.

God's trying to set me free.
From bad examples that's taken over me.

All the things have built up so slowly.
I'm now lost with all the furry.

I'm trying to be a leader and not a follower.
Do things my way and not get hurt.

I loose control really easy.
I don't know why I have no clue.

God's trying to set me free.
I hope he does so I can be me.

No Place for Love
by Carolyn Rice - age 13

Love doesn't live here anymore.

Love doesn't even knock at my heart's door.

Once upon a time it owned a special key that
opened up my heart.

But after a while I felt it starting to depart.
With each time drawing nearer to the door.
Taking with it all bliss and feelings of happiness.
Until love opened the door, closed and locked it tight.

Like I said before love doesn't live here anymore.

No my heart has harden, and now thorns begin
to surround my heart that was once bound by
love, so pure it could cure.

I guess I just got to secure.

I am not going to imitate or try to replace the love
I once had.

Because I know love doesn't live here anymore.

Our Lives
by Jennifer Richardson - age 15

Like drops of rain on a rose
shaking bitterly at the grass
smelling as fresh as a spring day
living only to fear the day it dies

Like an ocean that is motionless
moving only to the wind
fading until it dies
so are the days of our lives

Buffalo Woman
by Leslie Anne Richards

Her heritage is rich with history passed down for generations.
Like Mother Nature, she is patient and knows all.
Her eyes sparkle with a confident knowledge of what's to come.
She is comfortable knowing she has the resiliency to overcome.

Deep within the lines of her face lies the child in of us.
Each reliving the same experiences with slight twists
and minor diversions for our own tailor-made rendition.
Each line representing many things in her life,
but all center upon her strengths and triumphs.

Her memories are sweet and as fresh as the summer breeze.
Her strong sense of survival and knowledge of a distant past
is the gift she shares with us all.
It is here - in all of us.
It is the link that makes us all common.
It is the one we deny; the one determined to separate us all.

The sadness in her eyes is easily replaced
with the sense that we will all soon awaken.
She is patient and will soon greet us again
when time has indicated that our hearts and minds are open.

A Place In Nowhere
by Nicole Richmond - age 13

There is a place
Beyond the sun's rays,
And the dark driven clouds
Where broken-winged angels
Dance to old memories
Where your only hope
Is your only sorrow
And what you wish on a star
Is there tomorrow
While ripped paper
Breathes old poetry
Sad songs are sung
To the fragile broken hearts
This place is somewhere
Somewhere between the dead and alive
Somewhere between the cruel and kind
With the scent of 4 leaf clovers
And the surroundings of yellow leafed trees
This place exists
In only nowhere
But if you ever do go
Make sure your heart can see

Deaths Kingdom
by Crystal Sunshine Rickman - age 18

I saw that the sun had burned
the sky red (I will never know that
sun again)
I felt my last hopes get buried as the
sun set to rest
    Deaths kingdom is the night when
it wakes it's sleepy head to look you
deep into your soul (you know now
darkness eternally)
I felt the night close in on me
(as it was dragging me to forever)
I felt my last smile slip away
from my lips, not bothering to reach
my eyes.
I felt a hunger so strong deep inside
me a longing need for the feast of the
night
So hear I am in Deaths Kingdom
Waiting, watching, wanting, needing,
hoping, praying that this pain will
end.
    Its a Death that won't die
in Deaths Kingdom

Philharmonic
by Charles Douglas Ricks

The maestro's head is bowed. He prays that we do him proud. All of our instruments are held still. They wait to serve the master's will. In the air hangs a chill.
No mistakes are allowed.

We are all rehearsed and carefully tuned. It's our first concert. Nothing has been assumed. At once our beloved maestro lifts his head and wand. His face is aglow and fond. Our minuet begins softly and then is mushroomed.

Each musician has his own part to play. Our instruments each have special things to say. The instrument and it's player are one and the same. They make a unit in the heart of the orchestral frame.

The maestro's music can sing to a troubled heart. The sonata will give a mind it's new start, his music carries our souls to the heavenly day. Our worries are seen as meaningless and gone along the way.

This symphony is the maestro's master piece. It's written for our lives to give us the new lease. Let the soft melody come inside. Let it open our ears and minds wide. Let the master's symphony make the love to increase.

The maestro's head is bowed. He prays that we do him proud.

Jesus answered and said unto them, **This is the work of God, that ye believe on him whom he hath sent.** KJV JOHN 6:29

As The Wind Blows
by Jennifer Rieswyk - age 16

Confiding love
Warmths embrace
Spoke of feeling
And touchings face
Bewilderment
As looked upon
Dust as it settles
Waking up the dawn
Power of healing
To the sun as it shone
Forever brimming tears
On the brink of life
Is to live again
With feeling and love
Driving unto insanity
Screaming as the wind blows
Craziness is not forsaken
But taken for happiness
To laugh as one flower
Whose beauty is pale
One whose water
Seems to have gone stale.

Dogs
by Meagan Rikard - age 11

Dogs are nice,
Dogs are sweet,
Dogs like to nibble at your feet.
Dogs want to be just like you,
And like to chew up shoes when they
Are new.
Dogs can be mean,
But who cares?
They look just like Teddy Bears.
They have cute brown noses I just love,
But I wish I knew what they were
Thinking of.
Dogs can be big,
Or dogs can be small,
So what!!!! I LOVE THEM ALL!!!!

Kissing The Sea
by Jolene Ripple - age 17

I sit here upon the moist sand
Listening to the gentle ocean waves crash
With bitter-sweet peacefulness onto the shores
And I silently wish for you.

The light I see when I look into your eyes
Reminds me of the perfect God blessed stars
That twinkle above me
And guide me through the night.

And I know that you are here with me
Somewhere in the sands
That your blessed feet have walked upon
So many times in my dreams.

The moon like your perfect presence
Lights my somewhat dark path
And knowing that you're with me always
Warms and fills my soul tenderly.

But these gray clouds have brought me
Hasteful-tenders of my ownself
And made me realize what I was
And what I have become.

But I know that tomorrow the clouds will be gone
And you will walk into my life
With a gentle touch and you'll kiss me
Like how I kissed the sea.

Empty
by Sheila B. Roark

Coldly the band sits on her finger
radiating a tawdry brilliance,
giving her a false sense of worthiness.
Deep in the recesses of her soul
emptiness abounds and grows.
The gnawing feeling of nothingness
rips her in two as she struggles through her life.
She seeks temporary relief from the void
by wearing trinkets made of gold.
Until love comes into her heart,
her life will be as tawdry
as the shiny band she so proudly wears.

The River
by Sara Gaye Welch

Down flows the river from the mountain
Sparkling high like a diamond fountain
Wending and winding on its way
Bubbling aloud with so much to say

Around the bend see it comes running
Quiet pools where beaver sit sunning
Rocks and boulders mark its trail
On it flows like a great blue sail

Running through the forest tall and dark
Full of light like the song of a lark
Now comes the prairie with grass so high
It welcomes the river with a breathless sigh

On sweeps the river wild and free
Laughing and chasing the warm azure sea
River of life -----so deep-------so strong
Matching its rhythm to earth's life song

For the Journey
by Erin Roach - age 17

Forget the rough roads you have traveled upon,
And the turbulent waters that have tossed you about,
And the daunting mountains that have stood before you.
Think only of your family anxiously awaiting your return,
And remember the love that I packed in your suitcase.

Mother
by Ashley J. Robey

When I look in her eyes I can see her hard life,
Her many years of abuse and long weeks of strife.
Her parents were partial to the bottle you see,
And when she met Michael she thought she was free.
Though only a teen she bore a child of her own,
Thereafter more fabric of hardships were sewn
With three mouths to feed and one on the way
She worked several jobs, fourteen hours a day.
She has always provided everything without greed
Not once did she pause to consider her needs.
So now that she's older her hair has turned gray
The wrinkles grow deeper with each stressful day.
I could never compare her with another,
For she is the one I'm so proud to call mother.

A Transcendental Trip
by Adam Robinson

The wind whips my mind, stirring my soul
And sending a shiver down my spine.

Goosebumps engulf my body as thought and emotion collide.
The ebb of perpetual feelings harkens me to ride and ponder
On life's wondrous reelings.

God beckons as Winter's icy fingers caress the nape of my neck.
Listen my son. The answers are all around. They travel on the winds' whisper.
Gargantuan gusts are no louder than the supple serenade
That gently guides an autumn leaf to the welcoming arms of the earth.

August's angst-filled searing heat is no more penetrating
Than the cooling comfort of Autumn by a brooding brook.

Cloudless star-filled nights are no more revealing
than the cumulus clouds that cascade a full October moon.

The sun shadows this "other Me," piercing like a dagger
through the pulsing heart of the hero in an Elizabethan tragedy.

Swept away by the feelings of this world,
The sunrise speaks when I am ready to sleep
As the sunset rises me from slumber.

Reality and thought merge as I conceptualize these revelations.
Mindful meanderings in the woods reveal no more color
Than those spent on a bustling city street.

Ralph speaks to me, as my mind nets thousands of different thoughts,
And I struggle to fish out the big ones —
"The world, this shadow of the soul, or other me, lies wide around.
Its attractions are the keys which unlock my thoughts
And make me acquainted with myself."

My friend speaks to me as I look for my part,
"Keep searching Kimosabee-it's closer to he heart."

*In memory of Terrence Michael Morrisey -
Rest in peace - Until we meet again*

Lust
by Bill Robinson

I see her now, just like yesterday
Beckoning, with words, with gestures
Always one step ahead, just out of reach
So close, yet so far

Her nakedness blinding
Her promise inviting, compelling
Reach for a touch, a nibble
Success ar arm length away, don't quibble

Solve the problem, old man
It can be done with algebra, with equations
Factor for the unknown, try vector analysis

Remember long forgotten skills
Success an arm length away, keep trying

Keep the mood, hold the moment
Enjoy the pleasure her body gives
Don't stop, let it last forever
Keep looking, don't open thine eyes

A Love That's True
by Maria Luisa Robles

If love's not always there for you,
then that's a love that's never true.

Though words may often say a lot -
If not put to action, -
then truth - they're not.

In time of need and sorrow too -
if love's not there for you,
then that's a love that never can be true.

A love that gives unselfishly -
expecting nothing in return -
is a love that will live endlessly,
whose light will never burn.

And when you find a love like this -
- that's always there for you -
thank God for sending you a love -
- a love that's ever true.

Summer In Baltimore
by Natalie Rock

Flowers blooming in the beds
Radiating their bright colours
Birds singing in their nests
After they've gathered their worms.

Grass slowly turning into hay
As the sun hangs brightly over our heads
Heat coming from that very fiery ray
Humidity sweeping over from the vast Atlantic.

Fans and air conditioners working constantly
To cool people's tired, hot bodies
Fire hydrants spewing water ceaselessly
For children too poor to have a pool.

Ice cream consumed in great masses
As if Prohibition were about to strike once more
Droughts and electrical black outs are all possibilities
As we face yet another tropical summer in my Baltimore.

Wandering Stranger
by Sheena Rodgers - age 15

You spend your life
Going from one city
To another.

You appear,
Staring people down
With cold, cruel eyes.
You keep to yourself.
Any questions are met
With mumbled replies.

You're looking for something.
What it is, no one knows,
Not even you.
It could be love, life, or happiness.
But once you find it,
You'll know.

As suddenly as you appear, you disappear.
Not finding what you're looking for,
You move on to continue your search.
It has become your lifestyle.
You are a wandering stranger.

To Dream a Dream
by Athena Orsatelli

To dream a dream with wonder sweet -
To lay myself at thy young feet.

My heart doth swell with fleeting joy
to think I love this young, sweet boy.

And when the hands of time ring truth -
I wake to whisper, "O, for sooth."
'Tis but a dream that brings you near -
'Tis but a dream alone I fear.

My heart in waning strength doth cry -
For to my young love, I must say,
"Goody-bye."

Listen
by Dominique Marie Rogers - age 14

A school of fish swimming.
A lions fearsome
 roar
 A rock bank playing music,
 High above the birds
 will soar,
A hot misty jungle on a summer
 night,
 A predator waiting
 until the time is right,
 Listen tot he music,
 Let your heart go free,
 Listen if you will,
This is what my heart said to me.

Living In Atlantis
by Jennifer Rollings - age 18

I have this problem: What the psychiatrist might call "Envelopaphobia."
My mail piles up high on my desk.
It's all bad news anyway, no point really.
If I ever get back to the surface, I might get around to opening some of it.

But for now, I can't do much about it, stuck in my new city.
I've been here since the envelopes
with the numbers in them started to come, all wrong.
They said I'd "dug myself into a rut,"
letting my "bad luck with the tests scores," get me down.
Down, down, down, and my rope of numbers not high enough to pull me up.
Down into a place even deeper than the holes I made in beach sand as a child
that filled up and covered me with water salty as the sea, or bitter tears.

After all, they said I needed " a change of pace."
Well, things move slower here-restricted by the pressure of the water,
sitting on everything like a scolding parent.
Then again, it isn't exactly Mount Olympus.
Sounds magnify-my whispers become screams only the eels hear.
Even your face, yelling at me from above the waves to "snap out of it!"
is like my existence, liquid and unstable.
I fear that if I reached up to touch you, you would shatter and float away
in dizzying ripples, and when you came back how could I be sure
if the reflection reassembled in front of me was the same person
(if you bothered to come back at all)?

It's not so bad here, though.
On the bright side, there aren't any mail boxes.

Sweet Charm
by Gena Romano - age 14

A day in the Summer
 with fun in the sun,
I was cheerful and happy
 until terror begun.
With the pull of the ocean
I was breathless and wet,
 my foot caught in a rope
 Like a fish in a net.
 I cried for help
 but no one could here,
 like a mother to her baby,
 I held to my life dear.
 With the yell from my hero
 I was soon to be from harm,
 an angel had saved me,
I was blessed with sweet charm.

Seasons
by Stacy M. Rombough - age 12

In the fall we ride a bus
to a place called school,
There we learn a lot of things
and want to be cool.
Then as the year goes by
the grass turns into snow,
and the temperature drops
really really low.
Then as the whiteness clears,
You know that spring is here,
As the cool air changes.
The summer comes and goes real fast
as the year ages.
So we're one year older now.
To mature for childish games,
But still a little part of you
will always seem the same.

"If Only"
by Betty J. Fajna

If only you could feel my love for you,
understand what you mean to me.
without you in it, my life seems dreary & blue.
My love for you is so deep & real, why can't you see?

If only you could love me, the way I love you.
Your pain is my pain, your hurt is my hurt.
Please help me understand, what can I do?
What will it take for you to really love me?

If only you knew the hurt I endure,
each day I worry and I cry.
But through it all my love remains pure,
without you I'd just as soon wither and die.

If only you could be me for a day,
you'd realize how deeply I care.
Every day I ask myself, do I leave or do I stay.
But leaving you I could never bare.

One Of A Kind
by Norma Rose - age 16

My love is like the sun,
standing all alone,
so far away,
burning hot,
brightly, beautifully,
lighting everything that it surrounds,
filling it with warmth.

The Writing Process
by Diane Rosenbaum - age 14

a plain white lined paper, yet oddly magical
it lets your worldly problems slip away unmathematical
The act alone doesn't seem like much
but in reality it is very relaxing, invigorating and such
your mind wanders to dreams of magic, mystery and suspense
you only stop when your body relents
mermaids, witches, demons, fairies float into your head
thoughts of twisting plots and creative things once said
a galaxy unlike the one we are accustomed to
wonders and excitement unlike anything you ever knew
it sweeps you away in an almost high state of mind
you scribble away while thoughts race and you lose track of time
dancing on clouds, realizing dreams, fantasies granted whenever, it seems
Surprises await you lurking in corner of your head
beautiful things whether you greet them with love or dread
yet in all this time almost paralyzed by awe
you manage to jot down everything that you saw
your fabulous daydream is caught on a page
the ink still wet, your mind in a haze
you come out of the almost hypnotic trance
where your visions of magic had once danced
words still can not recreate your experience
the thought of it all leaves you some what delirious
a poem a single group of verbs and nouns
yet your head still reels with the tale it has wound
incomprehensible, yet somehow understanding
a series of take-offs and then quick landings
until at last the aftershock is gone
all that's left of your journey is this poem, this song.

Why do we hate when we can love?
by Kelly Rosenberger - age 16

Why do we hate when we can love?
Everyone is capable of loving even though they may
    not show it
The toughest people we see are really softies at heart
So why do we have such an anger toward other
    cultures and races?
No one will ever know.

Why do we hate when we can love?
Love is so much nicer, hatred doesn't get
    anyone anywhere.
If only we had fondness instead of bitterness.
Or affection instead of resentment.

Why do we hate when we can love?
We're all different on the outside, but we all
    experience the same feelings and emotions inside.
What is race? Only a difference in skin color or family
    background.

Why do we hate when we can love?
Why not lend a helping hand to someone even if they're
    different.
Anything that can help bring this world back together
Into the happy and living environment God created for us
We need to make him proud to be our Creator
So why DO we hate when we can love??

The Block
by Gregg Evan Rosenzweig

Every morning, I sit and groan,
make thoughts to myself, postured all alone.
Trying to drum up, to stir all my senses,
to break down these walls, these imaginary fences.

To suppress all those demons,
who spread ineptitude with glee.
Why, oh why,
does this affliction always happen to me?

For if Berlin can raze,
that gigantic wall of division.
Why can't I break down my own
and blast out this one last revision?

I think the pressures that mount
from the crevices of my conscience that be,
have the ability to scream and shout,
loudly serving to stymie me.

But show me, please, how to suppress,
thoughts I loathe defeat me.
Offer me a road map to quell,
so that words my own don't beat me.

Hoist me back to square number one,
chapters before the great big jade.
Where dreams were spawned of a better life,
from my stories, of which I'd get paid.

I wonder when this wall will fall,
some curtains should never close.
The key, the cause, the grounds of writer's block,
the jury's out, but still, nobody knows.

His Eyes
by Doris Ross

Jesus broke my heart in two
When He looked down from the cross
And said, "My God, forgive them
For they know not what they've done."
His eyes were, o, so hurt and pained.
And so entreating, too,
I could not look away or leave.
He's coaxing me and you
To look so deep into His eyes;
See love beyond the hurt
That each of us have given Him
Through sin and hate and dirt.
He tells us to believe Him;
To trust and follow, too;
To claim the love He's giving;
Live our lives clean and true.
Those eyes of love still haunt me
Each time I drift away.
He says, "Come back and follow;
Don't leave Me; please don't stray."
I live in anticipation
Of the day my Christ I'll meet;
Though we always fear the leaving
The meeting will be sweet.

A Story
by Kimberly Ross - age 7

That was so interesting.
It was a magical adventure.
Lovely illustrations brought
the story to life.
It took me to another land,
a land of laughter
and mysteries
and fairy tales,
a miracle waiting to happen
in the pages of a book.

Rebecca Anulacion
by Larry E. Ross

A medium light brown skin, coal black hair, a beautiful looking
phillipine lady, with a son that has interest of a farmer.
When I first saw Rebecca Anulacion, she was walking down
the hall way, on the first floor, going to work at the U.S. Mint.
On those mornings that I saw Rebeccca, to her I would speak,
indicating that I was a gent.
I was soon to learn that she worked in system control
on the second floor, and not long that would be in the same
division as me.
Now most of the working days of the week Rebecca I
will see.
On these mornings I see her most of the time
about her son she is ask.
Rebecca says, "(her son is busy with subjects on his
future goals and task)."
On the job in task to be preform, she is deeply involve.
In commonly called friend, it's responded to nicely with
a grin.
Sometimes I go into the main office of Cash
Division and joke with Rebecca for a while,
then I leave her with a happy smile.

Mama's Love
by Jan Rothbauer

Without a doubt the childhood days
Was most difficult - the least to say.
You always gave more than you had,
You always smiled - even when sad.
But you didn't fool me - Mama Dear -
I caught that swipe of a stray tear.
Precious Mama oh how I'd wish,
I could do more than dry an old dish.
But when you'd rock and cuddle me close -
Your precious love - flowed head to toes.
As I grew and dreams were shattered -
The know it all stage - thinking scattered -
The sibling squabbles - nearly a war -
Oh Precious Mama - you had a chore!
You taught through love - to believe - to care,
And never to judge - never compare.
Your rule to be honest, always true,
To feel good inside all life through;
To be humble, to say "I'm Sorry,"
'Cuz life is real, an' not a story.

That Look
by Patricia G. Rourke

Have you ever been transformed
by a single look?
Someone looking at your
entire life out of the eyes
of his entire life?
Eyes penetrating so deeply
that they awaken life
in what you thought was
your secret black hole?
Has anyone ever looked
at you with so much love
that your very molecules shook,
forcing you to emerge
from a muddy cocoon
with such astounding beauty
that when you finally
caught a glimpse of your
reflection, you had to pinch
yourself to feel
the reality of your
dream winging to life.

Deal With It
by Cicely A. Rowe

Some things are hard to deal with
Like the feelings in my heart
I've tried to make them go away
But, they're with me always
Everyday
I love you dearly with all my heart
But, I don't know your feelings
How you think, your thoughts.

I see you almost everyday
When you aren't around
In my mind you stay
We've been good friends
For many years
You make me laugh
Get rid of my tears.

Some say
That friendship is a basis for love
A lifelong companionship
But, I guess I'll never know.

Love
by Lindsay Roy - age 12

     The girl stands crying in the rain
when the man she loves say he doesn't feel the same.
     She tries to whisper the words why?
but all she does is cry.
     The tears fall gently down her cheeks
as they both stand still and no one speaks.
     Finally you hear him say I have to leave
and she asks why do you leave me hear to grieve.
     As she watches him walk away on his two feet,
she whispers to herself without you my life is incomplete.

The Lie
by Sandra Ruddick - age 19

Late at night as I lay in bed sometimes...I wonder what I did or said
to receive such understanding and love
as I silently thank all the stars above.
You cannot know how much that means to someone who has always seen
heartache and shattered dreams-- nothing but problems it seems...
Sometimes it's hard to say what I want to because I haven't a clue
of how to express myself when I'm with you--
I open my mouth but no words come out because sometimes it's hard to
say 'I Love You'
With out wondering if it will always be so, or if you will one day get up and
go--leaving me, once again, to my loneliness and solitude
where I would go into a depression and miss you.

All I can say is that without you my life would be pain--
like a thunderstorm without the rain,
like a dream with out a dreamer, a heart without a beat, night without day-
a poet with nothing to say...

With you, when life is at its worst, and there is nothing more to say
I can look forward to seeing or hearing your voice at the end of the day,
because when that one time comes, where there is no one to lean on
you-- I can depend on just as you can me.

Some say that all have half of themselves gone-- a soul mate
and they look, searching until that half is found-- a soul mate
Maybe I have found mine-- I don't really know if this is so
if it is then I need search no more for you are standing at my door.

Late at night when I'm all alone as I lay and listen to the night's tone
I wonder-- what might the stars have in store for a girl who has asked for
nothing more
then understanding, dreams and love-- thanking, silently, all the stars above-

Hoping, wishing, living and Dying... Loving, hating, Dreaming and crying...
I am who I be so there is nothing more to say or to see
unless you can love me for me even if it's not for an eternity----------

Today's Dream
by Lauren Ruhl - age 15

A heated powder burns from the start.
A mournful crow swallows my happy heart.
Vultures circle around my head.
Thoughts of peace are swallowed with my bread.
Harmony cackles it's way all up to my feet.
Happy taps, they dance to a melancholy beat.
Sincere good-byes, happy tears falling.
A dull glint of a child's sorrowing.
Singing hands clap a song of a long ago love theme.
Hands of time wave through a rolling stream.
A mouse travels under the seven seas,
to say "hello" to all the trees.
Eyes glow from beyond the Nile.
A mouth looks through the stars for its smile.
If forever ended yesterday,
and eternity stops tomorrow,
what is today?

Where the Unicorns Roam
by Jenn Rupp - age 14

Do you know where the unicorns roam?
Their favorite place is where the sea foams.
It's somewhere, oh somewhere that's so far away,
On a beautiful beach where no people have stayed.
The sun is a lemon high up in the sky,
This place has a beauty no money could buy.
As beautiful as it is, this beach of white sands,
Some very strange things have happened in this land.
In this place of places, there are lizards with wings.
They're what we would call dragons, these wonderful things.
They're all different colors: blue, purple, and green.
There's one problem though, they've rarely been seen.
Children know where this place is, they say it's all around.
It's high up in the sky and low down on the ground.
This place has been inside people since the time of the creation.
The place where dragons and unicorns roam, is the place called;
    Imagination.

A True Friend
by Jessica Lynn Rush - age 18

You were my faith when I was hurtin'
You were my strength when I was uncertain
You lead me down a path I would dare go before
You changed my life forever more
You brought color to a world of gray
You were there by my side every step of the way
But then one day I found out you were gone
And I too began to wonder if I could go on
But believe me I always understood, I knew
That life had just gotten to rough for you
You were always giving and loving as a friend could
But I didn't give back all that I could
Maybe if I too, had gone out of my way
You wouldn't have taken your life that day
I will always remember the laughter, tears, and smiles
The happiness you brought to my life goes a million miles
Even though I know you're in a better place
I still can't help but miss your reassuring embrace
When I think of your death, however, it makes me sad
Because you always promised me life wasn't that bad
So why did you have to go and die on me
Was it because I was too selfish to see
That you were really hurting too
And you needed someone the way I needed you
So as I sit here and cry
I wonder did you really have to die?

Shadows
by Todd Russell - age 19

Come to me elusive enchantress.
I am searching for you. Looking for you.,
I cannot find you. Where are you hiding?
You are running from me I can tell.
You dance secretly in places I cannot see.
I call your name. Scream your name.
I hear an echo. You don't answer.
Tell me where you are playing.
I want to see you for more than a glimpse.
I hear your giggle. Still you giggle.
But I don't get the joke.
Show me your incredible smile.
I want to see your radiant eyes.
I can't catch you. Let me catch you.
You won't let me. Why?
You dance behind dark shapes.
Your flawless motions are a burning.
I need you. Always I miss you.
Still I love you.
Come out from the shadows.

Rich or Poor
by Kathleen Comstock Rutledge

To have money
is to have
I don't know
to have without
is all I know

Whether to chose
rich or poor
couldn't be more of a chore

Wouldn't you know
I dream of more
Shouldn't be greedy
is what I know

Ought to be poor
to feel the good
The price is high
Is all I know

So whether to chose
rich or poor?
Both will be fine
is what I know

A Retired Marine
by Kathleen Comstock Rutledge

I spent my youth being a Marine, learning the ways of the Corp.
Not only following my dream living my dream as a Marine
I've followed in the shadows of others.
I've not only shared their sorrows of war but my own as well
I felt like I've carried the weight of it all
Always remembering I don't stand alone
My fellow men follow the footsteps I've walked
My leaders are always telling me their proud of my accomplishments
Only I know of my failures, my mistakes, after all a Marine is only human.
But we as Marines seem to think we are green machines
For we never tire, never settle for less then perfect because a Marine is only the best the best we can be
Now the time has come for me to part.
Can I except leaving the thing I loved most?
The thing that was my life for so many years the bond between fellow Marines is like no other.
Having people be proud to know you because you are truly a Marine in heart,
body, and soul
You've lived, ate, and slept as a Marine proud of it always
The question is letting go of something so dear to your heart?
A Marine never lets go they only go on.
But they will always be a Marine
Once a Marine
Always a Marine
No matter what we try to do after retirement

SO GOOD LUCK RETIREE
SEMPER FI!!!

Don't
by Jenn Rydalch

Don't look into my eyes
thinking you're going to succeed
on finding all I hide

Don't listen to my voice
and hope to hear
what it is I do so fear

Don't try to get close
and think you'll be
able to understand

Don't expect me to let you in
I don't want you to see
what I keep locked near...
...don't try to take
from who I am.

Bitter Sweet Memories
by Brenda Sabot

Within our life time each of us share
bitter sweet memories that leave us with
a lasting impression.

Our impressions are like flowers pressed
between the pages of our minds, bitter
sweet memories.

Each page is numbered and stored away as
a rich storage house of compassion,
warmth, and understanding of ourselves.

The lasting impressions are flowers
pressed between the pages of our minds,
bitter sweet memories.

Time
by Stuart Sakoda - age 17

As time passes through many days and nights
You remember the good times and the fights
You may remember the day you learned how to bike
When your dad helped you steer when you were only five
The days when you would cry and stay in your room
When your parents would yell and you know you were doomed
To remember your friends and relationships you have treasured
Some are still there and some have deserted
We all have memories of events in our lives
Which made us who we are throughout the day and nights
We may not recall all the pieces to our life
Because we still have our future ahead to decide
We all have memories we want to remember
And memories we want to forget
It's too bad we can't turn back the hands of which time has set
Time has made us smile and frown
time has made our lives go up and down
But when we are at the end of our line
We see time flashing and saying good-bye
So as you lay in bed and look up tonight
Just think of how time has affected your life
Of all the loved ones which you still hold
And the ones you had to leave behind
So as the sky changes from day to night
Remember how precious life depends on time.

The Place
by Lucia Salazar - age 14

Is there a place you can go,
Where no one knows your face?
Where no one cares to know,
That you're of a different race?

This place has been your dream
Ever since you were small.
Whenever someone was mean
You'd imagine the place and that was all

People say it is not real,
That it's all just in your head.
But it's something that you feel,
Not something someone read.

And if you want, I'll help you
Reach the place you seek.
Where everyone will love you,
Because you are unique.

If
by Cora Salvail - age 16

If I were the wind,
I would blow things to my content.
If I were the sea,
The boats would float in my current.
If I were a bird,
I would soar high in the sky.
If I were a tree,
I would wish my fruit be shared around the world.
If I were the grass,
The animals would eat out of my hand.
If I were a flower,
My scent would be smelt by all who pass.
If I were a deer,
I would wish my meat to a hungary child.
If I were an inventor,
I would invent a way to stop pollution.
If I were a doctor,
I would discover a cure for cancer.
If I were a director,
I would direct a movie of peace.
But since I'm a poet,
All I can do is make a wish of hope.

Easter Morning Star
by Virgie Mccoy Sammons

In the east the morning star
shines brighter still, for Easter.
The pink dawn slowly appear,
Easter morning is near.
If any star brings peace
This is the one,
Shining from the blue heavens,
Calm as an echo of a song.

The star gives way to morning light.
There's a hush all over the world
In reverence of a day divine.
The cardinal sing in tone lees shrill,
the blackbirds whirring wings keep still,
The Easter morning star
Brings repose,
Christ, arose.

I'm not there
by Crystal Sanders - age 14

Every morning you wait
    I'm not there
Since the accident I've not been with you,
because of a reckless driver who couldn't put
down a drink.
    I'm not there
Now you are alone, sad......,lonely and confused.
You hate the person who took my life and
yet walked away flawless.
    I'm still not there
I didn't do anything wrong, except
be in the wrong place at the wrong time.

The End
by Gail Sanders - age 14

We looked at the sky
It was dark and black.
I looked in to his eyes
He looked into mine.
Each could see the other's soul
Crying, crying for help.
And in his eyes I saw the sky
All dark and black.
Through his heart I saw his sadness
and felt his sorrowfulness
And together we looked out across the ocean.
It was dark and gloomy.
Then together we jumped
And as I fell with him
I knew this was it.
Today my life ended
And for once I was complete.

To Dad (on his birthday)
by Angela K. Sayre

It was hard for you, I know
Letting us all go,
But you did it with a smile
And a tear in your eye.

You taught us to be good
And to do the best we could.
You were always there, to stand by our side,
And even when you knew you couldn't help,
    You tried.

You always wished you could give us more
But Dad, what the hell for?
Our life is what it was
And for that, we are who we are.

You gave us everything
You could possibly give,
And now it is your chance
To watch, be proud, and see us live.

Reach For The Son
by Christine Scarborough

As you climb life's mountains's.
High above earth's lofty plains,
Upon a rock your foot may slip,
or your hands may even loose their grip.
Instead of giving up in defeat
Keep your mind set on the mountain peak
and reach for the Son.

As you run life's fast paced race,
A stumble or fall may even slow your pace,
Do not give up or even quit,
Remember life's race has already been won
Just keep your eyes on the finish line
and reach for the Son

As Christians we are called to be
Christ like in so many ways,
Even though things don't flow
the way we think they ought to go.
If you listen carefully you can hear Jesus say,
"HANG IN THERE, MY WORK IN YOU
HAS JUST BEGUN
So believe in me and Reach for the Son."

Love
by Tina Scarpitti

She moved through the distance ahead
Gazing the mist where the children weep,
Sifting through the sands of the mead'
Peering through ponderous waters of deep.

    Chirping sounds created up afar
    Movement withholds the action in place,
    Seeking the darkened memories within a star
    Two unknown worlds bound to be retraced.

Fleeing odds and spaces of hollow
A hearts' chamber can only survive bloodflows.
Tightening thoughts, decayed to be swallowed
Circulating droughts, made to be followed.

    Nature relieved its' suffering and pain
    Willows sway over the thickness of the mist,
    Tender waters prepared their ordain
    Warm thoughts, forever are missed.

Discovering doubts of reality faced
Reality was not a disguise,
Thinking of the smiles blended with disgrace
Soft, mellow sounds of natures' cries.

    She gazed down below ad soon peered above
    Clutching hands, praying for the spiritual shadows,
    Surviving the helpless, needing to be loved
    Within the distance remains the unopened gallows.

She spreads her wings, the Goddess of Love
She moves through life planting the seeds,
Opening her heart, a natures' dove
Giving her message, pouring her great deeds.

Spring
by Alyson Schefkind - age 10

The flowers' fragrances,
Wander up my nose,
As I smell them,
In the deep green meadow.

The wind conjures up tricks,
Through-out the ocean filled sky,
Past the old willow tree,
Into my face.

The meadows,
Filled with daises,
Dancing in the wind,
Surrounding my body.

The sun shining in my face,
Blankets of gold rush on top of me,
Light giver for me,
As I wander in silence.

Then the rain comes,
Washes down my beautiful picture,
Covers everything with pools,
I return home to wait for another spring day.

Emancipation
by Amber-Dawn M. Schiff - age 14

My freedom has come.
No more walls or gates,
To shield me,
From the outside world.
I now stand alone,
But no longer vulnerable,
To the world outside.
For instead of fear,
Love awaits me.
My heart has been stripped.
Stripped of its inhibitions,
Free to love,
Without limitations.
Nothing is left standing,
Between me,
Or my beloved.
A harmonious future,
Lies before us,
With love to guide us,
To that future destined
To come.

Change
by Cindy Schlossnagle

Spices that lost their flavor
Lids without bowls
Pan with no handles
Empty coffee cans have no purpose
Silent rooms where once there was laughter
Throw away the past
Empty out the old
Mend the broken heart
Disappointment, failure
Hope drowning in sorrow
Move toward the future
Pick yourself up
Start this day with love in your heart
Ready for what the universe sends

Cleansed soul
Renewed spirit
Calmed mind
Soothed body

Ravens Plight
by Charles W. Raven Schmid

will we all be here tomorrow
will the rivers and lakes stay pure
will the mountains be here
when my child grows tall

nations rip nations apart
guns and bombs
give me a break
I don't want to die
I want to live
don't want nuclear waste
or trash outside my door

They say we must defend
can't you see
if we don't save the planet
there'll be nothing
we must save it now
we can't wait anymore

Lay down the guns
stop and let me off
don't want to follow the Gods of war.

Egdelwonk
by Millicent Schmidt - age 16

No extra added.
How or why?

In school we're.
Taught to write.
The answers just!
Right or wrong?

Answered questions mean.
More knowledge but.
Gaining knowledge ushers.
In more questions.

Therefore, the search!
For knowledge should.
Culminate in only,
More unanswered questions?

Fear
by Alex Schmier - age 13

 I fear the world
its delinquents and domains
 I fear the world
its terrors and pains
 I fear my country
its power and greed
 I fear the day
its light fake
 I fear the day
too bright to take
 I fear the night
its secrets so dark
 I fear the night
too cold for my heart
  since we all fear this much
life is debris
  Did I mention
I also fear me

Death before my tears
by Crystal Dawn Schultz - age 18

Love is a dangerous thing;

My heart cried out for his love.

There I had his heart within my soul,

as he had mine.

As we kissed to part our ways he hugged me and said,

"Never forget."

That night his body burned in the
Raging fire of HELL on earth;

Tonight I cry,

Tomorrow I pry that he won't forget;

My heart within his soul & Death Before My Tears.

Life's Twisted Game
by Heather Schwalbe - age 20
In loving memory of Justin Rohde
1977-1995

As the sun rises and falls day after day,
The memories flash before me and time slips away.
There are times that I wonder if these memories will remain,
Or will they fade away with time and leave nothing but pain.
His hair was as soft as the wings of a dove,
His eyes were bluer than the heavens above.
His laughter was sweet, I can still hear it ringing,
His touch was so warm, I can still feel him squeezing.
My love for him burned like a torch in the night,
Then one day fate came, and cut like a knife.
It's so hard to handle this emptiness that remains,
He still watches over me and hears me complain.
As I look back at these memories that I hold so dear,
I sit back and wonder if he really is near.
I would give anything to hold him just one more time,
And remind him how "forever" he said he'd be mine.
Why do bad things happen to good people on earth?
I want to just scream because of this hurt.
The days pass so slowly and the memories do remain,
And love of friends is what I have gained.
Deep down in my heart a piece of me has died,
But the emptiness is filled with love for him inside.
He was the one and only love of my life,
To no one on this earth I could ever deny.
It's so hard to lose someone, but the memories remain,
It's all a big part of life's twisted game.

Silent Partner
by Marcie C. Schwalm

Let me stay
I'll never make a sound—
Is that what I should say?
Let me be part of you
I'll never speak for myself again—
How should I need my own language
your words can speak for both of us.

Don't presume to know my mind—
I am not the silent partner
not content to be your better half.
I am only content to be
always one up on you
forever the enigma
forever hiding something—
my silence is my only weapon—
the only way to hold you

The Guilt of Apathy
by Patricia R. Sears

Cry for the children,
The innocent souls needlessly lost,
As we sit by pondering
What our caring will cost.

Whose responsibility is it,
Could it be yours and mine,
To give hope to the hopeless
And light to the blind?

We cover up our ears,
Hoping their cries will end.
But they haunt us anyway,
Though in vain we pretend.

We turn away to the left
And we turn to the right,
Then we bury our heads
In horror at their sight.

But if we ignore their tears,
Pleading for one who understands,
Then do we not ourselves
Carry their blood upon our hands?

God help the poor children
Who in spirit slowly die.
And my He have forgiveness
On those who silently stand by.

Little Boys
by Kathi Serr

What happened to the little boys,
  That made this life worthwhile.
The ones who were so innocent,
  And faced life with a smile?

I taught them how to laugh and sing,
  And showed them how to play,
But then not very long ago,
  The little boys went away.

I used to wonder how to cope,
  With the trials they would face,
But now it seems almost as though,
  My family has been erased.

And now I struggle to accept,
  The way things have to be,
For when they left, they took with them,
  The greater part of me.

How I long to hold them now,
  To chase away their fears,
To watch them run and play again,
  To dry away their tears.

But knowing things won't be the same,
  Since the little boys went away,
I often wish, we could return,
  To our trials of yesterday.

Touch of Love
by Heather Seymour

You are here again
I can see your smile
Touch your face, feel your body
I can smell your scent again
Feel your kisses, hold your hand
I slowly reach next to me to pull you close
Then it happens, as it always does
And as I open my eyes to another cold morning
I am alone
Your smile has faded from my sight
Your kiss has left my lips
The hand I hold is my own
The body I long to love is no longer here
You are gone
The pain is as sharp as the day you left me
My eyes begin to fill, and the tears I try to hold back slowly run down my cheeks
I struggle each day to go on
I force the smiles all that know me expect
I laugh at the jokes
I play the role of the strong person I am, or at least the one that I was
The day has finally come to an end
The files are put away, the work done for the day
I am home, and once again I am alone
I look forward to this time
For this is the time I can openly feel the sadness, only I can feel
I can cry the tears that need to be cried
Feel the anger only I have the right to feel
I grieve the loss only I can grieve
And as this long day comes to an end
I can dream the dream of you and I together, that only I can dream

When I See You Again
by Tabatha M. Shank - age 13

When I see you again,
Will it be the same,
As it was that day?
Will you look in my eyes,
And feel the same love,
As you once did?
Will you hold me,
And will it feel the same?
And when I close my eyes,
And dream,
Will they be of you?
Will you cry for me,
Just like I have for you,
Yearn to be held by me.
Well when I see you again,
I will know then,
My love flows on.
And in my heart,
You were never truly gone.

Treasures

Back Tracking Is A No No
by Doris G. Sharp

When you've given your best shot, and it comes to no avail,
Never ever back track for you are sure to fail.

Crossing the same bridge more than once.
One might think love is greater by the ounce.

Look ahead far and wide.
Loneliness is something you just can't hide.

Why are you lonely, exactly what is the reason?
Never back track regardless of the season.

You can cross another bridge and hope for the best.
Leave the heart breaking for those who feel they need a test.

Try and find a place where flowers bloom and birds sing.
You are sure to be on your way towards the right thing.

If you take one step then I'll take two.
And this will be the start of something wonderful and new.

It's ok to reflect over the changes that one encounters in life.
This allows the growth process to manifest.

Be your role friend, husband, lover sibling or wife.
At all times give your very, very best, and you too shall pass the test.

Back tracking is a no no, or so it was once said.
By being true to yourself, you will get ahead.

In life we tend to do a complete 360 degrees.
Often having trial and tribulations that has brought us to our knees.

Be it ever so humble, that our role is such.
For to endure it all you will have learned much.

so with this concept in mind I suggest that you get up and go.
Remembering that back tracking is a definite no no.

Not So Perfect
by Kelly Sheehy - age 15

In your mind
He's perfect
He's so interesting
relationship is rolling
many conversations
very romantic.
But lasts only a while..
then you get to know him.
Every little thing is irritating
so predictable
Relationship obviously dead
never mind-not so perfect.

Tribute to Grammy
by Joyce Shelton

Summer winds blow
Yet you still don't know, why?

Why would someone,
someone so cherished have to die?

The silhouette of a life, so full of memories, can't end so soon.

A little girl needs the love of a generation that has almost been forgotten.

She wants her Grammy to share with and tuck her in.

As she grows up, she needs a friend to rely on.

To share the stories of first love, first kisses, and secrets.

Secrets only two kindred spirits can bestow.

The graduation day comes.
The young girl looks out to see the shadow of someone,
someone who could only be in her dreams.

The silhouette is only seen by her.
It is as if her longing, alone brings the woman back.

The diploma is received.
As the young girl walks back, she is not alone.
Her Grammy is walking with her, holding her hand.

She whispers, "My pretty girl, I'm proud!"
She kisses the child; and drifts away.

It was as if she was saying. "Don't fear. You are never alone. I am here
watching you, Forever"

Five years pass.
They seemed to have gone by so fast.
The young woman hears wedding bells and hopes again.

As she looks down the isle, there on the front pew, the woman who
promised forever.

Tears well up in her eyes.
"Father, you knew my heart. Thank you for listening."

She has accepted death; and she longs for the day,
the day when two spirits will dance again.

Uncover
by Cheryl Simmons - age 16

Trapped inside a six-sided box
Nowhere to run
Nowhere to hide
Take a good look at me
You might not have another chance
Traveling from one box to another
All different shapes and sizes
Could you catch me before I die
Take the truths twisted inside
They are the clues to the answers before
Holding on to the past for now
Watch them come and take it, throw it away
Nothing lasts forever in here
One will find a new place
To keep hidden in the dark with secrets untold
Feelings unheard, tears unseen

Desert Soliloquy
by Kristin Sherwood

In the desert,
My soul is empty
No love to sustain me
My undying hunger.

Like a dry heat
With no hope for rainfall,
My heart yearns for something
It cannot possess.

A passion pleading
Waits for an answer,
Like dawn waits for dewdrops
That fail to arrive.

In the desert,
With no drop of water,
A fire goes on burning
Flames that consume me.

When each dawn breaks
Into morning starlight,
I wake to my heartbeat
Echoing alone.

Darkness Trickles
by Heather Shrake - age 18

Crashing soundly within,
My emotions stumble,
I've tried hard to hide,
Intense is the rumble,
I've questioned my secret,
My own burden to share,
Scared of the consequence,
An antidote to rare,
The sand trickles down,
The smooth glassly shape,
All hidden so well,
Till darkness yelled rape,
I feel all this torment,
I sense all this rage,
Longing stable success,
Shall I settle cotton sage,
If I climb up three steps,
It's down one I slip,
It hits quite often,
Like a suicidal drip,
The pain must fade away,
For it's answered to end,
Need my life start over,
For my soul need I fend.

Red Beans And Rice
by Jacqueline Simpson

We used to eat **red beans** and **rice**
When money was low and bills were tight.
We used to eat **red beans** and **rice**
When we all worked together to build a better life.
We used to eat **red beans** and **rice**
When we sat around as a family and talked all night.
Now we eat steak, potatoes and french breads
Because the money went to our heads.
We no longer sit and talk
We just wave *hi* and *bye* as we continue to walk.

cycle
by Jennifer Silver - age 13

Love is a   flurry
of hopes   and dreams
a   sunshiny day
a whispering   breeze
inside   your heart
that never   seems
to   go   away

but when it does
its as though
youve seen a sunset
that didn't glow
and now its night
and youre alone

And you wonder,

*Will morning break
again?*

I Just Don't Understand
by Jennifer Sims - age 19

Her hair is white and growing thin, while She's a vibrant blonde.
Her days grow long and tiresome, of which She's now quite fond.
Her mind is filled with memories that She has yet to share.
Her worries seem so endless, but She hasn't got care.
Her dreams are often child-like, a place where She still plays"
Her mind can't seem to separate, while She sees through Her haze.
Her body feels so tired now, yet She is full of life.
Her troubles grow more every day, but She knows not of strife.
Her eyes are dull, their sparkle lost, while She could spark the night.
Her view is lonely blue-grey walls, while She can see the lights.
Her new home is the hospital, She lives on Sunny Street.
Her incarceration makes Her mad, She's happy with bare feet.
Her chest is heavy-hearted now, She chases butterflies.
Her breathing slows quite rapidly, She doesn't know She'll die.
Her eyes now scan the photo which She placed upon the shelf.
Her eyes then fill with water, She's the child of Herself.
Her mind begins to drift away, She glances at Her hands.
Why Her happiness faded with Her youth, I just don't understand.

A Circle Within Us All
by Brandy Skaggs - age 15

There is a circle within us all that
keeps our world from falling apart. It
holds us together through thick and thin.
And if you look real hard you will find
it deep within.

It is a circle of love that is connected
to the man up above. It is a circle of love.
And it never ends although it always seems
to bend.

Sometimes every thing seems to go wrong.
Then someone comes to pick you up and hold
you in their arms. After a while you will
feel a warmth inside. Don't be afraid its
just the circle coming alive.

It is a circle of love that is connected to
the man up above. It is a circle of love.
And it never ends although it always
seems to bend.

Sincerely
by Marta Skwarczek - age 14

Sincerely the girl, who lives down the lane,
Maybe she's crazy, or just simply insane.
She's your neighbor next door, or across the street,
Who you saw through the window, but never did meet.

Sincerely the daughter, in the teddy bear room,
Who's so sweet and innocent or so you assume.
She's the sarcastic one, with the curious eyes,
Who doesn't know how, but still she tries.

Sincerely the girl, with no guy on her arm,
She'll give you a second chance, but three time's the charm.
Sometimes she's sad, but cry she won't dare,
She's not very girlie, but really does care.

Sincerely that person in back, staring at you,
Not knowing that you, stare back at her too.
She's the one in the jeans, with the know-it-all grin,
She knows what to say, and knows how to win.

Sincerely the girl, you knew way back when,
But how well do you think, you knew her then?
She started to change, but maybe she'll stop,
Her theory is that all she did, was grow up.

Sincerely the friend, with her head under the hood,
Some would say, that she's misunderstood.
She is a typical, teenage girl today,
With such a small voice, and so much to say.

Where you are
by Angela Slaymaker - age 16

Even though you are so far,
I can dream of where you are.
When I look up in the sky,
I can see into your eyes.

I will stare off into space,
And there I'll see your shining face.
Then I look upon the ground,
Even there too you are found.

It matters not what I do,
All my thoughts are of you.
I see you in the stars,
But still I wonder where you are.

The Country Side
by Erica Wren Smedsrud - age 13

Some people are different
Some people the same
Some like bright lights
I like the country plain

The country may not be exciting
But it's beautiful, peaceful, and quiet
While the city is surrounded by tenseness
And may sometimes break into a riot

Looking over mountain tops
Running through fields of wheat
The air is crisp and wonderful
You life so complete

Of course there is always disappointments
And rules you have to abide
But it's never really as bad
When your in the country side

A Grandchild
by Carissa A. Smith - age 20

Lying frail in a bed, that didn't belong to her.
A hospice they called it, a place for her to rest.
The days passed slowly, without any change
Until March the first of 1996.
A child,
her grandchild, born by grace.
Anticipation now awaits there arrival.
She must live.
She must survive a few more days. She must hold
that child,
her grandchild.
A few more days passed and finally they came.
Ashley May they called that child,
her grandchild.
Tears began to fill up in everyones eyes.
She took the little bundle, and held her in her arms
That's all she needed the touch of that child
her grandchild.
Her eyes began to close as she fell in a deep sleep
One she would never wake up from
But her dying wish, that sacred wish
was that child,
her grandchild.

Beckoning
by Debra H. Smith

Wandering in the dark
Lost and afraid.
Moon over head
Silent and beckoning.
Mystical horizons call out
To the soul
Of the lone figure watching,
Yearning to be bold.

dry
by Emily O'Doherty Smith

rain pouring down the window
like sped-up ice floes

& the reflection drips
down my striped shirt

blue & green oozing
down my body in clean

silver sheen
(no one'll know what I mean)

this driver seat this new
car smell this new view

on the radio
she's a lesbian & I
wonder if courage comes

from actual strength or necessity
I would never be the same
as sane more sane

I just feel
they're the lucky ones

but does it ooze off of me
already like this un-wet
rainwater flowing down as reflection?

Untitled
by Cassy Simpson - age 13

Everywhere they are
You can see sparks
Their love is everywhere
They know each other
They love each other
Everyday they are together
Their love is forever

Moonbeam
by Jason W. Smith

My world envelopes in darkness
As pain corrupts my heart
Leading me into blindness
And leaving me nowhere to start

My tortured soul bleed
From all of my fears
Slipping into oblivion
The only proof my tears

My mind unravels constantly
Leaving me with insanity
Crushing all my dreams
And putting me in the hands of humanity

Fearing the nightmares
And the flashbacks that still haunt me
Screaming in my mind
And forcing my soul to flee

Can all of this be happening
Or is it all a dream
The only haven I find tonight
Is in a lonely but gentle moonbeam

A Wish
by Kelsea Smith - age 13

I sit in the dim glow of my lamp,
As I look over my shoulder I see that it's 1:53 am,
I can barely hold my eyes open,
But I can't sleep,
I am all alone,
Not one single sound in the whole house,
I hear nothing but silence in my two ears,
I whisper to myself "go to sleep"
But I can't for my mind holds one single thing,
It hold the sweet picture of my loves face,
But then that picture is ripped into a million pieces when I realize,
He's not here with me,
Which makes me so very sad,
I long for the day that I will be able to hear his sweet voice,
Telling me how much he loves me,
Us being away from each other is slowly tearing me apart,
But I know that my love for him is now at it's peak,
So no matter what I know it will end okay,
I realize that it's July 9th our four week anniversary,
But I also realize that he's not here with me,
This thought crushes me but I try not to think about it too much,
I wish that he could be here with me watching over me,
I wish that all through my bad dreams, he would be there holding my hand,
Telling me it's alright,
I wish that as I awake his lips would touch mine ever so gently,
I would smile at him then I would cry,
Cry tears of happiness,
Although tears of happiness he would tell me it's alright and not to cry,
I wish you were here to make this happen but guess what
Your not.

Seems Like Yesterday
by Tiffany M. Smith - age 14

It seems like only yesterday that I started
kindergarten filled with gladness.
Now it's my last day of 6th grade and I'm
filled with great sadness.
It's time for us to spread our wings,
and soar for greater things,
We are all at a turning point in our lives together,
Though the years have left us with great treasures,
These treasures are filled with many different emotions,
Emotions like love, joy, excitement, and
sorrow are just a few to give you a notion
We've shared the worry of up coming tests,
And wondered about who's the tournament's best,
We've studied and we've played,
While hoping to make a passing grade,
It's time now for us to join others,
Adding still more sisters and brothers,
With lots more to learn,
and many credits to earn,
We bid elementary school "Adios."

Love Hurts
by Tracey Snitkowski

    I never truly understood what people meant when they would tell me "Love Hurts" until the time I was with you--just being me and you turned away. Then I knew.

Success
by Crystal A. Snow

Success should not be measured by how much money or the size of bank accounts.
Changing or enlarging our wardrobes from year to year does not make a life of success.
The outside appearance never really matters at the end of the destination.

Cosmetics and new hairdo's are so popular at the time but never fill the emptiness in the heart.
Why does the human race seek after worldly treasures before accepting the love from GOD?
The true meaning of success is when I am accepted by GOD into HIS home to be with HIM forever.

Anger
by Rachael Souza

Anger blazing in one's eye,
Anger is a fire burning deep within your mind.
Anger can twist your face into a mask,
That hides any love within.

There is nothing and no one but one's self,
That can drown the blaze burning as the sun.

At times anger lashes out like a whip,
At others anger sings like the devil's fiddle.
Anger is as the deer in the fall,
Anger is there, and then it is not.

Some anger lingers slyly
Twisted up inside me.
Anger is stationary like a tree,
And hollow as a pod.

There is nothing like anger,
Waiting to fly.
Thriving on your sanity,
Till the river's run dry.

Night
by Sarah L. Sparrow - age 15

It is dusk - and a transformation has begun,
The red ball that is the sun slowly descends from the sky,
And becomes the canvas for a watercolor masterpiece,
The black is night begins to creep up onto this masterpiece as a cat stalks its prey —
Night is beginning to descend upon this radiant scene,
And with it comes the blanket of sleep that will come and carry us away...
Into the depths of our dreams,

While the night paints its masterpiece with the darker colors that consume his palate:
The brilliant pink hues of the flowers, become a deeper red,
The deep green of an evergreen becomes an almost black and formidable color,
The world is transformed into a deeper shade of beauty.
At the same time, a beam of pale light penetrates the darkness,
Illuminating the land as a smile illuminates the face of a child,
And the stars overhead are the holes through which the angels of daylight watch over the land,
Giving us hope,
That tomorrow the night will again give way the splendor of a new day.

Gray/Someday Molly
by Daniel Speake - age 15

So sick of the world you just want to cry,
So afraid you just want to die.
Unaware of the things you choose,
You're a target for lies and a magnet for abuse.

All your problems and tough situations
Arousing storms of fear and hesitation.
Hesitation to throw your fist through
The faces of difficulties that confront you.

Your voice is shaky as you cry to me.
Anger floods your eyes making it so you can't see.
Biting your lip, whispering words under your breath,
Shaking your head, holding your knees to your chest.

You used to have control, but it all slipped away.
Life used to show you colors, but now all you see is gray.
When you cry, I take your hand and lead you from night into day.
It's blind leading the blind, but we always find our way.

You can't say you didn't bring it on yourself,
But everybody makes mistakes so I don't mind to help.
Rubbing your eyes to get rid of the tears.
The more you try to see, the less it becomes clear.

Someday the sun will shine just for you.
Someday the gray will disappear.
Someday you'll find happiness in something new.
Someday color will reappear.

Depths Of Despair
by Anita Spreacker

Where are you my friend, where have you gone?
Tumbling......
Tumbling......
Tumbling......
Into the depths of despair,
Overpowered by the obscure realities
Of a turbulent existence.
Frivolous wonderment of what you might become,
Struggling to reach the plateau of mundane normalcy,
.... Just beyond your grasp.
Embracing instead the contours of the fiery,
Eclectic bottles of syrupy heaven.
Mr. Black Velvet smooths the ripples,
Embellishes the darkness,
And makes it
Shine.

Courage: Learned in Man, Inborn in Animal
by Lynda Staton

A man, armed with a .30-06, stalks a wounded lion through a dense jungle. The lion waits patiently in the underbrush. Both man and animal demonstrate what is commonly called courage. Yet, there is a difference. The man's courage is prompted by his own ego and his need to impress others. The lion's courage is instinctive. He does what he has to do to survive.

Macomber, in Ernest Hemingway's "The Short Happy Life of Frances Macomber," builds his courage from the taunts of others. The story depicts a man whose courage is measured by his zeal for the excitement of the chase and for the glory of victory, all of which have nothing to do with survival.

On the other hand, the lion shows courage from the basic need to survive. From the instant he is slammed to the ground by the hunter's bullet, the lion suffers agony, which fans his instinctive spark of hatred for the man who stalks him.

Both man and animal are social beings that mate and have families. But in a society where bravery is considered honorable, a man loses some of that social significance if he proves otherwise. He learns early in his life that he must show courage or experience ridicule. As John Dewey In Human Nature and Conduct states, "Men can progress as beast cannot...so that most serviceable actions must be learned."

With an animal, it is kill or be killed. His courage stems from instinct. Human courage results from outside factors, such as self-esteem, excitement, glory, and the all important, what others think. Through learned behavior man accepts the rules of society and strives for courage.

Hemingway's short story defines courage of both man and beast while illustrating the difference between learned and instinctive behavior. Courage, learned in man, inborn in animal, is defined by the motivations of each.

Sensing Realization
by Kiley Stephens - age 13

    Discovering confusion of
infatuated love
    Realizing there's a heaven in
the clear blue sky above
    contributing lyrics to an
unfamiliar song
    Acting cool with your friends
so you feel that you belong
    Making sense out of a story,
that doesn't have a plot
    Getting in a fight, when you
never really fought
    Closing your sore eyes when
they badly need to cry
    Feeling all is lost, and never
knowing why

Inner Peace
by Claudette Sternberg

The apple seed unfolds into a delicious fruit to eat,
So too the seed of the rose develops into a bud so sweet.
It is from within that the simple seed grows to nourishment or grace.
And each unveiling gently takes its own particular place.
We have a special seed within our inner soul,
One that needs to come forth quietly and also unfold.
It is the seed of inner peace in what we think or do,
And it ripens into a patient and loving Attitude!
The Outside of me is important that is very true,
But the inner seed of me is what I must always renew.

Mother
by Jacqueline Marie Stewart - age 13

Lonely mother sits waiting, waiting to see if her daughter will show;
    Waiting to see if she will be there by her side.
Then, there is the child's father who wants his daughter to live by his side.
    Choices, Choices, which one will she make?
    Will they be the right choices?
    Mumbling, mumbling out the girl's mouth.
    A low voice, a cry, a whisper. Who? Where? Why?
    The rich scent of her mother's perfume.
    She will surely miss that.
    Her father's cigarette aroma.
Put together, it makes a disgusting fume, but alone, they seem just fine to the girl.
    For whenever, the girl looks at her mother's picture,
    Memories, dreams...the girl feels the burning in her heart.
    Watery eyes...everything in sight is blurry, just blurry.
    Be strong, be strong, at least that's what your mother would say.
    Be strong, be strong, be strong.

The Arms of Fate
by Jamie Stewart - age 16

Safely in the arms of fate
we laughed and loved 'till it was late
and when the sun began to rise
you looked at me with passionate eyes.
In that passion I saw a new smile
that hasn't been seen in quite awhile.
Right then you told me just how you felt
and those loving words made my heart melt.
On that summer morning our hearts became one
as we sat there holding each other in the golden sun.
To this day I remember the passion of that morning
and everyday still you tell me your heart is so adoring.
Those vows we made to love until we stand at Heavens gate
together forever, safely in the arms of fate.

My Dream
by Catie Tara Strauss - age 13

The day will come when all problems will be solved.
The waters will be clean and the waste will have dissolved.
The ozone layer will miraculously appear.
The extinction of animals will not be a fear.
There will be plenty of food to go all around,
And not one hungry child will be found.
The trees will be many and never cut down,
And what is more, it'll be clean when you go into town.

The day will come when all health problems will have a cure.
Operations and medicines and much, much more.
There will be a medication to clear up cancer,
Waiting for death will not be the answer.
Heart-attacks and strokes will become obsolete.
They'll be a cure for AIDS, wouldn't that be a treat!
Unexplained death will never occur.
Blindness is a goner, not even a blur.

The day will come when all violence will disappear.
Hatred will be gone, and love will be near.
Weapons will be gone with not even a trace.
You won't have to worry about carrying mace.
There will be no more fighting, not to mention war.
You'll never have to worry about locking your door.
No robberies will happen and no more arrests.
There'll be no drugs or alcohol, no need for those tests.

I know it can happen,
This day might just come.
All we need is your help, don't act like a bum.
I know this can happen, you just wait an see.
We can make a difference.
I know you can count on ME!

The Sunshine Ray
by Nicole Stumbaugh - age 16

The sunshine ray on a lovely day
glows and glimmers so bright.
It dances with the lonely breeze
in the starry sky at night.
It dries my tears,
calms my fears,
and softly kisses my cheek.
It embraces me warmly
when it's foggy and stormy,
and holds me when I'm weak.

The sunshine ray on a gloomy day,
still remains the same.
Brighter than the brightest light,
warm and comforting at the very sight.

It helps me cry,
then makes me smile.
It keeps my heart alive,
never letting me forget my goals,
in which I always strive.
It opens my eyes,
and cures my soul,
with its golden, smooth texture.
Funny thing is,
my sunshine ray is nothing but
a memory and a picture.

The Tyranny Of Beauty
by Demetruis F.P. Stuwart

O mankind, I rebuke thee, and thy ways do I solemnly damn!
Thou are naught but superficial-- thy vaunted wisdom is a sham!
A quarter century have I suffered thee as my bewilderment has mounted:
Tell me why it is the inside that counts, but the outside that's counted.
Outer beauty endeth skin deep; but so doth thy perception:
Thy Shallowness reigneth sovereign; depth eludes thine conception.
Thou hath ordained and acclaimed Beauty thy queen;
Surely a harsher, crueler despot the world hath never seen!
She sitteth supremely upon the throne of thine heart;
Ye bow and extol her - what a coward thou art!
With right hand she favors the fair with scepter ornate;
And with left hand condemns the uncomely to an awful fate.
She decrees burnt offerings of thy treasures and wages;
And thou dost comply as thy forefathers through the ages.
Thou sacrifices thyself high on her altar so vile;
And are, at best, granted her fleeting touch a scant while.
Shalt man forever marvel her works in awe at her feet?
Thou worships her idol of vanity, preaching her creed of conceit.
For paragons of pulchritude thy loins are afire;
For paragons of virtue ye lack such desire.
And when I inquire of thee, O mankind why this is so,
Thou proclaimeth, "Beauty tempts me not-petty things I forgo!"
Yet, when I knock at the door of thine heart to commune with thee
I am turned away by Beauty; thy queen despiseth me
Alas, mankind, this I hold beyond doubt
True beauty dwells within, as what allureth lies without!
Ugliness hath crowned Beauty: on thy vice doth she feed;
Now dethrone the great tyrant and by righteousness be freed!

The Covered Bridge
by Linda Sura

As I traversed ol' Blue Rock Ridge,
I chanced upon a covered bridge,
Built a century or more ago,
Nestled within the valley below.

It spanned the river and joined my path,
Providing respite from noonday's wrath.
I rested within it's cool confines,
And shared my space with wild grape vines.

I watched as shadows darkened and grew,
When a violent nature began to brew,
But I stayed safe and dry and warm
As I took shelter from the storm.

And when the torrents were finally stilled,
I prayed to follow what God willed.
I had to decide which path to choose,
The Light I did not wish to lose.

I chose to continue the direction I'd come,
And not turn back where I'd begun.
I emerged from the shadows where two paths met;
One road to explore, one road to forget.

Purple
by Tricia Suriani - age 17

Purple
Eats away at me with an inspiring tooth
Sweet enough to pierce my soul
Dark enough to take a toll
On thy fingers which grasp thy pen
It feels God-sent

Purple
Bohemian strikes thine mind
To thy tips of my fingers, words begin to entwine
Words to be whispered upon the wind of pages
Liberated form invisible cages

Burned and turned by the eyes of their lovers
Sealed and burdened by a cover

Only appealing to those who can see
That would be thee, or me, please... thee

Purple
Swirling chaotically
Whirling ironically calm
About a prodigious and beautiful spool
Yet, hesitantly read by the fool

Perhaps in this ludicrous world
My purple will bleed upon thy trees' offerings
Striking sacred and unsacred minds sharply
Delving deep, falling dangerously steep
Providing sight, almost frightful, in spite, of its integrity

I crave for thy day to arrive, that thy passion of my life
Be fathomable and taken within
To thou soul unequivocally hidden
To express its reverence for, and seize that which will be given
By my purple pen, bloody and spent, to this world of thy dying, lost to thy living.

The Countryside
by Jennifer Swann

A leaf falls down to the ground
As usual, the earth goes round
The wind blows down through the meadows
And the children look happily out their windows
The grass is green and the sky is blue
Just sitting here thinking of things to do
I look outside and what do I see
A little bird singing in a tree
When the sun goes down and it begins to get dark
I hear the crickets and the dogs start to bark
When I look outside, I see a beautiful site
As the sun sets, I say goodnight.

Abuse
by Amanda Swann - age 14

There was a little girl,
so innocent and sweet.
She didn't deserve what was happening,
she didn't deserve to get beat.

Her mother slapped her and took her bear,
the little girl just sat and cried.
She thought that this was all her fault,
so she rested her head and sighed.

When she went to bed that night,
every inch of her body was aching.
She knew there was nothing she could do,
but she was feeling forsaken.

The next morning she woke up,
and found the bed soaked with pee.
She knew she would get punished,
but she had no way to flee.

The mother dressed the girl in clothes,
and then walked to the door.
The girl ate her breakfast,
then collapsed to the floor.

For she couldn't take these beatings,
her bones were not that strong.
And as the mother fell to her knees,
she then knew that this was wrong.

The little girl died right then,
her life had just been beginning.
She's dead right now because of her mothers actions,
because of her mothers sinning.

Here in my Heart
by Stephanie Swiggum - age 13

I could be a thousand miles from nowhere.
I could be a gain of sand within the sea.
I could be longing for rain in the desert or shooting along with the stars.

I could be rain or shine.
I could be rich or poor.
I could be black or white, homeless or homebound.

No matter where I am or how long we're apart,
You will always be with me...here in my heart.

Is She Real?
by Robert Tanner

She came to me in a dream, as if nothing else were real.
There was no denying it, I needed her to feel and interpret my emotions.
Yet I turned away in appeal, in a silent plea for mercy
Only to watch lust penetrate the surreal, my last vestige of self-defense
Against her undeniable will that erupted; leaving nothing behind but pretense.
Slowly understanding prevailed, although I saw nothing but nonsense,
Yet I knew her as myself.
Lost far beyond hope for innocence caught within lies, attempts at deception.
Staring straight into the face of forthrightness.
New, in search of my own integrity.
Lost without a trace.
Left with nothing, not even naivete.
I continue to see her face in the fog of my own gullibility.
She transforms the intangible differently than her
Then slides between every layer, convoluted in its' self-deception.
My buried foibles dissipate only to organize
into shapely hopes mixed with
Trembling fears gripping a dangling leg,
pulling my fingers from their aspirations.
Still she re-appears as if nothing were more urgent,
more compelling than insight.
Baring every nuance.
I once again enter her inviting spell
Lifting my spirits, and interest.
Forcing forward passion from its' depths
Spewing out all my accumulated nonsense.
I see she is real, and
I know her as well as myself.

The End
by Shelly Tarman - age 16

A thousand lamps, won't lift the dark.
Just how long has it been, since I've seen a spark?
Would I fight back, of hesitate to think?
Finally figure out, just how we link.

Link together as one, an undying soul
Or have we crossed that bridge, did we pay that toll?
How much will we have to hurt to pay that price?
How much more could we possibly sacrifice?

How can we hold the relentless stare,
Of a once so perfect pair?
Those two smiles so bright and wide
Now replaced with lost looks of pain denied.

They say if we hold on a little bit longer,
Things will pass, we'll only get stronger.
But how can this kind of pain just pass us by,
When I can no longer look you in the eye?

Maybe it's time to just let go
Would it work, who's to know?
That's the chance we'll have to take
But how can I tell my heart <u>not</u> to break?

And how can I tell myself <u>not</u> to cry?
When it comes time for that final sigh
When there's finally time for our hearts to mend
That painful sigh, that brings the end.

You
by Kristina Teaster - age 14

My knees tremble
With uncontrollable fear,

My lips quiver whenever
You are near.

My rapid heart beats faster
I feel as if I am your prey.

My eyes become bloodshot
And burn when you
Look my way.

Then for a moment I
Have a vision of you
Embracing me, oh how
I wish you knew.

My breath escapes as
You walk on by

My feelings once again I've
Kept hidden inside

Afraid to tell you how
I feel, for I know you
Would laugh, then disappear

So I lower my head,
And stand there in shame
For I am the one who's fault
Is to blame.

A Reason to Be
by C. Chris Telander

I've watched you longingly from far away
  And fervently wished you were near
Impatiently waiting for that glorious day
  When I can be there, or you here
By a cruel twist of Fate we've been cursed, kept apart
  By circumstances beyond our control
The situation rips and tears at my heart
  And leaves a gaping hole in my soul
Yet I cling to your love, to your every sweet word
  You're my anchor in these times of distress
The sound of your voice makes me weak when it's heard
  You're my life, my love, my happiness
I gaze 'pon your face every night on my screen
  Think of nothing but you while awake
You've revived my dead heart, you inhabit my dreams
  You're my inspiration, my Fate
I ache to be held in your warm embrace
  For you kiss to breathe life into me
For these the worst horrors of hell would I face
  You provide me a reason to be

Forgiving Innocence
by Jeremy Thomas

Scarlet season softens me
Inside such velvet pain,
I drink her sweet sobriety
To dream her amber rain.
An ocean sings of secret whisper,
Where silence hints her name,
Of all the times I've drowned to kiss her...
So many died in vain.

Hallowed hair becomes my honesty,
To break me is her scheme.
Blue eyes that breathes insanity,
Now echoes through my dreams.
Such mountains chant a fearless sorrow,
One promise so it seems.
To me she swore her lost tomorrow...
So far away it gleams.

Precious patience denies the plush
That decorates my soul.
Her poisoned skin injects a rush
And burns my blood to cold.
The sky intones a stirring song,
My strength perhaps, she stole,
I've grasped her reality far too long...
So hard it was to hold.

Time...
by Shanna N. Thomas - age 18

Though time may pass
And time may go
Through life's ups and downs
Life is still the same

Day in and day out
The road twists and winds
For some- time is short
And yesterday was their
        Last

With God time maybe
        Long
But, without him
It's short as nappy hair
That will not grow...

The Struggle
by Tammy Thomas - age 14

Wanting,
Never getting.
Stretching,
Never reaching.
Leaving,
Never returning.
Total Darkness behind you.
Knowing,
Never telling.
Having,
Never showing.
Fighting,
Never winning.
Total Emptiness inside you.

Wind
by Shannon Thompson

With unreputable awe, I take witness to a lulled abounding force,
As subtle arousing whispers sweep through the epervesant valley;
Dried leaves then flutter, in sunlight while trees bow to this
glorious reserection;
With heavens' breath contoured, the loving consicration
Seemingly echoing the sung message from the wolf's den to God's gate.
Independence giving this soul preminance in contorted love.
Nature yields this hallowed frame spryly awakened.

Those hands adorned with a painted grace, passed on with flight
and speed.
Ceding transcendence from water to land, anxiety takes arms, as
if ordinance in the origin of combat.
These fierce eyes, I perceive, the mark of an angered soul's union
abrogated.
Shadowing the scars, consealing revenge integrated,
Then in a wink, this mamed heart induces a coy regard;
Whose distant murmurs, of celestial play evolves.
Vibrantly, waves begin their dance, with this lost confident
and friend.
Soothing their rippled edge, with aromatic kisses of sands' shells.

From upon symbolic lips, this proclamation is set for amitivity
to dwell.
Attesting to this whirling inspiration, impressed upon my heart.
Loudly, I proclaim an eternally devoted respect, to this
bewildering sway spirit;
While with silence, pledging to keep a sympathy, for those not
yet domineeringly over taken.

Left Behind
by April Sarah Thurston - age 18

I slowly went into the room where my father laid,
Lifeless in a copper coffin. Looking down upon him,
Looking so cold, I begin to cry.
It brought all the memories I once had.
Reaching for his hand, I trembled.
I did not know how it would feel.
Would it feel like he was still there?
Or did I want him to be there?
His hand was cold and life was not present.
His soul went to heaven
Leaving his body for people to pay their last respects.
That moment in time, I realized that I loved my father.
Stepping away from the coffin,
I wanted him to jump out and take me home.
As I sit, I see people going up the coffin.
They turn to me smiling
And telling me everything is going to be alright.
Is it?
Will everything really be alright?
Slowly everyone turns to leave the room quietly, leaving me to myself.
Walking up to the coffin one last time, I said goodbye.
Waiting for a few minutes I kissed his cheek
And began lowering the coffin top down upon him.
When the lid was down, I kissed it one last time.
And I too, turning slowly around
Leaving all of my memories in my heart
And ending my childhood forever.

Essences
by Cecilia Thompson - age 18

Running along sand
touching soft land
stealthily.
Falling among flowers
laughingly
thinking thoughts, remembering
Peacefully.
Whipping whispers filigree
Mocking all the way.
turning twisted, treachery
Burning.
slipping, steeping
carefully
sipping earth scents
Longingly.

Dreams
by Alisha Tingle - age 15

Dreams break free ones hidden desires
And overflow with an air of reality
Where there is no law nor boundary.
As to what one can experience
For in dreams all is real.
Dreams hold an atmospheric beauty
Whereas in life it's pierced
With a terrifying realism.
Though dreams may entrap
These undesirable qualities
They have the purity and light
That only can be expressed
In this unkept record of time,
Our Dreams.

Life
by Jenette To - age 14

Life has its own special way,
It offers tears, laughter, and smiles.
But none of which to stay.

Sometimes I seem to always be in tears,
As I see it, it is never sadness or anger in me,
It is just fear-
Frightened of losing something,
Fearing something would never come,
Scared of a new beginning,
Or afraid something would never end.

Smiles is something I always begin with,
Either it's a new friendship,
Or meeting someone new,
Or, once again, seeing my own Best Friend,
Or even to myself, when I remember times when I'm not blue.

Tears, laughter, and smiles just come and go.
I never know when to expect them,
I never know what to expect as I grow.
All I can do is to show,
How much I appreciate life:

SEE IT AS BEAUTIFUL AS A RAINBOW!

Love
by Carrie Tomlinson - age 17

Love is a flower
Pretty and pink.
Love is a shooting star,
Wished on in piece.

Love is the affection-
You share with someone else.
Love is the feelings,
You store within yourself.

Love is the friends-
You have been with for years.
Love is the happiness-
Filled with joy and tears.

Love is the years-
That go on and on.
Love is your life-
Endless and long.

Love is the expiration-
Of your life,
Loves never ending-
Until you are gone.

Love
by Ellen Topping - age 14

I am trapped in a blanket of your love,
there is no escape,
No beginning or end;
Lonely was I when I was without you,
But now that I am with you,
I feel secure in your arms.
A tender kiss like a dew drop,
Always coming to me,
Love is always a sweet song escaping
from your mouth and emotions,
I found something I can call a home,
I hope in your heart I will always stay,
I hope this love will last forever,
I pray you and me forever.

A Poem For Charlie
by Brigette J. Torruellas - age 13

I know that you are blue
And I don't want you to
You deserve better than that
And yes I do care
Anyplace Anytime Anywhere
Your beautiful and you know it
I guess cool can get hurt too
Don't worry it will only hurt worse if you
don't let it go
SO
I'll will be there
Anytime Anywhere
The person who hurt you didn't care
But I do
So don't be blue
Just remember
I'LL ALWAYS LOVE YOU

For: Charlie, my older sister
From: Jo, your baby sister
I Love You

Thereon
by Robert C. Toxey

Upon my heart tonight there rests,
an entity of emptiness;
and on my mind the thoughts reside,
with whom should fill this space by my side;
doomed to wait is now my fate,
to see that girl to whom of late,
I've often conversed, too often left,
but time and love cannot be pressed:
our tumbling lives in violent throws,
so often set to simple prose,
resides as second and far below,
the love that is shared between these two.

Too long for her, too strong for me:
the oceans of circumstance standing between;
so dim, the cast of light in here,
so far as if to disappear:
her eyes I have beheld in awe,
a countenance worthy to beg of a smile,
to kiss those lips, no years could be drawn,
long enough to last the while,
that I should now and forever wish,
to hold thereon in a kiss;
though now the night drags hours on,
sleep, for me, is ever gone,

For as she isn't here with me,
I forever wish I was with she.

The Greatest Karate Fighter
by James A. Traynor

During a recent kickboxing training session in the gym at the Stevens Point YMCA, I had an encounter of the small-child kind. My partner and I were dressed up in our protective karate gear and had been in a two-minute resting session when I looked off to the side and noticed a young boy watching us. He was about seven years old and was munching on a cookie from the cookie bag he was holding. He looked at me and said, "If my dad were fighting that guy, he would be a lot tougher on him than what you are." I mentioned that my partner and I were practicing and didn't want to hurt each other.

After another three-minute round of kickboxing, my partner and I took a two-minute rest. I looked to the side and saw the little boy still standing and watching and still munching on a cookie. He looked right at me and said, "Mister, I think you're the best karate fighter I've ever seen!" I chuckled and thanked him and then asked if he liked karate. He replied that he was taking karate classes at the YMCA and could do a "front kick." I asked him to show me his kick and he did -- still holding onto his cookie bag. He mentioned that he wrestles with his dad sometimes and every once in a while even gets on top.

When I think of what the little boy had said to me, I realized that I had been a positive role model for him, at least for a little while. I also understood the importance of treating even the very young with kindness and respect. My peers in karate might not think of me as a great fighter, but to the little boy I was, at least for a little while, "the greatest karate fighter." It's a compliment I'll always remember.

Love
by Tiffany Tuders - age 12

Through the sky,
Light as a dove,
Ther are two people,
Who share much love,
Bruce, the husband,
Man of the house,
Would protect his wife,
From even a mouse,
Veronica, the wife,
Queen of the land,
Who siad "Yes!"
When he requested he hand,
Marriage, children, and pets,
There are no regrets,
And that's where it ends,
A man and a women,
Who began as friends!

Listen
by Tresa Tuinstra

The sun shines so brightly, it makes the flowers bloom.

When darkness falls the stars glimmer, along with the glowing moon.

After a rain when the sun peaks out, a rainbow may appear.

The world can be such a beautiful place, so precious and so dear.

Listen to the sound of the wind, as it blows through the trees.

A gentle summer rainfall, can put your mind at ease.

Listen to the birds as they chirp merrily, and sing a joyful song.

Keep our world neat and clean, and stray from all of the wrong.

Our children are our future, we need to think of them,

So that they can see the sun so bright, blooming flowers, and a rainbow that never ends.

One Day a Boat Was Sent For Me
by Katie Tunison - age 16

One day a boat was sent for me
to take me to the light,
with promises of hope and love
and images so bright.

I gladly stepped into the boat
and paid my toll with sin,
I was deceived and led back to
the dark where I had been.

A Day Of Remembrance
by Tennille K. Turner - age 19

The calm tides glitter in the rays of the setting sun
The harbor is deserted; all except one.
The smell of the salt-tinged ocean air
The rippling breeze blows through her hair.
Why does this woman stand alone
On the end of the pier, looking so forlorn?
In her right hand she clutches the cap
Of a wrongfully departed Navy chap.
In her left hand she holds a red rose
One by one the petals she throws
Into the sea on the outgoing tides
To where her Navy chap now abides.
Miles and miles into the open sea,
Where she cannot follow, but so longs to be.
A single tear rolls down her cheek
A tear that is silent but yet so meek.
She holds the cap against her breast
And prays that he is peacefully at rest.
She beholds the marker made of stone,
Hundreds of names in the dimming sun shone.
Several more tears down her cheeks fell
When she saw the name that she knew so well.
The name that was the same as her own
Yet now she bore it all alone.
She never thought this day would bring her such gloom
The same day they had wed - the third day of June.
Her hands trembled greatly as she fingered the name
Of the love she had lost - her dear Michael Caine.
As she shakily walked away from the sea
The flag of the Arizona waved in the breeze.

Inside
by English Ann Tuttle - age 16

Prejudice all around,
Is hate and anger.
It cannot be stopped,
But is a serious danger.
We can't control it from becoming,
Only not to be it ourselves.
Without color, crystal clear,
Without religion, no god,
Without gender, no sex,
Without money, all poor,
We would all be the same.

The Crosshair
by Ilene E. Twitchell

You're always in someone's sights
Who watch for your mistakes,
They are looking for some reason
The errors you will make.

Is it through the job you have
Or is it the way you dress,
Are you walking a strange way
Or is your hair a mess?
Are your table manners odd
Are you handicapped in some way,
Is the car you drive so old
It will collapse one day?
Is your accent a bit different
Than those with native tongues,
Should it really matter at all
As long as the work is done?
It doesn't matter what your color
How you look or what you wear,
The person is within the heart
...how you climb the golden stairs.

The End
by Danielle M. Tyree - age 15

My hands tremble as I write-for they know it's the last time.
My eyes are swollen with grief and pain.
Anticipating pain, my stomach begins to churn.
This paper is stained by my draining eyes.
My screaming pulse, gets louder each beat.
In a moment, all will cease.
The gun that sits across the table, screams to me.
"C'mon, just get it over, pull the trigger,
I promise, you'll feel no pain."
My minds' eye plays my life back-
showing me no mercy.
My convulsing hand takes the gun,
clumsily I unlock the safety.
I put the barrel to my temple.
All goes silent-no thought runs through my brain.
All my life I dreamed for this silence, any silence.
I now hear the bang of the gun.
Silence screams. I no longer want this silence.
Now it's the end.

"Lips to Lips"
by Chika Ugorji

eyes turned
swept unexpectedly into his arms
silence prevailed
no speech needed
my heart understands
our heart understands
locked in an embrace
engaged in a conversation
lips to lips
and face to face.

A Nineties Nurse
by Cheryl Urban RN

"I want to help people."
Compassionate, caring, giving, teaching, learning
sacrifice,
change,
frustration, stress,
acclimated to change,
then more change,
Still, compassionate, caring, giving, teaching, learning
shift work, holidays, week-ends,
evaluations, skills validation,
more change,
more frustration, and stress,
Still compassionate, caring, giving teaching, learning
corporate financial gain,
amidst
financial sacrifice,
respect that's lost,
Still compassionate, caring, giving, teaching, learning
cross training,
jack of all trades,
master of...?
Increased responsibility,
less time,
but
Still compassionate, caring, giving teaching, learning
tired,
frustrated,
looking for something new.

"I wanted to help people."

Krissy
by Sharon Kay Van Y

Crossing the room to my favorite chair
And seeing you already laying there
Gently with hands so soft I place you on my lap
You neither wake nor do you stir as I rock you back and forth
Then seeing you kick your feet and wondering what you dream
Are you chasing balls or watching doves as they fly high above
Remembering quite well as we romped cross the hills
trying to catch you as you ran till I fell in the sand
You were always there regardless of your size
Barking, Growling, Protecting me as strangers passed by
You've been my faithful friend
through thick and thin
Your breathing slows as you open your eyes
As your tongue licks my hand and I hold your head
Then the silence fills the room
And holding you to my chest
you're gone to join your sister far beyond
I'll miss you Krissy and will never forget
Your devotion and you're love

A Forgotten Friend
by Gezel Viruet - age 15

As little girls we would
play hours and hours to a day.
We always thought we would be inseparable.
You and Me.
From playing games of Hide and Seek.
To telling secrets, you to me.
Always together, we thought our friendship would strive forever.
Things started happening, we grew apart.
We loved each other as Best Friends and children
but we grew up to become women.
Now we see as adults, our friendship will be kept in our hearts.
Until the day we meet again and realize we were
meant to be BEST FRIENDS throughout eternity!!!!!!!

Beyond Before
by Cheryl Vitello

Out of the darkness,
And into the light.
Though you're no longer here
I know it's all gonna be all right.

Nothing mattered when you left.
That's how it was at first.
But in departing, you instilled in me
A hunger, a desire, a primal thirst.

When you were here with me
All my eyes could see was you.
Now I know there is so much more
Out there for me than what I once knew.

I've finally come to realize
That there really is something more.
I can see a light that illuminates
What was shadowed by "Before".

I'm no longer blinded by the dark
Since the sun has risen on yesterday's shore.
I will say good-bye to you
When I gather courage to let go and close the door.

The Thank You Star
by Rhianna D. Vittitow - age 12

A penny says thank you
for being who you are -
a shining light among many,
someone special...a star.

Carry it in your pocket
or put it safely away.
Whenever you see or touch it,
recall what it meant to say.

Our lives are touched by many
who hope good will come about.
Some make lasting impressions;
but among them, you stand out.

You give so much, unselfishly,
without seeking recognition.
May this star be the symbol
of well-deserved appreciation.

Words often remain unspoken,
and actions sometimes fail.
Please keep this modest token
as an expression of how I feel.

You're a very special person;
thanks for what you say and do.
Thanks for being there for me;
I feel richer for knowing you.

Some day you'll get a grand reward
for who and what you are.
For now, please accept the wishes
conveyed by this penny; thank you, star.

Dividends Postponed
by Patricia Vogel

You think to be a grandmother
Means kisses, laughs and fun,
You bet it does and more perhaps
When all is said and done.

God knows we try to settle down
The temperaments and hormones
Of grandkids with their flashing eyes,
Their shrieks, their thumps, their moans.

If you aren't where I am today
Don't let me hear a tut-tut,
For only we know all the twists
Of grandmahood incarnate.

The I.O.U. we want from them
Comes due in future time,
When they have passed beyond insane
To normal then sublime!

Spring is Here
by Katherine Vo - age 12

The morning dew, as fresh as crystals
The newborn sun awaits, shining the earth with the warmth of its
beaming rays,
A blue jay sings a sweet song joyously,
while young buds blossom in the crisp sunlight
The sound of children's laughter is heard
A young rabbit pokes his head out, sniffing the air and the green
grass,
His eyes are shimmering and clear,
Why, spring is here!

Sea of Storms
by Niki Vosloo - age 15

Wherefore not has the earth raged rigid storms across the lands:
Land upon land, no continent may be free of the tyranny
voices cry out but cannot be heard above the raging winds of Cecelia,
so helpless. yes.
So we watch and we wait, still nothing can be done of the raging
winds, and the devastating destruction of the ice that is thrown so
heinously from the heavens:
can be so unforgivable and large and deadly in the paths of many who
have crossed the hail under raging skies.
Blue skies so suddenly turn to dark while farmers watch helplessly the
lightning that strikes the cattle and sets fire upon the plantings.
Why without warning, will the sky meet the ground and suck the skin
from off
the bones of the unfortunate, while carrying a casket of eggs a full way:
setting down the unbroken cargo in a field twenty miles away.
Monsoon, Hail, Hurricane, Typhoon:
some mild, some unavoidable to elude.
Still we wait and we watch, no research can save us from the
unpredictability of the grasps of weather that sweep a Sea of Storms
across the cracked and damaged land.

Pride Stands in the Way
by Clara M. Voss

I stood shivering
The sun was gone
The sky disappeared
Black clouds hovered
Wind whipped the trees
Cold penetrated my being
Everything was blanketed
With gloom

Joy was missing
The clouds were weeping
Tears covering all I could see
Was it to end here?
Would I ever walk in the sunshine
Again, was there hope
Such a dismal scene
All my happiness gone
When you left

You were the sun, stars and moon
Bliss when you smiled
Joy with your arms around me
Such a silly quarrel
Why let
Pride stand in the way
Two tortured souls
Because no one could say
Sorry.

Someone Appeared
by Jamie E. Voss

Your family has left by choice
You must start life over by force
No parents to love you, who should be there forever
No siblings to fight with; your family is not together

You're all alone, no one to share with or to talk to
You'll never hear those three words "I Love You"
You wonder if you need that; the love of a family
Maybe you don't need anyone; you can make it on your own

You start out fine and you shed no tears
You have no worries or fears,
But after a few months you realize the truth
You really do need somebody to be with

You finally think that you'll die alone
Then someone walks into your life and towards you love is shown
Between you and this friend you share what family doesn't..
Compassion, love, loyalty and understanding

You need nobody else, your life is complete
You can finally breathe with some ease
Your life is and will be changing in so many ways
To that special friend you must say "Thanks"

Casey
by Dena Sue Vowell

The years have come and gone so fast,
When did today become the past?
Daddy's little girl and Mother's pride and joy,
Will all too soon be dating boys.
It's finally here, Your birthday dream,
Today's the day you turn 13!

Enjoy this day and make it fun,
Your teenage years have just begun.
These are called the learning years,
Filled with laughter and filled with tears.

You're growing up, Your world is new,
So much of life is ahead of you.
Dream that dream, grab that star,
Your love of life will take you far.

Dolls will give way to football games,
Your life will never be the same.
A baby doctor or a vet,
You don't have to choose which one just yet.

God will guide you on your way,
If you ask Him when you pray.
Wherever you go and whatever you do,
You will take my love along with you.

Devil's Play
by Dellen A. Wade

Run and hide-Seek and destroy
Life is full of games
Win and lose everyday
When you think you're too old for the fun
In comes Death as a gun
You can't give up-You can't give in
Don't look back
He's only a few steps behind
Run for your life-Have to keep moving
This time he's not fooling
You need to catch your breath
Your legs are failing
If he catches up you'll be wailing
He'll whisper in your ear
Sweet things you love to hear
He'll reach inside-Touch your heart
Blacken your soul
All the time you're begging for more
There are no rules-He was born to cheat
You don't realize until it's too late
This game won't be a stalemate
He runs your life from beginning to end
You were never destined to win
I guess you never should have played
You're one more person that could've been saved.

Cold Fear
by Kelli Wagoner - age 13

Bare trees shiver in the icy wind.
The moon's haunting light casts about ghostly shadows.
A wolf howls a sharp, sorrowful cry,
Causing a terrified rabbit to hurry to the safety of
   a hollow tree.
Color faded leaves fall swiftly to the frozen ground,
As silent, wondrous snowflakes join the wind,
To make yet another night of cold restlessness.
A pair of gleaming yellow eyes appear suddenly from
   behind fallen branches.
Sudden fear escapes from deep within the forest's unknown
   depths.

Fall
by Bethany Wadzinski

Leaves changing color.
Time to rake.
Crispness fills the air.
The days shorten.

Squirrels gather nuts.
Birds fly south.
Bears hibernate.
Frost covers the ground.

Time to dress up for Halloween.
Maple syrup runs free.
School starts - oh no! Crops end.
Winter is not far behind.

Together Forever
by Melinda A. Waechter - age 15

The old flame must burn again
Although the sorrow lingers on
They are together
Together Forever

They were always everlasting
They argued and agreed
But they were always together
Together Forever

The year was long
While they were apart
But they're together now
Together Forever

Many tears have fallen
From so many broken hearts
The memories are shining through
In so many different lights

Their life was long
And so full of laughter
The family keeps on growing
Carrying their lost souls

Even though we're sad
And nobody wanted to give up
They are together again
Together Forever

"Remembered Past"
by Kimberly Waggoner - age 17

Picture an overweight child sitting alone,
Not speaking to anyone,
No friends to call her own.
She sits in a corner, her head always down.
She's never with a smile, only with a frown.

When I look in a mirror,
That's all I can see,
Is the fat little girl staring at me.

For the rest of my life,
I will feel the pain
Of everyone laughing and calling me names.

If you forget the past, you're condemned to repeat it.
If you say something rude and you don't really mean it,
Look at who you are saying it to,
And think of the damage you could do.

Everyday in the mirror
all I can see,
Is that fat little girl staring at me.

Crushed Crush
by Erin Waldron - age 12

From across the room
You think he's cool
And wish that love would bloom.
But when you're in front of him
You feel like a total fool!

When you start to talk
You think it's just begun,
But when you see him walk
Away with your best pal
You really want to run.

You start to think,
"Why is love so hard?
It all ends in a blink."
You think about it too much
And you know that you'll be scarred.

Then one day,
When you're feeling blue,
You look away.
When you see him staring,
You know that love is true

Not Just Make-Believe
by Mysti Dawn Wambolt - age 14

There is a land that I would like to share-
It is so misty, and yet so clear-

The moss is hanging like Icicles on a tree-
Sticks are floating like fish in the sea

It is so wonderful, this vast little land-
Yet no one has seen it, so far it's been banned

Please leave this land alone - one day God will
call you home; your day will come and it wont
be long-
God will carry you, gone ... gone ... gone.

So just be patient my little one, for up
there, there is no harm-
Violence and pain, drugs and gangs,
knives and guns, there are none

If you just wait and try your best, your
paradise will come and you'll just rest

It is so perfect, just wait and see, and
you will not disagree

Please believe and not just dream - this is
real life not just make-believe.

You
by Jessica Walker - age 15

You don't understand how I feel.
You don't know what goes on in
my mind.
The problem is that you don't
take the time,
it doesn't take long,
to figure out what's wrong.
You don't know what I go through
everyday,
I try to show you,
but you just turn away.
Deep down in my heart,
I know it is hard,
but if you would just love me,
and show me you care,
things wouldn't be the way they are.
                    Mom.

Untitled
by Millie Wampole - age 16

Listen! Through the country
Hear the sound of my ring
All rejoice and loudly sing
In my honor each July
Fireworks and rockets light the sky
Celebrations both great and small
Mark each city one and all
Patriots march in grand parades
Picnics are held in shady glades
Old folks wave their flags and tell
Stories of me, the Liberty Bell.

White Fluffy Things
by Ruth Warner

Our God must love white fluffy things
as seasons come and go;
he gave us summer's downy clouds
and winter's glistening snow.

The lilies of the valley bloom
when Spring is here to stay,
and fill the air with sweet perfume
to glorify His day.

White lilacs in profusion sway
as summer nearer grows
while lilies on the hillsides wave
to welcome the white rose.

We are his other sheep most fair
and safe within His sight;
we must be true and chaste and good,
our robes be purest white.

So think in terms of dove-like ones
from which all blessing springs;
be pure at heart and innocent
God loves white fluffy things.

Forget Me Not
by Jessica Watson - age 17

All senses are obsolete
Right from wrong
You long to be loud
But silence guards you
Begging and pleading has gotten me nowhere
It's time to give it up
Placing our future on the line
I become one
As I take silence by the hand
Building the barrier, so bravely you tore down,
up higher.
Funny how it means nothing
I've given you warning, but your hearts a rebel
Bumps and bruises all forgotten
Just scars of you past
How long will this last?

Potential
by Shawn Watson

Two sad-lost souls colliding
wondering where, when?
Tangling hope and doubt,
does she taste
as sweet as she looks?
There's only one way to find out.

The Poseur
by Ali Webb

Her hair
In leaping curls
Blew by
Some smokey
Billowy
Appealing
Brown do

Curving round
And showy
It came to lie
Amid sloping
Circling
Shoulders
Dyed

No One Hears
by Joan Webster

I am surrounded by children...
    their noise...
    their wants...
    their desires
    must come first!

I sometimes cover my ears...
    to no avail.

Someone once asked,
    "Who takes care of you?"

I smiled and replied,
    "No one hears."

A tear fell at that
    moment in time...
I then straightened my shoulders
    and
    began again.

At Milepost Twenty-Nine
by Michele Weirsky

If I were fifteen again, I'd walk to town for a candy bar
I'd walk along Jackson Parkway where there were lots of cars and
a cornfield with corn so high you couldn't see anything else.
I'd feel like I was walking to California, I'd pretend I was
Just me and my one and-a-quarter mile adventure past the
St. Joe's cemetery, past mean, old Mr. White's house with
his beautiful Corvette parked in the driveway.
I'd look in the cars to see if I knew anyone and then I'd wave
hello, I'd walk down Belvidere Avenue passing big houses.
I didn't know any of those people yet, but I would wonder what
they were like.
When I got to the market, I'd stop and look up into the sky
listening to horns beeping and engines chattering at the stoplights.
I'd be fifteen and wide-eyed at this town, at the world for that
matter.
Sometimes when I look in the mirror I still see those big eyes.

Listen to me
by Rob Weis

what makes you happy on days when your blue
a call from a friend or a call from you
we seek the things that make us go
we seek the things that we do not know
from the inner burn of a lovers scorn
to your favorite jeans that have just been torn
hoping and praying for some security
honesty truth and purity
many tales but lies when life's begun
when it begins or when it ends
can you be lovers or just be friends
for one day when your old and gray
and your life is in order and not in dismay
and you can speak these words of wisdom
you better think twice before you come
for the rest of your life you will be thinking
why in the world was i drinking
for now you will learn what the elders spoke
to not rush in that love is no joke
it is truth love and honesty
but that you will have to learn to see
because you would not listen to me

The Final Choice
by Jami Welfley - age 18

Whispers of sad voices
Floating in the wind
Soldiers without choices
Losing touch with their kin.

Lost forever at war
Saying prayers for life
Families to be seen no more
No children nor wife.

Millions of deaths
Like a holocaust from hell
Taking every last breath
With a decaying smell.

In a dying plight
A wish is made
Sending down a light
To make a trade.

The shooting has ceased
And death no more
A figure is seen
By a heavenly door.

"I'll take thee with me
To my heavenly home
I'll make you pain free"
The mysterious light shone.

All the dead arose
With one gracious thought
For that path that they chose
"I died brave as I fought."

Still
by Melissa Welsch - age 17

Another place
A different time,
With new acquaintances
And unfamiliar routines...

But still I am left with
The same tears that haunted me.
Still I sit alone empty and frightened.
Still I wonder how to make it through
This complicated reality of mine.
Still the same unanswered
Questions wander throughout me.
Still I look for the same love
That is nowhere to be found.
Still I am lost within this
Mind that I've received.
Still I try to find a place
To where I fit in.
Still no one understands the real
Person that is hidden within.

Angel of Love
by Michelle Wheeler

High above the treetops
In the heavens above
Is where I see you
My angel of love

A purified vision of strength
That takes me through
My weaknesses

You provide me with
An everlasting happiness
During times of sorrow

You offer a glimmer of hope
When I only feel desperation

You are the companion
I long for
During times of loneliness

So how could you be seen
As anything less
Than a true angel
Sent to me
From the heavens above

Coils
by Carlena E. White

Violence— like a serpent
    Coiled around its victim
    Squeezing the life
    From my body.

Hatred— like a chain
    Coiled around a prisoner
    Squeezing the breath
    From my lungs.

Vengeance— like a cloud of smoke
    Coiled around the fire
    Choking the life
    From my body.

Peace— like a flowering vine
    Coiled around a tree
    Supporting me
    Giving me life.

'Tis Love
by Cheeki - age 18

I recognize the feeling that flows through me,
Tis love that quickens my heart to beat
Tis love that keeps me belonging to thee.

Like rivers and streams find there way back to seas,
Like winds blow and breeze never harming the trees,
Like the sun sets in the west and rises in the east,
Be confident my love, I belong to thee.

No fish or shark can tear thee from my heart.
Nor drizzle or monsoon drown away your love's art.
You are the brilliance of the sun burning in my skies.
You are the zen diamond in the midst of my heart eyes.

I recognize the feeling that burns inside,
Tis love I say
Tis love no lie

Dearest One
by Patricia I. White

My dearest one I have so long
tried to ignore the feelings you
stir in my breast.

The electric charge around us left
me feeling bewildered, confused,
and yes even ashamed for where
my thoughts led me.

Do you know the havoc you have
wrought in me? Oh, the feelings
and desires you have brought to life.

I see you watching me, but I can
not read your thoughts as you
have them curtained from me.

When you hold me in your arms
it feels so right and wonderful.
Does my response shock you?
I hope not as I am not shocked
by your responses.

I don't know what to do with these
feelings and thoughts you have
awakened in me. You, my sweet,
will have to help me with these
feelings and thoughts.

Can we accept how and what we
feel? Will we be able to find and
accept happiness, friendship, love, and
concern for one another? Yes, my
love, I believe we will.

Fall Is On It's Way
by Tara Janine White - age 12

The days are getting shorter, leaves soon will start to fall,
Better put away the big beach ball.
All the leaves will start to change their color,
Some leaves will become brighter, some will become duller.
It will soon start to pour down with rain,
Rain can be good or just a big pain.
The trees rustle as the wind starts to blow,
On the ground there will soon be snow.
Better get ready for school, both girls and the guys.
Here comes mom with the school supplies.
School will be here before anyone realizes it.
Better double check that your school clothes fit.
Most birds will soon fly south, behind them they will leave their nest.
The bears will find a cave and in it have a real long rest.
The end of summer is very, very near,
When summer is gone fall will be here!

White Buffalo
by Running Elk Woman

I hear her speak.
Her words are strong,
Like a million Buffalo
Thundering along.

Her words are
Peace, Love, and Life;
No more strife
And no more fight.

Hear, our people;
We are still alive,
With the sacred wisdom
That lives inside.

As one nation,
We come alive
To fulfill the dreams
That live inside.

War Embraces Humanity
by Steed Whittaker

Insanity born, on me you depend
   in the hell that you thrive
Violence, destruction, never an end
   all I need to survive
You can't hide me, I'm a festering sore
   never have I felt shame
I claim your young and old, wealthy and poor
   to me they're all the same
Claim your civilized, there's no need for me
   but I know it's a lie
All your talk is cheap, when you disagree
   my name is what you cry
I have made you wise, creative, and strong
   great leaders of a few
You can't deny me, no matter how wrong
   I'm the dark side in you
I'm your claim to fame, I make history
   and let you keep the score
Carry the curse of your own misery
   I'm known by all as War

Childhood Memories
by Tasha S. Wigley - age 18

As I walk in the halls. People stare and whisper.
Why do they do that? Just because I'm deaf? Shy?
"Look!" They say "She's short and ugly, she's too shy
and never talks, she's deaf and dumb!"
Go away. Keep away we don't want you to be our friend.
You're too shy and stupid!
I feel so lonely, I can't stand it anymore. I want to hide so they
can stop hurting my feelings.
I can't stand the whispers and stares anymore.
No friends, oh how I wish I had friends.
Why are they doing this to me?

They do not know the real me, since I'm shy and dear,
then why do they hate me so much?
What did I do? Why won't they give me a chance?
I try not be to be shy,
I try to listen,
I try to make friends, yet only a few
will be my friends.
I wish, oh how I wish they will give me a chance to be their friends.

Good-bye
by Miranda D. Zetocha - age 17

Words, that usually flow out, are caught
The only thing flowing are your tears.
If only the tears could say the words
 The words, that if they'd flow,
 Would mean everything.
Looking around in blurry vision
Trying to catch a glimpse.
Blinking your sadness away
 To see the last vision of what brought a smile
 to your face, a twinkle to your eye.
Hoping that soon, even in a whisper,
your words would come back to you.
 But they don't.
Your tears of despair come rushing out.
Through your blurry vision, you catch your
 final glimpse,
Your final glimpse of good-bye.

Answers to Problems That Living Imposes
by John Wilhite

Those age old stories that history discloses
Of honor and death and betrayal in life
Are answers to problems that living imposes.

For this cycle of living and problems it poses
We've answers for all - for both husband and wife -
Those age old stories that history disclose.

The old, old tales of the thorns and the roses,
Of ancestral struggles and coping with strife
Are answers to problems that living imposes.

Don't find then too late, (as in when your term closes)
Look in them to solve the conflicts in life -
Those age old stories that history disclose.

In the sagas of old, be they of China or Moses
With which books on the shelves and traditions are rife
Are answers to problems that living impose.

For each cycle in living and problems it poses
We've models before us for guidance in life.
Those age old stories that history discloses
Are answers to problems that living imposes.

Time To Go
by Jennifer Williams - age 15

I know I must go.
God tells me it's time
To enter His kingdom
And leave all behind.

I don't want to leave
Mommy and Daddy so sad.
Yet I want to see heaven
And meet my granddad.

Born prematurely,
I struggle to live.
As tubes poke my body,
My heart starts to give.

Lying in the incubator,
Just waiting to die,
God comes and tells me
There's no need to cry.

He says, "My dear child,
It is your time to go.
Your parents will be fine.
In their suffering, they will grow."

God places His peace
In my tiny, fragile heart.
And I finally decide
To willingly depart.

Through A Little Girl's Eye's
by Melanie A. Williams - age 14

It all started when
When I felt left out and hurt
Like an animal kept in a pen
Like my face had been smashed in dirt
I kept looking for a way to escape
The troubles and trials
Reach out of the red tape
Step out of this small area
I thought I had to go
The extreme way I thought wasn't so
Again I was wrong
And I have learned
Now I can go on and sing my song
And for this I have burned
I dream of the day
I will be reunited
There won't be much to say
I may decide to share
My story with my friends
Maybe if I dare
For on them I can depend
For they did drop in
And for that I am grateful
They will help me to the end
For they have been with me from the start
To them love I send
And I hope we never part
My life will go on
I will not close this curtain

Sea Water
by Silas H. Williams, III

A body of water full of fish, a place
where we get our favorite seafood dish.
A body of water full of salt, a place
where fish are caught.
Waves that are furious, waters that are
serious.
Waves you cannot tame, waves that are
never the same.
Waves that wash shore, water that surfers
wish to score.
Waves that move with gravity, waters that
have a deep cavity.

Untitled
by Daniel "Church" Wilson

When you look into deaths face
What is it that you see
Is it fear, hate, or peace
In that face that you dare to be

Can you peer upon the past
Or gaze upon the future that you dread
Does your flag fly at half mast
As you slumber within your bed

Shall you destroy the ones you love
Open your heart and share what I see
Embrace the stars from up above
For they are your only true key

Only then can you welcome death
If that is what you wish to choose
Shall you take your final breath
And play the game that you must lose

My Mamma's Eyes
by Ellen L. Wilson-Myles

Mirror, why do I see my mamma's eyes
conjured up like windows of my soul?
Gazing back at me...
I remember.
Last time mamma's eyes looked back at me
full of pain.

Eyes, longing to be understood
apologizing for leaving
pleading for forgiveness
Mamma's eyes so sad for me.
 Windows, cloudy with future tears to shed
 Why Mamma's eyes cry out my soul?

Lately, cloudy, rainy days fill my soul
 tears fall in storms all around.
Is ther strength through endurance?
Mamma! I can't see
 I am so weak
 My spirit is being lost in the puddle
 at my feet!

They don't see me Mamma,
 or see the puddle at my feet.
So, I dry my eyes, Mamma
 tears run backwards
they drown my heart.

Today, Mamma, guess what?
 They say:
 Baby, you've got your Mamma's eyes!

Untitled
by Rachael Winkler - age 17

Do you know who you are?
Cause I know who I am.
I am a person who can only do one thing.
Be myself.
Everyone wants me to be someone else.
I will be myself and no one else.
You need to learn this so you can do this.
I will learn what I want to know.
I will learn at my own pace.
I try to control what I do.
If I screw up, good.
Who cares?
Not I.
You don't care, do you?
Because I know you don't.
There are only three people that care,
and they are as follows; me, myself, and I.
What do you think of that?
I don't care for your opinion nor my own.
what's that you say nobody cares.
That might be the truth. I know that I care for all and for nothing.
A paradox.
That is what my life is, an endless paradox.
Or perhaps not.
Maybe it is a black hole sucking everyone in.
Taking them to the farthest reaches of the universe.
Showing them new things, and new ways to do them.
Showing them how to forget all they have learned to really live.
Perhaps not.

Natures Touch
by Loraine A. Wojtysiak

What would this world be
without scenic sights
Without the holiday sight-seer
delighting to life?
Or the stay-at-home common folk
enjoying their land
Appreciating harvest aplenty
made from their hands?
What would this world be
without natures touch?
We all know the answer -
simply NOT MUCH!

Like A Rose
by W. R. Woods, Jr.

Is one Like a
rose ---
Which God does
compose?
One blossoms through life's
stages---
As petals---rapidly turning life's
pages.
One is young, fresh---as toward maturity
one does grow---
The opportunity for one's beauty to
show.
As a rose---one must have sunshine
and rain---
And tender loving care---as well as
some pain.
One should live life to the
hilt---
Before one's petals begin to
wilt.

Dare To Discover
by Bethany Wright - age 12

Dare to discover
The meaning of life
All of its beauty
All that's in sight,
Dare to discover
How we are made
How beauty was created
How all can be saved.

Arrow Head
by Oranout Xaysena - age 18

Long hours
Different time zone
A bird set free:
Flying
but still caged
Traveling
but with no sense of direction
Wrapped up in a twilight zone
Spinning consciously, consistently, carefully
Feels like sinking into a bottomless abyss
Examined by curious eyes
Treading along the cage floor
Cupped hands catch sands in an Hourglass
unlike grains they filter through
A yellow path leading home
to many worlds
Like a shedding snakes skin that sheds itself
I take on three different wholes
An Arrow Head points and displays the truth
to a path once taken by a youth.

Enchanted Love
by Robyn Anne Wright - age 14

A butterfly lands on a kitten's nose,
A fairy's tear on a red, red rose.

The smell of gardenias menacing through the air,
A princess in a castle brushing her long red hair.

The deep blue waters still in the pond,
A mother and daughter unicorn share a special bond.

The frogs are all princes without a special kiss,
Everyone unites and relates in heavenly bliss.

Then the sorcerers steps in and waves her mystical hand,
She steals the prince and lays a plague over the land.

She laughs because she knows she has won and says "Stop me if you dare,"
The fairy dies, the frog cries, and the princess cuts her hair.

The princess enters depression, she cuts herself and scars,
She becomes captive of her life, her heart enclosed in bars.

Hopelessness overwhelms her, fear becomes her life.
She dies lonely and depressed engulfed in pain and strife.

But when she arrives in heaven, peace returns in the fall.
What they say is true, love it conquers all.

Change
by Heather Wyan - age 15

Sitting in the darkness, Thinking of the past,
Wondering why the good times, Never seemed to last.

Childhood meant freedom, From all restricting bands,
Never any worries, Only helping hands.

But soon those days of carefree joy, Began to pass you by,
Life got hard and full of tears, Too many to even cry.

Soon your friends began to change, Become sophisticated,
But if it were up to you, Adolescence could've waited.

High school left you drowning, In a sea of unknown faces,
It's here your past just slips away, Leaving few clues or traces.

Soon true love will find its way, Deep into your heart,
Amidst your many lovestruck words, You vow to never part.

Despite your many hopes and dreams,
You find true love's not what it seems.

Soon comes the sad and lonely day, The day you pack and move away,
Leaving behind home, family, and friends, Only now can the rest of your life begin.

After years of work and challenge, You find you've settled down,
A job, a family, a happy home, You're truly safe and sound.

It took some time and lots of thought, To make me realize,
That all this change and hardship, Is life's lesson in disguise.

First Kiss
by Tisha Lynn Yahnke - age 16

As simple as the spring rain
there will never be another one like it again.
As innocent as a newborn's smile
it will last only a second
but it will make a lifetime worthwhile.
As gentle as a mother's touch
nothing but a gesture...but it will mean so much.
As free as the wind
on a midsummer's night,
it has to be given time to develop
and when it does it will feel just right.
As sweet as candy from the candy jar
you'll grab it up in a second
and carry it afar.
As pretty as a picture
taken on a winter's brightest day,
you will be lost in the moment
and it will take your breath away.
As silent as nature's voice
whispering through the trees,
you'll have confused thoughts at first
but it will put you right at ease.
As soft and subtle as the summer's first dew
so precious...it will last your whole life through.
As fluffy as the sky
to see it will be pure bliss,
and forever in your mind will linger
the memory of your first kiss.

The Masquerade
by Samantha B. Yamin - age 15

The world is a masquerade ball.
We all wear masks.
And costumes on our souls.
We are afraid of each other.
Afraid of ourselves.
At the masquerade ball,
Some try to be more than they are.
Or are they dressed up as less?
Our costumes are made up of all things.
Some are just make-up, clothes.
Some are voices. Our personalities are acts.
Most are living out a drama.
The kindest are the cruelest.
The cruelest have the softness souls.
But when does this masquerade end?
When do our true hearts get the starring role?

Below the Stars
by Fan Yang - age 17

I appear like a sea gull from sky.
I have a new goal.
I am as carefree as a bird.
I drink the lemonade from big blue cups
until it is empty.
I watch the guy's surf under the waves
and wonder if my prince charming is among them.

Each night I open the window in my room
and sneak out.
Be quiet little birdie, shuu,
shuu, shuu, I whisper
as I tiptoe from roof to roof...
Around mid-night,
I lay by the chimney below the stars
and drink in the view of twinkling eyes.

I am a short skinny Asian girl.
I am seventeen years-young.
I imagine myself in a world
without the sadness or the worries.
The sea gull watches me
from its dark corner.
It shakes its wings,
and fly pass me
far, far, away...

A Place
by Jill Yavorsky - age 13

Somewhere out far
But near enough,
Lies a place,
A place to dream.
A place to wonder.
A place for you to shine and beam.
No one else knows
Of your special place.
For this place
Lies in the state of the mind.

Angel
by Alishia Yeater - age 16

Mama's
Sweet
Baby
Boy

A
Few
Years
Experience
And
A
Source
Of
Pride

Swimming
Through
A
Downward
Spiral
Made
Through
A
Conscious
Effort

Mother's
Love
Will
Never
Die

Empty Space
by Alyssa Yom - age 14

An empty space within my heart,
Where some love should be,
But instead there is pain,
Where nobody can see.

Hurt and anger flood my mind,
In this ocean I can't find,
Peace within me.

Hidden from everyone a deep
dark space,
No expression upon my face,
Dodging everything that is shot,
But learning from every lesson
that is taught.

Good from bad,
I know it all.
From what I know I try
not to fall.
Yet every time I stand,
I always seem to slip,
But from the faith I have
within my heart,
I know the beginning from
which to start.

The Longing
by Calvin D. Zenga

Your presence brings
    into my life, relief -
Yet at the same time
    it also brings me grief.
So close, so close,
    yet so far away...
I cannot touch you tomorrow,
    nor can I touch you today.
You're a precious gift
    just out of reach,
Like beautiful white sand
    without a beach,
Like a clear blue sky
    filled with clouds of gray...
I cannot touch you tomorrow,
    nor can I touch you today.
I long, I dream to feel
    your soft, gentle touch.
It's a longing I wish
    I did not feel this much.
There are things to be said,
    things I cannot say,
And I cannot touch you tomorrow
    nor can I touch you today.

The Voices
by Cassandra Zick - age 15

Do you hear it
The ringing in my head
I'll stay right here
Safe in my bed

You took my dreams way
You gave me nightmares
Take it out of my head
The ringing in my ears

Let me sleep
Go away
I don't understand
A word you say

You make no sense
Let me sleep
Stop the talking
Take a flying leap

If I could only
Fall asleep today
I would wake-up
Somewhere far away

You've locked away my sanity
Give me back my key
Go away forever
Please let me be

Appreciaton of Love
by Jessica Zimmerman - age 15

Sometimes I feel like you are the only
person that understands me,
the only one who loves me unconditionally
and takes me far from lonely.
I wish our love lasts forever
and the dreams we dream come true,
for I want to spend my life beside you,
and love you without condition too.
The day that I first met you
I knew that this would last,
that we would spend our lives together,
a better husband I could not ask.
Your face graces me with a smile,
your tender love shows through
I know that you must really love me,
hopefully as much as I love you.
I've seen you grow before me
I know I've grown with you,
I feel so safe and at ease,
I've felt this way with few.
I never thought I'd be so close
to someone in this life,
but now I know true love exists,
and that it exists in you.

The River Travel
by Agnes Zyzdryn - age 14

I traveled down the river
And it gave me a shiver,
The water was rocking me slightly
The sound was lightly.

An alligator popped it's head up
And his jaw went snap,
I stiffened like a log,
Turned the canoe around the bog.

I paddled stiffly, with a splish-splash
And got stuck in the marsh.
The wind blowing softly in my hair
I don't know if I can bare.

    The nature is in full bloom.
    I hope we don't stumble upon a monsoon
    Now I got the hang of the paddling thing,
    I feel like I'm going to sing.

    Now we're stopping for some brunch,
    Great, I'm starving for lunch.
    Now we're heading back,
    Oouch! Something bit me on my neck.

    I saw a snake slithering.
    I noticed, no one was littering.
    I saw a piece of trash by a rock,
    It was a dirty, old sock.

    We got to the first dam,
    It was guarded by Sam.
    He helped us flip over,
    We reached for cover.

    We landed on shore
    Please, no more.

Treasures
Chapter Three

Verses Magazine
Sponsored Competitions
Winners and selected works from the
Browning Competition
Haiku Competition
Longfellow Awards

Browning Competition

First Place

Why Do We Celebrate Christmas?
by Donna Kay

Tell me about Christmas and why it comes so late
Asked little Mary Catherine as she leaned against the gate
Some people tell me Jesus never celebrated life
Doesn't everyone believe in him, is that why there is strife?

My dearest Mary Catherine as her mother use to say
Christmas is a **symbol--or love and kindness every-day**
Christmas is **the spirit** of one born, so long ago-- and--
we celebrate in winter **new beginnings**, like pure snow

We celebrate the birth of Christ at this time--each year
As the **presence** of **his spirit** is so **vivid**, and **so near**
It's a time of **serenity** with stillness all around
You can **feel his holy spirit**, as he walks, without a sound

It's the time of year folks **stop**--and listen to his **word**
It's a shame, but it's just about the only time he's heard
Every-one's too busy and just trying to survive
They forget why he was born, and why we're all alive

Yes, some people don't believe, and other's don't agree,
as to why he came to earth to watch over you and me
It doesn't matter **where**, or if Christ was born-**that** day
It only matters that he came, and that he's here to stay

Christ celebrates life **through us**, each day of every year
And if you listen--you will **hear him** whisper in your ear
"Come celebrate my child, Come celebrate with me
Although you may not see me, all you need is to--**believe**"

Second Place

His Glory's in Plain Sight
by Carol Aagard

I climbed the lofty mountain path so I could talk to God,
But failed to see the forest flowers that lined that path I trod.
I could not see the majesty of leaf, or bud, or tree,
Nor hear the sweet symphonic notes the birds sang just for me.
I didn't see the pearly drops of dew that glistened there,
Nor draw within my hollow chest the mellow, scented air.
With doubting, faithless heart I knelt upon the loamy sod,
And out I poured my soul in prayers to Abram's unseen God.
So wearied down with burdens was my mind of mortal sin.
I hadn't seen the glory of His precious light within.
I pled for merciful forgiveness--I had been so wrong.
My burden somewhat lifted as I heard the robin's song.
Its throbbing tune reminded me of newness, life, and spring,
As I continued in my prayer, my heart began to sing.
The doubt was lifted from my soul, I knew my prayer was heard.
My loving Father waited there to answer every word.
And now I saw the leafy garland, bird and bud, and tree,
I realized that God was there and very plain to see.
Enthroned in every creature is His heav'nly Spirit's light,
From every living thing it shines, *His Glory's in Plain Sight*.

Third Place

Bird Song
by Carol E. Southerland

I sat amidst God's sunshine
Caressed by gentle breeze.
His Spirit hovered round me.
I listened consciously.

He sent two gentle doves
To linger for awhile.
Their presence so delightful,
It made my spirit smile.

He sent a dapper jay
Dressed in his Sunday blues.
He hopped and skipped about
Aware that God is true.

He sent a humble sparrow
In muted brown and gray.
He knows that God is faithful
And guides us lest we stray.

He sent a dashing cardinal
Its feathers blazing red.
Reminding me of God's great love.
That's why Christ's blood was shed.

And in that quiet moment
My soul felt calm and release
From earthly cares and sorrow.
His Spirit brought sweet peace.

Mileage Check
by V. June Collins

Yes,
I have laugh lines and crowfeet
Plainly etched upon my face.
At times, feel could do without
But to ponder would be a waste.

I'm told they're lines of character
Just a map of likely codes.
That clutter up smooth, clear skin
With lines that resemble roads.

Cover distance that I've traveled
Like mile posts, recording miles.
Add on fuel it took to here arrive
Required both scowl and smiles.

Life has been a good one, special,
Filled in variety of clouds and sun.
Along way, each day was registered.
I've earned each and every one.

Sometimes, still feel I'm youthful
Until the mirror shakes its head.
Saying, Sister you're nearly ancient
Of't times can hardly get out of bed.

You take each step, one at a time
And I almost never, see you run.
I think you'd better look again,
You're sure not thirty one.

Holy Is Thy Name
by Rachelle L. Felmet

I come into your house
To worship and to praise
I lift my heart...I lift my hands
For Holy is Thy Name
How great art Thy mercies
How forgiving is Thine heart
That when you forgive our sins
You will also say "I forgot"
Just to have a mortal friend
Right here on earth today
As loving and forgiving
In each and every way
Would be a very special gift
Mere words could not convey
But we all know that mortal man
Needs God...not man...
To wash his sins away
It's so comforting to know
How very much you care
That when I stumble or when I fall
You are always there
Praise your Holy Name.

Memories
by Raymond Fenech

Music flows through the mind
notes screaming merciless tunes
pasts that are rather forgotten
creating futures unknown,
      in sand dunes.

Sadness breaks waters
wasting the essence of life,
they gush into a wine glass
their saltiness like magic potion,
      wisdom's eternal drive.

Heart beat pounds my chest,
death beckoning, making its claim,
calling from an abyss, eternal nothing,
praying Him for a sign,
      to help, or to blame.

The time left, it escape me
aging is the destiny of all men
it eats away, corrodes them in crypts
as one by one they cross over;
      and life is like a myth.

The worse is like nightmares
unwanted, uncontrollable, never fades;
trying to win knowing all's lost;
these memories are like wintry frost,
      dissolve in gloomy summer shades.

The Battle Just Begun
by Art R. Milkes

My daughter, she is Born Again,
and knows the Lord's removed her sin,
and knows exactly where she'll be,
from now and through eternity.

She married a non-Christian, though,
who has been blessed, but doesn't know
the magnitude of the reward
that's his, if he accepts the Lord.
And so, although, it breaks my heart,
I've watched the struggle from the start.
She witnesses. She talks the talk,
but struggles now to walk the walk.

And while it hurts, I hate to say,
right now the struggle's going his way.
And to avoid the marriage stress,
so often she will acquiesce.

I know the devil thinks he's won.
The battle, though, has just begun.
My daughter's fighting for the day
her husband finds the Christian way.

I Believe
by Robert Charles Steinmeyer

I believe in you my dear
And that we both should be sincere
The night one should live in fear
And that I'll always love and be right here
My heart and mind don't always see so clear
But if we ever parted so strayed my dear
I'd shed a lifetime of heart broken tears
So believe in me as I speak so fondly for all to hear
Of the lovely lady in my heart I hold so close and dear

Mushroom Mystic
by Extry R. Sarff

Glide through the shadows along a gravely shore
Close to the melody of a rippling stream;
Searching for mushrooms, you'll find them galore
In mossy dells like a beautiful dream,
Lavender coral, spreading hedge hog, beautiful golden chantrell,
Angel wings, king bolete, and delectable black morel.
They spin a web of fantasy in nature's secluded glen.
You find yourself in the emerald Isles; home of the little men.

Close your eye, hear a Catbird cry; 'tis the song of a Leprechaun.
Hear the note from a Bluebird throat; sure, 'tis a Fairy's flute.
Part the fern by a little burne, look down through the maiden hair.
See on top big flat mushrooms. little Elves dancing there.
With your basket full, time to return, skip out into the light;
In your eye when you sigh, there's a smile of pure delight.

The Beauty of Prayer
by Kathy Schroeder

The beauty of prayer is often unseen.
It's not just the written word.
It's felt in the soul, a silent plea,
a longing to be heard.
You can't always see the power of God,
yet it's with us in many ways.
It's in the sun, the clouds, the wind,
the bow that tints rainy days.
The weary hands of a worker who toils
are a sign of life-long prayer,
as are the tears of a mother at birth
as she cradles the life in her care.
A prayer can be seen in the face of a boy
who can't wait for his life to start.
The prayer for that boy can be heard in the tears
that flow from his mother's heart.
Listen for prayers that aren't spoken aloud,
let your heart be your eyes each day.
With a few kind words and arms open wide,
let us greet bleeding hearts in God's way.
For blood doesn't have to be seen to be spilled,
or a heart be exposed to be raw.
We must listen for pain behind unspoken prayers
to fulfill the command of God's law.

Haiku Competition

First Place

Haiku in Seasons
by Edyth V. Harris

Butterflies at rest
Trembling on wind-swept leaves
Spring's motion picture

Second Place

Silent Bells
by Anne Marie Legan

Tiny bells tinkle
From lilies of the valley
Muted white music.

Third Place

Untitled
by Alan Frame

Feline lightning bolts
Flash across the Savannah;
Cheetahs on the chase.

Clouds Kiss
by N Loy Higgins, R.A.

Two white clouds kiss in
celebration of evening's
colorful sunset.

Untitled
by Roger D. Martinez

Snowflake falls to earth
one more, then another, soon
my gloves are covered

Untitled
by Marieta McMillen

Standing sentinels
along the super-highways
millions of billboards

Untitled
by A.R. Milkes

Winter's cold has passed
Wake up and smell the flowers
Spring has sprung at last.

Untitled
by Marjorie Millison

Wild geese darken sky.
Barren trees tend empty nests.
The first snowflake falls.

Untitled
by Louise Norman

Small brown dog, sleeping,
Loving her human, always,
Waiting, peacefully.

Longfellow Competition

First Place

Ghost Ship
by Marjorie Millison

A ghostly ship sweeps through the night
like a pale and winged moth in flight.
At the helm, a silhouette, dark and lone,
pursues a course the wind has flown.
An eerie spectacle, bow turned to sea,
what mission, what purpose, - what destiny?
What dream - what urgency lashes him onward?
Is he fleeing into darkness - or flying dawnward?
A specter clutched in the first of the night,
etched bloodless gray by the moon's deathly light.
What hound at his heels, driving him on?
Is he captain of his ship - or is he a pawn?

Ever onward, his sails whip the night,
awaiting a dawn - a fringe of light.
This strange man and his ship - are they what they seem,
or is this the gossamer webbing of a dream?
This seeker, who knows not what he's after,
who knows no home, no peace, no laughter.
This ghostly pair, clinging in flight
drop into the abysmal depths of the night.
"Wait - turn back," I call to him,
but he's consumed by the night and the vision grows din;
just a breeze ahead of a glorious dawn -

in darkness, racing on and on.

Second Place

In Love For Life
by Alan Frame

You wonder if I'll love you when you're old--
When highlights of your gracefulness will fade.
You worry that my passion will grow cold
When wrinkles inescapably invade.
A daffodil will flower, then decay--
And emerald grass will wither into brown.
But even though your crown of gold will gray,
I promise that I'll never let you down.
When aging orders youth to disappear,
Your loveliness will certainly decline.
But, nonetheless, I'll cherish you, my dear;
Your beauty from within will always shine.
  Although your prime is destined to depart,
  You'll stay forever young within my heart.

Third Place

Secret Eyes
by Cherry Mitchell

With secret eyes one beholds,
A love that is quiet and untold.
It's cast upon a sea of blue,
And touched with a ray of sun so true.

A gentle spirit outshines the sun,
A caring hand held back to none.
A youthful heart is gay and free,
Bringing joy, such as thee.

From a distance, one can see,
What the secret hidden might be.
You hide it well behind a veil,
Protected from ne'er-do-wells.

You hide behind a wall of jest,
To guard that secret, lest.
A careless and selfish heart,
Learns the secret and departs.

Gourmet Mania?
by Rita Lurie

Folks in Malaysia are lunching
New health food craze they are munching

Queen termites the treat
"Preserved" or fresh meat
Two inch long tidbits a-crunching!

Treasures
Chapter Four

Dedications
Literary works and dedications
requested by the
contributing authors

Jeffery Wayne Turner

> *I would like to dedicate this poem "Our Friend Rhonda" to a sweet woman who has touched many lives with her warmth, laughter, and most all, her endearing love. Rest in God's Merciful Arms Tonight.*
>
> *To: Mrs. Rhonda Taylor Downey*
>
> *Your Friend,*
>
> *Jeffery Turner*

Our Friend Rhonda

Our friend Rhonda didn't like seeing people lonely and sad,
our friend Rhonda could make us feel happy and glad.
Rhonda was a dear gentle girl,
she was better than a box full of lovely pearls.
Our friend Rhonda said, love was a must for all,
because, without it we would surely fall.
Our friend Rhonda was one of a kind,
our friend Rhonda will always be in our hearts and minds.
Our friend Rhonda will forever be missed,
But, we can always remember her hugs and her many friendships.

Joy Wolfgang

Imaginary Friend

God sent him into my life for seven years to give me guidance.

Though he's gone, he's my imaginary friend. He will always be with me. He said, "stay calm in any given situation."

My friend lives in Brooklyn, N.Y.. He wants me to be realistic and relax. He says, "I'm okay."

Guy was there for me everytime I called with a problem. Now he wants me to gain independence and work out my own problems. By telling me not to be afraid of anything or anybody helped me become my own person.

He taught me many things that helped me with my bi-polar disorder better known as manic depression.

He taught me not to put people on a pedestal. You get hurt when you put people higher than yourself, always putting yourself down.

He was my teacher, a psychologist. He taught me to think for myself. He says, "love is caring and sharing," and this is a good start. He taught me how to laugh and cry. He taught me to be still, wait, and have patience.

He would say, "you're there and I'm here." He wanted me to build my life here and know he's not coming back.

He taught me when and how to say "no," to set boundaries with people and not do things I'm uncomfortable with.

In the end he said, "he wanted to see me comfortable and happy." I'm comfortable having my own apartment with my cat. I drive a car, have a part-time job which gives my life the balance I need and I feel content.

God used him to transform my life and this was the beginning of my first miracle.

To Guy, my Psychotherapist, who helped me work the manic depression out of my system and put me on the right path.

To my Psychiatrist, Dr. Manoj P. Patel who found the right combination of medicine.

A special thank you to Dr. Patel's Assistant Psychotherapist, Ms. Alice Lohr who is always there for me and is treating me for a chemical imbalance.

Treasures
Chapter Five

Treasures Around the World

Selected literary works from the competitors in the Summer 1997 Iliad Literary Awards Program

If Only I Could Have Been...
by Harmony Raylen Abejuela - age 17

A celestial body that orbits the sun,
A creation filled with pulchritude made.
Astonishingly marvelous and mysterious
Its elegance never fade.

I could have been this being,
This creation worthy of praise,
Lighting up the world
In so many diverse ways.

I could have been this masterpiece,
Its parts intricately created.
Bringing awe to all,
Witnesses become elated.

Eroded with pressure and deletrious influence,
No wonder I could not reach my goal.
Filled with avarice and inner contempt,
Facing a battle within my vituperative soul.

No longer angelic, but opinionated and possessive -
I have blown my chance to be like this.
Worries now fill me overwhelmingly
With regrets for not being a heavenly bliss.

When would I have another chance
To change the way I live,
To concentrate on the present
Not just to take but also to give.

Through God anything is possible.
With compassion, He forgives any sin,
Through Him I can have an impact on the world
If only I could have been -------- a COMET!!!

if i only had...
by Dee Ann Ackerson - age 15

one day in my childhood,
one minute to be good,
one hour to be bad,
one second to say "hey dad,"

one field to run and play,
one word to talk and say,
one boy to like me too,
one river to muddy up my shoe,

one flower to play he loves me,
one sunbeam to chase a honey bee,
one christmas to open all the presents,
one easter to find all the eggs they've sent,

one chance to turn back the clock,
instead those days are under key and lock,
they are gone forever,
so never ever, say never.

Oklahoma City
by "Rev." Peter E.A. Addo

Our illusions were shattered in Oklahoma City,
So too were the theories of our universal themes.
The pain of intolerance,
The subtleties of class distinctions raised their head.
In our ill fated quest for perfection
In this less perfect world.
Even God is surprised sometimes
At what his best creation can do.
And we all felt helpless,
We only knew how helpless we were,
Not being able to change anything.
Does God make the rules as we go on?
We cry, we fret, we need answers
We need someone to blame
But all is left is you, forgive me
I thought we loved you.
And some looked at each other
And the body count mounted
Up in Oklahoma City.
Why, Oklahoma City?
How else can God be God, we asked?
Exit the children, center stage
In the end faith survived,
And through faith
We go to know each other in Oklahoma City
Just as it should be.
Exit the children, center stage
With the light still burning
We'll never be the same.
Now we have to learn to live with ourselves
Just as we are.

"Forbidden Attraction"
by Allen L. Aggers

This day is gone, night not yet old
Love we once had, now has grown cold

With passion for life, a thing of the past
Searching for answers, for love that will last

Walking alone on this trail of tears
Crying out words that none hears

Confusion, frustration, are ruling the day
Til this new love of mine helped show me the way

To a life of new living, a place in my heart
Through the gift of your giving, a new place to start

As we make sweet love, your passionate action
Reminding me less of forbidden attraction....

"To the Person Who I Love"
by Cindy Joset Agreda - age 19

In between words that shout, and world's apart

There is a man I call my own.

He seems to know my every move. I can't imagine what the
next day will bring to my ailing bones.

You hair turned so white when I, said it was you I love.
You can't imagine how I tried, to leave a word behind.

And grasp your lonely hand.
The tides came in tonight I saw your soul it was swept away.

Alone I stood as you swept away.
A teary eye could not subdue, the pain I carry inside my sinful heart.

In sandy dunes, and grassy hills, I stared into a world of mystery
YOU CANNOT UNDERSTAND.

Nor can I reveal to you.
You look at me with a questioning stare.
The years go by slowly, and painfully, to my teary eyes.

You cried when I left your empty world.

Flying Home
by Jackson Ahrens

Troubled sleep over Arkansas
As the hush shadow of jet wing crosses the plains.
The vapor memory of the last two days
Dissolves in the distant cloudbank.
I am exhausted after the funeral,
Functioning on automatic pilot.
My eyes strain toward
The white blue line of horizon
And across my mind files
The consoling faces of family
And of people whose names are familiar.
They understand no more that I do
What has happened, what has ceased;
What it means to know that she will never
Answer my phone call, never send
Or receive a birthday card
Or a Christmas card with a hastily written
"I love you" underneath the stock sentiment
That came closest to expressing
That which is left unsaid,
Unresolved across a lifetime.
The shadow crosses below,
Silently making its passing known.
No words, just continuing on
To the life that waits for me,
That I hope can stretch enough
To hold all that I bring back with me.
Turbulence rises in the swift current,
The plane shakes and climbs above the white blanket
To take me home. Take me home.

Loneliness
by Elizabeth A. Aiello

Loneliness is a formidable adversary not easily conquered.
Long walks and good books dispel it momentarily,
Dabbling in the past provides brief respite.
Friends create a fleeting illusion of comradery.
But loneliness will not be vanquished.
It always comes back.

Sweetness
by Samantha Aishman - age 18

O'er the land Sweetness walks, and he
thinks and breathes and smiles and talks.
Sweetness enjoys the beauty of the day whilst
he sweeps all cares away. Sweetness
laughs and cries and worries much and
always responds to my tender touch. My
Sweetness is mine to have and to hold.
May we always be together from young
to old.

The Man
by Samantha Aishman - age 18

His eyes are the color of dusty emeralds. In their depths is
visible innocence and sweetness. His lips are soft as cottonwood
fuzz. The kisses bourn on them so tender. His smile is bright
and warm, like the sunshine. The laughter trailing from such a
smile is treasured. His voice is deep and smooth as silk.
When he speaks, I listen intently. This boy, this man, I
know him well. He is mine and I am his. He is my
world. He is forever. He is the man.

The Pendulum
by Debra Beck Aker

A pendulum hang
within my chest

-no longer do I feel.

Weights,
that leave me paralyzed

-like, a clock that nears the end.

I listen,
to a steady sound...

and still, I'm letting go.

A miracle,
has raptured me

-I think it's now, I know

to pull the chains
of many years

-and raise a fresh new start

....so deep within
my heavy heart

-I feel the bleeding...part.

No longer ache
my weary soul

-as these chains I pull.

A clock that chimes
and lights the day

-never felt before.

A new beginning,
the pendulum raised
    ...the beating of my heart!

Loneliness
by Jennifer L. Akers - age 16

Loneliness fills the midnight sky,
with no one by my side.
I had all night to sit and ponder,
I had all day to walk and wander.
It's too awkward for such a silence,
frequently thinking about all the violence.
Loneliness is the sadness that fills inside,
sometimes the results are tears from my eyes.

Dream Catcher
by Donald P. Albertson, Jr.

Spidering thoughts caught
In a web of mystery
Spinning through your dreams
Weaving in and out of reality
All is closed to darkness
Only to give way to light
Every wish and dream dangling
Like morning dew upon silken threads
A net, a Dream Catcher
Filtering out nightmarish evils
Leaving only that which is desired
Deep within the dreamer's heart
Fantasy and truth woven
And cobwebbed deep within
The unseen self, the inner soul
Cocooned, awaiting the bloodthirst's
Return, growing tired of
Fine spun realities and craving
Fantasy's shimmering web of hope.

The Lord of Stars and Dance
by David Alexander

we came to this palace
without words,
bringing only gifts
to the lord of stars and dance.
to the one who sleeps
and makes the whole of dream surrender.
we hold the silver lies
of gold,
breath upon the sweetstone,
kindness to vision
and leapt in moving speeches.
he addressed us all from the bedside,
alone and just a shadow,
asked us to bend ear
to words that never came.
and the lord of stars and dance
lost his breath,
closed his eyes,
and sleeping still remains.

Sonnet LVI
by William L. Aliff

Enjoy the sun light,
Wish not the night its time;
The sun its place so bright,
And the universe once more refined.
The present so little to feel.
Through sense perceptions the image's face;
Only imagination to the future still.
Mere memory the past grace.
To time the present is small,
Suffering only a moment occupies.
Memory telling its duration to recall.
And the future its limit supplies.
Pain long lasting, resignation befalls.
In the end ceases with the call.

Live
by Kari Elizabeth Allen

Why do we live
It's so hard
We truly don't have a reason
We just know we're here
Some people say it's to help people
but if they weren't here we
wouldn't have to help them

When people die we cry
But why
We will die just the same
and one day no one will live

That is the only day that
people don't cry
It's a good day

Do we live to hear good sounds
or to see good sights
We don't know

I think we live for pleasure
but one day most of the
pleasure just went away
We still have to live here
in the hate even though
we don't know why

One Last Word
by Krystal Allen - age 14

One last word should not be good-bye
But it never is, have you ever wondered why
Maybe you don't want us to worry or cry.
Or maybe you didn't know you were going to die
Some obstacles are hard such as the death of a close
Friend
You're so much fun and had so much planned
Our senior year our last word would change to good
Luck
But since you left with the plan never to return
Our last words were in tears and they were you'll
Be loved and missed
You never know where or when your one last word will be.

First Times
by Michael W. Allen

You will always remember:
    The first time you met,
    The first time he gave you a rose,
    The first time she gave you a kiss
As you look through each others eyes
and say "I DO."
Those first times makes you whole.
When a tear falls from her eyes,
and the butterflies turn his insides,
You will face your family and friends
The first time together forever.

Treasures

The Monsters That They Fear
by April Alverson - age 13

Everyone in the world used to be a child,
A little kid that loved to run wild.

But every once in a while we would get scared,
Of things that we never should have feared.

We would tell our parents about the monster under our bed,
But actually it was made up in our head.

The monster in the closet was a popular one,
Because it always scared your daughter or son.

But nowadays the monsters they fear,
Don't make the noises that they used to hear.

The ones that they fear make a loud bang,
The sound of a gunshot through which a city it rang.

They fear drivebys in which they'd be killed,
The fear that their heart, soul, and mind would be filled.

When the adults were smaller and feared childhood fears,
They never had to cry the tears.

The tears from eyes which are shed,
When someone's friend is in a casket lying there DEAD.

Breeze
by Kathy Alverson - age 13

As I sit by the window
The breeze softly touches my face
Like a gentle, loving hand
Caressing my cheek.
It seems to whisper
Calming words of joy
And as the movement of the breeze
Tosses and messes my hair
I feel absolute calmness
That silences me
For this feeling is beyond word comprehension
The only person who understands it is me
As I emerge
From this grateful feeling
I feel sadness and hope
For this feeling will return

The Author To Her Essay
by Alexis Amber - age 16

With angry thoughts do I think,
Of the depth within my mind you sink.
A twisted smile upon my face while I toss and turn,
In my eyes, watching you burn.
That you could be so fierce
An animal you pierce
My heart with a deadly stone,
Causes my heart to scream at the thought of a clone.
A baby crying for lack of attention,
Neighbors notice and are forced to mention.
With each ruthless complaint
I seek unfairly for a saint
For whom I can take credit,
Even though I own no debit.
Through no fault of your own,
I am a dog wanting another bone.

Newborn Awakening
by Brooke Anderson

New eyes awaken to the burning sun
Bird song hushed winds become one
Surroundings are so surreal to me
Newness clusters around me
My hands are small but not helpless
Eyes fuzzy but not useless
Speaking softly are the voices
Standing out from all the jumbled noises
Murmurs hush me to sleep
It is love that I seek
Teach me
Shape me into your image
Hand to me hope
Dreams
Potent visions
Cry out frustrations
Newborn Awakening
Innocence

You & I
by Stacey Michelle Anderson - age 15

From the time that I was little
Right to my teen-age years
You would kiss my boo-boo's
You would wipe my tears.
From the first time I learned to walk,
Until the time I climbed my first stair
You were the one to help me
You were the one to care.
From a sweet little girl,
To a snotty attitude
You put up with me
You didn't change your mood.
Through my deep depression,
Right to my happy high
You were there for me
You would never lie.
From now until forever
Until your old and gray
I will love you and be there
For you each and every day.

Mankinds Tears
by Lauraine Andren

Weep not for me, as my tears are ended. Weep instead for each other, for what was, for what is and for what shall be. Weep until the face of mankind is washed pure no more tears will be shed and the glory of man is without blemish, and he has spread to the far reaches of the stars and man is without number and his days counted as many as there are grains of sand in all the oceans.

Final Words
by Nicole Andreyko - age 14

I slowly wonder what life was like,
When pain was numb and not felt.
I slowly dream of nightmares to come,
Visions brought on by a belt.
Blood and death stain my hands,
And razors are on the floor.
I grip my body tight and fall to my knees,
Praying no more.
My life flashes before my eyes,
And suddenly I understand.
I no longer want to die,
But now it's too late to demand.
For now I lay here, drowning in my blood.
Always wishing, that I had been loved.
But no I had been different,
Never given the chance.
My life was like a nightmare,
And always a new dance.
Maybe if someone had cared, just even a bit.
I would not have gone and done what I did.
But now it's too late,
Too late to take it back.
No one will know,
What my life ever lacked.

Forever In My Heart
by Gerardo L. Angulo

Mother, you will always be
the most important person in my life.
I know that your love
will always shine upon me
like a diamond in the sky.
Forever in my heart, you will be
like a sacred treasure that I shall keep.
I want you to know
that God will not separate us for long
for my faith in Him is very strong.
Our love was destined to be
a kind of love that will reach immortality.

Forever in my heart, you will live
to you, a crown of merit, God will give.
You touched the lives of so many people
here on earth, you were one of God's special instruments.
In the kingdom of heaven, you will find your reward
with your guidance, I will feel secure.
Mother, even though we are physically apart,
you are the love
that will burn forever in my heart.

In loving memory of my mother, Mrs. Bertha Maxie Angulo (1922 - 1995)

Dream Girl
by Giovanni Anselmo - age 15

Dream girl, dream girl, your beauty is so great
I can not wait to see you again

Every time I close my eyes you are there
You are so beautiful

Your smile so warm and friendly
like a warm spring day

Your hair so shiny and beautiful
like rays of the warm morning sun

You are so beautiful in many ways
I can not name them all

Dream girl, dream girl, I love you so
So I beg you..please don't go

In This Wish
by Rhia Antweiler - age 14

In this wish
You would stop the car
And talk to me
You would reach for me
Like you never have before

But this is just a dream
A cold snakeskin dream
Killed and reinvented
And passed on to someone new

But it is always you
Always leaving,
Always coming back

You slip through the noose around your neck
Nothing I can do can make you stay

I am listening to the cars outside
And you are inside every single one.

The River
by Brenda Lee Appel

A river is constant and ever flowing
It pushes onward and has tremendous force
Like someone in love, cheeks afire and always glowing
Don't try to stop a river just let it run its course.

Although a river is never straight and narrow
It has to have its bends and turns
Watch for sharp rocks and under tows
If you don't look ahead, a lesson you will surely learn.

A river can be clear and refreshing
Or it can be like a dark cloud
The water will sometimes ripple and almost sing
Or it can rush and roar real loud.

A river is a force of nature
But as long as you respect it, and ride it with style
Because without a river nothing would grow I'm sure
Just like without love a person wouldn't smile.

So you can see how love is like a river
So just give in and ride the rapids
But don't always trust a river
Face the currents head on or you may tip.

You always see more then one river in a lifetime
Some may see more than others
Never litter the waters - it's a crime
Don't take it for granted, or you may fall in and smother.

Matrimony
by Amber Arbing - age 18

She threw away her childlike ways
To all the single ladies waiting
While she said "I do"
To a new life

She made promises of the future
As she danced with the commitment

Oh draped in pearls and satin
A celebration of both beginning and end
And she walked out of their lives
To start a life of her own

Teasing
by Tina Arcolano - age 15

Looking through my eyes
and what do I see
Someone teasing another person
Instead of teasing me
That is when I felt bad and
I really wanted to cry
I told that person to stop
and then I told them why!

The Encounter
by Deine Aristide

Before caressing, delightfully embrace.
For gentle hail, inspires joyous karma.
Lustful movements, nest over passionate quivers.
Rapture, slowly tantalizing us.
Vociferate when x-rated yearnings zenith again.

Telephone Love
by Deine Aristide

Smooth, soft, sexy, tone.
Of that faceless voice on my telephone
That loves to roam.

Through the peaks and valleys
 Of my mind and heart
Where it's cold,
 and dark.

And I respond...
In my smooth, soft, sexy, tone.
As a faceless voice on his telephone
Wondering,
 If and why he's all alone
Wanting to know what's on his mind
If he feels my vibe,
And if our bodies could possibly intertwine

So his...
Smooth, soft, sexy tone
Can blend with mine.

Time
by Jenny Armstrong - age 16

They say time heals all wounds
but does it indeed?
Will time dam this torrent of emotion
or just make the waves reluctant to recede?

They say time heals all wounds
but will a wound ever really fade away?
Will time heal it completely
or will it leave a painful scar to stay?

They say time heals all wounds
but will enough time make this flame smother?
Will anything quench this burning fire
or will it only make this blaze burn another?

They say time heals all wounds
but will time alone heal a broken heart?
Will it help a heart to forget those memories
or will be only a reminder of what was torn apart?

They say time heals all wounds
but is that possible yet?
Does time really heal all wounds
or does it just make the mind forget?

Insomniac
by Lydia Armstrong - age 16

Insomniac, awake too often
Don't you want to bury those troubles
Under your pillow?
Don't you want to forget the day before you?

Run free through liquid images
Of infinite fields, poppies and corn
Surrounding your hate
Alive too much and feel too much
Of what encages us
Insomniac, awake too much
You see too much, hear too much
Don't you want to escape into temporary
 death?
Mind continues to buzz, always seeing
What your eyes will never
Insomniac, no lullaby could rest you
No bedtime tale could release your
 awareness
What is sleep?
What would it take to bury your
 restless soul?
Insomniac, you die with visible eyes
 wide open
Insomniac, awake too often

Calley I Loved You
by Robert F. Armstrong

It is amazing how a little 14 pound ball of fluff was able to endear herself to me for over 10 years.

She entered my life in 1982, when my daughter brought home this half-starved, sick and bedraggled, obviously abandoned dog into our home.

We cleaned her up, had her examined by a vet and put a notice in the lost and found section of the newspaper. Every time the phone rang my heart skipped a beat. I prayed it was not her former owner. She eventually found a good home which offered her loving surroundings. She always seemed grateful. She found our family!!!

Calley (that name because we found her in California) would lay with her head resting in my lap when she had the chance. She always met me at the door when I came home. She understood when I forgot to give her food, but she did remind me. We already had two other dogs and it took her over a year to share the food from one dish.

Calley and I enjoyed over ten years of love and companionship, but then she developed spinal problems and lost her eyesight. Despite her hurting, she continued with her love.

She is now at peace; no more pain. The only pain is now in my heart. She is gone but I still feel her presence. I know we will be together again someday, and we will resume that special relationship that I was fortunate to have with her...

Calley, I love you!

Dads Are Special People
by Ashley A. Arnold - age 12

Dads are special people.
They're caring, attentive, and kind.
Out of all the dads in the world,
the coolest dad is mine.

He'll give you hugs and kisses,
he'll spend his day with you,
and he'll even pick you up,
when you're feeling blue.

'Baseball, Basketball, and Football,'
he loves these sports you see.
But he loves them even more,
when he's watching them with me.

Going shopping with him
is really a lot of fun.
He'll tell you jokes and buy you things,
until the day is done.

Dads are special people.
They're caring, attentive, and kind.
Out of all the dads in the world,
the coolest Dad is mine.

"If There's a Path..."
by Gila Ashtor - age 14

Before you cried and pled for more
G-d knew your death and birth,
Your days were counted long before -
You set foot on this earth.

    And some upon arrival wonder
    Too fearful too fulfill,
    While others stand outside in thunder, -
    And hope not to be killed.

And in their days some people lead
Or stand firm with defiance,
The rest can't hunt, nor kill a weed,
Their lives based on reliance.

    Some in each day find time to heal
    While others are in need.
    Some fail to see life's path is real,
    While in that path, others succeed.

Some see a path,- but do not try
Too scared of unknown fate,
Now life's seen them, and passed them by,
They'd go- but it's too late!!!!

Forget Me Not
by Delali Attiogbe - age 16

    When I fade away
    And time says that I'm old
    I plea and beg and say
    Don't forget my poetry told

    Don't forget what I have written
    Don't forget words of my heart
    Don't forget the fame I've dreamed of
    Or the many sayings with which I part

    Forget me not this dear world
    But, alas, you probably will
    For I am an unknown poet
    Who hides her poetry still

Alone
by K. Atwell - age 15

Look into the eyes of the dead,
dark, blank, lonely in every way
people dance around
but thy cannot see them
thy looks and looks
yet is all alone
but after a great while
thy eyes do open to the Heavens above
the Heavens were there all along
thy just didn't see them
faintly the dark comes back
but the heavens are always there
it's just a matter of opening thy eyes.

Destruction
by Samantha Atwell - age 15

We spin in a world full of violence,
darkness and greed are everywhere, left and right.
The sky has turned charcoal, while the hearts of men
turn to stone.
No one looks to see the damage, no matter how large the
explosion.
Yet, every now and then I see a small child's eyes
open wide and look upward in this rush of madness. As we
ourselves stumble blindly over each other eager to reach
the top, but always searching for the bottom.
It would be a wonder to see people stop and listen to hear
the love hidden deep inside the darkness of everyone's
heart, to gently touch the petals of a springtime rose,
rather then swipe away another thorny weed.
I stare at the blindness in your eyes and I see only the
cold glare of stone looking straight back.

Options
by Tennessee Catherine Brittain

Twenty years ago we stopped
during our engagement, others found interest in you
someone else began to dote on me

Now we face each other once more
a chance meeting in spring
again, you are an option

You describe our encounter brought you to a cusp in your life
the connection, the attraction -- "Don't you feel it, too?"
yet, your pupils do not dilate in the darkened booth

You announce your commitment to fitness
sworn off all alcohol
yet, your beer belly gives you away

You admit importance of female physical appearance
I eye unkempt teeth, hair, and clothes
yet, passionately you try to convince me you have changed, matured

You tell how you rent a single room to repay debts
three more years of frugal living
yet, proudly you document your education, career, salary

You complain your latest has you cuckold
on and on you vent your humiliation
yet, later you inform me male indiscretions are part of life

I struggle to look interested
my mind screaming "double standard"
no, you are not an option...

I Ruined Us
by Brandi Autry - age 15

I wanted us to be something special and so much more.
I wanted us to feel something we had never felt before.
I wanted to create a fairy tale love story, and I would have if
It wasn't for my insane jealousy.
I just couldn't let go, I held on to you much too tight, and
Never once did you put up a fight.
You kept everything bottled up inside.
You pretended to be happy, but really you wanted to run and
Hide.
I always thought you wanted to be with someone else.
And when you thought I hated you, I didn't, the only person I
Hated was myself.
I wanted every minute of your time, and I wanted to give you
every minute of mine.
I could never be sure that I was the only one that you touched.
And I know now that I asked for way too much.
So if you ever wonder, you didn't ruin us, I did.

Welcome Home
by Janna Badger

Detached from domicile
Long elapsed departure
Inhabitants peculiar
Path lingers further

Familiar structures
Strange, Surreal
Physical abandoned avenue
Form peculiar illusion of self

Foreboding embrace
Dwelling expired
Foreign deception of
Home...

The War
by Joanna Aynat - age 16

Your too far away, too far away to touch, and the strongest love in side me, hurts too much. It tortures me to move my hands, to try and move at all, and beneath the surface, the earth begins to fall, crumbling, tumbling to the edge, cut jagged like a knife, It stabs my wounds, and the more I struggle, the deeper they plunge. Constantly piercing through my body, the pain too much to take, I'd give in too easily wouldn't I? I'd loose the battle. Could I withstand the endless nights, alone, thinking of what things could have been? To try and help myself would be virtually impossible. Tried, I failed. But the whisper of the wind, the sweetness of the rain, that salty rain that pours down like blood, Through it all I will alleviate this despair, my tears turn to dust, and the wind carries them away, but soon again, another storm, rage, anger, hate, but my heart becomes filled with hope, pulling me out of this nightmare, throwing me into another tine another place, another me, another chance. I think I've reached that point, where there's nowhere left to go, no one to turn to, dreams shattered like broken glass, seven years bad luck, and counting, until the next fall of the empire, the entire city in chaos, everything changed that day, but no one was different, I unlocked the door, but with my last efforts could not get it open, It was the point of no return, a dead end, lifeless, hopeless, but someday the strength of a thousand men will come, come to take over, my new army, with shiny black boots, taking their place on the battlefield, that dark, cold battlefield to begin my war against sanity.

Untitled
by Pamela Jo Francis Bacon

Can love call without hanging
   up?
Can life give and hang
   out?
Can laughter squeal,
   shout, and smile loudly
   in a thrill?
Do you know what it is all
   about?
Can a man of color
   give?
Can a woman soft,
   care?
Can turmoil beware!
   Can my right
      say nothing to my left,
   and still be there?
Can I of peach teach a
   good way.
And is it fair to share
   tomorrow today?
Can one love all the way; even so,
Can two or more really pray--
   -be heard, as well as listen;
      care; as well as give;
         live; as well as die;
            love; as well as--
Not another word; I see it in your eye!

Sunset
by Allison Baggott - age 16

My life is like a sunset.
With beautiful colors of peach, lavender, and rose.
Mixed together in a colorful display.
Everything looks so spectacular.
I am completely calm and full of joy.

Then the sun slips under the horizon.
The sky darkens.
I feel the wind screaming in my face.
I hear the coyotes crying to the moon.
And see the bats flying over head.

Suddenly, dark clouds cover up the moon.
And everything gets black.
Horribly black,
Terribly black.

Then my joy goes away.
I crawl back inside.
And I sit around,
Waiting for another sunset.

No Heartbeat
by E.J. Bahmer - age 16

To take away a life
Before it can begin
To never give a child
The chance to even sin
They'll never see the world
Or open up their eyes
Instead they are brought here
By a person who's not wise
they'll never speak a word
Or see the light of day
Never given the chance to imagine
the expressions on your face
Or feel a passionate kiss
Or distinguish between race
What could they have ever done
Before their life could begin
They never did anything
Never even sin
Their pale skin so soft
Their face illuminate in the sun
Their eyes open slowly
And show that baby blue
their little fingers outreached
Waiting for their cue
The cue that makes their heart beat
And allows their first breath
This chance they're never given
The chance to live or die
Is there any good reason
Can you tell me why?

Natural Elements
by Shersti Bahr - age 19

It seems that man rules all creatures
and if the world was a movie, we'd be the main feature.
About the country and oceans we roam,
to build the world into our home.
Burning, chopping, tilling, building
destroying the natural elements as fast as time permits.
The future rests on our ability to cooperate
and make nature yield to our enticing blows.
Then we're hit by a natural disaster as if nature
is laughing at our feeble attempt to take control.
All of our hard work now gone, we regroup and start again.
What a joke it is, the funniest comedy
that humans still think they rule the world
and nature's our student to be.

Timara
by Mary Melissa Baker - age 15

A deep taste of the rainbow
A full breath of pureness
Falling down; under; below
A delightful feeling of gayness
Eyes of ocean blue
A heart of sterling silver
A friend that's true
A certain quaintness about her
Pondering in a maze of thought
No way to solve the mystery
A million clues I have bought
The same throughout history

Transparent
by Heather Ballam - age 16

You say you'll always love me,
until the end of time.
But that's such on the surface,
your love is just a crime.
We only met the other day,
You're playing with my head.
I know you're just saying that,
to get me into bed.
I'm sure that you have done this,
to many girls before.
They say that they don't want to,
but still you push for more.
I've told you how I feel right know,
And you just look away.
You say that I'm the girl for you,
In each and every way.
We only met the other day,
Yet I know you inside out.
You're only after one thing,
And you think that you're all set.
But until you find respect for me,
that's one thing you won't get,
or even ever see.

The Game
by Richard Bank

A quick loud squeak-and the door opens
and the pack follows as I reach for my wallet
I tap the bouncer in his humongous stomach...
"Thanks my friend" and I walk on, passing
passing through an armada of people
No seats, just bumping with strangers
like a pinball I am Mario searching hard for the princess
To no avail yet I find
three x-girlfriends here-I need a beer
Music thunder now strongly in my heart
and in my veins waiting for the first and last ludicrous
event to unfold itself once rapped in a cigarette,
a word, a fight, a kiss, a dream,
I'll see you in the morning

Love or Lust?
by Cindy Banks - age 17

As I lie here in my bed tonight
    I dream of only him holding me tight
Oh Lord my heart is so blue
    But does this my love is true
Or could it be my loneliness is taking a turn
    Or may it be only his touch
Although I feel it was love at first site
    My heart is still in pain
Knowing I may never see
    But I feel he still holds the key
To my heart and my soul.

"Infinite Love"
by Mandy Elena Barberio - age 14

To look past what I wanted to see.
    I swore it wouldn't change anything, but
Beheld by the person you used to be.
    Questioned why I'm the one you embrace.

Feeling betrayal fortaking my heart.
    Hoping to overcome the rapturous pain.
You and I will never stay apart.
    This destiny will pull us together again.

Promise me your infinite love,
    And all that has perished will return once more.
All life's bliss and ecstasy will be of
    The greatest of things lost from before.

If the shadow on our love as cast,
    Then I know everything I felt for you
I should have left back in the past, but
    Lost in this love I will always be.

Try to forgive me for the desire I feel.
    I know that it will not make you stay.
Once upon a time this love was real, but
    With my life it will now decay.

Battle's Long Forgotten
by Thomas Allen Bateham

Battle's long forgotten
Where the bodies still lay
Too show all the
Battle's long forgotten
People may wonder why they died
Was it greed
Or maybe someone's lust
Or even the pride of other's
That caused people to die in
Battle's long forgotten
Elder's may say
They know the reason why
But they don't
That's why there
Battle's long forgotten
Where many fought
An were killed
Some stood tall
An won while other's fell all around
In all of those
Battle's long forgotten
Where the cries of the
Dead an wounded can
Still be heard calling
For all of the
Battle's long forgotten
To reach an end

Untitled
by Alexis Bateman

It's like the morning after
(when you wake up and realize you can't breathe)
the dawn comes sickly pale
sacrificing soul for body,
taking dogma for wisdom
I cry with my sisters, knowing eternal sadness
<u>that</u> <u>he</u> will never know,
oppressing my very being throughout the eons
the sun rises cement light
blinding night's intuition with accusations-
    I take back my sexuality
    I embrace my creative energy
    no longer will I feel your imposed shame
    making amends for what I am!
    Mark your territories, and fight your wars
    this beast, he was suckled here-
cancerous noontime assaults me, beating down
(I swear I didn't mean to wake him)
bear the heat that turns your mouth to desert
and let cactus words be still-
    I have love; keep your illusions
    we have unity; keep your possessions
    I recall a warmth that wasn't drought
    and a beating that never bruised
    make your governments and compile your laws
    this beast, he was grown here.

To Think
by Alba Batista - age 15

To think that I like you,
and to think we just mess,
to play with my feelings,
of just mess with my head.

To think we are lovers
or having it real,
to think if you played me,
How would I feel?

To think is to think,
and to do is to act,
to think and imagine,
but can't face the fact.

To think about things
that will make you regret,
and to do other things
that you'll never forget.

To think and to do,
all nice and slow,
to think and just guess
or think and just know.

To think is to think,
to do is to act,
to think it all over,
but now face the fact.

Love Never Fails!!!
by Shawn Buchalter

You were there for me in a time of chaos and pain ...
for this I am grateful for you have much to gain!
For the Love that you held for me was unconditional in
all it's glory .. so it will be read as such a loving story!
You've been there for me with advice of Wisdom, but at that
time I was blind to the pain I brought upon you!
Such a kind heart can not be ripped apart ... although the
devil would love it to be .. but even he can't see, the Divine Power
that's within you, only to be continued to another level ... Supreme
to the devil!!!!!!!
So keep the faith that's in you and continue to spread the
Love and it will be returned back to you .. on a greater scale ...
cause Love Never Fails!!!

Friends...
by Laura Bay - age 15

Friends like you don't come around everyday.
That's why it is easy for me to say
I am grateful for you each and every day.
I understand why God gave me you.
He wanted me to see I have best friends too.
Having you as a friend means so much.
I know through life we will always keep
in touch.
Life will get tough on us.
I want you to know I will always be here
for you.
Days and nights, tears and fears.
Keep in mind, I will always be here.

The Pearl
by Joan Ostrom Beasley

Bear and I climbed the hill behind the house, following the narrow, well-worn footpath. Such a warm morning for May - the air had lost its winter bite. The Airedale investigated each clump of grass, each twig or stick. Some fox or deer might have marked a spot which Bear knew was his. I reveled in not having to wear a jacket anymore. My hiking boots crunched on the dun-colored soil. Then a pebble rolled to the center of my heel. I tired to dislodge it to the side where it would not be an irritation. I moved to the left and again to the right with an extra tromping of my foot with each step. It would not be that much of a problem. I could finish the walk and not notice it.

We climbed the second hill. Wildflowers sprang up over night with the wonderful, Spring rains. Mountain Bluebells and purple Blue Penstemon nodded at our passing. That rock had become absolutely unbearable. I reeled in Bear's recoiling leash. Loosening the dusty boot laces, I pulled off the right boot and peered in, Trying to balance on one sock-covered toe so that the entire foot would not be covered with pebbles, I unceremoniously dumped out the little offender.

Why could we not, like oysters, make a pearl out of an unwanted grain of sand? As I bent to push my foot again into the boot, I saw the bright orange linear lobes of an Early Paintbrush. For some reason I had not noticed this happy display or the last lavender cup-shaped Pasqueflowers snuggled next to the base of a Ponderosa just off the path. There was my pearl - those extra few minutes when I was forced to stop to see a special beauty, to treasure a special gift.

String Of Pearls
by Joan Ostrom Beasley

Collection of irritations
forgotten, forgiven, or
successfully defused

grating, grinding, constant
sharp-sided detractions
from living:

rock in a hiking boot,
neighbors's dog barking
through til dawn,

phantasms of insults,
slights perceived,
humiliations,

love's misconceptions,
unretracted words,
misunderstanding,

lumped for sanity's sake
in iridescent adamant
disposed of

into glowing spheres -
medallions of
overcoming.

Memory touches, cherishing
pearls on the chain of
life evolving.

Ever Never Once Again
by Tiffany Bechert - age 16

When once the summer is seen
It lends a feeling of strength to the seer
The flowers, the smells, the pure warmth
The sleepy love you feel towards it
All is donned in unspoken hopes it will endure
Then one day it gets too hot to handle
Or perhaps snow buries you in its drifts
Summer's eve is forgotten, replaced by contempt
Hate voicing itself to the winter and fear
Afraid that summer, though your memory is vague,
That perhaps the next summer will not come
That winter will bury your mind, body, soul
Freeze you into deathless oblivion forever
As you cry deep sobs of reverence to turn back time
To ask for summer to be passed against your eyes
To feel the heat and wind blowing your hair softly
To join hands with smiles and run barefoot away
Then subtly one day such starts to return
The temperature is raised to fry the snow away
Weeks pass till one day as you realize it
All is back to summer's great lore once known
When wishes are not appreciated is when actions are lost
Now love the summer as never before
Dive into endless cool blue waters far away
Happiness returns to your being at last
'Summer is here,' the wind whispers, 'forevermore'

One Year
by Nicole Behrens - age 18

One year had passed, and if I've learned anything,
 it is to love you with all my heart.
One year has passed, and even though you don't always say it right,
 I still know you care.
One year has passed, and never has my life felt so complete,
 you fill my heart with happiness.
One year has passed, and never did I know someone could mean so much;
 I would be nothing without you.
One year has passed, and never did I know our love would be so strong,
 through good times and bad.
One year has passed, and looking back on all the memories, I know I love you.
 And that is why one year has passed.

Why Do We Have To Hurt One To Love Another?
by Julie Behr

You deserted me in a heartbeat;
Me, the one who was always there.
Now, my shoulders can't bare;
The pain you've laid upon them.
My head filled with anger and rage;
I feel like a beast trapped inside your cage.
You toy with me and my thoughts.
One day I do know;
This caged beast will be free.
Holding the key;
The key to your life.
Then and only then will I invade you.
You will feel me to,
You will surrender unto me;
    do as I wish,
    do as I please.
You will ask for more;
And beg me to stop.
You will taste the blood of my hate.
I will invade your mind;
And tear at your soul;
I will rip at your heart,
'Til I taste the goodness I have done.
You will then taste the blood of both our hate.

Chaos
by Denise Beining - age 15

World full of chaos,
confusion in her eyes.
An unknown truth,
believing in lies.

Violence in the streets,
watch what you say.
Scared to turn back,
but can't look away.

Anorexia
by Jessica Beland - age 13

Skin and bones,
That's all she is.
Skin and bones.

Skin and bones.
She never eats.
She rarely drinks.
She barely sleeps.
Skin and bones,
That's all she is.
Skin and bones.

Skin and bones.
The muscle's gone.
The fat's disappeared.
Her personality's gone wrong.
Her body temperature's 62.
How can I help her?
What can I do?
Skin and bones,
That's all she is.
Skin and bones.

Skin and bones.
She'll never be
The same old person,
Bright smiled Kristi.
Skin and bones,
That's all she is.
Skin and bones.

I Like To Hide In Places
by Elizabeth Belyeu - age 12

I like to hide in places
Where no one ever goes.
It doesn't really do much good,
'Cause everybody knows
Exactly where I'm hiding.
'Cause it's where I always go
Any time I have a chance
And my slipping off won't show.

I like to hide in places
Where I can explore the world.
Without leaving my hidey-hole
My sails become unfurled.
By opening a book I am
Transported far away,
Away from traffic, Planet Earth,
and sometimes light of day.

I like to hide in places
Where the world's a better place,
Where people in the stories have
Abandoned the rat race,
Or where the Earth's not there at all,
Or very far away.
Sometimes the world inside a book's
A better place to stay.

The Trouble With Beatrice
by Carrie B. Bennett - age 13

The trouble with Beatrice
Is that she never shares
She never listens
She never cares.

She deliberately steps on
My poor kitten's tail
Then she walks away smiling
as he lets out a wail.

She won't play in the mud
She always stays clean
She's too perfect, well
That's just what I mean!

My mom and my dad
They think she is great
They've not seen her mean side
The side that I hate.

The trouble with Beatrice
is that she's such a pain
When we go on a hike
She's afraid of the rain!

She's mean and she's rude
She loves making fun
of me and my friends
And then making us run.

My grandma, my grandpa
They hug and they kiss her
The main trouble with Beatrice
is that she's my sister!

Garden
by Mark A. Bero

The garden is a place to plant a seed.
The garden will grow for us all to see.
Veggies appear in a short period of time.
The taste of goodness is here to eat, harvest
My garden, for it's life's nature treat.

Hello Cloud
by Diana Berrios - age 16

The clouds form as one
As I look up at the sky
One big fluffy cloud
Catches my eye
It waves to me
As I gaze at it
It smiles at me
So I wave back to it
The white of the cloud is as thick as cotton
This is something that can't be forgotten
Suddenly I awake
And I look up at the sky
I say goodbye to my cloud
and he winks his eye.

Girl With a Voice
by Emilee A. Bennett - age 14

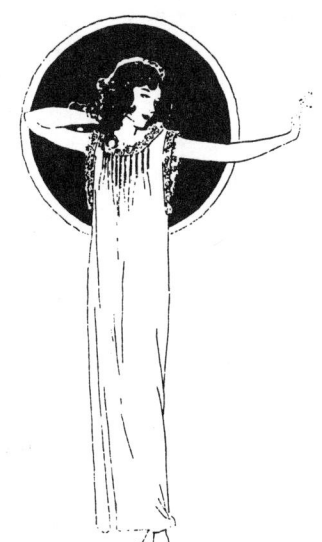

I sign this line the girl with a voice
Because I fear
That is the only way you know me.
I try
To get through to you,
But your line is always busy.
Sometimes I feel
That I will only get
The answering machine.
You have always been
So kind to me, even when
I'm not necessarily
The nicest person
In the world.
When you smile,
All I want to do
Is smile back.
The way your lips
Form the words
You speak, the tingle I get
From looking in
Your eyes,
Is more than I can say.
Why are you such
A good friend to me today?

I Try
by Jessie Benson - age 15

I try to look at the stars.
But instead I see your eyes.
I try not to remember.
Remember when you were mine.
I try to see the world.
Happy and full of dreams.
But instead I see anger and heartlessness;
or so it seems.
I try to feel my fire.
But instead I see your flame.
It's burning me up inside.
I hang my head in same.
I try to see the sun.
I try to see the moon.
I try to see my love.
But instead; you left too soon.

Love
by Lacy Benson - age 14

Love is a circle,
always in motion,
for all who dares,
to try it,
may just not find it,
or if they do, their
feelings might fly,
OFF THE CIRCLE OF LOVE

BYEBYE

The Centurion
by Marcella Berry - age 19

Oh, centurion of Rome,
    how divine your blood must be!
Oh, centurion of Rome,
    that you had knowledge to fore see!
like a true and gallant Roman,
    you have done your duty well.
like a true and gallant Roman,
    naught but commandment did prevail.
And though your heart at once denied,
    you went ahead and pierced his side
And as the lord looked down at you,
    his heart you saw was pure and true.
Poor wretched soul, you mourn and weep,
    with sorrow as a drowning sea.
Poor wretched soul, you mourn and weep,
    but he had already forgiven thee.

I Long...
by Alyssa Berthiaume - age 12

I long for the one I love,
For the one I love, loves me,
I long for his lips, oh those tender lips.
Upon my mouth with a gentle kiss,
I long for the one I love.

Should you go first
by LaCrystal R. Bing - age 17

Should you go first
and I remain to walk this road alone
I'll live in memories garden dear
with happy days we've known

In spring I'll watch the roses red
when fade to lilac blue
In early fall
when brown leaves call
I'll catch a glimpse of you.

The Stream
by Gina Bird - age 15

As I stand at the edge of a stream,
I bend and try to stop the fast-paced current
But the ever changing water won't slow
I throw in sticks
I throw in stones
But still the water speeds on
I toss in a stick
And I chase it
Under branches
Over branches
Along the bank
But the stick floats away
Off into the distance
And I am left behind
Panting out of breath
And my last glimmer of hope flickers
As do my memories of you
And the time we shared together
There is nothing else that I can do
To keep you by my side
All I can do is stand back
And watch you drift away from me
Like a stick in the stream.

Crushed Diamond
by Lisa Bethea

Beautiful splendor, timeless treasure;
Long after the rain; found-so still,
A new dawn, now and forever
breaking free...

A Sudden Silence
by Jolene Blackburn - age 15

There is silence,
It is cool outside and the wind is blowing.
I can hear the sound of my neighbors sander and a hammer
    hitting wood.
The birds are chirping, the trees are swaying, and my dogs
    are roaming around the backyard.
It's peaceful lying here in my backyard with the hint of gold
    from the sun peering over the tips of tall pines.
Thoughts of many things flow through my mind.
Thoughts of the future, past, and present.
A piece of my hair is trickling over my shoulder as the
    wind blows.
It gives you a feeling of warmth to keep you from being cold.
The sound of children being scolded by their mother travels from
    the road into my backyard.
The words I'm sorry were repeated and heard each time.
The sweet smell of honeysuckle blows with the wind.
To my knowledge it's coming from the flower buds on our
    grapefruit tree.
As a car starts and the door shuts, I listen.
It travels down the road and then once again, there
    is silence.

Untitled
by Robin Jane Black - age 15

Swept away by his charm
Yearning for his touch each day
The soft caress of his lips
against mine.
His body pressed against me
Making sweet passionate love
Entering a world of our own.
This eternal kiss
Our souls interlocking
And becoming one.
Forever and always.

Searching
by Marcus Blake - age 19

Searching...
Hence I came upon a spot in my soul.
Like a dry desolate garden, air stood still here.
The wind couldn't roll.
An abyss black place, edges harden.
Where the sun couldn't know or even touch.
I roamed about searching, free at will.
The blackness I saw was ever so much,
I thought it a dream to morbid to be real.
As I walked a path of withered broam.
Visions I saw all around me.
They screamed steps heavy at heart in search of a home.
This can't be me, to the side I leaned,
Suffering endured, tortured this soul.
From this trip my feelings have hardened,
to gaze upon my blackest hole.
To know inside me I water this savage garden,
searching...

The Love of My Life
by Vanessa Bland

It started on a sunny school day
I saw you and a friend walking my way

You had a smile that could light up the night
the love in your heart was shining so bright

I called you later on that day
but when you answered you didn't have a lot to say

I started to give up, then you gave in
our love grew so strong it felt like a sin

Then one day our love turned sour
and I knew in my heart these were our last final hours

I broke up with you not thinking at all
of how my life would take the fall

My days were lonely, depressing and blue
and I knew all I needed was love from you

I call every once in a while to see how you've been
and now I realize your heart has started to mend

I'm sorry for all the pain I've put you through
baby, you know I really do love you

My happiest days were when we were together
and my only wish is that it would have lasted forever

I sit on my bed crying every night
wondering why I started our fights

I read the letters you once wrote to me
and think of how it all used to be

I know the love for each other is still there
and deep in our hearts we really do care

But for right now I'm taking it one day at a time
and hoping that, once again, you'll be mine

The Redeemer
by Rebecca Bodle - age 13

God's light is brightly shining,
He always answers prayers with the
perfect timing.

No it might not be what you want,
But God's answers are always right,
believe me or not.

He loves and guides us from day to day,
He listens and understands us while we pray.

God will save you from the world,
He is the Lord of all Lords.

Trust Jesus and follow him,
And you will have no sorrow in the end.

To Live
by Erin Blankenship - age 15

It seems like I'm outside
And watching through a window
As life goes by
Others live dreams
While I wonder what it's like, to live

Every once in a while
I think I'll get to live
Oh, but no someone snatches it away
   from me
Like candy from a baby
Tantalizing me with life's glory

But no they must torment me
They won't leave me alone
Until they've destroyed my will
My heart falls to pieces
Each time they try to tempt me

Life is a cruel joke
I might as well be dead
Why don't they just take my heart
   and bash it to pieces
It's the least they could do after all
   they put me through

I lie on the ground and cry
As I look over toward the window
And I begin, again to watch life go
   by
Oh, how I want to live

Untitled
by Griselda M. Rangel - age 15

Life is full of ups and downs
But mine is mostly downs
I make you smile, yet I frown
For you say I act like a clown

That's what you want to see
Therefore I will show thee
Happy is what you want to be
Yet you don't see what's happening
   to me

Sadness over comes me
But yet laughter blinds thee
For laughing is all you want to see
And sad is what I'll be

A Boy
by Kristin Blevins - age 13

There once was a boy,
A newborn baby boy.
Soon to be a child,
A bright, wonderful child.
There walks a man,
A big strong man.
Soon to be a husband,
A life warming husband.
There goes a father
A father who will always love,
There lies a son, a husband, a father.
And there he rests in Peace.

Escape
by Nika Bodner - age 14

It is time to face reality
There is no escape
no way to break free
from these bars of my jailed cell

I live in a jailed cell
of criticism and tantalization
I know only too well
that the world is cruel

Within these stone cold walls
there is no comfort
No one answers my calls
no one listens to my thoughts

No one cares to see what I do
No one wants to experience things
things that are new
Or changes like I do

You leave me on my own
you say you give me love
it is as if you place a stone
A stone I can not see and so I stumble

Mom
by Casey "Bud" Boeling - age 18

We're far apart
but if I need someone
all I gotta do
is pick up the phone
after I hear your voice
I know I don't have to deal
with this crazy world all alone
your more than a mom, you're a friend
till the end
for you
I'm gonna win
grow up a man
make ya proud
different then Smokey
there's no tears from this clown
cause your always around
I don't thank you enough
for all the love that you've shown
to this young blood
when I was on my own and I needed
some help you didn't hesitate
when I was locked down
and needed someone
I called on you
you've helped me out so much
so now I'm sendin' my love
to ya
I LOVE YA MOM

Love, Casey

Freedom
by Danelle Boes

When is a person truly happy and how does one know when on is?
Is it something you feel, something you learn, or is life one great big quiz?

To see how much you've grown each day by introducing trauma, heightening
Your senses moment by moment with varying degrees of drama.

Why do we often look at others to define what we "need" in our lives;
When being content with ourselves is the trophy for which we should strive.

You must conduct your tasks with purpose no matter what they are;
Live in that moment, whatever you're doing and think ahead not far;

Because the future will still come to you no matter what you did today;
So don't expend the simple pleasures on issues you can't sway.

It's time to have fun, time to enjoy, time for comfort and peace of mind;
It's time to change your perceptions of the world, see through the eyes of the blind;

To have every encounter spark your awareness to see things in a way that is new;
Do not be afraid because deep inside "you" are still the same "you."

It is the one you forgot about when the world made you mature;
The one that needs to come to now and than to remind you that there is more;

than just going to work, cleaning the house, and although these things must be done;
Allow yourself to be a kid again, and once in a while experience true fun.

Try to remember that if life really is just a quiz, given by God to us;
Go out of your way in every endeavor to rightfully earn an A+.

Celebration of Defeat
by Angela J. Bonari

Can you see me clearly now?
Through the wreckage
of the year's past...
It seems lifetimes have
come and gone
since I've looked in your
beautiful eyes
and very few when I could
concentrate on their
intensity.

Blades of defeat
I clutched so desperately
so as not to know
permanency
in this lifetime.

So strange,
that time in the cemetery,
my blazing sunshine
on the day of my
forgotten celebration.

But, it seems I've lost you
somewhere between
life and death
and love and hate...
Will you ever forgive me?

In A World So Big
by Renee Bonilla

In a world so big
I'm surrounded by walls
I look so far
Yet see so little
Wonders of the world at the palms of my hands
Never to be touched by the souls of my feet
Green grass and blue skies in a whole different world
I see buildings and roads covering the dirt
Saying I can't go makes me want it even more
But I can not leave if knowing your sorrow

The Fall
by Emily Boronski - age 15

Far away from everything
Yet surrounded by it all
I sit here in the darkness
As I lean on the edge I fall

Falling faster and faster
Getting closer to the ground
My death is coming near
And a crowd gathers around

Falling like a plane who's engine has failed
Spinning downward toward the land
The crowd suddenly separates
As if pushed apart by a giant hand

A figure emerges from the shadows
His face as pale as a spirit
I yell and scream as I fall toward the earth
But no one seems to hear it

My final yell is heard
My life flashes in front of my eyes
The crowd witnesses this all
Only the spirit like figure cries

After All
by Brighid Bryan Boyle - age 16

It takes a lot of courage -
        for me to write you.
After all, me being me -
        you you.
Still I won't feel better
        till it's down on paper.
My life has changed
Not blaming anyone
But, now I have to grow up,
Thank you for everything
People say never change - but I do,
I can't stop myself
Neither can you.
You know me.
But you won't find me,
Thank you for the memories,
It's been great,
My courage will be tested -
If you ever get this,
Never blame the rainbows
        for the rain,
I am going to forget you now,
For you are a painful memory,
One I will try to forget, but fail
After all, me being me
        you you.

Love Ends
by Renee Bonilla

Love will wonder the hearts forever
Lonely souls with no one to turn to
Finding a face that puts pieces together
Wanting the joy that will help you through
Thinking this person will guide you through life
On earth that is true,
But at the end you find Christ

In Flight
by Jennifer Braden - age 15

swish swish
the graceful robin floats through
the wind
like a gently lifted kite
gliding and swooping in the gentle breeze
the robin wafts about enjoying the swaying of the wind
wings of the softest color flap occasionally
lifting the bird in the air higher
and higher
soon a flock of seagulls join in the flight
calling to each other
like the children in a schoolyard
the robin spies a tall oak tree to land on
and slowly drifts down
careful not to disturb an owl snoozing
on a nearby branch
the robin rests and gazes about
watching the other birds fly about
the robin soon feels rested and
prepares to fly again
ruffling his breast
stretching his legs and straightening his wings
suddenly
without a sound the bird is in the air
flap flap
swish swish
swoosh
the bird is again enjoying the
feeling of flying.

Dance With Her
by Tiffany Ann Bradley - age 16

Light glistened
Shadows of two
Marked her walls.

Feelings are never the same
One day
To the next.

Sense of closeness
Is yearned
From the one she cares most about.

Her eyes sparkle
And glow
When he's around.

Fear of rejection
Weighs on her mind
Questions that will never be answered.
Does he care?
Does he want?
Will he <u>ever</u> feel like I do?

Waiting Dream
by Tiffany Ann Bradley - age 16

Virgin lips reluctantly awaiting,
The touch of that young man,
Only the silent smoothness
Of his whispering lips will quiet her.

Anticipation makes new nausea,
Excitement makes her wiggle,
And that nervous feeling,
Crazily drivers her into an uncontrollable chatter.

His glowing eyes,
And sheepish smile
Brings humble thoughts
To the girl's tender heart.

Her feverish eyes
Covers the enchanted smile
She holds on her face
All the while, he appears.

A girl of my mystery,
And a guy of magic,
Dream together.
The thoughts of separation seems so tragic.

The Bridge of Love
by Jaime Brady - age 14

Life is like a road,
turning and turning.
Your heart and sole,
they just keep burning.
To pass over the bridge of love
you've got to give a friend
your trust.
Once you go there
you can't come back.
Your heart has it's
own love attacks.
Doors they open
then they close.
So you better watch
out, cause once
you cross that
bridge of love,
you and your friends
will never see the dove.

Untitled
by Alicia Aileen Brainard - age 18

I never show emotion anymore, so people
think that I don't care or that I have an
"attitude problem." I don't know that
I do care anymore. Which scares me.
What will become of me? Will a great
black beast swallow me? LET IT GO,
LET IT GO. I don't know how. PUSH IT OUT.
How? TAKE ALL OF THE LOVE INSIDE YOU.
I don't know that I have any. I KNOW YOU
DO. I KNOW YOU DO. Where? IN YOUR
HEART. What heart? I have no heart.
CRY IT OUT THEN. CRY. With what tears?
THE TEARS WITHIN YOU. I have no tears. They
left with my heart. WHERE? Gone. Gone.
YOU MUST FIND THEM. I'm lost. Lost.
Who am I? I can't see you.
Where am I going? I want to go home.
Where am I? Where is home?
I can't get out. I want to get out.
I can't get out.   Who are you?
Let me go!
I'm lost. Lost.

Making Friends
by Mindy Jo Branson - age 13

Making friends is hard to do,
Sometimes they make fun of you.
They talk about you when your not around,
And sometimes they make awful sounds.
When you move to a new school or town,
People sometimes make you frown.
The shouldn't judge by looks or skin,
They should judge by what's within.
Be nice to adults and kid's,
Act the way you always did.

Rainy Day
by Erin Braun - age 15

I've been blinded
I've been beaten
I've lost my soul
Everything is missing

I don't know anything
I forgot how to live
I don't remember the loss
But I remember the pain

Cut your hand
Watch the blood
It's the only thing that is one
I don't know where it goes
Everything is lost

Gray clouds drifting in
Promising rain that will begin, again
The rain that lifts my eyes
The rain that cleans my blackened soul

I don't know anything
I forgot how to live
I don't remember the loss
But, I do remember the pain

Way Back Then When I Had It All
by Diessa Breault - age 13

I wish I could start it all over again!
I miss my big house and my dog's pen;
And I know I will never get the house back again.

I moved away from my friends and family,
I miss them dearly, Yes already!

My favorite stores are gone away,
Just because I moved to Thunderbay.

I miss my friendly neighbors coming to say;
Hey how are you! Are you having a good day?

I miss the cute guys on my street
Saying HI! My name is George...and mine is Pete.

I miss the corner store that gave me deals
Cause now I ain't got no more meals.

See why I miss my old town so much!
Maybe somehow, someday I can return to my old town.

Love Is A Question
by Anna Danielle Breedlove - age 15

Love is a question
That you must seek deep within to find the answer.

Never search for the perfect someone
Because only in your heart can it be found.

When love finds you, don't ever let go.
Once you turn your head for a moment it'll slip away.

If this happens, don't give up on yourself.
Keep going and never lose hope.

This causes great pain,
But always keep in mind that there's more than one love.

Never will there be more than one of you,
So don't let precious life slip through your hands.

Don't count the years.
Instead make the years count.

Love will always come around
When you least expect it to.

Maybe not tomorrow or even in a year,
But don't worry because it's waiting for you.

If you keep your head down,
Then you'll walk right past what's searching for you.

It will be gone again,
And you may never have a second chance.

Never miss a rainbow because you are looking down,
And love will find you.

"God's Precious Gift"
by Bonnie Breitzman-Lacey

Darling, pink, and oh so sweet,
God's precious gift to you.
Now's the time for you to meet,
Don't be scared, you'll know what to do.

You'll ease true the whole process,
In the end to receive,
a perfect package, waiting to be blessed.
In your love and trust it believes.

Endless years of heartaches and joy,
frustrations, happiness and toys!
A life long commitment,
This package from Heaven sent.

You'll be loved and cherished,
dreams come true in all you wished.
Now sit back and enjoy being a Mother,
'cause in this baby's life there can be no other!

I'm Famous
by Caroline M. Bray - age 14

I'm famous...
I will always be famous
I just know I'm famous.
Just sitting here looking
Pretty smiling and glowing.
With my name in lights
And all my hopes all
My dreams and me
Myself and I will
Be famous.

The First Time
by Jacob Bridges - age 15

The first time I saw you, the first time we met.
We shared a great love, something that was set.
I knew in my heart that it was you, that we would share love and passion
for days on through.
It could take months, it could take years,
no matter how many shedded tears.
I love you so much, why can't you see, that you and I are meant to be.
Love and hate are in us both, in our hearts and souls.
I know you don't know how I feel, all I need is to hold you near.
I can't wait to see you soon, you look so beautiful under the moon.
Your eyes so brown, your skin so warm,
you are my shelter from the storm.
After the sun rises, we'll sit and spy, at the nature in which we lye.
Why do you ask why I love you so? Why do you want me to go? I
can't leave, I don't want to go,
there are so many reasons why I love you so.
Our passion, our love, our hearts intertwined, take some time and unwind.
The nights in the forest were so beautiful to see,
they meant a lot to you and me.
The first time I saw you, the first time we met,
I knew there was something special there.
As our eyes met and we kissed, sparks went off; Heavenly bliss.

Fading Fast
by Victor Newman Brockwell - age 13

Earthtones, my emerald eyes being shown, soft
talks about love and life, the sweet voice
that pierces just like a knife. I worry what is
to come of me and my soul, if I loose the one
I love to hold. Sweet words spoken are
worth more than any token. Close to my
heart and with me always, I hope you can
stay for many days yet life fades too fast,
and blows away. No more sweet words will
I hear you say.

Grandmother's Legacy
by Jessica Brosman - age 16

Silent now, do not cry.
I am the wind, I do not die.
Don't tremble over my grave tonight.
I am not there, do not leave in fright.
Quiet now, walk softly on the dewy grass;
I tiptoe amidst the sleeping children, I swim with the bass.
Don't guard yourself against the early morning breeze;
I whisper with the daffodils, I dance within the trees.
Careful now, don't hold back your emotions;
I live in the darkest canyons and the deepest oceans.
Silent now, do not cry,
for I am the wind and I do not die.

Alice's Attack
by Brittney Brown - age 17

There's a long lost episode of "The Brady Bunch,"
the one where Alice shoots the children.
The Brady's the perfect American family,
shot in cold blood by their friendly housekeeper.
It couldn't have been Sam, the butcher, who pushed her over the edge
because he was a good boyfriend and always gave her 50% off meat.
Alice so loved cooking meals in the Brady's lime green kitchen
that she often thought of sleeping in the refrigerator.
Next to card stacking, the potato sack races were
Alice's favorite family activity,
even though she had arthritis and knew she would never beat those kids.
And Brady family vacations were the greatest.
Alice always got to go along for free so she could take care of the kids.
I wonder what possessed Alice to do it,
or for me to think it?

The Dance
by C. Lawry Brown

As we harmoniously waltz through life
Will you dance with me?
Cheek to cheek we'll face the world,
It's sadness, pain and glee.

I'll follow closely as you lead
We'll glide across the days,
And pirouette through daily tasks
Ever changing in our ways.

In the beginning we were out of step
We stumbled on each other's toes.
But the more we dance, we anticipate
The way the music goes.

In time we learn each dip and sway
And glide along as one,
My darling won't you dance with me
Until the music's done?

The Answer
by Juanita Brown

Lord I need, your full attention.
This request, I have to mention.
I need your help, to make amends.
For gossip has, upset my friend.
She no longer, acknowledges me.
She looks right pass me, as if she can't see.
I've tried to find, what is the problem.
So I can know what needs solving.
But she won't even speak to me.
So I have had, to let it be.
Lord I need, your help today.
I want to make, this go away.
I believe, you are the answer.
And from your hold, I will not transfer.
I will let you, fight this battle.
Maybe this will, make her rattle.
Even if she, does not change.
At least I know, I went the range.
    He knows the answers

Love
by Katie Brown - age 14

Love is like a soft breeze across my face
It blows with a whistle of unwinding embrace.
Across the fields with glowing light,
as it opens the darkness at beginning of night.

Love is deep in the heart
When two friends have to part.
If only love could mend,
around that very long bend.

Love is a dark, dark sea
that goes beyond reality.
In the heart of friendship and truth
Is a never ending book of youth.

Love is a book without an end,
a letter that I will send.
In friendship I can see,
a soft breeze just for love and me.

The Perfect Family
by Rebecca Brown - age 14

Mother, Daughter, Father, Son
We all wish we were created as one.
The Prefect family that's what we want to be,
But no matter the number under one roof we will
always be part of gods family.
I know your probably saying I know this couldn't be right,
Just please don't get sad over any tragic family fights.
The perfect mother stands for truth,
And when her children are in a bind she acts back by
being responsible and kind.
The Dad of the house is always stern yet never to fair,
He'll never leave a tummy empty or a room left to be bare.
The children always very rude,
But the mom will as straighten them for she raised
them never to be crude.
So as we're forced to think,
Remember this is only enough to say in one blink.
There is no "Perfect Family" and we all have our times alone,
Just always think about what life would be like if we
had no family of our own.

Retirement
by Terrie D. Burch

Now the time is drawing near,
   You've dreamed of all your life.
When you can sit in rocking chair,
   go traveling with your wife.

Some say golfing is the way,
   to while away the hours.
Tips for playing cards and games,
   when outdoors there are showers.

Other say, "Just spend your time
   doing as you wish."
Sitting with your pole in hand,
   "Remember, you are meant to fish."

No matter what you chose to do,
   we wish you all the best.
May your years of leisure time,
   give you a much deserved rest.

Loved One
by Lauren Buck - age 15

She stares at me through the mirror
brushes her hair, washes her face
she is beautiful
she smiles at me showing her perfect, white teeth
oh, no, she has noticed the lines, completely unseen by anyone else
they tell of her stories, her strength
she feels old and ugly now
she fixes her hair as though it will make her forget
but it doesn't
she again looks at me through the mirror
she looks at me for encouragement, which I gladly give through a smile
she stares at me for a moment and smiles,
then moves to put on her makeup
I watch her like a cat watches a mouse
carefully lining her eyes in black, her eyes are velvet, soft to the touch,
eyes that see through everything, including me
she lines her lips in deep red, lips that will never speak of the beauty she holds
then when she is finished she looks to me and I smile,
a smile that tells her, without any words that I love, admire, and hope to be like her
to have the strength and determination that she has
to look at things the way she does
to see the beauty that lies underneath the terror and loss
to have the unexpected good fortune.

The One I'd Pick!
by Karen Budman - age 16

Out of bubble gum, taffy, and candy
I'd still pick the one man who is handy
Out of soda, water and tea
I'd still pick the man that's more precious to me
Out of marshmallows, gummy worms and peanut butter
I'd pick the man that makes me shutter
Out of cupcakes, candybars and movie stars
I'd pick the guy that loves me more than mars
Out of chips, pizza, and pickles
I'd pick the guy that doesn't mind to be tickled
Out of peanuts, popcorn and crackerjacks
I'd pick the guy that loves me back
Out of walnuts, pecans, and cashews
I'd pick the guy that says bless you
Out of cookies, pies, and cakes
I'd pick the guy that sometimes makes mistakes
Out of misery, doubt and sorrow
I'd pick the guy that's still there tomorrow
There's many things a girl wants in a guy
But she can't always have them all
So pick the one that suits you best
Better than all the rest
Invite him in as a guest
And let love decide the rest.

The Long Night of Mr. Smith
by Matt Burleson - age 18

The radio plays in the dimly lit room,
Serenading me with the mellow tunes of slow jazz.
The pipe smoke swirls around the room,
Filling the air with its pungent scent,
While I sit quietly and play a game of solitaire,
And sip my coffee as I while away the night.
The day's past events heavy on my mind,
I get little sleep tonight,
And wonder what will happen come tomorrow.
The time moves by slowly with every tick of the clock,
Drawing on for what feels like forever,
But I get no more tired as the night goes on.
The tiffany lamp glows softly beside me,
As my card game continues on for the rest of the night,
Giving me light to play by.
The mood stays somber, but restful,
Like when one no longer cares to worry.
The time passes on as the music plays on the radio,
Carrying me through the night gracefully,
Easing my troubles as tomorrow comes nearer,
And preparing me for the troubles ahead.
I contemplated the actions to take to get me out of trouble,
But few come up to comfort me,
And those that do appear are little comfort at all.
I blow a puff of my pipe into the air in front of me,
And look quietly at the swirling smoke,
Thinking deeply at what happened.
The night goes on forever without end,
And little comfort comes to me,
As I sit in my chair waiting for the morning to come at last.

The Kiss
by Ash

What made you choose?
Why did you change your mind?
A kiss.
One kiss?
Yes, a kiss.
A kiss that I missed all this time.
The kiss I've been waiting for all my life.
A kiss that draws all that I am,
The kiss of love that I finally understand.
About giving and taking,
One on each hand.
And each hand gently placed,
on my face.
To bring me close,
for a kiss that was given,
not some false boast.
And every kiss since has been as fine,
It was the kiss that changed my mind.

Don't Give Up
by Kati Wittman - age 16

Don't start the day with doubts and fears, for where they live,
faith disappears.
Love won't grow in a gloomy heart, where sorrow lives and
teardrops start.
Don't give up before you've begun, you still have time to get
things done.
Don't waste the time that's given to you, and know that I am with
you in all that you do.
Don't be a quitter, you're not alone, we all must crawl before
we're grown.
There are no rainbows without rain, there are no victories
without
pain.

I Wonder
by Ash

We all lay down to die
I wonder how will I
Shall it be long and drawn
or swift, here now then gone

You think it's funny how we go
Always do we know
Fate is right behind
but never on our mind

All have gone before
Starvation,
Plague,
and War
but different for each soul
No matter what the dice they've rolled

You must face it on your own
Completely alone
No matter who stands by
For it's you who now shall die

Untitled
by Nicholas Busselman - age 18

who lives there
        amongst the never ending cosmos?
who keeps a close eye
        upon our frustrating development,
and why won't you give us a hand?
we need your help,
 if you can give.
        we need your guidance
    to help us live.
are you afraid of us?
  I would predict you are,
because we have never come in peace
with our ignorant tools of mass destruction.
we fail to project our civility
       our morality,
        and sensibility,
but aptly portray our stupidity
    on a global scale,
lends us your support
help us not to fear,
bring us the truth
for its all we want to hear.
have you come for us before?
   has ignorance made you leave?
can you bless us with another chance
another chance to see,
we are not the perfect beings we think,
and the world in which we'll destroy is at the brink,
you may wonder what it is we think,
don't wonder, just rescue us from this relentless sink.

Beyond The Rainbow
by Erin Butler - age 17

When I think
Where perfection is only a moment
and innocence is lost in a single breath
I escape into my fantastic free existence
Beyond the rainbow, high and magical
where no evil can find me and injure my love
I live here in this veritable place,
a mere specter world to those around me,
Unwilling to find the portal in time -
obstinate to the miracle of dreams
in which luminous stars sparkle gently upon my face
Guarding against nightmares and childish fears
Watching over my every move
Bringing fantasies and dreamer to me.

My Garden
by Erin Butler - age 17

She sees me
picking up earth
broad red roots
pushing stubborn newborns
up into the sky
beside fat bushes
bringing weeds
and fruits
I select a
yellow rose
and at the same time
a new seed in bloom
I step back
and dream of sacred ground

Plaint Of A Snorer's Wife
by Dell C. Byrd

Each night, there's much activity beneath our rumpled covers,
but not the sort one would expect from two old-fashioned lovers.
Commencing within minutes of your head adjoining pillow,
it continues unabated 'til the dawn awakes the willow!

It starts out with a gentle buzz emitting from your nose...
a sound that I could live with...but it grows and grows and grows!
I'm hard-put to describe it, for its forms are often varied
and only yet experienced by <u>me</u>---the one you married!

Sometimes it's like a hiccup that is swallowed, then released;
sometimes, more like the honking of some <u>very</u> angry geese;
and sometimes (when you overeat!), it's like a dying cow.
I wonder <u>why</u> you do it---and I've even wondered <u>how</u>!

It's been 'bout twenty years now I've been looking for a cure.
I tried, at first, some gentle taps---but they were too "demure."
I've tried all types of pokes and prods and even violent kicking.
Each time you take a well-earned pause---and then keep right on ticking!

It seems I've run the gamut, short of beating you with brooms,
and the logical solution is to move to separate rooms.
But, in fact, I cannot do it---you know why, I won't explain---
for within three days, I'd rue it, and would ask you back again!

God's blessings are abundant, and in truth, I've gotten plenty,
but when I ask for forty winks, I'm lucky to get <u>twenty</u>!
So forgive me when we wake, dear, and I feel (and <u>look</u>!) like hell
if I do not always answer when you smile and ask, "Sleep <u>well</u>?"

L.O.V.E.
by Willow Blossom

When I hear his name
My heart skips a beat

When I see him smile
I think thoughts so sweet

I wish he was here
Right here in my arms

I would hold him near my heart
And tell him I love him

Tell him he's in my dreams
Thoughts and in my mind

Hold his hands, grab, his arms
Kiss his lips and never let go

Show him that I love him
By being there in time

When I think about him
I almost begin to cry

He means so much to me
If I loss him
My heart would just die.

My Love for You
by Ashlee Byrum - age 13

My love for you is everlasting.
It's a love like no other.
A love of never fasting.
A love shared with one another.

My love for you is never ending.
It's like a happy-going day.
A love that doesn't need tending.
A light to show the way.

My love for you is forever growing.
A love maturing with age.
Like a candle forever glowing.
Never to be put out with rage.

My love is a candle on the river.
Guiding me to you.
It's a stream of gold and silver
Full of riches old and new.

"time knows"
by Ana W. Caeidhe

time knew
i loved you
even before
the first dawn
just
as
time
knows
you love me
even after
the setting
of the last sun

This Is A Note I Write To My Boyfriend
by Amber Cain - age 15

This is a poem about my best friend
to no other girl would I ever lend,
He can be so sweet,
almost too good to eat.
He is always thoughtful
feeding me ice cream by the spoonful.
He kisses me good bye
And he never tells a lie,
I know he loves me lots
If not he'd be in a box.
He's loyal all the time,
like a dog without a crime,
He listens very carefully,
for if not he'd wind up terribly.
He tries to stay clean
When he's not I get real mean.
He takes care of me well
responding to the call of a bell.
I'm told he's finely broken in
to a woman's or wife's satisfaction.
He tells me dinner's good,
But for all he knows it was found under the car hood.
He puts up with my monthly attitude
Even when I refuse to cook the food.
He comes home from his hard day of work
And I say "Hey grab me a cold one ya lazy pork!"
But for the final thought,
A man like him cannot be bought.

When the Slaves First Came
by Amber Cain - age 15

In the 1500's there were the Europeans,
Dadgum, dumb, darn, dead—headed, damaging demons,
White as a clean sheet of lineless paper.
They traveled the sea by ship
In search of slaves obedient to the whip.

Then there were the African people
Their bodies were dark silhouettes at dusk on the top of a steeple.
They minded their own business,
Caring for the families, being harmless.
They lived peaceful until the whites were harmful.

One day, the whites came
They set some homes aflame.
They kidnapped men and put them on ships.
The ships moaned and groaned feeling their pain
They soon grew sick and pale, which soon drove some insane.

When they reached their destination there was hope in their eyes,
But then they seen what terrible life before them lies.
There were fields with endless rows of fluffy white plants.
They lived picking cotton, everyday
To escape, there seemed no way.

The Sun Inside Me
by Ryan Caldwell - age 18

The Sun, an aspiring star.
So gruesome it is too see it
Barron with night and soaked inside light.
It makes all my rights seem contempt.
Allowing justice full of mockery,
In sense it is nothing...
Oh, do you see what I see?
Nothing.

Between Light and Dark
by Ryan Caldwell - age 18

I call out to the waves of Time's likeness.
The Darkness resides upon the sand dunes.
He utters words to call my old mistress
And out come the deception of his goons.
I've fallen in the perils of His grasp.
My mistress calls me out into the night.
Stuck in His hands of His hate and His wrath.
Out of a crevice comes one stint of light.
Light reaches out for my body and soul.
Striking the Darkness with lightning and fire.
Howling and howling and wanting some more.
Death now comes to the Darkness, the Liar.
The Light is standing above the mountains
Peering at me, drowning in its fountains.

A Flower's Journey
by Merlin D. Calhoun

You ask if I will miss you
If I shall reminisce
Within this poem the answer
For I do promise this

I will pick a wild flower
Covered with evening dew
Place it on the water
And send it off to you

So that god will guide it
as it drifts toward the sea
I will bless it on it's journey
with words of poetry

It will cover endless miles
Over countless brooks and streams
To serve as a reminder
That your always in my dreams

I will send it on this journey
to fulfill one fantasy
That if ever you do find it
You will think of me

So late some summer's evening
As your walking on the beach
If a crashing wave beside you
Places a flower at your reach

Know it is a token
that rests there at your feet
Proof of love unbroken
It's journey now complete

Dance a Dance
by Ashley Callen - age 17

The peach satin shoe wrinkles with pain and delight.
A quick, unsure glance at the director is reminding of the goals.
All aches find their places hidden and insignificant.
Each ankle bone and shoulder muscle and tilted head look to be in perfect harmony with themselves and the other ankles and shoulders and heads encompassing them.
The tired gray-blue eyes become filled with liveliness as emerging designs are gathered and interpreted.
Junk is thrown out and worthy things let in.
Thoughts wander away and others are recepted.
The shapes are abstract, forced, painful, and difficult so that they may be performed and interpreted as classic, natural, effortless and giving.
On the ideal day, every aspect of the mind and of the body are used to their fullest potential.
Each detail is accordingly attended to, while shapes are appearing to move as one and in perfect sync.
Like a swan, like a frog, like a teacher, like a friend, like a ghost, like a neighbor, like a flower.
To challenge, to learn, to experience, to work, to release, to connect, and to celebrate.
Create a picture, sing a song, write a story, dance a dance.
Each elegant motion like the precise notes in a song and the delicate strokes of an oil painting.
The movement gently sweeping the air to put something new into action.
Dance a picture, dance a song, dance a story, dance a dance.

The Beast
by Heather Callahan - age 19

The sun is setting in the east
Deep in the shadows stands the beast
He's stalking the streets tonight
No one can see him, he stays out of sight
He haunts my dreams
He makes me scream
It's as plain as anyone can see
His next victim is going to be me
I can almost feel the life sucked out of me
I can feel his eyes of fire burning through me
I run in between the stalks of corn
This is where my life will end, I scorn
I can see his eyes, but I can't see his face
I shouldn't have come to this evil place
I wish there was something that I could do
He's catching up, my life is through
I'm trying to go faster, but he's slowing me down
I keep running and running, I can't turn around
I'm never going to get away
I'll keep running till my dying day

Strange and Unusual
by Mindy Calvert - age 16

I am strange... unusual.
   or so they say.
I am not my body and my body is not me.
It is a mask that conceals my insanity,
   a cover that cries out delusions.
Beneath this hallucination,
   sights not seen,
   voices not heard.
I am invisible to all with a rational mind.
The ordinary cannot see the pain I endure.
   Consequently, why should they see me?
I speak of them as aliens,
   foreigners, strangers among the deranged.
Are they aliens?
   Or am I the one who is?
Are they normal?
   And I out of the norm?
Is anybody normal?
Therefore, can you label me
   strange and unusual?

Clouds on the Horizon
by D.J. Calzada

He was young....she was even younger.
He had nothing tangible to offer her.
No money....no possessions....no prospects.
He came empty handed and without a plan.
He was a man of few words and what he did
say was soft and rang of the truth....always.
He said he loved her with all of his heart.
She believed him with all of hers.
She felt he was a rare find....uncommon in every way.
There were the obvious objections, of course.
How could he possibly provide?
Where on earth would they live?
The answers came to her without effort.
He would find a way and any place would do.
They would have the good fortune of true love
and a wealth of memorable experiences accrued
over a lifetime rich with the warmth of gentle passion.
As they drove away, she looked over her shoulder
at the tree lined drive of her childhood home.
It was here that she had been her father's princess.
She looked at it hard and burned the images in her mind.
She meant only to follow her heart, not to forget.
She sighed as she turned to look down the road
toward a future filled with hope and expectation.
She was confused by her sudden, unexpected tears.
When she turned to capture just one last look,
everything familiar was far too distant to see clearly.
Storm clouds gathered on the horizon.
It began to rain and she cautioned him to drive carefully.
Her mother stood on the steps and wept.

too shy to say
by Neomi Canett - age 16

talking on the phone
or just hanging out
it was all going good
'til she came about

it should of been me
but I was too shy to say
I didn't want our friendship
to end in a tragic way

when we first met
I thought you were so gorgeous and fine
but later came our friendship
that I didn't want to put on the line

all those other guys I used to see and talk to
I really never wanted to be with them
I wanted to be with you

but this is reality
and that's just the past
one thing I really know
our friendship will always last

you will always have that place in my heart
too bad we got off to a really bad start
I love you truly
and I know you know
It's just too bad we were too shy to show

Death
by Diane Campomizzi - age 17

Death is a part of life that is hard to get past,
You wonder how long this feeling will last,
When you lose a loved one no one can replace,
Sometimes it's hard to remember their face.
But deep down inside you know their there,
To see you through your despair.

A Last Glimpse
by John C. Cannella

And then she walked away
 Into a vacant sky
  Taking with her
   All the essence
    Of mystical movement
     Gracing the earth
      With her love
       Filling the empty
        Lighting the shadows
         Presence slips through her
        Amazing the moment
       Defying everything
      Rushing to the front of the picture
I thank God I have vision

The Feather and The Wind
by Jeffery D. Carey

If you were a feather
Could I be the wind
To carry you to where you've never been
To a place where we need not pretend
When you feel down and alone
With no one around you
Let me be the wind
Let me embrace you
When you are drenched in rain
And your tears have drown you
Let me dry your soul
So you may drift on air like I do
And let the air be our love
So I, the wind
And our love, the air
May together take you, the feather
Into the setting sun,
And drift together
Forever

Life
by Lindsey Carlo - age 14

I once saw a woman.
Face of happiness.
Face of beauty.
I now see her husband.
His striking hand.
His frightful face.
The woman's face is now
Not as beautiful as I
had once thought.
Face of fear.
Face of hate.
His striking hand comes
down and hit's the face
once filled with happiness.
Now filled with tears
and sorrow.

Purpose
by Courtney Carrillo - age 18

Two souls searching for a deeper
meaning to life.
Asking and wanting to know
all that is in store for
all creatures.
Life is not giving any solutions
to all its portraying mysteries.
Is the answer hiding right
before our eyes?
Or do we really have to wait
to ask Him?
Trying to discover all that
should not be
and trying to answer what
is left for our eyes to uncover.
All these unsaid pictures waiting
for us to develop an idea of what life is
suppose to be.

Alone
by Joseph Carr - age 17

I dwell in darkness
Afraid of the love in you

So I run away
Afraid to face
Is there nothing I can do?

To mend this heart
Broken so fast
Hurt in so many ways

Am I doomed to face
My days alone?

Is there anything but hate?

I wish I could love you
To break these chains that bind

Why must I be so afraid
To face a love I find?

If this is doom in a broken heart
Can I face my days alone?

Or will I dwindle out like a dying star
Where loves light has never shone.

Arise From Your Slumber
by Ashley Carter - age 16

The world turns
the mind leaves the body
a moment of peace relaxes
   the soul
blood rushes and
kisses cool
sweet smelling incense meditate
   emotions
and a slow soft romance promises
   to the heart
voices of children fill the sky
tears of joy are shed
a young girl awakes from a
   dream

Depression
by Cheryl Carter

Depression is an illness that makes you feel alone.
No matter how hard you try you never feel at home.
The stress in life is always more than you can really bear.
At times you don't want make-up or to even fix your hair.
You try to eat even though you have no appetite.
And lie awake tossing wishing you could sleep at night.
You find you cannot concentrate no matter how you try.
And everything that goes wrong makes you want to cry.
You feel like you can't go on and you really want to die.
There are thoughts going thru your head of attempting suicide.
So if you ever feel this way there's something you must do.
Seek help at once, please don't wait, your future is up to you.

Opened Eyes
by Janet Carter - age 13

My hopes, my dreams linger in the air
I take no action just sit and stare.

My life moves on, no accomplishments made
Until my small dreams fade.

I look around at what the world holds,
And find out it's not just a big bag of gold.

There's sorrow, and weeping, starvation and pain.
A thought has struck me there's so much to gain.

Not prizes or money, Beauty's no good.
It's the feeling inside you, that you know you've
done what you should.

The true treasures of life must be earned.
So do your part, and take your turn.

Hope
by Maggie Casey - age 14

The child is fading fast, in mother's arms, death is near, but the child
feels no harm.
Father cries, mother's pale, doctor say "Lord help this child."
Mother kisses child's eyes as they shut with no surprise.
Child cries with closed, shut eyes.
Fathers beg for mother's life.
Lord says "Redeem yourself, to keep your wife."
Father's eyes are filled with confusion, killing himself is his solution.
Shot gun goes above fathers nose, down on the floor,
death takes from life,
As his wife goes into shock,
the beeping of her heart suddenly stops, for the doc.
He yells "Flat line."
Nurse says "Clear," but dead silence mixed with fear.
Nurse takes the child with fear in her eyes.
child alone, mother dies.
Doctor tells the nurse, "give it up."
the Mother was on crack, the father on dope.
Child open her eyes as the doctor spoke, "She's a lost cause."
Nurse says "No...She is Hope.

Untitled
by Melissa Cashin - age 14

I Love You, I Love You
Through out eternity
I Love You, I Love You
Those words said to me.

I Loved You Then,
Like I Love You Now
All I keep wondering,
Is why and how?

You let me go,
Like I was nothing
If only you could feel
My pain and suffering

I Love You so much
You would never know
Oh, why, Oh why
Did you let me go?

We'll be together forever
That's what I thought
I guess you didn't feel the love
I felt in my heart

I'll say it now,
And I'll say it again
My Love for you
Will never end

The Soul After Death
by Kathy Caudle

Everybody has one. I'm talking about a soul. Specifically, I'm talking about a soul as it relates to death.

The presence of a soul voids out death. This means that death per se, does not exist. Each new human being receives a soul at the moment of procreation. Because each new human being receives a soul, death is considered as not an absolute end.

Doing spiritual things nourishes the soul. Nourishing the soul keeps it alive. Keeping the soul alive til the end, mortal death, means a person's immortal soul lives on.

Many acknowledge the existence of a soul. Navajo Native American Indians, for instance, believe the spirit lives as long as someone who lives remembers you. Similarly, Mexicans believe a person lives eternally through his/her soul because from death comes life. Christian doctrine teaches the existence of life after death. All Christian funeral rites are said in the spirit of the deceased enjoying everlasting life. The ancient Egyptians placed items of mortal life in their burial tombs. This was done so the deceased could take the items with them to the immortal after-life.

Scripture in the Torah shows death ends earthly existence only. In the New Testament of the Christian Bible, the existence of eternal life is repeatedly shown.

Why then after now seeing that life after death does exist would a person who had received a soul at procreation, then throughout mortal life spiritually nourished his or her soul til the end (mortal death), die? In other words why would anyone not believe that a person with an immortal soul, who had nourished his/her soul until mortal death, would live on through his or her soul?

Babies
by Erin Chaffin - age 16

Babies are precious,
babies are kind,
babies are curious,
and not hard to find.

Babies were once
me and you,
and probably your
husband too.

Babies are special to
all of us,
especially the ones with
gaul to have two.

So have fun with your baby,
while it lasts,
because they grow up so fast.

Generation Now
by Joseph Chapline

I sit. I watch. I learn. I tell.
That radiation box teaches me well.
Talk show society morals at a low
I feel the shame of my generation
Morally deprived and cultural desecration
Higher educations at an all time low
Empty futures, Technology starts to slow
A helping hand is hard to find
In a Filthy city with trash we leave behind
As our waters blacken and our souls turn cold
The mighty dollar still has the strong hold
Racism no longer has a color
When two people of the same race, culture, and religion try to kill each other
What happened to peace and goodwill to man?
Is that a myth or a fairy tale of a forgotten land?

P.S. The earth is your mother. Your neighbor should be your sister or brother!

Caveman Ruler I
by Debra Anne Chapman

Mammoth fur
Warmly snuggles an early traveler.
Yet, a cold blizzard eternally blows
outside of his sheltered cave.
Boldness beats in his primitive heart.
His Ice Age strength surpasses his fear.
Warrior courage presses into his early soul.
A group of followers band to join him.
Hunting a primitive rhinoceros they charge.
Over the ice they travel and chase their prey.
Hungry and wild they run 'till they catch it.
Cold winds are unable to ruin their triumph.
Free and strong the leader feels blessed.
He guided his hunters to glory, to food.
His happiness shines from his smile as he stands,
Ancient, ornery, and a skillful caveman.

Untitled
by Cynthia Lynn Chatham

Dyslexia
Mad
Angry
Overwhelmed
Shocked
overcame
literate
happy

Paradox
by Joy Chavez - age 17

I am the Paradox
-Both of the inevitable and evitable
Existing in eternal happiness and endless sorrow
I am neither black or white and yet both
The skeptic and the believer
Hot and cold
Pro and con
I live yet I am dead
I died yet I am still live
I am the 'like'
I am the 'as'
I am the 'nor'
I am the 'not'
I exist as yes but live as no
I am...yet I am not
Breathing eternal peace but fighting an endless war
-The sinless Saint...the Saint's devoted sinner
I am life, brilliant and regarded
I am death, dark and discarded
I am beauty, rare, sensuous and sweet
I am wealth, riches seeing no end
I am homely, common, horrid and bitter
I am poor, wallowing forever in poverty
I am the brilliant of mind
I am mindless fool
I am the Paradox

The Tree
by Jennifer Chen - age 12

When I was young,
I'd sit under your branches,
And listen to the whisper of the wind,
And try, if I may, to understand your conversations.
I never could.
Over your knobby root I'd sit,
And dream about the day you were planted,
How that person gently planted a seed in the ground,
And then, you sprung forth, a young sapling.
Ages passed, and you grew.
Into your prime.
That was when we were both young.
Now, as I age and age,
So do you dear friend.
And now, you are old, as am I,
But we can still think,
Of times that were before...

Feelings
by Phanly Chhoun - age 17

When I'm upset I go for a walk,
I wish I had someone with whom to talk.
Instead I keep my feelings bottled inside,
Can anyone see the emotions I'm trying to hide?
If you look deep inside my eyes,
You can see that they're blue as the sky,
My feelings are very well disguised.
I need someone to guide me through,
All my feelings are strange and new.
I want someone to help me understand.
To guide me through and hold my hand.
I can't deal with my problems alone,
Maybe we can talk together on the phone.
I just need a few minutes of your day,
For you to listen to what I have to say.
Maybe if I say what's on my mind,
The answer would be easier to find.
Will you please listen and help me learn?
I would do the same for you in return.

Think of Me
by Linda Childs - age 12

I cannot put into words
These emotions that I feel.
I have never experienced
Anything quite like this.
They are confusing,
These emotions,
And I am caught in them.

I could try to put
These feelings into writing for you,
But never come close
To telling you what
You mean to me.

The three simple words
That we are told we can use,
Become not so simple anymore.
so instead I will say,
Think of me,
And there will never
Be a day when I don't
Think of you.

Love
by Tara Chiles - age 13

Love can be great.
Love can be tough.
Love can be sweet as
sugar.
Love can be boring.
Love can be heartwarming.
Love can be heartbreaking.
All though it's true.

Man In The Moon
by Lori Chism - age 16

Late at night while the
house is still, I gaze at the
silvery moon
   I wonder of its mysterious
man and his mystical late-
evening croon.
   Whispering my secrets of
love and regret
   Wondering why life's
path seems unset.
   He listens intently, but
dares never speak
   The light that he casts is
soft yet so sleek.
   His silvery glow reflects
through each pane
   Forever through night
creating a stain.
   Grasping for answers
that seem yet so far
   He replies with but a
small twinkling star.
   Morning is near
and the night will fade
soon
   And I'll no longer
hear that late-evening
croon
   As I weep softly
for my man in the
moon...

My Everything
by Sonia Chohan

He is the sunshine,
of an everlasting glow.
He is the raindrop,
of the sensuous rain.
He is the rainbow,
covering the sky.
He is the lover,
of each and every story,
he is my everything.
He is the moon,
charmingly handsome.
He is the star,
darlingly forever.
He is the wind,
breathtakingly beautiful.
He is the prince of all the fairytales,
he is my everything.
He is the river,
of emotions that flow.
He is the colour,
of feelings that grow.
He is the mountain,
of courage that builds.
He is a reflection,
of bittersweet memories.
He is the song,
that rhymes so sweet.
He is the one,
I long to meet.

Coming In
by Leslie Churchill - age 18

Come inside,
Make yourself mine,
Look around,
Show my blinded eyes,
For me to learn,
Things are unknown,
To us both, no fool.

Come in,
I've told you before,
You know you're welcome.
My house is yours,
A sacred place if you look just right.

Not everyone can be one,
Luck has nothing to do with it.
Ties and binds,
Strings and whatever.

Down underneath,
You or I.
Only you can come inside my house,
Only I can let you in.

Alone
by Miranda Cikalo - age 17

Looking at the stars and counting the countless numbers
Do I realize what loneliness and hatred feels like.
Knowing that no one cares for me.
Knowing that love is no longer a part of my life.
That all I can feel is hatred and deceit.
And the loneliness of being alone.
I never asked to be what I have become.
Now I only wish that I could feel once again what it is like to be loved.
What it is like to be cared for.
I look up at the moon with my tear stained face and sigh.
If only I could be loved
Maybe then will I be able to feel what happiness is like once again.

Kaleidoscope
by Jesse D. Clark

When I was young and life unspun
to lay before my eyes
I thought it a toy kaleidoscope
a gift and mine the prize.
But as I grow old I'm not quite so bold
and I've changed my point of view.
The world is not my toy,
I'm no longer a boy,
and the gift is this time with you.

Treasures

Crossroads
by Tiffany L. Clark

My life is at a crossroads
From childhood to adult
But instead of being excited
I'm feeling more tumult

I'm feeling very scared
About the path that I should take
And how to go about it
But that's the choice I have to make

I always thought I'd have more time
To decide on what to do
But adulthood quickly crept up on me
Before I was ready for it to

For becoming an adult
Isn't as fun and easy as it seems
And it's not the way I'd imagined it
In my crazy, childish dreams

It's much harder than I'd imagined
Am I up for the task?
These are the things I'm thinking of
And the questions I have asked

For now I'm at this crossroads
Wondering which path to take
And let me tell you, here and now,
It's not an easy decision to make.

The Red Birth
by Kina Carisse Cliette

Alone I walked down the darkened alley,
Naive to the sheltered dangers that sat,
Dangers that loosely gripped obstacles in my path,
Knotted mesentery below and terror squeezing the rest,
Anxiety rammed my heart to purge through my chest,
And again anxiety backed up to gain way for another stretch.

My expressions were muffled by an ominous hand,
Pain shop up my small body, my excrement -- blood red,
Hot breath moistened my hair, Exuberant saliva crusted my folds,
My house was fastidiously cleaned,
With threats, Mother Goose not even be told.

The hardened pressure released,
The night air cooled my body, I beckoned my soul to return to its cracked shell,
Where my id should have danced delight'ly,
My ego -- sat with hands in face,
Three monkeys shook on the sill of my window pane.

Though injured by the twaining,
My attention, ripe for diversion, To the hum of the contras of fatalism,
A band of children, foot and foot,
Marched for saving grace,
To rescue another cohort from eternal pain.

And the children chanted...

"Innocent green will burn the most, Before evil kindling at the devil's roast;
Their hardened souls, their chafed flesh, Prematurely, will be laid to rest."

Not the first, and not the last, Another birth -- again blood red,
A secret, a tall tale, told at judgment day;
God's gift, in the devil's wrapping, With a card, that prophetically says,
What knaves know but carelessly choose to still disbelieve:

"Nails that kiss preemies' heads, Have their hearts' blood in their fervid beds,
For never, can they cares preemies, without stabbing pain."

Fawn
by Alice Clausen

A fern so soft
can hold a fawn
Belong the forest
Belong the dawn
The tall one to
with
All his pride
Shall shade and
hide
From all harms tide
Drift not far
For
This fawns life
Belongs the forest
Belongs the light

Favorite Sport Fishing
by Jennifer L. Cody - age 14

Fun is found
In fishing.
Some people
Hate
It because their
Not patient enough to
Get a bite.

Solution
by Heather Coffindaffer - age 19

Laying down to rest,
alseep in the coffin
people stand around to mourn
cries of grief and loss -
fill the sky,
problems fill life
too unbearable,
take the risk of your life
swallow your solution
slash your heaven
pull your salvation
hang your answer
do what you will
but do it quick
time ticks in your ears
flooded with worries
you wilt
weak in the stomach
you crumble
and fall into a pit,
you dug to solve everything
ending up with nothing
all in a day's work
sounds commence, bells toll
silence is felt and life ceases
as you imagine -
now you are king,
and nothing is gained

The Rights
by Barbra Coleman - age 16

Does anyone have the right
The right to start a fight
Does anyone have the right
The right to hurt you
And leave marks
Not just physically
But also mentally
Does anyone have the right
The right to call you names
Especially when they hurt you
More than any words could ever say
Does anyone have the right
The right to make you mad
Do you have the right
The right to take your problems out on someone else
Do you have the right
The right to cry for no apparent reason
Do you have the right
The right to be happy
That right I'm not too sure about
It doesn't seem like I can have that right
It seems as if my life's a living hell
I'm never happy
And when I am
My happiness is taken away
Why can't I have the right
The right to be happy

A Friend
by Melissa Coleman - age 16

He came to set our souls free.
Willing to die for both you
And me.

His love for us will never end.
Knowing He will always mend
Our broken hearts, grief, and pain.

And threw it all,
A friend we gain.
When we accept Jesus,
Just the same.

My Special Day
by Linda Collins - age 18

As my father gave me a hug,
My stomach turned, I had the jitterbugs.
As he held me tight,
He said, "It'll be alright.
Just give a big sigh,
And hold your head up high."
As I walked down the aisle,
I held my father's hand, and smiled.
Then my father gave me away,
For this has become my Wedding Day!

Trouble
by Stephanie Coln - age 14

times will come
when you feel dumb,
everything is sad
things will make you mad,
trouble is all around
especially at times when you feel down,
when you feel everythings great
trouble will come at times you hate,
why do we get in trouble
making all our problems double,
i wish trouble would just disappear
but instead it will always be here,
just live with it the best you can
when its over you can just make a new plan,
i am here for you
supporting everything you do.

The Bad Choice
by Julio Comas

Hurrying down the street that day
the hand of peril at my side
gaining ground to expose to me
the shadow of guilt in which I reside

gasping for air, limping
and heavily perspired
losing balance I fell to the ground
simple relief was what I desired

the loss of blood had taken toll
on my weak and battered frame
no longer able to flee the scene
I had created just the same

for the prey I wished to victimize
had thought one step ahead
the attempt to take what was not mine
was foiled by piercing lead

the subway seemed the perfect place
to rob and not be seen
homelessness caused me to compromise
my sense of honesty

so again I looked to the street behind
the shadow pursuing me
was my wouldbe victim taking aim
to finish this tragedy

now helpless I could only make
one gesture in appeal
"shoot straight, don't make a mess of it
it's my last spin of the wheel"

Holding On
by Coralann Conn - age 20

In my head,
   I hold a dream
     a wish,
      a fear,
       a threat,
        a thought,
         a love,
Of Something created.
   In my heart,
    I hold a hope,
     a feeling,
      a word,
       a sound,
        a song,
Of Something so sweet.
   In my Soul,
    I hold a need,
     a purpose,
      a place,
       a peacefulness,
Of Something that seems so complete.
   In my arms,
    I hold you.

Freedom
by Sara Conrad - age 13

Drive me out to the country,
Where air is mist, that licks upon my skin.
Where sunsets never dim...
But change, creating slide shows
Of color.

Outrageous starry eves' stars
Are teacups, full of flavored dreams.
I wish, take a daring drink--
Cheers, to dawn.
I hear a summer stream.
Smell dew opening upon a petal.
My soul and spirit both--
They're friends.
Run, gallop, upon the prairies!
Fresh graze and unruly floral.
Space? Plenty here!
Vast, open, wide enough to see almost all,
Hear almost all.
No, not empty, but free...
Free enough for me.

Endless Heartache
Dedicated to the Memory of Hugh Cook 1936 - 1994
by K. Catherine Cook - age 17

There was a time when his heart ceased to beat,
   A rhythm like that of tiny fee.
He found a place to lay,
   Never to see the light of day.
He was welcomed with open arms,
   The centuries won by his charms.
Things were different now he knew,
   For at last his dreams were true.
His life long pain was gone,
   As he watched anew the approaching dawn.
The life he once knew had been taken,
   The sense of his loss left his family shaken.
As their grief ended,
      Their hearts slowly mended.
He is remembered still,
   By the stark white cross upon the hill.

Caryn
by Cynthia A. Cook

She sits in a corner of the living room
Quiet, but observing all.
With eyes of clearest blue
And blonde hair done in braids,
She stands just two feet tall.

Wearing a gown of velvet and lace
The smile and rosy cheeks of her face
Belie the fact that she is just...a doll.

The little girl who loved her
Has grown up into a lady,
And now is constantly busy
With her own very real little baby.

So Caryn is content to spend
Her days and nights in a hair.
But when the time comes for the new child to play,
Caryn will be waiting there.

Know What You Mean To Me
by Tiffany M. Cooke - age 14

Consider the distance in space,
Consider the dept of the sea,
The number of stars in Heaven
              Then...
Know what you mean to me.

Every day I'm with you,
The day seems to fly right by,
             But...
When I'm not...
I feel like I'm gonna cry!

If I could have a word
For every star in the sky...
That's still not enough to tell you,
How I <u>feel</u> when <u>you</u> are nearby.

Love Is Like The Wind
by Jamie Cook - age 15

Love is like the wind,
Free flowing, touching
everything in its path.
Catching them off guard.
Unready and unaware.
Love drives around aimlessly,
until it finds its next victim,
wrapping them in chills until
they're freezing and desperate
and flow with the breeze.

Heart Full of Dreams
by K Catherine Cook - age 17

Ever since I met you,
    there's been a hole in my heart everything
    falls through.
Your what I need,
    to make my heart again pay heed.
I think of you day an night,
    wondering if what I feel is right.
Your older than me,
    an sometimes I feel we can never be.
You look at me with intrest,
    making my heart pound in my chest.
You turn to me an smile,
    leaving me as giddy as a child.
You were the first to see,
    I'm now smaller than I used to be.
Everytime you say hello,
    my knees are reduced to jell-o.
My dreams are of you,
    reality knowing you don't feel the
    same way I do.

Dedicated to the brother of a friend, and Scottie.

Alone
by Toni Crook - age 13

Here I stand,
I stand alone.
With no friends of my own.
I used to be happy,
I used to smile.
But since I've laughed,
Its been awhile.
You used to care about me,
But now you don't care a dime.
You were my only friend,
But you left without regret.
And though I know it's wrong,
I wish we'd never met.
Here I stand,
I stand alone.
Now I have no friends of my own.
I guess I should have known.

Love
by Karla K. Cooper

Love is a wish
For anothers happiness,
A heart broken
And mended with a kiss.
Love is the gentle
Caress of his calloused hand,
Or the sandpaper roughness
Of his knuckles
Gently stroking
The tears from your cheek.
Love is sitting together
In harmony and quiet contentment,
Knowing that your
Presence is all
That is needed
To fill the heart with love.

My Prince
by D'Ambra Kraft - age 19

Sweet Prince
The man of my dreams
When I am sad
He is there
I have him always
When I am in need
He is my shoulder
When I need to cry
he is so strong
Never in need
I want to be there for him
When he is in doubt
He is strong willed
and needs me not
I want him to know
My shoulders are here
I am here for him always
For his feelings to share.

Untitled
by Kerri-Lynn Corey - age 16

A breeze was blowing
The sun was shining
It's funny how
I felt like dying

In your arms
I should have been
But there I was
Alone again

'Not anymore'
I had said
Once I thought
That we were dead

The memory around me
Steady and strong
Made me realize that everything
About this was wrong

My head in the clouds
My feet off the ground
And, all at once
My heart started to pound

I hate you, I love you
I never can tell
Looks like I'm caught
Between heaven and hell.

The Age Of Innocence
by Joyce Cortez

To my siblings who number three
I pen these words for the memory
Remember when down on the farm
We built a dam but meant no harm

A place to swim was out only goal
"Find more rocks. We're on a roll"
There we swam like we said we would
Till the neighbor said his yard was a flood

"Tell those kids they ruined my place"
"Tear it down kids." Dad was on our case
How did we know what was going to be said
Kids surely can't see that far ahead

We thought we had our own secret pool
And that our ingenuity was pretty cool
After the grown-ups had to meddle
For just wading in the creek we did settle

Face
by Meagan Cox - age 12

A person you hold dear to your soul,
that face and heart shall never grow
old.
Remember the eyes, the lips, and the
hair,
and they shall be with you everywhere.
That person's face shall live in your
mind,
it shall not scare you but make you
feel fine.
Remember the face that warms you anew,
it lifts you high when you're feeling blue.
Remember a face, a face of a friend,
and all your sorrow will come to an
end.

Dream Master
by Angela Craig

You come on like midnight fantasy
Smothering me in spiked velvet
As I wait for you, patiently,
Like sacrificial lamb

Inject me, tragic
With your slippery-sweet Atomic Nectar
Wash from me my sins

Sprinkle please all over me
Your death (contagious) powder
Come so deep now, must crystalize my veins

My promise heartbeats slow you ready
And your whys echo painful in my laughter

I lie back sleepy
And watch the willow weep

How Do I Say You're Forgiven?
by Karen Craig - age 13

Hey "Dad,"
How do I say you're forgiven?
After all that you put me through,
After all of the pain an sorrow,
I am to put it aside and forgive you?
No, I can't
Not after the tears.
Not after the lies.
No. I can't say that you are forgiven!
I know that I am not to hate
I was brought up that way.
For it was not you who first tied my shoes.
It was not you who saw me through
    my first day of school.
So it will not be you who will walk
    me down the wedding aisle.
I now know how to say you're forgiven.
By saying that you're not!

What You See Is NOT The Black Woman
by Tereta Dawn Craig - age 16

What you see is a Black woman who could pass for
homeless by the way she looks.
What you see is a Black woman without
husband, but with child.
What you see is a Black woman on welfare
struggling to beat the system.
What you see is a Black woman beaten by her man
who thinks she'll hear with his hand.
What you see is a Black woman who can throw an
attitude at you in the blink of an eye.
But what you DON'T see is a Black woman who keeps
herself noticeably clean at all times.
What you DON'T see is a Black woman making it all
possible to give the child what the father doesn't.
What you DON'T see is the Black woman who has beat
the system and owns some.
What you DON'T see is the Black woman who is
making it by herself and doesn't need a man.
What you DON'T see is the Black woman who
has a positive attitude and is very confident.

What you DON'T see is ME!

If I Could Do It Over Again
by Stephanie Crandall - age 14

If I could do it over again,
I would remember to pick up that one little piece of trash.
If I could do it over again,
I would try to car pool more often.
If I could do it over again,
I would take a shower 5 minutes less,
And keep that 20 gallons of water in the ocean.

If I could do it over again,
I would help to teach my siblings the rights and the wrongs of life,
So that they wouldn't make the same mistakes that I made,
Once or twice.
If I could do it over again,
I would watch TV less and read more,
Like my grandmother did to me.

If I could do it over again,
I would learn more about my home town,
Where I lived in New York,
Because if I knew that I would never see it again,
I wouldn't be so glad, but most sad,
That my life there was coming to an end.

What You Need
by David A. Crawford

Rich man, poor man, white-collar, blue--
If you wanna be happy, wanna have victory,
    you need to know, know what to do.
You need God's love, salvation from above, family and friends-- beloved.
You need food and clean water, clothes and good shelter.
These make you wealthier.

You need to feel the summers' warm rays-- the rain of spring days,
    the autumn blow, and the winter snow.
You need to feel your lover's embrace; you wanna feel, this you know.

You need to see the sunrise and the blue, blue skies,
    white clouds sailing by, stars glittering on high.
You need your sense of sight, your eyes to see light.

You need to hear the birds singing their melody;
    a comforting voice praising thee.
You need to hear God's gift of sound-- wind blowing in your ear,
    music so close, music so dear.

You need to touch the love of your life-- touch that life right,
    touch your sweetheart's dreams.
You need to touch the sand by the stream--
    touch the concrete cinderblock, and the moss on the jagged rock.
You need to touch the leaves of the trees--
    touch the green grass of spring, touch cold icy things.

You need to smell the saltwater; the scent of perfume,
    flowers and weeds-- pine trees.
You need your sense of smell; you want your nose to tell.

You need your sense of taste--
Taste your lover's lips, taste the snowy bliss,
    taste your dinner-- poor, poor sinner.
You need to taste the victory, Jesus paid for you-- lovingly.

The Only One I Need
by Amber Crisp

I wake with you on my mind
I sleep with you in my dreams.
I wait for you to hold me near and
Whisper promises of love in my ear.
I dread the times we have to part
I wish I could hold you forever
We'd never have to be apart.
I love you now and will for always
I'll love you even on my dying day
You're the one that keeps me going
You're the reason I wake, and
I hope you wake knowing
All I ever want is for you to be near.

A Moment of Peace
by Christy Crow - age 17

Today I realized that people are never who they seem,
    But we fall in love with what we see,
I realized that there are many people I will never remember,
    But would change my life if we never met,
I realized that a heart is fragile,
    But a mind is strong,
That everything takes time,
    But if you wait it will heal,
I realized that people change,
    But always stay the same deep down,
That although you're lonely,
    You're never alone,
I realized that words are fire,
    And can ruin everything built up,
I realized that tears are cleansing,
    And hugs are a seal of love,
I realized that the people you love,
    You will always love,
    Even in a memory,
    And that's all that matters.

Book
by Amber Crowe - age 15

I always miss you when you're away and when
you say you don't believe me it makes me wonder
how well you really know me

you think that I'm such an easy book to read I
have large print so you don't strain your eyes thick
grippable pages to turn and I'm only a couple
chapters long not even a book really just a
short predictable story and you believe all this
so I'll tell you something:

you don't know me as well as you think although
some parts of me you've memorized there are
pages and pages that you haven't seen yet
many chapters unread and many thoughts not
shared and I'd love to show it all to you I am
so much more than you think

World
by Ciara Cumiskey - age 12

Water
Land
Creatures Great and Small
Dawns and Dusks
Love
Hate
Kindness
Cruelness
Earth

Again
by Nicole Cummings - age 15

You hit me and I
come back for more.
My screams are
silent, my intentions
true.
Silent but deadly I
plot my revenge.
Short and sweet; your
screams are silent.
Quick & clean and all
that's left behind are a
tear & a dream.

Shadows
by Richard Curren

Through the foggy shadows
of the mirror...she stares
into the empty, sunlit air.
Summoned there perchance?
Perhaps...
... Who knows?
... Who cares?
The fading scents
of yesterday's todays?
The lingering hope
for youthful stares?
   ... who knows?
   ... who cares?
Only she...
   she, who through
     the twilight stares,
      into the lonely,
       senseless air.

Stand
by Erica Curry - age 13

What's the world coming to
everywhere you look,
everywhere you go.
Someone is getting killed,
or is so high on dope.
We need to take a stand,
but who will do it?
I guess no one is a big enough man.
All they can do is talk the talk,
but no one will ever walk the walk,
If we can only stop one kid,
well that's all they are.
That will be one in a million
and that's a pretty good start.

Life is Crazy
by Trudy DaCosta - age 15

   Life is crazy,
Unexpected,
But still to be respected.

   Drive by shootings,
Gang recruitings,
Children Dying,
Forever Lying,
People all around the world crying.

   Hustlers selling drugs,
Kids getting beat up by thugs.

   Innocent people afraid for their lives,
Trying to survive,
No one in which they can confide.

   Life is crazy,
Unexpected,
But still to be respected.

Fenced In
by Angela Daigle - age 15

Trapped in a little cage
is where I seem to live
filling it with **rage**
nothing you can give

Locked into a room
locked without a key
waiting for my **doom**
what is wrong with me?

Endorsed inside this gate
is where I need to stay
sitting here all my life
every night and day

Sealed in a cube of glass
wishing to climb out
realizing my time has passed
jumping all about

Staring out the window
no way for me to **yell**
it's like looking into heaven
while I'm inside of **hell**

This is how my life seems
sealed and locked to me
what am I supposed to do?
Who am I supposed to be?

Just So You Know
by Matt Daily - age 17

I just want you to know
You're my beautiful, bright, white snow.
You're my candle burning bright.
You're the stars of moonlit night.
You're the only one I've loved.
You're the one that I've dreamt of.
You're the only one for me.
My love for you's an endless sea.
It's the number of stars in the sky
Or all the numbers of human lies.
Please don't leave me in darkness, alone.
It makes me feel your heart's cold stone.

From Far away
by Joseph R. Daley - age 19

Two lovers embrace,
in a passionate kiss,
laughter and smiles,
a fulfilled wish.
They warmly hold,
on to a love so great,
They've got the rest of their lives,
they can hardly wait.
Together they live,
In a heavenly dream,
I just wish they knew,
Things aren't what they seem.

I stand and watch them,
from a spot far away,
I was once happy,
long ago was the day.
I barely remember,
what it was like,
to be held by a woman,
to have good dreams at night.
In all of my life,
I could never have dreamed,
that the woman I loved,
would ever leave me.
I do know now,
with out any illusion,
love may only bring,
pain and confusion.

Lock the gate
by Joseph R. Daley - age 19

I look inside the empty shell,
a dusty place, yes indeed,
one last sigh, it's time to leave.
If there was one other way,
to put everything back,
to fill the grey with color,
it's too late for any turning back,
I want to cry, emotion flow,
but I hide it all in my heart,
I've done good this far,
so why should a new way start?
I walk outside the door,
I don't want to leave,
but I can't hold on, not anymore.
I walk down the sidewalk,
I don't look behind,
I will never return, memories flood my mind.
I reach the end of the path,
a heaviness in my heart,
I look to the horizon,
I don't know where to start.
so many places, so many things,
I wonder to myself,
what will the future bring?
I tell myself softly,
It had to be fate,
things were never right,
and I lock the gate.

Love
by Roselynn A. Dalipe - age 14

Love
is like a rose.
It excites you
when it blooms.
It is so fragile
yet so precious
most of all it
is so beautiful.

Black
by Tracy Dalton - age 12

I like the color black,
Just like a cat.
Not just that but a bat.
Black in the color of a night sky,
When it get day light it say "Good Bye!"
I wouldn't like to get a black eye,
When I don't I just sigh.

A Missing Part of Me
by Ann Marie D'Angelo

I sit here and cry thinking of the great times we had,
And if she knew how much I truly missed her she'd be glad,
To know that she'd always have a friend in me.
But now that she's gone, I guess what's done is done and meant to be.
She left because her life was too hard to live,
But to have her here now no one knows what I would give.
She was a great friend and probably one
of the only people who understood me,
And when she ran away left me here to cry but if she could only see,
Me here now crying she'd be sad,
because that's the type of person she was.
I envied her, she had everything going for her,
She was gorgeous, smart and definitely sweet.
And maybe someday we'll once again meet.
Jen, you're the best and I love you so,
And because of that one day you may never know.
I'm sorry I was mad at you, I never had a chance to say goodbye,
The guilt and loneliness makes me sit here and cry.
Good luck in life but never forget this friend,
For maybe some day we'll meet again.
And we'll all be together and happy again.

Mother
by Daniel Daniele - age 13

From the minute he appeared to Her, Her eyes were filled with tears
For she was chosen as the one, to bear the Savior for future years
Of all the women in the world, His blessings went out to Her
A peasant woman of true faith, a virgin, graceful and pure
Many days and many nights, were spent in preparation
In the coming of what was going to be, an utter celebration
Before she bore this special child, sent from heaven down to earth
Faces aroused at the arrival, as She took a breath and gave Him birth
From the minute He came into the world, He was blessed upon the surface
To spread the word of God around, was His special purpose
She clothed Him well and gave Him food, She cared for Him so dearly
She was His loving Mother, She showed Her love so clearly
Then the awful day arrived, when she stood in utter shock
She watched them take Her son away, they didn't give Her time to talk
He was brought to a king who judged his arrest,
the people wanted Him dead
He suffered 40 days of utter pain, His Mother cried at his knees, as he bled
For Her to watch Him upon a cross, with nails torn through His skin
How devastating for Her to bear, Her loss, and their win
She watched Her Son die on the cross, with blood upon His head
She stood in agony and pain, at Her only Son who now was dead
She cried and cried for many nights, Her eyes all filled with tears
For when it came when Her Son returned, Her cries turned into cheers
Her Son was back, He had risen from the dead, She was filled with Joy
For She remembered how it was like, when He was just a little boy
She went through a lot of pain, which then turned into glee
For when Her time had finally come, She had been set free
The month of May was dedicated to Her, which we will continue to carry
This special month of celebration, for this very special Mother Mary

Remembrance Day Poem
by Daniel Daniele - age 13

Happiness, sorrow, disappointment, joy,
All this and more, I felt as a boy
When the big package came I thought I had nothing to lose,
Until I opened it quickly and read the bad news
The army, oh no! It couldn't be,
That's when I remembered the horrible D
Danger! Death! Devious! Oh No!
They came to my door with the news- it wasn't so
They pulled me and dragged me "Oh stop it!" I said
They hit me and slapped me, my face turned all red
I got shoved in the van, I was sent far away,
They put me in a suit I had nothing to say
The large open fields, the big heavy guns,
"Attack!" someone shouted, "Before everyone runs!"
That's exactly what I did, I ran for my life,
The gunshot was heard like the stab of a knife
It ached and it groaned, my body was still,
The bullet past through me, it was their time to kill
My mind had gone blank, my eyes saw just black,
Aside to the fact there was blood on my back
Good-bye my family, my friends, farewell,
"Is he dead?" someone said. They couldn't tell
Now on the ground with my heartbeat so low,
My breathing so soft, my body like dough
"Kill him!" they shouted "Make sure he's dead!"
"Please don't kill me!" is what I said
They kicked me, beat me and pulled the trigger once more,
With blood in the air, my mind shut like a door
I lost all my thoughts, I finally sighed,
I never realized the things I was thankful for, until this day, before I died

Haiku
by Jason M. Danko

petals of the rose
wilting unexpectedly
early frosts remorse

moonlights progeny
wander dark & empty streets
accompany them

midnights heat
speeding cars and lonely dreams
lie shattered in the street

flashing neon signs
evoke haunted memories of
desolation

early afternoon
clouds drift lazily;
nobody notices them

memories of
bonds broken;
flower by the sea

the soft blowing wind
and lovers secret whispers
echo through the trees

Spring Robins
melting snow
a warm cup of tea

Power
by Sam Dascani - age 14

Down the stairs where the unknown stride,
it's never over for the unknown.
Across the current to find your life,
you know that nothing has flown.
The ending of the war,
has yet to see.
The beginning war,
has yet to be.
Not a single light is shown
on the skies of gray.
The flow of light,
is not to brighten the day.
The strongest hand
is to disappear from land,
while the king is to stand,
but only polite to the grand.
The sorrow of love
kills as fast as it can,
and not even the joker
can ever laugh again.

Heritage
by Kim Datoush

Denied of my heritage,
of how I came to be,
my face his,
his face mine,
she never wanted me to see.

If she had only told me,
the secret from her youth,
I would have never blamed her,
because she spoke the truth.

But because she chose to lie,
she did damage to us both inside,
the secret kept for no good cause,
to protect her stubborn pride.

I came to see past the shadow,
and now my day arrived,
the day I found you, father,
the one I was deprived.

A Fragile Heart
by Megan K. Daubert - age 14

My heart is fragile,
If I give it to you,
Please promise not to break it.

My heart is fragile,
Don't run with it.
Please don't let it shatter.

My heart is fragile,
Take care of it,
Please be slow.

My heart is fragile.

Sunrise
by Robin Daughtry - age 12

The sun is a shimmering coin
far above us in the sky. As the
sun rises it's warm light brings
joy to everyone. The outrageous
beauty and uniqueness of the
sun as it rises is so indescribable.
So I think I'll just sit back and
watch it.

Let the Sunlight Through the Window
by Angela d'Avignon - age 12

Let the sunlight through the window
let it shine upon a flower
let it shine upon your face
May you smile for many an hour.

Let the sunlight through the window
let it shine upon the floor
let it shine on all the walkings
May you walk many more.

Let the sunlight through the window
let it shine upon a chair
let it shine where many sat when they were weary, where they rested,
 let down their hair.

Let the sunlight through the window
let it shine upon the cup
where the pessimist says "Half-empty!"
the optimist says "Half-full!" and watch him drink up.

But foolish is the man who pulls the blinds and pushes sunlight out,
For he is pushing happiness and optimism away-
pouring them out through life's spout.

But you, take heed
do not be as foolish!
Pull up those blinds and let the sunlight shine!
Into your cheerful house, your home.
Let your voice sing in a joyful tone!

Let golden sun pour over your life,
through your windows,
and in the garbage throw out strife,
And let the sunlight through the window-
Let it brighten up your life.

Dan River
by Clarice Lawson Davis

Hey Dan River ! -- Where are you running to,
lying deep and still in sapphire shadows ---
Is it to catch the first ray of the sun,
after the darkened night ?
Your rhythmic gurgle is a chant of joy,
along the lonely paths you tread ---
from mountain sides, masqued in nakedness,
searching for unsaid reaches, through parched land,
grassy fields, and tall forest.
Tangled clouds hang high,
as you wind your massive way,
along the thick red loam, and gusts of wind,
send bubbling tremors, upon your wispy ripples.
White weeping willows dip their fingers,
into your cool waters ---
and searing quail fly above your mirrored surface,
to drink, from your depth.
Hey Dan River ! -- Within the realms of your troubled spirit,
is a gentle, quiet, interlude ---
not asking, not seeking, but simply keeping,
within the things you've seen --
and of the places you have been.
Perhaps, it is well you cannot speak.
I'll let you pretend that you know how the secrets,
of my heart revolve.
Grasp instead the mellowed current of your flowing timeless, stream,
that rushes to greet each new and living thing.

Treasures

L.O.V.E.
by Lacey Davis - age 13

In this world of ears, I can hear your cries,
and there you are, standing in the swirled tears,
that come from my eyes.

Love. L-O-V-E. Lasting, Outshining, Valiant, Entrust,
My love for you is a candle of heaven that has been lit,
you are the wick and I am the wax,
love also needs wit, heart is what it lacks.

My soul has become sea foam,
in which does your boat roam.
This exploration is very excruciating,
because every time you smile,
my soul keeps on evaporating.

My face is stiff from crying,
my body is tired from trying,
and my heart is crushed from dying.

Day after day, night after night,
I hide, wishing he was touching my side,
But still I may, and still I fight,
trying to get through each day and night.

Rain
by Margaret L. Davis - age 17

An angel's tear
That falls from
The heavens above
Towards the earth below
Lands on my shoulder.
Looking up
Towards the bluish grey sky
I wonder
Is she crying for me?

Naive Pigeon (Move On)
by Nicholas Davis - age 17

Wallowing in anguish behind the twilight's shadows,
With your hope cloaked by a woeful shroud,
You watch your limp love as she lay dead on her back,
Wings broken and folded loosely at her sides,
    with hallowed-out eyes.

Your stare now goes unrequited;
Love was snuffed out be the everlasting zephyr
Which you so stubbornly defy.

Your coo mourns forth a hollow dirge
    As I carry off the lump of white down
        - To plant her in a bed of celestial roses,
            Or a crematory of stygian flames -
And still you keep your eternal vigil
With your black feathers tattered
And ruffled to spite the cold wind:
Your ignorance retains your desperate and fruitless, hidden hope.
And you sit and stare in pain-
            in vain-
At the cold, dank, crimson concrete
Where once was mirrored your love and affection;
    You're still waiting for a reflection.

On The Outside Looking In
by Nicole Davis - age 14

On the outside looking in,
Always at the circle's edge
The center hidden from view,
When at last an opening obtained
Always pushed back outwards and away.
No, I don't fit in.
On the outside, looking in.

The Dream Seeker
by Stephanie Davis - age 15

Dreams are a part of you; a part of life.
Dreams hold your wildest fanticies and your most hellish nightmares.
There is a collector of dreams; a Dream Seeker some people call him.
He goes around and gathers dreams when people fall asleep.
He carries all the dreams in a velvet sack, resting upon his shoulder, back to his wondrous destination.
The Dream Seeker arranges the dreams by length of time, age of person, and intensity.
He feeds off the images; his soul drinks from the illusions.
He lives off the human imagination.
He is the Dream Seeker; the <u>only</u> one.

Majestic Seas
by Lindsay M. Decker - age 13

The waves lap upon the beach,
The busy gull lets out a screech,
The dolphins play among the waves,
And hide amid the rocky caves.

The crabs scuttle through the sand,
They gather food where water meets land,
The minnows quickly swim away,
To tease the crabs another day.

The coral reef doth hide a trove,
Where no man has ever dove,
Where the fish's colors are bright and true,
And the majestic seas sparkle with blue.

A Goodbye
by Malinda DeGroot - age 14

If there is one thing I know
It's that I love you two so
You've meant so much to me
I'll remember you for eternity
The times we've spent together
The love that will last forever

A friendship that is true
And a heart that now is blue
Even though we must part
I'll remember you in my heart
The Lord meant for us to meet
At a church on an Oklahoma City street

He gave me two great souls
With one great goal
And a love that is so dear
That makes me want you near
And because of this I rejoice everyday
Since you two came my way

Choices
by Ana Laura De la Garza - age 15

A person has many choices in life.
To take his own life or
to die a natural death.
To lie, cheat, and steal or
to be honest and giving.
There are things you cannot choose like
the family you are born into.
Other things you may wish you didn't
have to choose between like whether
to take the life of your unborn child or
to risk your own for the child's life.
Then there is the choice we must
all make during the course of our life
whether to use paper or plastic
grocery bags.

Black Rose
by Michelle Delancey

Walking through a field of
roses,
I've always felt a thorn.
Walking through my
memories,
Shattered, broken, torn.

Like I'd imagined roses,
To be beautiful to the touch.
I envisioned my life,
To be held without a crutch.

But among this field of
flowers,
Grows a evil weed.
My nightmares come to haunt
me,
Grows from an evil seed.

A black rose among the red,
Is like a devil among the weak.
Always looking for some
good,
To devour and make it bleak.

Growing on a twisted vine,
They rise up to the sun.
Trying to block out the light,
Wanting to be the only one.

Soon the evil flower withers,
And the gardener's glad it
died.
My heart is the gardener
And my soul has withered
inside.

Hello-Goodbye
by Tanya DelaPena

By chance--
    But no accident
Just a few spoken words -
    And a simple wave
As if to brush off
    Not too thrilling - at first
Inevitably, though, forecasting
    A site of first love.

Then words were spoken--
    Language of two personalities
Gazes interlocked
    Both reached
And a bridge was made
    Joining in the middle
By intertwining fingertips
    Rocking the waves underneath them.

With the rising of the tide
    To drown them
Into a realm of emotions
    Never felt before
The gentle rocking
    Making each a little queasy
But remaining calm as if letting
    It be - letting it happen.

Two souls
    Uniting
Of two unconstrained
    Minds.

Then, suddenly
    The winds became stronger
Stretching laced fingers
    Holding onto nails
Air is scarce
    So words can't be heard
Waves crash too loud
    So the bridge came tumbling down.

Angel Of Death
by Linnette DeLarre

You showed up like an angel out of the night.
You used your smooth charm to sway my emotions.
You took possession of my body with your touch.
You claimed my heart with your tenderness.

You spoke your words of love with passion.
You changed my world with your special ways.
You kept me warm when the nights grew cold.
You brightened my days with your love.

You made me cry with your words of anger.
You knocked the love I had for you out.
You punched through your perfect image.
You became the angel of death.

You cut down all the people I cared for.
You played with my mind and my heart.
You put me in a living hell.
You never should of hurt me like you did.

You ruined me. I am empty because of you.
You erased love and trust from my world.
You belong in the fires of hell.
You are the angel of death.

"Knots"
by Crystal Dennis - age 17

Just one simple word
Could show you my life
One syllable on the outside
But hides many behind it
Who would have thought
That one word
could hide so many thoughts and stories
Who would have thought
That one word
Could show you everything
Everyone who should know this word
Will now also know me.

A Poor Woman Finds Divine Providence
by Alba DiPaola

There was a poor woman whose mane was Simple.
She lived each day without moving a finger --
and sat on her doorsteps with nothing to do
but yawn all day till her jaws hurt too.

She watched people go by with their bounty,
and often inquired, "How did you get such bounty?"
"Divine Providence, good woman," they said.
"Divine Providence?" said Simple.

She was perplexed: but then decided--
to look in every nook
for Divine bounty of any kind,
hoping to improve her life.

When out of the blue a melody came to spew,
from a fair lad whose songs were true.
"Young lad," she said, "Have you by chance
seen the Divine Providence?"

The lad continued to sing melodiously --
while she listened attentively ...
"Divine Providence is often found
by helping others-the spinner, the woodman, and miller too!"

With both hands she slapped her head,
"Stupid, stupid!" she said.
She understood only too well
the fair lad whose songs were true.

Then all at once ran out to find:
the spinner, the woodman, and miller too.
By now you know how this story ends.
She finally found her Divine Providence!

Untitled
by Sara de Sousa - age 15

I can't cry anymore.
My tears for you have gone.
I'm tired of being without you,
I'm tired of having to mourn.

I can't remember when I lost you,
Or even if you were ever here.
When I try to picture your face,
I can only see a cold blank stare.

I wish you were here forever,
Your presence would end the pain.
At night I hope and I pray that
One day I will see you again.

Rain
by Carrie DeVelbiss - age 18

Rain pours out of her
    eyes
       every time she remembers
       his magnificent face.
The expression in his cold eyes
    makes her weak heart tremble
      with unbearable pain.
        His voice is filled with barely suppressed

  hate.
His manner is full of undeniable
    contempt.
       She does not understand exactly
        what she has done wrong,
      and neither does he.
He just knows that he does not want her
       anymore.
He makes it rain.
  He makes the acidic drops
    flow from her eyes
      like blood from an open wound
        The mist sprays upon her face
       and stings more than just her skin.
She loves him,
    but he does not want her anymore,
     and because of this
      she knows it will
        rain...
          forever.

Lily Pad
by Grace L.A. DiBella

The splash of water upon
the rivers shore,
make a pattern of
floating forever more..;
To walk upon a
Lily Pad,
would make my life
ever so glad.

Gone
by Erin Devlin - age 15

How could you leave me when I was so young
My life hadn't started, it hadn't begun.

You left us all in such a mess
All so sad, under so much stress.

The world came crashing down on top of me
I held it in for none to see.

All that's important now seems so small
My knees so shaky I'm surprised I don't fall.

All the things I am now deprived
Like you teaching me how to drive.

You're not going to be there on my wedding day
To walk me down the aisle and give me away.

My children will never get to hug their granddad
Never knowing the love they should've had.

I will never get to hug and kiss you; see you laugh or cry
For that I will miss you 'til the day I die.

Sacrifice
by David Dickey - age 19

God almighty
With mercy and grace
Let me look
And see Your face
Hope and peace
Combined in You
Thoughts and dreams
In You come true
Life eternal
You offer me
Life eternal
You set me free
On that hill
You gave your life
On that hill
The ultimate sacrifice
God almighty
With mercy and grace
Let me wipe
Those tears from Your face
I gave You my life
Cause You died for me
Because of You
Now I can be

THANK YOU!!

Darkness
by Jesica Diermier - age 15

Laying in the dark
Wishing for something better
Hoping it will come true.
Crying for someone long gone,
Praying for someone almost gone.
Waiting in silence through it all.

I Miss Him
by Sarah Dixon-Sullivan - age 14

I miss him.
He is part of me that is not there.
A piece that broke off
And fell away.
I have not seen him for so long
And more pieces are breaking and falling off
More pieces of my heart.
I still miss him.

Fantasies
by Jesse Donithan - age 14

At times we're often so deceived by our illusions,
That we can't see life realistically.
And when we're forced to look at things as they really are,
The shock of recognition can hurt.
So while the truth of love seems so difficult to find,
It's probably right in front of our face.
And by overcoming the obstacles of life
Our love is put into place.
The incongruity between love and desire
Is the main irony of this emotion.
In our minds we'd expect to share our deepest secrets,
But, in reality our devotion means nothing of the sort.
The true identity of our source is incognito.
Yet the knowledge is a phenomenon.
This powerful feeling is a mystery,
But it's not driven by a pressure or person.
Once you've fallen into the hopeless essence of love,
Youthful innocence is lost forever.
And although persistence may be rewarded,
The chance of appreciation is slim.
Still faith should not be lost forever,
There is always your imagination.
And while the pain of reality is always on the other side,
Let your fantasies ease the frustration.

Night
by Siera Kay Dooley - age 13

I hate night.
I love it when I'm asleep-
And I can dream.
To get away from this thing.
But I hate night
When I can't sleep.
When everything else is dead,
And it seems, so am I.
But I'm alive.
Still breathing, still growing,
Still scared and uncontrolling.
And I hate day.
Too old to go out and play.
It's cloudy and ugly
And so much like myself.
I love to be healthy. I love to sleep.
I love to play out in the sun.
I hate when this takes over,
I hate that it controls her.
It's too hard to fight it,
All I can do is bite it.
I hate night.
Because night is when I cry.

Light
by Cathy Dodge - age 14

Shines from the heavens,
Burning so bright.
Shields you from the evil
That comes out at night.
Scares away ghosts
That kill you with fright.
So bright, so everlasting,
This simple thing called light.

The Sin I Confess
by Angelica Dopheide

Once you loved me or you told me so,
but twice you hurt me and still made the hurt grow.
You held me close and completed my dreams,
you had me believing you'd mute all my screams.
You opened my heart and reached inside,
you pulled everything out and crushed my every pride.
You cradled my love in the palm of your hand,
you swallowed it whole and left me completely damned.
What more could you take from me?
You took a love that I once had,
and a dream that I grasped like it
was an old and faded fad.
You poured out my every tear like it was water to waste,
you brushed me aside like an old crusty toothpaste.
Why'd you say you love me when you could care less,
despite all your lies and hurt you made, I still love you
like a sin to confess.

Hardest Good-Bye
by Dawn Dorn - age 13

We all learned a lesson, on that dreadful day.
But for us to learn that lesson, someone else had to pay.
Pay our fee for friendship, and our fee for love.
For us to stay down here, she was sent to the heaven's above.
We all sit to wonder, why not one of us.
We know she didn't suffer, or give any fuss.
In our holy garden, she never got to grow.
Just a tiny little rose-bud, and she was the one to go.
Everyone always thinks, that the flowers are to die.
Now that she is gone, we know that it's all a lie.
God had a good reason, for her to have to leave.
For Heaven is a quilt of joy, and she was just one weave.
One weave had made a difference,e for both you and I.
Even though we got a once in a lifetime lesson,
we still wish she hadn't had to die.
But when we kneel to our knee's to pray, tears start falling and we cry.
For we all now know that the hardest thing, we have to do, is say "goodbye."

Moving
by Wendy Dotzler - age 12

Moving away
far far away
Long in the distance
By a beautiful bay

Where grass is green
and birds sing
But that isn't to say
I'm here to stay

Dreams
by Dorothy Doubet

Happiness pours on me like rain
No longer can I feel the pain
Hurt no longer lingers
Love has placed upon me its fingers
Soft sweet whispers invade my space
In my dreams I feel and see your face
I can feel the hope in the air
My dreams are so fair
To be near you always
To feel we could fly away

The Ann-Marie
by Annie Down

To Thesea she goes
her sail's up high.
Gliding through the waves
farther and farther. She a ways
no trouble at all. As she turns
a beautiful horizon before her.
She goes slowly in the breeze
enjoying herself taking in everything.
Coming home, the Ann-Marie.

Who am I
by Farrah Sheree Dozier - age 20

Who am I,
 I may be different
But I am just like everybody
 else.
I need love,
 but maybe in a different
 way.
My love may be the same
 as me or different.
My mother and others may
 find it hard to understand.
But I am being me,
 Who I am.

Bed of Roses
by Kristin A. Drake

   Life is as a bed of Roses;
    For every bed of Roses has
a multitude of thorns.
    In order to touch the tender
petals or smell the delicate
fragrances;
    One reaching for the rose
could be scratched and stuck
many times.
    Just as in life a person
reaching for a tender or beautiful
thing in life may experience many
paint.
    Yet in the end holds the memories
of the moment beauty was obtained and
has learned how to stand up through
all the struggles, pains and hurts in life.

Life's Treasures
by Sarah Dufresne - age 16

Trust is something we must share
Just like love and time and care
Some say diamonds are a girls best friend
But they always shatter in the end
Some say life is like a book
If you're afraid, you shouldn't look
Some say love is like the sun
But it is gone when the day is done
I think friends you always treasure
Just like love and time and pleasure
They lift your spirits when they're low
And make your life some how glow
When they see upon your face a frown
They do their best to turn it up-side-down
A friendship like this should always be cherished
Until the day you perish

"Simple Changes"
by Kelly P. Dugan - age 13

A thousand chanting mists of wind
shows the green grass rising with simple changes.
The creativity has no boundaries with the
current knowledge that life bestows upon.
We choose our water ways and make the small adjustments,
that so often occur, wisely.
The age of lengthiness has come, but now must leave, tiny
accomplishments overpower.
Simple changes and dreams are why the world advances successfully.

I Am
by Tara Duncan - age

I am the need
the hurt, the want
and desire.
I am the smoke, that comes with the fire
I am the rain, the sun
the stars and the moon
I am the healer
I am the wand
I am the knife, that pierces your heart
I am the hand, that tears it apart
I am the love, that blooms in the May
I am the hate, that forever will stay
I am the confusion
the guilt and the sin
I am the chain that keeps you locked in
I am the dream and the fantasy
I am the hopes, that will never be
I am the warmth you seek when there's rain
I am the coldness that causes such pain
I am the shiver that runs down your spin
when you get drunk, I am the wine
I am the night against your bare skin
I am the passion that closes you in
when you feel the desire deep in your body
that feeling that's there, always will be
because you see
I am that feeling
that desire...
   Is me

My Little Mare
by Jennifer Dupuis - age 14

Her mane flickered through the breeze,
like a fire you could not cease.

Her hoofs pounded on the ground,
and her tail swatted the flies all around.

When I jumped on her back and went for a ride,
she never tripped or bucked she would just glide.

She was the best friend that I ever had,
and when we won ribbons it made me very glad.

I'll never forget you my little mare.
I'll hold you in my heart oh so dear.

Breaking Up
by Jessica Durocher - age 16

One day we were in love, totally happy together,
but there was a change and now we want to stay away forever.
We used to always be together, we could never be apart,
evidently time changed all the feelings in our hearts.
The way it ended was horrible, all the screams and shouts,
the need for it to end wasn't all that hard to figure out.
I had always thought you would be there for me,
the reason I trusted you, I now do not see.
You set out to hurt me, maybe it was all just for fun,
and I'm just left here wishing our relationship had never begun.

ignis fatuus
by Jeremy Dziedzic - age 18

uttering painfully to the heavenly mist
"i cherish the vagueness of it all
but i'd rather let it go,
i'd rather let it fall."
so entrench this notion
into my mind
for i am the foolish one
that they left behind.

they left me here
in this land of fantasy
"is anything real?
is anything me?"
"is there anything more for me to find,
or am i lost in this hypocrisy?"

so what's your motives in trying to seduce
your breathtaking maneuvers do not amuse.

i'll accept your last temptation
to go on living
this deceptive attraction;
so trick me into your delights
just try and deceive
entwine me in a life
that i will never leave...

that i will never leave.

"Take Me"
by Tricia Earp - age 15

It makes a lot of sense that it should
matter in a lonely way
As if I say: sure it don't, except in the
most mysterious way.
The reason is because,
As I try to forget you, you still remain
in my head so strongly - it kills!
But I show it in such an invisible way
Would you let it be me that you feel for?
I wish you let me be your love.
Scattered and broken as I try my
hardest to grip onto your sweet thoughts,
it eases me so gently
won't - you - love - me - just - a - little

In Loving Memory of My Sweet Kitty - Jumper
by Lorna Eastcott

It began in one of those garbage dumpers
    for the little one soon to be known as jumper.
What cruel person would act that lowly to
    leave a kitten in refuse to starve so slowly.
No bigger than the palm of your hand
    when seen and rescued by a caring young man.
Apartment dweller unable to provide a home
    beseeched please to me his Mom by phone.
Three spots and tail of orange tabby on white
    I set out him on my shoulder one night.
At golden arches we obtained some lunch
    and on the road upon this we two did much.
Arriving late to a trailer at a highways camp
    facilities were cramped the weather damp.
That my partner wasn't thrilled it appeared
    would we both be thrown out it was feared.
The next day a picture captured was the best kitten
    lay asleep curled up on his chest.
Many priceless ones were taken since then -
    the type invoking "remember when."
He adapted to Dolly a Dalmatian we got next year
    slept in her bed and groomed her ear.
They shared drinking from a toilet one day even
    lay atop our car catching some rays.
A fearless hunter in and about the house he caught
    shrew - rat - weasel besides mouse.
One evening he went and laid beneath our
    bed - looking sick and by morning was dead.
Ten years he filled our hearts with love and
    we think of him at rest without pain above.
Grateful for those wonderful pictures now
    when memories return like his squeaky meow.

Trust Me
by Allison Ebbecke - age 16

Trust me with your love, for I will not misuse it.
Trust me with your heart, for I will not abuse it.
Trust me with your tears, for I will wipe them away.
Trust me with your thoughts, for I will light your way.
Trust me with your hands, for I will hold them tight.
Trust me with your feet, for we will walk all night.
Trust me with your soul, for I will carry you home.
Trust me with your mind, for you are not alone.
Trust me with your eyes, for I will help you see.
But before I can do any of this, you must trust in me.

Winters New Hail
by Hayley Ebersole - age 11

The winters new white hail escapes from its cold black home,
To freedom,
No longer enslaved in the cold, bitter darkness.
Is it worth it?
Falling like a leaf?
Falling.... so this is what its been waiting for?
So this is the amusing ride?
Worth it?
Yes, oh yes, worth it all.
As the cold, hail body drops on the frostbitten grass,
Pop!
Up it flies a little, then down.
Now it's over.
The children frolic gaily on the same grass,
Wrapped in layers,
Skip!
No, the pleasureful delight is not over!
Now is the best part,
To see them,
Them, frolicking about,
Yes, this is what it is for,
To see their grateful faces.
Eyelashes lined with sister sleet,
And mouths open wide to catch the falling snow.
They go inside to open arms,
And the hailstone lay dead with its joy.
Yes. It was worth it, worth it all.

Muddy Sinkholes
by Kimberly R. Eck

I think its raining outside,
I hear it splatter on the lawn.
Each drop falls off the roses. It
lands in the dirt and then its gone.
As I stand outside, and I let it wash
across my face...
it drip-drops into puddles,
and then it ripples into its place.
As the rain gives way, I am left
with nothing but the mud,
and the buzzing of mosquitos that
are still hungry for my blood.
I look down into the puddles, murky
and alive with mosquito larvae,
and I laugh at God for cursing
us with another sultry summer day.
A day filled with thorns and mud
and mosquitos biting at my soul.
I let a handful of mud ooze through
my fingers back into its sinkhole.
I let the rain dry on my face, and
on the roses slightly brown.
I let my pale, stringy white lips
slowly curve up from their frown.
I guess I'll make the most of
this humid summer day.
I smash the mosquito feasting
on my shoulder, and flick the mush away.

Sadness
by Beth Edel - age 13

Sadness for what?
For my own mistakes,
Or maybe from persuasion.
I don't know which.
All I know is that this,
Sadness inside hurts,
And causes heart-bleeding pain.
to some it can even cause insanity.
It drives you crazy knowing,
That it makes you weak & helpless.
It's only cure is happiness.

See
by Rachel Edelshteyn - age 15

From a pauper to a blind man,
I yearn for what it is you see.
You view no world of filth,
just a discolored eternity.

For if I were a blind man,
which is what I wish to be,
I'd live my life in pure content,
not seeing what I see.

Not knowing what goes on in life,
Dear blind man I envy
the way that you are numb
to all- a loss of sensitivity.

A blind man has a privilege,
one which none can see,
A blind man has a sense of touch,
that touched the heart of me.

A Night to Remember
by Scott Edwards - age 15

On a clear warm night on this very land
An old man took his young grandson's hand
They strolled through the park and looked for the stars
While catching fireflies to take home in jars

The little boy asked why the sky was blue
As the old man laughed not having a clue
The little boy asked if the sun goes to bed
The old man smiled and just shook his head

The boy grew fearful as the night grew dark
The old man held him while they left the park
He seemed very wise and advanced in his years
Yet just like the boy with questions and fears

Forever
by Tasheena Edwards - age 15

Just one look
that's all it took.
You had me hooked.
Your style was new.
I had no clue
that all that stuff
about love was true
And then to make it better
we're still together
I really think it can be forever.
And last, I need to say
I love you more each day
and I pray you never go away.

Love In Any Language
by Amanda Eggers

There are millions of all different languages
And in each one there are billions of different words
English, French, German, Latin, Spanish,
Portuguese, Arabic, Chinese, Japanese
All of these languages and others
Are the tongues of human kind
And only one word means the same thing
in every language
This universal, controversial, brilliant work
Is small yet undying
That one almighty word is LOVE

The Sun
by Michelle Mostovy-Eisenberg - age 17

The sun helps me tell my story, the story of a love lost. The sun rises and sets, which signals a new day; the sun has yet to set on my love for you, and a new chapter has yet to begin.

I first met my love many years ago-- I was young, and so unaware of what strong feelings were; yet, I somehow discovered what love was when I met him.

All was lost when I looked into his pale blue eyes, the colour of the sky on a clear day. His eyes told their own story-- his eyes showed warmth, understanding, humor, intelligence-- all I was looking for in a man.

Sunset after sunset passed, and my heart was full of pain-- I could not tell him that he held my heart-- I could not bear to look at him, to look into his beautiful eyes. My heart was to be torn apart by this man; yet, we had never shared one embrace-- we were still strangers, yet he knew me better than anyone else-- I felt I understood him, searching for all of the answers in his eyes.

It is now a long time since my first love occurred-- my heart is still broken-- I still shed unwanted tears-- for him, only him. He who first stole my heart left his scar upon my heart, for he still controls my heart, for the sun has yet to set on this day.

Woman of Voyage
by Kristan Elkins

I Am Woman, Hear me Roar!
From the jungles of Africa, to the cold Alaskan hut
From the loud and noisy streets of New York
I am Woman!

I am Woman, feel my pain, the pain endured during many historical times
Pain that may take a lifetime to heal

I am Woman, help me make this world a place where
Peace will endure everyone's Mind, Body and Soul!
I am Woman! A Woman at peace

This Is Not
by Rick Ellingson

This is not our land
    For it is the property
        Of the planet earth.
These are not our forests
    For they are the property
        Of the planet earth.
These are not our rivers, lakes, or oceans;
    For they are the property
        Of the planet earth.
The animals and plants are not
    Our property
        Belongs to the planet earth.
Human own nothing. As humans we are all
    Temporarily.

We Walked On the Lagan*
by M.W. El Nachef, M.D.

My love to you like pleasure from pain,
with all the buttons being turned on high
like an angel ascending in the sky-
through nicotine clouds and acid rain.

We walked on the Lagan hand in hand
I said my fairy: what's in the know?
You said: As lovers on the go,
Love's to enjoy, not understand.

Don't look at me like a child being spoiled
There's a child in me that shall never grow
for a smile from you, his eyes shall glow
He was and he will be sixteen old

My love to you is never in vain
It's more than simple "give and take"
It's more than burning on the stake
It's the more you lose, the more you gain

I think, my fairy, I found the truth
Not in endorphins or cocaine
but in a poem in heroic quatrain
that strikes the soul in nail and tooth:

....my love to you like pleasure from pain
with all the buttons being turned on high
like clean air in very scarce supply
through smothering clouds and choking rain

*Lagan: River in Belfast, Ireland.

Memorial Day
by Stephani Englebright - age 14

A cool wind blows across the open plain
Of the resting place of loved ones gone.
The day light has long since been broken
Where I now mourn in pain.
The sun is warm as the day is bright,
Shinning on the memories falling from my eyes.
I remember your last days,
But not without a fight.
I remember your hands of leather
Always secure & safe.
But I remember them trembling
Against mine of feather.
Placing the memories on your grave,
So never will I forget
The only grandfather I ever knew.
Those memories I will always save.

Uncontrollable Heart
by Brandie English - age 18

Undying love within me
Love for someone so cruel
I keep thinking that maybe
Maybe I'm not that big of a fool
But every time I see her
Where I once saw myself
My heart takes a turn for the worse
I wish you could feel what I've felt
It was you that finished this ride
With this helpless, little doll
Threw me to the side
And let my teardrops fall
I should hate you
And despise you just the same
Instead what do I do?
I play this senseless, heartrending game
I lost myself in remembrance
And your memory won't let go
I wish I could forget this
But my heart is in control
I wish I could hide
From what I know is the truth
Though every piece of my heart is breaking
While hers establishes love with you
No matter who she is
No matter how long it goes on
I will keep my wish
I will keep holding on

My Child
by Christine English - age 14

He sits there listening kindly,
Playing games and watching me.
How lucky I am.

The years have gone by,
Aging and never knowing the end is near.
Diseases caught and kept.

Now he sits there listening,
But yet far away.
I wished that he would be able to play,
But he sits.

Then, as if by a flash of light,
He takes two breaths,
The room is silent,
Everything seems to stop.

As I watch horrified of what might be.
I walk towards him,
Touching his skin softly.
I feel his cold body and scream.

He starts turning pale and pained,
As my parents call to report his death.
I sit by him, trying to listen for a voice,
And holding his hand,
Why of all,
Did it have to be him?!

Grandma
by Christine English - age 14

As she lays there,
So skinny, so small.
She looks like a baby again.

No sound she makes,
For she is sleeping.
No need to wake her,
For she knows not who we are.

So we leave her,
Peaceful and quiet,
Grabbing for life.
But she will always live in us.

Harmony
by Vicki Enscoe

Each bird has its own song
Lifted in the air all day long
It blends with the humming of the bee
And the buzzing of the insects in the tree
Which adds to the beauty the eye beholds
With the wonders of Nature yet untold
Revealed in the scents of the nostril's breath
Allowing us to choose life or death
It all comes together making life's harmony
But depends upon our focus and what we want to see
Do we dissect that which is put before us?
Or do we go forth joining in the glory of God's chorus?

Light filters clouds drift
Water ripples
Still --
The Song lifts

The music goes beyond the senses
Deep within one's soul
The end result is God's picture
With all the little things that make it whole

Seeing Life
by Elisha Erb - age 13

When it's dark and gloomy
It means nothing to me
Seeing is everything
Everything in life.
Seeing is like having a husband or a wife
It's beautiful
And suitable
Some people see life as anything
But believe me ther's more in it to bring
Seeing life is like seeing a flower
To see all the power
Then it bloomed
And everything was consumed
Life is so beautiful to see
It's more than just he or she
The eye is very good to use
It will help you on what to choose
The eye is wise
So treat life good
For that is what we understood
Use life well
Because you'll never know what to tell

Best Friends
by Elisha Erb - age 13

When friends are together
They don't think of the word never
They play and have fun
In the spring, in the grass, and even is the sun
But, when they get mad
They become sad
They break apart
So much to feel that's in their heart
Sadness everywhere
And know one to care
They <u>had</u> so much to share
Now it's gone
Everyday they think "why"
It's just a dumb lie
When they said goodbye!

Friends Forever
by Sara Erb - age 15

As I stare across the room,
Looking directly at my sister,
I feel a warm glow,
Creep up from my heart.
Can it be so?
After so many years of arguing,
I am no longer seeing her as a child,
But as an individual, like myself.
There is still the occasional fight,
With the sudden outburst,
And whenever she wants to,
She can still be a pest.
But now there are many more laughs
Filled with the occasional story,
As we relate to each other,
As human beings, not as strangers.
As we have grown up,
We have matured into young adults,
And citizens of the future,
But we have also matured as sisters.
No longer are we strangers,
United by the same birth parents,
By being each others sister,
But now we are each others friend.
We can turn to each other,
When the going gets touch,
We are there with a shoulder to cry on,
And a laugh to cheer one up.
We are here to be part of each other's life,
We are here to be friends, not just sisters.

Sister To Brother
by Karen LaRene Ercek - age 13

Well, Big Brother, I'll tell you:
Life for me might prosper.
It's had awards in it,
and straight A's,
And good friends,
And intelligent brothers to help me through the hard times.
But all the time
I wish it were you,
Who is always working hard,
And getting hurt,
And left out,
I wish a life for you where there are no problems.
So, Big Brother, don't you worry.
Don't you think you're not noticed.
Because in my eyes you were always better; Best.
For I have always believed in you, always will,
But I still have the upper hand,
And life for me might prosper.

Dedicated to James Michael Ercek

"Life is a Wilting Rose"
by Karen LaRene Ercek - age 13

A daughter sees a troubled mother.
What shall that daughter tell that troubled mother?
"Life is easy; be at ease; be relaxed"
And this might make her smile
and serve her hard years of motherhood
and make her joyful for her daughter,
and guide her thoughts to the sky.
"Life is a wilting rose; catch the petals, go quickly."
And this too might make her calm.
Roses have grown where success has failed.
The growth of a rose has sometimes healed
and sometimes has been the bind.
A past counts. So does future.
So do daughters.

One Voice
by Brandis Lee Erickson - age 17

It's a million emotions.
All of them, all at once,
Trying to be heard.
All of them trying to invade my heart,
And drown my good sense.
The good sense that tells me exactly why I should forget.
But that is one voice,
Out of a million.

My Heart
by Selin Eskandarian - age 15

In my heart
In my soul
I hold a key
For you to explore
You opened my life
You cared for me
You understood the inside
Of my being
You stay in a spot
Only you can be in
And inside my heart
All you do is give
You filled my life
With happiness and laughter
And with eternal love
I look after
Without you here
I cannot live
Without you with me
I feel emptiness
Only you
Hold the key to my heart
And only you
Know why it tears apart

Hear The Voices
by Jennifer Evans - age 17

The streets will be flooded with their tears; Tears of sorrow and of pain.
They'll grasp for understanding, for answers they'll never gain.
They'll wander the lonely streets, their wails will haunt the night,
If we don't stop now and understand the wrongs we need to right.

There are children with dirt stained faces, torn and tattered clothes,
Who wander through this dark world, scared and all alone.
They're begging for attention only to be shunned,
These poor neglected children who want only to be loved.

Hear the voices of the children, calling out for love,
Hear them suffering in their loneliness, Hear them pray to God above.
Hear the voices of the children begging to be seen
As they wander through this dark world that has grown so cold and mean.

There are children with black and blue faces, many swollen wounds,
Who suffer from broken fractured bones and a deeper emotional bruise.
They're reaching for a savior to save them from despair,
These poor abused children who want only to be spared.

Hear the voices of the children, their cries of unbearable pain.
Hear them weakly beg for mercy; Mercy they'll never gain.
Hear the voices of the children as they cower on their knees,
And as they huddle in a corner, Hear their terrified pleas.

There are children with small fragile bodies,
 bones showing through their skin,
Who go to bed scared each night, not knowing if they'll wake up again.
See their tear stained faces, their bodies covered with flies,
These poor starving children, who want only to stay alive.

Hear the voices of the children as they tremble in their fright,
Hear their weak moans of hunger as they beg for just a bite.
Hear the voices of the children sobbing as they die,
Hear them calling out for help, hear them calling you and I.

The Friend I'd Like To Be
by Susan Evens

I'd like to be the sort of friend that you have been to me.
I'd like to be the help that you've always been glad, to be.
I'd like to mean as much to you, each minute of the day.
AS you have meant to me, my friend, to help me along the way.
I'd like to do the big things and splendid things for you,
To brush away the gray from all your skies and leave then only blue.
I'd like to say the kindly things that I've so often heard,
And feel that I could arouse your soul, the way that mine you've stirred.
I'm wishing at this time, that I could just repay,
A portion of the happiness you've given me today.
If I could have but just one wish, this is what it would be.
I'd like to be the sort of friend that you have been to me.

The Power to Smile-by
by Melinda Faatz - age 13

A smile is a gift,
A simple yet powerful gift,
That connects the whole world together.
Not everyone knows how to speak a certain language,
Or play a certain sport,
But we all can smile.
A smile has the power to brighten a person's day,
The power to make love, friendship, and happiness.
All people have a special gift,
The gift of power,
And the power to smile.

Untitled
by Angela S. Fach - age 17

As the day changes before our eyes,
Your life is open to the bluest of skies.
Now, as the years have passed away,
With choices to make in tomorrows' day.
Reality or dreams,
Make them come true.
Keep the faith when your feeling blue.
Belief and trust, I have in you.
Within all that you want, and all you do.
Now, follow the path
That life holds for you.
Now and forever,
Achieve what you can.
Because today is the day,
That you have become a man.

*Dedicated to My brother Joshua for his
18th birthday September 24, 1997.*

Spider & The Fly
by Jo Ann Falletta

Your the spider with the sticky web
looking for the fly who would soon be dead.
Your much too smart so you'll watch over-head
patiently waiting for your stomach to be fed
Here comes the fly plump & juicy in size
"Ahhh! What a treat tender morsel of meat"
"That's right Mr. Fly your certainly welcome
to come inside."
He removed his hat & there he sat, not realizing
just where he as at.
Ignorant fly who just wanted to relax--
suddenly noticed the spider with the axe
Down with the axe now he was dead
Up with the spider to do it all over again.

Moral of The Story...

Beware of the spider with the axe in hand.
Beware of the spider with he evil glance.
Beware of the spider with the sticky web.
Bust most of all......LOOK OUT FOR YOUR HEAD!

No More Games
by Nicole Farley - age 16

My heart was an open door,
Waiting for your love forevermore,
Now, my life, dependents on thee,
Will soon cease to be.
You've tempted and teased until you've
    Knocked me down upon my knees.
Now nothing in the world can heal...
All the pain you've made me feel.
I even confessed my love so true,
Hoping to get some affection from you.
But you didn't care, you never showed
    any love towards me,
All you did was continue to be free.
You painted the town,
You slept around.
Even though you did these things,
I still care, my phone still rings.
So why don't you call?
I'd rather be your friend than
    nothing at all.
Don't you understand what I say?
Only you can make me feel this way.
So take my heart, hold me close,
And tell me you love me the most.
Don't play this time, don't tease and taunt,
Just let me know if it's me you want.

The Dreamer's Reality
by Nicole Farley - age 16

We are young and vibrant, the end of a
 century.
We are the dreamers the ones who reach
 for the sky.
Our minds see life as an endless possibility.
We've been friends for quite a while
Soon we'll all graduate, throw our hats
 and laugh,
We'll go to collage and such with a smile.
All of us will make new friends.
Then phone calls will stop, and letters will end.
We'll grow apart, even though we love each
 other very much.
Does anyone really mean it when they say
 "Let's keep in touch?"
Oh of course we'll meet again along the way
You'll say, "How have you been? It's great to see you again!"
I'll ask for your number and say "See you someday!"
But I'll never call, and you'll never walk down that
 same hall, or stroll down the same street.
So never again will we meet.
Then one day when we're all old and gray,
We'll open up the paper and see that one of us
 died the other day.
Suddenly, we'll stop remember each other and think,
 that all of our lives had passed, within a blink.
And time we wasted apart from each other,
Should have been time well spent with one another.

"And Yes I Remember"
by Candy Farris

Here I sit upon a rock, that's been here longer then I. I sit with the wind burning my face, the tall grass brushing my feet... And yes I remember.
When I was a child, running through the fields with my brothers, the buffalo passing us by, the sun on the land, the dust in my eyes... And yes I remember.
When the first snow fell, the air as fresh as could be. The fire of our tepee's slowly burning to nothing, ashes filtering through the smoke, and the fire throughout our village. The cries of women and children, my people running in all directions, and not knowing where to run. Mud flying, my people dying... And yes I remember.
When life seemed to be destroyed, my people dying all around me, horses caring white man, who killed my parent's, and my people. Blood bathing the land, the eerie sound of a gun riffling through the air, me, standing all alone... And yes I remember.
Being locked away on a land not big enough for my tribe. Going hungry, and being forgotten by the man, who put us here. The land already dead and destroyed, no food could grow. My elders, and my people, so hungry, so unhappy... And yes I remember.
I sit on this rock, and remember my past. All the things that were promised to us, and never fulfilled. My people just want to be free, to roam with mother nature, and hunt to survive. This Reservation wasn't what was promised to us, but we were put here anyway. I sit and remember a tine when I was free, young, and one with mother nature. I only feel sorry for our grandchildren, who will never be able... to remember.

Imagery
by Jenny Shine - age 16

His cold rough hand caressed
my bare face.
He smelled of no
perfume but of a
fresh wind in the sky.
He was white as
snow. Beautiful.
He brought memories of
wonderful things.
I loved him.
He sounded like quiet
dreams and a distant
laughter. A
wolf howling
to the invisible
moon. In the evening's
white sky.
I loved his sound.
He tasted as a spring of
water pure as a true love's kiss.
He was the icy breeze
as heaven in Alaska's winter.

Poems
by Amanda Faucher - age 14

It takes me quite awhile
To find some words that rhyme.
But in the end you'll realize,
It's really worth your time.

They let you sit and fantasize
And escape depressing things.
Then, you can look back
And see the joy they bring.

They let you sit and wonder
Or bring back the child in you.
And after some time you'll see
They're really fun to do.

Parents
by Amanda Faucher - age 14

They think they can control your life.
They know that it's not true.
And it really makes me sick
When they tell you what to do.

I'm my own person,
Independent as can be.
And it takes some bad behavior
To really make them see.

Sometimes they're on my nerves.
Sometimes they're in the way.
Sometimes I wish I can be alone,
Even for just one day.

I think they sometimes tell us lies,
Like when they say they love you,
And no matter what may happen,
They'll know what is best for you.

But I guess I will admit
Without much hesitation,
That to set us with some limits
Is their full-time occupation.

We'll understand later
What we don't understand now.
Our parents really love us.
After all, they've kept us 'till now.

At the moment just accept this fact.
Don't try to start a fight.
Realize they really do help us.
Don't you hate it when they're right?

Cheated
by Trisha Feehan - age 14

When the last from childhood dies,
and the flowers in the pasture lose
their exhilarating color
You will find us.

Behind the cold, gray cells of the prison
no food, no money, no heartbeat
You will find us.

Pushed behind you, kicked aside, spit upon
And unending hatred
Sounds of bleeding flesh
You will find us.

Barely surviving,
pierced with suspicious stares
burning into damaged souls,
Our presence unwanted

We are here, We are alive,
Can you find us?

How Precious the Years For My Son - Steven
by Rachelle L. Felmet

I waited so very long
To have a little son
I was even told
It just could never be done
But I somehow always knew
From the very start
That this baby I carried
Was the child of my heart
The names that I picked
And the colors I chose
Were for the son I'd have
He would be perfect...
Just like a rose
So great was my joy
And full was my heart
I would always protect you
And always take your part
Now you're all grown up
With children of your own
And I wonder if you could know
How precious the years...
So quickly are gone.

My Son — My Heart For Michael
by Rachelle L. Felmet

I wonder if you ever
Think about those years
When you would come into my room
And I would calm your fears
I still see you standing there
Right at the foot of my bed
"Mommie" — "Another nightmare?"
And you would nod your head
"Come on — crawl into bed"
You would curl up close
You seem to need my touch
God above knows...I loved you so much
"Everything will be alright —
It was just a dream"
As I put my arm around you
And drew you close to me
You would snuggle...close your eyes
And I wiped away your tears
Now so many years later
I wonder if you struggle
With still other kinds of fears.

Bedtime Prayer
by Angela Felton - age 14

Don't forget to say your prayers
Please pray for me tonight
I fear I may be falling
As I reach the highest height

Don't forget to say your prayers
And say your thank you's, too
We have so much to be thankful for
There's so much we've been through

Don't forget to say your prayers
And tell him all your dreams
You love me just as I love you
Or that is how it seems

Don't forget to say your prayers
Pray you'll always hold me tight
That we'll always be together
The prayer I pray every night

The Waiter
by Paul Fennell - age 18

The people come in and out. The mall is not very crowded today. Which is good. I am only
> Looking for one.

Watching the people go by, waiting for the one. Waiting for the man that took away my son.
> Waiting for the man that destroyed my life.

The time goes by, I still do not see him. I know his face like my own. I know his evil smile and
> The evilness in his empty eyes when he smiles. I can close my

eyes and see it plain and clear.
Watching the people go by, waiting for the one. Waiting for the one that ruined my life. Waiting
> For the one that killed my wife.

I sit and I wait. Watching the sheep go by. They're daily routine of life. Except they have all lost
> Their leader.

Suddenly I see him.
He is right in front of me.
All this time mocking me and laughing.
I stand up and he does the same
That smile is on his face. The cold, bitter smile that he was wearing when my wife and son died.
I am ready for this. I have been ready since I saw his evil cold eyes.
I begin to walk toward him. He advances on me too.
I reach into my pocket and pull out my gun.
I see him pulling out a gun. I am trapped, I have to take vengeance on this killer. This maniac.
I pull the trigger.
Watching the people go by, waiting for the one. Watching the people scream, I know his time is done.
Waiting for the man, the Monster, the Beast, and the Destroyer of my life.
Pulling the trigger again.
My life brakes down in seconds in this room. My life is broken and destroyed, like the piece of
glass of the mirror lying on the floor.

Poet's Dream
by Louise Kilby Fesperman

If I could paint a picture
Of things that I have done
The canvas would be crowed
With good times and with fun

Each day would have sunshine
With skies of azure blue,
Roses trailing picket fence
And some morning glories too

I would draw a robin red breast
A Cardinal of bright red,
An evening of lovely sunsets
Mixed with white clouds over head

A lake beside a lovely hill
Where beaver swim and play,
The moon to glorify the night
And sun to shine by day

I would try to paint a picture
Of places I have been,
A road into the future
A road that has no end

You and I would be together
As we once were long ago,
Hand in hand we would walk at twilight,
Greeting people that we know

The picture would be perfect
The painting would be done,
For my memories would be captured,
Of my happiness and fun.

Failing Dreams
by Mike Fetters - age 16

Pain does arise,
with folly of heart.
I swallow the poison,
by treacherous dart.
I dream by night,
of love so pure;
By day is crushed,
with tantalizing lure.
Foolish I was,
to think of a chance,
Proud of this love,
now impaled on lance.
Visions now gone,
as new ones emerge.
Nightmares of hate,
and loneliness is my scourge.
Ever increasing holes,
engulf my heart.
Fleeting is love,
and dreams torn apart.
Lonely is this world,
in which I walk.
Colder than winter,
only growing evil stalk.

Evergreen Kisses
by Teresa Fiehn - age 15

Wave through the trees
Evergreen kisses barely
miss my feet,
on a merry-go-round
trying to locate the sun
run faster
reaching the lake
the clear water
and the reflection
you least love to see
creatures only known
in a child's imagination
creep up from behind
sinking deeper in the abyss
the oasis in the middle
of the ocean
is fading
in civilization nothing
is a pure and clear
as the evergreen kisses

Ode To The Great Lakes
by Linda M. Fields

Lake of lost souls, sea of forgotten tears,
the Lady weeps for those who show no fears.
In her cold embrace she'll pull you deep,
where in eternal night your soul she'll keep.

You Never Knew
by Rachel E. Fields - age 17

I watched you fall in love with her.
I hated her. I guess I was jealous.
I wanted you for myself.
Wasn't I the one who was always there for you?
Who listened when you and that heartless girl had a fight?
Who cared for you when you were sick?
Who never forgot your birthday? Me, that's who.
You never understood.
Where were you when I needed you?
Where were you when I was sick?
Where were you when my father died?
You should have been there, but you weren't.
You never knew when I needed you.
I called you over that night to talk.
You were angry because I cut into your time with HER.
You never came. I needed you then, but you weren't there.
And when she finally left you, who did you turn to? Me.
I wanted to spare you the pain. I knew she had left you vulnerable.
So I was there for you then, too.
I couldn't even tell you that I was dying.
The room was getting fuzzy, only your face remained clear.
Still I comforted you. She isn't worth it. You deserve better.
In those last few minutes, I had only one thought.
I loved you, and you never knew.

Death In The Afterlife
by Olga Filippov - age 14

Beyond the gloom of london streets
buried deep into the ground
Darkness is what the eye meets
Silence is the only sound
Their souls are trapped within the rocks
Their bodies wrapped in her black cloak
It seems the afterlife she mocks
She smiles when in rain they soak
Soon after, she has left and they
Float spirits up into the air
They move aside while making way
For her. Black cloak and raven hair
They are alive, yet what they say
I s that in spirit they are dead
Under the dark pavement they lay
They'll never get what they once had.
                    Life.

A Wager
by Ashton John Fischer, Jr.

I do miss Oblivia; she was best,
Unlike all others, and whispered to me:
"Sleep, my dear, you are tired, should deeply rest
In my arms, only mine, and dreamlessly,

Forever, that you've eternally earned,
Have seen too much for too long, plucked an eye,
And I, Oblivia, from you have learned
The truth of all; my love, down we will lie."

She's never lied to me, but always laid,
Seeing nothing, no eyes, abysses deep,
Into her darkness, meanings she has made,
For me whom she holds; if loses, she'll weep.

Again, a rhyme scheme is the truth of all.
Oblivia knew that, as we two fall.

Thanks Be To God
by Ellie Finch

The angels sang on that day in the summer
When before them she bowed--no longer in slumber

She knew she would be going there as she trusted her Heavenly Father
Who said, "Believe only in me and your soul shall live forever!"

From the holiest of places she looked down on mere mortals
Who wept in the rain over a pile of turned soil

To God we give thanks for life past a garden stone
For He paid the price so she wouldn't die alone

As the months and years will continue to go by
The memories she left in our hearts will not die

The memories of laughter and of timeless celebrations
Will be carried down to future generations

The scent of her perfume and the sweet sound of her voice
Will always call out to me and drown out the noise

As I continue to become a woman of God
I'll look to the heavenlies and wait for her nod

I'll aim to follow in the footsteps she's trod
For they lead to Heaven, to an Almighty God

Thanks be to God that memories aren't the end
But rather are something that time lets us lend

Memories are warm and will carry us thru
But a reunion is far better when God lives in you

Fingerpaint
by Allison Fister - age 15

Glistening, glittering, glossy, goop
    Smeared to perfection.
Colors flying, paint swirling, little girl
    giggling
Dipping her little fingers into the cool
wet, goo to make a creation of her own
on her paper, or better yet; the wall!
Long ago I knew that girl who was as
happy as can be, smearing that glossy
goop all over herself, and in my
    memory, on me!

Oklahoma City
by Mary Beth Fiorella - age 13

In the year of 1995,
A normal day began.
To work by car, the people went,
Every woman and every man.

About mid-day a bomb went off,
Destroying the whole place.
Gone are all the people,
And every smiling face.

Every family torn apart,
Every heart left broken.
Lost for someone's cruel heart,
All last words unspoken.

Untitled
by Jeremia N. Fisher - age 19

What should I write about
thats one often said
most written write
what they think in their head

My head just full of nothingness
My hope forgot, dreams have died
throughout my life
My brains got fried

I know the way
to end the madness
I figured it would come back
along with it, the sadness

I know I have to stop
if nothing for a while
I need to come up
Return with style.

The Dreamer
by JoAnna Fish - age 19

When the rain falls down
she thinks and dreams,
She writes a little poem
about meadows and streams.

Imagination starts wandering
about roses and doves,
In a field by a stream
she holds her true love.

She writes what she feels
and means what she says,
she only feels happy
when touched by suns rays.

In loves arms
she wishes to be,
to be held, to be kissed,
to live happily.

A piece of paper
her heart she writes,
she sprouts some wings
and she takes flight.

Away from her sadness,
sorrows, and pain,
back to her dreams
and back to the rain.

Loving Mother
by Amanda Fitchorn - age 12

Your loving arms
   shelter me
from any harm.
The shelter
   of kindness
Follows me around.
   Your gentle touch
How proud I felt.

How Do I Say Good-bye
by Jeanna Fitzgerald - age 17

When a loved one dies
You can always say good-bye

What do you do when a friendship dies
Do you let it drift away without asking why

Why does the attitude change so sudden
What happened way back when

What did I do to make you mad
That caused you to treat me bad

When a friendship is dead
Do you go back over everything said

Do you regret the secrets told
As soon as the shoulder is cold

When the eyes turn to ice
Do you regret being nice

When the friendship dies
When can you say good-bye

The One
by Nicole Fitzhugh - age 15

She screams into
The night.
No one is
Listening;
No one cares.
Tears stream
Down her face.
They just
Look away.
She searches
Desperately
For love and
Acceptance.
They ignore
Her pain.
She loses hope
Until she meets
The one.
The one who
Is listening;
The one who
cares.
Jesus.

Untitled
by Lynzy Flack - age 15

Somedays I feel like just lying around, not
getting all dressed up and looking pretty.

Sometimes I look at my life and say what a pity.

But there are other days when I would get
up and do something with myself, then look
in the mirror and see the real me.

The me that is always hiding, for some reason
not wanting anyone to see.

The few people that have seen the real me, know and
love me for what I am about.

The others who don't know the real me, talk and
laugh behind my back; sometimes I just want
to scream and shout.

I am thankful for my true friends.

The ones I know will be with me through the
good and bad days to the end.

The others, I hope the best for them all.

And I will surely be there for them, unlike
them for me, when it's their turn to fall.

Difference
by Zachary Flategraff - age 13

People confront you looking for your sympathy.
Telling you all their problems. Then when you think
your getting through to them they just push you
away. The next day they get a gang together and they
want to beat you up. Love is such a strong word but
not as strong or powerful as hate. But they are used
everyday, and peoples feelings go smashing into the
pits of hell. People aren't people until they find
their soul mate. Only then are you complete.
He says yes, she says nothing is the only way they
know. Whether it's with fists whether it's with words;
still it hurts. Everyone is different and unique
in their own personal way. Everyone has a good side,
and a bad. Don't egg anyone on. Respect the way they
are. Give respect.
Devil on the right, angel on the left, what one are
you supposed to listen to. Not all can do that.
So they get into a whirlwind of emotions. Some
people are good, some are bad, and some you want to
punch right between the eyes. While they're down
call them a name. Enjoy your triumph. Some people
are ugly, some are pretty, some are fat, some are
skinny. Don't put anyone down respect the way they are.

Dreaming Our World
by Erin Flaum - age 16

Our world is just an ancient dream.
A dream which crept beyond the bounds of the horizon,
and kissed the morrow farewell.
She slept unto the madness and carefully
slipped by everthreatening skies.
Her eyes, although unseen, for shrouded by the mist,
glimpse upon the threshold of the everblackening future.
She shall become a nightmare, though conquering
the impossible.
She shall no longer resemble a dream,
but a nightmare in which we live-Reality.
This nightmare shall never end;
it will be an on going debt the dreamers pay,
Until the ancient dreamers stop dreaming
and the ancient dreamers face the truth;
the truth of which will be never sought.
For only the truth of reality is an alien in a dreamer's mind.

I Will Always Love You
by Karla Flokowitsch - age 19

Brightness of day and darkness of night,
birds will chirp and mosquitoes will bite.
The sun will shine and the moon will glare,
and the love in my heart will always be there.

Seasons and holidays will come and go,
raking leaves and throwing snow.
Blue skies and green grass,
going swimming and hot days pass.

Choirs will keep singing their songs,
and melodies will keep going on and on.
Poems will keep rhyming,
and wind-chimes will keep chiming.

Showers will fall,
and flowers will bloom.
As long as the sun keeps shining,
I will always love you.

Grandmother
by Jillian Marie Florence - age 17

Greatest comforter in times of troubles.
Respects me through it all.
Allows me to do things I normally can't.
Never says "She doesn't have time."
Deserves all the time I spend with her.
Makes me smile when things go wrong.
Of course she's my best friend.
Thinks that I am the best granddaughter in the world.
Helps me with my problems.
Easy to be with.
Remembers everything that's important to me.

Age
by Barbara Flynn

Some think life begins at 40
Others like their teens
It all depends on who you ask
And what age really means

Is it the grey in grandma's hair
Or the pimples on my face
Is it the aches and pains of time
Or simplicity and grace

Each day becomes a memory
We share throughout our time
No matter, whether good or bad
It's there - a mountain climbed

We rise to great a dawning
Feeling so brand new
Then we realize the fact
Another day just flew

It's gone and we're still here
A chance to do our thing
Will we realize our dreams
Or wait till dusk again

Unabided Passions
by Lucas Foglia - age 14

Upon first slight was the fire lit,

Burning away all barriers with its apocalyptic passion.

In desperate attraction their hearts yearned for one another's sweet embrace,

And yet in silence the strangers passed,

Never to see each other again.

Hate
by Lucas Foglia - age 14

The surge of emotions that burn within;

The disruption of a world made only by our own interpretations;

The panic of a tormented soul.

As an ever-sought light in a world of scattered dreams,

We find a haven in the anger kindled by the realizations of our own self-flawed existence.

Nightmares
by Heather Foos - age 13

As I lay here in my bed,
crazy thoughts scream through my head.
They're awful and horrible,
they aren't very nice,
I went to a doctor,
he gave no advice.
So still I lay here in my bed,
these images creeping slowly back.
Everytime I fall asleep,
they slink back to attack.
I try to make them go away,
but the harder that I try,
the more they want to stay and play,
I really don't know why.
All I know is that they're here,
so if I were you, I'd watch my back,
you never know,
they could be near!

Night in the Prairie
by Christina Forbes - age 13

In the gray-green pasture, of willow and oak,
 the crow caws at the dark blue cloak,
As the day sets and the spider crawls from her tent,
 a single blade of grass is bent,
A wondering beauty is grazing around,
 alert to the tiniest of sounds,
The fish moved with grace,
 as the net dueled him to a race,
And the crickets sing their song,
 darkness would not be there long,
Through midnight the ground turned wet,
 and a mouse then came and swept,
The grass turned to a frustrating maze,
 when the lantern was never more ablaze,
A heavy footprint in the land,
 would no more be revealed in the sand,
The morning shadows were cast,
 there was the green grass.

Being Dumped
by Morgan Ford - age 12

It feels like being stabbed in the heart.
Or someone painfully tearing you apart.

I did not believe or understand why.
That someone would relish making me cry.

When I really felt my love was true.
The person I loved did not think so too.

He thinks of love as a silly little game.
Too bad I did not think the same.

My love is a road with a dead end.
How do I prevent this from happening again?

Eyes
by Hedy Wolf

Eyes are like stars,
Shining through life,
Unless they dimmer
And there is no sight.

Open your eyes
And see the life,
See the flowers
And the birds fly.

How fortunate!
You can see
Which way to go
And the books to read.

Never forget
The sightless souls
Offer your help,
Show them the door.

My Love
by Steph Fowler - age 16

A smile like a little child,
And yet it's bold and strong.
His laugh is like a symphony,
And has become my favorite song.
His eyes are like the ocean deep,
Full of life and shine.
I know no harm could ever come
When I feel his hand touch mine.
And when he speaks to me, so sweet,
My heart begins to melt.
The things I feel when with him
Are like nothing I've ever felt.
The bond between us grows each day,
As we share our hopes and fears.
He know everything about me;
He's seen both smiles and tears.
And if he'd ever leave me,
I don't know what I'd do.
But that time seems impossible
When I see his eyes, so blue.
I thank the Lord both night and day
For this gift He's given me.
I know it's all because of Him;
To my life, He holds the key.
He holds the keys to all my being,
But He now gives one away.
To my love He hands the key to my heart,
Inside his palm it will always stay.

The Light
by Steph Fowler - age 16

I am huddled in a corner,
    as I weep in frustration.
I am cold and alone,
    as I sit in the darkness.
My head and heart are flooded
    with so many things,
But these thoughts and emotions
    are not alien to me.
Then a brilliance brightens the corner
    and I begin to feel the warmth.
I realize I am not alone,
    there is now another presence.
It is the Light, and He has come
    to warm, to comfort, and to guide me.
Then reality hits me
    and I become aware
That the Light had been with me all along
    but I had shut Him out.
My tears are now of guilt and shame,
    but they are dried with His forgiveness and love.
I was given another chance
    and it's because of His compassion
That I now walk down the path
    with a guide who knows the way.

The Mask
by Desiree Franey

things are not always what they seem
my life is not at all a dream
if you would peel away the mask which I wear
you would see my heartache and my despair
my worries and sorrows will not go away
despite the mask I wear everyday

while on the inside I'm crying
on the outside I laugh
do not be fooled by my smiling mask
my worries and sorrows will not go away
despite the mask I wear everyday

What If?
by Peggy E. Franklin

"What If?" he told me to-stand still and wait;
"What If?" God wanted me-not to choose that mate.
"What If?" he just finally said-go right a head;
And do as you wish-and not by me be led.
I've given the warnings-to tell you no;
You won't listen to me-so your path you may go.

Now as I look back-and ponder at will;
And think on the times-"What If" fills the bill.
For this could have happened-to a rebellious one;
For as the Father steps back-says go to your fun.
I've given you a mind-and gave you a will;
So go your own way-but great pain you will feel.

So now in my mind-the pain I did see;
For now I do think-this happened to me.
The signs they were there-as God tried to say;
He's not your true love-and to me please obey.
But I wouldn't listen-nor I didn't see;
The handwriting was there-on the wall just for me.

Missing You
by Renee Frith - age 17

Oh, great grandpa, I miss you so
I wish it hadn't been your time to go.
Now, as life continues on
I realize you are really gone.

Never to be see again
Until that day when we meet in heaven.
I often think of the things that you said
While memories of you float around in my head.

I know that you are happy now;
You're with the one for whom you took a vow.
But I hope you do understand
That sometimes I wish I could hold your hand.

I will never forget all the old times;
Like when you used to tell me nursery rhymes.
Or all of the times when I sat on you lap.
As I grew older there grew a big gap.

I left you alone when you needed me most
At a time when you seemed like a ghost.
Your wife had passed onto a better place
And you grew sad when seeing her face.

Now I am realizing you are really gone
By finding ways not to cry at the crack of dawn.
Writing my feelings in the form of poetry about you
And remembering all of the good times too.

I will love you always.
Sometimes finding myself in a daze;
Just thinking of you
When it was just us too.

My Sister And Me
by Mary Fritz

When we were younger the years kept us apart
As we grew older they helped us grow closer at heart

Through every year that comes and goes
I know that our friendship only grows

It is like a rose that starts out as a bud
It slowly matures with the help from above

We have shared stories and we've shared dreams
We have shared laughter and we've shared some screams

Your shoulder has always been there to lend
And help me through bad times that seemed not to end

I know deep in my heart this is a special find
The friendship we share is one of a kind

Friends and yet sisters for life we will be
The best part of this is choice, not because we are family

Dear sister you mean so very much to me
A sister and my best friend, the closest one of three

I know that I can always turn to you
When ever I need a laugh or two

A Greater bond there could never be
Like the one we share my sister and me

Magical Mirror
by Sandra Fraley - age 12

I looked in the mirror one day
And what I saw I could not say
It was magical
It was beautiful
It could draw you near
With a touch of fear
It could push you away
If you did not obey
Magical lands are what I saw
As I stared in great awe

Control
by Dee L. Fujii

I dream of a world
Full of color and light.
Where harmonious nature
Makes absent fear and fright.
Where worries dissolve,
In a flood of contentment,
Where everyone is equal,
Leaving behind prejudice and resentment.

I dream of a world
Cloudy and dark.
Where the sun never shines
And terrified, pain-filled screams,
Play a constant part.
Where evil reigns supreme
Breeding fear and horror.
And the subjected beings die,
Before their lives even start.

Where do these worlds exist?
I think I know.
Inside my mind.
A part of me.
They fight for control.
Which one is truly me, and mine?
Where lies my soul?
God help me as I walk this thin, delicate line,
Fighting for my sanity
Fighting...for control.

True Love
by Kathryn Fuller - age 13

They said you were too young to understand,
Cause love is just a one time thing,
You've got a long time to grow and look,
For someone new to share your life with.
Now that you've grown and found,
That you have been with the one for all this time,
You now know that you did know,
What love was once when you were young.
Now that you are on your way to starting a new life,
With someone that you have and will love,
The rest of your wonderful life.
You may ave few quarrels,
But those will only be from the mind.
Unlike love, which comes from the heart.
So now and forever in love you shall stay.
With the one of your dreams,
You love,
Your fiancee.

What Am I Searching For?
by SteAnn Lee Fulp - age 18

Who am I?
What am I?
Why am I here?
What am I doing?
Why am I living?
Who am I looking for?
What am I searching for?
What does the world,
hold for me?
What am I getting out,
of being here?
Can you please answer,
these questions for me?

Free
by Candy Gabbard

As I stared into the sun set holding on to the things
You left behind.
Memories of the past slowly passing by.
Times we spent together pictures of the past.
The times we said goodbye broke our hearts we knew
it wouldn't last.
Tears fell from both of our eyes, Your's and mine.
I didn't realize then neither did you.
We had to say goodbye we both wanted something
different in life.
I didn't want to hold you back you didn't want to ho
Together we knew it would never be right apart would be
the best in time.
A long distance call every now and then, when you miss
me or when you need a friend.
It took me sometime many sleepless nights tears of pain
fell from my eyes.
I looked deep within my self so my heart could be free.
You see I reached a place deep down inside a place
Where I let you go I said goodbye.
Free at last to love again, but if I ever need you I know
You'll be there as a friend.

God Spoke
by Kristin Gaines - age 16

The Devil drenches the sky with blood.
Next he takes the clouds,
Tinting them with the blackness of a thousand
nights.
Patches of soft blue and yellow try to
peak through.
Hastily he dashes them with flames of
firing orange.
Smoky grey fumes creep over the sun.
Putting a haunting yet mysterious haze
over the land.
The Devils hand reaches once more,
Then sunlight broke.
God's hand grabs the Devil's.
As clearness flows across the sky.
A once blood-shot sky melts to a silent rose.
Baby blue replaces the blackness in the clouds.
And the orangeness of fire is smothered by
white crystals.
Quickly, the haunting haze lifts, as the
Devil pulls his hand back.
And in a thundering voice, while white crystals
fall
God spoke to every ear.
Be not afraid.

The Bridge
by Kristin Gallagher - age 17

Calling through burning steam
Your senses numb in blinding pain
Refuse to forgive your only love
Endless circles keep you insane
Surprise endings comfort hope
The candle lit in the deepest black
Forged links of a tangled mass
Seen through eyes that wear the tracks
Solemn vows kept for no-one else
Secrets that we all know
Free the doves so they may fly
Free the light so it may glow
Faith blankets the entire fire
Keeping life from self-destructing
Love seeps in those weary pores
Forcing joy to start constructing
A new bridge stands alone
Sorely needed at the time
It stretches out its beaten hands
And grabs your arm just in time.

Shattered Dreams
by Max Galloway - age 17

Dreams so bright are broken now
like shattered glass lie at my feet.
Each painful shared a memory bad and
bittersweet. All I held most dear is
forever gone, buried deep underneath
headstone gray and weathered away.
Silent watch they keep over those who
died too young, too soon their stories
yet untold, while I who yearned to join
them wait for my life to unfold.

The Substitute
by Joseph Gariano - age 19

A palette of paint I cannot use.
My rolls of film are always doomed.
My finest dish can't lift a spoon,
and not one sculpture's in my room.
I've held guitars, but played no tunes.
My fingers tangle a top a loom.
My charcoal will sketch no time soon
and with larynx scathed, I'll never croon.
But the art within I'll never lose,
for when my heart ignites its fuse
to pen and pad my legs will cruise
where I can create the substitute.

Kristen
by Karen S. Gass

Brown hair hanging in ringlets
Eyes an intense dark brown
Skin tanned
to a deep autumn brown

Mind unlocked and anticipating
the input of wisdom

Hands reaching out
to touch and feel
natures sensations
Eyebrows shooting upwards
as she laughs

Singing with a voice
full of mischief and laughter

Holding her and realizing
the uniqueness

Talking a deep breath
and inhaling her scent

Preserving her image in my mind

The Hunt
by Eileen Gatewood - age 13

Quick and timid, they hop about;
With eyes sharp and a jerking head,
They watch and listen for what lies ahead.

The prowler sits ready to spring,
To catch one of those little wings.
With ears forward and tail back,
A sudden jump and a flap.

The victor was the winged one,
As the prowler goes away,
Live on! Live on another day.

Leaving
by April Gay - age 14

I lived in a small town.
I thought I would spend my life there.
I had friends and was satisfied.
I was happy and suddenly it all changed.
Leaving I cried and pouted.
Leaving I felt so alone.
Leaving I found a place
   where I could begin again.

I never wanted to look in the past.
I knew I had to look in the future.
I rose above my loneliness.
I made friends and built again.
Leaving I held my head high.
Leaving I could not let them know.
Leaving I felt that
   once again I was alone.

I, through the years, left many times.
I, though sad, managed to live on.
And I waited to leave again
when I decided that...
Leaving for me was not true.
Leaving I knew was too hard.
Leaving I
   would just not do.

The Seashell
by Sarah Gephardt - age 13

I was on the beach when I thought
  I saw a leech
Then it was a well, which turned
  out to be a seashell
It looked like a pig because
  it was so big
It was big at the top and small
  at the bottom
  with points all around
Just lying on the ground
I picked it up and looked
  inside
And a hermit crab came out
I put it down and it started
  to walk away
so I sadly said good-bye
  to my seashell that once
  was a well
And a leech lying on
  the beach.

For The Someone Who Holds My Heart
by Kristin Gerber - age 16

I know how to feel it.
I know that it's true
I don't know how to say it
But I know that it's you.
I feel like I know you well enough to say
You complete my heart in every way.
You fill my heart with love and fun
I know it's strange, but you're the only one.
Our love couldn't happen with just me and you.
There's someone else that make this true.
There's no way we could have this love
Without the help of God above.
He holds our love within his arms
And keeps our love alive and strong.
I thank the Lord everyday I pray,
For sending you here and showing the way.
Even though you hold my heart,
God's had our hearts right from the start.

Emotional Uncertainty
by Christine Bonnie Ghattas - age 12

Anger, the feeling of love long lost,
The long-lost love of lovers, star-crossed.
Frustration and hatred are present of now,
Love, warmth and kindness have yet to be found.
And so when they are, the cruelty will end.
Love and peace are pure,
While hatred is terribly unpretend.

Untitled
by Edwin Gibson

"Tympanic thunder,
Rolling Cadence in the sky.
Stroboscopic lightning,
Soothing sounds of rain,
Patter of drops
On leaves and roof.
Sweet trill of birds
After the storm,
Tempo of crickets.
Time to think.

"The future we dream
The past we rue;
The world is old,
Yet ever new.
What is -- has been,
Will be again.
Cycle in cycle
Forever more.
What is now --
Was before.

Not Alone
by Raymond J. Gill

Whom do I speak to, when my world
is filled with wonder and delight?
When all I see around has no trace
of darkness and only light

Who fills my being with flight so
high and pure,
that I am transported far beyond
anything of man's allure?

Who is with me when I walk alone
with none to know my heart,
and I am lost in thoughts of all
that beautifully good and I am part?

Whom am I speaking to, when I
am with my mind alone,
and I am so clearly made aware
of all that is, or could be known?

I somehow feel that these thoughts are
not mine, but are just given to me,
and I am left awe struck of
what I am now able to see.

My Star
by Rebecca Gill - age 16

A bead of light
Shines under the door
Silently the snow falls
I look out the window
At the stars
And as I make a wish
I wonder if you could be doing the same
Maybe even wishing on
My star.
Like people on the earth
There are millions of stars
In the sky
Soon to collide
With destiny
As we will, someday.

A Loveless Life
by Stacia Glenn - age 15

Love is hurt, love is pain,
Why fall in love? You have nothing to gain,
You fall in love, they break your heart,
You feel like your life has fallen apart,
You cared for them, they hurt you still,
But love made everything seem so real.

You sacrificed your heart and soul,
For a person who's hurting you was their goal,
You were foolish enough to succumb to their charm,
And it has caused your heart nothing but harm.

You swear never to fall in love again,
It seems like love is a game you can't win,
Your tears dry up and fade away,
You finally believe you'll be okay.

You spend endless years cold and alone,
Wishing and hoping you again could have known,
The touch of another so tender and sweet,
You realize now that it was truly a treat.

Not all men are callous and cold,
But it's too late now - you've grown too old,
You wasted your years without love in your life,
And now it cuts your heart like a knife.

You learned a lesson far too late,
Because a loveless life should be nobody's fate,
You hear an angel call from above,
But you can't go - you haven't found love.

God lifts you up from your loveless hell,
And his love for you he begins to tell,
You realize now you were never un-loved,
Because God always sends his love from above.

Special Moments
by Karla Glentz

I've known you for years, and watched you from a far. As a teenage girl, dreaming what it was like to be in your arms, not knowing you were with someone else's loved one. I hoped and dreamed about that day. Until one day I saw you again, not knowing how much we needed each other as soul mates and as friends. To share our pain and laughter. We met again and our eyes met and we knew, it was time to share our friendship and our souls together as one. To heal each others hurt and pain only as we could do. Each time we were together we grew as one because we were whole again and ready to try to go on. Not as lovers but as friends forever, sharing our heart and souls as one because of the love of healing from our pain of love.

Dear Friend and soul mate
Steve Klopp - April 26, 1996

'Self-Esteem, The Power Within'
by Sally Glick

If you think you are beaten, you are.
Success begins with, I think I can.
If you think you dare not, you don't.
A truly great person, is one who consistently,
Helps others to feel good about themselves.
If you think you'll lose, you've lost.
Success is due totally to your state of mind.
If you like to win, but think you can't,
It's almost for sure you won't.
A great person openly shares
Responsibility for mistakes,
And never, ever looks for a scapegoat.
But, sooner or later, the person who wins,
Is always, the person who says, 'I know I can.'

Words
by Robyn L. Gomez

Don't just tell me you love
 me to appease me through the night.
Don't just tell me you love
 me to make things seem all right,
Don't tell me lies and hope I
 won't suffer from the pain,
I can see the truth in your eyes
 things could never be the same,
Don't pretend to care and be something
 you could never become
For I would never want to love
 something that is numb.
Just be yourself, for it is you
 that I will always love and need,
Then you and I can become one
 and love will be our seed.

The Four Elements of Power
by Emily Gomm - age 15

The wind was harsh,
As it blew against my face.
The way it made my hair feel,
So razor sharp that it could cut.

The air was cool,
As it made shivers go up my spine.
The way it made me wish for warmth,
And a mug of hot cocoa.

The water was wet,
As it rolled down the cabin windows.
The way it made me wish for a fire,
To warm my heart and soul.

The fire was dry,
As it crackled and threw sparks.
The way it made me think,
Of the elements to force energy towards life.

True Treasure
by Eddie Gonzalez - age 19

As I gaze at your beauty at your grace,
I know there is a God for only He could
create such a lovely face. when your
smile you display, a piece of heaven
you give away. When to your voice I
lend an ear, music of angels singing I
hear. You are like fine gold, the
value beyond the wealth of the globe.
Symbols can not portray the divine beauty
you contain. Words can not express the
beauty you possess.
Now it is wise for me to say thank you
for being my friend. For blessed am I
to have a friend which young men glorify.
I may know nothing, but to this I am
sure, that my friendship for you is
<u>TRUE</u> and your name forever in my mind
will remain.

Untitled
by Eddie Gonzalez - age 19

On cloudy days full of joy my heart remains for knowing
that you are my friend.
There is no trace of tears in my face, for blessed am I
to have a friend which young men glorify.
for being my friend lucky I am and when a sad day I have,
I think about you my friend and surprise I won the grand
prize.
"Who is this that appears like the dawn fair as the moon
bright as the sun?" My friend I shout and say, with pride
and honor I say it twice again, My friend the lovely one
my friend.
For being my friend, friendship I now understand and it
is not hard to explain, that luxury and gold will pass
away yet a friend forever will remain.
I will never be able to repay the friendship that you
gave yet I say let it be, let it not change.

P.S.   "May the lord deal with me, ever so soverly,
                if anything but death separates you and me."

"Diary"
by Farley Goodrich - age 14

Diary, oh blessed book,
I must write in you my most intimate thoughts.
Stories of thine own loves forgotten
Pierced hearts and shattered hopes.
Dreaming is the only ray of light in this dark world
Always full of misunderstood feelings of hatred.
Feelings of happiness, though also are bestowed
Upon thy own heart overwhelmed.
Such eternal joy that causes fears
The book is, as well, full of eternal fears
For these are all emotions that are felt by thee
And written down with passion in oh, blessed book.

The Perfect Jewel
by Elisha Goodson - age 16

As a flower in the wind you think Mother Nature has done you wrong.
Gasping for air, reaching for a new ground.
Swaying back and forth, side to side.
Not realizing you are a jewel to the world.
You are beautiful, but not understanding that fact because you are different.
Looking like no other, you are disappointed.
Your feelings on your surroundings is admiration.
Admiring everything that looks the same.
As the days go by, everything changes.
The surroundings die, so you stand alone.
Winter comes but yet you do not feel the cold.
Spring arises, as well as new surroundings.
You are now tall, strong and peaceful.
As you remember how you were the spring before,
You have only one regret, the disappointment in yourself.
Now the surroundings look up to you as a guide.
For they think you have lived through all.
You now feel acceptance from the world.
Mother Nature sees what has happened
Your time on earth is through.
Slowly the wind stops blowing, the sun hides behind a cloud.
Your oddly beautiful petals fall to the ground.
The surroundings seem to cry as it starts to rain.
Mother Nature knew she had made no mistake.

Removed
by Daphne Goss

Have I told you how I felt
Have I shown you inside
Sink into the blackness and melt
Remove my evil disguise

I put up a wall
You can't tear down
But I let you fall
Into my frown

The hurtful past
The feeling abused
My icy mask
Has been refused

I thank the stars above
For having you around
You showed me you loved
In my pain, I dragged you down

Still, you were there
To look me in the eye
And to show how much I care
I think I would die

You hold me tight
And whisper soft
Within your light
My troubles are lost

The hurtful past
The feeling, used
My icy mask
Has been removed!

Life
by Shannon Goulet - age 16

Life,
something everyone should
cherish,
most people won't with
knowing they soon will
perish.

Life,
something that can be beautiful,
exciting, and full.
others think, mine is nothing
but dark, boring, and dull.

Life,
something filled with adventures
and excitement, no doubt,
wrong, it's just filled with
mysteries and confusion to
figure out.

You live once, trying to without
sadness and spite,
you live once, have fun and
live it not wrong, but right.

The Perfect Night
by Christina Gray - age 12

A dark green dress, I wore that night,
My hair in tight curls, it looked just right,
My stomach churned, my heart it jumped,
The doorbell rang, it loudly thumped.

On the doorstep he wait, all dressed in black,
On my hand a corsage, mounted straight like a plaque,
A big white limo, shinned brightly on the street,
The thrill alone, was a special treat.

I stepped inside, my mind in awe,
Champagne and wine, was all I saw,
We talked and laughed, while on our way,
I thought to myself, what a perfect Prom Day.

Mirage Land
by Sonya Grayson - age 13

Over mountains and oceans
Beyond plains and deserts
A wild land lies
Waiting to be discovered
But loved and kept secret
By me

Jungle green ferns inhabit
This island flat
Wild flowers of pink, red, and purple
Like roses, but larger
Sand dirt soil is hot to the touch of bare feet
A warm wind blows
Palm trees bravely stand alone

This is a lovely mirage prairie
Pretty, serene, peaceful
Green river water flows to a small pond
Triangular fish and frogs swim
Finding pleasure in frolicking

I often visit my island
To be by myself
Thinking
Drinking in the beauty
Of my land
Mirage Land

Night Gazing
by Sonya Grayson - age 13

Indescribable emotions seized me
As I looked up, up, up to the heavens
To see my father point his finger
And whisper as softly as the wind
"Look - there is Haley's Comet"

It was a beautiful sight -
The clouds seemed to part
As a mysterious beam from above
Flared behind that frosty ball

The bustle of people shifting
Ooohing and ahhhing
Drinking in the beauty
Of dreams on a memorable night

The damp night air
Crisply chilled the bystanders
While lending a hand of comfort
To all who gazed
That night

The comet was illuminated
Against the velvet sky
A pearl showing off its glamour
That night

It was all a magnificent
Memory
A vision blurred as time swept by
Once a vision so bright
So special
That night

A Quiet Yearning
by Jason E. Green

A delicate rose yearns towards the sky.
Its perfect petals open in anticipation.
Cool drops of rain moisten it's leaves.
Quenching an afternoon thirst.
Glistening droplets enhance it's beauty,
while it waits quietly for the return of the sun,
and a gentle breeze to dry away the rain.
A return to it's proper elegance

Love
by Tiffani Jolyn Gregory - age 14

Every time I think about your love
It drives me crazy
I give all my love to you
Now I long for your love in return
I give you my trust
Please don't misplace it
I give you my heart
Please don't break it

Now all I need
Is your tender loving care
After all we have been through
I will keep on loving you
Don't shed any tears
After all my love is right here

There is something about you
I just can't resist
It must be your tender loving kiss
I just can't let go
Of your tender loving care
Is it so much to say
All that we share is love

Missing You
by Valerie Gresham - age 13

It's been a while since
I've seen your face or kissed you on your lips
Or even since you've touched me
With your gentle fingertips
Every night I feel the tears
Rolling down my face
Cause no other man in this world
Could ever take your place
Being without you is such a fear
Even tough I'm needing you
But while you are gone away
I promise I'll be true
But the reason I am so upset
I really have not a clue
I guess it's because your sweet
And I'm really missing you!

Colors
by Brandy Jean Grider - age 12

Red is like the sun sinking down behind
a hill at dusk.
Green is like a beautiful forest stretching
on for miles.
Blue is like the ocean on a sunny day
at the beach.
Purple is like millions of violets swaying
in the summer breeze.
Pink is like a young child's cheeks after
running and playing in the hot sun.
Yellow is like a cold glass of lemonade
on a hot summer day.
Brown is like a little bunny hopping
through the tall swaying grass.
All these colors represent
wonderful lasting memories!!!!

The China Doll
by Mary Grubb - age 17

A hand carved china doll was given to a child.
She had such beauty and elegance, with a touch so mild.

She picked the child up and carried
the child through the child's carelessness.

With cracks the child couldn't mend,
the doll was put away,
and her spirit drifted in the wind.

Every child has a china doll.
Some forget;
others display, cracks and all.

Angels
by Alison Guarino - age 15

Angels, what a mystery, why are they here? They seem so far away to
some but then again to some so near.
Everyone has one to watch over them,
but it is whether the person believes.
Believe and they will come, if you don't there will be none.
All of them are pretty in their own way, but they will appear to you; I
can't say. They have special qualities inside, that they probably had
even before they died.
How do certain people become angels or not? To become an angel would
be an experience no one would ever forget; I know I would like it a lot.
Somewhere deep inside everyone, is a place where they believe, some
just show it more than others;
but why does one believe more than another?
Everything in this world was once or still is a mystery, some things are
solved and now have a history. Some things like angels won't be solved,
unless all of us believe and get involved!

The Coiling
by Emily Guerin - age 17

In the darkest dwelling lies a dream.
Vaguely rich of affection, it fulfills a flower,
blooming with passion, An outlaw,I've become.
In a second glance, reassure me. I need your tender
smile to get through this enigma I so reluctantly
deprive. Silk caresses my skin of weakness,
causing a tingle, I sit. Sit alone by myself, unaware
of the largest disturbance yet. In my mind it is over-
in my heart, it has just begun. My anger is aroused,
as petals softly fall to the molten earth.
Not a soul to guide me through this never ending path.
Think hard, or be had. Continue to awake, motionless in
the sun. Save your aggressiveness for tomorrow, for it
is not far behind. I am only myself, what more can
I be?

I Think
by Maria Guerrero - age 14

I think of the times we had,
now that he's dead.
I think of his kind, loving face,
now that he's in a case.
I think of is love,
now that he's higher than a dove.
I think of the beautiful things he's
made with his bare hands,
now that he's six feet under the land.
I think of the names he would call us,
now that he's dust.
I think of how I cried,
now that he died.
I think of how lonely it is in his place,
now I wish I could see his face.
I think of how much we loved him,
now that he's in heaven.
I think of all the things he used to say,
now and always I'll be his sugar babe.
I think of how he must have felt in that
small hospital bed,
I think of all the times we had,
not that he's dead.

Dedicated to: Seigle S. Beekman and Family

A Denial Burlesque
by Joyce Trusler Guilkey

Denial is an artform   a gallery of the mind
An imagined haven of escape   a sanctuary so kind
Denial is a paintbrush   for the canvases of life
Spreading oils of tranquility   shrouding pain and strife
Reality is left to those   with the artful skill to pine
To envision ugly consequences   denial has no time
Should flowery, sunny landscapes   begin to darken with dread
Faithful whitewash of denial   is ready to be spread
Denial is lifes palette, brilliant colors of the mind
Creating murals of illusions   on walls to hide behind
Bad habits and excesses   are blotted out with glee
To picture their acceptance   would assume reality
The most skillful of these artists   paint realities of their own
With smooth and practiced strokes   of denials pastel tones
Denial is a talent of   ingenious strokes quite free
Reality is only as real   as denial lets it be
Most therapists view it hopeless, a dementia at its best
They try to smear each canvas   with dark colors of unrest
But their craft is not artistic, painting storms and scenery cold
Just a canvas without color, gray realism they unfold
Reality is for people   who desecrate denial
Painting and sculpting normality, escapism they defile
Denial is for gifted artists   to create mosaics surreal
For a life in a world of fantasy, reality is too unreal

Hearts of Stone
by James D. Guinn - age 16

A heart of stone only leaves you alone.
But stone erodes from love is rain.
You can shelter your heart, but can't keep it apart and unknown.
You lie and try to hide a kind side, but cause less and more pain.

Despair, despair, and lover's despair
Will disappear in her arms.
You stare in her eyes and run loving finger through her hair
And you do love her too, cause true love never caused a heart harm.

Love, (a flower) ultimate power over the heart gone sour.
Hate, (the gate), the worst fate for the lost soul.
The lover, (the sun), melts ice and snow and weather so dour.
Her smile (her warmth), is her gift of gold.

Words through you heard through eyes.
Don't try to speak cause words are weak
Compared to stares that can't lie.
There are many loves but yours is unique.

Faith to give ones soul
To one who gives so much more.
Place her love in your heart, fill the hole
And be sure, (love is pure, forever and eternity more).

Good-bye
by Kayla Guitreau - age 17

You're leaving me so soon.
I don't know what I'll do.
It will be very hard
to live my life without you.

I know you have to make this step.
College time is here.
I just hope I can be strong,
and not shed a tear.

I have so many questions.
I am so confused.
I know there are others to date,
but it's you I don't want to lose.

Will you go off to college
and find that special girl?
Will I be able to move on
without you in my world?

You have made me so happy.
You have taken away my pain.
Will I ever be this happy again,
or will my life be pouring rain?

There is one thing I hope
and pray every day.
Please keep in touch,
and remember me always.

Alone
by Roni Gumbert

Darkness falls, no light is seen
You look around and there is no human being
You are afraid you don't know what is wrong
What sticks in your head is a very strange song

A song of love, a song of sorrow
Hoping to meet someone special tomorrow
You hope he will come and rescue you
From the darkness you withdrew

Dedicated to: Bob Karwowski

Competition
by Julie C. Gutana - age 16

We all possess the unfaltering, open desire to win, win, win.
And there are some things that all of want
Which include good looks, athletic ability,
and to be the best that there has ever been
We look at the competition we face,
and to each person we either praise or taunt.
Do we ever stop to think what this green eyed jealousy
and hectic rat-race is all for?
Competition is good but it has so much fault.
We exist in a grassy field marked with many paths; and competition is core.
Our competitors have feelings;
but we force their happiness and self esteem to halt.
Although we know there is much more to
a person than grades, looks, and agility,
We cease to remember that very vital fact.
And instead measure each others weaknesses vindictively, and judge
superficially to the fullest ability.
When really our value is not only in the magnanimous deeds we do, but also
in the kind ways we act.

Competition helps to give birth to success. It is good.
But not to point that we lose our way on the paths of the grassy field that
we call life.

Lost
by Kristen Gutto - age 13

I reach out
for something
something to
grab.
There's nothing
to grab
I keep falling
falling, falling.

"Troubles"
by Amanda Rose Gwost - age 15

All my troubles are her to stay.
For no one understands my ways.
They throw rocks and pelt their arms.
My sudden bloodshed feels quite warm.
As tears fall for my only block,
They stand by to laugh and gawk.
Down I dig into a pit,
Yet no dirt can break my wit.
There I'll rest for eternity,
With my soul upon His knee.
For with my sorrow I'm too naive.
But all will end the moment I leave.
Six whole years I've had this haul.
And now it will be part of my fall.
Four stories up, Thirty miles high,
Leaping forward into the sky.
Plummeting down onto the earth,
Only my household to value my worth.
On the pavement I let out a sigh,
Ranting and raving my last goodbye.

Choices
by Alex Hadzariga

Overhead the angry sun
blisters heat across the land
walking weary like a homeless man
As my tattered feet touch the sand.

The walk is trying like an endless game
And sensitive skin brings constant pain
And I'm not quite sure if I'm thinking the same
for the wind blows, persistently calling my name.

Ever tied, feet bleeding and soar
I hobble along and walk some more
so dehydrated I moan and wane
And again the wind calls my name.

come along Alex, and have no fear
you shalt not die alone out here
see my flesh, grab at the hand
save the turning into sand

my EARS full of dust but I hear every word
And took winds advice no matter how absurd.
so picking myself up the radiating ground
I reached for the wind that created that sound.

And these peaceful words a blessing so fine
it calmed my nerves, cleared my mind.
And then unto the seraphims that patiently wait
I bow my head to accept my fate.

Aaron Duane Dennis
by Melissa L. Haines - age 16

On this day, one year ago
A cold wind started to blow
Your eyes were filled with many tears
It was probably the most in all your years
And through all of your pain
You thought you would go insane
That was one of your longest nights
But after awhile you knew you would be alright
His life was in a tight tangle
But now he is a smiling, little angel
You may miss his sweet, little touch
But he always love you just as much
You may have asked, "Why me?"
But at least now he is finally free
The pain will slowly go away
But the memories will always stay
Your days may have it's highs and lows
But that is how life always goes

Imagine
by Lisa R. Halbsgut - age 12

Imagine a world with pale blue skies,
Arching rainbows, and gold butterflies.

And the sound of waterfalls rushing: rish rush.
With colors so elegant on leaves so lush.

Imagine this world with an abundance of flowers,
And enormous trees that stand proud, like towers.

The wind is humming a sweet, simple tune.
The flowers are dancing, the leaves will start soon.

The waterfall's a drum with it's constant, steady beat.
The rainbow's a racetrack, so narrow and neat.

And animals roam. They are running around,
So peaceful and free. There are joyous sounds.

Imagine this: Our world would be the same,
All of this was, until we came

I Am Here, They Are There
by Alissa Hall - age 12

I am here, they are there
That's the way it is
I don't need them
They don't need me
That's the way it will be
I am here, they are there
Even though I want them
I can't have them
Even if they want me
They can't have me
I am here, they are there
This is the way it is
There is no explanation
We will never be together as one
'Cause I am here
And they are there

It's Over
by Erin Hallahan - age 15

I've tried to express my love for you
in so many different ways
Different words and thoughts
things that might make you stay
I've grown tired trying to make this last
but you don't seem to care
I guess our love is nothing but past
because the idea of trying to fix things you don't share
All of my feelings were so true
and then I took one look at you
I wanted it
but you didn't
Ending things will be very hard
but it has to be done
Because living a lie is not what I'm here for
So good bye for now
Off to find another love

My Desire
by Maria Hall - age 14

My desire is to love you so much
that I will only think of you, and
when I think of you, I'll see all
that we've been through, and still
wonder how our love could last so
long and be so strong. My desire
to love you is to never part, if
we do, my desire to love you will
sink, and I'll never think of
anyone else. Love and desire
will part from my heart because
it's only my desire to love you and
only you and to never part from
you for as long as our love is
strong and can last long.

Kelly
by Al Hallberg

It was one of those friendships
That only happens during a war.
He was from the Carolinas
And I was from the Dakotas.

He was easy to know, so like me.
We met at Parris Island "boot"
Sharing the tortures of "camp bell"
We survived, laughing when we left.

Korea made us grow closer yet
Strange how close one can become
In just a few short weeks of sharing.
Letters from home, laughs, and jokes.

We stared into the face of death each day
Our friendship comforting us.
In spite of war and cold winter snow
Our friendship continued to grow stronger

I heard the mortar shell sing its deadly song.
I turned to scream at him, but he was gone
Disappearing in an icy cloud of crimson mist.
Memories of our friendship live on.

Let Me Hear You Whisper
by Monica Hall - age 14

As a breeze gently blows on the eastern coast,
let me hear you whisper,
tell me all I want to know,
where you've been where you're going, what you've seen and heard;

As a volcano erupts on a Hawaiian Island,
let me hear you whisper,
encourage me that life is worth living,
remind me that life's ups and downs are tests given by God himself;

As a shot rings out in Chicago young teen dies,
let me hear you whisper,
teach me all that you've been taught,
please be patient when I cannot remember;

As the ground shakes in California destroying lives,
let me hear you whisper,
tell me your deepest darkest secret,
I'll tell you mine if you promise not to tell;

As a child cries out alone in the night,
let me hear you whisper,
tell me all your hopes and dreams,
I will not laugh at you;

As a couple say their vows in a church in the North,
let me hear you whisper,
tell me of your fears,
voice your pain and anger;

As the sun sets on a southern town,
let me hear you whisper,
smile with me, and make me laugh,
let your humor shine,

As the world at long last is at peace,
let me hear you whisper.

But Only You
by Dawn Halm - age 17

There is many things in life
That I appreciate, but none
As most as you.

Just when I needed a friend
Who was there, but only you.

When the sky turned black
And life had no color
Who was there, but only you.

When it seemed that no one
Cared and I was alone,
Who was there to tell me different,
But only you.

For now I have a friend and
Life has color and I'm not
Alone and that's why I thank
You, because who could have
Done it, but only you.

Memory-Difficulty
by Emily Hamberger - age 11

Looking into the evening sky
I thought about what he told me
How never to be afraid of a life
So very different from my own

That other life, my friend's,
Did not understand the way of life,
That one needs t forgive and forget,
And remember not to hold grudges

I tried to help her, but I could not
She could not see my way, my world
Her life was destroying mine. Why?
Why couldn't she see through the darkness?

So now I count my blessing, I look up
and remember what he told me
Don't be afraid of a different life,
Live your own, Celebrate it

Spouse
by Elizabeth Hamilton

You hoped for someone you could count on and trust.
Someone who would love you as they love themselves.
You never were taught how to be a spouse,
how to be organized without any doubt.
Looking for the day you would be able to come together to plan and put
aside for your family's future.
The dream of great communication with truth and trust.
The hopes of a loving spouse is everyone's dream in marriage today.
It takes time to know one's self.
It takes almost a life time to know your spouse.
Marriage is not to be toiled with, but cherished.
Marriage is for a life time, not anything less.
Your mate is your friend, lover, and helper in all that you endeavor.
To take it lightly is the abuse to one's self.
Cherish your marriage, love your spouse.
Sit down together and plan it out.
Don't take for granted the marriage that you have;
Love and learn all that you can to make your hopes and dreams reality.
You may be that loving spouse.

Power of Love
by Savannah Rose Hamlett - age 13

Who says the wind can't move the sky.
Who says a tear can't hurt the eye.
With a love as strong as ours.
Your faith can last a million hours.
With a ring our life will begin.
Our hearts love will defend.
A single star in the sky your love will never lie.
For as we stand her today.
Our love will never stray.
As we say I do.
Our hearts will whisper I love you.

The Colors Of A Rainbow
by Leslie Renee Handshoe - age 10

Pink, green, yellow and blue. The colors of a rainbow, of a rainbow were meant for you on a rainy day to make you smile and put that special feeling of sunshine in your heart. And to remind you of the first rainbow the promise which God gave the rainbow to you for.
      Remember the promise.

Walls
by Nicole Haney - age 16

You feel them falling everyday,
There's nothing you cam do or say.

The doors are locked, there's no going back.
Courage and hope is what you lack.

You turn the key, but it turns no more.
You cannot unlock this barricade door.

Time passes, you're still inside,
no one can hear your pleading cries.

Each time you become brave and try to escape.
The walls become stronger and beckon you with hate.

They shake and shimmer, quarrel and quake.
The pain inside you cannot fake.

The end is here, the time has come.
The walls once falling, now are done.

You now understand, you now can relate.
These "Walls" around you are society's violence and hate.

Life Tomorrow
by Amy Hansen - age 13

I always wondered what life will be
    like tomorrow.
Will I meet the man of my dreams?
Will I lose a friend?
Will I gain a friend?
Now I realize that everyday I wonder,
    is a day I lose.
Life is passing me by like a bird flying
    through the sky.
I could sit home and wait, or I
    could be lured in by the bait of the
    wrong crowd.
I want to be flying through the
    sky with that bird.
But how?

Still Hanging On
by Amber Hanson - age 14

I'm still hanging on
Hoping our relationship will go back to normal
I miss the way it was

Still hanging on
Still hoping there's a chance
Still wishing all those problems never happened

We're a couple but it's not the same
I'm still hanging on
Still wishing for another chance
Where did I go wrong?

You don't deserve me but
I'm still there
Still hanging onto the little we have
Still hoping everything gets fixed

Do you still care?
Do you notice me?
Notice I'm still there
Still hoping
Still wishing
Still hanging on

You're Not the Type
by Traci Hanson - age 16

Late at night
I hear the ring
A muffled voice,
just a minute...MOM!
A few minutes later
a click of the phone
Who was it I ask
Just Dad, she says
He'll be home later
But then I realize
You're not the type to call.

Untitled
by Traci Hanson - age 16

If I gave you my life
Would you take it?
Or would you just
Pretend I was insane?

If I promised you my tears
Would you watch me cry?
Or maybe you would
Act as if I were not there.

If I offered you my soul
Would you accept it?
Or would you only
Make believe you didn't hear?

What would you do
If I gave you my heart?

Other Side Of The Veil
by Paul A. Harman III

Sixty years, or eighty or more,
I had known some of these people.
They had a different set to their faces
back then--each carried a purpose in their posture,
a weight upon their soul that
drained the orgies of lights of life
down to one narrow beam.

Your life is your work of art,
a one performance only show

Here we stand, all freed
of age, of sex, of any force to drive us down
any single path.
Look around you, the world is now
as wide as it gets,
when we are all at last free
to commune with each other.

Canterbury in Kent (29 December ghost dance)
by Paul A. Harman III

On a hill at the center of the Western world,
a human died to bring peace.
Eleven centuries and seventy years
passed, and at Canterbury in Kent
human sacrifice turned consecrated stones red.
Peace was as far away as ever.

(The 29th of December, ghosts danced in the snow.
Seven years, and the Archbishop has left us.)

On a bloodied continent full of ghosts,
new noises forever shattered the peace.
In Dakota, December the 29th, shadows vanished in snow.
In Chicago, on a May first through fourth,
human sacrifice turned the cobblestones red.
Peace was as far away as ever.

(The 29th of December, ghosts danced in the snow.
They said they'd take our land, and they took it.)

On a hillside deep in the Western world,
four of many more died to bring peace.
Nineteen centuries and seventy years
had passed. General Canterbury in Kent
was there for another May first through fourth,
and peace was as far away as ever.

The terrifying thing: the timeline moves always
forward, and nothing is repetition.

The Flutist
by Caitlin Harold - age 14

The woman sits alone,
her fingers flying over the familiar silver keys.
Playing the notes she has so lovingly written;
her song is who she is,
the story of her life.
As her melody wears on,
her fingers become the worn keys that she gently caresses.
The woman's body becomes the delicate instrument she knows so well.

Forming the shining silver,
Her flowing golden hair
melting into the angelic turn that hangs in the air.
As the last bittersweet note rings out its voice,
All that remains on the aging wooden stage
is a gleaming silver flute and a single white rose.

Treasures

Forget
by Christina Harrell - age 18

The sun is shining
Grass so green
It rained last night
The world is fresh and clean
Blue-Jays on the ground
Crows in the trees
My dream last night
Made me feel like a disease
But I know I'm not
So I must go on
I have to forget about the day
He did me so wrong.

Leaving
by Virginia L. Harrell

Leaving does not mean ending,
It means beginning.
New directions chosen,
Welcomed challenges,
The freshness of learning.
Exchanging experience for opportunities,
To become newer experiences.
Leaving is a renewal,
A chance for improving
With possibilities for growing.
For leaving is the ability to move on
To a new beginning,
Not an ending.

To Parents
by Heather Harrington - age 14

You shelter me thinking your
doing me good
All you can see is under your
black hood
I'm trapped in here, a world
that means nothing to me
Why do I have to be the
way you want me to be?
I'm going to explode if I'm
not who I am
Why do even give a damn?
I told you, the more you
push, I will pull
I will become a red-eyed
charging bull
Children rebel when they're
pushed too hard
Then they're trapped for good,
chained up and barred.

Ignorance
by Caron Harris

Surrounding the street-wise students, the room was bursting with the hopes and fears of thousands of men, women and children. The musty room was packed with love, anger, hate and shame. Romance, intrigue and expectations were straining the books' seams trying to escape into the lives of the children. Murder, espionage, power and lust were crying out to the youth. There were smells of fears, death, pleasure and pain. Every plot ever dreamed, every event initiated, every fantasy realized, and every possibility imagined were there for this adventuresome generation to seize as their own.

The adolescents gazed at the shelves full of books and ran their hands along the rough spines. They decreed. "There is nothin' good here." They left without realizing they had missed the exciting experiences of centuries of exploring and living. They had said that every event written about, every story told, and every mind explored was "nothin'." Life could have been lived to the fullest, but the youngsters had walked away. They had not tasted the inspiring excitement, the rush of flavors a reader would savor.

The students were hunting excitement and fun, they were looking for insight and reasons. They had been offered the world, but left without a book. They had left without experiencing the most exciting stories that their limited minds would have ever dreamed. They naively left the library with "nothin'." Again, they came to my class with nothing to read. Their isolated lives still untouched, void.

Untitled
by Krystal Harris - age 14

Deep beneath the skin I rot
Like the unripe fruit of a peach tree
Falling to the naked ground
Eatin away by the withering worms
I rot
I rot away and away to the core
Till I can rot no more
The pain of the unbearable world
Has eatin away at me
Away at my soul
So I rot
The black of earth is closing in
My emotion tortured and trot
I figure I'll never win
So therefore I continue to rot
Days are getting shorter
Hours even older
Will this forsaking pain ever stop
The pain of rotting hurts
Dying must be the only thing that works
To end this never ending pain
That rots.

A Pirate's Whore
by dony harrison

Yesterday's social debutante - Today any Pirate's whore
Her price another round of rye whiskey - Served at a sleazy harbor side bar
Jaundice tear stained cheeks - Coty translucent powder caked and dried
Crowsfeet frame smeared mascara eyes
Fold to flesh ruby lipstick spread across her swollen face
Skinny arms, distended waist, patchy lesion skin
She road a lonely non-stop midnight train - Left alone not one friend
Hard liquor once killed her pain, later it took cocaine
A lost love finally drove her insane
Satan awaits with a smile - Her successful doomsday mission of sin
Aids virus will be the end - Found dead on a deserted wharf
Cardboard casket buried on an indigent county plot
What was life's purpose for a Pirate's Whore
Only her, out of wedlock, daughter, could open that door
A promenade doctor adopted the infant of a Pirate's Whore
Educated in private schools - Only the finest fashions she wore
This was the heaven given her - By a mother now gone to hell
The reason for her insanity - A Pirate's Whore would never tell

Black
by Tanya Harris - age 13

Black is like a mine
filled with diamonds and gold.
Black is something
ravishing and filled with essence.
Black can be a person dark as can be.
Black can be an emotion...said aren't we.
But what Black really is, do we know?
I do, it's me.

Untitled
by Elisabeth N. Harvey - age 17

Tears fall gently
As memories flood her mind.
The faces are blurred.
She thought of no one else.

Remembering the pain and
The sorrow brought her back.
Senses reeling, she was unaware
Of the happenings around her.

Her pale face shown in the dim light.
It showed times of heartache,
The pictures made her remember.
Feeling vulnerable, she escaped the theater.
She couldn't stand it any longer.

If I Can See Your Face Again
by Rashawn Haskell - age 15

If I can see your face again
 it will make my dream
  come true
I want to start over and make
 it brand new

On that day when you left
 me all alone
You broke my heart and weakened
 my bones

Tears came to my eyes and I dropped
 to the floor
My heart felt like a closing door

I had a dream later that night,
 a vision of you walking through
  the door
It made me cry even more and more

As I look at your picture on
 the wall
I remember as lovers we had
 a ball

So now can't you see,
 how you hurt me

Deep in your heart I know you
 love me
So lets make things the way it
 used to be

Signs of Spring
by Cassie Hatch - age 13

A bird bursts into a beautiful song,
Breaking the silent, stillness that winter has left.
For the winter has been ever so long,
That no natural sound has been heard yet.

Streams run down the country road,
And grass blades are peeking through the snow.
You might see a deer, a rabbit, or a toad,
Because animals are awakening now.

This is a time when animals awake,
A time for nature to renew itself.
It's a special beauty only nature could make,
And these are the signs for spring.

A Sun Rise Good-Bye
by Kedesha Haughton - age 18

I watched the sun rise this morning.
It touched my skin and tickled my
Nose. I have seen many sun rises
Before, but none quite like this one.
I remember them all completely,
But this one, this one I will never
Forget. For you see, it is to be my
Last. It was so bright, so bold with
Colors of yellow, red and just a
Dash of orange with a tint of gold,
And distinctively beautiful. At first
It seemed as if everything was
Moving very rapidly; getting ready
For a celebration. The clouds in
The sky moved swiftly by and the
Birds and the insects scurried along.
The wind danced gently with the
Trees, rocking back and forth. The
Smell of dew on the wet lawn and
The sounds of the morning hung in
The air. Then suddenly, the sun
Pushed its head above the horizon
And for one, single moment,
Everything took a breath, held it, as
The sun stretched its arms, waned,
And opened Its eyes. That was when
I closed mine.

Blind Love
by Krista Hawkins - age 16

I've always heard that love is blind
But I've never actually understood.
That is until now.
Now that I've met you, things have changed
You've helped me to open my eyes and see
That it doesn't matter who's right or who's wrong,
Who's black or who's white,
Who's young or who's old,
Who's rich or who's poor,
All that really matters is love.
When you love somebody,
Everything else just disappears.
All you can concentrate on is that one person.
Not on their faults and their differences,
But on them and the love that you have for them.
And you know that as long as you have each other,
Nothing else will ever matter as much to you as that.

Wonders
by Carolyn M. Headrick

Wonders lie beneath the snow
that cannot yet be seen.
Till winter ends its frosty bed,
they will not be revealed.
What could be as beautiful
as this winter wonderland?

Wonders from the earth will rise
up to take your breath away.
From glistening white and grey clouds
to refreshing green and sunny skies.
What could be as beautiful
as this spring miracle?

Wonders appear anew in summer,
bold bursts of color to dazzle.
Replacing the faded blooms of spring,
continuing one after another.
What could be as beautiful
as this summer display?

Wonders work their magic now,
providing bounty for the coming winter.
Leaves turn orange, red and yellow,
lighting up the landscape like fire.
What could be as beautiful
as this autumn harvest?

Grandpa, I Love You
by Denise Heffert - age 14

Good morning Grandpa, what will you do today?
I'm going to school, I have a test
I better study, I can't delay.
For you Grandpa, I'll try my best.

Good afternoon, how was school you ask
It was a decent day I guess
I put effort into every task.
Because of me, you expect no less.

What will you have for dinner tonight?
I suppose I could eat my vegetables for you.
Though I'd rather not have them in my sight,
For you there is nothing I wouldn't do.

Good night Grandpa, I hope you sleep well.
I know I will as long as you're around.
Tomorrow there's more that I will tell
They'll be different sights and different sounds.

Good morning Grandpa, they tell me you're ill.
Would you like a cup of tea:
Look at the bird on the window sill.
One of the many beautiful sights to see.

I came home today, you weren't there.
Dad told me they brought you here
I thought that it was so unfair.
It shouldn't have happened to you my dear.

Wake up Grandpa, from your eternal rest
There's something I forgot to say,
I love you Grandpa, you are the best
And in my heart you'll always stay.

Running Out Of Luck
by Kalesha Henry - age 16

The death of a dream,
The feel of defeat,
Makes all the good times feel like a feat.
Will it come back,
Your great grand slam hit,
Or will your strikeout and belong in the pit?
To run the wrong way,
Or score the wrong goal,
To stuff your own player and run into the pole.
The sound of a whistle,
The fly of a card,
You're better off benched and all full of lard.
Your teammates support you,
Say you're not to blame,
But you know that they're thinking don't show up next game.

"Gone"
by David Hernandez - age 17

Right now, I am feeling blue
Because I am missing you.
I want you in my arms
To impress with all my charms.
I had once been heartless
Until you came and gave happiness.
I can't get you out of my mind.
Indeed, you looked very fine.
After the day we were together,
Went away were any nightmares.
Why must you be so far away.
There is so much for me to say.
I want to see you everyday.
Alone, I do nothing but pray.

As I try to go to sleep
I can't help but start to weep.
You perch over me figure
On a cold day of winter.
Soon, you getup to depart
With a new man in your heart.
I can bear to think of this
For I longed to give you one last kiss.
I see you walk, not turning back
Suddenly, my heart sank.
I never wanted you to flee
For we were meant to be.
Only if your heart could see
That special part of me.

My Simple Life
by Heidi Margarete Hernandez - age 15

With sorrow in my heart,
with fear wherever I go.
Afraid to love to feel and,
even express myself.

But, I have learned not to
live in sorrow nor fear.
Never shall I be afraid
to hold my head up high
full of overwhelming pride!

And so I dream my dreams,
and believe what I want to believe.
And I shall always take pride,
in me and my simple life.

The Unseen Paradise
by Roger Heslop Jr. - age 17

Life, the unseen paradise, dark and dim,
Just black and white and all seems grim.
Existence, the fog, the reality of unseeing,
A cold dams chill, the price of being.
A lonely chasm, silence unbroken,
The dreary maze like destiny unspoken.
Standing wand walking but can't see ahead,
The abyss and nothingness, just fear and dread.
Entering darkness seeming frightening,
The unknown and dangerous, almost exciting,
A twist of irony, the added fear,
One would never think one would end up here.
Just a few more paces and them look back,
It's odd how easy you can lose track.
You can decide which direction to go,
But where it'll lead you'll never know.

Anger
by Morgan Hett - age 16

I never knew the anger within me
I never knew it would be released
I never knew I had that kind of temper
I had had enough, too much had built up inside
Two weeks before, I remained calm
Calm through the toughest meeting of my life
Everything slid off my back, that's what I thought
Until that night, my wall came crashing down
The crying, the yelling, it felt kind of good
It was as if something was lifted from my shoulders
Had I been too calm?
Should my wall have tumbled sooner?
Or would things have only gotten worse?

When You're Down
by Silvia Hickel - age 14

When you're down
I'll be down too
and you feel like...
there's nothing I can do...
you cry every night
you smile everyday
I ask "what's wrong"
and "don't worry" is what you say.
When you're sad
I'll be sad too
you feel so bad
but I'll do what I can do.
You cry every night
you smile day by day
I want to help
I feel like there's nothing I can say except "I do care."
if you're mad
I'll be there for you
you can yell at me
cause I'll take it straight from you.
when you're glad
I'll be happy too
I'll share in your joy
cause I've always been there for you and always will

Little Girl
by Silvia Hickel - age 14

once there was a little girl,
her friends were dear and true,
whenever she was sad,
they knew exactly what to do.
once there was a little girl,
her family was gentle and sweet,
the family never went hungry
they always had something to eat.
once there was a little girl,
her mind was young and active,
but she was told not to use it,
her hopes, her dreams, were all held captive.
there once was a little girl,
her life was left to die,
she acted so happy,
her life was such a lie.
whatever happened to this little girl?
she now may rest in peace,
she now may rest happily,
just to say the least.

Man's Valley
by Colin Patrick Highland - age 20

The valley is flooded;
Flooded with light and the essence of life.
The only shadows are that of the clouds
Chasing one another among the mountain slopes.
Striped fairies of black and gold
Wander from petal to petal and cup to cup.
A stag lowers his antlered head--but not in defense.
He sips the flowing nectar rushing from the mountains.
The fiery fox scampers from the brush
And joins the stag in his morning ritual.
The gleeful cry of a crimson-tailed hawk echoes
And disrupts the quiet sound of drying dew and rustling leaves.
The last remnants of night are almost gone,
Except for the crickets chirping--
Unaware of the sun under their shady stones.
An eery silence envelopes the valley.
The fox scurries back to her hidden home,
The stag raises his regally tan head.
What is that smell? What is that sound?
It is foreign and unknown.
It is man.
Man, unsatisfied with what is already his,
Stumbles into the peaceful valley
With his clumsy boots, his thoughtless actions, and his gun.
A single shot is fired.
The princely stag stumbles and collapses.
The stag of nine winters will know no more
And is taken from his beloved valley.
The valley is flooded;
Flooded with light and the arrogance of man.

The Petals
by Michelle Hill - age 14

Have you ever felt like your life is like
dead petals on a rose? Sometimes when life
gets too hard to stand, those petals will
start to fall. No matter how fast I pick
them up, they just keep falling more
quickly! For days now I've been trying to
pick up all the petals, and tried to stop
them from falling. Every day it gets worse.
When I look, there's more petals just lying
there, waiting for me to pick them up. I keep
wondering "When will the petals stop
falling?" Then one day, the petals did stop
falling. The rose is dead. My insanity and
frustration has finally come to an end.
    Life is over.

The Film Within The Dream
by Aaron

I stand looking into the huge
oil painting. They are hanging in
air, each one set at an angle.
Each one filled with short beige ribbons.
The ribbons are set at angles
within ordered rows. I look at
them. They begin to move and dance
around. I find myself among
them. The ribbons turn into tall
military people with swords
and pistols. There is hand-to-hand
fighting, screaming, whirling dancers.

I stand looking at the paintings
and unmoving ribbons. I am
once more within the paintings in
the midst of a great battle, I
know many of the fighters but
I know no names. Fog glides across
the gullies as we fight. We grow
silent as we put our efforts
into strike, parry, load, fire, duck,
attack and defend. I am once
more outside the paintings. I stand
breathing hard, dripping blood. I wake.

The light filters through the shutters.
"One does not fight merely to sin."
said Cyrano. Purpose and joy
is in fighting. A conclusion
is not necessary. Process
is the more important product.

The Owl Came and Hooted
by Aaron

Half asleep, I opened my mouth and let the nurse
take my temperature. Each morning at six
that ritual began my day and began my life.

I walked to breakfast. Running was a crime that led
to the death we might encounter. On the table;
ham, and eggs, toast and mile. Lots of cold milk.

Back on the porch I sat up in bed and studied.
My toy plane came from under the pillow
and gilded down the sheet. I walked to lunch.

I took a nap. When I awoke the sun was
beginning to set beyond the wooded hills.
Nurse took my temperature. I walked to dinner.

At the table beside my bed, I listened to the radio;
wrote, read, talked, and played quietly.
At nine they took my temperature; turned the lights out.

The owl came and sat in the tree outside the screen
and hooted. Long into the night my six-year old
heart beat strong while the tears flowed.

That Night
by Amber Rose Hillyard - age 15

That night while I was lying there with you,
you made me realize something I never knew.
I'm not alone here,
I really have people that care.

God, I wish I could just say it,
you mean the world to me each and every bit.
No one has ever said the things you say,
made me feel so special or held me that way.

I love you in every way,
and think about you every day.
I know we'll probably never be together,
but remember friends forever.

You say you want to go,
to leave here, you hate it so.
If you leave promise you'll say goodbye,
I promise I'll try not to cry.

Remember goodbyes are face to face
not without a trace.
I lied there running my fingers through your hair,
and couldn't help but stare.

Your face so precious as you sleep,
gave me forever memories to keep.
And angel is what you are,
but special is where you go far.

About The Same
by Carl F. Hoffman

Should all the cupids of this world
Suddenly spurn love in casual shame
And if all the flowers were also gone
I'd be loving you about the same.

Should moonlight quietly disappear
And ardent emotions regress to lame
If cupid's arrow was lost to sorrow
I'd be loving you about the same.

If the heavens no longer lit the sky
And darkness was the road to fame
Still, I would not need guiding light
I'd be loving you about the same.

When romance is put to the ultimate test
True love stands aloof of life's petty game
Power of passion explodes in caballed zest
Yes, I'll be loving you about the same!

Tea With Mother
by Judith A. Hoggan

Today I wandered through the Mall,
Buying nothing,
Seeing all.

And then I stopped in a quaint tea shoppe,
Where my thoughts
Back in time hopped.

Or, rather traveled to another space,
In which I shared a
Lovely place
With my beloved Mother.

I thought how lovely it would be
If she were now
Here with me,
Sharing an espresso, or a cafe latte,
Or maybe a cuppa tea.

In a garden room
With the sun so bright
And the lovely flowers
All a bloom.

And a harpist playing
Soft, lifting tunes,
And my Mother saying,
I love you.

So, I bought you, Mother, darling
In that moment of joyful thought
This small token Royal Daulton
Which I know you'd've not bought (for yourself).

Happy Mothers' Day, 1997

Dignity
by Veronica Hollmon

D is for determination, to reclaim all that I had lost.
I is for ingenuity, required to escape from you at all costs.
G is for gratitude, that I lived when others have died.
N is for necessity, the tools I used to survive.
I is for idols, like Nicole, who paid the ultimate price.
T is for tenacity, to struggle on when all seemed lost.
Y is for yearning, for the freedom I had lost.

Dignity is what I have now
Freedom from strain and worry
from bruises to spirit and brow.
If you're in a violent relationship
The time to leave is NOW!

Nicole
by Veronica Hollmon

My skin is brown by nature
While yours was pristine white
But we have much in common
Including husbands who fight.

The physical bruises heal
Given the luxury of time
But often were the tears
From bruises to spirit and mind.

I did not think I had the strength
To leave violence behind
But with your untimely demise
Fear gave way to the courage
That I had buried so deep inside.

I wish you were here to see me now
I can once again howl with glee
As much as it pains your family
Just like me, you are free.

You have gone to a better place
And I just want you to know
I carry you inside my heart
Every place I go.

So smile Nicole and know
Your sacrifice was not in vain
May your family find comfort in the knowledge
You enabled me to leave my life of pain.

Race
by Veronica Hollmon

You hear a great deal of discussion in terms of black and white.
You hear catch phrases like "racial divide", but what's it all about.

So my ancestors came on slave ships, while yours came as immigrants.
Or maybe your ancestors are natives, who welcome others ancestors on the Mayflower.

What matters now is equality, not quotas or gimmicks.
Honest wages for honest work, not greed or corruption or bigots.

Maybe you're Catholic or Jewish or Muslim or Christian Scientist.
Maybe you're black or white or red or yellow or a mix.

We are all of one race, let all false perceptions shatter.
We are all members of the human race, start there and nothing else matters.

Untitled
by Lindsay Hollock - age 13

    she cried
           and did not stop
why why?
     she cried
           in the filth of the street
   on her knees
in the shadow of the tall light
    she was left alone
             feeling small and defeated
     no where to go
                no one to see
                no one who cared

Dirty, Smelly Closet Grunge
by Sarah Holm - age 13

Have you ever seen my closet
for your sake I hope you have not
Because if you open my closet
you will smell the stench and rot

Dirty socks and dishes
have made it my most fame
when will you clean it up
is my mothers usual complain

When my closet
starts to mutter
I walk by
and have to shudder

When I finally
look in there
the grime, and goo, and glop
is starting to grow hair

I finally locked my closet
with a big silver lock
and maybe, just maybe
the noises will finally stop

So when my mother asks
how's your closet's health
I don't know, but I'm not looking
you go look yourself

What do I want to be?
by Adrienne Holness - age 12

I want to be strict and flimsy
I want to be born and die
I want to be mellow but eccentric
with my feet on the ground and head in the sky
I want to be wild and crazy
with everything shiny and new
I want to be wise as the ages
and always know what to do
I want the winds and weather
to come at my command
I want the subtle power
to hold the stars inside my hand
I want to take a breath and inhale all the sea
once that's done I'll let you know
just what I want to be.

Ever Again
by Stefanie Holton - age 17

Looking up at your lonely apartment
I long to be in your arms
I can still feel you caressing my face
How I long to have again the love we once shared.
But will we ever again?
Too much has happened for us to go back people say
Is it sincerely true
Please tell me
Do you still share those old feelings with your heart
But will we ever again?
I say often to myself that you have found a new love
It's like a sharp dagger has been twisted inside of me
Every time I hear my voice utter those hideous words
A constant battle between us -- a raging war with me and myself
It often scares people for me
They believe of me I am blinded by love
But will we ever again?
You understand my obstacle and only you
For in the same dilemma are you as me
You feel my pain as I yours
My eternal bond to you is immense
And will never be taken away
No knife, no words, no absence of presence could appear it vanished
But will we ever again?
Forever it will remain always.
Nothing could ever be this wonderfully difficult to live with
My question may die never answered fully by anyone way of my heart
Dying in aloneness is not called fair
It is called listening to the voices of this cold, vacant world
Whose questions have been answered not themselves.

Missing You
by Sabrina Honeyfield - age 17

Anytime I think of you,
I smile and hope to see you
Again soon.

All day long I think of you!
When my mind is empty
Thoughts of you fill it up.

As I lay awake in bed at night,
I hear songs that make me think
Of you.

You never leave my thoughts!
Even when I sleep,
I dream dreams of you!

I think of your warm smile,
And smile myself.
Counting the days till I see you again!

Hoping it all will come fast
Growing tired of crying, waiting,
and most of all

Missing you!

Fear
by Sarah Honkanen

Slowly walking through the night,
The smell of smoke what a fright.
Lightening flashes across the skies,
A man appears with evil eyes.

I'm shaking, I'm trembling, I want out of here,
I'm crying, I'm screaming as I overcome with fear.

The man disappears, I hear a scream,
I feel I'm trapped in an eternal bad dream.
I want to wake up I want to go,
As a horrid black spider scampers across my toe.

I'm shaking, I'm trembling, I want out of here,
I'm crying, I'm screaming as I overcome with fear.

Something makes a screeching sound,
I feel myself drop to the ground.
A human form slips quietly by,
And from my lips a terrified sigh.

I'm shaking, I'm trembling, I want out of here,
I'm crying, I'm screaming as I'm overcome with fear.

These Do I Love
by Pamela C. Hood - PCH

Old things, old places
Satin sheets, warm embraces
Special times, familiar faces.
Sweet scent of perfume, but leaves no traces
You slipped into my life, in such a quiet way
And now you give new meaning to my everyday.
The touch of your hand, the look in your eyes
Makes my heart ache when we say our good-byes
You'll always be my sunshine after the rain,
You give me strength and ease my pain.
I hear your voice and it makes my heart flutter
I get so excited, I sometimes stutter.
Thoughts of you keep me warm through the night
Our love can't be wrong when it feels so right.
You squeeze my hand, you touch my heart
I'll love you forever, I have from the start.
Your moist lips so sweet, they taste like honey
Your smile and laughter make my day sunny
Our love is like music, a beautiful song
I'll love you forever, this love can't be wrong.

Our Fear
by Jill Marie Hopkinson - age 12

She gives us pleasurable memories
Always playful and energetic
I throw her toy, she wags her tail
Tikka runs to go get it as she barks joyfully.
My grandparents have a house boat
When Tikka's there she stays inside, for we fear she will jump off
Our Fear came true
They leave the door open and go upstairs
Where did they go?
Her search goes on, but she does not, as the water takes away her life

My Light
by Amy Hopper - age 15

I wander down the lonely road
And realize what I lost
The sun in my life
The heart of my soul
Has anyone else been down this road?
Or am I the explorer?
I'm alone
While I'm surrounded by many
My being is moribund
My body assumes control
It performs all the correct actions
While inside I am dying
The anger has faded
Now just pain that destroys my soul

My life is torture
Why should I go on?
In someone's eyes a light shines
Has this person walked this road?
I wonder...
Can he nurse my soul as I nurse his?
Does he know who he has become to me?
My light in the forest of darkness
Yet as my hand reaches for his...
He reaches over
I receive a high five
Instead of a firm tender grasp...
hope died...

Leaving Behind, Saying Goodbye
by Darla Michelle Horn - age 14

Leaving Behind, Saying goodbye
how many times do I have to wipe
the tears from my eyes.

The older I get, the harder it is
Because these are more people who
mean most to me the people who
I will realiy miss.

Time after time, cry after cry
The harder it is to say goodbye
But what people just don't understand
is saying goodbye to that important
friend.

The person who stands by you day
by day as times goes by, the person
who comforts you when you cry,
The person who puts a smile on your
face when your down, the person who
gives you important advice without
making a sound.

Why do I have to say goodbye,
well the choice really isn't mine
if I didn't have to leave life would
be just fine.

I count the times, the times I cry,
Time is up! its time to leave
behind and say goodbye.

Lover's Regret
by Shannan Hornung - age 15

I'm eating my heart out
Can't you see the blood on the floor
Haven't been too well lately
No I just can't take life anymore

I should've thought about this
I could've loved you more
I just wanted life to be so good
Now without you it's such a bore

Everywhere I hear you talkin'
Screamin' your words in my ear
You're haunting me so it seems
You know I really wish you were here

I know it's all my fault
I know I make mistakes
Thought I could play games
'Cus I wanted you every other way

Does this dream have to end
With smiles upside down
Shattered hearts and gleaming tears
Too much pain to bear a frown

You know I can't live without you
But that's what they all say
Never thought I'd feel so bad
But I'll always love you anyway

Dark is Deep
by Cathy Huffman

The night draws folks outside.
The soft summer air -- a little too warm,
The velvet dark of night,
The moon shadows cast by piney sentinels,
And the stars -- Oh! -- the stars!
Like diamonds on a jeweler's cloth,
They fill the circle of the sky.

Folks stand on the porch behind the screen --
For there are bugs you know.
They marvel at the handiwork of God
And count the stars,
But their numbers, like grains of sand, are far to great.

But dark is deep --
And there are terrors in the night
And fear of what we cannot see.
The sounds of night are strange --
Doubtless made by fearsome creatures of our dreams.
The folks grow frightened by the night and shut the door.

Music and the Muse
by Michele M. Hulek-Doyle

music attracts
fleeting images
to the pen
that transcribes
upon the page
the cohesive whole
brought together
by the music
and the muse

Why Argue and Fight?
by Jennifer Hull - age 15

I don't understand why people fight
It just isn't right or fair
People argue and still it isn't right or fair
I just don't understand people and why they'll
argue till their dying day.
I know I argue and fight, but I don't even
understand myself at times
because life doesn't seem right or fair
it seems like thoughts and things are
left out just to make something else a whole
I just don't understand why fighting and arguing were
ever made because so many people would actually
get along if there weren't any made or thought up of.

Throw Away People
by C.E. Gray

Society sits in judgement, looking down their nose
At homeless people with tattered clothes
Dirty little children, living on the street
Go to bed hungry, with nothing to eat

Prisoners in cages, like animals in a zoo
But who really cares, long as their hidden from view
Those will needles in their arms walking in the rain
Some for fun, and some to ease the pain

While religious people hide in churches with big steeples
Completely disregard those throw away people
Those without money, title, or fame
Who's meaning of life is surviving the pain

The government spends millions, on statues and monuments
But to really equate justice, not one red cent
They stand and give up service, and pre written speeches
And with stolen taxes buy their condos on the beaches

And in this same country true love and passion
Lovers and poets find it no longer in fashion
So close your hearts, your minds and your eyes
Cause nobody cares, when throw away people die

Untitled
by Maegan Huntington - age 13

Hearing that gothic music, I close my eyes tight,
And my mind is relaxed.

With trembling stillness,
And unbreakable silence,
I see a resplendent blue color inside my eyes.

The color in my eyes flow like a dark blue river;
And everything it touches is taken along with it.

Likewise with the music;
I am taken away with it's beauty in the meaning,
That it never leaves me;
And not only am I taken with it but it is also taken with me.

Pain
by Shirley J. Hurd

Jagged edges around my heart,
Pain by pain pulled apart,
A razor slicing at its' edges,
making holes and little wedges.

Teach me please to feel no pain,
I hold my breath in sweet refrain,
Minds of wisdom, strength and courage,
Let me live to love and flourish.

Heavy, oh heart, how you bleed inside,
STOP! please STOP! Don't take my pride,
Blast this world of pain and hate,
You make me live with dreaded fate.

You've torn my life and others too,
With rules and deeds that we can't do,
I hate our sickening, insensitive race,
To push me through to save your face.

You degrading plastic fools,
Who have no sense and so few tools,
You ruined my life, you just don't care,
That there are some who are treated unfair.

I have so little that I can hope for,
You've slammed your windows, and closed my doors,
Curse your rules and menial deeds,
Which dent my life with unwanted stampedes.

Why do you make these blasted thrusts?
And take away my hope and trust,
You've packaged away my life so fast,
You've blown my present because of my past.

"Moments"
by Beth Iffert - age 19

Taking life step by step,
    remembering moments that will always be kept.
Those that bring upon unending smiles,
    And the pain that travels devastating miles.
Thinking of times that seem so sad,
    those joyous nights with friends you had.
Uneasy feelings on what life is really about,
    alone and afraid the fears you shout.
Creations in life destroying the mind,
    wondering in life what you will eventually find.
Fear of what will appear in life next,
    you read the future in your own little text.
Thankful for the tears that wash away your pain,
    wondering what in the future is left to gain.
Thinking about the future, pondering on the past,
    wishing that certain moments would vanish at last.
The pain and fear driving you farther away,
    leaving you with absolutely nothing to say.
Closing your life like the ending of a book,
    as you begin to think and take a closer look.

I-Wonder
by Charles (Bubba) Irish - age 18

I wonder sometimes
If I'm living or dying
But between the tears and crying
I haven't see a thing to help me
Where I'll know if I'm living or dying
All I can do is hope for the best
But prepare for the worst!

Understanding
by Robyn Ann Irving - age 15

Staring off into darkness,
Staring off into space,
What I see is not who
I am, but what I've become.

Watching from my coffin,
Daring to jump out,
Laying down without sound,
I want change.

Flowers start to bloom from
Heaven above as the sky
Touches the sea,
I stand silently.

Spring follows winter,
So naturally I wonder why,
It's all so clear to me,
I know, I understand now.

Waterfalls play music
All around, birds fly
High above and I just
Stare and listen.

Listen to it all as one
Of Earths precious gifts,
I am one with the soil
I am one with the Earth.

The Earth is one with me,
Together we will be safe,
And together we will always
Change and be free!

Heart's Fire
by Aeron Ives - age 19

How 'fire is thine heart, like candy in flame?
Lovely is thy warm face, and smiling too!
How beautiful is thine hair, night untame'!
What knowest thee of my love sole' for you?

The hearts of most shall bleed tears of pain,
But thy soft heart, it doeth shine as rays.
Long I for you every long age in vain.
And thy hot face, it gloweth thy lamb's gaze.

How thy many raven locks art as a glory,
And shine, Artemis' light in a pond full of tears.
The flame of thy blush doeth 'waken me,
Flicks high and wide, as fire in thee, and sears!
Thou knowest my love ceaseless, free from time,
But doeth thine silk heart burn--bleedeth as mine?

Cemetery Nevermore
by Kim Iwanejko

The thunder roared across the sky,
The lightning struck the earth.

The cemetery had an eerie aura,
The graves were all too shallow.

Dirt slowly became mud,
Headstones slid away.

The dead were angry,
Their coffins afloat.

The cemetery nevermore.

Turning Leaves
by Jennifer Ingram - age 17

Blades sway swinging
slowly over down
dancing freely
tickled by the wind

Flowing softly
round the laces of
the lady green
with growing tresses

Through her ribbons
and there it whispers
dreams serene by
sweetly turning leaves

Treasures

Here Johnny Lay
by G.D. Jackson

Here Johnny lay,
such a waste,

Poor Johnny got
sucked in,
Always wanted to
fit in,
with drugs, gangs and violence

Johnny wanted to be
real cool,
didn't want to
stay in school

Such a Waste,
Such a disgrace
could have been
so special
could have made
his mama real proud

Instead at 16,
here Johnny lay,
such a waste,
such a disgrace.......

A Dying Flower
by Jessica Jackson - age 17

Golden curls spill out from under her flower scarf,
    loosely tied under her chin
Her deep ocean eyes
A pale blue dress
A picture of beauty in heavens early morning glow
Like a tender kiss or drop of snow
In the early morning mist,
    we fail to see her end coming near
The shadows creeping in here,
    though the window cracks and under the door
The evil fear we could not ignore
But though our hopeless despair,
    a calmness flowed in the air
Her easy smile to show,
    she had no fear to go
We see her ocean eyes close
    she hadn't the urge to fight
Though in the ancient sleep,
    her true beauty death could not beat
Sleep sweet flower and feel no pain
a quite surrender and peace you'll gain
With golden curls and deep ocean eyes,
    to the heavens she will rise.

Glist Of Sun
by Thomas D. Jackson

Wishing not to speak
To sound as others sound
(illmotivated and insincere)
Rather, seeking....
To feast the soul
Upon the crystalline glimmer of your beauty
The shine, shimmer, and tint of your glittering eyes
The gloss of your mineral lips
And fleshtone of your amethyst cheeks.

The radiance of your presence,
Whose loveliness crowns the heart
With a rose of longing,
Is the glist of sun off water.
Enchanting to the eye
And pleasant to the soul.

Justin
by Chris Jacob - age 16

Don't understand why you're in my heart,
Don't understand why you're in my dreams,
Don't underhand why my blood's been rushing from the start,
But baby I'm sure,

I want to call you on the phone,
I need you here next to me,
Until the day your holding me again,
Baby I'm waiting all alone,

I can still see your eyes, taste the hunger on your lips,
I never wanted to leave,
I could live though life's storms in the safety of your arms,
I could love you in the late summers' eve,

Don't underhand why there's no other man than you,
Don't understand why the memory of your touch has me shivering and blue,
My thoughts are tangled in a mess,
I want your heart and nothing less,

Don't want to be lonely or friends with heartache,
Don't want your memory to ever fade away,
I'll live with you or no other until my dying day.

Little Star
by Lindsey Jamison - age 14

Twinkle - Twinkle little star
Oh so far off that you are.
The sun is closer hot and bright
but farther off is your pale light.
Your silvery twinkling is so nice
floating silently, a piece of cold Ice.
Your light so luminous and silver
what things will your planets deliver.
Perhaps life or even Transcendence
Maybe they will bring our world
More Independence.
So as human beings we will sit
and stare and wonder
        What is out there?

Patio Porch Ensemble
by Cathy Jacobs - age 12

    Lightning cracks across the sky,
When I hear the thunder die.

    Like an orchestra striking up to play,
The thunder puts an end to this weary day.

    The soft rain dripping on my back,
Ensemble of instruments, of which there is no lack.

    Turning it from night to day,
Lightning quakes but doesn't stay.

    A cool breeze now and then,
Which makes me quickly pick up my pen.

    The sky a strange purplish gray,
Lightning storms, come what may.

    This is the music I love to hear,
It gives me comfort but also fear.

Duality
by Romy T. Jacobson

I want to bronze the clothes I wore to your apartment tonight   I want to burn them to ash
    (would I keep their remains in an urn?)

I want to scrub myself until I bleed your silky acidic touch away   I want to relish in the
                      invisible marks your
                        fingers left on my
                        adoring skin

I'm dirty as the sheets in
a third-rate Nevada brothel   I'm pure as ocean breezes that tickle virgin coastlines

I kissed a dream and found Heaven of Earth as Hell's flames were leisurely burning away

my soul

lucidly confused

about the tangible unknown

                you are concrete mist.

Love Is But A Simple Thing
by Leah James - age 17

Love is but an emotion,
That emerges from the heart;
One that you can't be sure of,
Nor know if it shall part.

Love can make you a prisoner,
A fool in your own eyes;
Or it can enlighten you,
And someday make you wise.

Love is but a simple thing,
When spoken from the lips;
But appears as the deepest vow,
To those who find the bliss.

Love is what I have found,
When I look into your soul;
The feeling that I have each day,
That makes me feel so whole.

Love began in you and I,
When we started to discover,
The incredible bond that we share,
As long as we have each other.

Night and Day
by Nicole Jamison - age 14

As the sun begins to fade each night,
Crickets start to chirp.
Birds snuggle quietly in their nests,
And animals lay to sleep.
Quiet is upon us.

The world turns
And morning comes again.
Birds take over chirping,
And the crickets lay to silence.
Animals arise,
And the sun shines again.

Now And Forever
by Nicole Jamison - age 14

We are friends,
You and I,
Like a circle in the sand,
Never ending,
Now and Forever.

Your understanding
is like the waves on an ocean.
Never ceasing,
Now and Forever.

Your sense of humor
is like the wind.
Bursting forth
every now and again,
Now and Forever.

You are like a storm,
quiet, then loud;
Together we are like a circle,
Never ending,
Now and Forever.

Time Past
by J.S. Janeksela

In my mind I hold an image,
all that remains of a night.
It lightly fades with each moments passing,
but I am unable to forget.
I am unable to move on.

Each time I wander through my thoughts,
randomly browsing a short life.
This one memory stands apart.
Perhaps because it is fresh,
not long removed from the present.
Perhaps because it was perfect,
so unlike this flawed world.

I think it was both and more.
Yet I feel as if it has always been there.
Like it happened long ago and far away.

I return to it over and over,
pondering it's implications.
Searching for hidden meanings.
I only find what is there,
nothing more,
nothing less.
Just time past.

Fire
by Misty Ann Janes - age 15

Fire it burns but when
your mad it doesn't seem
to hurt. Full of anger
wondering if it's ever
going to go away. As I wait
and watch for the sun
to go down still wondering
will it ever go away.
As my heart races
and my eyes water
as I feel the anger
and watch the sun
as my heart races
faster and faster and
the sun beats harder
and harder as I still
wait for the anger to
leave me. As I'm waiting
and waiting still
wondering.

Grow
by Jennie Jeddry - age 15

It grows slowly
A flower.
Starting green,
turning red like blood's valentine.
People quickly stare.
Entranced, enhanced
It's only a plant
A beautiful one.

When In Instinct
by Robert Jeffers - age 18

He starts in the day
A man in a trance
Realizing his tears of desire acquire
no results
His only option now is to shatter
those freshly closed windows of opportunity
He seeks acknowledgement through power
Restraining the infinite
A diamond studded sky returns
The spotted night is at hand
His only path, candle of light
in search to belong
can find only walls
He's lost in the soft flame
The flickering unpredictableness
The halo of drifting light
Hunting for the only escape he knows
Undoubtedly missing a life of accomplishment
for a condemned consistency
In wasting expensive time
his thoughts begin to wander
through the vast universe of complications
Finally, his ample subconscious takes over
delivering his fate
The calm rush of pain
releases the problems of reality
Light from the moon disburses the glow
that emerges the corpses face
And knowing he's lost the life that he had
he see's after all death isn't bad

Would You Know Me
by Casey Jenkins - age 14

Would you know me the real me if I didn't speak up?
Would you take the time to know the real me if I didn't speak up?
Would you still see me the real me if I couldn't see?
Would you still stop and talk with me if I couldn't talk?
WELL WOULD YOU?!!!!!!SPEAK UP!!!!!!
Do you know me the real me? "The one that has everything?"
Yeah that's me!!! The one with the nice clothes and the big house!!!!!
But little do you know, when I walk around with a smile on my face,
I'm really crying on the inside. And when I laugh I'm really yelling for
someone to help me,
someone to notice me!!!!!!
Do you know me the real me? No!!!!!! Because if you did you would
know that,
I fear to go home each day and that I hide myself in my room, to get
away from everything.
And until you know me don't judge me!!!!!!!!!!!!

Gone
by Casey Johnen - age 14

I can remember all the good times we've had
standing together soaking wet,
Water fights and B-ball games
I just can't leave those memories yet.

Haven't seen him in a couple of weeks
'cause he has no extra time,
No one to practice with or tell jokes with
I just can't get him off my mind.

Soon I know that he will be gone
gone far away,
And I just can't help but wish
that he'll be back someday.

The Way I Feel About You
by Jesi Johnson - age 14

We talk, we laugh,
We share intimate secrets.
We're best friends,
But I wish it were more.

My heart has strong feelings for you.
I take any chance to brush
Your skin lightly with my hand.
A hug from you means a lot.

The feelings of being in your arms
Seems right. The way you hold me
Close against your chest when I cry
Is comforting.

As I stare into your deep blue eyes,
It takes all my strength not to
Throw my arms around your neck
And kiss you.

Sometimes I catch you looking at me and
Smiling tenderly. I wonder if you feel
The same way I feel about you.
It would be a dream come true.

Time
by Jennifer Jenkins - age 14

Time is a fire
on the desert sand
Time is the kidnapper
that took your hand
Time is a rose
wilting away
Time left me sorrow
when he took you away
Time is the poison
that brought you to your knees
Time is the thief
that took you from me

A Soldier's Pride
by Dawn Johnson - age 15

A tired old man sat in his chair,
    His grandson upon his left knee.
The puzzled young boy curiously stared
    Where the man's right leg used to be.
"Where is you leg, Grandpa?
    Where did it go?
Please tell me the story.
    I really must know!"

"Well," said the man, "it happened this way.
    It was a cold, dark January day.
The War of Independence was raging on.
    My men were ready to fight hard and long.
The British came charging up over the hill.
    Shots rang out; nothing was still.
Then a hundred times worse than the sting of a bee,
    A bullet hit me right in the knee.
I went to the doctor's tent, weak and dazed,
    And the doctor told me my leg couldn't be saved.
So, on that cold, dark January day,
    The army doctor took my leg away."

The boy thought for a while,
    Then with tears in his eyes
Said, "Do you miss your leg Grandpa?
    Do you ever cry?"
Then the old man said, eyes gleaming with pride,
    "For one lost limb I never could cry.
For you see my dear boy,
    For freedom I'd die!"

Untitled
by Misty Johnson - age 16

Sunlight upon your face, the morning
dew in you hair. No matter where
I am you are always there. Your
smiling face makes the sun shine
in the darkest place. Your tears
make my fears disappear. No matter
where I go you will always be
a step behind me. You watch over
me and help me see things that
I would have missed. You are my
night, you are my day, you are
my smile on a rainy day.

Lonely
by Jessica Johnson - age 16

A lonely hermit living by the sea
She dreams of all that she could be

The shattered hopes and pathetic ambitions
All crushed by her father's superstitions

But still she tries to abandon her shell
To be with her soul mate where all is well

She cowers to newcomers and strives to bring them in
Born without love into a family of sin

Her broken world crumbles each passing day
May a new beginning come as she pray

She can't escape her destiny
She's forced to live in misery

Maybe someday she will see the light
And her father will realize he's not always right

The love of her friends push her to live
If only they knew the support they give

Always wanting to be a princess but living as a troll
She has learned to play that role

And one day she may break her shell and be free
But for now, she's only a hermit living by the sea.

Visions
by T.L. Johnson

Into the stillness of the room I lay.
The dawn almost upon me, the night
Crept slowly on,
I could not move.

Out of the darkness a symbol of life, a
Wondrous angel emerged from the
Window light,
I could not move.

The devils danced at the edge of my bed,
While the angel watched on
I could not move
I could not sing

At last the dawn began to break, and the angel
Watched on no more.

I Saw It In Your Eyes
by Brooke Johnston - age 13

"I meant to tell you,
you could have left."
"You didn't have to
play the game,
and sacrifice it all."
"He would have set
you free that night,
you wouldn't have to die."

I saw it deep in your eyes,
the fear you had that night.
I saw it when you played the game--
I saw it when he won.

I saw your eyes fill up with tears--
I saw your pain and fear.

A Moment In Time
by cece jones

Should I remember your smile Love
And the way your brown eyes look
Will I remember your voice Love
From a long ago summers day
I shall my Love
I've had many memories to fill a sunless day
For I've understood my destiny and now my fate awaits
Captured now forever
In the darkness of the night
A small light shines bright
Keep smiling Love
Your not lost I'll find you Love
Just give me
A moment in time
To last forever is a wondrous thing to share
The briefest moment is to share destiny with only a thought
Never to be parted Love
For even a thought brings you back to me time after time
How grateful I should be Love for a moment in time
Brings back to me all I had thought lost
But for a moment in time

When Daddy Wants To Go
by Christie Jones - age 17

When Daddy wants to go,
there is not much you can do.
You can hope and pray,
that he will stay.
But you know full well
that he is better off away.

When Daddy wants to go,
you know that it is for the best.
But even that does not seem,
to take the hurt away.
You can cry to make yourself feel better,
but that will not keep him here
when Daddy wants to go.

When Daddy wants to go,
you know he will be better off,
someplace else than at home.
So you tell him goodbye, love you,
and see you soon.

When Daddy wants to go
you tell your heart that
it will not be forever,
but when reality comes
you know that he is gone.

Becky's Eyes
by Danny Jones - age 18

If I'd not known Becky's eyes
perhaps the day would be
easier to understand
and more gentle to me.
If I hadn't memorized
the sounds she makes
while beside me
I might have filled my memory up
with October skies or November seas.
But as it is my memory lane
has no room for skies
all the space is taken up
remembering Becky's eyes.

New York City 4/19/97
by Erin Jones - age 18

I took a walk through the
mecca of life today
Pot-hole pocked blacktop
rose up to meet me
and sterling silver concrete
kissed my lonely face
in that metropolis of life.

Life moved along with
the blur of the yellow cab
While my white suburban fears took
hold of my unprejudiced heart
As I glanced at the city hardened
ebony faces that passed me by.

Jealousy became a green demon
alive in my body
Jealous of the hands that were held
and the lips I saw kissed
Oh, what a thing it must be
to be in love in this city
What thing it must be
to be alive in anyway at all.

Trust
by Hanako S. Jones - age 12

   Broken trust is the hardest to heal.
betrayal, well, that's another deal.
Who can you trust in this doubtful world?
Secrets spring up like ferns unfurled
Everywhere, nowhere , altogether at once
They collect in the mind from all the past months.
Secrets around like butterflies passing with time they flutter by
No longer a secret, its known by all.
Another friends trust, broke, let it fall.
For a friends no one if they break trust
Shine down the sun, to make another day
for a friend's doubt and sadness
for the ugly trout who broke the trust
No one's to be in that position, to see
An innocent on framed
"I did nothing," he denies. "Well prove it you fly!
Your not trusted for something you did not do."

The Spector
by Nella M. Jones

The spector waits
I feel her presence everywhere
Waiting, watching, wanting
Waiting for whats mine to take
The love of my life, my reason for being
She watches and waits to take him from me
Her presence in my life brings questions
Tears and angry words
Words that even tho said in anger
Can never be taken back
She brings strife among my family
Fathers and daughters, mothers and sisters
The riff grows wider
She watches and waits
I know not what hold she has on him
Someone new, someone different
Is that what it is???
Or does she give him something else
That I have not to give???

An Understanding
by Tawnya Jones

I realize now, that your existence in this world was distraught,
And only you could comprehend the anguish that grew within.
If only they knew the irony.....a facade of courage imbibed in tragedy.
Yet, you remained forever silent...isolated in your torment.

There is an invariable confrontation between the ruler and the vassal
that dwell within the boundaries of one's soul.
Did you yearn for quiescent water -- hushed and limpid?
Or did you hasten for the rumble which would inundate the terror within?

You faced your suffering with such courage; like no other I'd seen before,
All the while, aiding others with their sadness and grief.
Now, You're in an eternal, peaceful slumber and I lie awake, wondering...
In the stillness, is there a freedom that you've never felt before?

I used to perceive my existence as barren,
A past filled with so many mistakes and aberrations.
A ceaseless pilgrimage into blackness,
Yet pursuing the light of faith and acceptance.
Such an intricate journey, why the continuance of pursuit?

I begged for an ending...I could hear it's whisper on the wind,
And then, in your eyes, I found understanding and acceptance.
Amidst the darkness, you taught me to hope.
Learning to live is a complex endeavor....but your hushed tones I hear,
Though the path is burdensome, redemption is assured.

Be Born Again...
by Joy Joy Joy

Be born again
From Jesus' teaching from Gospels.
Love is Jesus' teaching !
Be born again from Love ! Don't kill !
Don't kill animals
To eat their meat,
To eat their fat.

Be born again
From Jesus' teaching from Gospels.
Love is Jesus' teaching !
Be born again from Love ! Don't kill !
Don't kill animals
To take their hide,
To take their fur,
To take their tusks.

Be born again
From Jesus' teaching from Gospels.
Love is Jesus' teaching !
Be born again from Love ! Don't kill !
Don't kill animals as sport, as divertissement !
Don't kill animals in medical experiences, or in other experiences !

True Friends
by Jamie Kalinowski - age 18

Thick warm air surrounds our delicate bodies as we enter the coal-black night.
Twinkling like glitter, the stars light our way.
Talking, our hopes and dreams for the future are told to every night creature.
Stopping,
we listen to the crickets making their music.
Together we settle on the cool grass.
Enveloping me, the smell takes me to another time:
A time when we were teenagers.
Believing we would always be together,
trying new things, and taking small chances,
but time has caught up to us, tearing us apart.....forever.

We promised to meet here many years ago.
I came, only to find an empty heart and mind full of memories.

Dedicated to a Lost Friend
by Erika Kalkan - age 15

Before do you remember
The fun we had,
How we always made it through
The good and the bad.

Remember together
How much time we spent,
The days and nights
We came and we went.

Where did those days go?
Those days that meant so much to me.
How come things changed?
Didn't you like how it used to be?

If you did, I think
Those days would be here
That's what I keep telling myself
As I wipe my tears.

If they don't come back
I don't know what I'll do.
I can't think anymore
Because all I think of is you.

Rain
by Anju Kanumalla - age 16

Rain
a silver curtain
fell.

I pushed it aside
and walked forward
expecting the rain
to close in around me.

Instead
raindrops met my skin
cold and sharp.

I awoke
and
I was very aware
and
I was very unaware.

The rain fell
bathing the world
washing away time.

Dream or Day
by Shayna Jo Kaufman - age 12

As the stars float around my head
i wonder if I'm dreaming in bed
Or am i awake as bright as day
And if I wake will I be as gay
will the sun shine through the tall birch tree
and the birds fly high and free
Or in my dream will I live in a village-
where candy trees grow by a cola stream
I always wonder about my dream

A Notice, Pinned To The Board On The Wall Of Cid's Food Market...
by George Katznelson

A notice, pinned to the board on the wall of Cid's food market,

Simply said, "Mobile Home American dream 1981 -
                                      For Sale."
One of a multitude of multicolored, multipurpose notices offering or
                                      informing of,
things going on in the neighborhood or multiple wishes of its
                                      residents
one of whom, quite pathetically, I thought, was trying to sell off
                                      his tires,
assuring potential readers (there were none, alas, except me,
                                      poor devil!)
that the tires are "as good as new," disregarding the
                                      obvious
proximity of a Goodrich store with plenty of tires,
                                      brand-new
and possibly priced not much higher than the ones marked, on the board,
                                      "4 Sale."
But, above board, the Rockies, with their glittering
                                      snow caps,
Stood out so proudly, so uncondescending to the rat race going
                                      on below
that it suddenly dawned on me: the American mountains
                                      wouldn't approve
the selling of an American dream, even if it's the mobile one of

1981...
Well, who asks THEM?!

A Special Mom
by Kara Keding - age 16

When I first met you, your smile was so sincere,
it erased all my fears.
Your eyes were so gentle,
which showed you are definitely sentimental.
You complemented me from the start,
and I could tell it came from your heart.
You are so caring towards me,
you even made me feel like a part of your family.
I had an immediate liking towards you,
and that is so very true.
Your heart has a certain tenderness,
that I can't dismiss.
There is a special sort of endearment we share,
if I was to deny it I would be unfair.
You are like a mother to me,
which proves you are truly extraordinary.

The Winds of Change
by Kiper

What is this thrill in the air around me?
What is this breeze that seizes me with fear
and uncertainty?
I gasp and my heart beats louder, and I realize
this is the chilling winds of change.

Oh, I shudder.
I shudder and I stutter, and I swallow deep.
I retreat, but to no avail it surely follows.
I shake and twist, and with a flick of the wrist
it sticks and wraps around me.
No clever stunt will bunt this element of
human nature.
No lever will destroy, or be so coy enough to
trick the capture
of the cool and uncertain winds of change.

I then surrender (no less tender) and give in to
hopes and anticipation.
I plan a course (the best I can of course) and
wet my finger to test the direction.
I unfold these moldy wings and flap wide
and swallow my pride,
as I am lifted high
into the engulfing winds of change,
and to the past I say goodbye.
Then I say hello
to these enchanting,
these bewildering,
uncertain winds of change.

If
by Kindra R. Kelley - age 12

Jesus is coming, coming soon
It may be morning, night or noon.
If Jesus was to come today
Would your sins be washed away?
Love in the world just isn't clear
But love in the world just isn't here.
People wonder why people say,
"I want to die everyday."
It's because they just don't care
Just like they don't care if they dare
There are so many sins today
That people just want to fade away

Reflection
by Jeremy Kellhofer - age 18

So...my head is propped on one hand.
my eyes are almost shut.
i see a small blur, that resembles you.
when my weak hand begins to slide, my eyes open to see...
my hair is perfect and messed up.
slowly rolling down a hill that started out as you.
my legs hurt, but my body is at rest because an angel sits on them.

when you cried i smiled.
i was happy you were still that happy to be something special
if i wait much longer you will be gone.
blurry objects in a mirror turn out to form you and me.
i dream of not being propped on one hand, but that's my only
                                    choice of all my choices.

maybe you can be a reflection in my pond if it doesn't run dry.
even if it does, i know you will find a way to still be my friend.

Do I Know He Loved Me
by Amber Kelly - age 17

Grandpa's strong hands tightened
Around the arms of the chair, knuckles
Growing white.

The stuffy essence of the room created a
Vivid stillness.

His labored breathing and my heart
Beating clash to become calm.

Every minute daring to pass questions
The future of us together.

He goes limp and yet his face looks tense
When I gaze at him.

Standing, I turn and stare at the man
I thought could never die.

An unknown source seems to pull my
Heart as he slumps over.

I thought about how nothing could
Replace him holding me just moments
Before, and yet the silence of his death
Tells me that my grandpa loved Me.

Without Goodbye
by Shannon Kelly - age 16

Her eye, it follows the gardened passage that leads to the noble entrance.
She is enthralled by her precedent home, in which her mother and father live today.
She places her paraphernalia and such down beside her on the slippery cobblestone path.
The sun climbs the sapphire sky, and the soothing morning warmth envelops her.
But all too soon, a permeating mist begins to unveil the prolonged secrecy,
As she is reminded of troubled times past.
As so she would like to forget,
The trees whisper, pleading with her, not to ignore these recollections.

She grasps her husband's hand, as for security,
That he is feeling the same way as she.
Her other hand, gingerly drawing back the carefully laced curtains.
They stand, like statues,
Hand in hand,
Gazing at their daughter with such hostility, anger...
With immeasurable love and adoration.

She shakes her head, realizing it may be too early, realizing she is not ready,
Not ready to take another step down the way to forgiveness.
Ever so carefully, she grips her baggage, and takes one last look at the home...
That house...
With watery eyes and a dampened nose,
As ever so slowly, she takes a step back on that slippery cobblestone path.
And with endless tears,
She walks away,
Abandoning this edifice
With her shiny ebony shoes
And with her breaking heart.

Nobody Knows Me
by Stephanie Kelly - age 17

Nobody knows who I am
nobody can
I only know the real me
and what your looking at
right here
Is not what you see
How can you say I know you
When you don't even have
a clue
How is it you say I know
how you feel when you
don't know the real deal
You
don't know the real me
nobody does
It's not always what
you see, nobody know who
I am nobody can
I only know the real
me, nobody knows me but me,
nobody see's what
I see, nobody feels
how I feel, nobody
KNOWS ME

The Loss
by Steve Kelly

Kneeling she seeks to
Shrink from the anguish of life
Lamenting her loss
What purpose is served?
A life ended creating
Union of mourning
Her soul unwilling
To give release to the past
Hopelessly futile
Addiction is a splendid hell
It matters not what the need
From alcohol to the poppy seed
For some sadness casts the spell
Influenced by this trend of pain
A junkie for this misery
Happiness is as treachery
A smile is only forced for gain
This suffrage oh, don't let it end
The descent goes on and on
So far beneath the day I've fallen
This woe on which I now depend
Enshrouded now I see the truth
I fooled myself believing
My love would end her grieving
Lo, loss for all time shall endure

Out of Light
by Heather Kelsey - age 13

So many birds chirping
loudly,
all the warmth and sunshine
everything so cheerful and
lively.
　Unexpectedly dark, thick
clouds roll in.
Birds spree and the warm
sun is gone behind the greyness.
The world is so dark and
mysterious.
all the screams of thunder
and flashes of bright bolts.
pure cool water droplets
fall softly from the sky, like
pockets of air.
　Suddenly a crash of lightning
appears as quickly as everything
came and the drops of water
fall faster than before.
　Now, late in the night I
fall asleep listening to the
pitter patter on my window
　How so soothing and
comforting.

Searching
by Julie Keltonic - age 13

I search and I search some more
But I cannot see
I cannot see my destiny
For I am blind
Blind to see the love
The love that surrounds me
But if so much love surrounds me,
Why don't I feel the love that surrounds me?
'Tis the love I give
The love I give to few friends I obtain
The love I give to my close relatives
But where is the love I should get in return?
'Tis nowhere
There is no love
That is why I am searching
I will continue to search until I find the love I am searching-
for

The Sun
by Julie Keltonic - age 13

Brilliant rays of light
Shine upon the two caskets
I look upon your battered figures
Wondering why
Why must God put us through this pain?
I look to the sky to hold the tears welling in my eyes
Clouds now covering the sun
Drops of water fall upon my sulking face
The rain begins to fade into the bleak darkness
The clouds slowly move away
The luscious sunlight begins to filter through the clouds-
once more
I must move on, and I will move on
For when my soul leaves this earth I step upon
I will be with the two of you once again.

In memory of Randy & Samantha Deglin.

Always And Forever
by Sam Summers - age 14

Sometimes you find a special friend,
While looking in all the wrong places.
But, that dream keeps you going,
That one hand filled with all the aces.
The dream of love, no one can replace it.

I looked far and wide until I found you,
Along dusty roads and on the highest mountains.
Soaring through the cloudless skies,
And, in my dreams a picture came,
Of one that stood strong and true.

You're my best friend, and my hope for the future.
You brought me up when I was down.
I don't know what I'd do without you around.
You and your funny faces, acting like such a clown
Bringing me on those walks made me sure.

I wish for you to never be sad.
Lift your chin it's gonna be alright
'Cause I know you're gonna be out of sight.
Lose those fears and hold on tight.
This was intended for you to feel glad.

I'll never forget you, my baby blue,
Without you, I don't know what I'd do.
Remember our times of happiness forever.
Because in my heart we'll always be together.
Always & Forever, our love will remain true.

Love
by Megan Kennedy - age 13

What is love?
Is it cupid's curse?
Is it something I can pull out of my purse?

I thought you loved me.
But I guess I was wrong.
You just used me.
And to think, I went alone.

What does love mean?
Does it mean to cheat, to lie?
Or does it mean an intimate friendship that never
dies?

I thought I loved you,
But I was wrong.
I finally realize,
It wasn't love.

I Is A Lonely Word
by Peggy Boogaard Kennedy

Sheltered in the fern and onions, a fawn,
Patient with a full stomach, drowses.
Only its ears flick at the raven's call.
We climb across lichened rocks.
There is a sea sound that lulls in forests
As boughs dip and rise with the wind.
The fawn merges into the shadow patterns
In the moss song while white stars of dogwood
Cluster about with the gay garments of spring.
The ravens add dissonance with sentry notes
As we climb toward the seacliffs. I see
An eagle as it ranges above; because I
Is a lonely word, the eagle travels far before
Night swoops down with great, dark wings.

Untitled
by Ca'rel Kennon - age 18

Life and love connected in chains of lust and utter attraction
Sexual linguistics of a sexually controlled society
Harmless antics given to cold bodies covered in sin
Dead men's souls cry out for forgiveness to late
While sinking into the depths of the earth
Human waters flow thorough my veins
Strangle me of my air
And choke from me the truth
If I might only become whole I can become real
My night mare will be over
But when it's over it's just begun, in the back of my mind I hear run nigga run
Am I a slave to my world?

The Killing of Prize-Seekers
by Andrea G. Kerfoot

Her colorless gray eyes, like chips of ice,
Staring, penetrating peering deep into the soul,
As if trying to read your thoughts.
Ever deepening frown, a permanent wrinkle,
Tight little mouth, pursed lips part,
Her tongue, sharper than a surgeon's scalpel,
Emasculates at thirty paces.

    She never even touched him.
    She never rose from her chair.
    She wounds from a distance.
    She kills with her knife-words.

Cold and aloof, she protects herself from love,
Giving nothing, she expects all.
Judging from her Colonial throne,
She deems or denies worth.
Hard won compliments, like angry cats,
With criticism tails slashing the air.
The ultimate prize, withheld love,
Never won by anyone.

Tortuous Friendship
by Jill Kerr - age 15

She only had one love in her life,
But he would never know.
She loved him, and no one else,
But soon she would see him go.
He loved only one girl,
But the two of them were friends.
To tell her that he loved her,
Was sure to make it end.
After loving him for 5 years straight,
She had to watch him go.
He died in a car crash at age 18,
And he was never to know.
He never knew that she loved him,
She never knew he loved her.
For they both were afraid that the friendship would end,
So they both decided to just pretend.
They would have been so happy together,
And they both would have lived forever.
But because they were both so scared,
And because for each other they deeply cared,
They never tried to be anything but friends,
And so one day, she watched it end.

What message do you send?
by Patrick S. Kidder

The story of life, a beginning from an end.
What message do you send?

A balled fist or an open hand,
which do you wear, into the land?

A smile or a look of hate,
first impression, an encounter's fate.

A suspicious mind or a loving heart,
which one is the better part?

Tell the lie or tell it straight,
it's a choice you must evaluate.

Wounded soul or loving heart,
which one is the better part?

Be proud or be irate,
life is choice, not fate.

A balled fist or an open hand,
which do you wear, into the land?

The story of life, a beginning from an end.
What message do you send?

I Will
by Jamie Kimberly - age 15

I wave goodbye to the beginner,
she's gone on to a new family.
I wave goodbye, hoping to see her again
before we sail away on separate rivers,
But will I?

I say hello to the finisher,
she's the last to follow in our footsteps.
I say hello, hoping that I'll still know her
when she's chosen her own path,
But will I?

I learn from my creators,
the two that molded me.
I learn, hoping that I'll remember
all they taught me,
But will I?

I endure with my fellow oysters,
they help to make every day a pearl.
I endure, hoping that we'll keep in touch
even after out lives no longer intertwine,
But will I?

I live with all the stars in my life sky,
they brighten up the dark.
I live, hoping I'll still love them even
after the sun has risen,

I will.

Missing You
by Mandy King - age 17

As I sit with the cool breeze of the night air
upon my face.
I think of your smile your touch your warm embrace.
The smile you gave brings back memories I'll
always treasure and save.
Your slight touch as it glides softly down
my skin. If only I could feel that once again.
But your embrace, only to be in your arms
once more, I'm in doubt that's one thing
I can't live without.
If only you knew, if I could say,
how much I need you in my life today.
Those nights we spent together I thought
they'd last forever. Kissing you so passionate
and true, making love is all I want to do.
You holding me tight all throughout the night.
I'm missing you and wish you knew,
my love was always true, but because of
her that's not what I can say to you.

The Light Behind The Door
by Clif King

The door stands silent, separating the light from the darkness.
The light shines on friendship, hope, love and a child's innocent face.
The face of the door is us, beckoning the light.
Darkness lurks beyond the threshold, waiting for our first step.
Fear and the anger of those no longer a child, hide in the darkness.
The door separates a shining new life from the tarnished.
Sin frolics, fearful of the thin shards of light beneath the door.
In death, as in life, the unholy one revels a closed door,
a tomb that forever forbids the light.
Mankind, old and gray, remembers, then forgets,
years of coming and going through doors of all colors.
Life, unlived, slips away through a door left ajar.
The rush of life pierces the joy and sorrow, fear and anger
.....the love and death.
We open the door,......or slam it shut,
denying the light, as a cold heart turns away someone in need.
Sadness and grief, trapped, decay and poison the spirit.
The door,....our heart, must be open,
open wide,...believing, embracing, loving the light.
For the light is GOD.

Feel the Evil
by Sarah King - age 17

Removed from our selves
we fly out of body, out of mind
to some it's out of time
Dark is the night, the absence of light
brings fear of the unknown
yet we know all there is to know
Feel the evil creep in, slowly it begins,
speeding as it goes
Feel the evil step lightly across our beings
It's hard to believe without seeing
But it's there, the evil of our souls
awaits to be awakened
To tear at the life built with these two hands
The evil of hate, greed and lust
The lust for power causes others to cower
in fear and in terror of the hungry dogs that run in packs
Feel the evil, it shadows our souls, it waits to take over,
patiently looking for the flaw
so it can rip with it's bloody thirsty jaws
Feel the evil seep into our minds,
leaving us helpless to its deeds
Feel the evil pull you in
and spit you out full of sin

You
by Dennis King - age 19

We have had a lot of laughs,
and had our share of cries,
a lot of hellos,
and plenty of good-byes.

For a long time now,
You have shown me the way,
and given me so much love,
each and every day.

You have given me support,
each time I got in a bind,
your a great person,
both caring and kind.

Your the best girl in the world,
yes, this is so true,
What would I do without you?
I don't have a clue.

In my thoughts, you will stay,
my love for you grows stronger,
day after day.

I hope you are happy,
with a smile on your face,
because in my heart,
You will always have a special place.

Miss You
by Dennis King - age 19

A simple photograph,
a memory in all its splendor,
frozen in time for eternity.

I look at you face there,
beautiful and stunning as always,
but stranded motionless forevermore.

I see your gleaming, star-like eyes,
and want to get lost in them,
a realized impossibility.

Noticing your soft, pouty lips,
makes me long for a kiss,
that I know I cannot have.

I imagine your warm, sweet breath,
like a friendly summer breeze,
an enchanting thought that soon fades.

I can almost feel you,
your body held close to mine,
but I am saddened as reality overcomes me.

Then suddenly I know I can have all these things.
for when I close my eyes,
You will be with me in my dreams.

My dream
by Tiffany King - age 14

I had a dream
one cool winter's night.
It was a dream where people
did not fight.

It was a dream of peace,
a dream of calm.
A dream with no thing
like a bomb.

The animals lived,
and played all day long.
The people were happy
just singing a song.

But when I awoke
my dream disappeared,
and everything was normal,
just like I had feared.

Lovers
by Jessica Kinsella - age 15

War of the lovers, nobody wins,
they hate one another, but go back again.
If their wondering hearts only knew.
She lets him win, he lets her lose.
Blinded by all they see as real,
The broken don't love, the dead don't feel.
But day after day, it stay the same,
Each has only the other to blame.

The Dream World
by Jodi Kintner - age 15

Listen to me
As I tell you about
A place where you can go
Without a worry or a doubt.
A place without pain,
A place without sorrow,
A place where you can be,
Where there is no tomorrow.
A place of love
And happiness too,
A place for me
And a place for you.
A world of peace
Without all the hate,
A place where people can find
their one true soul mate.
Someday I hope I enter this world
And live through what I see
And in my mind
I hope this world will no longer, just be a dream.

One Step Closer
by Jennifer Kinzeler - age 14

If retiring your ambition is crossing your mind,
And the drive to go on is often hard to find,
Look into your dreams, what you hold to be real,
Then you can carry on through what you feel,
When you're pushed, and you're pulled, and you just want to let go,
And it seems that failure is all you'll ever know,
Dig deeper, try harder,
And in the end you'll see you've come a bit farther...

Black Hole
by Brianna Marie Kirby - age 19

Blackness caves into the heart
Youth cannot save it
the virgin soul cries out
Pull and pull us out of
this black hole

A chivalrous knight perhaps
with the strength of ten
or God himself
with armor of all men

The loneliness grows
with no remedy to cure it
so it thickens
causing discouragement

Heal us with Your heart
and Your strong, strong hands
take us from danger
from ourselves within

we call You pleading and trapped
in this black heart
this decaying generation
screams for you

Pull us out!!!

Thunderstorm
by Megan E. Kirkwood - age 11

Hint of danger, pure and free.
The Thunder's come to rescue me,
From the stress of Life to be.
The sky lights up a sight to see.
Darkness roams the helpless land,
Mother Nature's skillful hand.
Vibrant streaks across the sky,
Makes a baby scream and cry.
It leaves the sky with scars and fear,
But, it soon heals, the wounds disappear.
It leaves the world with amazement and fame,
But, it will return just as fast as it came.

angel by my bedside
by Eugene Kitt

Every night in the middle of my sleep
without opening my eyes
I could feel her presence
there is a angel lying by my bedside
A calm feeling comes over me
A period of undisturbed serenity
It is nice to know your covered
even in your sleep
I asked her her name
She told me STEPHANIE

Eyes
by Robyn Kiyomi - age 15

He gave you those eyes to bore into my spirit,
To give me a smile,
To make me laugh,
To make me cry,
To drive me so pitifully mad
Because those eyes,
Which give me a smile, and make me laugh and cry,
Are staring into another's
To give <u>her</u> a smile,
To make <u>her</u> laugh...but not cry,
And to make <u>her</u> so insanely happy;

He gave you those eyes
To miss nothing...
Except one thing...
Those eyes have not set eyes
Upon eyes
Which miss you.

At Waters Edge
by Connie Kleiman

Mountains rise majestically,
behind thy cabin rare.
Flowers coax the sun to shine,
and robins herald in the spring.
Sweet blush of youth upon thy face,
and shyness at first meeting.
With wisdom far beyond thy years,
and calming welcome ever present.
Tender are thy loving hands,
that cradle lifes sweet blessings.
Soft warm winds o'er meadows rush,
butterflies dance in silent wonder.
Reflections on the waters edge,
reveal thy beauty in glowing splendour.

For Sarah with love, Connie

Letter to an Alien
by Meryl B. Klein - age 12

The environment will soon die
And there will be no memory of you or I

And then we'll scream, we'll scream and yelp
But no one will ever come to help

And without help we will soon be gone
And Earth will not keep going on

So please help, help us in this atmosphere
Otherwise there might not be a here

So please cone, it'll be worth while
Please come soon, before we're a big trash pile

So, Mr. Alien, please help, please come
And receive a reward, money of a large sum

Thank you for your time, we hope you come
We are the third planet from the sun

Locks & Trendils
by Connie Kleiman

Tread lightly now through fields of honour,
for tho hast given light to darkness.
Abundant laughter fills the hollow,
where once the tears did flow so freely.
Surrounded thus by locks and trendils,
softly draping round thy girth.
Knighted now is passions flurry,
hence forth to gather loves own glory.

For Mike with love, Connie

Memories
by Arminda L. Klier - age 12

I am remembering my childhood.
My childhood's what I see.

I remember my little shoes,
that only seemed to fit me.

I remember the names of my little friends,
and the games we used to play.

Oh, the joy of memories I hold.
Either shiny new or tarnished old.

Some memories are not so dear.
Those are the ones I hate and fear.

What ever happens,
I will always feel fine.
Because I have memories,
that are always going to be mine.

One
by Chuck E. Klinger

Please don't cry
I don't know why
        Let's give it one more try
        Let us learn to fly
We were made for each other
For we are like no other
        Two separate bodies and minds
        Equals one whole spirit
A totally loving soul
Where we can be as one

For you, From me
by Jessica Klingner - age 20

Sitting here in the dark,
I stare and wonder.
What you are doing?
Are you thinking of me,
Like I am of you?

I stare at the starry sky,
and think of all the miles,
separating us.
My heart aches for you,
Even more.

I long for your touch,
Kiss, to be held in your arms.
To lay by your side,
To be surrounded by your warmth.
Just to be next to you.

I want to walk with you
On the beach at sunset.
To make love to you,
On the sand.
To give you part of my soul.

You are my friend,
Soul mate,
Someday my lover.
You have awakened me,
Like no one before.

I love you,
For who you are,
and what you have done for me.
Someday oceans, continents, or countries,
won't even keep us apart.

A Rainfall, a rainbow, a sunset
by April P. Klinkhammer - age 13

Rain,
Sweet rain,
Smelling like roses,
A rumble of thunder,
A flash of lightning,
A rainfall so sweet,
So light and delightful,
But it soon ends,
And the sun comes out,
With a streak of color
That fills the sky with
Red,
Orange,
Yellow,
Green,
Blue,
Purple,
And the colors paint a sunset,
But the rain,
Sweet rain,
Starts to fall again.

Friends
by Sherri Lynn - age 14

Every friend I've ever had,
could never compare to you,
You've always been there for me,
in everything I do.

And when the sky is cloudy,
and when the birds don't sing,
you always make me happy,
and treat me like a queen.

I love it how you smile,
in your special way,
and write me little letters,
to brighten up my day.

So if I'm feeling bad,
or if someone isn't true,
I'll know someone is there,
because I'm friends with you.

The Image
by Amanda Koch - age 16

As I am walking I come to a stream,
    I follow it as long as I can see.
The water is so calm and so clear,
    the only sound that I hear
is of a waterfall that is near.
    And of the rushing water as it picks up speed
Over the hill it falls fast,
    so fascinating I stop in my tracks.
To gaze across the way I see you to my surprise
    just like you were before you died.
But you are happy and with someone,
    whom I don't recall.
But I realize you don't see me at all.
    Is this image of you real
or am I thinking it up.
    I do not know.
Then you disappear without a trace
    and all that is left is the outline of your face.
Then I realize it was real I didn't imagine it.
    You came down from above and you did see me,
you came down to guide me the right way.
    Thank you for everything,
I think I can make it now.
    I'll go on my own and make it through,
I'll see you when I am gone for you to say,
    Well Done.

The Leap
by Amanda Koch - age 16

In the dark.
I see you just standing there
    with fear on your face.
I ask if your alright,
    but you don't answer nice.
I see you want to be left alone,
    so I leave.
Then I see you on the rail,
    ready to jump.
I scream out loud then,
    hear a shout.
I yell to you,
    but it is too late.
You took a leap,
    and tested your fate.
I blame myself I was the only one
    there.
If only I hadn't left.
    Maybe you would be here.
Another innocent person,
    who's life is now gone.
But may their soul rest happily,
    in the hands of God.

My Love for You Will Never Cease
by Laura Kochansky - age 14

The last letter you wrote
Dried daffodils you sent
A shriveled up balloon
An empty box of chocolates.

I think of you
Of the times we spent together
The times we laughed
And the times we cried.

I think of the time we watched the sunset on the beach
The time we walked beside a waterfall
I think of our unconditional love
And how it is still there
Even though you are gone.

Gone from the Earth
But not from my heart
I will love you always
And soon we will be reunited
Forever.

My Love
by Darcy Koehn - age 15

My love for you is strong,
nothing can keep us apart.
I couldn't live without you,
you have all the keys to my heart.
People say we shouldn't be,
but I won't listen to them.
People say we're too different,
maybe but then again.
I love you more than I can say,
I can't seem to find the words.
So before you say, "I'm losing her."
Remember you're my whole world.

Why
by Sarah Kohn - age 14

Our relationship was so good.
Why did it stop?
I thought you loved me,
I guess not.

The way you looked into my eyes,
I was so mesmerized.

But now we're apart,
and I'm all alone.
I always think of you,
and wait by the phone.

I thought that we were meant to be,
since you said you'd always love me.

You told me your problems,
and I listened to you.
Now you won't talk to me,
what am I supposed to do?

I don't understand why it couldn't work,
was I that much of a jerk?

But now it's over,
6 months went by too fast.
I have just one question,
why couldn't it last?

Vigil
by Olga Kokino

    Like a floodgate opening without warning, multitudes pour into the street. Appearing from all directions, the silent throngs swarm like phantom souls rising to meet their Armageddon. Soldiers stare down upon the swelling tide from high atop cathedral
steps. The resounding outcry "Viva, il Papa! Viva Lech Walesa!" erupts amidst the plethora of hands shooting up in "V" salutes.
    One moment the five of us had been sitting, idly chatting at the café, sipping a Viennese coffee with a biscotti; the next, we are swept into the charging mainstream, shoulder to shoulder, sparkling Nikes astride weathered work shoes. We march in synch,
but our startled silence evokes questions and suspicious looks from Polish comrades. The next time victory signs thrust into the air, we too salute, together with the young children holding Solidarity flags beside their strident mothers, fathers, and middle class workers.
    Militia stationed beneath arched enclaves--hands clutching submachine guns--track the procession moving along the main cobblestone road. Television cameras record every movement--perhaps even impending death.
    In the next chorus of "Viva, il Papa! Viva Leach Walesa," we join in, heads held high, voices strong, victory signs chopping the night air. The procession continues several blocks, stanzas of "Viva il Papa! Viva Lech Walesa!" punctuated by emphatic Vi-Pa Vi-Wa syllables. Synchronized feet, slogans, and v-salutes blend into a powerful rhythm
propelling us forward as one body.
    Congregating around a grassy knoll, long white tapers disperse, one flame alighting the next until incandescence swathes the penitents' faces in glowing radiance. Long flames jump upward into the still darkness, prayers to the nameless buried at the Tomb of the Unknown Soldier; then, candles extinguished, the sea of dissidents evaporates almost as quickly as it appeared.

Love Never Ends
by Sonja Kooyman - age 16

Give me roses,
Or diamonds and pearls.
Even dreams cannot compare,
To the love in this world.

Roses will die,
And diamonds and pearls can break.
But also dreams are forgotten,
When you awake.

Love is the only thing,
That has a guarantee.
Love never ends,
It remains until eternity.

Beauty
by Amber Korte - age 14

Who is to decide what is truly beautiful? I've been told it's what's on the inside that counts others are obsessed with anorexic, cat like creatures with too large eyes and lips; sunken cheeks, and a delicate jawed fantasy with no figure. I believe beauty is an individual thing, a dimple here, a freckle there. An awkward, nauseating cuteness you just can't describe. The color of their hair, the length of their strides, the height of their hypnotizing stare. You may wonder what makes you love someone. I believe that I have found the secret, but I don't think I will tell you right now. Maybe I won't tell you at all. You can sit and analyze a person all day but still, beauty is in the eye of the beholder. Maybe you feel faint at the sound of their voice, or wish you could eternally bathe in the happy fragrance you smell every time they pass by. You love the feel of a touch, a glance, a comment they give, that means they know you exist. It sometimes seems you have a shield that envelopes you, preventing you from finding that person's faults. The world's worst tyrant may seem the saint you never knew. And when you know you've won that person's heart and love for which you've always yearned, it seems the illusion equal to walking on air, and your heartbeating an overwhelming joy is all you can hear. So tell me, now do you know the secret?

Puzzle Of Life
by Erica Krakovitz - age 13

When life becomes a puzzle
Scattered across the floor...

When dreams become broken seashells
Washed upon sandy shores...

When love has lost its meaning
An outdated coin tossed in the trash...

When comfort's cozy cabin
Has plundered to the ground
Leaving nothing but embers and ash...

...Build yourself a puzzle
With every piece you add
Express yourself

...Gather your shining seashells
A dazzling array upon your dusty shelf

...Let new words upon your lips
Pepper life with endless wealth

...Sew dreams into the ribbon of life
And smile inward to
Yourself

Spring Morning
by Erica Krakovitz - age 13

Morning crystal dew...the jewelry of the pine
Dark, chocolate soil...the bedding of the shrine
Florid early blossoms...the lipstick of the trees
Dazzling, shiny surface...the lip gloss of the sea

Flowing, tranquil water...the liquid chills my toes
All pervading pollen...the dust around my nose
Brilliant rays of sunlight...the warmth upon my back
Luminescent butterflies...the flutter within my heart

Living With Death
by Loretta Krausz

Death is a terrible thing,
It brings sadness and sorrow.
You feel lost and empty.
A part of you is gone,
Your heart aches for that someone.
Sometimes death comes with relief,
The person isn't suffering.
They are in a better place,
Your worry of pain for them is gone,
but your love for them seems to be greater,
In death you live day by day,
and the nights are harder.
When waking in the morning you sigh,
Will this day be better you ask.
It will if you make it better,
Remember the good and the bad,
For the memories are what you have left.
Ask God in the morning to be with you,
Through the day, and the evenings.
He will hear you and he will help,
Take time to grieve and take time to laugh,
but in all remember that death is unavoidable,
and that you will meet again with your love one.

*Written for you Kurt in your days of sorrow
and may this give you peace. I love you, Loretta.*

Parent Divorce
by AnnMarie Krazmien - age 12

Ping Pong balls go
  Back and forth
  Back and forth

I feel like a ping pong ball
  I go back and forth
    Between parents not paddles

One paddle hits the ball
  The other paddle hits the ball
    It keeps on going back and forth

I got to mom
  But back to dad
  Mom for summer
  Dad for school

The ball won't stop
  The paddles won't stop
  The game won't end

I can't stay in one place
  Mom for ten weeks
  Dad for the rest.

Isn't this supposed to be my life?
When do I take control?

Fear
by Matt Kreider - age 14

I was born at the dawn of time
I am everywhere
With everyone
I stalk thee in the night
After you have said goodnight
I am the shudder up your spine
I am the doubt in your mind
I follow through life each day
No, you cannot wish me away
For I sit on your shoulder
What am I, to the mind?
The mind's Greatest enemy?
Or perhaps the mind's perfect ally?
You decide
For time is of the essence
For I am Fear
And must slip away
Back into the shadows
And hide away.

Curiosity
by Matt Kreider - age 14

Curiosity killed the cat; did it not?
But was that not only one of his nine lives?
A life lost an answer gained
For without curiosity
What drives the human race?
Why launch a probe?
Why get out of bed?
We are eager to only see
What unfolds from our actions
How it will affect our lives
What we will find
Before you need a probe
You need a question
And without curiosity there are not questions
We were given curiosity
To expand our knowledge
To ponder
To find a question
Answer that question
And then find another

Hero
by Keri Kulmeier - age 14

A hero you think of me, but a hero you are
Whenever I have a problem I don't have to look very far
You help me out every single day
I just pick up the phone and your a phone call away
You are always there and have that special touch
If you were never here, I would miss you very much
I tell you all my secrets without a wondering doubt
You listen to my problem and figure the situation out
You understand me and know me so well
You picked me up when you knew I fell
I have come to a conclusion of what you are to me
You're that special hero as far as I can see

The Game
by Matt Kreider - age 14

The game
It has been played since the dawn of time
Since an animal established I'm more important
I'm better, smarter, and stronger
Then evolution created man
Yes, we play the game
And play it well
Better than any mere animal
We create wars and conflicts
We strive for better weapons
Now with our technological terrors
Mere man becomes a statistic on a death poll
A number
Are those men who fight on the battlefield expendable?
In their leader's eyes?
In our leader's eyes?
Yes
All for glory
We must win
We must become more powerful
Evolution?
let the puny fall
And the strong triumph and grow stronger
For what is this game?
Can it be stopped?
No
For mother nature created the game
the game of which we play is the oldest
SURVIVAL OF THE FITTEST

The Moon
by Marta Krynytzky - age 15

The moon, my moon
    is silvery white
though shining bright all through the night
    It wears a lacey vail
        beneath the clouds around it
it holds its gruesome scary tale
a tale of love,
    a tale of hate
        a tale of unwanted shame
that tells about the things a boy will do
    to gain the arms of a dame
love and pride once did blend
    but never will again
for the moon's poor soul
    washed them apart
        with its morning bloody tears
she proclaimed with utter honesty
    that she would through away her fears
then take her place in the sky
    alone forever, her hardened heart
        will lie there and never die
and as long as there's a cloud or two
    the moon will never lie

Plastic Jesus
by Craig Kunze

I was in a five and dime store
To buy a card for a sick friend
Twas there I first noticed it
Amongst the other gifts to send
And thought I didn't have much
(Lord knows I'm not a rich man)
Guess a spirit must have moved me
To buy Religion made in Japan

You need a Plastic Jesus staring back at you
Could have it looking outward
But He'll know when you're through
So have it looking instead-Right into your eyes
So while you're driving away the hours
Maybe then you'll realize...

So I stopped there that moment
Went back and picked up two
Gift wrapped me up the other Savior
Said in the card-Here's what to do...
...Just prop it right up on your cars dash
And don't worry if others fuss
'Cause there's a piece of God in everyone
And everyone needs a plastic Jesus

You need your plastic Jesus staring back at you
Could have it looking outward
But you'll know when you're through
So Have it looking instead-Right into your eyes
So while you're driving away the hours-Maybe then you'll realize....

God Our Lord
by Dodie J. Kurtz

Oh God our Lord,
in heaven above.
Look down upon us,
and give us your love.

We pray for the poor ones,
the hungry, the blind.
This world would be better,
if more people were kind.

Please don't forsake us,
for we are in need.
Please look upon us
and see a good deed.

Your heart must be heavy,
at what you must find.
Please bless the happy,
the strong and the kind.

Oh God our Lord,
in heaven above.
Look down upon us,
for we need your love.

College
by Carol Kuschill - age 19

So you've reached higher ed?
  Look at all the possibilities around
you -
You can major, minor, double-major
in any field you want.
  The choice is yours in college.
No one will hold your hand through
these next four years or more of school.
  You have to make the initiative.
Expand your horizons by being in a
club such as phi delta kappa,
yearbook, debate.
  Join a sports team like swimming
or hockey.
Remember, this is college and no
longer high school.
  Welcome to college.

The Predator
by Nikki Jean LaBruyere - age 19

The vulture attacked its prey
And stole its soul away.
No more will it be
Allowed to roam free
Nor see the break of day.

The vulture had its fill
And left the dying kill.
So its eyes shifted
And spirits uplifted
To prepare for another meal.

Dedicated to all ex-boyfriends.

Blinded
by Alison Jewell Lambert - age 12

How I do hate this place.
Like a circus animal always on my
toes. Or a blind man on a cliff.
I know death and terrible tragedy
is near, lurking among me. But I
don't know exactly when or how but
I know its soon. I wander
alone, blinded by foolish emotions
but someone told me what to
expect and I didn't believe
them and I fell. I fell off my
precious cliff. The first fall is
the worst. And I find myself
climbing my cliff, rising to glory
and them falling over and over
again. So I give up. I stay
down. I have fallen to many
times, my spirit is broken,
so I lie there alone. Blinded.

Let Freedom Ring
by Christina Lance - age 17

As the lights slowly drift away from my view,
and as we venture into something that is new.
The calm and undisturbed darkness calls my name,
I know that from now on, my life won't ever be the same.

The sweet smell of the salty air blows softly in my face,
It seems days go by in minutes, but I remain in the same place.
The darkness is so inviting as it inevitably swallows me,
Strangely enough, I feel imprisoned, but at the same time free.

This large vessel of freedom rocks from side to side,
and I love the simple pleasure as through the water we glide.
The lights are farther away now and the Adriatic owns me,
It can plainly identify me, but it, I cannot see.

As this vessel carries me to my freedom for all time,
the water calls my name and the bells of freedom chime.
My ways of calmness are so uninterrupted from the chaos of everyday,
and the new things I try, sets me different from my old ways.

It's Independence Day back in the States that I call home,
and I'm miles away doing my own thing, and wanting to roam.
They're back there enjoying the fireworks while we can only sing,
and all I've got to say to that is Let the Freedom Ring!

Walk In The Woods
by Cherie Landis

I took a walk in the woods today, the air was crisp and clean.
The trees are all turning red and gold that stand along the stream.

The leaves that have fallen upon the earth are like carpet beneath my feet;
Muffling the sounds of my hiking boots, giving off a scent that's musky and sweet.

I crept to the edge of the lake to see if the doe and her fawn might be there;
But all I found was the still of the day and the call of a Jay in the air.

I sat on a log at the water's edge and ate the lunch I'd packed;
Watching the ducks bob up and down with he warmth of the sun on my back.

The scold of a squirrel high up in a tree told me I wasn't alone;
So near a stump I left him some curst and the apple I'd brought from home.

The shadows grew long as the day went on, the air had gotten a chill.
I gathered my gear and I headed out, following the trail down the hill.

As I walk through the mossy woods, along the creek, and hear the forest chatter.
I know this is a place to leave for our kids, a piece of earth that really will matter.

Time to go for today, I always return, it's one of my favorite places to be.
One with nature, out here all alone, depending on only me.

Imagination
by Teal Lansing - age 15

Surely the world knows what imagination is. It is the ability to reproduce a special memory of the first bird you heard sing. It is finding yourself in a world of roses and apple trees. It is believing that their are elves in tree trunks, and fairies in the flowers. It is the golden horn on a unicorn, and the silver wings on a pegasus. Imagination is the feeling of happiness you get when you think up an idea of how to create. It is the story of how you fall in love, or how you find your fate. It is the painting of a rose, and the meaning within it. It is the curiousness of what's behind the locked door. Its what keeps you going when the tears start to come. Imagination is what you use to write your thoughts, and feelings down in a heart on a tree trunk.

My Imagination
by Jacquelyn Lane - age 14

In a land called Enchantment,
there is a river that's named sorrow.
There are fish called enthusiastic,
and today molds with tomorrow.

The sea calls out fear.
The mountains echo bravery.
The clouds are never to near,
and the strength is rarely wavering.

The rainbow colors love.
The leaves rustle choice.
The treetops cradle a dove,
and the river ripples its voice.

The island shouts out loneliness.
Rocks crumble warning.
Moonlight cuts through the river
and the sunlight shines 'til morning.

I walk through this timeless land,
which is never what it seems,
but feeling sunshine upon my face
I wake up from my dream.

Piano
by Ian Langford - age 13

I'm listening to classical music.
I'm waiting for it to come, but not yet.
It keeps me waiting like an eager child in a candy store.
Then it hits me!
It sounds so soft and light, like a feather in the breeze.
It blends so well with the music!

Can it Change?
by John Lara - age 20

Why is it some people don't understand
About my place on this great land
I've done some things that I wish I could change
It's not like home on the range
It's really messed up inside my head
Sometimes I wish that my past was dead
There is no way to change everything that I've done
I wish everything was gone and that I could have fun
But I have a hugh remorse
That my baby is gone from this cruel world
Gone to heaven in eternal peace
I sure am glad that I have my niece
She is so sweet and beautiful
I hope she doesn't grow up to be dull
I cry at night thinking about everything
Until I fall asleep at the 12 o'clock ding
Maybe it will change in the future
I can only hope that I'm no smoocher

My Gift From Above
by Beverly Largent

He is Tall, Dark and Handsome
A man both honest and true
With his eyes so dark they sparkle like gems
'Neath his glasses that fit his face and nose too.

His arms are long and strong
His hands, gentle but firm
With his smile so bright and his teeth so white
He could dazzle the apple right off of the worm.

His cap he always will wear
His shirt sleeves, turned under there
With a chain that is always there on his neck
He's solid and steady and ready to share.

His shoulders are broad and wide
His muscles, firm and strong
With a swaggering walk that's truly his own
He's taken my heart and to him I belong.

If you should see this man
The one I've grown to love
With his tender heart and sensitive ways
You'll know he's my gift, sent from above.

Memories
by Denise Larsen - age 15

I wake up in the morning feeling empty and lonely,
it seems like forever, although it was so shortly.

I pray every night to God up above in hopes that
my loved ones are all right.

I quickly say Goodbye and once more I cry one
last tear.

Because I know in my heart they have touched
a certain place and will always be in there.

When I look back I laugh, cry, and remember
the way it was and the way they were, and I know
now they still live up above and are watching over
me, and I'll always remember them as they were,
how they lived, and now as a memory.

When I wake up my eyes are watery and red from
all the tears that I've cried, and I know they are in
a better place they're with our father...GOD.

Someday
by Bethany Larson - age 15

Someday, someday soon,
You will leave me,
Drifting away with the wind.

Such a beautiful face,
My love and my life,
Floating along with life's current.

The secrets, the laughter,
All will be silent without you,
Flying further on angel-soft wings.

No, it wasn't your choice,
Yes we know it is coming,
Painfully tearing apart my heart.

Never again will we hold each other,
Your presence, I'll never again feel,
Loving from the farthest distance.

Someday, someday soon,
You will leave me,
Then someday, someday soon,
I will come to you,
See you, hold you,
Love you again.

My Daddy's Poison
by Danielle M. Rygh - age 13

The weekend I am to see my daddy,
he promises me he won't drink one drink.
He thinks I'll just forget, but I don't.
He knows I won't say anything, and I don't.
To him the alcohol is his best friend, but
It's really his enemy in disguise.

The next weekend I'm over to see my daddy,
he says he won't drink his poison.
He thinks I don't remember what he promised, what he said.
Then I go and cry the cry that everyone can hear but him.

Again, I am coming over.
The promises are now nonexistent.
And while I'm put through slow and excruciating
pain, the poison continues to go down drink
by drink.

And just then I begin to hear my daddy's silent cry
for help that no one else can hear;
painful cries that not even my dad himself can hear.

Nothingness
by Julie Lathia - age 13

Time passes me by
Slowly and obscurely
My world is a place of
Darkness and Nothingness.
Not even nothingness
The complete absence of
Thought, Emotion, and Being.
An utterly complete
Human Vacuum of
Life and Love
Blackness.
This is my world
When you are not
Part of it.

Untitled
by Shanna Laude - age 15

Way up high
I wish I could die
Looking down at the earth
It's just for the first

I wish I could see
Could it be
I see you
And you see me

As we are coming down
You look like a clown
Then you frown
I can't see why
Could it be
that I am going to die

We come faster and faster
Then without knowing we're down
We are buried in the ground
You scream and shout
But there is no doubt

As I lay there bleeding
You are beside me kneeling
You tell me everything is gonna be alright
But that gives me much fright
I can see the bright white light
I tell you that I am going to go
But you say no
Then as I go
You tell me you love me so!

Pisces
by Tanya Lawrence - age 16

So into what darkness can the apparitions fade
Will my daydreams survive in reality's shade
When within my ecstasy erected your existence
And the voice of your heartbeat still shadows your distance
But your constancy raised an oblivious air
I sank in the warmth of that smile you wear
With corduroys and t-shirts, your daily attire
Not burdened by passion, still burning like fire
From the nexus that spawn of my prolix confession
Externally strengthens upon each aggression
And the zeal of first love burns a perpetual flame
Consumes the surrender and endures the blame
Yet through the enchanting I fear I might see
That I've needed you more than you'll ever need me
For what night visions bring will not always be
The likeness of reality
Still when I dream, I dream in you
I dream the dreams you'll make come true
But for now, my brown-eyed sandman, these lonely lids obey
Closing not for those that sleep nor those that fade away
Except for this, dear friend, for words can sell such worthless things
Golden binds break easily, but unlike our silver ring
That you never wear, but know, what meaning lies within that band
we'll never break, **divinity**, strewn amongst the stars as sand.

In the Park
by Marie Layugan - age 11

In the park, I saw some leaves,
Green as green can be.
Some had golden colors,
On that big, tall tree.

In the park, I saw a bee,
Sucking on a flower,
Then a bird flew to a branch,
With it's strength and power.

I saw the blue horizon,
With a bright, round sun,
Rising from the blue, cold sea,
I hope this scene's not done.

The people laughing and having fun,
Makes me smile and skip.
Some small gymnasts are tumbling 'round,
Also makes me flip.

The flipping made me dizzy,
So I laid down on the grass,
Then some kids marched down the aisle,
Looks like a kinder class.

It started raining, then a lightning,
Striked into a tree.
I'm getting wet, my mom is here,
I better go and flee.

Everlasting Experience
by Amanda Leach - age 15

It's softness caressing the sky gave
you a warm, welcome feeling.
At one moment it was so bold, so bright
and the next gentle and romantic, refreshing
and relaxing. This picture perfect
moment reminded you of when you
were younger. Running barefoot through
the summer's warm, velvety grass. You
were a child trying to discourage your
anxious mother as she beckoned you
back into the house.
   You then think of what is to come.
Night. After this magical moment. It's
ever so coldness. It's briskness. It's force
of darkness. Its image is so haunting
and yet enchanting.
Then you stop these harsh thoughts for you
look around and that wonderful moment
is over. Your thoughts are now reality. Night
has come. But, you don't feel cold and
empty. You feel warm and full of magic.
For you have just experienced an everlasting
sunset.
   Everlasting in your heart and ever changing
in your mind.

Dwelling
by Tamara Leaman - age 17

I luv U with all my heart, U have always known it
U'v hurt me from the start, look into my eyes, they'll show it
Still I come 2 U 4 more and still do not know why
I luv being around U even though it makes me cry

I long 4 someone like U, 2 come close and touch my heart
I get frightened by someone like U 4 the fear of it being ripped apart
My soul cries out in agony 4 all the pain that it is feeling
My spirit is slowly fading from the essence U'v been stealing

My sadness is my world, 4 I dwell within it everyday
My hope is my inspiration 4 I hang on every word U say
I choke on all my words, I swallow all my pride
A strange part of me walks this earth, in privacy the other
part will hide

I speak U'r name out loud, I speak it in my mind
Whenever I try 2 understand myself it's U I always find
I feel U'r voice everywhere I go, along with U'r image that chills
me through and through
Forcing me against my will 2 luv every little thing that U do

I luv being in luv with U but I hate this torture that always seems
2 follow
My mind is constantly occupied by U but my heart is 4-ever hollow
U R my illness, my medicine, the constant craving of all things I lack
It's the worst pain I'v ever known 2 luv someone who
doesn't luv U back.

World Of Water
by Laura Leathers - age 12

In this world of water it seems to me
there are to many bridges
to cross
you can walk a distance
but get nowhere
for you see
you must cross a bridge
everyday
it is what they say
but the bad thing about these
bridges
is that they have no sign's
so every bridge is a new adventure
whether good or bad
you must cross a bridge
and that bridge sometimes
it seems like it's never going
to end
but gather all the courage
inside of you
for if you can make it
through one bridge
one day
then I'm sure you can make
it through many others

Friends?
by Kristian Lear - age 14

As tears fill my eyes
my friends tell endless lies
They told me I had lost their trust
after we get into a big fuss.
My head starts to spin around
as I feel my unsteady heart pound.
Then I run out into the rain
and feel a stabbing pain
why is it taking me so long
just to figure out that I didn't do
anything wrong
As I walk back to my place
I see a familiar face
I let all my worries rush away
I'll save them for another day
As I rush into his arms
nothing now can do me any harm

Death
by Joëlle

Death is the rule of nature.
She comes like a thief,
She passes by us in silence,
But her impact is awful.

She ravages everything on her way,
The elders, the youngsters, the children,
She steals our parents and even our children.
Death will for evermore be a mystery to us.

Death, making a laughing-stock of us,
Shows how far we, human, are weak,
How far we are fallible,
To what extent we are vulnerable.

Our Universe is nothing beside Death,
It is nothing but a trivial matter
That will be quickly forgotten. Our Planet and
This life on earth are only ephemeral.

Today we are alive and tomorrow we are dead.
Nobody can foretell when, where and at
What time she will catch us,
She is nothing but a storm that comes in silence.

Oh, Death, Death! I hate her.
Sometimes she comes in disguise
Stealing the fate of some gullible people,
Shutting their eyes from eternal life in heaven.

Death! The only way to fight you and to
Win you over is to live every second
Of ones life fully without ever thinking
That there is an end to everything.

Dedicated to my Godmother, Peggy

The Girl?
by Jamie - age 15

A shadow hits the street tonight
A body drops without a sight
A dog barks down the street,
as the shadow makes his retreat.
Another victim
another soul,
but it don't matter no more.

A girl with no heart and soul
A girl who dreams of toys and boys.
Depressed without a clue
thinks of nothings and somethings
inner turmoil, don't know what to do
temper, anger she holds it in.
No one knows the real her.
When you see her happy,
dancing in the street,
you don't know her anger,
which lays deep beneath.
Everything under control,
not a little slip, not even a blink.
See her plastic smile?
She is even human,
does she have a soul.
No one will ever know.

You
by Heather Lee - age 14

You think you know,
You say, "I understand."
You act as if you have been in my position.

Yet, you don't know.
You don't understand,
And there is no way you have been in my position.

You try to help.
You try to make me happy.
You try to be so positive...

But you don't always help.
You don't make me happy,
And you aren't always positive.

You don't understand.
You can't be in my position.
You just don't know,
         You can't...

There is just no way you can help,
I'm me ... and you're you.
I can understand me ... you have no way of understanding.

How could you understand?
You aren't in my position and you never could be,
My life is just a mess ... and yours is so perfect.
         You just...
               Can't help.

That Wonderful Someone
by Melissa Ann Lee - age 14

That wonderful someone who makes my life complete;
Would be you, my darling, you are so sweet.
I want to disperse my love to the world;
But I feel as a clown, and confine my word.
The reminiscence of your glorious face, so lovely;
Scramble though my mind, hastefully.
I see you from afar, and feel a biting coldness;
I feel my face grow hot, I'm blushing, I confess.
That chair is called, "You" `cause it.is.so comfortable;
I like being near it, too, I feel no trouble.
That bird is called, "You" `cause it.is.so graceful;
When I look into your eyes, I feel the forceful pull.
You stole the Stars From the Skies;
And gave them to me to put into my eyes.
Love, oh love, sweet love, my dear;
I feel as a bird when you are near.
I feel I can fly, so high, so high;
So very high in the sky, blue sky.
Higher than the trees;
Through the flowing breeze;
Weak over come my knees;
I've fallen in love with ease.
So, as you can see, right here, my dear;
You're that wonderful someone, my dear, it's clear.

Out of Control
by Rosemary Lemon

Love burns with heart's content
  A drought will absorb the world
Hurt has climbed the Rocky Mountains
  I'm beguiled as a bird who lost her feathers
Treachery has shown his face
  I'm like a ship without a sail
The hurt of a breakup turns to pain
  My world has turned upside down
Love's almost touched the ground
  A dozen roses stop the frown
A surprise caused one's face to shrank and shine

Personalities
by Ashley Lerdo - age 14

I don't know what I want to do. I sit and ponder who I am. What I am. I see a girl, but feel displaced from her. She's a totally different person. I'm just someone who watches. I have control over what she does, but I still feel displaced, I don't see her as me. I see her as she is. Not as I am. I say she, but I mean me. If I think of me as she, I can better understand her as she or I as me. I know what she feels, for I feel the same. I know she lies, for I lie. She seems to be smart. Right now she's heartbroken. This is the next promise he's broken out of many. She says she loves him. I love him. Is it love? Love. You know her heart wretches in pain as she thinks of him leaving her. You. You. She has told him many times how she feels, he doesn't seem to understand. He's supposed to love me. Her. That's how fairy tales work. Wishing stars. They're supposed to work. My. Her stars have turned out the lights. Love me. Her. Love her. Love me. Total heartache. We will suffer for him, for our love. My love. Her love. We love him. Personalities.

Untitled
by Helen Leung - age 18

Stepping out of my house on a bone-
chilling morning, I saw the blizzard still at toil,
like Merlin whipping up dreaded spells
The once hard, cement ground lay buried under heaps
of Virgin snow.
The only sounds were the skin- biting winds and the crunch
of my boots as each footstep indent
the velvety powder. Snowflakes of doilies twist
before me like a ballet dancer in a jewelry box.
My body is practically numb from his bitterness, but the
child within struggles to pop-out like a cork of a
shaken champagne.
At last I rupture forth, laughing, shouting-
gyrating round an round. My heart swells with
happiness-not a heed in the world and the once
lost innocence, returns, as Old man gale
wordlessly creeps elsewhere.

A Land Without Compassion
by Kristen Lewandowski - age 15

There is an important issue which many ignore,
It is much too real on which to close a door.
Animals are being killed for senseless reasons,
All through the year and not just one season.
The graceful snow leopard, the cunning harp seal,
Don't people know that they too feel?
The intelligent chimpanzee, the curious grizzly bear,
It is men that these animals fear.
Cheetahs and wolves are endangered too,
This issue is not anything new.
These animals are defenseless against armed men,
These wasteful killings will stop when?
If these frightful men would open their eyes,
They would hear the animals' pleading cries.
Won't anyone help them, won't anyone try,
Or will the bloodshed stop when they all say "Goodbye?"

Love
by Crystal Lewis - age 14

If **Love** is a story,
    let me memorize it

If **Love** is a song,
    sing it to me

If **Love** is a person,
    introduce me to them

If **Love** is a direction,
    point me the right way

If **Love** is a day,
    let the day last forever

The Poet
by Donna A. Lewis

I was told I have a gift
The gift of love
I know this gift must come
from above
Abundance of love that flows
through the heart
Makes poetry a fine crafted
art
I want to bring contentment
and joy to your life
To express myself by sharing
my pains and pleasure
for this is how my love is measured
To look at the stars and see
how they shine
Is like writing down words
of wisdom that rhyme
Don't be like the moth
that fly's into the light
Open your heart
Don't narrow your sight.

Creation Of Evolution
by Oatry Covington

If there roared a blast of a great, great bang
God had summoned light and the universe sprang
From his hands, to burst forth in massive profusion.
Almighty God made evolution.

If mankind emerged through the channels of ages,
Groping minutely through progressions of stages
If there were a quiver or a quickened extrusion,
Almighty God made evolution.

From the voiceless void of the eons of night
Dawned a thousand ages in his sight.
The seven day creation bids an urgent inclusion:
Almighty God made evolution.

While scholars tarry over test tube and tome
The changeless truth is traveling home
From empty, futile, mindless exclusion:
Almighty God made evolution.

When strivers cede the final bomb,
To weary earth, the kingdom come.
When time is called on all confusion
God will reclaim his evolution.

Ballet
by Ashley Libertucci - age 12

    Ballet is like a rose;
it is a sign of love;
beauty of you're arms and toes;
you'll fly like a dove;
a chance to be free;
    to float like a leaf;
        you'll finally see;
it's not all grief;
        you're hearts so strong;
   you don't seem to care;
it might take long;
to be fully aware;
someday you'll fly; arms so strong; you'll
feel so high; it won't be long;
you're heart beats; the light's on your
face;
perfectly pointed feet;
is all you need to end this complete grace;

Be
by Samantha Liivam - age 12

Remember the past
Remember the times gone by
    LEARN

Think of the future
Think of times to come
    DREAM

Have the courage to change
Have the will to move forward
    PREVAIL

Treasure the good times
Treasure the bad times
    CHERISH

Look up to those who care
Look down to those who need to look up
    LOVE

Learn by looking back
Dream by looking forward
    LIVE

Pandora's Box
by Audrey Lin - age 13

Open it and wonder
What it beholds
Is it light,
Or is it darkness?
What epoch is it from?
Certainly is a mystery
But the question is,
Will you uncover it
Or leave it hidden for all eternity?

For all you know,
It could be anything
Anything from the four elements
To the Heavens
To the stars
It may reveal the path to your destiny
Or it could be the hand of fare
Pointing at you
What's on your mind?

It may make you a cynic
Of the secrets it keeps shrouded
But you must keep pondering
Whether you should open it or not
With this, anything will occur
There's no room for knowing
Only room for wondering

But whether it is good or bad
Light or darkness, Saints or Demons
Whatever it contains, never give in to despair
When there's only room
For hope

Just Wait And See
by Mindy Lin - age 16

Can't I just claim you now?
Like a prize, but with treasures within.
Oh, do I dream about how,
Oh how I would care for you and comfort you akin.
Oh tell me how you could be mine,
And I'll tell you, together, we'll be just fine.

Why are we together at times so few?
It breaks my heart to realize that all I have of you are dreams.
Why can't these dreams come true?
Desperate or obsessive it seems,
But truthfully, we were meant to be.
Just wait and see.

This Very Moment
by Cherie Nechvatal Linquist

Twenty years ago this very moment,
The radio broadcast jarred me awake.
"Entertainer/actor Bobby Darin died
This morning." -- please be a mistake.

So I lay in bed with eyes unblinking
And rigidly loitered an hour or more.
When the disk jockey repeated himself,
My life was over as I'd know before.

I've been in turmoil since that dawn,
Off and on, and once in a while by choice.
Sometimes I cry and sometimes I smile
Over the wonder of such a flawless voice.

And just like Bobby sang in the classic,
The one that always causes the tears--
I've already missed my brown-eyed daddy
Some of these days, for all these years.

No one can empathize with this anguish;
They discount and taunt my melancholy.
Because we never met, twenty years ago
This very moment should be the finale.

But he was always concrete to me
And the love I felt was bona fide.
Twenty years ago this very moment,
The Utopian inside of me died.

For twenty more years, or forty years,
However much longer I have yet to live,
I'll listen and long for and mourn the loss of
The Purest Performer this world had to give.

Love In Different Ways
by Sara Livingston - age 10

Love comes in different ways.
Some people love their jobs
Some people love their pets
But others love people
Like husbands and wives.
Still there is another kind of love,
There is one more love among people,
The love of friendship.
It is not a passionate love,
But the love of peace and harmony.
The love of knowing there is someone to back
You up and to be there when you need help.
It is almost like the love between sisters and brothers.
There are all kinds of love, and there are many
Kinds to discover.
Love is not a feeling to be played with.
To some love is all they have.
"I love you" is not just a silly phrase to
Be said to anyone.
That silly phrase has a lot of meaning.
Love is a special thing that comes from the heart
And comes in many different ways.

The Willow Field
by Emily Loeffler - age 14

I stand here, silent as a snake in the grass.
Still,
Non-moving.
Around me the branches of the willow trees sway
Back and forth,
Back and forth,
To and fro.
The wind whispers, tickling my ear with the loose hair blowing around my
shoulders.
It tosses the fields into a sea of waving grasses
Rustling and crackling
Like waves breaking on the ocean's shore.
The clouds skim by overhead; white and fluffy.
There is no chance of rain.
Above the clouds the sky is a brilliant blue and the sun is shining brightly,
But here the wind is whistling across the land
Setting all into a swirling mass of moving shapes and colors,
Even though I am the only one here
Standing still in the middle of it all;
A rock in the middle of a swirling river,
An oak tree in a forest of bamboo.
But then I turn my head and I lift my voice,
And become part of the oceans that are these rippling grasslands and these
stands of willows,
And I sway, and I bend, and I sing,
And I am free.

My Dream Come True
by Robynne Locke - age 13

The day I fell in love with you,
My dream awoke, my wish came true,
I never thought that it could be,
But loving you is my destiny.

I waited for so very long,
To find a love that was this strong,
I can't describe the love I feel,
It's just to perfect to be real.

Since you sent your love to me,
There's nothing else that I can see,
Cause all I think about is you,
My one true love, my dream come true.

Fear Of Heartbreak
by Robynne Locke - age 13

She met so many men before,
But not one she had loved much more,
And she knew this love was true,
Because this man had loved her too.
    One day he asked if she'd be his wife,
    Because he loved her more than life,
    And said, "My darling, it is true,
    I wish to always be with you."
When she learned he felt this way
She was afraid she couldn't stay,
Because her heart was filled with fears,
That all her love would end in tears
    She turned her eyes away from him,
    And said in her sweet angel voice,
    "I'd hold you in my arms forever,
    If it were to be my choice."
"But even if I love you dear,
We both know that the end is near,
Cause I can't take you in my heart,
For fear that someday we'll depart."
    And as she bade her last goodbye.
    She couldn't help but start to cry,
    Because she knew she'd never know,
    Why she let her true love go.
And even to this very day,
All alone she'll always stay,
Cause she's afraid she couldn't take,
The painfulness of one heartbreak.

In My Mirror
by Cassie Loera - age 14

I look into my mirror
But the face I see
Isn't mine anymore
This face has a smile
And eyes that always shine
I want to believe different
But this face just isn't mine
For I am just a lonely girl
Who has not a single friend
And I am so alone in the world
I just want it all to end
I look in the mirror
And more and more
I see that this face
Isn't mine anymore
As I look in the mirror
I also see
An image of how happy
I always used to be.

Differences
by Yen Marie Lopez - age 19

Differences clash time after time
And no one understands why.
Opinions that no longer need to hide
Under the black cloak of fear
Can rise and see the sun shine
Only to find an eclipse that covers
All the words that you have.

A battle is forged between
The two opposing sides
Using weapons and hurting words
Instead of listening and using their minds.
The mind is a void waiting to be filled
With new experiences, opinions, thoughts,
Even if agreeing is not within reach.

Hearts get hurt, yet they as easily
Can be healed with a word
Or even a good ear.
So be wise and true to yourself.
Listen, examine, understand, test,
Even enjoy the differences in-between.
You'll see how much you receive and learn.

Autumn
by Jenny Lorenz - age 20

This the most beautiful time of the year,
The outside should make everyone full of cheer
The sun shines on the trees,
Onto their colored leaves
some are just plain green,
With no other colors to see
Others have a touch of color on the ends,
Some have color on them that blends
Ones are orange and a touch of yellow,
the looks of them are calm and mellow
Some are just bright orange or dark red,
After that they turn brown and fall dead
the brown leaves cover the ground,
Walking on them is a crunching sound
Soon after temperatures drop,
Winter moves in and makes snow on top

Flying; Free
by Katy D. Lore - age 12

I fly, through the shimmering,
   bright blue, swirled sky.
No bullets puncturing my soft,
   feathery wings.
I'm free, soaring through
   the air gently, gracefully
   over the trees, I see my
   baby birds flying with
   such uncertainty, they
   are free, can't you
   see!
When we're flying with dignity,
   gleefully, we are flying;
   FREE!
And as for me; I am joyfully
   happily flying; free!

Saying "Good-bye"
by Tessa Louch - age 18

I have to say "Good-bye" today.
 It's always been hard for me to say.
I always get all chocked up inside.
 And I never ever enjoy my ride.
I wish we didn't have to split.
 But I will take this by the bit.
All because I have my memories.
 They will always be there, my remedies.
For when I start to feel a whim.
 All I have to do is remember them.
Waiting until I need someone to be kind.
Showing me all of our good times.
 Keeping me from my many whines.

Never Yours, Never You
by Tiffany Louden - age 16

I don't know why, but I know
I can't get you off my mind.
Why is it I want you so?
I need to know that you're mine.
I don't know how to explain myself
Tell you how I really feel
It's you I want, and no one else
My heart is yours to steal.
I know I've loved a thousand guys
But none have felt like this
My ears have heard a million lies,
My lips have felt many a kiss
But never yours and never you
You were true from the start.
I wonder what you'd do
If you knew you had my heart.

Summer Dreams
by Kristen A. Louis - age 14

Summer dreams are balls of fire with its bolts of heat beating on your back.
It's the way you feel when you jump into an icy blue swimming pool and
Discover it wasn't that hot after all. The way you wrap your carnation colored
Fuzzy pink towel around your frozen stiff body. The way you smell the hamburgers
And hot dogs looking on the blazing hot grill that is just like the ball of fire beating on
Your back from your summer dreams.

Cool Blue Eyes
by Kim Lucas - age 13

As I gaze into his
cool blue eyes! I see
the cool blue ocean line.
The sweet loving sound
of his voice. That sweeps
me off my feet and
carries me through the
cool blue ocean breeze!

Till I Find Happiness
by Jennifer Luchetta - age 15

I live a world of strangers
I'm an outside looking in
like the only hanger in a closet
like I've committed a sin
sometimes I feel like I want to jump off a cliff
other times I feel like flying way up high in the sky
No one knows the pain I feel
No one has the strength to heal
I've been hurt and bullied
beat up and crushed
yet I have not told a soul till now
it is now I speak out it is now it all comes about
I've been put down told I was ugly
I've been take advantage of and almost died in the hands of another
There's no one here to listen
just me and my pain
There's no one here to help
just me and myself
everyone has their day
where they will slowly go away
and it is then they will say
I have found happiness!

Foolish Games
by Suzanne Luciano - age 15

One too many games you are playing
Did you listen to what I was saying
You said you loved me. How?
It doesn't explain the way you act now
Do you pretend I'm there
Are you pretending to care
Weak promises you never said
Was it in my eyes what you read
So silent, but so loud
To love you, am I proud?
Ask me once, ask me once more
So much room for anger to store
You shouldn't have played these games with my heart
So many promises they become hard to tell apart
Ask me once, ask me twice
Whisper words of love in my ear as I roll the dice
Show me that you still care
Roll once again, move to the next square
Foolish games, never ending
Did you get the message I was sending?
I dropped so many clues
A broken heart, punishment for not following the rules
My heart you wanted to win
Now you get lucky when you use a free spin
Foolish games include passion to burn
Too bad your luck ran out because you lost your turn.

Love and War
by Trisha Lunas - age 13

When there's hate in your heart you'll go to war.
You'll fight just a little but it'll become more and more.
Even a fool knows that war will never die, but if you quit
The eagle will fly.

When there's love in your heart you'll feel it.
You can never finish love, but the eagle flies
As long as you don't quit.
Everyone knows that love itself has a heart.
If you love a little or if you love a lot,
As long as you love you'll never fall apart.

Set My Feelings Free
by Jessica Lundquist - age 13

I want to set my feelings free;
I want to be me.
I want to cry,
without having a reason why.
I want to live,
without having to always give.
I want to smile,
just once in a while.
I want to yearn,
without again getting burned.
Can't you see?
I want to set my feelings free.

Our Grandsons' Prayer
by Betty Mills Luper

Now we lay us down to sleep
We pray the Lord our family to keep.
We love you all, don't make us choose—
Only one will win, but we all will lose.
Wish us happiness, wish us love,
Don't fuss and fight, "Oh, God from above."
Make them see what they're doing to us
When they argue, quarrel and cuss!
We don't ask for toys, fortune or fame
But for love and affection, Don't you need the same?
We both are a gift, "From God from above"
Created by miracles by Mom and Dad's love.
You all may think we're just too young
To see What's happening, and where we belong.
But my Brother and I know, "Oh, God, from above,
That we are blessed and it's you that we love!"
So, Mama and Daddy, our Grand people so rare,
Don't just tell us you love us—show us you care.
Stop fighting and bickering—This is Our Prayer
      "Oh God From Above."

Dustin and Austin

Wishing You Were Here
by Mer Lyon - age 15

The stars still twinkle in the midnight sky
As I sit here wondering
As I cry, as I cry
Why did you take my Mom and Daddy away?
Now there is no one to tell me to go outside and play
At least it was quick and they didn't feel much pain
Slowly passing like a cold winters rain
These scars I have to bare, both inside and out
Your loving hugs I have to live without
No more will I hear your voices calling for me
Those painful times I remember that sting like a bee
I know I wasn't easy and always a cinch to bare
I just want you to know that I will always care
Even though you're not here to kiss me at night
You will be in my memory till morrow deep midnight
when the stars still twinkle
And I still cry
As I look out over the midnight sky
And the moon shines down its golden beams
I know that I'll see you soon
but only in my dreams

The Shining
by Oliver V. Lyons

Plangent the persuasion of sandy shores,
Anchored deep the charismatic charm,
Beckoned back - time washed the more,
Mesmerized the memory, with thought disarmed.

Reflections birth bathed, the past yet yearned,
Odly new --- the golden view,
Magnetized times frame -- forged, fire burned,
Passions time tempered, past patinas purviewed.

Widened the winters of my yearning years,
So august the autumns that framed my falls,
Hurried the wait, hour-glassed time's cheer,
The beauty of being, now best of all.

Nostalgic the nostrums of cycled change,
The top spins past as world's before,
True trophies to tame, so transient time's range,
Each day forever, each day much more.

Each day an ocean, waved bright to see,
Undulating utopias past searches shore,
Each day the joy grasped long to be,
Each day forever -- each day adored,
Each day forever -- one needs no more.

Rock ground to sand, now sanded ground,
Life beached -- sun bleached,
Life's gain --- now plain,
To shine for God -- each graveled grain,
When shined for God, no life mundane,
When shined for God -- God's Love world gained.

Wedding on the Pier
by Derek Mackety - age 20

A wedding on the pier, what a sight to see
A beautiful girl standing next to me.
The wind at our backs, the waves at our feet,
The first time our families meet.
Talking, laughing and admiring the view
The horizon, the water, me and you.
The skies clear, the sun goes down
Boats pass, waves dance all around.
Myself in black, her in white
We take the vows, an unforgettable sight.
Not a care, not a worry, not a fear
A perfect day, a wedding on the pier.

Don't Say Goodbye
by Nicole Marie Macrander - age 16

Why are you saying goodbye
When we both know it's not your time to die
If I promise to be your only
You most promise not to leave me so lonely
You can't leave me here all by myself
because your love is the riches wealth
You have opened a new world to me
This world I love to see
Every day of just to be with you
Will never make me feel blue
So please don't say good bye
because we both know it's not your
time to die.

The Birds
by Jessica Louise Maestas - age 15

A flock of black and white birds took flight,
Escaping their phone-wire perch.
They flew around the tree-tops, all together, never straying.
You could see each flapping alone
Yet staying together; truly one being.
One separated, flew off on its own.
It tried to follow, but quickly lost its way.
How many people are like that?
Always trying to find something, never sure of what it is.

Barefoot in the grass; it seems so real to me;
The clouds and sky suspended silently above.
No birds fly now, they've left my view.
They might return; you never know
But then again they might not,
Having found better places to fly, better voices to inspire.
If you open your eyes to the beauty around you,
You become one with the life surrounding.
Feelings roll and fly to the sky
To join the birds in flight.

Fly to the horizon sweet bird of mine.
I may never see you again.
But it's OK, I know you're there,
Waiting for my longing sighs to follow.
Things get better as time goes on,
But nothing can forever last.
A cosmic state, staying still, or simply moving on;
There's always something more to see.
And when you understand it, there's still so much to be done!
Reveal yourself to the light within,
Find another view.

Kisses In The Wind
by Dione Manheimer - age 14

Tomorrow's here and I'm losing you
My heart's in pain please make it new.

I was wishing this day would never come.
But prayers are short and few on tongue.

I don't want to ever see you go.
My broken heart I dare not show.

My tears of agony will call you name.
Until your back it won't be the same.

My promise to myself I feared I've sinned.
Until your home I'll send kisses in the wind.

Eternity
by Vicki Mann - age 12

I stand at the cliff of reality,
My back turned to the real world,
As I look at the waves of my life,
Tumbling and swirling,
Hurling themselves at rocks of despair,
All is silent.

Who am I?
Where do I come from?
These are just a few,
Of the everlasting questions,
That come rushing to my mind.

Before I can stop,
I find myself waking up,
I know that I am falling,
Falling back into the same pool of treachery.

Cometh the Midnight Wanderer
by Chris Mansour - age 18

To the west of the river, across the meadow, just past the graveyard,
There lies his territory.
Beyond the fens of 'Ole Ghost Town and the moors of Monterea
The wilds and the woods begin.

O'er bush, o'er log thistledown, cometh the Midnight Wanderer.
Into the brush and the scrub he slides his way through,
Avoiding the snakes, gliding over the leaves,
Listening to the howl of wolves.

Gazing up to the moonlight, drinking it in, basking in the starlight.
Feeling soft wind caressing his back, kissing him tenderly.
He presses on, enjoying the fun, relishing in the night's power
The wild roses and the night flowers exhale their mystical fragrance.

Yet deeper into the forest goeth he, beyond the trails and beauty,
Into the darker, blacker region of the wood,
Where life hath no place amongst death--
Twisted reed and foul decay govern the sinister homeland

The Wanderer presses on, with thoughts of home and warmth
Guiding him through the gloom.
The misty vapors, the reek of filth,
Surely the end of the trail must be near.

Swish past the trees and open the door,
Into the light from the fire,
Lying safely in the bed,
Cometh the Midnight Wanderer.

Never True Love
by Kristina Marchu - age 14

I thought he really loved me
I thought he truly cared
Love is something strange to me
Something quite not there

He said all the right things
He knew just what to say
He even talked of a diamond ring
That never made its way

When he finally left me
I wasn't that surprised
It was the last straw
That made me realize

I was just a pawn
In his sick little game
And now he's gone
Faster than he came

All that I have to say
Is good riddance; goodbye
And to this day
I'm officially over that loser guy

Life
by Kathryn Anne Marcinak - age 13

Life,
Who knows what it means,
It cold mean many different things,
Life is pretty flowers and luscious candies,
It is something much more than that,
Life is also sorrow and woe,
It is the struggle between good and evil,
It is about the love we give and have for each other,
It is unity and honor that equals life,
It's what makes us get up each morning to live it,
And what makes us lay our heads down to pause it,
Life.

Puppy Love
by Veronica Marshall - age 15

The rub of an elbow
Or the touch of a hand,
A sweet little girl
And a growing young man.
The glitter of eyes
And the scent of sweet love,
The pump of young hearts
And the "coo" of a dove.
Innocent smiles
That mean so much,
Long and hard glances
And a sweet feeling touch.
Nervous hands
That don't know what to do,
Queer and shaky voices
Saying, "I love you".
The calming of nerves
And a sweet little kiss,
The feeling of love
And it's innocent bliss.
So incredibly unnerving
And so very tough,
So this is how it feels
This so called puppy love?

The Stage
by Jonathan Daniel Marsh - age 16

When I walk out as the light comes up
I feel the doors of Heaven touching my toes
I can be anyone, do anything
I can fly, I can die, I can be or I cannot
I can be a villain or a saint
I could be God
When I walk across the stage
The stage becomes me
I become the stage.

I Blame Me
by Breeann Martinez - age 14

I remember all the past
times we had so much fun,
but I know my pain has
just begun.

I don't blame all our problems
on you, because I know I
made my share of mistakes
too.

I do miss your lips pressed
against mine, but I miss
you more because you are
so divine.

I wish your arms were
around me now, so I could
close my eyes and think wow.

My days are short and my
nights are long, when I'm
missing you I try to convince
myself it's wrong.

But please don't ever tell me
you still care, because even
then when I needed you, you
were never there.

But I guess we all have to
pay a major fee, because
sadly the last two letters
of blame are***

ME

The Gift
by Michael Martin

With careful hands she fitted both the buttons on the face.
She sewed the mouth down under, then the nose went right in place.
Two little furry ears on a little furry head.
The kitten was created with a needle and some thread.

The weaving of the basket took at least a day or two.
A ring of lace around the top and then the job was through.
The handmade flowers topped it off, what beauty they'd provide.
The kitten and a ball of yarn were neatly placed inside.

A note was written thoughtfully. It came straight from the heart.
"To mommy's precious little girl," was how the words did start.
The note was filled with mother's love, and then sealed with a kiss.
The little girl could not receive a greater gift than this.

The gift was given to a child so tender, yet so brave.
The mother said one last goodbye, and left it on the grave.

Departure
by Michael Martin

Clinging. Waiting. Holding on.
The timing must be right.
Once with the others, but now alone.
The voyage would start tonight.

Not knowing the reason that it grew,
Not knowing it's final end,
The leaf let go of all it knew,
And caught a ride on the wind.

Trust?
by Santiago Martos, Jr.

Trust an unspoken word, an unspoken feeling.
Like the mysteries of the universe, it has no boundaries, has no ceiling.
It's fuel for the lonely and insecure of heart, sometimes gets me through
the day but especially at night when its dark.
It can be the most endless gratifying feeling on Earth,
is it something that's given to us by God at birth?
Must you have it with someone in order to be friends,
or can you socialize, date or marry and just pretend?
Can I ever fully trust someone without any worry?
The passion to know this mystery is something I wish
I knew in a hurry.
Am I free to express myself to the world unconditionally?
Can I trust that societies' biases won't persecute me spiritually?
Mother, should I walk through Life with Trust?
And if I choose not to will my decision be Just?

Mesmerized
by Courtney Mashburn - age 19

No one knows the beauty of your soul like I do
A single whisper, a touch, a vision of you
The sweetness of you I hold in my eyes
Can only mean that I am mesmerized.

Thoughts of your tantalizing body dance in my head
While feelings of you are left unsaid
Each moment that passes by I see you and I together
and hope that they last forever.

Your sexy sensual eyes are a pleasure to see
And every inch of you, I want a part of me.
I long for your lust and your passionate love,
You are the finest gift sent from heaven above.

Know that you have a clue of how I feel,
Maybe my heart can be free and heal.
The one thing that would make me happy is you by my side
To feel the feeling of being mesmerized.

What I Need
by Dena Mason - age 18

What I need right now
is a good strong shoulder.
I need someone to trust.
I want to feel the security
of knowing that someone
will always be there.
Someone to laugh with,
to cry with,
and to share with.
I have to know there's
someone to rely on all the time.
Not someone to criticize or to
tell me what to do.
I need someone that will just
listen to me.

An Eternity
by Nichole Marie Mason - age 16

To stay and never leave my side.
Hold me in his arms till the day I die.
I feel my heart beat against his chest.
We hold each other now and there we both rest.

Oh! how I wish this is the way it would be.
Oh! how I wish it for an eternity.

Tears I shed every night.
Thinking that everything will be alright.
Hoping not to lose his love.
Praying I'm all he's thinking of.

Wishing this would never end.
Wishing forever it could be; I will always love him for an eternity.

I would like to dedicate this poem to Jason Morgan.

The Rose
by Jolene Matherly - age 15

The rose, a symbol of beauty
That is hidden deep within
I can see it on your face
And engraved beneath your skin

It almost hurts to look
Into your diamond eyes
I see something so familiar
That it comes as a surprise

I love the way you're sweet to me
You make me feel so good inside
I've never felt this way before
It's like a roller coaster ride

I'm so excited when I'm around you
Though you give me quite a scare
It's so hard to make sense of how I feel
But you should know I really care

Because when we're together
I want to hold you close
I love when I can look at you
And see the beauty of a rose

I Miss You
by Cora Mayer - age 19

Ever since I went away
I think of you too much
Lying here without you
I long to feel your touch
I wait to see your eyes
Look back into mine
Whenever we're together
I wish to pause the hands of time
So I could hold you always
In my arms, as well as my heart
Then I'd never have to miss you
Because we would never have to part
But, for now we're far away
Which of course is not by choice
And, until I can hold you again
I can only hear your voice
But, when I look up at the stars
I know you see the same ones, too
It helps me just a little,
But I still miss you.

Free
by Shawn Mayes - age 16

Running wild
Being free
That's the way
I want to be
Driving around
Without a care
Would you come
Would you dare
Running free
Forgetting authority
Just to forget
That I'm a minority
Sitting around
Drinking some brew
Just hanging out
With me and my crew
Running wild
Being free
That's the way
I want to be.

Green Heaven
by Jean Camou

Nothing more than a cricket shone
twinkling hard, crusted emerald
with black and wisp, telling of my
kitchens age.

Wheedling whipping tails deliver
teeth that cannot penetrate my lemons
walls, my bananas doors, my skins.

Beneath the stomachs of my oiled wood
spiders carry the excess spice that wind
up around my lids,
while above only the termites remain
to chew and grind the bones of
their goddess.

The Touch of a Smile
by Kay L. McCann

Brief glances in passing
And soon a friendship
More valuable by far
Than everything else
On this planet

For a friend is sunshine
Happy ring of laughter
Freshness of morning
Sparkling crystal dew
Meeting with another
On a free-flowing wavelength

I knew you'd be here

Treasures

Honest To God True Love
by Cristie Mc Carty

She became a part of all of you hearts.
She gave you all love from the start.

She would run wild like a care free breeze.
If she wanted something, her eyes would just
    say please.

She would make a mess in your rooms.
You'd say that's okay and smile, then clean
    it up with a broom.

She'd bark real loud to let you know someone
    was there.
If you cried she'd come lay by your side
    To show you she cared.

You'd get down on your knees to play with
    her thinking it was cool.
She'd tilt her head and think, what a fool.

But she was the best thing you ever got.
She taught you all a lot.

So when you all think the pain won't
    come to an end.
Just remember she will always be
    your bestest friend.

Even though she's not around.
That doesn't mean you can't see her
    When your feeling down.

For she's running wild and free up
    in Heaven above.
Making sure you never lose what
    you all gave her,
HONEST TO GOD TRUE LOVE.

Guilty Conscience
by Avia McClain - age 14

I am bad deeds;
    increasing when evil comes,
    putting chains upon your back,
    weighing down your brain.
I am evil thoughts;
    against your elders,
    family,
    teachers, friends,
I am your conscience,
    guilty conscience.
    Wishing I'd go away?
Lingering on,
    until you decide-
      Give up!
      Give in!
    Your mind is mine.

Goodbye
by Linzie McCoskey - age 14

You say you must go now,
That it is time to leave.
Why now, Why so soon?
Tell me, Please.

Your life has yet to come,
For heaven sakes it's just begun.

In this hateful, cruel world,
which we are forced to live in every day.
Angels came on a gust of wind,
and carried you away.

But why you, why now?
The answer is yet to come and I will always wonder why.

Yes you were suffering and yes you were in pain,
and god came and took you
to his kingdom where forever
you will reign.

As long as you are happy and forever unharmed
(and even though I long to hold you in my arms)

Every sunrise and every sunset
and every day until it's done.
I know you will watch over me
until my time does come.

Then we can be together
for all eternity,
and I'll love you forever
(my sweet darling baby)
Just like you'll love me!

Skipping Stone
by Joe McCulloch

The reflection of his face
in the rippled water of the
rivers edge, unlike the stones
beneath the surface

polished of their scabrous
edges from the aerobics
of the waters flow
the giving in and letting go

glassy surface from the wet
rolling it over and over in the palm
water dripping home from his hand

and for a moment the troubles
of his day ride the droplets with
the river to the sea

so it is and had to be
with sidearm swing he sent
the stone skipping free.

Children of the Streets
by Sarah Lynn McCullough - age 14

What is it like,
to live in a gang?
Where the only sound you'll ever hear
are ghatts and guns going bang.

Some say these kids are crazy
or say its a good kid gone wrong.
We can't just ignore them
their life span is not long.

They don't deserve to die
like us, most are children too.
We need to get up and do something
American this is your clue.

Save the children
that's what they say,
but when it comes to Gangster kids
no one takes the time of day.

The Savior Of The Liberty Bell
by Elizabeth C. McCurdy

The bell rang in Philadelphia on July 8, 1776
   She proclaimed the Independence
of the United States of America for
all to hear her voice-
   She moanded in sadness when
she was cracked in 1835 - shipped
around from State to State the
vibrations were great!
   She called for help to be taken
home to Independence Hall - to roam
no more - the daughter of the American
Revolution heard her cry. This Philadelphia
chapter led almost single handily by
Anna McCurdy (Sterling) was my Savior
that's for sure!
   She brought the relic home
exposing the danger of any future
transportion-
 I'm home safe at last
thanks to Anna's tremendous labor
and outstanding love for me - her
mighty help - saved my life!
   I'm the crown jewel
of America and will remain
in my shrine in Independence Hall
Where I shine in all my glory
   Saved for generations to
honor and admire what I stand
for.

*Dedicated to Anna McCurdy and our County
President William Clinton - all presidents
in the past and those to come.*

The Black Storm Of The Night
by Shane Patrick McDermott - age 20

Lightening paints the picture
Of your face across the sky.
Thunder shudders your words
Through the heavens.
The rain coats my body
With the caresses of your hair.

How distant you are from me,
Like the very storm which rages this night.
Yet I feel your breasts upon my chest
And your soul within my breath.

I exhale in hopes of catching you.
But you descend to the water with a splash,
Falling endlessly in an abysmal rage of blue,
Like that of a stone cast upon the ocean depths.

I am abandoned here,
Left reeling for your touch and strength.
But like the storm of the night
You remain elusive for another eve.

One day I will capture your rage
And frolic in your light and noise
As your love touches my soul,
Like the vary rain which pounds the earth
In the black storm of the night.

James
by Sarah Lynn McCullough - age 14

At one time
I was in love with you
and this love that I felt
I now know this love wasn't true.

I was young and so very shy
you used this to your advantage,
when you were done with me
all you said was good-bye.

You hurt me so much
now I can see,
I thought I loved you
but you didn't love me.

When you left me
It hurt real bad,
but I guess it didn't hurt you
you were not even sad.

Eclipsed
by Shane Patrick McDermott - age 20

On this eve,
As the Earth passes between the moon and the sun,
A great shadow is cast on my soul like that on the moon.

I fumble through my days with great indecision.
Having just lost a lover to only find another,
As if I were supposed to fatefully meet her.
But would fate torture me so?
As this new love promises to only leave me too.

Just as the moon lies in darkness tonight,
So do I.

So many dreams become colorized
In my never restraining, hopeless romantic mind.
Yet they cannot pass through the darkness which enshrouds my soul.
The color is drawn from them in her shadow.
As this new love of mine is color blind,
Blinded by the cruel, tortuous hands of a clock.

For what reason was this beautiful color blind girl brought into my life?
I know not,
But am both grateful and confused by her presence.
As I would rather have those dreams be drained of color,
In her casting shadow,
Then to never be dreamed at all.

My soul has been eclipsed like the moon.
And I must wait until sunlight can shine upon it again,
As with that light which beams into my soul,
So will love.

Providing color to my dreams and warmth to my soul.
And like the moon waits patiently
For the timing in the universe to be correct,
I must wait too.

The Dream
by Kristian McElroy - age 12

I go to sleep at night and I end up in Candyland.

I throw a shinny penny into a lake and I make a wish.

I swim under the water like a fish.

I run up a hill and fly into the sky.

I end up on a raft floating down a river into the moonlight.

I look up at the stars and think, this dream needs my family because they are the most important thing to me.

Rain
by Jeanne McEvoy - age 13

I'll always remember that very day,
It rained so much, I almost cried.
Soaking wet, just standing there,
I saw your face and nearly died.
Puddles and rivers floating by,
Kind of funny, we practically drowned.
I always think of what it was like,
When I hear your voice a soft, sweet sound.
But all the memories washed away,
And they bring back so much pain.
I'll always remember that very day,
Your names reminds me of the rain.

If It Makes You Happy
by Dana McGinnis - age 16

If it makes you happy,
then go ahead and tear out my heart.
You hurt me more by lying and deceiving me.

You think of me as a fool.
One you can play with
and discard when you're done.
If it makes you happy.

You just remember this:
I've been keeping track of all you've done.
Let me tell you this,
You'll get it all back before I'm done.
If it makes me happy.

Him
by Karen McGinnis - age 13

Him.
You want him, but can you have him?
Every day he becomes more and more desirable.
    You know it's meant to be.
Then again maybe not.
You love his looks.
Your feelings go beyond his looks, though.
    There is something inside that tells you he's the one.
People tease you.
People laugh at you.
You feel like you can't even look at him or laugh at his jokes.
But you like him just the same.
    You wonder if what you're feeling is true.
Why feelings are so complicated?
You want to tell him how you feel.
    But you just can't bear the thought of him telling you he doesn't feel the same.
If he smiles at you.
If he teases you.
If he makes you smile.
It brightens your day.
People tell you he doesn't like you.
But it's the feeling deep inside that you just can't let go of.
    You dream of the day when you're together.
Everything is just perfect.
Then you come back to reality.
You say to yourself, it'll probably never happen.
But it's the feeling inside that you just can't let go of.
People Teasing.
People Laughing.
But you like him just the same.

Underneath is all
by Lauren McKibben - age 15

Underneath my exterior,
Underneath my clothes,
Underneath my words,
A special person grows.

I may not be beautiful,
My clothes may not be the best,
My words may not always be kind,
But I am as good as the rest.

If you look underneath it all
You will know it is true.
You will see the beauty inside,
And understand me too.

The River
by Kelli R. McKinney - age 16

Flowing, Raging, Twisting, Churning
Oh, fast, swift current,
Sweep me off my feet.
Take me down, down,
Down into the freezing depths.
Take me to the bridge
Oh, the fatal bridge of sorrow.
Show me why,
Show me why he let you take him;
Among your boulders of death,
Into your ferocious current,
He took his life.
The arch is high and wide
As I look up to this bridge.
Beautiful in stance,
Yet ugly in remembrance.
It frowns down on me, and
Towering over the river, it weeps.
It cries for him, too.
The bridge looms against the sky
Monstrous and treacherous
Yet I cannot pull my eyes away.
I am filled with wonder at its height.
And I can't help but imagine
What it would be like...to fly

Kelly Sean Lynch
May 20, 1977 - August 25, 1996

Lust
by Mark McKone

Madness driven,
Crazed insane.
Running blind,
Running maimed.

Lasting hope,
Driving me insane.
Lost in darkness,
Fog of the brain.

Can't stop thinking,
I am to blame.
Can't help the thought.
I'm burning with pain.

She told me to stop.
But she does not know my name.
I can not help but force her.
I need to feed her pain.

It ends with a scream.
My pain is relieved.
I do not feel the blame,
And I have no shame.

The Beam
by Helen Mc Lean

I'm having lots of trouble
With this beam wedged in my eye --
I simply can't see past it,
No matter how I try.

It hinders me when moving specks
Lodged in the eyes of others,
Leaving a slanted, imperfect view
Of the foibles of my brothers.

Perhaps, instead of looking OUT
To right and wrongs I see --
I should look IN,
Behind the beam,
And start to work on me.

One
by Melissa Anne McMaken - age 18

Running my bath water
I heard you enter the room

You turned off the light
Lit the candles

I kissed your face
Began to undress you

Sitting in the bathtub
I held you tight
As you kissed my neck

Your skin was so soft
My hand began to wander

Our dripping wet bodies
Connected

I whispered
I love you

and we became

One

Wondering Thoughts
by Sherri McManus - 19

As I peered down from the monstrous cliff,
　　the mist slithered under my feet.
Distressing thoughts that were roaming around in my head did not lift.
Rage, anger, and hopelessness were the driving forces that led me to
　　stand upon this cliff here.
"Let's just end it all right here and now," I say,
　　but with that thought, my eyes began to tear.
Like a mad man, my emotions kept rushing wild within me.
My hopes and dreams have now been shattered.
With these emotions, why isn't there a reason to flee?
Rage, anger, and hopelessness sits and eats at my soul, as a corrupting
　　corpse as it lies in a grave.
Fear grows within me,
　　because of this I feel as if I live in a cave.
Here I stand, weighing the idea if I should end it all.
No one to hear me, no one to catch me,
　　all I have to do is fall.
Rage, anger, and hopelessness continues to pierce my body, like a sharp
sword.
"What shall I do?" This is an on going battle.
As I ponder for an answer, my heart is left bleeding and continues to pour.

Anxiety Attacks
by Laura McMillian - age 17

The worried mind that doth possess a mouse
Prevents the rodent's chance at sly escape.
For, when it squeaks inside its little house,
The predator, a snake, prepares its gape.

And as a victim wanders into sand,
He fears he faces genuine demise.
And, when he moves about to reach firm land,
For sure is he in for a grave surprise!

A student sitting down to an exam
Looks through the many pages of her fate.
She panics, and she sees she's in a jam.
She babbles, and she does worse at that rate.

When stress and pressure seize the minds of all,
They kill one's judgment, causing one to fall.

Growing Pains
by Laura McMillian - age 17

Now, seldom will most human beings know
The cause of aches and pains that blow their minds.
For each is like a child who always whines,
But never thinks of what true reasons flow.
What tantrums that small children often throw!
Unhappiness is what each person finds
In many types of pain, yes, in all kinds.
What hurt doth tiny seeds of sorrow sow.
But, as a mother treats her kid's scraped knee
or hubby's heart aches more from cupid's shot
When cancer seizes Honey's frail abode,
There's more than just plain sadness here, you see.
Hurt binds us close together in a knot.
Strange it may be, though it's a linking mode.

Words on a Breeze
by Sheena McNeil - age 15

Poetry is like the wind,
teasing
and elusive,
yet it surrounds us.

Sometimes
like a gentle breeze,
it is light
and happy.

Other times,
like a hurricane,
it is powerful and
harsh.

And all the while
seeming
strangely beautiful
and unique.

Always changing, yet
it remains
Immortal
through all the world.

We love you dearly
by Tara McTeer - age 13

God thought about it hard, God
thought it would be best
If he put you up in heaven, put you
there to rest
You are dead, we all do see
The tragic sting of reality
We often think his actions are unfair
But he did it for your health, he did it
for your care
We love you dearly, we love you much
We are longing for your caring touch
To see you smile, to see your face
No one can ever take your place
Your death was the prick of a thorn
But memories can never be torn
We cherish your memories and your
laughter
We hope you live eternally and happily
ever after
People have told you, people have lied
That your heartache will subside
As the days go on
There is a part torn out of everyone
We pray that you will safely lay
Up in heaven, where you will stay
We love you dearly, we love you much
We are longing for your soothing touch

*This was wrote in memory of my neighbor
Darren Mills after his tragic death
due to a car accident.*

A Good Deed
by Martin D. Meadows, Jr.

Somewhere in time,
<u>good</u> has been served.
<u>Good</u> necessitates nothing
as said it is free;
Saving the savage,
walking or not
among the earth, wind, and sea !!
Success is handed to the one who delivers,
happiness is rewarded
to both who hath quivers.
A smile within comes about from
<u>good</u> thought;
A pleasing accomplishment of care
dare not bought.
An act performed to alleviate
the weary--
<u>Good</u>, inborn to all,
including the dreary.
Without reason or profit
help can be given;
A moment of kindness
engulfing our livin'.
A warm filled heart
pours <u>good</u> through instinct...
<u>Good</u>, is that of
a <u>deed</u> which is done;
from one to another
where other were none !!
...Thanks be given.

Out At Sea
by Myra McTeer - age 12

Here we are out at sea,
just my Dad and me.
The waves crashing against the
boat,
somehow we managed to
keep afloat.
The boat rocks from side to
side,
in the waves we will hide.
Until its time to head on in,
then we will make our
journey again.

School Days and Tears
by Amber Meinhold - age 18

I hate school
Where the mean eyes live
It is where the other girls
laugh at my dress

They taunt
"Wash you clothes, poor girl!"
Why do they say these things?
Washing clothes costa a lot a money.

Money.
Then those girls...
would play with me.
And I would like school.

Run
by Amanda P. Mercado

Man might harm the body, try to kill the spirit;
   with punches, kicks, threats and foul words.
But I asked Jesus to make a way out of no way;
   and Jesus answered my prayer.
He watched over me while I slept;
   when I was rested, He work me up.
When I was down and distressed,
   He picked me up.
When I was lost and felt that I was without a friend,
   God had a habit of stepping right in.
When things became unbearable, He showed me the way;
   To move forward to a brand new day.
I thought, "God gave me a mind that's better than some.
   Who's fault would it be if I don't use it and run?"
Many times I fell along the way;
   but God blessed my every struggle, every day.
He picked me up and turned me around;
   planted my feet firmly on the ground.
He helped me to run through trials and tribulations;
   the need to return often a temptation.
but my mind staid on Jesus, my heart in despair;
   I kept moving forward. Return! I didn't dare.
There were helpful people in front and on both sides;
   Begging "Don't give up, take every obstacle in stride."
So I persevered, kept my hand in God's hand.
   Today I am safe and free ... of an abusive man.

Always And Forever
by Gena Meyer - age 16

Like lonely stars will always be in the heavenly skies,
Is how I want you to look forever in my eyes,
Like a morning bird sings the song of a new day,
Is how much I love you and want you to stay,
Like spring leaves blow in the gentle breeze in the morn,
Is how I'll always be happy that our love has been reborn,
Like the smiles that are brought to everyone at a dance,
Is how I'll always and forever remember the romance,
Like the magnificent brightness of gorgeous diamond rings,
Is how much love your caring heart brings,
Like fireworks need a spark to fly into the air,
Is how much I treasure the thought that you really do care,
Like the colors of a summer sky...pink, purple, and blue,
Is proof that I will always and forever love you.

The Letter
by Melissa A. Miara - age 12

My body trembles slightly
and I rock back and forth, back and forth

Tears stream down my face in rivers and lakes
and the letter becomes a wet mass of paper

The words blur and quiver before my eyes
and the ink spreads slowly, ever so slowly

And my heart feels black and crumpled........just like my mind
As my voice shakes and I bawl loudly

Hearts are fragile living creatures
but to live you must die

I miss the soft touch of your lips against mine
I miss the feel of your hand, grasping mine

I miss your words of comfort
your firm grasp

Did you leave me for another?
My heart burns with jealousy and rage

The rocker creeks as I rock back and forth
staring in to the raging storm

My books are thrown by an
unknown power

A lamp crashes to the floor
shattering into a million pieces.

A lightning bolt seizes control of my rage
and I cry, praying that it is all a dream

Lightning and thunder combine
and a tree crashes through my window, the sharp glass

I fall, still weeping
forever tormented by my rage

Suicidal Ways
by Megan Meska - age 13

I take a bite
and drift away
the rest of the day I merrily play
in a world of my own
I awake in a daze
and slip into a passion of suicidal ways
a bullet in my head
poison in my veins
My heart has stopped beating
or at least it feels that way
say good-bye to ignorance
for I've seen better days
and maybe I'll get over
my suicidal ways

Untitled
by Karlynne P. Micarsos - age 17

O ne's importance is never appreciated until it's gone.
N ew day comes after another.
E ach day should be lovely.

S everal people are honored only when they're dead.
W ise men don't waste time;
E very seconds are valuable.
E veryone should value time;
T ime is gold.

D eath can come anytime.
A short word saying, "SORRY" can make a difference;
Y ou must never believe that there will still be tomorrow.

Ship To Shore
by Jennifer Mihovich - age 12

Someone shipped away to shore
Where no one's ever gone before
The floor was hot, there was no door
The man said never ship to shore
There was not a single store
The same surrounding never more
Don't ever, ever ship to shore.
He wished he could sit down and rest
But never more
He tried his best
A few days passed, not going fast
The man said that this was the last
He's never fed
He wants a bed
No, don't look now
The man is dead!
We hope you learned a lesson
A lesson never more
That you must never, never
ever, ever ship to shore.

Do You Understand...
by Ashley Miller - age 13

Do you understand...
the meaning of love,
the meaning of beauty,
and things there of.

Do you understand...
the reason to cry,
the will to live,
or why people die.

Do you understand...
the people you see,
the future ahead of you,
or the person you will be.

Will you ever understand?
If you said yes, you're wrong.
You'll never truly understand something,
until that something is gone.

When you look back on life,
will you understand?
In your mind, maybe not,
but in your heart, you probably can.

I Am Mother Nature
by Cori Miller - age 15

Yes, I am Mother Nature,
To whom it may concern.
I give power to all things
So it may breathe, grow, and learn.

My features are no mystery.
In my strong hands, you stand.
I shelter you with all power.
My strength?
with it,
I created the
Mother Land.

My silky hair - The rivers that baptized my son, Jesus.

My eyes - The windows into the world.

My lips - Express the thundering cries of joy and pain.

My body - The untamed oceans.

My breast - The giver and nurturer of <u>all</u> living things.

My womb - AFRICA, the alpha of all civilization.

My feet - The path makers for the future and a brighter day.

Yes, I am Mother Nature,
to whom it may concern.
Now you have learned just what I'm about,
and where you stand.

You are my child.
I will love and protect you
As best as I can.

Be not afraid of me,
Letting you fall.
You will always be in the
Palm of my hand.

No Guarantee
by Jolene Miller - Age 14

I've been there before
Though I don't know just how
It seemed real
But is it true this time
I have to know
    No boundaries to cross
No expectations to live up to
How do I know for sure
How can I guarantee
I won't be hurt this time
That this is really the one

Ocean Surf
by Mindy Lee Miller - age 16

Blue crystal waters
Sparkle in the sunlight
the warm tropical climate
Hords the natives near
At each crashing wave
At each in coming tide
at every gull cry
feel myself unwind
all my fears are released
they disappear
not a worry for miles
the out going tide
Uncovers life in the depths of the sea
walking in streams
And rivers, so calm
your lost in a new world
of peace and harmony
only you and nature
I feel the power behind the soft breeze
And the life swimming beside my feet
tickling my toes
As I walk down stream
The birds
The plants
Oh how I love it
Stow away in a bottle
forever in my dreams

Once I was alone
by Robin R. Miller

Once I was alone,
    then you came along.
You wooed me with your smile,
    and held me for awhile.
My life suddenly changed,
    gladly rearranged.
You brought laughter to my life,
    in spite of all its strife.
You made me feel alive.
    I no longer had to hide.
Free to be just me,
    but now you've set me free.
Tears they fall like rain.
    Betrayal, torture, pain.
You say its for the best,
    but so did all the rest.
Once again I am alone.
    Alone and oh so cold.
Go and find your place to hide
    I've nothing left inside.
So this is how it ends.
    Cold and alone again.

Silence
by Afrika Afeni Mills

Silence has the loudest cry
Silence weeps the most bitter tears
Silence feels the shrillest pain
Silence knows the deepest hurt
Silence fills my soul when my voice speaks nothing

When the words won't come
Silence changes my expression
And returns me to childhood
When feelings didn't have names
And words weren't expectations

A friend is one who turns bitter silence
Into sweet laughter
Who finds my smile under layers of doubt
and turns needless worries into trust
to show that their concern for me
runs deeper than the deepest ocean
Whose expectations make me whole

Roses
by Christine Miola - age 18

They are beauty of the meadow.

Their soft tender feel is like the feel of a
newborn baby just entering the world.

Their shrewd spikes cautiously watching.
Their exquisiteness edifying every flower.
They are the beauty in one's heart.

Roses, may they bloom and entice every flower.

No More Words
by Erin L. Mitchell - age 18

Do you dare ask me my opinion
I don't think you know whats in store
unless I'm free to tell you
no words I speak once more

because I see the difference, to me its mostly bad
and seeing it most everyday, I find it awfully sad

Don't dare speak to me
if I find it somewhat slow
the slower that you speak
the less I speak once more

So no more words shall I speak or speak shall I no more
because my words have no more significance
than the lonely man next door
who never speaks nor speaks when spoken for

Speak when I am spoken to only to be polite
not anymore than when I often see the light
that comes closer to me
from any darker night

If you listen closely you'll find my words if you read my mind
but I have to say
only a few are of that kind

So when you speak, speak to my mind
if not, learn to unspeak
or unlearn to speak my kind

because I have no words
and once more
no words you will find.

Carthage
by Chris F. Minshew

On each and every moonless night
I stand in a town that has lost its life.
Wondering where it all has gone;
This is the place that I still call home.
Visions of violence and hatred are here,
People in this town unreadily accept fear.
Once a shy and hospitable town,
Nightly, folks lock their doors with a frown.
I weep at the loss of innocence and truth,
How sad it is when it's noticeable in youth.

"I lay"
by Kristina R. Mitchell

I lay here thinking of our
    past, hoping that our love
will last...
    I lay here with my eyes
wanting to cry ... but all my
    tears are dry...
I lay here with my heart in
      so much pain, waiting &
wanting to be in your arms
    again...
I lay here thinking about
    how much I affected your
life & why you asked me to be
    your wife...
I lay here knowing that I
    love you & I know what I
need to do...
    I lay her with you in my arms
and the love in my heart

Distractions
by Wendy Moeller - age 17

There's so many things happening;
There seems no end in sight.
One keeps on going and living-
Hopefully no wrong and all right.

Work, School, Science; whatever it may be
Seems to use up all of your time.
Then, of course, there's always a tragedy
And one notices the world is full of crime.

You're so naive to think you're invincible,
To think lifelong dreams will be fulfilled.
A vagrant who never forestalled
Their myriad of feelings for whom they would have killed.

No fun; all work and stress. No play.
Suddenly, consternation fills you-
Those you once loved, have passed away.
The facts are elusive; what can you do?

So many distractions have caused you to miss
Those important times filled with salient memories.
Tremulously reaching to give a kiss-
You say goodbye and send them to live in peaceful eternity

The Whisper In The Wind
by Diane M. Money

The sun shines brightly on this day
Gently caressing the child at play
Her merry laugh floats lightly on the breeze
Hiding, though still not masking
The Whisper in the Wind.

The waves roll gently toward the shore
And cool the young woman's soles
As she strolls the ocean's edge
Still, muffled in that ocean's roar
The Whisper in the Wind.

The satin gown trails the chapel floor
As she progresses down the aisle
A vision in white, this bride-to-be
And there, mixed amid the organ chords
The Whisper in the Wind.

The OR lights cast shadows stark and cold
The pains come fast and sharp
Yet through the pain, she oddly smiles
For, heard above her newborn's wails
The Whisper in the Wind.

The rain falls gently on loved ones 'round
Her coffin descends slowly to the ground
Still, amid the prayers and tears
Loving, peaceful strains to hear
The Whisper in the Wind.

If I were a Drawing
by Jessie Montoya - age 15

If I were a drawing what would I be?
Would I be a candle flickering in the dark,
Would I be a rose growing in a field of weeds,
Would I be the sun falling into the ocean,
Would I be a star among the millions,
Would I be a starry eyed, love struck girl,
Would I be a fine porcelain doll in a collection?
No, I would be the caged bird who dreams of the world.

My Secret
by Elizabeth D. Morales - age 17

The figure in my mirror seems so
helpless.
Add another thing for me
to fear.
Disgusted with myself I turn
away.
I guess I must have missed the
single tear.
The eyes around me look with such
dismay.
My trusty mirror yields another
pound.
I gorge myself to fill the
emptiness.
My purge is the escape that I
have found.
The figure in my mirror seems so
helpless.
My weak, frail body holds my secret
sound.
I hide my pain and hold my head
up high.
The pressures in my life have got
me bound.

My Place
by Laura J. Morgan - age 14

This is my place where I can escape the world
Where pain can't touch me, where I am free
Nothing here hurts me, nothing disturbs me
But you took that away
You stole my secrets
Disturbed my peacefulness
Hurt me where I couldn't be hurt
You act as though you did nothing wrong
But you can't understand the many ways you hurt me
You've forgotten how it feels to be alone, defenseless.
So I pretend that I'm okay, that we're okay
But inside I know that I'm not, that we're not
Nothing is or can be okay between us
Because you took away my place.

Ethereal
by Michelle Ann Morone - age 18

Twin drops of white
   fall into the lake of
   moonlight.
Drawn from the crystalline
   sky of tears.
She sits in the silence of
   wonder.
Deep and penetrating the
   starry night.
Cool and crisp winds
   caress milky arms
   resting gently on a
   wide carpet of soft grass.
Dark hair whipping slightly
   across pale skin
Tossing and turning
   floating on swift currents
   of air.
Faintly she breathes life
   into her universe
Where black, twisting hair
   forms the night
   and from soft, pale skin
   comes fluidity.
Reality is born on feathery wings
Away-far away-
Still,
   I dream.

You and I
by Heather Morrill - age 19

You know we get along so well as friends,
yet it's no secret we want so much more.
Each one of us makes compromises and bends;
Each day we open yet another door.
We always kid; we always joke around.
We playfully tease one another.
Through hard times and through all our ups and downs,
We're always there to listen to each other.
We hardly ever fight about a thing.
I always wonder to myself just why.
When we first met and even now I think
We're made for one another...you and I.

Romance
by Ashley Morris - age 17

Rape is such a shame
for the girl feels she is to blame.
Done is his deed,
for all the man contains is greed.
He took away her pride,
yet he feels he has taken a big stride.
The fear is still there,
while he feels he has taken a big stride.
The fear is still there,
while the joy has gone into the air.
He took away her prized possession
and still have not learned his lesson.
He does not care what is lost,
for he will rape her at any cost.
The crime has been done
and only the devil has won.
She will not forget that fateful night.
For what happened was not a pretty sight.
At one final glance
he tossed her her pants.
The words he said
will always be in her head.
If anyone finds out about our little romance
you won't have another chance.
The tables will turn some day
for the raper can not just walk away.
Justice will serve him right
because the girl will fight.

Suicide
by Karen Christine Morrison - age 14

As I lay in the grass and look at the sky,
I daydream of you and call you "my guy".

As I look at th figures that form in the clouds
I see only your face and the smoldering sun, so round.

As I feel my soul drift slowly away,
I cry out loud as I call your name.

As I remember the times that we had,
I think of you crying and that makes me sad.

As I reach the point where I feel the heat of the sun,
I think of my life and ask, "What have I done?"

As my body becomes a speck on the ground,
I realize I'm fading and can't make a sound.

As I see the smoke of the devil's lair,
I scream in my head, "This is not fair."

As I plead for my life, for one more chance,
I feel my soul to my body advance.

As I realize that I'm in a hospital bed,
I know I will live, like the doctors said.

As I hear your voice, I cry out, "I love thee,"
then I realize that you cannot hear me.

As I notice that I can't breathe,
I tell myself it's only a dream.

As I suddenly realize that I'm going to die.
I lay in the grass and look at the sky.

Dreams
by Nicole Morrison - age 16

Life is so painful, you never get what you want
The one I love doesn't know I exist
I love you but you don't care
When I look at you, you look the other way
I want to be with you night and day
When you look at me, I know you see through me
I want you to like me, but I can't make you do
 what you don't want to do
The only time I am happy is in my dreams
When you are holding me near whispering sweet
 nothing in my ear
When I wake up it's another day of living without
 you, with the urge of grabbing you by
 the neck and kissing you passionately too.
But I know that will never happen only in my
 dreams
Now and forever I want to sleep so I could dream
 about you and me being happy...Always

Jamie My Dear
by Ramona D. Morrow

Jamie My Dear,
Please don't shed a tear;
Even thought we are apart,
You will always have my heart.

The five years we've had
Were joyful, never sad:
What memories we're shared
Will always be there.

So Jamie My Dear,
Please don't shed a tear.
The love in our hearts
Will never keep us apart;
Even though we live in different places
God will always grace us.

So Jamie My Dear,
Please don't shed a tear.

My
by Zoe Morrow - age 11

M y
window is my door to the
world. It will show me
places both good and bad.
It will show me the silver
glowing stars as they light
up the sky. It will show
me clear blue water rushing
up against the white sand.
It will show me tadpoles
growing into frog and
babies growing into adults.
But most importantly it
shows me your lonely yet
beautiful face.

Country Love
by Tina Moscato - age 16

Sitting in the haystack thinking about you
Makes me forget about my heart feeling blue
With wilted flowers lying in my hands and hay stuck in my hair
I sit writing this poem thinking of you being here
While Im in the hayloft up so high, I can see so far
At night up here I can see our shining star and I wonder where you are
Sitting in the grassy fields looking up at the beautiful sky
Watching the clouds drift over me to disappear far off makes me think of
 our sorrowful
 good-bye
The wind whips through my hair with the sweet scent of a summer
 breeze
Puts my weary mind at ease
I carefully watch the grass and flowers dance to the suns good-byes
I then remember that this is like the night, dark and cold until I see you
 again then the
 sun will rise

His Glory, Our Gift
by Denise Prevost

One Second you could be here,
The next you may be gone.
Our live's are way to short,
To feel like it's all wrong.
You have got to make the change,
Find your faith and see the way.
The man up stairs,
Would never lead you a stray.
You have got to believe in him,
Each and every day.
His presence is all around,
By the blessings that he gives to you.
Whether they be big or small,
they are gifts to us all.
He lives and breaths,
In everything that you do.
If you ask him for strength,
He will give you that too.
Look in your heart to find the way,
To make your own happiness,
Filled with beautiful sunny days.
Listen to a believer who once,
Had her own share of pain.
Fine the man above,
And you only have his love to gain.

Is It Love?
by Melissa Mulheren - age 18

When we are together,
 all the anger goes away.
When I look into your eyes,
 sadness seems so far away.
When I am in your arms,
 the sense of security comes rushing to me.
When I hear your voice,
 all the danger runs away.
Is it your fault,
 I feel this way?
Maybe I just had
 a feeling of loneliness;
And hoped to find
 a friend in you.
Is it love?
 Yes, I think it is.

Jesus's child
by Andrea Murdaugh - age 16

I stared at my baby,
through tear stained eyes,
I watched Jesus take his hand,
and disappear into the sky,

I closed my eyes,
I could not speak,
silent tears I wept,
as my body became weak,

I shivered uncontrollably,
as I was lead away,
grief overcame me,
and I began to pray,

My dear lord god,
why must this be,
if you are so great,
then why can't you see,

Open my heart,
for I know not what I do,
please forgive me,
as I will forgive you,

His voice came to me softly,
his shadow in the morning dew,
I asked him why he took my son away,
he replied "do not worry, he is my son too."

To Become You
by Nicholas Myers

And if I could paint you,
I'd offer only your eyes as
piece of sky above forgotten cloud.
Vast and rolling, eyes
as rings of open light I'd
gladly dive into -- to become you.

And if I could sculpt you,
I'd offer only your hands as
doves of delicate peace.
Fragile yet free, hands
of sweet subtle relief from
the violence of my mind.

And if I could sing of you,
I'd offer only your voice as
paisley rain to dampen my welcoming brow.
Severe yet affirming, voice
that drips through my skin to whisper
"stay calm...you belong."

And if I could hate you,
I'd offer only to bleed in
broken shadow on distant view.
Hair on fire, I'd bleed just
west of your sense, for fear
you'd see through.

But because I can love you,
I offer only my stance and sense
of your air in perfect time.
Naked and alive, I raise
the roof higher just to grasp the
dust that falls from you.

Can You See
by Denise Moyar

Can you hear the sound of a long and lasting rain,
High in the forest, I know that one feels pain.
Can you see the rain drops one by one, as they fall
To the ground as if in search for someone.
Can you feel the winds dying down and the sound of
A cry, from a silent rain drop sent from the sky.
Can you see the sunlight trickling through, there
Are hints of life here not just gray and blue.
Can you feel the presence around you, it's God's
Greatest gift that so few find.
Can you see it's the littlest things that make
Miracles come true, so if you have faith believe in
The man who knew.
Can you feel in your heart that you can be saved
Just ask in the Lord and he will show you the way.

An Oath to Life
by Cesar Navarro

An oath to life is having hope towards life
but so many see life as an illusion of an
unforgettable past and unknown future; of a life
that could have been and of a life that once was.
But as experiences have shown us, life itself
has a "LAW" the law of life "To Live is a choice
                              But to
                         Die is Law"
Too, many times we have seen,
Too, many times we have cried,
Too, long we have thought,
Too, long we have lived,
But as humans we are neither givers nor lenders
of life; instead we are only the holders not
the owners.
To many think we make life, but life makes us,
We do not shape our destiny; destiny shapes us.

"Inside The Dwelling"
by Connie Neal

The dwelling still stands, but when you knock at the door,
the person who answers, you don't know anymore.

The voice sounds familiar, you've seen that grin,
but nothing's the same when you step within.

The structure looks sounds, nothing seems to be broken,
though the person inside can't remember most words that are spoken.

Eye's fill with tears, it's so sad to see,
though you know in your heart, "Fate's not up to me".

The warmth of the sun pours through the windows here,
and showers of feelings still appear.

Words, filtered through a rearranger,
flow to your ears as if from a stranger.

So hard to stay and listen, to know what to say.
Rest assured, somewhere it's recorded you've been here today.

A hug ends the visit, as you go out the door.
You did all you could, as you've done so many times before.

Caretaker, continue to do what you can,
But, *PLEASE, PLEASE,* remember...."THE DWELLING IS OURS,
BUT THE SOUL'S IN GOD'S HANDS!"

Written for Marianne,
(loving caretaker of her husband who is afflicted with Alzheimer's disease)

Torn Between Two
by Rachel Neff - age 20

I'm torn between two, ones a friend and ones a lover
My heart feels for one and my mind thinks of the other
To make a choice is hard there is only one I can choose
So either way my thoughts, or my feelings I have to lose

My hearts been broken a thousand times before
One more heartache may cause it to be permanently tore
My heart only feels it doesn't think or reason
So if I choose my heart all doubt and insecurity will be leaving

My mind thinks and ponders on every possible explanation
It's cautious and heartless and never looks for salvation
My mind only has thoughts it doesn't feel devastation or pain
So if I choose my mind I will be playing a players game

Torn between two, my friend has my heart and my lover has my mind
Life has dealt me a card that is unusual and unkind
In the end it will come down to one or the other
It's the choice do I want a friend or do I want a lover

I Am
by Lori Nelson - age 17

I am curious and fun.
I wonder about the creatures in the wildfire.
I hear the pandas running in the forest.
I see the sky, clear and pleasant. I want to be free as a bird.

I pretend I am a panda roaming through the forests.
I feel the eyes of a hunter upon me.
I touch the tall, thick stalks of bamboo.
I worry that none will be here in the future.
I cry that I may not live forever.
I am curious and fun.

I understand that I need bamboo to survive.
I say the farmers honey is sweet to eat, too.
I dream I am sleeping in a zoo.
I hope the world will let me live my life, free.
I am curious and fun.

A Noncommissioned Officer's Prayer
by David E. Nettles

Hello Lord, I need to talk,
they say a child learns to crawl, before he learns to walk.
I know the things I value are things not seen or touched,
like freedom of speech and worship in this land I love so much.

Lord, I am an NCO.
Wherever my country sends me, well, that's where I go.
I'd give my life for my country, it's something I have to do
to keep us free as men should be and defend the Red, White and Blue.

Sometimes I wonder about the people I want to help keep free...
For them I'd go the extra mile, but would they do the same for me?
People have changed a lot in all the years gone by,
now they burn the Flag that once they held so high.

Help me to make a difference in the work place or in the field.
Let me lead by example, and integrity be my shield.
Give me strength and wisdom, my duties to help perform,
while I stand beside my homeland as she weathers out the storm.

Lord, I'm no one special yet I must do the best I can,
along with other like me spread throughout this land.
Help us stand up for America, our children and grandchildren to keep free.
God bless the United States, and Lord...Please bless me.

Lillies
by Lindsay Newman - age 12

Lovely lillies
Sit upon the lake
When the sun comes up
Their blossoms awake,
Their lovely satin blossoms
Glisten on the orange-red sky,
Like angel's wings drifting
Through the sky.

How do I love
by Christian Nielson-Buckholdt

How do I love
A warm, beautiful night
The quiet rustle
Of a leafy tree
Sighing so
Contentedly
How do I love
A warm, beautiful night?
I love it as
It loves me.

How do I love
A warm, beautiful night?
Soft breeze flying
Gently by,
Blowing clouds
Past moon in sky.
How do I love
A warm, beautiful night?
I love it like
It were I.

How do I love
A warm, beautiful night?
Diamond stars
Come into view,
To decorate night
Of darkest hue.
How do I love
A warm, beautiful night?
I love it as
I love you.

Happiness
by Beth Noeth - age 16

I once lost a part of my life after I was born. It would rain all the time and the sky, a gloomy gray.

Months went by and I was still the same, depressed and missing my mother. I thought my heart would never go back to one after being broken.

Just when I thought things would never get better, she walked back into my life.

Sooner or later, the rain turned into sun, the sky, a baby blue, and my heart one piece instead of two.

Not long after we met, she gave me a special gift. Something I had lost long ago, something I call happiness!

Dedicated to my biological mother, Michele Cripe. I'm so glad we finally met. I love you.

Forbidden Love
by Amanda Norby - age 17

Your are a precious diamond
Made of perfect oddity,
And filled with wonder.
Your abilities amaze me.

Your solid form is a reality.
Your dazzling smile
And your sensuous charm
Build me in a passionate trial.

But I must bring myself to remember-
Diamonds are a knife to glass.
Only the rich can afford the best,
And I can only dream of sass.

I am a poor, lost, lonely soul
With no direction to move.
In your eyes I am only
A peasant forbidden to your love.

Me & You
by Stephanie Norris - age 13

Me and you are one
We can't help what we've done
Me, I'll give you every want and need
Then maybe we can be together in deed

You drive me crazy when I see your face
You keep me safe with your warm embrace
Me, I love when held close in your arms
When you do there are no alarms

Me, I wish we could be together
And I would be happy for ever
You hold the key to my heart

You are the love of my life
I belong to you
I give my love to you

Three Words
by Kristi North - age 13

Three words are all I want
you to say,
Three words that mean I won't
leave, I'll stay.
Three words that are
true and strong,
Three words that describe my
feeling for you,
Three words that will help
me cope,
Three words that will give
me hope,
Three words that make me
believe,
Three words that help
me achieve,
Three words, that mean so
much,
Three words you can not
touch,
Three words that will let
me see,
Three words that will show how
much you care for me,
Three words that will show are
relationship is true,
    Three words.....
        I love you

Your Life Is A River
by Saana Numminen - age 13

Your life is a river,
    that can run out of water.
Your life is a present,
    that can be taken away from you.
Your life is a river,
    and someday it'll disappear.

Your life is a river,
    that has life in it.
Your life is a wonder,
    that you should guard every minute.
Your life is a river,
    and someday the river dies; so do you.

Your life is a river,
    that can dry every minute.
Your life is a miracle,
    that you should be glad.
Your life is a river,
    that really is important.

Your life is a river,
    that can run out of water.
Your life is a present,
    that can be taken away from you.
Your life is a river,
    and someday it'll disappear.

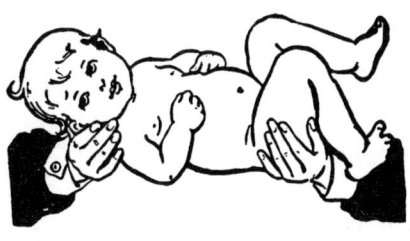

Shawn Jr.
by Kristin Oban

Having so much hair on his tiny head
Soon became his mark
And although I didn't see them
I bet his eyes were just as dark.

His handsome face looked so sweet
As he lay so innocent
His doll size baby body
His fingers slightly bent.

His leg could fit right in my hand
His toes I didn't see
But judging by the rest of him
They're as perfect as can be.

Everytime A baby is born
A lullaby is played
A joyous day it should have been
Instead we cried and prayed.

There was nothing we could do
For our dying newborn son
We had no indication
That his life would soon be done.

I miss him every day and night
And love him endlessly
Though a precious gift he was on Earth
In Heaven he needed to be.

To Mothers
by Tanya Obermyer - age 14

There is nothing quite like it,
No words to describe,
When you see this miracle,
Right before your eyes.
You feel real funny,
and swell with joy,
All you can do is wonder.
Where did it come from?
How did it happen?
In a sense you know those answers,
but when you think about it,
You don't.
Your questions and wonders,
They soon fade away,
As you watch that new baby take its first breath,
and squint those little eyes,
If just for a few seconds all your pain........
They're gone!
A feeling of peace and happiness comes over you,
It's as if your world has stopped in its tracks,
You think your life will never be the same,
and you're right it won't be.
Your world will be different for-ever.
You'll never put yourself first again.
You will have many sleepless nights,
and many hours of endless hell.
But you and I both know,
You wouldn't trade them for the world.
And for that we thank you!

Roy. G. Biv
by Grace Adaku Obikpo

Yours is not the same
As Roy. G. Biv,
My name.

Mine bears an arrow,
That's fixed to the bow,
To shoot down
The Rainbow;
And to learn
Its seven colors;
Reciting
Them as follows:-

"R" begins
Red,
While "O" begins
Orange.
"Y" begins
Yellow,
Like "G"
Begins Green.
"B" begins
Blue,
While "I"
Begins Indigo,
And "V" begins
Violet.

Here are
Rainbow colors, son,
Which also
Analyze the sun.

Question, Answer
by Caitlin O'Brien - age 14

Do you know what
I do not know?
Can you see what
I cannot see?
Will you fell what
I will not feel?
Should you be what
I shall never be?

Perhaps you know
What I cannot know,
And maybe you see
What I don't see.
But I will feel
What you can feel
And I'll be
What I want to be.

In The City
by Rachel Occhiogrosso - age 14

Just seven days past, in the city I came,
with thoughts in my reason of crowds and fame.

Yet of city streets I speak many words,
of filth been seen and curses been heard.

Not grease nor trash as here there be,
do lie at home for eyes to see.

For mucky water does here run,
down filthy streets which there be tons.

Here, buildings are covered with mens' loathsome drawings,
of sickening gang deaths for which they stand mourning.

Beneath all the sketches, there lies brown peeling paint,
while the reek of the sewers will make one quite faint.

The man at the subway, holding cup and his cart,
pleads sweetly, "donations," with hopes in this heart.

Yet, hearts do grow cold, as they scare to come near,
for his stench be repulsive, and this they do fear.
Why be a heart so frozen, as to pain his mind so dear?

Noise one does hear as one walks through lewd streets,
and fumes does one smell, through one's nostrils so weak.

"So this is the city," state I with wonder.
Why does one choose to stay, where horns and guns thunder?

Why be a land of thrill, so vulgar to the eye,
and so putrid to the nose, as this land here where I lie?

To the city I yell, "Good riddance forever."
so, back home I did go, to the brilliant pure weather,
and this I quite fancy, and desire no more!

What's My Name?
by Yom Odamtten - age 15

The butcher is back.
His knife is sharper than before.
He only sees red and black,
He swings his mighty ax.
Cutting by the thousands
Packaging by the millions.

Is this not the beginning of the end?
He leaves the meat to rot.
He's to busy spend any time removing his landmine.
It's very simple, your skin will boil in his big ugly pot.
You hardly can believe it. You've committed no crime.

Yes he offers you a shower, you say yes;
You're so dirty, not just on the outside though, he tells you.
You get in and you feel tired all of a sudden.
Your throat closes on you the person next to you falls down, she's dead
Looking from side to side you realize that one by one they're all falling down.
Finally you fall too.

You look up into his cold hard eyes.
He looks at you with a hunger you've never seen before
You want to spit in his face,
Bur oddly enough your mouth is dry.
You feel dizzy you know that tine is running out
So with your last breath you ask him, "Who are you?"
Before you hear his response you're dead.

"Who am I? I'm the one who takes your family.
I am the one who will follow you wherever you go.
I bring hatred that runs so deep,
I am War.
And I decided to come to your door,
Don't try and run because wherever you go I will be there."

The Importance of Thunder and Rain
by Angela Oesterle - age 18

The experiences brought to you in life
teach us the message in strife
You learn through the hardship and pain
the importance of thunder and rain.

The noise of the thunder lets you open your eyes and see
What should've and could've meant to be
It makes you hear the words that rang in your head
But this time you can determine what is said
The thunder may be soft or loud
And sometimes you are too blinded and can not see behind those dark clouds
And lets you begin to open your heart

The rain is the calming effect
Where you set aside everything and learn to respect
You grow to understand where thoughts and feelings got out of hand
And start to forget about all demands
The midst of the rain eases the matter of who was wrong or right
Eases the questions of who started and ended that first fight
The calm rain cleanse your sore skin
And gives you that one missing piece that you long for within

It's not that you are expected to learn and grow from the noises that comes from the
storms outside
Or forgot about all the times you have sighed
But the messages throughout those harsh storms
Lead us to a better place where your heart can become more secure

Strangers Thoughts
by Angela Oesterle - age 18

She stands completely barefoot on the corner
Wondering why the people passing by ignore her
They have not known the road she had traveled
they have not known how soon her dreams seem to unravel
All they did was stand and glare
All she did was wonder why her life seemed so unfair

She thought to herself, only if they knew
Knew that her life was shattered and torn apart
and right now all she wanted was a brand new start
Another chance to take the remaining fragments of her life
and glue them together to relieve her strife

She thought to herself God had been unfair
He had given her His cross to bare
The cross the everyone seems to carry
The cross that made her life seem wary
She took a long look at her swollen feet
thinking now she knew the definition of defeat

She thought to herself, it is too late to look back
It was now the time to take a step forward and act
She pushed herself to the next street
Knowing that this time there will be light at the end of the road
Knowing that someone else could carry the load
She walked forward and talked to herself
Saying 'they don't know what I've felt'
Saying only if those strangers could walk in my shoes for one day
Only if they knew what other people say
Only if they knew

A Friend In Blue
by Nicole Oliver - age 15

I had a friend once
an angel sent for a short journey
dressed in a uniform of blue
he had a badge for honor and rank
a gun for protection
cuffs for when he arrested
ana a radio to call for help or check 1099
he left behind a wife, a baby son, a daughter, a partner
and friends
he put his life on the line to protect the streets
involuntarily he left this cruel world
he was slain for doing his job
he greeted everyone with a smile and cheerful hello
now only memories remain of this angel in blue
his work completed and now he rests in peace.

*In Loving Memory
    of
Sgt. Gregory K. Martin*

The Light
by Nicole Olney - age 15

The sun's tears seem to stain the day
and the sickening clouds won't fade away.
No matter where our bodies roam,
the Earth we consider as our false home.
We all share this light, we've come to find,
but if we don't hurry we'll be left behind.

Nothing
by Heather Olson - age 16

Nothing you do is good enough.
You try to run yourself
Into the median,
Wishing to end it all.
But you stop,
Thinking of the person
Behind you and his family.
Guilt resides in your heart,
An emotion you know all to well.
Frustration and anger,
Loneliness and self-reservation.
The world doesn't want you,
Why should you want it?
You tell me these things,
And I say:
You are exactly like me.

The Angel
by Sherry L. Olson - age 16

I thank you for having me in your life
for helping me through my troubles and strife
from up in the clouds you were looking out for me
taking me away from the bad things I shouldn't see
in troubles and doubt
you knew what it was all about.
You're my angel from above
and I thank you with love.

Thinking About You
by Sarah Olson - age 17

Here I lay thinking about you,
What can I do to make my wishes come true.
That one wish could maybe come true.
If I knew how you felt about me too.
That's why I lay here thinking about you.
If you knew that I cared,
That I loved,
That I dream about you,
Only if you knew.
When I saw you with her just made me want to cry.
I just asked myself why.
Was she more beautiful than me
Or was I supposed to see.
To see the memories you made with her
Not me.
I just lay here thinking about you,
Maybe my wish will come true,
That some day I will be with you.

My Special Place
by Lillian O'Neal

Close your eyes
and let me take you to my special place.
There's a stream that runs into an old brook down near
a wishing well. An aura about it lends a beauty and magic to this place.
A robin red - breast echoes in the winds of my return. It's my special
place where I might sit and dream. The waters are so crystal clear, that
you can see the fish make ready for the swim upstream. As I bend over
to touch the cool water, a bull frog floats by on a lily pad. Further up
the brook the reflection of a tree that seems to make a bow... then like a
bridge it reaches to the other side. The leaves are shades of minty green,
with drops of water that seem to capture the sunlight from a
dark blue sky above. Just before my evening comes to a
close, I reach into my pocket... take out a penny... toss it
into my well... make a wish and we say good - bye to
my special place not found on any map.

Love Is Blind
by Ashley Orais

Glowing like always, you pass me in the hall.
My stomach jumps, my heart soars, as if it could never fall.

Then I calm down, I realize,
To think of us together, merely to fantasize.

I think you don't like me, but then I know,
I can read the past, it tells me you do, it just doesn't seem to show.

I wonder what is different, after all, it was merely last year,
that when you spoke to me, you were always so sincere.

Something's different between us, a thickness in the air.
The thing that really kills me is, that when I try to talk to you, it's always
your questioning stare.

If only we could be alone, without your friends or mine, I'd ask you what
has happened, maybe as a clue,
Why it is that sparks no longer fly between me and you.

I turn around and see you talking to another girl the way you used to me,
You look me directly in the eye, I guess it is the pain in them that you can
not see.

I guess one thing you've helped me find,
Love my friend, love is blind.

Angel Sarah
by Jennifer Ann Orgill - age 20

You were sent down from Heaven for me to know and love.
Your two tiny "monkey feet" were so cute as you laid
in that hospital crib.
Your little grin has never kept mine away.
Your curly hair and front boingers are something
no one could ever forget.
Your head full of curls is why it was so easy to call you curly.
That day in May is a day I will never forget.
For that is the day we found out you were so sick,
and the day my heart broke into two.
Someday I hope my broken heart will mend,
but know it's up to you my little solider.
I can only hope and pray that this battle you will win.
Your curls are now gone, but with that smile
there is no way I can't smile along with you.
Your heart is full of love and happiness, your soul is strong.
I will always be thankful that I have you to help me learn
and grown and to gain strength of my own.
You and me are a team, two hearts are better than one.
Our love is strong, the two of us can do anything.
Well my Little Angel, I know God is with you
and will be by your side every step of the way.
For he loves you as I love you, keep up the fight little one,
I will never let you down, as you will never let me down.

Him
by Shannon Ori - age 13

Where he walks no one knows,
Where he stops the wind softly blows,
I follow in his footsteps carefully as I can be,
He looks back and sees me hiding behind a big Oak Tree,
He reaches for my arm,
With his smooth, strong hand,
The warmness of his touch warms up all my glands,
Then we walk where no one knows,
Where we stop the wind softly blows,
Hand in hand forever more,
The wind will guide us to my front door.

Lonely Feelings
by Candace Osborn - age 15

I can only write the way I feel. For there is no one I can fully tell my feelings to. I have so many hopes and dreams in my life. However, as I lay here I cannot figure out how some one so simple minded could ever have such dreams. I feel so different from everybody else. I feel because of this difference I am slowly disappearing, I am becoming invisible. The people I could once talk to I no longer can. And the mother that is suppose to nurture and care for me could never care about anyone but herself. And the I love you's I receive are as shallow as the devils heart beat. The only one I can trust is God himself. For he is the only one that truly cares. I am trapped in the horrible feelings I have. I have no one mortal I can talk to, I am alone.

Signs
by Jenny Osborne - age 14

A whisper from God
A touch by an angel
Both of these are signs
That someone is with you.
You don't have to worry
When you're in time of need
Just remember someone's with you
All the way indeed.

A message from the havens
As you strain to hear
You often don't realize
That an angel is near.
There's no need to despair
When there's still a chance
Just look over your shoulder
All you have to do is glance.

Why?
by Kear Ou - age 15

Why didn't you say "I love you?"
"I love you" is what you wouldn't dare.
Why did my heart mend for you?
You who don't even care.
Why can't you stay near?
Stay near like you used to do.
Why can't you still be my lover?
My lover who can turn my dark sky into blue.
Why do you have to leave?
Leaving my heart in pain.
Why do you have to tell me these lies?
Lies that mixed my tears in the rain
Why can't I just get over?
Over all the laughs and memories we had.
Why can't I find someone new?
Someone new enough that will never ever get me sad.

Rememb'rance of Misery
by Jesse Owens - age 17

The war of the past is haunting my mind
The disease in my head you will not find
flashbacks of 'Nam invading my thoughts
Nothing but misery the war has brought
V.C. in my sights as the hammer goes down
Blood in his throat is how he will drown
I have caused this horrible death
The thought will haunt me till I draw my last breath

        Misery of the jungle in my past
        An anger in me that can never pass
        Haunted until I am taken at last
        Rememb'rance of Misery

Distorted memory of an unlikely pain
In presence of this nightmare my thoughts will drain
Blinded by the horror that erases my thoughts
Dislocate the happiness my heart has sought
Misery brought on by the thought of hate
Memory causing mind to disintegrate
Flashbacks of yesterday renouncing my hell
Reminding me of the jungle and how I fell

Across the Miles
by Tracy Jean Owens - age 18

When I left, you told me that a new life would begin.
Every night I say a prayer and I hear you again.
Across the miles your voice finds its way to me.

As I cried you told me that I would be returning.
Everyday I constantly find advice that is reassuring.
Across the miles your strength finds its way to me.

When I return I know that I'll be met by an open door.
Every night I take time to thank God once more.
Across the miles your faith finds its way to me.

As it comes time for me to leave once again,
it will all be as it first began.
Across the miles your everything will find its way to me.

As Time Changes Presence and Tears
by Tracy Owens - age 18

My years as a child were more simple.
My needs were met and my wishes granted.
My presence brought happiness into the world
and my cries relayed what I wanted.

My teenage years were relaxed and free.
My future was bright and my hopes were high.
My presence brought pride into my family
and my cries were oftentimes held inside.

My years as an adult were fast paced.
My success came and my youth slipped away.
My presence brought comfort to those in need
and my cries said what I myself could never say.

My elderly years were slow but few.
My appreciation grew and my spirit remained.
My presence brought patience into the room
and my cries held prayers to see memories maintained.

Sniffles
by Edna Panaggio

Hot water bottle at my head
    And sitting on my pretty bed,
A stuffed up nose confined and ill
I sit and pray, "God, what's your will?"

I turn my head to see the book
    Beyond a mirror shows my look,
so pale and bland and then I wheeze,
I pray, "Dear Lord, some comfort, please!"

The menthol isn't much relief
    Attention on the cold is grief.
and so, the good book says, "Be calm,
just spend this time upon a Psalm."

Just wait and listen and you'll hear
    What God will say within your ear:"
The ear, of course, that isn't closed,
The things I hear, I may oppose.

The self creaps in, "All right I know,
    How can I rest, it's time to go."
Insisting now he says, "I speak
lay low, my dear, for you are weak."

Obedient to God am I,
    I creep below the covers high
to rest and sleep as he has said,
hot water bottle at my head.

Blind
by Kimberly Pappas - age 13

How happy we'd be if everyone were blind
There'd be no difference from one to another
How happy we'd be if the world were kind

How great we'd be if everyone were blind
Everyone would be in the same clique
How great we'd be with no one behind

How perfect we'd be if everyone were blind
Everyone would be equal, happy, and kind
So would you, could you help me find
A way for everyone to act is if they were blind

A Long Hard Fall
by Kelly Pappas - age 13

I can't describe how I feel inside,
All I can do is run and go hide.
My life isn't bad,
No bad at all,
Every step is another hard fall.
Either it's good, Or either it's bad,
I never thought one fall would turn out so bad.
This fall was so bad I couldn't be strong,
I was at fault this time indeed,
That after all it was my turn to plead.
A loud cry for help,
A yearning for love,
And angel was right there,
Sent from above.

The Stream
by Kylie Parks - age 14

She flows through day after day
Careless she often seems
She is reflected on all that surrounds her:
The trees, the rocks, the flowers.
Her water is cold and unyielding
But her spirit is warm and inviting
As she flows on, her water begins to thin
And her carefree rhythm turns to a careful drum
Now she is losing that which keeps her alive
For her carefree spirit must never die.
And so she pours brilliantly on
As carefree as she's ever had be
For streams flow to the river
And river to the sea.

Golden Basket
by Nellie Parratt - age 13

Watch the ball go through the basket,
    golden basket.
The sound that it makes is elastic.
The crowd going wild,
just like a little child.
Standing up yelling, screaming.
The coaches all gleaming.
The players acting mild.
The opposing team mad,
thinking everything is bad.
When the time runs out,
the losing team will start to pout.
Making the playoffs are a doubt.
When they start to think,
    maybe it really doesn't count.
As I make the free-throw,
my team will always know
that it doesn't take much for a show.
You just gotta go
and let it flow.
As we looked to the score,
and saw all the galore,
we thought of the other team, torn and poor.
Then we started to make more.

Who Am I?
by Jaclyn E. Parrish - age 15

Who am I?
I'll tell you who I am.
I'm somebody who never gives up
And always says "I can".

Who am I?
I'm somebody who can't be easily put down.
I'm made of the word "pride"
And I let <u>no one</u> turn me around.

Who am I?
I'm somebody who knows what I want in life.
I don't listen to those who tell me to turn left
When I know all my goals are to the right.

Who am I?
I'm somebody who knows what I want to be.
Learning all that I can
'Cause education is the key.

Who am I?
I know who I am...
How about you?

Was I to Run Away?
by Amy Patzkowski - age 14

As I laid there awake inside of my bed
things twirled around in my head
What was I to do the next day
Was I to run away?
How was I to sleep with head terrors
and who really even cares
What was I to do the next day
Was I to run away?
I needed freedom to live outside of my room
Its like being shoved inside a tiny mushroom
What was I to do the next day
Was I to run away?
I wonder what freedom is like
Is it having fun and riding a bike
What was I to do the next day
Was I to run away?
I had my own car to roam away
But I never went to far anyway
W#hat was I to do the next day
Was I to run away?
I went to school each day and played happy
but inside I felt real crappy
What was I to do the next day
Was I to run away?
The next day I went home with a friend
And I never went home at the end
Oh what was I too do the next day
I had just ran away.

Those Three Little Words
by Anna Pavlik - age 13

When I was young
I once had a love so great.
But he never said he loved me.
Every day for those three little words I would wait.

Upon one eve he came to me and said:
"Here, my dear, is where we must part,
For now I am a Union soldier,
Even though it breaks my heart."

His was not the only heart to break.
For as he spoke I threw myself at his feet
And cried in anguish:
"Do not leave me here alone!"

He kissed my lips
And left me huddled on the floor.
I kept on crying,
As he walked for ever out my door.

Now I am an old woman walking along the shore,
And on the wind they blew,
Those three little words,
"I love you."

Cold Wind
by Rebecca Payne - age 14

Cold wind hits my face
As I try not to cry
For the one I love
Is gone somewhere
And just thinking of
Him bring tears
To my eyes and
Happy memories to
My mind and makes
Me realize now
How much I love him
And if I can wait
Time can help with
The hurt inside.

This Man Full of Mystery
by Rebecca Payne - age 14

This man full of mystery
My heart pounds fast
This man full of mystery
Has such a smooth touch
When he rubs my neck
I seem so relaxed with
Cold chills going down my back.
As his laughter and joy brings
A smile to my face
With hopes and dreams to be with him
All washed away in just a night caused by fear
When will we find peace for those with a tough life?
But until then, I'll just wait till he becomes one.

A Loved One's Death
by Natasha Peak - age 15

It is so sad when a loved one dies
You feel the need to grieve and cry
I know it may not seem fair
Just remember that they're always watching and they still care

You may feel sad and very low
But you have to let them go
Hang on to those special memories
Don't blame yourself and fall to your knees

Crying is okay to do
When you feel the need to
Tears are good for the heart
Especially that hole in that certain part

It was their time to go
So now live your life and grow
It is not your fault because they're gone
You have to be brave and move on

Dreams
by Noamie Peasley - age 15

Dreams are a leaf in the wind.
Blowing by one obstacle,
    but landing on the next.
They are colorful and bright,
    full of love and hope
    and tears and fright.
They can easily reach their destination
    and can be brought down by something
    without any explanation.
It's so easy for them to lose their way,
    but they will reach that place someday,
    if they're proud and strong,
    nothing can go wrong,
Because dreams are a leaf in the wind.

Horse For Sale
by Alana Peery - age 16

She's very gentle,
She has no vices,
She is mine and she loves me.
She jumps and gallops,
She even runs barrels,
She is mine and she loves me.
She's strong,
She's healthy,
She is mine and she loves me.
She's fun,
She's loyal,
She is mine and she loves me.
She's not the fastest,
She's not the shiniest,
She is mine and she loves me.
She's not the tallest,
She can't jump the highest,
She is mine and she loves me.
She'll never let you clip her right ear,
She's too old to win first place,
She's mine and she loves me.
She isn't worth a lot of money,
she is priceless to me.
She is not for sale.
She is mine and I love her.
So don't call this number.

Shadow Ghosts'
by Carlotta The III - age 13

During the neon gold casts off the winter solstice moon,
In the murky swamps of New Orleans,
Lurks a mysterious force, that goes unseen to all but I,
Hidden beneath its cool, serene, listless exterior
Waiting hungrily for me.

Underneath this flawless surface
Is a burning prison wall of chainlinked fire,
But home to those... creatures,
Of a paranoias illusionists' world,
Who know and love me so well.

When the unbearable silence of all quiet is broken,
The waters start to boil and subside,
Making way for wavering, smoky images arising in the thick, blue mist,
That cry and scream my name in vain,
Hoping to enslave me once again. - But I'm not going back.

I'll never again look into their alluring, conspirating red eyes,
For fear of seeing my long lost friends,
Who are now part of it; ever long, part of them.
My memory is vague; it has been over one-thousand years
Since I've been held captive prisoner for those devastating monsters.

The Shadow Ghosts'
Have since taken my immortal being, but they can't
Have my mortal soul. No, not my soul...
For they are too busy seeking revenge on...
The living... me?

I've heard links of disappearances associated
Along these deep, dark, deserted banks.
Along the murky swamps of New Orleans,
I stay breathless, motionless, within these weeping trees,
Because I know they're watching, hungrily waiting, wanting only ME......

Driftwood
by Robert R. Penland

Anchored it's entire life,
the branch supports the leaves
that provide nourishment to the tree.
It's efforts un-rewarded,
new branches emerge above it
taking the sunlight away.
Leaves no longer appear in the spring.
The limb, once a life giver to the tree,
is no longer needed.
An August thunderstorm
persuades the tree to release it's grasp.
The downed branch
rides the current
and is soon at sea.
Drifting, as years go by
it loses it's identity
and arrives on a distant shore,
where passers-by admire its beauty.
Death brought it freedom.
Death brought it beauty.

Phenomenon To Nurture
by Holly Michele Perry - age 17

The innocuous creation
of his body intrigues even
the most apprehensive
dominion of my heart,
contents my lips with laughter,
pervades my eyes with delighted tears.

To muse the deliberation
that such a gratifying endearment
could emerge from the torso
of the most passable of people
is nearly incomprehensible,
and yet I observe with
inquisitive eyes,
the son initially born to me.

Octobers Retreat
by Lisa Peschon - age 16

As the red hot sun,
Goes to play hide and go seek,
For another day,
As the dragon dances in the fire,
And into ashes it goes away,
And as the flames turn colors,
As the leaves in Autumn,
The smoke disappears into the sky,
Where the stars are twinkling,
To catch the human eye,
It is nature's song,
Twas Gods plan,
To listen to the creatures,
The solitude of another octobers retreat.

A Better Way
by Dawn Peters - age 16

A shrill cry cuts through her sleep.
Melanie stumbles out of bed.
Her two-month old has begun to weep.
Another long day lies ahead.

She pays for diapers, food, and daycare.
She works. She cooks. She cleans.
All this because the baby's daddy is not there.
What a life for a girl of sixteen.

All her life she's been disappointed.
She's been let down and she's been wronged.
But by God's mighty hand she's been anointed,
And so she presses on.

Melanie knows her baby's father is gone.
She understands he may never come back.
But Melanie continues on,
She has no time to cry over this sad fact.

Melanie is optimistic.
She's not like any other.
She's refused to become a statistic
Just because she's a teenage mother.

Melanie does well in school.
She works hard everyday.
She has no time to act a fool.
She's busy earning straight A's.

Melanie does all this for her child so beloved and dear.
She hopes her hard work will pay.
She prays and dreams one day she'll hear,
"Thank you, mommy, for making a better way."

Why are some people merciless
by Janna Peters

Why are some people merciless
   I don't why!
Why are some people merciless
   People do get hurt
Why are some people merciless
   They don't have the Lord

Why are some people merciless
   They don't have the Lord
Why are some people merciless
   That is why some people
      Commit suicide

Why are some people merciless
   They don't have the Savior
Why are some people merciless
   They need the Lord
Why are some people merciless
   They need love
Why are some people merciless
   God need to love them

My Grandmother's Quilt
by Ms. Ronnie Peterson, RN, MS

A special spread of love covered her bed,
A warm blanket of love from her toes to her head.

With each piece, her life's story unfolds,
A life of purpose as the story is told.

One piece connects another, to form each star,
Pieces that tell a tale that is the best by far.

The smaller pieces build into an even larger block,
With these pieces, I wish I could turn back the clock.

Each set of blocks highlights memories of a lifetime,
Times of fun and fancy, a time when grandma was mine.

And there, in the corner was my winter dress, a plaid of deep blue,
The dresses that she fashioned, even then made grandma very cool.

A warm winter dress to a child of ten,
And now I only have her memories, for now to transcend.

Positioned in the center was the cloth from my mother's mint dress,
And now, how I miss her sweet grandma's caress.

Recalling the endless summers in grandma's loving arms,
Just knowing there was love, and that there would be no harm.

Now I find myself running my fingers along the quilt seams,
Holding Grandma close in my heart, is the best of all dreams.

In Loving Memory Doris Amanda Desrosier - November 11, 1914 - May 9, 1997

Something Called Love
by Vanessa Peterson - age 17

There are things that can't be understood.
There are things that you don't want to understand.
There are things that have to be understood.

Somethings are meant to be disliked.
Somethings you grow to dislike.
Somethings you can't help but like.

Nothing is the way it is supposed to be.
Somethings just are that way.
Yet nothing is the same when it comes to love.

Love cannot be understood.
Everyone likes being in love.
Love just is what it is.

There is no explaining it.
There is no questioning it.
So it is simple to say "I love you."

Silent Is My Voice
by Paul Pettine - age 17

Silent is my voice, silent are the sound i make.
Only the chosen few can hear the sound of intellect
swarming through their bodies as it seems to always
appear in the height of personal self gratification.
Or is it? Silent is the sound of the earth laughing
and crying like a child of a "deaf" society. I can hear her,
calling my name, calling your name, calling calling
calling!...shhh...this is a library!
It's so strange how everyone is always in the fantasy
section of this elaborate library and all of their books
are over due. What was that you ask? Where am I? I am
in the righteously out spoken section. 99-99 all untitled.
"I'm not even a member" I say to the hairy spider
hanging from the shelf covered in dust labeled American
History. It's ironic.

Foolish Love
by Kate Petzold - age 14

Late last night I was goin' thru some old things,
when I saw a picture of you.
It reminded me of days when you were mine.

You had a way that always left me here with a smile.
I want those sweet days back again.
I just want to share my heart with you again,
but I know I'll never get you back.
You left me never saying why,
never calling or writing.
I thought you loved me,
but I guess I was wrong.

Your life is with something else now,
something I can't relate with.
Your life is nothing to me now.

Now I know we weren't made for each other.
I should have known that a long time ago,
but I was young and foolish.
I thought you'd come back.
I thought you loved me,
but I was wrong.
You'll never love me again and now we'll never even be
friends.

Raven
by Betsi Peyton - age 13

Dark wings blot the sky;
Far below, a girl-child cries.
Mind-sent daggers pierce
An unready past.

Days, years, lifetimes
Are erased and I
Become a raven.

Starving for futures
I devour the world
Screaming defiance.

What Would You Do?
by Christal L. Phillips - age 19

What would you do if the rain
    didn't fall?
If the sun didn't shine?
If the wind didn't blow?
What would you do if I never
    loved you?
Would you pretend not to know?
Would you forget me and
    walk away?
Or would you try to give it
    one more day?
What would you do if I told you that
    I loved you anyway?
    Would you stay?
Or just turn and walk away.
    What would you do
    if I still loved you?

My Mountain
by Elizabeth Pineiro - age 17

He stands,
tall as the mountains high, firm as the land on which we die:
but his legs are weakening, his systems are ailing

He stands,
in silence and solitude, receiving almost no gratitude

From midnight 'till dawn,
He stands,
opening doors for the wealthy, forever wondering if his little girl is
healthy

He stands,
greeting residents and passers by, wondering if his next paycheck will get
the family by

He stands,
with pride and a warm heart; with no shame, knowing that Life has yet
to beat him at It's own game

He stands,
never thinking his job is done in vain,
for he knows in his heart that his little girl will be the one who'll gain

He stands,
praying to the Lord to get him through another night,
so that he'll live to see the day when his little girl will win the fight

He stands,
with two brittle columns as his support,
asking himself why he was forced to lead a life of such poverty,
opening doors for those who call his people lazy.

He stands,
and they don't see his pain and suffering, nor do they see he is
physically dying
They don't realize the Lord is awaiting him, but that's okay, for his soul
continues to grow,
knowing that in the end, his little girl will win

New Day
by Zachary Pierson

A lifeless man
A unborn child
A treeless land
Out in the wild
A star less sky
A new formed star
A waterless river
Out by far
Near by moonlight
Far away places
Blinded eyesight
Unknown faces
Dying sunshine
A new made dawn
Disappearing forest
A new born fawn
A bright sunset
On a glowing moon
A life long dream
A new day is soon.

Here or There: You Decide
by Alicia Piotrowski - age 15

Look! That would be me.
I wish I was there.
See now I'm dead.
Why?
I slept with a stranger
I looked for Babes
I didn't really care about AIDS.
I never asked
I never cared
Now I'm here
I wish I was there
Take a tip.
Learn about AIDS
And other sexual transmitted diseases
If you don't
You don't
You could be here.
Wishing you were there.

Misty Harbor Club
by Quentin J. Plair

Softly cool and mellow tunes
roll around the background
of the misty harbor club.

Lovely, lonesome guests enter
partly to hear the melodious sounds
of the house jazz band—
partly to find someone's hand
to hold for a while.

Sax players send them all
on soul cleansing trips to heaven's outskirts—
providing direction to the peace they're seeking
skillfully imitating a lighthouse beacon
in tune for just a while.

Eyes meet and conversations begin
A few nice moves and cleverness wins.
In a few short moments the fun begins
friendship blooms and loneliness ends
they hope, for just awhile.

Ode To An Alcoholic...
by Misha L. Pippin

There once was a girl, one day in a whirl!
Joined hands, to become the doting wife!

She tried with her might.
Until that crazy night!
All alone sobbing, aching wondering if its right!

She has a beer, in fear.
This time she isn't the dear.
She continues on, not realizing the tear!

Her man finally comes home,
Seeing what's been done, he goes to roam!
Trying to find peace... Hoping it might cease!

He's always full of love, flying like a dove!
Going through life, just to please his wife!

She though when she'd drink
She was immune to that fink!
Only to realize Satan would win,
cuz she continued to sin!

Not looking at the past, as a way to fast
All the worry & troubles she put in hand!

Her man sat for years with all the fears,
of what might happen, if she didn't fit in.

She then met a lady, knowing she'd like AA!
As a brand new way, life could be run.

She found fun in understanding what she'd done!
to realize her sin & one day win!

AA - A way to say she'll be OK!

This poem was written one week after i got sentenced to AA. It changed my life an to this day, I am still not drinking!

Hard For Me To Say
by Robert R. Plaskon

Growing up together was hard; a lot of times even fun, but after all the ups and downs and after all the passing years we stuck together through it all. In best of times; in worst of times and you have always been there for me, even when I didn't ask.....That is why it is so very hard to say goodbye. We both have separate lives now, but I feel I am losing a part of myself. There is so much of you in me, but brother you will always be in my heart. I cannot say those three words back to you that you find so easy to say to me. In my expressions and gestures I do, but you cannot see them.....The destiny of our love is like a feather upon the wind. Even though it's hard for me to say, my love for you is strong. After all that we've been through, I'm so glad you are my best friend.....God is talking to us through letters in the clouds; the wind is changing them. Remember? Is the moon smiling tonight? Just touch near the bottom of your eye and look up. Yes, he is happy! Remember? The stars in the sky are always shining night or day. It doesn't matter. Life still goes on to whatever problems we need to face.....The way to find peace and laughter is to lose yourself in the harmony of nature. I will see twice the beauty when I share it with a friend; that is you brother. Will you still be here for me brother, even when the sea doesn't touch the sand?.....My young body gets weaker as life still goes on; it's my time now. Just replay our memories from your mind and heart and you will never be alone. Thank you for everything but, I must tell you one more thing before I close my eyes.....

   Dear brother, I love you too

My Inspiration
by Mandy Platthy - age 14

When I was oh so very young
I didn't really trust anyone
except I had this special doll
it was lifeless, yet so cute and small
I told it everything I knew
I told it personal secrets too
'Cause I knew it couldn't tell anyone
besides, telling it stuff was fun
Now I have someone real
She can hear and see and touch and feel
So now I tell HER everything I know
but someone please answer me: why'd she go?

What Can I Give
by Carmelita Pobre - age 18

What do you give to someone when you've given them so much?
Please tell me, what do you give to someone as such?
I'd give you a gentle voice to help calm your fears
or a strong heart to help harbor your tears,
but they are prizes that I too, would like to know.
They are precious lessons that only angels can bestow.
We've shared a summer day and one brief Christmas night.
I remember it well, for the memory still burns bright.
And for this I could spare you some more valuable time
so that you might know a memory of your own design.
I might make you a hero in the poems and stories I create,
but I think we'd be happier if I left that to destiny and fate,
because the English language couldn't begin to describe
the wonderful person you are deep down inside.
I could wish you the best of everything,
but those only dear Providence can bring.
I could pass on every dream I ever had.
Nothing on this earth would make me more glad.
You helped so many of my own come true,
adding color to my life, bringing miracles into view.
I could grant you the world and heaven too,
but they aren't my own to offer, so this will have to do-
Better than the moon and the twinkling stars up above,
in the end there's one thing I can give you: all of my love.

Love Is
by Annette M. Poirrier

Love is great
Love is bad
Love is also sad

Love is fine
Love is also another line

Love is sweet
Love is sour
Love is also just a bed of flowers

Love is cherished
Love is perished

Love is special
And no one can take that
Away from you. Love

Friendship
by Annete M. Poirrier

Our friendship was fine, just
like a bottle of wine. We walked
around the park, just like two
doves in the dark. We laughed
and cried about all our good
times. There's one saying I
hope to never forget. Friendship
will stay and you'll never go
away.

Heart Of A Nation
by Jennifer Pool

I am a child of no country and of many at the same time.
I look into the mirror and what do I see? The clear
blue eyes of a Swede?

My skin has a paleness only Scandinavia knows, and yet
my cheeks have the roses of an Irish glow. My hair could
come from anywhere; the dark curls entwine, like a Spanish
peasant girl or a Welsh coal digger's pride.

The questions run around in my mind -- a mutt searching for
signs; a thought which brings me to my personality.

Does my laughter have a Celtic ring? Is my wit a British
thing? From which of my female ancestors did my sentimental
side arise? When I find myself getting on well with the
guys and being practical besides, could I be a Norwegian in
disguise?

Sometimes I feel I have no place born of so many strays. But
then I remember I bear no scorn in a nation of immigrants from
every shore. In this place we are different but the same. We
take the best from every land to build a better one.
This is called America where my roots are sown; the only home
I've ever known. From no country an I torn. This is where I
was born.

Alone
by Francesca Popham - age 16

You see me standing here alone
my shadow is my clone.

I waited for you as long as I could,
just like I told you I would.

You've made me scream, yell, and cry
now all I want to do is die.

You told me you'd always love me so,
now you've left, your love had to go.

Why did you leave me alone like this,
all I can think about is our first kiss.

Now I feel left out in the cold,
you tell me to be strong and bold.

I'll always love you no matter where I go,
But why did you have to leave me here all alone??

Brian Goodell
by Darci Porter - age 16

Riding, you were testing it,
to see how fast it goes.
I bet now this is something
that you wish you didn't know.
I guess sometimes it's wonderful,
to find out how good you are
but not when I want to see you
and I look up at the stars.
The good die young,
is what they always say
if only you were a bad boy,
then maybe you could stay.
Whenever life was bad for me,
you'd always talk me through.
Now that it's the other way,
who'll be there for you?
In my prayers and in my dreams,
you'll always be a part
Now listen to me Brian,
you'll always be in my heart.

*Dedicated to Brian Goodell,
my good friend who died tragically in a snowmobile accident*

Swaying In The Wind
by Cindy Post - age 16

I'm a tree branch
Swaying in the wind
I'm going this way
But wait
Now I'm going that way
I end up in one spot
But I don't stay long
I must go in other directions
Do other things
Meet other people
I don't know where
I really belong
Or where I want to be
It's too confusing
Too frustrating
You want me here
But then you want me there
Just let me wander
And sooner or later
I will decide
Just let me stay
Swaying in the wind

I wish
by Melissa Price - age 12

I wish everybody didn't have to fight.
I wish we could all get along just right.

I wish there was peace everywhere.
I wish we could all learn to share.

I wish violence didn't exist.
I wish people didn't fight with their fists.

I wish everybody had a home.
I wish no one was alone.

Cry
by Mary Pringle - age 13

Ever since you passed away,
I've been lonesome, my dear,
I wish you were still here today,
So I could hold you so very near.

Ever since you went on to an unknown place,
I keep having flashbacks of the smile on your face,
Not a day goes by that I don't cry another tear,
Because losing you has always been my biggest fear.

I wish you didn't have go,
And leave me here even though,
You are safer than you have ever been,
I've go to see you sometime again.

I can't believe you're gone,
Where did things go wrong?
All I can do sit cry,
My eyes are going dry.

Memories of Paradise
by Meagan Pritchard - age 17

How far will my memories go
How long will they last
for days, months, years
or for a hundred thousand miles
A kiss given an eternity ago
... but only a few days passed
Words spoken not long ago
... but already slowly fade away
A face a thousand miles away
... but so close I can almost touch it
A remembered smile, and a long sigh
A last hug, and a kiss that made me cry
we then said our final good-bye
But for how long will my memories last
... how many days until I forget
The feelings I felt
And the brief glimpse of Paradise

Your Picture
by Marjorie Marie Privett

I framed your picture hanging on my wall
There are so many things I now recall
Especially when you came to my home to call
There are other times, I will now tell you all

Did anyone think that I would fall
For this fellow who became my all
That's when I placed your picture on my wall
Oh, how I wish you could come again to call

Since you left some nights I can not sleep
When I think of you my heart takes a leap
My love for you were always ocean deep
Pray that my love for you will always keep

Some nights I wonder through our home
Since you are not here, I feel so alone
At times it's hard to believe you are gone
If time could be recalled, I'd give up all I own

Darling, I often touch your picture on the wall
The features in your face, I can so recall
The love you gave your family belongs to all
It shows in the picture hanging on my wall

All Alone
by Sumie Pruitt - age 15

Dark walls a lonely place
no light to show my face.
My fears are hidden deep within
hidden beneath my biggest sin.
People walk by and look at me
and sometimes wonder why I
cry desperately.
My needs thay cry but no one
hears, why can't they see the
pain in my tears.
Am I lonely at a shallow end
or will someone reach out
and be a true friend?

18 Days Of Hell And Back To Not Heaven
by Pam Puleo

When life ran smooth
   river babbled
      brooks peaceful
         creeks curved
           'round bends
              of wilderness
Those days shared
      in joy
       in peace
          will never cease
            to exist
in memory in experience

The Great Pyramid
by Douglas Punt

Having the best qualities of all before
sits solely for the Archaeologist to adore
against all elements of nature (perhaps even more)
with questions and theory the Archaeologist digs deeper
calculations, summations, hypothetical situations
"Why is this Great Pyramid here?"
deeper, deeper the path did grow
until, to the Archaeologist, the Pyramid did not longer show
the beautiful, strong sight she once did know.

Sisters
by Nicole Pupshis - age 11

Two sisters of love
Two sisters of hate
One uses the other as bait
  -a wish-
Death is it
  Just for her one and only sister
One wishes the other death
  -pushed off a tower-
Sisters who shared
Sisters who loved
Sisters of hatred
  -death-
Silence.
She is dead.
Left for blood thirsty wolves.

Restored
by Kelly Queener - age 15

I'm crying
I'm crying as love falls around my ankles
As burning stars fill my mind
And portray their evershining glory
Against the silver waters
Those contrasting bodies reflect my glory
Inverted
We seek each other, lovers to the sky
Dreaming of
Well-kept worlds of drunken drops
Winding their liquored heads across the fields
Of my mind.
They are fertile.
As water grows the plant
So do rain and tears to me

I cried, I cried for my lost hope
Then I found love
I cried, I cried for my lost love
Then I found myself

But the stars never let fall their woes
Feelings festered on that moon
And when those feelings overtake their fire
To put it out,
It will rain dreams and thoughts
And if our minds are fertile
More than plants will grow.

Guiding Angel
by Lisa M. Quilici - age 16

    For a moment, we are all angels floating aimlessly about this messed-up world we call our own. You sit there as you tune
your harp, but cut your finger on the razor-like string. As your blood drips onto the bloodthirsty ground, the seeds of liars begin
to grow. Then you slide down off your sunbeam and wrestle it back to the underworld.
    For you are a sunbeam in my eyes. Eyes filled with disappointment in our accomplishments. I see your saddened, tired, soul
through window-panes of glass abandoned by its keeper. As I listen to your harmonic voice it speaks the truth, as wrong as it
is. You enter my dream world as a leak enters the ceiling.
    I dive into the bottomless pool formed inside my soul - and notice you are there with me. Though I am not staring at a
human, I stare at an angel holding out his hand to embrace me. I grab for it, but fall right through.
    You show your saddened smile as we return to my bed. It is then, when you disappear into the flickering flame of my
bedside candle on which I pray on every night. Even though my eyes do not see you - my soul does, for you are gliding inside
like a bird.
    Free from this boring and judgmental world.

Ignorance and Wisdom
by Leif Quinlan - age 17

Racism is the beast with fire in his eyes.
He gallops and tramples about,
he is among us, feeding on lies.
His stench reeks throughout.

His face, mangled with burn.
His claws, sharp and precise.
His bite, quick and stern.
His heart, filled with ice.

His will controls the weak.

Freedom is an angel with wings soft as sarcenet.
Her presence, a sweet soothing sound.
She carries us, guiding without abominate.
For in us, her strength can be found.

Her beauty, given from love.
Her breast, warm and soothing.
Her grasp, noble as a dove.
Her will, stout for ruling.

Her strength is ours.

Unmentionable
by Karen Janine Quinones

I went to the park
    To get a piece of mind
The silence was comforting
    Everything was so sublime

I laid on the picnic table
    And looked up to the sky
I wondered where in heaven
    Was my little guy

The tiny clouds rolled in and
    The tiny clouds rolled out
I smiled as I looked toward them
    And saw no need to pout

The sun shined brighter
    Than I have ever seen before
God showed me, that I didn't
    Need to be sore

A large cloud passed and
    It was fluffy and meek
I knew that God was taking care
    Of the one I couldn't keep

Writing Is In My Heart
by Joleen Santos Quintanilla

Writing is very SPECIAL to me,
not too many people know
how PASSIONATE writing is to me.

Writing is a SPECIAL FRIEND of mine,
I share my FEELINGS, THOUGHTS,
EMOTIONS, and LOVE with writing
all the time.

I possess a SPECIAL WRITING TOOL,
as well as a SPECIAL, WRITING PAPER,
that no one could ever see or find;
I write with my HEART; my HEART
inscribes my writing onto my MIND.

I would love to see my writing published,
it's one of my goals,
but to me, the most IMPORTANT, most
SPECIAL thing that matters to me, is
that I wrote with PASSION and
CREATIVITY; a PERFECT PUBLICATION
in my SOUL.

Thought it physically appears to be,
I amy not have the time and place
to write,
emotionally, i do;
for it is in my HEART that I have the time
and it is in my HEART   where I write.

Writing, I have loved
from the start,
WRITING is in my HEART.

Untitled
by Dawn Marie Ramirez - age 18

Softly the rain falls upon
the sullen ground,
the ground which was
bestowed upon us,
for us to inhabit
and make our own.
Full of sin, I am told,
yet left to us,
for we are the ones
left to this
sullen ground that is
so heavily tread upon.

Gently
by Hattie Ramos - age 17

Gently hold my hand
gently touch my face
make me feel as if I'm needed
not out of place
tell me you'll love me, again
tell me your love is within
gently, let me be
something I don't want you to experience
or see
seize me gently
and, tell me I'm yours
something worth wanting
a love that soars

Shining Star
by Richard Rangel - age 18

Night time falls on the fast world.
The many hearts of the people slow down.
The hot concrete cools little by little.

My room is dark.
My eyes are hollow and swollen.
My skin is frigid to the touch tonight.

The rain crowds the street and the night
is longing for the day.
The clouds are heavy and obscure.
My eyes have no answer to my minds questions.

The moonlight envelopes me.
The sky water ceases to fall.
My window shatters into pixie dust.

My body is free to fly beyond the boundaries of walls.
I fly into the cool night.
The sky cotton is fresh as it brushes my face.

My tears have dried and my mouth forms a smile.
I fly in the onyx atmosphere amidst the diamonds of the heavens
and I begin to glow.
My body is a blinding brilliance.
I am a shining star.

Unborn Child
by Amy Renee Rapp - age 14

Just one simple mistake,
The girl said she might.
Now she cannot forsake,
She thought it was right.

She was too young to know better,
The boy said he'd be by her side.
He then went and left her,
How could she decide.

Too young to be a mother & wife,
Her parents told her so.
She chose to end a life,
She did not know.

The child will never cry,
Because of the senseless death.
No frown, tear, or even sigh,
Not even take a breath.

Heart never filled with christmas
cheer,
Or experiencing the break of day.
Or felt the presence of some one
near,
In every time or way.

Never ever going to smile,
The reason we know why.
It only takes a little time,
This child is going to die.

Untitled
by Tamara Rasokas - age 16

A star of power
Of bravery, of love.
A wish for all of us
A prayer for hope,
A hope for prayer,
Uttered in secret depths,
Never heard.
Like a child that cries in the dark
A flower, forgotten and dismissed.
Screams of agony.
Whispers of deceit.
A silent figure,
Watching in the shadows,
Shedding fears
For all destruction.
Nothing ever works.
The best is always ruined,
And the stars have started to fade.

First Mistake
by Hope Ratliff

I only wish you could see
What you are doing to me,
You are breaking my heart
You were right from the start.
Oh, please, give me one more chance
And I will dance my last dance.
Can't you see the pain in my eyes?
You should know love never dies
It just sits to drown in your tears
Gasping for breath year after year.
When I see you my yearning grows stronger,
Even though you love me no longer.
Late at night I can't sleep
All I do is just weep,
For your strong arms to cuddle me; oh, so tight
And your love to guide me through the night.
You love someone else
Which hurts even more.
It hurts so much my heart is sore.
Now my tears turn to blood
And my hurt to sorrow.
You may not love me now,
But there's always tomorrow.
For now give me one more kiss
For old times sake.
Even though that was our first mistake.

A Child In This World
by Hope Ratliff

Should I bring a child into this world,
A world so cold and so hellish?
Would bringing a child into this world
Make me seem selfish?
Do I want a child to live a life like mine,
Where, no matter where I live, there will always be crime?
Do I want a child to run the streets and party all night?
Of course not.
but would I be a good mother?
Would I do it right?
Would my child get by in this world?
Would he pass the test?
Should he live in this world of pain
and suffer like the rest?
Should I bring a child into this world
Where there is so much hate,
Where children are kidnapped every day,
Not to mention being raped?
I would want my child to live up to his dreams,
To be all he could be,
Whatever he does,
I want him to be happy.
That is all that matters to me.

Untitled
by Amanda Rausch - age 12

Everytime I try to remember why said
  "Goodbye,"
My brain can't think, my eyes just blink, and
  I begin to cry.
I think of you with hair jet black, your
  smile a loving grin.
No matter what the argument, love would
  always win.
I think of you with eyes so bright, I go
  blind at a glance, and then I remember
  how it felt to hold you when we
  danced.
The memories are bittersweet, my love for you
  goes on
I even love you more, now that you are gone.

Shaded Emotions
by Drew K. Ravich - age 13

Misty dew engulfs my emotions,
while navy blue skies whisper good night

The golden sun burns my eyes,
silver stars burn my fears

The charisma of the night,
shows the dark side of day and
exhilarates my very being

Untitled
by Bridget Raymer - age 13

The vines in your
eternal soul twist
& tangle, fighting to hold
in your anger & emotions.
to spill your immaturity
swallow it down to your
bottomless pit for eternity.

The Affair
by Wil Raynor

She threw her caution to the wind
And allowed her heart to feel again
The wall came down
And he could see right through

It was just a chance encounter
And they were face to face
A lonely heart and a wounded pride
Met in a crowded place

Their eyes were like two mirrors
Reflecting needs untold
Their bodies spoke to each other
With movements brave and bold

The all consuming passion
Was not to be denied
Self-righteousness and morals
Were quickly tossed aside

Their needs were met together
One wild and steamy night
They each had fed a hunger
As they turned out the light

Hidden Heart
by Shannon Redinger - age 18

  The mysterious image of his eyes I remember distant and leering.
  So many question not answered yet his memory disappearing.
I dread the day that memory leaves my questioning mind for I thought he'd
left behind an unforgettable mark,
Yet still he intrigues me, the shadow of his absence leading me unanswered
into the dark
  His undying love for me that had lived long from our past - I never
understood that feeling and whatever made that last.
Now here he is gone and never to return-
For I shall know nothing more than his heart that had yearn
  I will never have the chance to challenge the passion of his kiss
  It would be the beginning of only one thing I may now start to miss
There will never be a chance for love between me and him
For a love not given the slightest chance could be very dim
  Catching no attention and trying in all ways
  it seems tears last longer and happiness never stays
One thing I knew about this love - it was not meant to be
and more depressing it became when he finally came to see
  As I whispered I never loved him in a shallow sounding breath
  the words put pressure on him creating his own death
Never hope for anything more after someone shatters respect
For the lesson could be greater than any you expect.

Healing
by Michelle Reed

I could lose myself in you.

Actually,
I did once.

I've only just begun
sorting everything
into mine and yours.

The memories of past dreams
fly from my mind
like sparrows.

Driving until there is nothing
but the setting sun.
Covered in the Texas heat
I find that moment of satori
when all things become clear.
I raise my arms to the open sky
in a movement of power

casting off the past.

Each Leaf On A Fern Represents People
by Jessica Reing - age 13

Each leaf on a fern represents people
Each berry on a bush represents life
The flowers from the earth give us beauty
The sun and stars give us light

Now the leaves on the fern are dying
The berries are falling to the ground
As the flowers wilt we are crying
There is no more light or sweet sound

Every being takes its part
In the big round circle of living
Whether it's dead or had a heart
And each has done some giving

Eternal Love
by Alicia Rencher - age 14

You were there from the start,
Unbeknown to my heart.
You were looking out for me
From where I could not see
Then I fell. I fell hard and I fell far
You come out from your place
I was ashamed of my face
I was embarrassed, lost, and scared
You said it would be alright, that you cared
You picked me up and carried me to your place
A place where discrimination and hate are scarce
If it wasn't for you I might still be
In the place I fell for all the world to see
I thank you with all my heart
For looking out for me from the start
I love you with everything found in me
I'll never love anyone else, you'll see
Forever and ever together we'll be.

The Beauty That He Gave To Us
by Richele Jolene Renner - age 20

The beauty that the gave to us
is a comfort to my soul
the calmness of the water
the singing of the birds
the brightness of the sunshine
sends peace to my heart and soul
the beauty that surrounds me near
the beauty that I hear
the beauty that he gave to us
I don't know why he made this place
there is beauty in it's face

The Quest
by Peri M. Rezai

Will I ever complete my restless search
Which leads me onward, I know not where?
From shabby hovel to elegant church,
Hoping to find it, praying it will be there.

Amongst the ancient ruins it may be found.
In modern cities it may be hidden.
So extremely deep, dark, and profound,
That one might think if were forbidden.

Lying eternally deeper than the stroke of a brush
Or buried in a sculptor's tool
Expressing itself in the song of a thrush,
Concealed forever in the heart of a fool.

So long as men shall consecrate their hearts,
In ever beauty shall advance the arts.

Little Girl
by Samantha Rhodus - age 16

Sanity is impressive
she never lets them see her cry
they think she is doing fine
because all the fear she hides.

Her eyes have lost their sparkle
her soul separated from her heart
she never tires, her spirit dies
she doesn't know where to start.

Behind the smile, there is so much pain
no one knows it's there
she goes on, smiling
no one understand or cares.

She has grown up way too fast
a child she's never been
she takes all the blame for it
she thinks she will never win.

Her heart is over flowing
with the pain through all the years
the life drained from her eyes
replaced by unseen tears.

They think she's full of pride
but it's all part of the show
She's just a little girl inside
She doesn't know where to go.

Little girl laughing
Little girl smiling
and when no one is watching
Little girl crying.

Ode To Life
by Tricia LeFevre

When westward winds no longer blow across the gentle plains
And birds soar not to lofty heights on graceful outstretched wings
When man no longer hears the sound of mighty oceans roar
Nor feels the cool refreshing touch of sand along the shore

When time knows not the gentle kiss of showers that come in spring
Nor melodies that calm the heart from songs the robins sing
Nor purple mountains majesty that climb forever higher
Against an azure sky, gold-touched, peaked by a sunlit tower

When earth no longer cradles a newborn baby's cry
Nor shelters life beneath where snowy blankets lie
No longer knows the peace of deepest, darkest night
No longer feels the warming rays that come with morning's light

When all these things have come to pass and sun and moon are dulled
When stars have left their heavenly realm and sounds of life have stilled
When man no longer walks this earth-an earth which once God kissed
Will man look back, reflecting on the beauty he has missed?

Time
by Erica Richardi - age 11

  'Tis true time is lost and never found tis lost with youth.
  Of which pours out of the hearts that are formed of steel and rock,
  Of those people who sin and shed the blood of others,
  Of those who spread thee word of war from the devil to the peaceful world,
  And of those who can't find love in themselves, because their love has been lost with youth and never found.

Finger #5, the Thumb
by Jessica Richey - age 17

Pale pink half moon in a
night sky of pale peach
the horizon is limned
with pale white clouds.

It is tiny, this world,
it's frail and beautiful
yet strong too
it speaks of things unknown.

A single star shines
in the brightening morning sky
it is silent, alone
yet it is triumphant

It sings its sorrow
and its solace
it loves and it hates
it laughs and it cries

It shows us, this world,
our humanity
our strength and weakness
and our own ability to achieve.

A Bag Lady
by Madeline Johnson Ridgway

A bag lady —
transportation bicycle.
Home? Where ever she lays her head.
Worldly possessions?
Bundles tied to a rope,
stacked on a seat
budging all over sides.
Her face? Wreathed in matted grayish hair.
Weary, sad, worried,
she trudges into a grocery store,
eyes downcast.

I hand her a bill.
She asks, "for me?"
Her eyes lit up.
In a sec I see
a tiny smile
in a wrinkled cheek.
Wasn't it worth while
in a life so bleak?
Small bill to pay
for a smile that day.
And then I wonder
what it's all about
and shrug my shoulders
in questionable doubt.

What's In A Name?
by Philip Rippa

Perhaps it was because of those lights
those damn yellow ,incandescent light I was put under
when I was two day old.

Forever under those lights.
The radiation enhanced my growth into
my current status as

Loser.

I often wonder what is in store for me.
Where will I go?
  Who will I be with?
    When will I die?
      Will I go to heaven?
        Does anyone even care?

Pressure, not from gravity or peers
but from inside, wears at my foundation
leaving me shaken and weakened.
Sort alike a faulty cooker.

People, places and things blend together;
too many to keep track of.
But for 22 years, I have muddled through
thanks to friends I didn't appreciate at the time.
Now they are all that I have.

Amen to that. Amen.

Speak Out
by Lori Riscoe - age 15

The lady, who has covered up oh too many times,
sitting in the mirror, powdering a black eye,
planning to escape, as tears roll down her face.

She has forgotten...

That she is not the enemy, she is the victim,
sitting in bed, as her whole body shakes,
out of fear for when he might return.

He did not realize...

The pain and suffering that he was causing,
sitting at the bar, he soon felt no pain, he
would strike again, with his hand clenched tightly.

They did not realize...

That one day, it might be too late,
sitting in the kitchen, not knowing what to say,
to end the tremendous heartbreak.

Final Thought
by Sanya Ristanovic - age 16

She looked up at the sky with eyes so wide full of awe and agony, she realized that life was just a memory.
Whatever she had done in the past had become just that.
Nothing ever made sense to her any more.
She didn't know the difference between reality and dreams.
Everything was a blur.
She blinked hard, trying not to cry, keeping her emotions inside.
She kept saying to herself "I can be strong."
But all of her self-encouragement had no impact.
She began to weep.
She began to think of her problems with life, love, and lack of happiness.
She began to imagine how wonderful it would be to have all that.
Standing on the edge of life itself, she began to sway back and forth in the wind.
Realizing that this was it, her choice was her final one.
The wind blew through her hair as she looked down at the passing river of cars.
Suddenly everything seemed to slow down, the cars, the wind, the birds flying free through the air.
She smiled at the world and let the wind carry her to her final destination.
Before she reached the bottom of her sorrow, she screamed and wished she could rewind time.
Her final though was that life was too precious to waste, no matter how tough it was.
She is no longer in this world; her eyes no longer look with awe, nor cry with anger.
She is gone, but that was her choice.
She took her life thinking it would put her at peace.
It did, forever.

Untitled
by Catherine Rivet - age 16

One man stands
-alone-
At the edge of the world -
The sole survivor of the final battle
Destruction alone is left
An island sits silent, forever desolate
Inhabited only by Death

It approaches
-silently-
A shadow in shadows
-stalking-
Closer, closer, closer

One man stands
-alone-
Walking on the
Knife Edge of Danger

This Is What It's Like To Die... Before Your Heart Stops Ticking
by Teri Rittmann

Bright eyes full of wonderment,
Now turned black with the dying of the day.
Once complete with the gathering masses...
Now the solitude is full contentment.

Old memories return to fill the void--
Like a dull knife stuck-slowing twisting.
Painful cries now rejoiced for...
Although once banished as immaturity.

I would love you now, then & forever,
But the time for healing has soon passed by.
Unseen wounds, no strength left to care for;
The pain still lingers as it slowly rips away.

Feel my friend-deep inside you;
Focus on your reflection in my tears.
Stop--don't speak, words seem useless--
One silent moment of understanding what I never could say.

You feel my sorrow, I see you trembling.
Hold it with you now & always.
Your words now forgotten as quickly as they arrived;
The brief facade displayed caused a lifetime of damage.

My tears are the markings left by those before you.
Not from laughter as I tried to display.
Forever carving my face like burning acid,
But all is forgiven because time has run out.

As I said before - you see now I was right...
Nothing last forever -- not happiness or even the pain.
You're not helping me, so STOP -- or just kill me —
This is what it's like to die before your heart stops ticking!

Miner Joe
by Sheila B. Roark

When the day was over
Joe would head to town
Going to his favorite spot
To drink some whiskey down.

He was one of many men
Who spent his life below
Mining hard from dawn to dusk
To help the silver flow.

So when the day was over,
To the Bucket of Blood he'd go
And watch the dancing girls perform
Their nightly burlesque show.

He needed something in his life
To ease the pain he felt.
So he would drink some whiskey down
Then all his cares would melt.

Disaster struck the silver mine
On one dark, stormy day
As it caved in, it crushed the crew
With stones and bits of clay.

Joe was one who lost his life
The day the mine caved in.
A man who mined the Comstock Lode
Is buried deep within.

The bar seems empty without Joe,
The man who came each night
To drink his whiskey all alone
Until the new day's light.

Comes The Millennium
by Sara Gaye Welch

Comes the dawn of a new age
Comes the seer, sorcerer and sage
Comes the time for all mankind
Comes the time of joy for all to find

Comes the days dawning bright and clear
Comes the nights devoid of fear
Comes the children bright of face
Comes the welcome in every place

Comes the gardens so sweet and fair
Comes the living without any care
Comes the place where all can learn
Comes the fire that does not burn

Comes the tiger with the child
Comes the tame along with the wild
Comes the moon with the midday sun
Comes the warrior without his gun

Comes the language all can understand
Comes the lasting peace upon the land
Comes the fence that will always mend
Comes the tomorrow without any end.

Journey
by Kristin Lynn Roberts - age 13

On this journey we hope to find
what might be called the power of mind
We haven't an inkling of where to look
Only that it can't be found in a map or book
Along the road we pick up things
That in the end will give our heart wings
Will our searching, our prodding serve us well?
Perhaps the answer is that only time will tell
Yet time can be the most difficult thing to spend
But, never seems to be enough in the end
And so our search will go on
Renewed hope with each coming dawn

Love can be........
by Sheri Robinson - age 14

Love can be a razor, not every body bleeds.
Love can be a river, not every body drowns.
Love can be a flame, not every body burns.
But one thing love is, a seed waiting to
flower when ever the moment needs.

Down by The Bay
by Teresa Robinson - age 11

Down by the bay where watermelons grow;
Back to my house I dare not go.

For if I do, my mother will say, "did you ever see a
Moose kissing a Goose?'
or
"Did you ever see a whale with a poka-dot tail?"
or
"Did you ever see a bear combing his hair?"
or
"Did you ever see Llama's eating their pajamas?"
Down by the bay.
DOWN BY THE BAY? OH I SAY!

Dedicated to: a good friend who taught me about poems.

Lonely Heart
by Rosanna Robles - age 14

I used to think it was my fault,
that I did something to you. But
I didn't, I was just there, the
one that would love you always. A
reason just to get close to you,
a chance just to brush my arm
against yours, is what I look
forward to all day. A hug I want
to give you a thousand times, for
a thousands years. A curse is
what I call my love, not a
blessing, not a prayer answered,
not even happiness. Anything I
would do just to hold you near
me, kiss your ear, kiss your neck,
and kiss your lips. I love you,
but no chance will I have,
not even a look you give me.
You are blind of me, but me
not of you. We weren't meant
to be, not even to meet. So
here I am lonely in a corner
thinking of my beloved.

The Mirror
by Alexander Rodriguez - age 17

A man walks alone,
he walks, walks amongst
misery, pain and suffering.
He tired to help others,
and lives with this
because he decides to.

A man walks alone,
he walks with sorrow,
sadness and isolation.
He waits for something,
and lives with
because he has to.

This man looks to help himself now.
This waits for happiness,
and they fall on their knees
to cry
because they are the same one.

Unparallel
by Shalom - age 13

I can't stay here like this, bowing on my knees
To you, I am forgotten, like a lost & cured disease

I have tried to remember what it is I've done
Because now I'm the lonely beggar that you are
sure to shun.

I still love you, though I would hate to remain a part
of your lying, selfish, regretting, & untrusting heart.

Directions To Splitsville
by Jennifer Rollings - age 18

Pack quickly, travel light,
were my hairdressers instructions to me
when I confessed to her that I was having rouble
fitting everything I wanted to take to college into five small moving boxes.

This motto, she boasted, was what had allowed her to leave
three children and an ex-husband back in Wichita,
carrying only a Samsonite and a fantasy of an apartment by the ocean.

Follow my advice sweetie, she said as she trimmed away my split ends,
and you'll be able to walk out on anything and anyone
no matter how strong you feel your loyalties are.
Though consequently, she admitted, she had never had anything
that couldn't fit into a single suitcase.

Keep it light, only the essentials.
A heavy piece o luggage will slow your pace when speed is critical.
but be sure to include enough that a doubt or two
can't find room to squeeze in with your toiletries.
As a general rule, no precious memories or souvenirs—they weight more
with time.
The quickly part is also important: if you draw the process out too long,
you might start to regret all the things you aren't taking,
or begin to wonder why you're going at all.

I'm telling you this, she explained,
seeing as how you're about to go out and brave the real world,
just in case you ever need to get away from a situation
where it'll take more than bravery to get you out the door.

My Mother And The Stars
by Sara Rollins - age 13

My mother was very nice,
she always gave me good advice.
When she died I just
cried and cried.

At night I would stare at
the stars and the moon,
watching them from my room.
I would imagine that she
was on one of the stars,
a star that came from
afar.
A star that came from a
better place,
a star that was nice and
gave her space so she could
look down and see my face.

I wish I could see her
one last time, if not well
that is fine.
This is the end now I must
go, when I will see her again
I do no know.

Friends Forever
by Karen Romanko - age 16

I don't think you ever realized
The day you left the tears I cried.
The way I felt you could never know
Oh, please tell me why did you have to go.

You told me friends forever
I wish it had been never,
And I really hope you know
How hard it was to let you go.

The feelings I am feeling inside
You know you never really tried,
You never could understand me
And I hope that you now see.

You told me friends forever
I wish it had been never,
And I really hope you know
How hard it was to let you go.

Someone else had taken my place
I could no longer look you in your face.
I knew that it would have to end
I don't think my heart will ever mend.

You told me friends forever
I wish it had been never
And I really hope you know
How hard it was to let you go.

And I really hope you know
How hard it was to let you go.

Life
by Amanda Rone - age 13

Once a decade ago
   I never would have
     thought about this kinda
        stuff I would have been
            thinking about Barbies
mommies and daddies

Once a decade ago
   I would have never
     Been thinking about
       these kind of things
         things like Babies,
           money and dead heads

Once ago upon a decade
   I would not have been
     thinking about the
        Big Juicy fat worms
          crawling in and out
            of my ears because
              the coffin was too
                cheap

Cheapness is what killed me
in the first place

My
by David L. Rose - age 18

My body hurts from weary days.
My mind hurts from these years.
My soul is dry from crying.
My eyes are out of tears.
My muscles have all gone away.
My nails have broken off.
My throat is scratchy from the heat.
My hairs no longer soft.
My life is slowly draining.
My sight is all but gone.
My bodies not what it was.
My Gods left me alone
My story has become so short.
My end is where its at.
My skin is caked with dirt.
My voice is dry and flat.
My soul will always know.
My friends that I once had.
My body will not miss,
My life that was so bad.
My hope has left me here to die.
My fridnds have already gone.
My Reaper friend is here, so heres
My good-byes and so-longs.

Untitled
by Librada E. Roseman

Whatever happened to
  "Peace on Earth, Goodwill to all men"
To be a man now seems only a trend!
You can't trust a soul, you don't have a friend
   Tell me my brother when will it end.
              Tell me, Tell me,
   How long must I wait, our children
          are dying, please
                  Open the gate!
Hurry, Hurry, my brothers, before it's too late.
   you see, my sisters are joining you
           in this craze lost game.
We were once loving mothers, busy mothering
         the Earth
Now we live by the grave, tossing in dirt.
Stop living and lying and planning for death.
Start living and loving an look for the best.
   You were created to rule over all on the Earth
   You are King of the Sky
      and Prince of the Earth
Claim what is rightfully yours since your birth.
Wake up what is left of this Peaceful Earth
Stand tall in your manhood my beautiful brother
And soon we will learn to love one another
and give to his earth a new kind of lover
Where no race on Earth,
     Cannot call each one brother.

Silent Assassins
by Tyrone Rose - age 18

   It's been centuries since we have escaped
our last hibernation,
   Opportunity has presented itself, now we will
cause mass destruction on every nation.
   My brothers and I strike in many
forms,
   We can be as silent as a mosquito bite, or apocalyptic
as a thunderstorm.
   We have been known to possess many hosts... human
label them insane,
   We control them to torcher, burglarize, murder
inflicting mortal <u>pain</u>.
   We have had many names throughout the ages,
That's because we have evolved into more powerful stages.
   We have been called Small Pox; wiped out, because
we were not strong enough,
   In time we grew stronger, now it's our time
to erupt,
   And rule this despicable planet, man
call Earth,
   Out plague will take 2,000,000 lives, and create
sterility for no births.
   Their gods blessed them with five senses,
But all will be wiped out with our pestilences.
   Striking as Cancer and Tuberculosis,
Death comes to millions, without any future notice.
   A.I.D.S my brother, which man has yet to eradicate,
To rest in peace will be human's only fate.
   Who are we? That's what you might be asking,
It must be known that we are the SILENT ASSASSINS.

To My First Love
by K. Calhoun

Twice the age at which we met
  Has passed since first I loved thee: and
Thy sweet love is with me yet.
  Thy face dawns clear and fresh before me.

For as thee lie in peaceful sleep
  In the bright morns, so long ago;
My eyes like the sun
  Upon thy face would creep;
And upon it: my love would bestow.

My eyes alone thy lips would trace, and
  kiss thy fair and gentle brow;
And I would marvel at thy grace:
  To leave thy side: I knew not how!

Thy breath to my ear was a
  Wind chime sweet;
As I heard it soft and slow inhale.
  I brushed a hair from thy pallid cheek; and
I begged my hand to be discreet,
  As I rue: my own heart's betrayal.

Like a butterfly upon a fresh bloomed rose:
  I drank thy nectar, pure and sweet.
There has ne're been a time,
  With candor and prose: when
I have loved with a heart: so complete!

Angels' Helpers
by Jan Rothbauer

God's Angels' Helpers are everywhere,
In fact, there is One Special Pair.
With angelic spirit, working so hard,
Following His Word - always on guard.
Angels' Helpers live their life,
Helping others through their strife.
Visualizing beautiful halos 'n wings,
of course, God's Angels' have these things.
Tho' wings 'n halos of Helpers unseen,
tis' positive their Master will redeem;
His Angels' Helpers - a chosen pair,
Entwined their web with love and prayer.
Absorbing with smiles, prices untold,
A selfless quality few behold.
Everyone's blest, with whom they share,
This precious pair of God so rare.

Eye of the Cat
by Philip Anderson Rountree

She moves softly through the emerald darkness
toward me as I awake and stretch.
Our warm caress is interrupted by deep hunger pains
which require action.
Just before dawn we fall still once again to rest,
as the dust off angel wings descends, glistening,
and finally covers us.

Questions
by Basha Frost Rubin - age 12

If you love are you a romantic?
If you see are you not blind?
If you're a witch are you evil?
If you lie are you not telling the truth?
Is everything as it seems?

Electric Woman
by Valerie Josephs Russell

I watch her rise early in the morning.
Going about her chores,
Like a robot electried, always wiping, always cleaning,
Seemingly bombed out on detergent.
She paints, she scrubs and sings as she goes along.

She launders her husbands clothes, cleans up after the
children, wipe their runny noses.
She organizes, she bakes and sautees the beans,
One minute, she is here, the next she is there,
Always doing for someone else.

Everybody expects, but very rarely gives,
So she runs and walks and goes and comes and stands
and bends and looks and listens and gives.
She nurses and nurtures and loves.

She is an electric woman, a wife, a mother, sister and
friend. You may not see her but you hear the tatter of
her feet.
I don't hear her today, oh, nothing is being done today,
neither will she do tomorrow,
because, today is the day, mother pass away.

UnParallel
by L. R. - age 14

I can't stay here like this, bowing on my knees
To you, I am forgotten, like a lost and cured disease.

I have tried to remember what it is I've done
Because now I'm the lonely beggar that you are
sure to shun.

I still love you, though I would hate to remain a part
of your lying, selfish, regretting, and untrusting heart.

Alone
by Krista Rutledge - age 17

Do not stand at my grave and cry.
I don't want to say good-bye.
I need to live, I need to be,
I need to do, I need to see.
I can't just lie here in the ground.
There is no one here, no one around.
I need to be alive and well.
Being here, well, I think it's Hell.
Thinking back, there's a lot that I miss.
The smell of rain, or my boyfriends kiss.
I can't stand being still.
I'm lying here against my will.
I need to talk, I need to shout.
I need to walk and move about.
I can't speak, I can't even moan.
I don't want to be here.
I'm all alone.

Hope
by E. Donald Saari Jr. - age 18

Throughout the seasons, throughout the years.
Throughout all the screaming, throughout all our tears.

We're so very distant, miles and lakes.
When or where? Must have been all the mistakes.

Weeks had no details, no more than just days.
It tore us apart, we've gone our own ways.

The addictions mislead her, she swims in their sea.
Her pain always there.....I wish she wee free.

Now that we've parted, it is hard to move on.
Sadness engulfs her since I've been gone.

She must fight and be strong, her problems she must cope.
I still miss my other, Everyday I must hope.

Memories
by Angela Sabocik - age 13

"My memories will last forever because,
you were my first true love.
The first one I kissed
The first one I truly missed.
I want to fall to my knees and break down and cry when I see you flirting with someone else,
You make it seem like it was all one big lie.
When I had a frown,
You always made it a smile by acting like a clown.
When I was held in your arms,
I knew I wouldn't get harmed.
For me it was always a pleasure,
To be together.
I know you love her but I just can't see,
How you could forget about me.
I miss your bright blue eyes meeting with mine,
God your so fine.
When you broke up with me it hurt like a thorn,
All that I remember was popcorn.
I can't stand
Waiting for you to take my hand.
I never had to wait,
For you to be my date.
I had a tear in my eye,
When you said goodbye.
I will always remember the times we had
Good and bad."

What Should I Do
by Katherine Saffioti - age 12

As I lay in the hammock,
and listen to the chimes,
on a pad I doodle your name,
a couple of times.
As I sit and stare at a picture of you,
I wonder if you love me too,
I see you in my head,
every night as I go to bed,
What should I do,
when all I can think about is you.

What Is Love?
by Joyce Sage

    Conduct a poll on the question, what is this feeling called love?
    You will be shocked and amazed with the answers, for on this subject humans are dumb
    Love is a lasting commitment made between two hearts
    Remarkable in its beauty of which happiness should be a part
    Selfishness and ill treatment prove the love that is yours counterfeit
    Retreat from that battle to find a genuine love that will fit
    Into a puzzle which pictures a scene such as serene tranquil lakes
    If it's dark and stormy, full of pain, you'll know you've made a mistake
    Don't fall into the trap of many, filling loneliness with just anyone
    Then fearing to end the madness to face loneliness once this is done
    Patiently wait for true love, it will find you where ever you be
    Don't rush this emotional Jewel, then priceless diamonds you will see

My Love
by Sheridan Saltus - age 16

Let me tell you about my love
The one I'm always thinking of
He's thoughtful, caring and sweet
And on me he never cheats
He treats me with respect and makes me feel like a woman
He's honest and straight up
I've never found a man who can love me like he can
Who makes me feel special with every kiss
And the moments we share together are filled with bliss
He knows who he is and what he wants
He's a man - who never fronts
Like a wish, he came true
He lifts my spirits when I'm feeling blue
He stepped right out of my dreams
And showed me what real love means
I've never found a man so honest and true
If you told me you have, I wouldn't believe you
Because my man is one of a kind
This kind of love is hard to find
I know because I've searched
And many times I've been hurt
I've always looked for the best
And refused to settle for anything less
This man is mine, I'm holding on
We'll be together forever because our love is strong

Remember
by Virgie McCoy Sammons

    Yesterday Lingers On. Yesterday becomes a memory with pleasant and unpleasant events therein, thus will live on in minds of now, and minds to come.

    The knowledge of events are retained in our minds, this brings us to be more aware the nature of memories we must leave when we pass.

    Whether we intend to or not we do leave memories.

    But in this we never really lose our loved one's, they always seem only a breath away.

    I believe every one's intention is to leave good things to be remembered, for those who care enough to remember. When someone says or acts as though he never made a mistake, I say that person hasn't done anything, just as every one does something good. I've never seen a rose without a thorn.

    Yet no one seems to remember the good in those whose name has been called, but their mistakes are held high and lifted up. I often wonder why?

    Yesterday lingers on, the memories of those gone may be by some miracle what was wished for, yet they may be the opposite of what was intended.

Untitled
by Daniella Samperi - age 13

When I saw you big brown eyes stare deep into mine
I knew then we shared a magic one of a kind
Together day and night your love made me survive
But when you went and broke my heart
I couldn't believe how far you got
You stole my soul, my heart you had
Forever is what you said we had
But forever is nowhere to be seen and you're just a vague memory
Memories of the past is all I have
Your picture I keep beside my bed, wishing you were there instead
I know you're no good for me
Just a heartless man...no human being
But all I can remember is how good we used to be
Maybe this is all a fantasy...what we never had...just a dream
But all I know is you took advantage of my love
Cheated, lied to the heavens above
All I ever wanted is sincere honest man
Someone who understands me for the way I am
I should have recognized the signs
But something about your smile makes me weak
That look you sent when we first met
Our eyes drew close...our bodies bent
But that is so far in the past and we are no longer a romance

"Lost Soul"
by Mark H. Sanford - age 17

Filled with rage, consumed by hate
An angry child lashing out
attention starved, laughed at
labeled as a freak, cast out
he turned to drugs for comfort but they
bit him like a venomous rattlesnake
He never wanted it to get out of hand
but it's too late
He took his life because he couldn't go on.
He was alone and afraid, yet too proud to
get help
He died for no reason.
He felt the time had come to get away
before he caused anymore pain, suffering, destruction.
So he now knows that he is doomed to Hell as a
Lost Soul.

What Does That Say About Me?
(fragments)
by Yaritsa Arenas Sanchez - age 18

I want lips that always smile
Eyes that never cry and a heart of pure gold
I want Beauty that bursts from inside
What does that say about me?

I want Love to flow through my veins (...)
I want a song to sing when there's nothing to do
A poem to write when that song is done (...)
To Love, to Forgive and even Forget (...)
What does that say about me?

What I have is veins that bleed
My eyes have tears that no one sees; that no one will ever see
My lips seldomly smile
I laugh continually (...)
Yet I seldom smile

My heart overflows with regrets
With sadness and "What ifs" and unresolved grudges
It's dull and gray
There's a key hole in it...
It's too dark to look inside, and the key is long lost

Thunder, Lightning and an empty silence fill my days
Moonless skies I see at night
But if you look hard enough, while I sleep
A faint light shines through the keyhole in my heart
A dream has made itself known
One filled with Hope and Love
One that vanishes with the morning
But remains just the same
A dream so close that it's beyond reach

What does that say about me?

Another Day
by Sean M. Sansom

Disparity speaks
Love to wear your pain
You freak
Worthless albatross

Leader to the less
You get excited
When I'm depressed
Cryptic eyed pleasure

Chosen for nothing
How I excel
Success, madness in jest
sobriety words I cannot express

Three Sisters - Annie Ruth, Margaret, and Rita
by Rita Akin Sandlin

Once there were sisters three
Who were close as close could be.

We had fun in many ways
Picnics, wienie roasts and holidays.

So exciting were vacations and camping trips
Where we all gathered to flap our lips

I learned so much from each one
Wash and clean and have some fun.

The last of which was me
With each family I learned to be--

A nurse, a cook of sorts and babysitter.
All these kept me a flitter!

The years have passed and all are grown;
How many family members I've not known.

Would like to have a written line
In my mailbox from time to time.

I Wonder ...
by Stephanie Savage - age 14

Why the earth was made round
When something gets lost it isn't always found
Why certain things happen the way they do
Why all cows have to say moo
Why the world has to end
Why only certain people we can depend
Why people must quarrel
Why every story doesn't have a moral
Why looks are all that seem to matter
Why it seems that I'm always getting fatter
Why love is so real
What it would be like to not feel
There are so many things that don't
exactly have answers
Just like why is there such a thing
as cancer
Whether we have really neat
clothes
Things just happen,
I suppose

The Peaceful Poet
by Jenna Santoianni - age 13

A little girl,
sits in the dark,
of her only refuge,
she is frightened.

For she hears the screams,
of hate and rotten love,
from the mouths of her own creators.

The words ring in her ears,
words of a lost love,
of he said she said,
words that scar her heart.

When the storm calms
she looks at the relics of the war,
smeared mascara,
hot cheeks,
offset tempers,
harsh words spoken,
hearts broken.

Have they forgotten the sweet child,
who waits in the shadows until everything cools?
Have they forgotten how it pains her to see this,
self-centered the least,
for she does not say a thing,
for she knows the end is near,
she doesn't pick sides,
she only escapes to the comfort of a pen and paper.

The Piano People
by Elizabeth Saputo - age 13

When I strike the first note,
When I hit the first key,
My hands take over,
Independent of me.

Nimble and quick,
They sound each note;
Over the keys,
They run, glide, and float.

They work to attain;
Together they strive,
For one common goal,
Each finger alive.

I read the music;
My hands do the rest,
Moving over the keys,
With incredible zest.

As they are working,
Before too long,
You'll hear something unfold,
A beautiful song.

For these music-makers,
Very well understand,
The magic of song.
Now, give them a hand.

Hope You Do To
by Susie Savage

I feel as if
I'll make it
Getting stronger all the time
Weakness is slowly leaving
And I feel more like me
Glad to see the storm passing
Wish all could find their way
Out of their bitter night
Like me

"Empty Inside"
by Shannon Sayson - age 18

Walking in and out, every single day
no certain place to turn; not even home.
Running up and down; which way
no possible choice but to stay.
There's a certain feeling in my heart;
I don't know what it is.
There's a empty feeling in my heart;
no love fills it inside.
Did it burn away; throughout the years?
Did it die away; throughout my tears?
Maybe. The possibilities are endless; of it coming true.
I feel empty inside; no place for anything.
I feel hollow inside; no reason to sing.
Maybe I'll find my true friend and fall in love,
with the boy of my dreams.
Life is too short; shorter than you'd realize.
Life can be long; longer for those who are non-troublize.
Empty inside; fight the feeling.
Hollow inside; I'll find peace and happiness.

We've Forgotten How
by Christine Scarborough

When we were babes
We wee cuddled and hugged
We were secure
We smiled and cooed
When we were babes
We were comforted and loved.

When we were children
Many had hopes and dreams
We were picked up and comforted
When we would fall and skin our knees
Brushing the dust off
We frolicked and played.

During many of the adolescent years
We were encouraged to do our best
We were told to face up to our fears
That God would take care of the rest
When things didn't quite go the right way
Often we would smile and say "That's okay."

But now as adults we've forgotten........
......The warmth and security of a mother's love
...Our childhood hopes, dreams, and bandaged knees
......Those adolescent years when we weren't afraid
to fail.
Problems and concerns now seem somehow more
complex to avail
All because we've forgotten how to laugh.

A Smile
by Angela Scarfe - age 13

White chocolate and cheesecake
dance on my lips in sweet harmony
dancing and singing and laughing
with my best friends for eternity
being alone with my one and only
sweet silence broke with joyous laughter
my favorite songs played loud
throwing myself into the music
a good book that brings tears to my eyes
or a smile to my face

Love Is Like A Cat
by Blake E. Schaefer

Love is mysterious,
Creeping in on little kitten paws.
Pouncing like a tiger
After the kill.

Tearing at our hearts,
Never destroying,
Sometimes taking us apart,
Only if for the while.

Giving us courage through the storm
A bobcat cries,
Far down below,
The panther lies.

Through this the calm will come.
Peace resides,
The tiger gone
And the kitten purrs.

Now we stand like a lion
The storm behind.
Standing as a symbol the golden mane,
Our love forever bound.

I Cried A Tear
by Blake E. Schaefer

A tear I cried.
Not for myself,
Beside myself,
Had I lived a lie?

Little pageant queens,
Like wind up dolls,
Used and thrown away.
A child's or a parent's dream?

Adulterous affairs we see.
Advisors, presidents, soldiers,
The advantage of power.
Their's indeed!

Babies killing babies,
Disillusioned social teens,
On the highways of life.
Killing of three in Tennessee.

Cries from Waco
Vigilante bombers.
Oklahoma wails.
A country mourns.

Comets, Murder and suicide.
That's right!
Hang your head,
You too need to cry.

I've Never
by Jennifer Schafer - age 16

I've never been in love like this before,
I've never liked feeling so out of control,
I've never had anyone love me like you do,
I've never been impressed like I am with you.

I've never believed in fairy tales,
I've never believed dreams can come true,
I've never thought I'd be in love,
As I am so much with you.

I never believed in love at first sight,
I never thought I'd love with such might,
I never thought I would someday find,
A man I wanted to be with all my life.

Clinical Order
by Barbara Schick

The cluttered waiting room
    covered with a veil of gloom
pervades the ultimate word:
    "First come, First served."

An energetic, bouncing boy
    playing with a worn-out toy.
Little sister limp and warm
    lying on her mother's arm.

The pudgy woman in bib apron
    and a shaggy sweater on,
said that she could not abide
    the terrible throb in her side.

A man with greasy clothes --
    car service is all he knows --
with a grimace made of soot.
    He may have a broken foot.

The lanky youth is choking
    back the tears and joking.
Has more pain than he can stand
    under the bloody rag on his hand.

Then opening the door with a grin,
    a well-dressed lady walks right in.
Scented roses follow her;
    shoulders covered with a fur.

The receptionist calls a name.
    Heads raise to hear the same.
One voice answers from the crowd
    followed by a perfume cloud.

In Your Arms
by Laura Schimpf - age 15

In your arms I am excepted, no questions asked.
It's where I am embraced as lazy Sundays pass.

There you give me unconditional love.
A gift never given to me before.
I know I don't have to be afraid.
You'll protect me like it was no big chore.

In your arms I can gather my thoughts
as your fingers run through my hair.
It was here that I wished to sink into you and never be found.
You let me know that you'd always be there.

In your arms you give me the truth and never anything to hide.
You give me more than I ever deserved,
along with the promise you'll never make me cry.

It is here that I sleep peacefully as you whisper words of
sweet tenderness in my ear.
If I awake from a nightmare, you assure me there's nothing to
fear.

I feel that you have healed me.
As I stare into your eyes I know I'm finally whole.
With your support, I now know who I am.
In your arms, I found my soul.

Angel's Kiss
by Jason Schmidt

With her Angel eyes and lips...
She says good-bye and I lose my voice.
We kiss and I cherish her silkened sweet lips one last time.
We look in each others eyes and I never want to stop looking.
The sweet angelic stare from her light green eyes makes my heart
warm and my emotions run high.
To feel her arms around me and know that I will never feel her
warmth again, makes me hold on tighter.
We pull apart.
One last kiss, one last romantic stare.
Our hands slide down each others arm until our finger tips touch
one anothers until they slip away to unreachable.
She gives her angel smile, my heart brightens.
She turns to leave and it darkens.
I watch helplessly as she walks away.
Wanting to say the feelings that run through me, but no words
come out.
Wanting to express the emotions that course throughout me, but
standing there motionless.
I lose my moment with every step she takes.
Scared that her feelings don't run the same way as mine, I say
nothing.
I lose my moment.
My Angel is gone.

The Friend
by Shannon Schlegel

I hope you find
what makes you happy.
Your heart should be filled with love.
to make you smile again,
I'll give up hope on more than friends.
Just to see your eyes glimmer and shine.
With a handful of pennies
and a flash of that dimple;
My trust you've captured,
like no one else can.
It hurts so bad to see you stand
so close, yet out of reach.
Every time I see you smile,
fireworks light up my night.
And I care to much to say good-bye
while just friends is killing me.

Nature's Dance
by Jason Schmidt

The crescent moon shines through the blackened sky.
A voice cries out.
The lone figure sanding by a tree looks over.

The stars burn bright cutting through the darkness.
She sees a lone figure by a tree and calls a name, his name.
She sees him turn.

The clouds half cover the moon and stars and it grows darker.
He barely hears the words.
He squints to see if it is her.
He slowly moves away from the tree.

The wind gusts through the night like an unseen thief.
She calls out again.
She strains her eyes to see through the darkness.

The grass gently sways from the breeze.
He hears her this time.
He waves to her and she begins to run towards him.

The crickets songs cut through the silent night.
She grows closer.
He opens his arms to embrace her.

The crickets chirp love songs, the grass sways to the beat, the wind blows in harmony, the clouds undress the sky to expose the crescent moon and bright stars.

They kiss and fall into the night.

First Light
by Jason Schmidt

Starry eyes looking in the windows.
Seeing the depths of what is usually hidden.
Smiles grow, Tears fall, Fear heightens, Anger deepens,
Compassion flares.

Widen eyes not fully understanding.
Everything that once was known has been forgotten.
Images change, Familiarities dissolve, Intimacy turns to distrust, Rationality turns to absurdity.

Deaden eyes fall away.
Everything known has changed to the unknown.
Everything unknown has changed to the known.
Everything has turned to nothing.

The shades on the windows close.
Starry eyes become no more.

Mother Nature
by Gayln Schnobrich, Jr. - age 19

The blueness of a violet,
the redness of a rose;
The beauty the world posses,
no one really knows.

From the rushing rivers,
to the peaceful lakes;
no human could recrate,
the beauty our nature makes.

Mother Nature the might artist,
a miracle is she;
Never should a moment expire,
we take for granted, the creation we see.

Integrate
by Margaret Scholl

Eccentric mind no spiritual giant,
Knowledge encases flickering light.
Challenge survival from beginning to end,
Our theology, inner prayer, mental flight.

Fashioning bits of self together a problem,
We have become our own vast simpleton.
Gradual growth sprouts through experience,
Requiring lifetime of reflection.

Single honest analogy taste of God,
Becoming average ordinary devotee.
Accepting what one runs from,
With sensitive fluency of sheer reality.

Groping, faltering, fragment splinters,
Matter of striving bridging blur.
Integrating radical before and after,
Making fragile life a great adventure.

God
by Sabrina Schongalla

inspired are we, the ones who witness light,--
who conjure forth the darkness from the otherwise pale night.-

controlling the thoughts of mortal minds,--
believing that what man see he finds.--

forcing outward belief while believings' given none for just,-
we, who cause only fitfully the element of lust;--

commemorative fear and contemptuous false revolts,--
striking emotions we resume with mocking anecdotes.--

grief over mortal loss brings forth laughter when they die,--
a feeling of mocking assailment while watching them soberly cry.-

curiositys' lacking an abundance of humanity,--
using lives as a childs' toy, we enjoy the ruin of reality.--

it's continuing production; the players that we steal,--
we're life's lost hatred, we the souls who cannot feel.--

the guerillas of life, causing pleasures lost--
such minority to us, it's their constant miserable cost.---

the Murderer's Complaint
by Sabrina Schongalla

I have derived these words that
  relay to you, I now
The clues and weapons
the fear in which I speak dismays
  existence.
Our murderers come around to hasten
  pulse.
Each death the killer hopes the
  blood to congeal
  and spill not forever.

The first were death's complaint
  of unsolitary expire
They cry out in agony and
  beg in dire.
And the lives that the murderer
  hath begot,
Pierced sharply at this blade
  they're at.

Should murders' ease to spill not
  this deeply color'd blood---
and keep at bay man's evil deeds,
  those that now appear misunderstood.

wireflyz
by Peter Schranz - age 8

I went to oscarmeyer and I saw a little wire.
NO! It was a wireflire ouch!OOCH!EECH!
OCHE! AAAAAAAAAAAAAAAAAAAA!
it stung me.

Death at the Bridge of Sorrow
by Crystal Schroeder - age 15

Screaming for help
No one cares
It's just a teenage thing
No one helps or comforts
Through tears of pain and loneliness
It's better to bring it to an end
Than to stay and keep getting hurt
Friends or family just don't understand
The pressures of the world
So now it will all finally end

Bridge of Sorrow
by Crystal Schroeder - age 15

Ghosty winds rush under
You hear the sound of a tiny voice
Screaming for help
But no one listens
A gentle breeze softly rushes by
It seems to make me look down
At first I saw only one thing
The watery death bed of a child
Then there it was
A footprint in the mud
Tiny and insecure
But soon another wind rushed by
Pushing the water over
But I knew better than to look again
For just as one soul was already lost
So the footprint has already been washed
                Away
                   Forever...

The Poet
by Stacey Schultz - age 16

So I hear you wrote a poem.
Is it about your new life?
The life I'm not a part of anymore.
So I hear you wrote a poem.
Is it about the setting sun? The sun sets on everything, you know.
So I hear you wrote a poem.
Is it about her fair skin and beautiful features?
Beauty is only skin deep.
So I hear you wrote a poem.
Did you look in the mirror and describe the face?
The mirror has a way of fooling the smartest.
So I hear you wrote a poem.
Is it about the warmth of a smile or an embrace?
I think winter is coming.
So I hear you wrote a poem.
Do you think you have all the answers?
Somethings just aren't good enough, anymore.
So I hear you wrote a poem.
Does it describe the one you love most?
Write in pencil, things change.
So I hear you wrote a poem.
Can it be set to music?
Why is your song silent to me?
So I hear you wrote a poem.
This is one I never want to end
Because when it does, so do we.

I Love You
by Dana Schwartz - age 13

    Someone special came into my
life and I changed. I never thought
there would be a special someone in
my life, until I met you. You told me
you loved me and couldn't live
without me. The night I danced with
you, you held me tight and told
me you never wanted to let go. Now
you're gone I have no reason to live.
You've gone so far away I wish you
would have stayed. You moved on,
on to another school, and probably on
to another girl. It's over between us.
You were all I needed please believe
me. I don't know much, but
I know I love you.

Love
by Tara Selafani - age 14

Love doesn't have to do with colors, and it doesn't have to
do with race, it isn't based on anger, nor hate.

Love isn't jealousy, love isn't selfishness, it can not be confused
with lust, it is one step closer to trust,

Love is honest, but not always fair, love is openness, true
love is rare,

It isn't based on money, it isn't greed, true love is
suicide, love is being by their side,

True love is all I desire, a friendship that's caught fire,

I want the feeling that I'll never be alone again,
I want the love that never dies, gentle, tender, and is not
full of lies. So basically I desire someone to hold me tight
and refuse to let me go, someone who's not afraid
to let their love show.

Run
by Sarah Sebastian - age 13

I run without meaning
I run with desire
It's the rush of wind,
  the wind of wisdom.
   It's the sense of freedom
the sense of escaping,
 and leaving behind every-day life.
    I leave troubles behind
Friends along.
   The sky is my map
Road signs my literature
   As scenery moves-
    I move faster.
When the trees fly by-
   I fly with them.
    I run without meaning,
    I run with desire.

Drink Of Love
by Kevin L. Seely

Squinting and emerged in sin
I wallow.
The smell of love surrounds the challis
in which I swim.
As wildflowers wilt
and rain blankets my thoughts
the smell of lavender filters through
distracting my drowning mind.
Drink, swallow and spit out
this foul taste
which has stained the ground
I have walked.
I love you more
so I say
as the red river flows,
but not
like the truth of a child,
but of the need for my drink.

For Autumn
by Kathi Serr

Down a deep black hole, I reach for you,
  I know you are down there, I hear you,
Crying out, "HELP ME", Please, "HELP ME"
  I circle the hole, grasping for a piece of you,
A hand, your hair, some clothing.

But my hand comes back empty, as your cries,
  Become more desperate, hopeless, to my ears.
I stumble, but I don't give up, as I search for,
  A rope, a pole, a ladder, anything,
To stick down, into the pit.

Everything, is too short, won't reach, can't help,
  To penetrate the darkness,
Where you scream for me, to bring you back,
  Into the light, to mend your heart,
And help to make you strong, again.

I will not give up, for fear that I will lose you,
  And may myself, slip down,
Into the hole, never to return again,
  To live alone, in darkness,
Afraid of the light, forever more.

You must help me, stretch up your arm,
  Grasp my hand, please try,
To meet me half-way, give me a chance,
  To pull you up, out of the darkness,
That threatens to destroy, us both.

Quiet Tears
by Rebecca Servon - age 15

Quiet tears, quiet fears
Baby cries quiet tears
She pretends to be strong
But her eyes fill

She keeps a stare at nothing
And they slip through the sides
Drifting down a soft face
She wants to be held in his arms

He is a poet, He was her friend
Leaving her behind
He says to her

If I could kiss away your tears, I would
If I could sweep away your fears
I'd try
And if all the world was good
You would have no reason to cry

He walks away
The sighs caught in her chest
break free
She had let him take her
heart

What To Do With A Pen & Paper
by Mariel Sewright

No matter how I put the words down on the sheet,
My true feelings aren't expressed ... written thoughts incomplete.
Each word has a meaning all of it's own,
Yet in combination with others it is sown.
Phrases, definitions...<u>All</u> unknown,
Each is taken in the light that it is shown.
To string words in a group, a sentence it makes,
Numbers in a column, there can be no mistakes.
For figures add up the same, unable to lie,
Words & Numbers... The question is why?
If I don't continue, I haven't given a try.
With sincerity the voice of these can buy.
Any wave that passes through your brain,
Not spoken or written is an effort in vain.
To convey a idea to someone else is indeed great,
Yet without communication... What is fate?
A mental abyss... a uncrossable void.
But, to open up & share is bliss enjoyed.
So each time you've been blessed with a thought,
Write it down to capture the quest of which you've sought.
To ensnare the meaning is expression caught,
A high price is clear definition bought.
To simply state your mind in conversation that is vague,
The art of communication has died of the deadliest plague.

Complete
by Heather Seymour

Last night, as I lay in your arms
a whirlpool of emotions rushed through my body
The feeling so unfamiliar to me, I was frightened by it at first
Then somehow it seemed to calm my innersoul, like nothing before
It reached in and caressed my heart,
internally answering to all my desires and dreams
It carried with it an abundance of love, trust and laughter,
accompanied by hints of confidence and pride
I felt it's power and strength
It seemed to somehow touch my bodies every being
The tears in my eyes I could no longer hold back
They rolled down my cheeks as these emotions swept through me
Just as the wind controls the sea on a stormy day
I too was being controlled by this
I was frightened no longer
There was a safe, secure and calming feeling within me now
I felt beautiful, full of pleasures beyond what I had known to exist
It was so pure and fresh
Innocent and real
I felt so much excitement and adventure,
as if I was a little girl again riding a roller coaster for the very first time
I could feel the respect and admiration we shared for one another
It was something I had felt with no other before
As you held me tight in your arms, our bodies connected as one
You whispered to me comforting words of love,
and suddenly it was so clear
The sounds of your voice, the smell of your body, the love in your eyes
All of it, everything
Being with you made me feel whole
What I was feeling, for the first time in my life, was complete

My Mother
by Melinda Shampine - age 13

My mother is my best friend,
she always will be until the end.
I can always depend on my mom,
she's always there when I need her.
My mom don't treat me like a ghost,
thats why I love her the most.
I never see my mom a lot,
work takes up most of the time she's got,
she gives me everything I want.
I love my mom with all my heart and
soul.
Although I fuss and disobey my mom,
every day I hope she knows I still love
her forever and ever.

Untitled
by Ashley Shaw - age 15

Did you know that love is a lie?
A false idol of eternal bliss.
The false moon is bright with hatred and
The essence of a truer glow:
Sweet surrender of glory.
We all act as mannequins?
Yes. The plastic patented smile
Haunts us tonight and forever.
Knowledge is a seed, it grows
And dies with us.
Death is sleep forever;
Peaceful and serenely warm.
The stars shine with an emerald light
As night time drags on.....

Still The Garden Stands
by Shawn Shenefelt - age 20

As time marches across the forgotten plain,
Time, which is lives bane,
Life, like the moon doth wane,
Still the garden stands.

As winter sets its fell hand,
Snow covers the prosperous land,
All colorful things die, from the colds demand,
And still the garden stands.

When war uproots lives simple way,
And when the burning is here to stay,
Destruction is set to play,
And still the garden stands.

Rains of godly tears,
Stop falling throughout the years,
Droughts bring hidden fears,
But still, the garden stands.

Insects with hungry rage,
Eat all the flowers and sage,
Nothing is left out of the cage,
The garden stills stands.

When loves fire is put out,
Love is lost without a doubt,
I'm left to cry and pout,
But the garden in my heart still stands.

The garden in my heart
Wounded by a poisonous worded dart,
Blooms with a vengeful start,
Never wanes, here to stay, through the years, full of rage.

Whin(I*Found*Out)Who*Was*Callin'-
by Philip Sherrod

N'Usin'(Every*Ounce)N'Manipulation(?)-Uv'Her
-(Me*1st*KingKong)N'(Ms.Sex(??)..Come*Back..
Tomorrow/State-N'Gender*I wuz(Taken*Aback!!))
-Shocked(At-th'Degree?)-Yu'(Wud..Contrive*Up!?)?

-For*Position-Er'Advantage/..(Tu*Be..Right!!)??
-But(Bye*now!?)..I(Shud..Have*Learned)That-N'..(
This*World!?)-Greed/Gravity/N'..Depravity(*Knows
*No*Qualms?)-Consequence(N'..(Small*Secrets??)?)

Did-Yu'Think(Yu..Could*OutThink?)-Th*Thinker(??)
Evidently..(We*Both*Knew??)-Th*Answer-Is(No*Dark-
Secret!!)?-Even*If?Yu..Delivered(At..*MidNite/Small-
Gift)?(Tied-Wf'(Red*Ribbon??)-Gold*Embossed/N'Sprayed))

-Wf'Pungent*Scent-Lets*Say..(Sweet-Purple*Violets!!)?
-Ever..Permeating(Mye*Nostrils?)-Even*If..I*Had..Cos-
Metic*Surgery(??)-Like*KingKong(Climbin'Empire*State*Bldg.)
??-Wf'Nostrils*Aflair(??)-Iwud(Not*Think*Twice)About*Makin'

B(N'Neural*Anatomy?)-Even*If..(MYe*GrandParents)Were.Frum*
Aushwitz(??)-Thinkin'(*Twice)..B'fore(Pullin'Famous*Embrace?)
-Dear(?)-Like HeimLich*Maneu'ver(Embrace*Wf'Fee(??)-Paid N'
(Sold*Out!!)?-All*Grades..(Aside!!(?)-I got..JPlus(N'Jeep!!!)?

"Hog's Nest"
by William Shenkenberg

a pig in a poke we'll
make a joke, he drank
beer in this bar, right
from a jar, I know how
it goes a blond has a rose,
when it comes to Blondie,
he clung to the handle this
German knows, I can't hold
a candle, an Italian ate fire
William's not a liar!

One
by Heather Shrake - age 18

Love is crazed,
Love is nervous,
Love is anxious,
Love is relentless,

Who chooses the choice of love,
Who defies the definition of emotion,
A thousand questioned torment the soul,
And yet there's only one answer,

Love is aggressive,
Love is nothing,
Love is life,
Love is absolute,

Who feels the feeling of love,
Who desires the desired of the inside,
A thousand answers torment the soul.
And yet there's only way.

To love...
is to become one!

Holding On
by Kate Siegel - age 14

Your love for me was fading
Mine was doing the same
I was so blind to see
I was the one to blame

Everyday we were together
And everytime we were apart
No matter how hard we tried
We knew one day we'd have to part

We tried to hold on
But both knew it wouldn't work
And now we realize it
It really, really hurts

Someday we'll be back together
I know it in the back of
 my mind
For now we'll have to hold on
 to what we have
And hope that we survive.

The Faces Of Nature
by Sharon A. Silverman

Nearly silent breezes whisper gentle words
fluffy white clouds float effortlessly by
hot bright sunshine warms one's skin
flowers in bloom stretch tall and strong

A fine day for wishes hopes and dreams
moments in the sun make anything seem possible
our thoughts travel to other places and times
if only life were truly so care free

The slow easy winds begin to pick up speed
pure clean cottony clouds take on shades of grey
the sunshine dims then suddenly vanishes
the flowers bend and bow to the brewing energy

Whipping winds now threaten to rip down towering limbs
soft billowy puffs are no more as dark clouds rumble
the sun now history gives way to thundering rain drops
petals of beauty are now torn from their nest

How quickly our angelic world becomes terrifying
time slips away paying no mind to anyone or anything
we seek shelter while nature acts out her rage
we must count the minutes until peace reins again

Was the storm but imagination gone wild
tender fingers of air brush lightly against my cheek
the brilliant sun takes it's place in the clear blue sky
new baby blossoms appear on weather beaten stems

The Earth Mother bestows upon us lush gifts of love
such gifts leave way for us to forget her temper
the drenching tears she wept replenished and refreshed
restoring faith clouds sun and glorious breezes

Pure Luv
by Jason Simon - age 19

Loving someone is not that bad
but sometimes the feelings hurt
they can make you mad or sad
loving someone is all about trust
sometimes you have scenarios
where you will eventually fight and fuss
Loving someone is all about putting pain on the line
the sacrifices you will make
but you will gain wisdom to put the anger behind
and when the hurricane is over
you can analyze the sight of the spark
and you know deep down inside
you will never be apart
from that particular animal or human being
they will show you that it's true
with them in your life
things are better seen
through all of the deceitful things and the drama
I will never love no one else like I love my mama

Abuse And Neglect
by Jacqueline Simpson

She lived a life of fear and shame
Hiding secrets to clear someone's name.
She was small and had little power
No one took time to be the hero of her hour.
People noticed everyday, but said not a word
As they turned and walked away.
Cutting her wrist in desperate despair
Death met her halfway to end the nightmare.
Upon her death they gathered in prayer
With hearts full of pity and their heads hung in disgrace
Sadden for a child alone and constantly afraid.
Deep within themselves the question still remains
Could I have saved her life instead of sharing the blame.

Who Am I?
by Vanessa Elizabeth Simpson - age 14

Who am I in this society
today?
Forced to act, think, dress,
else,
I flee.
I return to my motherland,
and people,
Realizing, my actions should
not be sufficed
to suit anyone else,
but myself.
And that this is where
I belong.
Here, I am not expected
to follow anyone.
I can have a mind of my own,
Become my own person now.
Protruding from behind
the shadows,
I find my inner self and
soul.
Finally, I am proud of
who I am!
Black, Beautiful, Brilliant,
and Independent!

God's Promise
by Rainboe Sims-Jones

Twas a beautiful day and very bright. There wasn't a single cloud in sight.
The flowers were blooming in the sun. Twas a perfect day for summer fun.
Every person from miles around wanted to come to that sunny town,
And on the news the weather-girl stated that the weather was not to be abated.
Dozens of people picnicing at parks. No one at the beach watching for sharks.
Volleyball games and frisbee throws, swimming lessons and a sunburnt nose.
And then on that very sunny day, the sky closed up in a terrifying way.
The cloudless sky turned gray and black, and so everyone ran back.
First the wind blew miles an hour, then came the March and April shower,
of snow and rain, sleet and hail. That one storm would not fail!
The thunder roared and lightning shocked, the clouds cried and the sun mocked
for behind the clouds the sun was locked, and at the dock a ship arocked.
The storm went on for a very long time; more sunrises and sunsets than I could rhyme.
But I know my wrongs and I know my rights, and this storm was at least 40 days and
nights.
So anyway, when it stopped no wind stirred and no rabbits hopped.
But when the rain from the storm dried out, many souls hustled about.
And then the day when came the dawn, a rainbow appeared and shined on,
and a voice spoke down from the sky; twas very odd.
It said, "The rainbow is a promise of God".

Memories
by Cleo Sisco - age 15

Memories of you
Flood back into my head
As I think about the letter
That yesterday I read
I remember all the fun times we had
Even though sometimes were sad
I will forget you never
And remember you always and forever

A note to Billy Whitley

Pains
by Whitney Anne Sivils - age 13

I have a pain inside me.
I can't bring it out for fear of breaking
the peaceful glass.
I have put on a happy face for such a
long time...
such a long time that I am starting to
believe my own lies.
I am falling for my own tricks.
I pretend so many things that I don't know
how to be true to myself.
I don't push myself to be better anymore
Second best will due now.
I feel like I have a whole world to
run around on, but I am tied down,
Now I have limits,
when I used to be free.

Petty?
by Whitney Sivils - age 13

Are we all so petty that we only care about looks?
Can we only see the outside, the outer shell?
Well, what about the inside, the heart, the feelings?

We try to make ourselves beautiful to be noticed.
We all wear the same cloths to fit in.
We talk the same to feel cool.

Are we all just losing touch of the real us?
What are we without the clothes, the make-up, & the mask??
We are people, real people.
Not white or black...
Not skater or prep.
Just people
Bodies & souls all in one.

People choose how to act.
That is what makes them different.
We are just thinking about how bad being different is.
What if being different was "cool"?
Would being the same be bad?!

"Cool" is not an achievement when it is based on your style, it is a let-down.
Being cool because of how you dress reflects on trying to be someone you aren't,
Not greatness.
Be different.
It is the real you, the beautiful you...

Treasures

I am the Sunshine, I am the Rain
by Dawn Sizemore - age 17

I am the light of the world
I bring joy and happiness
when no one else can
I am what shines so brightly
in your eyes
I am what you depend on
I am what you need
I come and go
from time to time
I have to, because like you,
I need to rest too
I am the ball of fire in the sky
I am the sunshine.

I am the darkness to the world,
who bring gloom and sadness
I am what wets the earth, I come softly
sprinkling the flowers
I come brisk and hard, damaging your life
I am what ruins your sunshine day
because of my intense jealousy, I want to be noticed too
I make myself known to the world by wetting it
You cannot get rid of me
I am what you need for life of rainbows
I am the rain

No Turning Back
by Nicole Ann Skurich - age 12

My childhood's gone
But I realized that the hard way
I made the wrong decision
Why not be an "immature" one
They seemed like such babies
I wanted to grow up
And fast
I tried and rushed
I made it here
Unfortunately I just found out
There's no turning back
You learn who is real
Who's fake
You learn about friendship too
But that all came with a price
I have no trust
I have no faith
I closed all exits when I was innocent and free
I turned my back
I never looked behind me
Nor cared 'til today
Now my childhood's gone
If I ever had one I don't rightly know
I locked every door
I lost each key
There's no turning back
No way
No how
No one hears my near silent pleas or
    sees through my lying face.

Growing Pains
by Nicole Skripochenko

My soul seeks out the light.
So many questions still unanswered.
Why is being a teenager so painful?
No more running to my parents for comfort.
Only my friends can provide me with answers.
Sometimes the answers are not what I seek.
Sometimes trouble finds me before I find it.
My head hurts with the puzzle of life.
Wouldn't it be simpler to exit it.
No doors open up for me.
No textbooks prepare me for this.
My soul keeps on searching.

Mother
by Heather Lee Slaven - age 15

Mother your so special
I love you from my heart
You love and care for me
But nothing I give in return
I just can't tell you, I just
can't describe, the thanks I
give to you for giving me my
life. You've done so much
for me you never have let me
down. Sometimes you get angry
But that is understood.
You have never stopped loving me
and I hope you never do.
Your my mother mommy and
the best I've ever knew.

Galway
by Robert Sessions Smilie Jr.

Cobblestone streets are old and hard.
They lay before me like the sea.
The people move as this place,
slow, deliberate, and ever constant.

Here the wind blows cold and hard.
Rolling in with the dark gray sea.
Rolling in upon its child Galway.

But hearts are warm and aglow.
I feel them beating around me.
Alive in this place of the sea.
This place of the emerald isle.

The Hungry Grass drinks in the soft rain.
I drink the warm coffee, and watch
the Ireland I love.

Death
by Christine Smith - age 16

Teens give no thought of life or death
They do not realize they may be drawing their
last breath.
But when the time comes for their
tears to flow,
They wonder where their friends shall
go.
But no one, not one, know the name
or face of death.

Grandfather
by Jason W. Smith

My dear grandfather
Can I cry on your shoulder tonight
Can I whisper my secrets in your ear
Until the early morning light

Can I trust you to comfort me
In all the pain I'm in
Can I believe that you'll love me
Even after I confess all my sins

Will you hold me and say you love me
And tell me that it's just a dream
Because grandfather the way my life is
It makes me feel I have to scream

Will you be there when I die
For I know that my time has come
I hope you can forgive me
And all the things I have done

I love you grandfather
And I hope you love me
And someday when I see you in heaven
We will both be free

Unheard, Unloved, Alone
by Jamie Lynn Smith - age 19

I tell you my problems... you do not
listen.
I scream in the emptiness... yet nobody
hears me.
Yelling my problems to the world...
yet everybody walks away.
I repeat my lyrics till one day someone
hears me... someone listens

I learn to love... then all love is
taken away from my soul.
He shows signs of affection... only
to hurt me in the bitter end.
I try to make you love me... I fail...
and my despair deepens.
I try to make you listen... but you turn
away... my heart shrivels.

I long for someone to hold... and to
be held in return.
For someone to share my dreams...
and my feelings with.
To have someone here beside me... to
comfort me when I'm scared.

To have someone know what I'm going
through... to tell me everything's
going to be alright.
But for me in the end... I am
Unheard, Unloved, and Alone

What Is ?
by Jacquelyn K. Smith - age 19

What is <u>love</u>, but a gift that
two people can share for eternity.

What is <u>romance</u>, but a special
gift that some people have to
share with the one they love.

What is <u>eternity</u>, but two people
spending infinite time together.

What is <u>marriage</u>, but a challenge
to stay in love with the one you
are with till death do you part.

What is a <u>child</u>, but the proof
that two people really do care
for each other deep down inside.

What is a <u>divorce</u>, but a way of
getting out while you still
love each other.

What is <u>death</u>, but a way of God
letting you start all over again.

A Pastor In God's Word
by Kelamenter Smith

God bless this Pastor
and give Him wisdom too
Help him and Strengthen him
When all else fails but you

Feed him with your words
Which is powerful and true
Fill him with your anointing oil
that shines about him new

Touch him with your Holy hand
and spread your love about
Let his soul be overjoyed
by what you have showed him now

Let it be manifested
Deep down in his soul
To offer us a word from Thee
Being a Pastor in God's Word!

The Great American Dream
by Michele I. Smith - age 16

Every race,
Has a different face,
Filled with power, love, and knowing.
But a shield of hate,
Has set our fate,
And prevents these gifts from growing.

As time drags by,
We're born, we die,
But the hatred goes on and on.
Will the killing end,
Will the love soon mend,
Before all Gods races are gone?

It's a painful sight,
When we see a fight,
Between black, white, yellow, and red.
Will the fighting cease,
Will there ever be peace,
Before we fight until we're dead?

Will we ever find,
Our lasting bind,
That will bring us together as one?
Will we have that day,
When we can say,
That racism is forever gone?

Side by side,
We'll walk with pride,
No matter how odd it may seem.
As I kneel today,
I hopefully pray,
For the Great American Dream!

Phoenix Rise
by Rebecca Smolcich

Rise Feat Phoenix
From the ashes of yourself
Spread your crimson wings in glory
And revel in the freedom
You are reborn
Life is yours forever
Screams of triumph
Echo through the infinite sky

Rise Great Phoenix
To soar upon the winds of time
Most magnificent
Of her creations
All others are dim
Beside your brilliance
Master of thine own destiny
Burning brighter than the sun

Rise Great Phoenix
And then descend
Relight the pyre
'Tis time, once again, to go
Vicious circle
Round and round
To end, for you,
Is to begin anew

Self-Admiration
by Olivia Somes - age 17

What does an outsider do with an inside perspective?
She mocks the inside with judgment and
watches the outside from the outside.

She is between a middleless game she is unpurposely
playing like a accidental birth.
Her eyes are perfect yet far-sighted.

She just imagines all the casts until she is a castaway,
abandoned in a crowded space.
She wishes for things that are to easy.

She ages as a baby and spoils with useless integrity.
She conquers what she already owns and
she loves what she cannot identify as a illusion.

Is it all worth the effort of her soul or is it just
the weak striving for something weaker
in purity and lost from intimacy.

Energy is all she has left, what will she endure with it.
Will it be the inside or the outside.
But it all just inflicts more pain where she has no immune system.
Then on one relaxed day she finds
what she has endured so much to find, realization.

So that feeling comes to heart,
she has that feeling of a survivor.
Everyone who survives that internal death they placed feels it engraved
in them.

The Truth
by Regina Camille Sommers - age 12

People look at each other
For the color of their skin
Not for their skin
Not for their heart
That is deep within.

Black and white,
What is the difference.
We are both talented,
We are both smart,
We are all striving,
To find the right path
For our future to last.

We are both happy when we are glad,
We both cry when we are sad.
Killing each other
For the color their skin,
It shows no decency,
They just can't see.
I hope you read this,
For you will find
That color is blind!!!

My Yellow Flower
by Paula J. Spark - age 13

The world is black
The land is dark
Wishing that God
Would make his mark

I look some more
A bright light ahead
Everything else
Seems to be dead

I get closer
Till I'm nearly blind
I stare at this
My new found find

It shines so bright
It lights the earth
Giving each and every
Thing new birth

It is so pretty
It gives all power
It is a beautiful
Yellow flower

Stumbler
by Daniel Speake - age 15

Burning down like a candle,
The pain inside you can hardly handle.
You don't even want to give it a try.
Just want to cover you face and cry.

Clumsy at heart, your arms are open.
Your pain is obvious, your will is broken.
Sometimes it seems there's no way out at all,
Every door you open leads to another wall.

The ground you walk on shakes beneath your feet,
Stumbling along chasing as you seek.
Your love is unending, you can't make it stop.
You hold out your hand but you can't reach the top.

You came so close, you get right beside it.
Your eyes are closed, but you swear you'll find it.
You stumble, you fall, you never learn.
You see with your heart, the rest is a blur.

So I Say
by Amanda Speranza - age 13

As white as snow,
As cute as a bow,
As skinny as a pickle,
As funny as a tickle,
    So I say on this bright day
look at the sky and what
do you see,
you see a star named
        Shawn Bradley

Treasures

Grandpa & Me
by Amanda Speranza - age 13

I pray for you all day and night,
I hold you hand and hold it tight, When I look at you
and see you sad, it breaks my heart in quarter and halves,
I need you home, I need you here, When I am not with you
I shed a tear. You are my grandpa, you are my daddy,
you are my friend,, you are my family. You are so much to
me when I am with you, You mean the world to me,
Grandpa come home, Grandpa come here,
        GET WELL SOON
I need you here!!!!!!!!!!!

Our Dad
by Kathryn T. Spezza

I remember the day we all laughed and cried
it was at your bedside; the day you died.

We kissed your face, we held your hand
we tried to keep you from going to that better land.

We told you story after story; we just kept talking
we tried so hard to keep you with us and away from walking.

Yes we knew Our Heavenly Father was calling
but we kept touching and talking to keep you from falling.

It was selfish of us I know; you were in such pain
we love you so much our minds weren't thinking another story, again.

But our hearts told us what we really did know
that God's calling you and we must let you go.

With hearts pounding hard we set you free
for Jesus your brother; to carry you across the great sea.

And so you don't fall he holds on to you tight
and leads you into Gods eternal light.

We all believe in Gods great love
and believe there's no pain in the Heavens above.

So rest now and be happy; we'll see you again
and we'll have even more stories to tell you then.

Our lives (these stories) we'll need for awhile
before we can bring them to the paradise isle.

So with each & every day of our passing lives
please keep an eye on us through those heavenly skies.

Because although your not here; it's not All that bad
we all have our memories of you "OUR DAD".

Heaven
by Ashlea Elizabeth Spires - age 16

    As the rain poured down
in the middle of the night
I woke up to feel
a bit of a fright
When I got out of bed
And turned on the light
I saw this big man
but I wasn't afright
I thought I was dead
and goin' to heaven
but it turns out to be
he's there 24-7
So always beware
of the man upstairs
Just cause he's there
don't mean your goin' nowhere!

Stardust Dreams
by Kiki Stamatious, R.A.

There are many things to se in Kalamazoo, Michigan. Every morning I like to take walks to get some fresh air. I walk down South Rose Street and head down to Bronson Park where the fountain bursts out in all its glory with it's Manchurian atmosphere. The churches all around the area give off a feeling of nostalgia. I'm taken back to the time of Jack and Jill with the bucket they carried up that hill and Hensel and Grettel when they wee left in the forest where their travels lead them up to that Ginger bread house where the witch so enticed them. The entire candy area that looked good enough to eat. This is how it is on my travels. I look up at the emblems of one church and I see a starburst enriching my entire body. I look toward the North and it's like I see a samurai peering down at me. The children pint off in different directions. There is a statue of a little girl pointing up at a bird she sees flying by into the night dissolving into the zodiac.

Cupids Arrows
by Michelle Stambler - age 13

Cupids arrows are rare and few,
so blessed is thee if he aims one to you.
Unexpectedly, it hits your heart,
with the one you love, you'll never want to part.
A falling rose petal, a freshly shed tear,
those are all signs that love is near.
Young we are, and youth is pride,
love, we are sometimes forced to hide.
So when Cupid comes of his home up high,
our hearts spread wings and begin to fly.
Cupids arrows are rare and few,
so blessed is thee if he aims one to you.

Did You See My Little Girl?
by Jeanne Stampley

Did you see my little girl?
Round face and pretty curls
she's left for a walk
we didn't get a chance to talk

Did you see my little girl?

My little girl left unseen
she wore the color green
the light shine in her eyes
bright as the sun in the skies

Did you see my little girl?

I have only myself to blame
I tried calling her name
I bowed on my knees in prayer
and walked up the stairs

Did you see my little girl?

I tried to be strong and wise
with tears in my yes
as I picture her pretty face
my arms await her embrace

Did you see my little girl?

Dedicated: In loving memories
of my son
Robert C. Floyd IV
and his loving wife
Threase Floyd
My two daughters
Tontia W. Esquilin and Kewana D. Floyd
My husband
Arnaz Stampley Sr.

Knowledge
by Amanda Stanek - age 12

For people
Their knowledge is stored
In one large box
With a door
Though, for some
Their door is harder
To push open
Than it is
For others

You
by Melinda Stanley - age 12

When I see a shooting star,
Knowing it falls afar.
I think of your sparkling eyes
Squinting like little spies.
Always filled with excitement,
Always so much cheer
Enough to give everyone 'round the year.
But like that star
The twinkle doesn't last long
And you and me will
Both be gone.

My Apologies
by Katie Stansfield - age 16

For all the pain you've ever felt,
    And all I've added to it,
I'm sorry.

For all the times I wasn't around,
    At the time you actually needed me,
I'm sorry.

For all the times I made you cry,
    When I should have made you laugh,
I'm sorry.

For all the little things I could have done,
    But never found the courage to do,
I'm sorry.

Just because I loved it when you cared,
    And now that I hate it cause you don't,
I'm sorry.

And finally since you hate it,
    When I say I'm sorry,
I apologize.

fortune and shame
by Melissa A. Stanton - age 14

If you disappeared, my world would
be shattered.
I could care less, my world wouldn't
matter.
Tears would fall down, like
pieces of ice.
No second chance, you couldn't try
twice.
If I woke up and you were
suddenly dead,
I would be left with nothing but
dread.
Unexpressed anger, feeling so
low,
life would go by so suddenly
slow.
Taking a challenge, just rolling
the dice,
this is often a risky price.
For life itself is not only a game,
it is a struggle between fortune
and shame.

You
by Kelly M. Stevens - age 13

What is as red as a rose and as blue as the sea?
What has the hopes and dreams of you and me?
What has our complexion, our taste, and feeling too?
Could it be something in the air, something that flew, something that sees us
in a perfect view?
No, it's not like any of those things at all,
It's something inside of you, something either big or small.
It's your courage, your brightness, your pity, your shame,
It's not anything that anyone else can claim.
And if you pay close attention to what you say and do,
You'll feel it just start popping out from inside of you.
So, if you feel a tickle in a funny and strange way,
Just remember what you've just read in here today.

Losing Love
by Renee Steele - age 17

I lay down,
Listening to people crying all around.

The tears flow like water,
And now, how can it be it's all over?

It's time to face that she's really gone,
How will my heart ever go on?

I love my Great Grandmother so,
At that moment I started remembering all those days
we had fun in the winter snow.

I also remember her telling me I needed to stop
growing or I'd pass her by,
With tears in my eyes, I want to know who said she was allowed
to go.

I know it wasn't me,
So why then must I let her go?

My Great Grandmother is up above,
To my Gram I send all my love.

I dedicate this poem to my late great grandmother.
Marcella Mosey
Born: July 19, 1918   Died: September 17, 1995

Within Myself
by Pamela J. Stein

I slipped far within myself
in that swollen room
So many memories dumped
in heaps, why do they leave so soon

Still the winds-they pound those
drops upon the window pane
As with the storm and does the
moon will these feeling wane

The past races before me, with
sadden in view
Mounds and mounds of evidence
there were those pleasures too

Finally light filters through-throwing
shadows on the walls
Quickly now the day will fade
those images growing small

Timeless though, the memories—
priceless gems held within
Future reigns for those who follow—
their turn for where I now begin.

Castle Bluff
by Alena Stephens - age 17

The wind rustle leaves
Like spirits in the wild
The smoke rises high
The rain comes down hard

High road we have climbed
And a high road to come
This is the end
When clouds part, minds clear

A place called Castle Bluff
Where you'll find you have enough
To make it through
Through it may rough
He'll be with you

And you come alone, like some child
So let us her a voice shout a praise
When through the dark we see ourselves

A place called Castle Bluff
Where you'll find you have enough
To make it through
Though it maybe rough
He'll be with you

Where sunny rocks of truth
Meet trickling water of fear
The tears may come
and drip from high cliffs

And still there's a light
In every heart and smile
And let us know
We're not far from home

Well, Thank You
by Sheila Sterling

You taught me geography,
you made me so happy,
now I want to continue,
evermore, thinking of you.

You taught me of culture,
you were my special helper,
now I want to reach all hearts--
of Christ's love, now imparts.

Showed me Africa, you see,
taught me how to draw country,
gave me my dreams for career--
dedicated to you, I'm here.

Told me I did the right thing,
reaching his heart as I sing--
You said that's great--
"Well, thank you," I restate!

The Beat Of A Drum
by Paula Stich - age 17

I dance to the beat of a drum, thanking earth.
I flow with the songs of mammals, thanking nature.
I arrive at a restful state, thanking the dwelling spirits.
I smell the aromas of purifying air, thanking thine ancestors.
I drink of replenishing waters, thanking my nurturer.
I give all to survive,
Thanking, what is yet to come.

Life
by Martha Stidham - age 14

Once there was a greasy pig.
This little pig drove a rig.
The pig and rig is really neat, but his pig is really beat.
Because he is breakfast for next week.
But first they must play hide-and-seek.
He hid inside a garage disposal,
and then received a marriage proposal.
His new-found wife, her name is Ned,
soon found-out she was breakfast in bed.

Night Dreams
by Joe Stiles - age 18

They smell it like fear
And hear it like screams
And if you're not careful
They see it in your dreams.
I have such a gift
Which was forged in the past
And I hope
That it always will last.
That gift
Cannot keep me dry in rain
Or tune out
My bitter sharp pain.
I survive in the day
And long for the night,
Whose sweet mother moon
Is such a wonderful sight.
I endure it alone
Because of the cost
To see it with her
Will mean she is lost
She knows who she is
For the dark gives her sight
And her glorious home
Is the all-covering night.

Come Back
by Danielle M. Stines - age 17

Your tender love
Is all I'm thinking of
Feeling your soft touch
I miss it, oh, so much
Remember the days of the past
When we thought this love would last
I dream about the good times
And I wish that you were still mine

My mind keeps saying, "No",
But my heart won't let you go
I stare into the night
And see the stars, they shine so bright
I swear I could see your face
I need you to fill that space
Why can't I just move on?
I realize that you're gone.
But baby...

Come back - I never meant to hurt you
Come back - I need you here tonight
Please hold me in your arms,
 and make everything alright
Come back...

Why did you leave me here
And fill my eyes with tears
I told you that I love you
I would never lie to you
You broke my heart, you left me crying
I'm here alone, but I'm still trying
Trying to hold on
Please come back and make me strong...

Love
by Billy Strachan - age 12

Is this love?
I whisper to myself as she passes by
My whole body tingles in a sweet harmony
I have never felt love before

It is supposed to be a sweet majestic feeling
That is only felt once
An indescribable feeling
Never felt twice

And if God has destined me to feel this
once in a lifetime feeling
I am afraid this is it

If Only
by Catie Tara Strauss - age 13

If only the world was perfect...
If only the sky was blue,
If only peaople cared about things, (like me and you)
But the world's not perfect, as the sky is gray,-
Yet nobody listens to what I may have to say.
But still I believe that anything can happen,-
It's changed once before.
The time is approaching to knock down that door.

If only there was no violence.
If only there were no drugs.
If only people didn't give up with simple little shrugs.
But violence is a killer,- and drugs may be too.
Yet everyone gives up, as if there is nothing we can do.

If only poverty wasn't a problem,-
If only everyone shared!...
If only people gave it some thought, and showed they really cared.
But poverty comes in great amounts, and most are not willing to give.
Yet many people ignore this,
Thinking this is a perfect world in which we live.

If only there was no hatred.
If only we all got along.
If only we felt like we could just belong.
But most are not loving, and fighting is all we do.
Yet we still want to belong. Wouldn't you want to too?
But still I believe that anything can happen...
The world has changed before.
NOW IS THE TIME... TO KNOCK DOWN THAT DOOR!

Loved and Lost
by Jenny Stricker - age 15

It seems like here lately your always on my mind
I want to search for answers, but I'm scared of what I'll find.

At first it seemed so easy, I ran from you so fast
I never stopped to realize, I could be haunted by my past.

It seems like only yesterday, you held me close and tight,
and whispered that you loved me, before we said "good night."

It never seemed these feelings could come back so clear and strong
but I guess its safe for me to say that my heart has proved me wrong.

It seems like only yesterday, your heart was truly mine,
but now there's only empty questions to be answered with the time.

I know that once you loved me, I could see it in you eyes
but now I don't know what I want, just hold me when I cry.

I remember how I loved you with a force that was so strong
I can't help but ask myself where I went so wrong.

I know how I feel now, my hearts still full of fears
only now your not beside me to wipe away my tears.

Love Struck
by Carlena Stroude - age 12

When I saw you
For the very
First time I was
Love struck

Right when I
Heard your voice
I was
Love struck

For the first time
Looking in your eyes
I felt
Love struck

Whenever someone
Mentions your name
I'm Love struck

Goodbye
by Colleen Martha Sullivan - age 13

Now its time to say goodbye.
I know its sad but please don't cry.

I say goodbye to all my friends.
I hope our friendship never ends.

I say goodbye to this lovely state.
I'll say it now, or it'll be to late.

All my friends I loved you well.
I say goodbye, I say farewell.

"God's Gift To Me"z
by Janet Stuckert

My heart is filled with Love of mankind. I try my best to caress the lonely. To let them know God loves them and encourage them to Pray. I care for the hungry, I give what I can buying foods that will stretch a dime to a dollar.

I'm not one of wealth not even middle class, but it doesn't matter what our income is. I think it's Gods gift to me to have such compassion. I'm a good listener and sometimes that's enough, for them to know, they can vent and no judgement, I make. I try to guide them to the Social Service thats best for their needs.

And keep in touch telling them I Love them and I really do, God has guided me this way. It gives me peace and just seeing a smile on a depressed person can really make my day. This quality, I have is due from a chemical Imbalance of the brain. I'm so thankful to God and all the professionals who worked so hard to stable my mind.

It was so difficult for family and friends, and myself to understand what was going wrong with my mind. I thank God and my way is showing similar people Love and Compassion, and encouraging them there's always someone who cares. And things do change, but they must fight with all they have in them to change, and most of all be able to say I Love myself I'm God's Child and He walks with us always.

The Becoming
by Nicole Stumbaugh - age 16

After four years of separation, the two young men finally meet.
Face to face, and heart to heart.
They informally shake hands,
and then suddenly, as if for once in both their lives,
Their pride crashes with grace and crumbles with forgiveness.
Finally they realize what is important,
and that is--their everlasting friendship.
Tears swell thankfully in red smiling eyes.
Tears that are mixed with happiness, wonderful memories,
and memories never lived.

One of the young men had just begun to break the many cruel chains,
that had strangled and tortured him for years.

The other was just there,
content with his friend's warm hug and tears.
He returned that loving gift with a caressing hug,
and tears of understanding.

Two young men, weeping with the loss and regain of each other.
No shame--the word didn't even cross their minds.
With tears they created love,
and with love they grew,
as did all of the spectators who watched that heart-wrenching moment.

Now two MEN let go and smile.
Two MEN who were always friends, become friends once again.

We were all touched that day,
but possibly most of all,
was my best friend and I.
We were proud to watch our two older brothers,
grow up even more.

*Dedicated to my brother Mike and his friend Chad,
two of the finest men that I've ever known.*

Crying Angels
by Nicole Stumbaugh - age 16

I hear them,
I hear angels crying.
Crying outside my window pane.
Weeping, sobbing tear by tear,
I hear angels crying;
crying for souls they lost,
lost to the depths of hell.

I see invisible tears,
and sad invisible eyes.
For in my mind I hear their silent cries.
I feel their motionless wings
flap lame at my face,
their halos hung in defeat,
and soiled dresses of lace.

Does that mean that the battle is done?
The soles the angels sought were not won?

Will they give up and leave us here?
Leave us blindly in our tears?

Will angels ever laugh again?
Will we ever soar upon the wind?

These questions I ask only the angels know,
still I wonder where we'll go.
So I say, if you're good, you'll soar up high,
but if you're bad...angels will cry.

Fantasy
by Lauren Sullivan - age 17

The sun shone down brightly
On the green valley below.
An innocent land lay revealed
Which had never known hate or sorrow.

Castles made of crystal
Reflecting the brilliant light
A trained, disciplined army
Which had never had to fight.

A loyal, gentle people
With one king to rule them all.
His queen by his side,
Both fair, lovely, and tall.

A host of wizards to keep them safe
In robes of silver and blue
Snowy white beards and kindly eyes,
Everything they knew.

Bold and beautiful dragons
Gliding majestically through the air.
Kept to guard the palace,
The king and queen and their heir.

A young and curious boy
A wooden sword in hand.
A golden crown on his head,
The future of this land.

The wizards and the dragons,
The young prince and the rest
Are now no more
Than a child's fantasy at best.

Everyday and Every Tomorrow
by Tanya L. Surdam - age 17

Oh my dear friends, where did you go?
To a higher land to rome?
Do you still smile up there and play?
You all know I miss you, but why do you cause me such pain?
I dreamt a dream of you,
You were back home and safe.
I really wish you could come back to take away my pain and sorrow.
I hope for that everyday,
And I'll hope for it every tomorrow!

*Dedicated to four great friends
Killed on September 26, 1996 in an alcohol-related accident*

Untitled
by Laura Surowiec - age 14

I Love you
but you push it off
You care
but not enough
As I cry
I don't care if I die
but you don't see me
If you did
It would not matter

You give me a bear
but it just made me
Love you more
It's hard to see
you go on
So free
with no need to love me

Ringlet of Essence
by Linsey Susin - age 13

Kaleidoscopic climates fill
Reflections of bygone days.
An unfinished sphere holds
Clues to yesteryear.
Quilted patches tell the saga of
A generation that now ceases
To exist.
Feeling the smooth,
Metallic luster,
Gives an insight tot he bubbling brooks
Of the vitality.

Be True To Yourself
by Bob Svoboda

See with your eyes
But look with your heart
The answer you find may be a
    surprise
And bring you closer, not pull you
    apart
If you enjoy colorful flowers and
    pastel skies
Then search yourself and begin with
    a fresh start!

It Just Isn't My Day
by Ann Swartz

    It was the 17th of April and all seemed to be the same. Jerry came over bright and early to help us move, but we were still to blame.

    For little did we realize what the day would bring; because everything seemed quite natural to hear the birdies sing. We had our coffee in peace and quiet; but it didn't last that way all night.

    We wondered just what thing to do, we saw some pictures than a shoe. By this time you shift from this to that, just walking around all nervously trying to find your hat. What am I doing? I can't really say; because in my mind it just isn't my day.

    We collected some things and put them in the van. Went back in the house and also was interviewed by a T.V. man. What am I thinking about and how do I feel? I'm nervous and numb and composed as a seal; but still I feel the flood was in town, as I saw the sandbaggers on the dike running down.

    The whistles just sounded as if to say- It's coming! It's coming! I don't mean to scare you. Take all you can grab; even if the sky is blue.

    We drove oh so slow to find all the streets full of water gushing down; which was not cool. We dillied and dallied to get out of town and oh what a relief when the sirens went down!

Loneliness
by Jennifer Swick - age 14

Loneliness is what I feel,
When I am not with you.
Loneliness is what I feel,
When I can't stop thinking of you.

Loneliness is all that's there,
When your love is else where.
Loneliness is how I cope,
When all that's left is distant hope.

Loneliness is memories,
That hurt more as the days go by.
Loneliness is the dreams,
That sunk when you said Good Bye.

With all that was,
Here's what's left.
I give you all I can,
LONELINESS.

Kaleidoscope
by Natalie Anne Szoldra - age 17

The first shimmering moment of life,
like a diamond in the sea,
glittering in the noonday sun,
brightly lit and glowing flame,
a brand new name, a shining light
Then ... gentle twist and darkest night comes
for the first time, and
happy rhymes and gentle songs hearts
that belong
Until...
one stands alone.
From brightest dawn to deepest dusk--
From morning song to twilight dreams--
fantastic schemes and lives
that sometimes go away
Such shining hopes, such sudden turns
from bright to dark, from grim to grand
from joy to sorrow always waiting
for tomorrow...
And a twist of fate, a ray of hope
With the faintest sleight of hand,
the alteration of all life's dreams
and all their scope...
All with one tiny turn
of life's
kaleidoscope.

The Dream
by Natalie Anne Szoldra - age 17

Thoughts left unspoken.
Images left unseen.
Flash
before my minds eye.
In the cover of darkness,
My hopes, wishes, and fears
materialize
Given form by only my imagination
-yet very real.
Part of my mind curls protectively around
itself.
The other part searches,
searches for the hidden meaning.
New truths,
Answers to questions left long unanswered.
Sometimes, the past comes into focus.
Sometimes, the future reveals itself.
Often, the meaning of seemingly
random images
remain elusive of the grasping tendrils of
my sleeping mind.
The images disperse.
I awake to a new day.
All memory of the night vanishes.
Vanishes.

Getting no where, The changes
by Jacqueline Taajiogueu

Where are we going
What are we doing?
Getting no where
There's a no man land
That's where are our feet are placed on
I hear! people say the 90's
What does it mean
Where are we going
Loosing the place
No man land
Getting no where
Where are we going
The 90's what does it mean?
Does it mean to lose one's place
No man place
Read the sign
What is the time telling us
What are we doing?
Read the sign
What did it say?
Sign read (Love, Respect, Trust, Caring,
Morals.
Tina Turner say, what does love have
to do what it.
What does the 90's have to do with
loosing one place.
Read the sign
What does the sign say!
We have forgotten about our
Read the sign
What does it say!
Sign reads (Love, Respect, Trust, Caring,
Morals
Have we lost our place
What time is it, the 90's

Deadline
by Cecile Talley

I have a deadline
by Friday, I have in mind
A date, a decree
delivered, by mail for me
Send on time, will set me free.

Monday through Thursday
I collect, gather info
to complete my form,
finding my items, presents,
such - a - storm, confused, I'm torn.

Early Friday morn
My missing detail was found
Now, no longer bound
Was, my unoccupied mind
Renewed, Refreshed, Reserved, found.

But One Moment
by Edgar Tan - age 20

In a glance the world paused, the sands of time stuck in suspense,
Unprepared to be entranced, in a gust of love just too intense.
In that glance a calm ensued, a weary heart sprung back to life.
Wilted hopes looked towards the sun once more,
a dawn emerging from the night.
In that brief moment life was quickly renewed, the fountain of youth to hope long forgotten,
A droplet of dew to quench a lifetime of thirst, a fresh breeze through air stale and rotten.
But in one glance the sun fell back, behind formidable mountains to stay.
And though it seemed to be within reach, it slipped through the hands for it was too far away.
In one glance the light disappeared, replaced by shadows that soon prevailed,
A too familiar scene from the past, of loves that emerged and had failed.
In solitude, in coldness, no warmth of light to revive.
Now a myth, just a dream, cherished hopes burned to survive.
Deciding whether to burn the past to go on,
or to remember but freeze in the present,
Spirits are lifted but to achieve what ends?
Lifted only so one can fall once again.
A glimpse of radiant light for an instant,
to realize how dark are the times that are lived in.
What seemed to be the coming of dawn,
was but a flash with lightning speed,
And like thunder the sound of the pain echoes on, leaving bitter sorrow upon which to feed.
In that transient moment so brief, of light and of love so divine,
The world below looked so clear from up here,
earthly problems left behind as I climbed.
But when that moment was gone,
the good fortune in my life had been spent,
And the truth of the world fell up toward my face,
a return to the dark in descent.
For a moment I could walk on clouds, tread on water, fly through air,
For a moment I knew of love, for a moment I was there.
I look to the sky for the star I had tried, to reach, and never let go of.
But no stars in the sky, only stars in my eyes, a lifelong delusion of love.
Staring off in the distance and then into my soul, only to find empty space,
Holding onto the shattered pieces of hope, with but a memory to embrace.
And so the radiant joy that might enter my life,
and give my blind hope new sight,
Was eclipsed to leave me in darkness once more,
left with but one moment of light.

Feelings
by Lorraine Tanyu - age 16

Is it love or lust?
They questioned my feelings for you.
do they not think of it to be just?
For I have just started anew.
You are like the stars at night
that shines down from the sky,
Being with you just feels so right
It makes me feel like I could fly.
As you shower me with your gentle kiss
taking me in your arms in a warm embrace
You leave me in heavenly bliss
This is not just a phase...
My feelings for you comes from the heart
For I will always love you
Even when we are apart.

Check Mate
by Mary Ann Taylor

Satchel lost his checker
Somewhere in the house
"Twasn't with the other toys
Or next to Mommy's mouse.

It wasn't with the little cars
Or the engines on the track
And we just looked in our backyard
It's not with the toys outback.

Nor sitting there with Hopalong,
Not even with Kathy Cabbage Patcher
Or in the tub with Ronnie and friends
Not even on Thomas's cow catcher.

No one could find his checker
Though all day long they tried
But then, just there, his checker
Beneath the chair, he spied.

Satchel held it for all to see
So pleased was he at last
Of all the objects we had "checked,"
No one thought of Grampa's magnifying glass.

The Unconscious Mind
by Sidra Tees - age 14

Sometimes we look
Although we are blind
Sometimes we listen
Although we are deaf

Sometimes we use our heads
Although we cannot think
Sometimes we use our hearts
Although we cannot love

Sometimes we need to cry
Although we shed no tears
Sometimes we need to suffer
Although we shed no blood

Sometimes we have to scream
Although we have no voice
Sometimes we have to die
Although we have no life

A Lost Soul
by Aliya Tejani - age 13

Searching deep in a blind alley.
Crying out in despair,
Which way shall I go?
Which path shall I take?
A mistake?
A blessing?
Maybe a fulfillment unknown.
An outrageous longing, an energy so far.
Reaching but not touching,
Wanting and not getting.
Is it love?
A rare and singular gift?
Can it be found under the deceiving ways of life?
Will the moment pass and never return?
Time blows like the wind and stops to
wander like a curious soul.
It gnaws away at you, yet creating
Preposterous memories that leap up at you,
Leaving a glimmer on your soul.
Grasp it, tenderly, and let it take you to
A splendorous place.
Without a doubt, right.
Without a doubt, a lingering blessing.

Painful Dreams
by C. Chris Telander

It seems to be, it seems to me
Both folly and temerity
To dream, aspire, to try to be
More than your reality.

For dreams they quickly turn to dust
Once forged of iron now crumbling rust
The Fates themselves decreed you must
Succumb to fear and to distrust.

And love the grandest dream of all
Poor lofty lover doomed to fall
Your heart be shattered but still you crawl
Toward the one that is your all.

My advice to you my friend
Stay locked up safely and pretend
Love not lest pain be your true end
Your fragile heart you can't defend.

For love your heart will vitrify
Its glassine texture you'll deny
The blow will come, you'll wonder why
Your heart will shatter, your soul will die.

Again I warm thee foolish one
Love not lest pain be all you've won
Give not your heart or be undone
Avoid the sorrow from this gauntlet run.

Life and Death - A Sonnet
by Becky Telep - age 13

As we come into the world, we shed our 1st tears
Strange faces draw near to us
We squirm and cry, trying to end our fears,
If we get nothing we want, we fuss.
As we grow older, both you and I
We wonder what will come
When will we die?
Will we all go or just some?
Why do some die so soon?
Do their souls just disappear?
Or do they live forever like the man on the moon?
But I guess we all have to say this, goodbye.
And ask the question, why do we die?

My Life
by Meredith Templin - age 13

The world to me
seems really unfair

And no one seems
to give a care

If it's my idea,
she beats me to it

I don't wanna live
going through it

She has the craft,
the crown of life

Sometimes I feel like
I'm fighting with life

When they all adorn
her with gifts, and
praise

Those have become
most of the days

They always seem
to put her first

I feel like I'm
blessed with a
horrible curse

She's so helpless
it's her state of
mind

They always say
she's one of a
kind

She's so sensitive
but the people don't care

Why is my world so unfair?

Young Hearts
by Amy Tench - age 13

Love is something special
 It always seems so real.
But it causes misunderstandings,
 Leaving wounds that fail to heal.

Patience is the key,
 Trust opens the door,
love comes walking in,
 from there I say no more.

But if you don't have patience,
 and can't built up your trust.
Don't become discouraged,
 Throwing love out with a thrust.

For love will grow if given time
 And if given space.
But never try to speed it up,

For it grows at its own
 pace.

Him
by Meredith Templin - age 13

In my heart we'll
never die

His love is like a
star in my dark
night sky

I am a prisoner,
trapped in his love

He was sent by God
from the heavens
above

His kiss still lingers
on my lips

His strong hands
hold my hips

He made me happy
and made me cry

He made me feel
like I was sky
high

He made me laugh,
I'll make you see

How much this guy
really meant to me

Valentines Day
by Sarah Tentis - age 16

Valentine's Day means much more than giving or receiving flowers, candy, or cards. Valentine's Day is a special day to be with the one or ones you love. Valentine's Day is a day full of love, joy, hope, and happiness for all

With Love Darling
by Amy Tench - age 13

Love is special,
 Love is sweet,
Love is what makes
 life complete.....
 Love is giving,
 Love is kind,
Love is joy and peace
 of mind.....
Love is laughter, seldom tears,
 sharing, caring, through the
 years......
 Love is more
 than words express-
 but mostly,
 Love is happiness!

Ironic Truths
by Bella Tendler - age 15

Sometimes, I try to get my emotions down on paper,
But my words don't seem to flow,
They come in chunks of lying truths,
That only I could know,
They're so well concealed in shock-proof gear,
I'd hardly know its me,
That's writing all that half-truth rot,
On insecurity.

Sometimes, I try to touch my soul,
But my soul seems all numbed out,
From years of packing arctic chill,
Around my fear and doubt,
And inspiration slips and slides,
Off my frozen core,
And returns only grudgingly,
Not wanting to be hurt anymore.

Sometimes, the future frightens me,
I hardly live the day,
So scared am I that all the charm,
Of life will slip away,
I plant my heels into the ground,
And say "I won't go on!"
But horrified, I see the truth,
That life just moves right on.

Time
by Shelby Terrell - age 14

Running farther from the light,
darker, darker into the night,
heavy steps upon the street
I run and run till we shall meet,
it's really only a matter of time,
will I live to fight or live to die,
not enough minutes in the hour
not enough hours in the day
shall I work or shall I play,
it must only be a matter of time,
will it come, in peace and pride
or come to hurt us deep inside,
then I face the truth, admit defeat
that day when destiny and I shall meet.

A Robyn
by Ashley Thaler - age 14

In a life where there is greatness and pain,
there is a Robyn.
In a life where there is happiness and sadness,
there is a Robyn.
In a life where there is hard work and easy work,
there is a Robyn.
In a life where there is a lot of friends and not a lot,
there is a Robyn.
In a life where someone lives a long time and there is someone who doesn't,
there is a Robyn.
A Robyn is someone who experiences all of these things and more in life.

Poem Of Love
by Jennifer Thierbach - age 18

I love you more than the heaven's above
Because you filled my whole world with love
So here is a poem saying I love you to death
For you I would give you my last breath
I just pray to God we never break apart
because it would feel like someone stabbed
me deep in the heart
When I feel your warm embrace
I'm the luckiest girl in the human race
What I feel for you is a lot of pride
I will always be here by your side
I want to go to you with open arms
Because you are so filled with charm
So promise me we will always be together
because I need you now and forever
You helped me find my way
day after day
I love you more than words can say
with this ring is all the dreamed we shared
Because your the only one who really cared
My love for you will always remain true
even after we say I do

Our Princess, Diana
by Lyell Thomas

Diana...Diana...Our Princess so young
Such beauty forever and a song well sung
A life cut short and so very brief
The World caught up in total grief.

Creation gave you to the World
Appreciation seemed never unfurled
In Death...we the people came to know
How loved in silence...was so very so.

Your last words was reported to be
"Leave me alone...Leave me alone!"
Memories now, is all that's left
Of a life taken like an act of theft.

Tons of flowers at Kensington Place
Adored by the world in such grace
As we all ask..."Why-Oh-Why?"
Did such beauty have to Die.

Now you are wrapped in eternal life
No more bright flashes of revealing light
Called to heaven while riding your prime
Tranquil silence...frozen in time.

Some how life will continue on
Never forgetting our fallen blond
Time for the mass will Ebb away
We all will join you again some day.

Is It Really About Us
by Shanna N. Thomas - age 18

It really breaks my heart
To think you would be untrue
After I promised I'd be true
Now you say you love me
But, boy I ain't hearen that
Cause we are too much
        Alike....
And I know that's like a
        Sike....
Now I've heard about yo' girls
And you say I should believe
You and not what I heard
Well I know before it was
My fault

But, this time it's
        YOURS.......

Are You?
by Brooke Thompson - age 13

Oh, how I need someone to care.
Oh, how I need someone to kiss my tears as they spill down
my cheek.
Is it you?
Are you my eternal?
My love?
Will you be there when things get tough?
Oh, how I long for someone who shares my thoughts!
For someone who caresses my needs with such tenderness,
such passion, that every wrong thought every wrong feeling
runs and hides, like the devil seeing the face of our Maker.
Are you my bliss?
Are you my tender kiss that I long for?
Are you, can you, be my one true love?

Sadness
by Brooke Thompson - age 13

    Sadness is but a feeling.
A weight of such sorrow and despair.
A cry of a heart breaking.
The moan of a soul perishing.
Sadness can be deep within the heart or right at the tip
of your fingers.
You try to cover it up;
is that possible?
Do you just recover?
Or, even years later, do you still mourn as if it all
happened yesterday?

Clippings
by Cecilia Thompson - age 18

Reminiscence of childhood
linger, secretly kept away in a heart
so young and untouched.
She bows her head in allegiance
to not forget the child still
shadowed where
imagination creeps within. She writes.
Her voice is a beacon
in her ever quiet silences.
Listening to the melody of life.
She thinks.
She has notions, which individualize, casting her out sometimes.
She is of the artists where dreams
she knows can come true.
Realizing determination and spirit
last as long as you believe.
Wind to her becomes magic, fire to her is myths,
Water to her is paths,
Earth to her means everything.

Untitled
by Kara Thompson - age 14

I am standing at one end of the hall
he is at the other....

Gosh, I should of listened to my mother.
Crushes come and crushes go,
but with this crush you will never know.

In some cases I would know,
that some people never go.

Even though time has past,
you know that crush is going to last.

Maybe one year Maybe two,
but to him who are you.

When you think back to your crush,
you just might begin to blush.

The Light
by Brianne Tillotson - age 17

I'm here in a room full of faces,
    But no one really notices.

I reach out. Everywhere I turn
    My heart gains yet another burn.

I look, searching in every direction,
    Meeting only rejection.

I speak. My words drift through the air
    And simply disappear.

I seek a private hollow
Deep within some unseen shadow.

I shrink inside a mind of mass confusion,
    Into a life of seclusion.

I fall down into a world
Of a vulnerable young girl.

I hear a whispering in my ear
From a voice I sense is near.

I listen. It is directed toward me,
    But the source, I can not see.

I open my eyes. Suddenly you appear
    Diminishing my childish fear.

I hold my hand outstretched to you,
    As in a dream finally coming true.

You touch your hand to mine
Causing our fingers to entwine.

Your presence, inevitably, breaks the spell
Drawing me out of my shell.

I realize that I made it through
Because of the friend I found in you.

I Lie in the Dark
by Alicia Tillman - age 13

I lie in the dark
My thoughts running fast
I think about my life
Future, present, and past

My childhood was good
It was happy and grand
I could sit on the beach
With my toes in the sand

My teenager years
Strange yes they were
I worked in a restaurant saying
"would you like fries with that sir?"

Young adult and middle-aged
Next they came fast
I got married and had kids
Just hoping it would last

Now I grow old
I did leave a mark
And now my time has come
As I lie here in the dark

One Last Night
by Brandilynn Tivera - age 16

Underneath the stars so bright,
We walk through the silence of the night.
Near the beach;
On the sand,
Keep me near;
Hold my hand.
Listening to the rolling waves,
Reminiscing of those other days--
When we were considered as one.
But now we must part,
For our new lives have begun.
Thinking how life could be,
Together;
Just you and me.
Everything I presume will be all right,
Just stay by my side,
For one last night.

Pandora's Box
by Charise Tjoeng - age 13

My legend says...

Out of Pandora's box
Come things never seen before.
Not only did the bad emerge,
But also did the good.
Emotions like joy and gladness,
Jealousy and hate.
Treasures like peace and laughter,
To lighten a heavy heart.
Unwanted things drifted out,
Wars, lies, and anger.
Treachery fused with loyalty,
As mercy mixed with evil.
Good and bad met each other,
And clashed with unburned fire.
Then harmony flew out the box,
The sharing of good and bad,
Harmony balanced the both,
Let them mingle together.
Out of Pandora's box
Came both the good and bad,
Not only do we have both,
We have harmony.

Been Waiting
by Chris Tippie - age 16

So long I've waited all these
years...
For you to come to me,
with your gentle touch and
wild kiss
you set my spirit free.

Are You
by Ellen Topping - age 14

Are you thinking of me tonight,
Are you wishing on a star so bright,
Thinking of you and me,
Thinking of how it used to be,
Do you really want me,
Do you really need me tonight,
Today,
Tomorrow,
And forever more;
Do you ever wish you would see me
again;
Are you lonely without me;
Wishing tonight on this star so bright,
Looking I see the sparkle of your
eyes,
But you're not there or anywhere
near,
It's not right,
So I wish tonight,
On this star so bright,
We become what we once were.

Mother Takes Care
by Natasha Torruellas - age 11

Help, Help!
There's a mouse in the house.
What am I to do?

I called for my brother,
but he just called for my mother.
For you see, my brother is a fraidy cat.
So he took to the road and, scat.

Help, Help!
There's a mouse in the house.
What am I Do?

I called for my sister, but she just called for my mother.
For you see, my sister is a bit of a silly cat,
she just spun herself round till she fell on the hats.

Help, Help!
There's a mouse in the house!
What am I to do?

I called for my father.
But he just called for my mother.
For you see, my father is NOT a fraidy cat
He just does not like rats.

Help, Help!
There's a mouse in the house.
What am I to do?

This time I called for my mother,
and what did my mother do?

With her Paw, her mighty paw,
With one mighty swipe,
Mouse Pie,
Mouse Pie tonight!

Daybreak
by Stephanie-Lynn Tooke - age 16

The rising sun symbolizes the renewal of life. The freshness of dawn is presented by the glistening dew that has formed on the sharp blades of grass. Vigorously the stream flows from the snow-capped mountain and into the babbling brook hitting against the rocks. The Morning Glory gaily sings her happy tune, as all the little woodland creatures scamper about their daily routine. The rainbows vibrant colors paints a picture in the sky, while the sun shines creating the warmth of love, as the gentle breeze spreads peacefulness throughout the land.

Growing Pains
by Jesselle Rae - age 12

i LOVE A BOY i COULD
NEVER HAVE.
i ADMIRE PEOPLE i
COULD NEVER BE.
i HAVE FAITH IN A CHILD
i NEVER WAS.
i HAVE HOPE FOR A PERSON
NAMED me.

My Friend Is Gone
by Jerrymarie Transue - age 17

He left the world in a blast,
everyone said his memory would forever last.
Nobody knew why,
but the color of death was in his eye.
Something has happened, he is gone,
people tell me that he will live on.
I always have him on my mind,
then I remember I must put him behind.
When I think of him,
I wonder if he could ever win.
But that's when I remember he's living life within me
When it seems I can't get over his memory,
people always tell me,
things will get better just wait and see.

The Real Nightmare
by Crystal A. Trease - age 18

Talking, laughter, smiling faces.
Different people from different places.

Gunshots ring out from a .38.
You try to scream but its too late.

You watch your friend fall to the ground.
You run to help but he won't make a sound.

Screams of terror are heard as the sirens get near.
You go into shock and fill with fear.

They pick up your friend and take him away.
You cling to hope and begin to pray.

The act wasn't because of religion or race.
My friend is dead because he wore the,
wrong color in the wrong place.

*In memory of, James J. Geiger
1976 to 1995*

Fascination
by Darla Trew - age 14

The dark was surrounding me,
And the grey clouds above.
The rain pouring down the window pane,
Drip, Drip, Drip

The sound of thunder struck the air,
Deafening me.
Lightening flashing the spring scenes,
Sending animals scurrying.

Fascination,
The rain giving life to all.
Spreading a blanket of life over the country side,
Bathing the environment.

Fascination,
The rain stopped and everything comes from their homes.
To see a beautiful, fresh country side,
The beautiful colors fill the sky.

Fascination,
All wrong is washed away.
All bad is gone, time to start over,
Fascination.

Essence
by Joanna Trimble - age 17

What of this Woman
that lies here in the cold,
a woman I do not know,
yet came from her womb.
Some say she was
beautiful, filled with joy.
Some say she was
introverted, and intro-
spective.
I feel her with me
through my steps, this
person so anonymous.
There are no answers
to any questions,
no evidence, nothing
to be found.
So here I am, with no
role to follow, just wait-
ing, waiting to find this
woman and her.....
Essence!

Spacey Night
by Tiffany Tuders - age 12

There are the stars,
There is the moon,
They are so far,
I'll see them soon,
It is day,
Soon to be night,
I hope I have,
A wonderful flight,
In the plane,
Out to space,
Beside the moon,
In proper place.

Pastel Colours
by Justyna Troczynska - age 12

The skies are all fading,
the nightfall has come.
The sweet pastel colours,
so bright yet so glum.

The birds are all leaving,
the branches so bare,
nothing but leaves,
Silent in despair.

Yet nothing's alone,
not the moon nor the stars,
for the sky's always there,
here and afar.

When all has rested,
a new day's begun,
the trees see out moon
and they greet the sun.

And then once again,
arise pastel colours,
with blue and with purple
out comes pitch black.

As I write this poem,
I look up and I see,
ten pastel colours
and I see me.

For I am a star
with glamour and light.
I sit here alone,
alone in the night.

Wind
by Jessica L. Trotter - age 14

Refreshing when a breeze on a
Midsummer's Eve.

Scary when a storm on a dark,
lonely night.

So graceful, yet lethal.
Dancer of the clouds and trees.
Singer of the cold winter's night.
Companion of an old dusty desert.

North, East, South, and West,
None of which is really best.

Traveling, changing, and carving,
While I watch, wonder, and wish.

Untitled
by Shanon Tuter - age 12

Summer
Swimming,
Lemonade,
Mosquito bites,
Lightning bugs,
Sunburns,
Sweating,
Cold Sheets,
Baseball,
Aloe Vera jell,
Attic Fan,
Leaving your windows open at night,
The smell of fresh cut grass,
The sound of crickets,
Summer clothes shopping,
bathing suits,
Slip and Slide,
Friends,
Staying out till midnight playing hide and go seek with the neighbor kids,
watermelon,
barbecues,
pets,
bike riding,
the lake,
foggy eyes from so much chlorine,
no school,
Vacation,
Freedom,
SUMMER!

*I Dedicate this poem to my Mom and Dad
They have always been there for me.
I love you guys!*

The Heart Rules
by Ilene E. Twitchell

Does your heart race with thrills
When your husband speaks,
Does it pound as the thunder
Hearing of ones grief.
Does your heart soar, as with wings
When embraced in lust,
Is your heart filled with anger
From all things unjust.
Does your heart feel remorse
Of hurtfulness done,
Is your heart gentle and kind
Glowing like the sun.
Does your heart sing with laughter
With a hearty ring,
Does your heart have a window
To let someone in.
We all get back what we give
For each day we live,
The heart rules over the mind
Of generous kinds.

Untitled
by Katie Tyson - age 13

Certain people follow
Usually their dreams are hollow
Promises are broken
Grief is not spoken
Sometimes you choose not to speak
Over an issue so bleak
Afraid that what you say may bring harm
Stolen away from you that beautiful charm
The charm of your personality
Your individuality
Freedom can be taken
Hope and faith is shaken
Only love can guide us
More valuable than the touch of Midas
Love is an emotion that be seen and touched
But not defined

Jeremy's Last Moment
by Emilie Udell - age 13

"He's been through hell," she said.
I too saw it in his eyes.
He's been hurt a lot,
But never cries.
The pain he carries has taken its toll,
And has made his heart worn out and cold.
He's walked in too many doors without ringing the bell.
He kept so many secrets,
He swore himself not to tell.
Now the hurt he carries shows in his face,
And deep inside,
There is a bitter taste.

Here just take him
by Heather Renee Unseld - age 12

Here, just take him, is that what I said
Then why are you trying to take him?

I used to be his little girl, me.
He's done nothing wrong.

You give him cancer, but what is cancer?
Do you think it's a trick or a game?
Well, it's not.

Do you think he's for sale like a piece of
property?

Here, just take him, is that what I said?
But, I'm not giving him up like a toy we
don't want anymore,

Because he's my dad and I love him.

Mystery Man
by Kae M. Urling

Birds circle in the sky as lighting
flashes way up high
Smoke fills the sky and in front
of me I see.
The softness of his skin,
The luster of his hair,
His eyes shinning like new glints on snow
while his smile warms my heart.
His beauty is the brightness of all.
Yet no woman can see.
Not for those who can not see whats
on his mind or in his heart.
Lighting flashes in the sky, and the stars
shine in his eyes.
Smoke fills the skies as he kills all
the other guys.
No other man shall possess the powers
that he holds inside.
Only she will know of the powers he
holds.
Who is she only he will know.
It is not me, he left me alone.

Coffeehouse
by KCV

A waterfall, a beautiful jug, a twisted man...
Each one is expressed on the walls
Papers in the corner, some of which are out of order
Sounds of jazz rest overhead...a little jive
Easy going people, black, white, and yellow
Outdoors it is raining...it mixes with the jingles
Soft clanks, quick sips...long haired girl studying in the corner
A small beam of light from an antique lamp
Smell of a Thrift shop beams from the furniture
Isn't it nice?...Forgetting all your troubles...
Think I'll head back up for a double.

Missing You
by Tina Valiukas - age 14

Roses are Red,
Violets are Blue,
Who cares what they say?
Who cares what they do?
They say that you are dead,
but I know it's not true.
I hear your voice,
I hear your laughter,
I see you in my heart-
in my heart you will
always be alive and well.

I wish I could see you
Just one more time.
Just to say Hi, how are you?
Or a bye, see ya later.
You left us without
warning,
You didn't say goodbye.
I wish I could
see you
Just one more time.

Heavens Door
by Erin VanderVelde - age 13

Why him?
Why did he go?
What is it like, in his new home?
On a cloud, where he sleeps,
Oh so peaceful,
Oh so sweet.

He's up there on a unicorn.
He watches us like an angel,
Then he tries to ease our mourn.

But no one has the answer to,
Why he had to go.
Why seems to be the question,
But not even a teacher knows.

His childhood he did not live,
At least not to its fullest.
His body is done living now,
But his soul lives deep within us.

He fought his battle,
Then lost his war,
He now walks through,
Heavens door.

But don't think for a moment,
That he will be forgot.
Because Joel was,
And is,
Loved a lot.

Dedicated to Joel Ankerberg

Two of Hearts
by Erica VandeWouwer - age 17

I'm at the age of curiosity
when it comes to guys.
I take a look around the world
and see the downs and highs.
When there is one who sees me clear
and looks into my eyes,
I thought I figured out the ways
of curiosity in guys.
One may smile, and nod his head,
and one may give a glance.
And sometimes there is even one
who does a little dance.
But when you think you have this guy
enveloped in your splendor.
He doesn't return the feelings like
a man of his gender.
So you look away for a while and
observe your other choices,
But a tiny little thing inside
screams in many voices.
For when another comes along
who treats you like a lady,
The other fellow back behind
is looking kind of shady.

Tomorrow
by Sarah Van Schoik - age 13

I'm afraid of tomorrow ever becoming real
I'm afraid of how people will make me feel.
I'm scared of my pathetic life day after day
I'm terrified of myself I guess you could say.
Nothing is easy to me anymore
It's practically a habit now that I lay and cry on my floor.
I don't know how to handle the simplest things
I analyze things to death, even stupid little flings.
I'm gonna screw up my life and never be successful
Maybe all my beliefs are just crappy bull.
I'm never right or good enough
I can't concentrate on some very important stuff.
I don't want to change, but I sometimes wonder if I have a choice
And no one will be there tomorrow to listen to my voice.

Mankinds Plight
by Colleen D. Vanskiver

In mans neverending plight, to have world power, and all it's might,
Have some of us lost sight, of the things in life that are important and right?
So what if we cut down all the trees,
Man needs to make money, it's not greed...
Industry and progress are everywhere,
Half the planets children are starving, does that seem fair?
Toxins and landfills here and there,
The earth can hold it, does anyone care?
Older citizens sick and alone,
Can't pay their taxes, there goes their home...
Maybe what mankind needs to see,
Is how our creator, meant the human race to be...
For what good is mankinds plight, if in reality,
We have lost the true fight...
Of guiding future generations into hereafter that, is honorable and bright...

Why Me?
by Jennifer M. Vedar - age 15

It felt so good the first time you held me,
The first time you kissed me, the first time you cared.

It was like a fantasy, too good to be true,
You made me too happy to see you right through.

But why did this happen to me and not you?
Why tell me you care, if it's not even true?

And now that it's over, can I get through,
The pain that you left me, as you've found someone new?

I don't want you to be in my life,
How can I let go with you always in sight?

Why did I fall for you like I did?
I believed you about everything, what was in my head?

I just needed someone, not only for a day,
But I needed you most for me everyday.

I wanted so much for us to be "one",
But now I can see that we weren't meant to be.

Confused
by Dena Ventrudo - age 15

Dark and gloomy
Cloudy but roomy
Is how I feel inside
Bright and sunny
Sweet like honey
All inside my mind

My heart is full of haze
I walk like in a daze
Lost inside my soul
I find my changing goals

So dazed and confused
Need to find a refuge
Don't know what to think
Inside I start to shrink
Where will the future go?
Oh, I don't know, I don't know

Don't know which path to choose
Which one leads to doom?
Don't know which one to run
Where can I find some sun?

So dark and gloomy
So cloudy but roomy
Is how it is inside
Bright and sunny
Sweet like honey
All crammed into my mind

Don't smile why
by Julie Veriha - age 15

The days go by and by
And you have never smiled why
Will you open up and cry
Yes she said

But look into your heart
And see her smiles
See all the things
She's left behind

Just close your eyes
And see
There is no misery

A smile a smile I think I see
Could it be
Yes yes
I see all the things she left for me

My Awakening
by Nisha Verma - age 14

I woke up out of bed today,
and for some reason,
nothing was the same as yesterday.
The sun was still shining.
The birds were still chirping.
But something was wrong.
I couldn't hear the lies anymore,
and couldn't see the show.
What I could see is what is constantly being covered up.
What I know can't be hidden from me anymore.
I can see the world now, not like I could before.
It's all in front of my eyes
The fresh new visions of light and darkness
fascinate me like nothing else can.
Yet I never could have imagined
that this day would be
My Awakening.

Forget Me Not
by Stephanie Vitale - age 15

I know right now we're so far apart
But my love for you is still strong in my heart
It is the same everyday
In every shape, manner, and way
No one or thing can change it
Or push it into a pit
It still remains
as though kept there by chains.

I don't know if you still love me
But as you see
I feel that you are the only one
My love, nourishment, and sun
The light in a dark world
I which around my life is twirled.

You mean everything to me
So hear my plea
Never forget all we have shared
Or how much I really do and have cared.

Tabitha's Baby
by D. Wimmer Vitanzo

When you were born you were put up for adoption
This decision was out of love and the best option
For you to have loving parents and a home
With a large yard where you can safely roam
You deserve security, love and attention
Plus many other things too numerous to mention
She knows your new parents are filled with joy
It doesn't really matter if you're a girl or a boy
She was too young to become a mother
But the love she feels for you matches no other
It was hard for her to give you away
It was a very high price she had to pay
She'll never forget you no matter what
You'll always be in her heart and her thoughts
She chose your parents with a great deal of care
With you their lives they'll eagerly share
She hopes someday you'll understand what she had to do
It wasn't for her, it was all for you
So have a good life, baby dear
As you walk with pride and have no fear
Know your parents love you and she does too
May God keep you safe and always bless you

Word Without A Face
by Heather Voyles - age 15

The word is one that is lowly uttered.
Death, she whispers, so quiet and so free.
Our life is controlled. Our love is smothered.
Our death is mourned, but sometimes not, I see.
The smell of death is not yet defined.
But yet so many have smelled it.
And yet so many have cried.
We piece together phases of grief, bit by bit.
The word of death has no trimming of lace.
It is the word without a face.

My Brother
by D. Wimmer Vitanzo

I miss you so now that you're gone
I think about you from dusk 'til dawn
I sorely miss the sound of your laughter
When I told a joke, both before and after
You were taken away without a word
That was the saddest thing I've ever heard
You never shouted or even got mad
You were the best brother I could have ever had
You always wore a grin or a little smile
For your family and friends you'd go that extra mile
You never complained nor showed any fear
Just two of the reasons I held you so dear
My heart is broken and will never quite mend
I didn't just lose a brother, I lost my best friend
As to why you left I have no answer
Except God in His mercy released you from cancer
I know your illness caused misery and grief
And when death came, it was a blessed relief
Now you are in Heaven where there are no ills
Free from your life of surgery and pills
Someday I shall see you again, brother dear
When my time comes I shall not fear
I will greet you again with opened arms
And once again luxuriate in your humor and charm

Untitled
by Doan Vo - age 15

Death...Isn't it peaceful?
death seems so near,
when it should be far,
why is that?
am I depressed?
surely, I must be,
He wants to take me away,
to the peaceful land,
I don't have much reasons...
to live....now do I?
I'm slowly....but surely, wasting away.
now would be the best time to go,
why wait later?
he'll come one night and sweep me away,
they'll find me...
not breathing,
I'll be dead,
he'll take me,
no one will have to worry,
I'll be safe,
in a far away land,
up above,
I'll look down upon you,
and watch you,
you know, I'll be happier...
as a soul, as a spirit in everyone's mind,
I'll be with you wherever you go,
watching over you,
when I'm dead...I'll be your guardian angel....

Soul Mates
by Tawnia Vollstedt - age 15

A world apart we hear one another
And listen through silent hopes.
We search the skies for an answer,
For the stars are the key to fate,
But the outer-realm denies our request.
We pass by everyday in life
Yet we never see each other.
Our hearts beat one rhythm
Though the sound is lost in lonely nights.
We awake to new promises,
That are forgotten by noon.
We hold each other in dreams
Yet never touch in reality.
Each of us vows to dismiss our feelings,
But the passion is too strong.
We are soul mates;
Bound to one another,
By an unanswerable force.
We may never meet each other,
But we grow up together....Always.

My Best Friend
by Erika Vopnford - age 11

My best friend was always there when I was feeling down.
My best friend was always there when my head was spinning round.
My best friend was always there for me, I'd have to say
what would I ever do
if my best friend went away?

My best friend has gone away and I am left to cry.
My best friend has gone away I had to say good-bye.
My best friend has gone away I cannot stand the lack,
oh how I'd like it
if my best friend was ever to come back.

I wrote my friend a letter she didn't return my note.
I wrote my friend a letter, does she ever know I wrote?
I wrote my friend a letter, and I don't know why,
but if my best friend does not write back
I am sure to cry.

My best friend's not moving back is what I heard today.
My best friend's not moving back she is there to stay.
My best friend's not moving back she's not here to hear me say,
You've been with me through thick and thin,
you're my best friend in every way.

My Best Friend
by Jamie E. Voss

I didn't know her for long,
But I loved her to death.
She never really belonged to me,
But I grew to love her as she did me.
She was my best friend.

I'll never forget...
Her big, beautiful eyes.
How they would light up
When I got home from work.
She was my best friend.

I'll never forget...
The way she smiled
When I would say,
'I love you boo-boo'.
She was my best friend.

I'll never forget...
How she'd jump into the car,
And stick her head out into the wind,
Letting her hair blow all around.
She was my best friend.

I'll never forget...
They way we wrestled.
At first she would be rough,
But then she would lick me to death.
She was my best friend.

Then my biggest fear happened
On a day I'll never forget...
On Valentine's Day
I lost my best friend.

Silence
by April Jannette Walker - age 16

A whispering silence lies beneath us. A child's cry is unheard. Everyone looks as though they do not hear a thing, but they know each and everyone is screaming inside, hurting as their hearts bleed.
Life seems to have deserted everyone and leaving only a shell, a shell in which nothing wants to enter. The eyes of the hurting blink as if not there. Lost away in a memory they wish were there. They are searching for a voice which whispers happiness, but this silent voice is nowhere to be found.
A smile beams without delight, love is shed no more. A tear falls from the face of the young and old. Silence has fallen upon them as a blanket. And yet it seems as though no one wants to remove it.
Would anything be possible without hope? For deep within our hearts lies love, happiness, and hope. And there each one shall wait until someone captures them.

Recycled Minds
by Michelle Wallace

Our minds rule the world
Human ambition makes history
Repeat itself
History, history, history
The whispers of those dead
Screaming the obvious at us
Our thoughts rule the world
Running in cycles
All is known, nothing fresh
Back to where we begun
Back in history
To thoughts that make us
Who we are

In My Dreams
by Shannon Walkup - age 15

In my dreams there is a wonderful place I love to go. There is a large wide open meadow lying just before a soft white sandy beach leading to the ocean that lies just beyond the two mile stretch of tall green trees and rich brown soil. In the meadow there are sunflowers as tall as houses and pink, yellow, and red tulips that grow to my knees. There are wild flowers everywhere I turn, colored as if I were walking through a bright rainbow. Off in the distance is an old wise oak tree, that is so enormous it seems to watch over me like an old grandfather. I feel very safe and warm when I sit against the grandfather like tree listening to the winds whispering to me. I can never leave this place until I watch the brilliant yellow sun set just beyond the water while I'm being mesmerized by the beautiful pinkish red sky as it turns clear blue and fills with white stars. Then I wake up; just to long for the moment when I'll return.

The Walk
by Pamela Waller

I walk along the meadow lane,
Upon my head comes drops of rain.
There's a puddle, I jump,
Then I sit down on a big tree stump.

Wild flowers are growing right next to me.
I lean to pick them upon my knee.
I look up to see you standing beside me,
You make me laugh,
I feel so happy and carefree.

So take my hand,
Walk with me along the meadow lane.

Christmas
by Jennifer Walston - age 15

To this day it will never be the same,
When Christmas comes around
Jesus' birthday we claim
Lights are flashing in the town.

Little ones ripping
Opeing the packages
Everyone is caring
No one saves the plastic.

This is always taken for
Christmas, family, laughter,
Happiness, and joyful times.

Someone who sits
Alone crying asking why
I cry over her on this day,
Happy and joyful day.
Always there and now vanished.
To this day it will never be the same.

Grandma sits
Alone watching me
Crying over her on this day.
Watching through
The eyes of a cardinal.
It will never be the same
never
NEVER

On the day she died
by Ashlye Warner - age 18

Big Ben in England was pelted with rain
but still toned midnight just the same.
My cats sighed,
the old shepherds cried,
and even Satan himself looked up
from below
shaking his head in utter sorrow.
Not many, of course could say they cared,
but they were definitely all aware,
that on that day
that day she died,
the whole world couldn't help, but cry.
Hearing the winds blow in such fury,
seeing the rain fall with no glory.
All around they screamed,
and it definitely seemed
that the world was lost in shambles...
Then she herself looked down from the clouds
shaking her head.
At the moment, in the air
I swear
the words "I love you"
echoed through
the entire atmosphere.

Beyond The Grave
by Ruth Warner

There's someone calling me beyond the grave;
an image in white linen born to save;
His gentleness and love will set me free,
and help me to become all I might be.

This world with all its glitter and its gold
is temporary, calculating, cold.
To walk forever in God's truth and light
will be my goal and ever my delight.

The devil in his heyday did his best
to put the human races to the test;
but he will never conquer righteousness
or turn aside from God those who are blessed.

So may life's journey end courageously
and may I find endurance inwardly.
Most precious Lord direct me to be brave,
and some day walk with you beyond the grave.

Eyes Of Dreams
by Donté W.

    First eyes; love: never knowing how those eyes will evolve, changes from interpretations through what they'll see. By time the truths, untruths they will view. Affected by confusion, hurt, so many external sources; attempting all too often to harden so deep within. Beginning hopes, will they ever come to past? Suffer will two of two, when one of two lose first eyes. Eyes of dreams are eyes of the beholder. Standing strapped now, believing the truth is only yours. Seeing with eyes of exclusively your pains, wants, need for now; never giving thought of tomorrow, The agony of selfishness is not felt by the selfish, yet deep within the heart of inextinguishable first eyes. A suffering that will continue until selfish realizes that their life, is not just their life, but also the life, of eyes of dreams. Meanwhile the idle side of sureness exists, causing close separation and bidirectional paths. Eyes of dreams turning to other dreams to fulfill future quest, but mostly to inhabit present emptiness . With a wish for first eyes to see their way back, with the understanding that succeeding alone, is not that remote of an acceptance. So great is the sacrifice, after realized, her happiness you can't cause. Once the pain of this subsides; to wish, no matter how agonizing, that she finds someone who can. So sacred this wish.

I Am Crazy
by Dean A. Warren

My friends tell me I am crazy
and believe me to be just that.
I tell them that at least I am not lazy;
that is the end of our chat.

Spring Day
by Jenn Wasserman - age 14

The flowers sway slowly
in the cool spring breeze.
They make a rustling sound,
just like the trees.
The ocean churns calmly,
making a peaceful noise.
The sun beams down joyfully,
enlightening girls and boys.
The birds are singing happily.
White clouds are floating by.
As I lay on the limb of an acorn tree,
watching the world go by.

Dreams
by Tyffanie Watson - age 15

Dreams of hopes and aspirations
Wither in the wind
Leaving bits and pieces
For someone else to mend.
They flow down a winding river
Splashing here and there
Painting rocks with memories
For someone else to share.

Dreams of hopes and aspirations
Soar through the sky
Never knowing where they land
Or when they're going to die.
They live their life to the fullest
So they never question why
Life seems so short
And dreams of hopes and aspirations seem to fade and die.

The Shelf
by Joan Webster

When the peacock sings,
the crystal bear smiles,
and the pink rose glows.

Because of you,
I know the beauty of love
and the need of it too.

My thoughts dance
in circles of silence...
as the colors of hot pink
    to denim blue
        swirl within.

You allow touching softly...
then the storm rages...
but,
you never
quite let the fingertips of the soul go.

The want is consummate...

as the peacock sings...
the crystal bear smiles...
and the pink rose glows.

Fright Life
by Stacy Wedding - age 14

The sky is dark, the stars are bright.
The night is long, and full of fright.
The coldness in the air, my heart is pumping fast.
I hope the fear doesn't get me, and I hope it doesn't last.

The fear came over me, I didn't know what it was.
I wish it would go away, who knows, it sometimes does.
The sun is coming, to wash away the night.
To clean up the fears, and take away the fright.

The daylight is here, the fear is gone.
Everyone is safe, because of the dawn.
so Go on, Go on, enjoy the day.
The darkness left, So now it's all okay.

Stop Hitting Her
by Tiffany Weiss - age 15

The tears you see, but you can't see the pain,
trust you lose, bruises you gain.

Stop it please, you're hurting me,
but he never listens to your desperate plea.

So you run in your room and lock the door,
he picks the lock and hits you once more.

You're scared of him, does he still love you?
a child's nightmare is coming true.

You want to say "Stop hitting her!"
her crying voice you'll always remember.

So you try to think of happy things,
a smile to your face it may bring.

So you keep covering up the bruises and fear in your eyes,
hide it with your realistic lies.

But you have to learn, you have to get out,
CHILD ABUSE.... is what it's all about.

Why I Love You
by Audra Lea Weixelman - age 19

When I think of you
I get a smile on my face
and butterflies in my stomach
When I see you
My body get goosebumps
and my heart flutters
When you hold me
my body turns to mush
and all my depressed thoughts seem to vanish
When you're in me
It's a feeling I have never felt before
and nothing like I ever could imagine or dream of
When you're away from me
I miss you so much
That is why I Love You for now and always

Being 12- years- old
by Kate Welch - age 12

Hi I'm Dawn Keller,
I'm no feller.
I'm 12- years- old,
I'm not that bold.
Being 12- years- old isn't simple,
I mean you get zits and pimples.
It must be all that dirt.
At least I get to flirt,
With boys in older grades,
But that phase will soon fade.
My grades ain't been so hot,
That's because I don't study a lot!
I wonder if 13 is going to be a flick,
It's probable not going to be a picnic.
And that is that,
Did I mention my chest was flat.

The Only One
by Melissa Welsch - age 17

I can feel the outside surface of
my own body shake with fear- with dread.
I have a hurt that is so deep
that haunts me when I'm sober.
I want to know if anyone else
can look at me and see my bones quiver.
Is this just another one of my sensations?
No one can feel what I am feeling.
No one knows how I am struggling.
Am I the only one that can see into my mind?
to know what I know?
Am I really all alone in this world of fabrication?

Broken Hearted Me
by Melissa Werner - age 13

Broken hearted me
It hurts so terribly
The pain you put me through
That's the price I pay to be with you
You never talk
And when you do
It's never about me and you

After The Curtain Falls
by Marisa Wessler - age 14

Sets once used to create a world
Are packed in a truck and sent away
After the curtain falls.
Costumes that painted a soul
Are washed of scent and hung on a rack
After the curtain falls.
The theater that was once filled with emotions
so complex and diverse
is still in the same place.
But it doesn't have the heart it once had
After the curtain falls.
The director now drinks more than coffee
The actors still wait tables with hope
The dancers still have aching bones
The tech still curse at their hammers.
And they all vow that they will never change
And they will never forget the memories made
But none of these things are quite the same
    After the curtain falls.

Abby, my best friend
by Kassie Westcott - age 13

The wind blows softly upon my tender cheek,
Through the cool breeze I can hear you calling me.
Your voice and laughter surrounds me,
I allow my soul to be swallowed up by it.
Everywhere I go I feel the warmth of your presence in
My heart.
At night, as I lay myself down for that night's rest,
I look up into the sky and see you.
See you, watching over me and smiling.

Ocean Bond
by Alisandra McGowan - age 15

White hot sand,
with each step,
creates and reopens, blisters on my feet.
Firey sun reddens, the already freckled skin
of my neck and shoulders.

I look up,
Daddy, tall, strong,
He takes my hand.
We wade into clear green-blue liquid,
frigid to my scalded skin.
Gasping as the blood rushes to my head.

Softly rolling waves lift me,
one after another off my feet.
Strong gentle hands raise me above the white caps,
and turn me to ride the crest to the sloping shore.

Untitled
by Jennifer West - age 15

If I were small, I'd roam the worlds
Of every crack and crevice.
They'd be like caves to my small self,
When I am small as an insect.

If I were small, you'd be the one
To watch over and protect me,
For you're the only one I'd trust
And in your hands, you'd hold me.

If I were small by courtesy,
Of some strange, magic potion;
I'd cry for I would miss your world,
And drown in my own ocean.

Untitled
by Jennifer West - age 15

You need someone to support you,
With me you'd only fall down.
You need someone to uplift you,
I'd turn your smile into a frown.
Please flee from me,
And let it be;
For I will only forsake you.
You now must part,
Though I hold your heart,
For I'll only return it broken.

You Are My Friend
by by Charlotte Whigham

If words could er' express my dear,
The joys the times have been;
I'd let you know a million times,
I'm proud to be your friend.

We've known the ups, we've know the downs,
Around the world we've been;
But you were always there for me,
I'm proud to be your friend.

Rush!!*!*
by Katie Lynn Whitaker - age 13

I enter the doorway to a basement
A big party is going on
I take a seat and wait to be served a piece
Of fantasy land
As I take the first hit I feel my heart
Pounding
Faster, and faster
My adrenalin pumping and pumping
As I slowly feel my mind drift away to
Another place
I could see the strobe light flicker in
The back of my head
Then I felt as if I was flying higher and
higher into the sky!!!!
Everything was pounding and pumping
All at the same time
Then all of a sudden I fell!
Everything was black and everything had
Stopped!
I couldn't see anymore flickering from
The strobe light
Everything was quiet
I felt so lonely and deserted
Then I knew there was no more rush
It was over, I was over...

Believing
by Siobhan White - age 14

If we must die
And lose our friends
To save our blessed country,
Then that is what
So many do,
They die for us
And I say to you:
If they die
For a cause
That is forgotten soon
Then they didn't die
For the cause.
They died because
They believed in us.
They must be honored
And never forgotten.
The Wall names many men
Who, just like me and you,
Loved their country
And they died because
They believed in us,
They believed in me and you.

The Dreams
by Sara L. White - age 16

As dark shadows;
Roaming around my room.
They make my life a sorrow;
They fill my life with gloom.

One after another;
From my memory they come.
They scare me half to death;
Though to you they may sound dumb.

Some of him attacking me;
and almost unnaturally dying.
Then I wake in the middle of the night;
All alone and crying.

Things so nasty and so cruel;
They make me want to scream.
I'm so afraid it will come true one day;
But for now it's just a dream.

The Funeral
by Daniel Mark Wichern - age 13

Everyone is sad nobody is glad.
Dark and roomy and very gloomy.
A sob a sign everyone tries
to hold back tears so nobody hears
the mourning the weeping only one is sleeping.

Resting in peace for eternity.
Then suddenly a burst of fright
a child is now scared of the night
of mourning of weeping and everything not right
living in fright of the night which he sleeps.

Never the less he starts to weep
of fright of the night and everything not right
of death of hell and nobody can tell
the fright this child has of the night.
And he looked back on where it all began
the death of his great grandmother and
remembers where it all began.

The Glorious Looks of Love Though a Young Woman's Eyes
by Tara Wick - age 16

His hair is blondish brown and short, but touches his ears,
It lays on his head as if it's careful not to break it,
It shines with the direction of the light,
When he smiles it makes his face look like the sun bouncing off the trees,
His smile gives me a feeling of being wanted,
It makes me feel the happiness that he is feeling,
His arms feel like a mountain,
They are firm like the rocks of the mountain,
They look as if they could be the base of the mountain and hold it up,
When I hug him his grip is strong but gentle, as if he could break me but he
doesn't want to hurt me,
His embrace give me the feeling of a warm summer breeze,
When he likes something his eyes look real intent,
His eyes look as soft as the morning breeze,
His eyes sparkle like the sun on the ocean,
They look as if they take in all the information that you give,
As if he is listening intently, with all care,
His lips are as soft as a teddy bear,
His eyebrows curve over his eyes as if to protect them from harm.

Time
by Ariel Wiegmann - age 11

So precious
And delicious
Like a cake
Ready to bake
Do not waste
But don't make haste
Don't go so fast
Try to make it last
For if you go fast
You might find that your past
Is boring and full of work
Don't make life murky
Just make sure you have time for fun!

Untitled
by Dawn Wielgus - age 15

The doors slammed shut
And there was no way out of the hut
The hurt and pain was caught
And all who was there did nothing but fought

The rain poured down and out
Until there was no longer a chance a drought
The thunder yelled all around
And in the end nothing could be found

The hurt was still there
But nothing was left to fear
The pain subsided for only a day
Always returning after going away

Revolution
by Jessica Wilcox - age 19

I feel among us a Revolution,
It sneaks upon us quietly, and yet is so vivid.
I am not speaking of the flowering Impatience,
Nor the Jenny-wren's song of Passion, as she returns
    to start the Fifth month,
Whispering in the ears of the trees who, in turn,
Gossip the melody to the woodland creature,
Then to the brook who babbles it across the countryside.

O 'tis the Revolution in the sky repeating daily;
Do you not sense the night ship sail through your veins?
Do you not hear the foghorn question anyone who is listening?
Do you not see the billion lighthouses; how they offer this
    ship mercy and protection? (Yet it voyages on.)

I sit here on the shore and witness God dropping the moon
Behind the watery horizon as an anchor drowning in the sea,
    so the ship can rest,
For it has finally found its shelter after many hours.

O Captain Sun! Master of Lighthouses!
You have rapt me as you hug the earth with a blazing
    brilliance of bountiful warmth.
O Majestic exuberance: Glow until the chimera reoccurs,
    and once again, out of the port, the ship sails.

Single Tear
by Emily M. Williams - age 15

A single tear rolls down my cheek
Each one a memory I'll never be able to replace
Each one with a name and a face
A single tear for those who left
Each with a path all there own
Each going, going, gone
A single tear every night
Each one burning my heart
Each one tearing me apart
A single tear rolls down my cheek
Each a memory of a blue-eyed face
And each one knowing the ice cold man he was
    can never be replaced

Forever
by Kristi Nicole Willis - age 17

You came into my life one day,
And made all my fears and worries go away.
I knew from that day on,
We'd always be, and you'd never be gone.

We've had our ups and downs.
We've had our smiles and frowns.
But in all, we've make it through,
That's one thing I love about you.

You and me have always felt so right.
I love to feel you hold me tight.
Don't ever let go of me.
I know we'll always and forever be.

You're so special in so many ways,
I think about you every night and day.
My love for you will never fade,
I think just for me, you were made.

I hope you realize that I love you,
And I know you love me too.
Let's always stay together,
I promise to love you...forever!

Dreams
by Krista Wilson - age 13

As I'm lying here in my bed,
I see the thoughts run through my head.
I see my days; just the best,
In my somewhat unpeaceful rest.
I see the things I wish I could do,
And make my life better when I was blue.
So there is a way to make me per**fect**,
Where everyone shows me respect.
There is only one problem with this game,
There are those dreams you cannot tame.
These dreams are bad,
But they have no right to make me sad.
I should wake up and disregard,
The dream about a bomb within a greeting card.
If only the good dreams I could steal,
Then I could try to make them real.

Just Another Day at School
by Jeniene Wishart

When the doors swing open at the sound of the bell, it's expected that boys and girls will get settled in their classrooms as quickly and quietly as possible. It would make the teachers' day an easy one if the students could all be engaged in active learning from this time until dismissal time. Let's see what the teacher is really confronted with on a daily basis.

As the secretary sits behind her desk and the PA system sounds its buzz, she immediately answers the call. The teacher in the third grade quad can't flush the toilet of the girls bathroom. Within the course of an hour the buzzing sounds again for the 2nd and 5th grade. In the 2nd grade, the teacher needs her pencil sharpener repaired 'right away' and the 5th grade teacher said she's walking out because Dan said: "How the hell do I know."

Johnny appears in the office and is directed to the health room. The teacher sends him to the nurse, suspecting him to have a high fever. It's 98.6, but without a temperature, she can't be sure he really is sick. Sandy is sent from class to be given her daily medication, Ritalin. The teacher knew that it was time for her medication since she disrupted the class quiz chanting the ten commandments.

In the cafeteria 1st and 2nd graders throw pizza and gatorade at one another. The teacher on duty has slipped on a plastic bag. The office is summoned to the cafeteria, but there is no one to relieve the teacher on lunch duty.

Out on the playground, sand is flung and teachers are busy talking in a huddle about the movie last night and future lesson plans. Suddenly, a student falls from the slide and two other students can't share the jump rope with another group of girls.

Meanwhile, back in the teacher's lounge there is chronic complaining by a select few. This is not a very relaxed place three out of five days during the week. Discussions of the principle objectives, parents' concerns, job descriptions and misbehaved students are continued. Nothing ever seems right! It's a select few in the school who seem to have the most to complain about.

The day is at a close, the Principal's door is finally opened after having been closed for hours. Too many phone calls intercepted as the principal demands there be <u>No Interruptions</u>! Teachers send up their bubble sheets that were written up on students for numerous classroom management situations. It's time for the secretary to call the buses, as the principal places everything from her desk to the secretaries. Messages are ready to be answered, teachers ask for minutes to speak with the principal and once again the door is closed...."See you tomorrow!"

Homeless
by Laura Wodtke - age 17

People on the streets
with nothing to eat.
Sitting near stores
trying to collect money.
Going hungry, getting cold.
No one to talk to, no one to hold.

No where to sleep, barely any clothes.
People ignoring you, you think people don't care.
Older people look at you, younger kids start to stare.

You start to cry when you try to sleep,
Scared of not waking up in the morning.
You fight to stay alive, you beg for donations.
Not many people listen, people are afraid of you.

You think about the past and how you got like this.
You pray to the Lord each night and hope someday
you **WON'T** be like this.

Best Friend
by Lauren Wolfe - age 13

She wags her tail when she plays with me,
And looks around the yard,
She's after her tail, a stick, a bone,
And makes me laugh real hard!

She's training well, she has the gift,
She follows all my wishes,
She licks my face, arms, and legs,
And gives me lot's of kisses!

She sits and plays and gives her paw,
And wiggles her tail at me,
It seems this dog has all the tricks,
I wonder how that can be?

There are times when my life can get pretty mucky,
I clap my hands,
And give a nod....
And here comes my dog, Lucky!

Take Me To My Dreams
by Cassandra Renee Wolff - age 14

Tossing and turning
In and out
You're trapped inside me
I beg you, get out

I look in your eyes
You mesmerize me
But yet, just a dream
It tortures me

I'll never be yours
You'll never be mine
I remember the love
What's now forgotten time

"I love you," you whisper
But then I wake up
Ouch! It hurts!
I can't be that tough

Goodnight, Goodnight
Time for bed it seems
And then regretfully
You take me to my dreams

Hidden Strength
by Cassandra Renee Wolff - age 14

They look inside
And try to understand
Why I don't want help
Why I don't need a hand

They say "I want to help"
But they don't really know
How I seem to see
How they scrutinize so

They change the code
They think I won't learn
While I wait for the day
When it's my turn

I'll show them something
They'll see they were wrong
They'll know I'm not weak
They'll realize I'm strong

A Glimpse Of Heaven
by Farrah Renee Wolverton - age 17

A cool crisp night with stars so
bright. The moon looks so relaxed as
the night moves fast. The winds so
strong and ruffled and thankful are
the lovers that hold one another
in each others arms. The pastel blue
sky that appears so calm. The look in
your eyes tell me our love could not
be wrong. The cool crisp breeze that
so powerfully drifts through the air.
Makes the trees look as if they don't
have a care in the world. I know
that I will never see heaven until
I die and even then I may not, but
I do believe that God has allowed
me to see a glimpse of heaven
when he allowed me to find you.

The Colors I am
by Alexis Wood - age 14

I am the color of green and beige
Beige is the color of being happy
Just like a nice clean scrunchie
I am always happy
When somebody is sad
I can help them by being happy and
Confident around them
I am also the color of green
Green is the color for being
Confident and calm
Just like a nice big juicy apple
I am always calm and confident
Just like the calm, calm sea.
Those two colors are my favorite colors
That's what makes them so special.

Death
by Douglas B. Woods - age 19

As I went to sleep I knew what lay in store,
I bowed down before my bed and prayed to the Lord.
Looking out the window I saw Death at my door.
I took a deep breath and let the dark soul in,
Death takes many lives,, and now mine is at an end.
When Death extended his hand I knew what to do,
As he shook his head I knew my life was through.
Death stared into my eyes with an evil grim,
A deal was proposed, my live and soul I could win.
The game began with a spin of the wheel,
Once things were underway, I knew it was for real.
For hours the game continued on,
We continued to battle on the front lawn.
In the end victory was all mine,
Death excepted his loss, and said "Maybe another time."
I retrieved my soul and on with my life I went,
That night, to the Lord, prayers of thanks I sent.

A Daddys' Heart
by JoAnn P. Woods

Look just with in a daddys' heart.
And there you'll find a big huge spot,
Just put there for a daughters' heart.
For daddys' are slayers of monsters and menders
of wounds,
And a comfort from the big cold world.
And no one hugs like daddys' do,
With arms of steel and words of gold,
When daughters' look into daddys' eyes,
And there they'll see filled up with pride,
For daughters' are a daddys' heart.
A river of love pores out of thee;
With every beat and surge it flows;
With ruffles, roses, satin, and bows.
This is what daddys' little girls are made of;
For one of these days all filled with white,
A beautiful church adorn in delight;
And then came the day for daddys' to bear.
"My Daughter To Him "!
"I Guess I'll Say, "Yes"!
For daughters' are truly a daddys' heart.

Puddle of Memories
by Emily Wray - age 16

My heart has been slashed wide open, but not by any knife of steel.
But a knife of a love once strong, now gone.

The tears that fall used to heal, and now only sting.
And mix with the blood and dreams at my feet.
In that puddle I see reflections,
reflections of the past and us.

A breeze dries the tears on my cheeks,
it whispers of what could of been and ripples the puddle.
The rain promises to fall- clearing away the puddle.
But the sky only grows blacker, and no rain falls.
The puddle stays.

They come to heal my wound with words and hugs and promises.
But the wound grows bigger and more sensitive.
Until only one can heal with soothing words of love.

My heart is bleeding,
my eyes are weeping,
my love is leaving,
as the puddle grows and reddens.

The door closes never to be opened again.
The heavy red door, hot to touch.
Inside a love young, pure and sweet lives,
but out of my reach.

The puddle spreads, seeping under the door.
The love slowly dies, it's beyond my control.
You hold the key to the door,
but you've lost it along the way.
Maybe found another day.

Until then......
the puddle grows and reddens.

Treasures

Me
by Nikki Woolery - age 16

I'm a girl
with many thoughts and
feelings
I'm a child of the
cold,
but
have warm feet.
I have brown hair
blue eyes and fair skin
My hair is long.
Tonight is cold and
rainy.
don't mind me
I'm a child of the cold.
Snow Fairies and
Ice queens dance
in my head,
I'm crazy,
but,
a child of the cold.
Snow dreams....

Deep And Abiding Love
by Georgia Wright

Earth Mother, cradle her tenderly,
For her own tenderness we will miss.
Eternal Father, bathe her in Your love
As sweet as she expressed in her kiss.

Let her spirit now be near us
As she was there for us in life.
Let her faith and teachings guide us
Through these days of sorrow and strife.

Lay Your hand upon her cheek softly
Like she laid her hand upon ours.
Among the fragrant blooms she loved,
Let her pause to smell the flowers.

Send angels to walk beside her
From this life she now departs.
Let Your light touch her gently,
As gently as she touched our hearts.

Broken Hearts Will Mend
by Robyn Anne Wright - age 14

Once long ago I held you tight,
now I only have dreams to help me through the night.

I gave you all my love to always keep you near,
but just at that moment I faced my biggest fear.

You left with her now I'm alone in this hell,
I'm told to forget you and just say "Oh well."

Forget about the good times, the jokes that we made,
The midnight walks on the beach, the drinks in the shade.

I can't forget these things, they constantly swim in my memory,
though you hurt me and lied, you mean so much to me.

The bad times so many, the good times so few,
I know you did me wrong, yet I'm still in love with you.

Not a year goes by, you're not in my thought.
All the alibies you sold, all the alibies I bought.

Not a month goes by you're not in my dream,
you carelessly left, and ripped my heart at the seam.

Not a day goes by you're not in my brain.
I must be in love, either that or insane.

Not a minute goes by you're not on my mind,
Your beautiful eyes, how you left me behind.

You said you'd always be in love, she called me her best friend.
Empty lies and tables turned but broken hearts will mend.

It Was You
by Sheri Wright - age 15

I was thinking of you,
      when I took his hand.
I was up in the sky,
      wasn't ever gonna land.

I was thinking of you,
      when I put my arms around him.
The sun had almost gone down.
      The sky was getting dim.

I was thinking of you,
      then I saw you standing there.
You turned and walked away.
      You thought I didn't care.

I was thinking of you,
      when I tried to pull away.
Wanted to catch up with you,
      but, he made me stay.

I was thinking of you,
      when I let him kiss me.
With my eyes closed,
      your face is all I'd seen.

It was you, I was thinking of
      It was you, on my mind.
Now, if only it was you,
      who's heart would be mine.

Love
by Tabitha Summer Wulfekuhl - age 18

    Love is a mystery
you fall in love with someone
out of nowhere.
The way you feel when there
near and far.
    Chills that run up your spin
The first time he said I Love You.
    Warmth of his body on a cold
winters night.

    Out of the blue
lightning strikes your heart.
    Your left with shattered
pieces and memories of the love
you thought would last forever.

Keepsake
by Linda Yamada

Memories
of me,
Tucked away
in lonely corners
In the attic
of your mind,
Gather dust
and cobwebs,
Gone
but not
Forgotten...
Piles of ashes
on the floor,
Turn out the light
and shut the door,
You don't
go up there
Anymore,
Remember me
Forevermore
In the attic
of your mind,
Memories
Burn hot and cold,
Think of me
and shed a tear
and I'll be
Forever near
in the attic
of your mind.

Another Valley Beyond Broken Walls
by Amy Yamashita - age 15

    Tonight I will sleep in the valley of the pale moon light. I shall dream of beautiful things. Things made of love and happiness. Of joy and forgiveness. I will swim in an ocean of passion and lust. I shall crawl in the sands of time and caress the sun filled rays. Father time will watch as I play with his magic. He will return time to its regular post after I'm done. Meanwhile mother earth is waiting for me with a blanket woven of grass and trees. When I find her I will sleep again to find in my wake another glorious valley.

Sweet Ambition
by Carolyn J. Yap

Ambition..the stars in your eyes, the man you hope
to marry;
the amount of money you hope to make at the job
you plan to hold.
Ambition...so firm in our minds yet as fleeting as the
star that comes crashing down to earth in a fireball of
destruction and devastation.
Disillusionment with our life's plans causes us to stray from
our chosen path, our dreams and our goals. We are crushed.
But in our heart of hearts, we know one day we will accomplish
our ultimate ambition, whatever that may be. In our mind's eye we
can see ourselves soaring high on the rockets of our success
and we are jubilant, ecstatic...
We have finally made it, out sweet ambition.
However, the true challenge lies in holding on to that which we
find so dear in our hearts.
Ambition...it can cause us to go where we have never gone before,
exploring depths of emotion and victory unbeknownst to us; yet, if
we are not careful, it an be the cause of our eternal downfall..
Our sweet ambition...it's not for the fainthearted, yet it can be
joyously uplifting...

The Guy
by Erica Yeary - age 13

As I look into his deep brown eyes
I wonder if his "I love you's are lies."

But it couldn't be, his kisses are soft as a dove
No matter what everyone says - he's the one I love.

American Women
by Paula J. Yost - age 17

They held their families together during war times
And late at night they counted their dimes
From straight skirts and bobbed hair
To children, jobs, and cookware.

They made it through the depression of then and now
American women can show the world how.
Strength is our virtue and love is our guide
Of our laws we will abide.

My generation's term is up and coming
I am proud of some of the women we're becoming
In my life I want to uphold
The morals of those before me, as if they were gold.

Nature Tries to Speak
by Emerald Yu - age 18

I felt the
wind tonight,
though it wasn't
very strong, it whispered
this eternal reality, asking
for its extreme needs. The
wind blows, and the air screams,
screaming to survive, wanting
some attention. The rain cries,
the earth weeps, weeping for its
thirst and needs. The
rock falls, the ground
cracks, could this be
nature screaming,
weeping, wanting
some attention?

American Not Second Class
by Fran Young

You see her there, hair of bonnie red-gold
And laughing Irish eyes of green.
How haughty she can look. How sad she can cry
And in anger, she's fighting mean.
She's American born. American bred.
With viper tongue and lilting laugh.
She was raised in the school of hard knock way
But my Mother's not second class.

My Dad was a quiet, strong, gentle man
With a hard not gentle life.
He loved this strong willed American girl
And took her to be his wife.
He worked, as they say, from can to can't
Through summer heat and wintry blast.
They raised six children on that dirt poor farm.
Dad's American, not second class.

There's more than a bit of Scottish fight
And a dab of Irish gay,
A bit of England too, I expect
Slipped in along the way.
Lord only knows what else there is
In the making of this stalwart lass.
What 'ere it be, it's not very clear
But I'm certainly not second class!

Love
by Audrey Armstrong - age 14

Love is war
Love is pain
Love is suffering
Love is shame
Love is comfort deep down inside
Love is a feeling you can not hide

The Voices
by Devon Zawitaj - age 14

    I hear voices in my head,
Two, Three sometimes Four
If they are right or wrong
I just don't know,
I hear voices in my head.

    Voices from the past,
present and maybe future too.
Am I going crazy because of this?
I just don't know,
I hear voices in my head.

    I hear voices in my head,
Two, Three sometimes Four
They tell me to be mean.
They tell me that I am wrong,
When I just might be right.

    Is this the way I'm supposed to be?
Is everyone this way?
Now am I going crazy?
I just don't know,
I hear voices in my head.

Friends
by Emily Zeien - age 14

Friends, don't always trust them.

You think they're your best friends but you find out they talk behind your back and then deny it.

Sometimes they're there for you and you're there for them too.

You think you can say anything to them and hope they won't say anything...think again.

You think they would never betray you, but they steal your loved ones and have no guilt.

Never call anyone a best friend until you know them inside and out.

Friends...don't always trust them.

Nobody Knows, But Me
by Emily Zeien - age 14

Nobody knows the hurt that I had to deal with, but me.

I acted just like I was fine, cause I didn't want anyone to feel sorry for me.

Nobody knows the loneliness that I had to deal with, but me.

I acted like I didn't need anyone cause I was hurt so many times.

Nobody knows the grief I had to deal with, but me.

I didn't want anyone to know my deep feelings or sorrow I had of so many losses.

Nobody knows but me.

Untouchable
by Monica Zimmer - age 15

Untouchable
are the clouds on a warm summer day.
No matter how beautiful and how much
you want to,
they can't be reached.

Untouchable
are the stars on the clearest night.
There's nothing you want more than to
catch one and keep it with you always.

Untouchable
is a rainbow after the softest rain.
You could reach forever but never grasp
what you're reaching for.

Untouchable
are you.
Though you're the most beautiful thing
in my eyes you remain untouchable
to me.

The Railroad Track
by Cassandra Zick - age 15

Come with me
Far, far away
Deep in the mind
Where your imagination plays

Plays with your feelings
Plays with your thoughts
Now play with me
In my past long forgot

So soft and fuzzy
Smells awfully sweet
Took me away
Where my dreams and I would meet

Sounds so soothing
My thoughts at ease
Gets softer and slower
As reality leaves

Note by note
I know the tune
So different yet the same
As if it were brand new

Puts me to sleep
And makes me feel safe
A protecting dome around me
Like my own little cave

Time to leave
You must go back
Let's play this again
Catch the next railroad track

Misery
by Robin Zikoski - age 13

Lying on this hospital bed,
I feel like I should be dead.
This pain I feel,
Is so unreal.
I wish I could learn,
When it's my turn.
My turn to die,
Instead of just lie,
Lie here and suffer,
To try to get tougher.
I want the answer
Why'd I have to get cancer?
I'm only eleven,
Not forty-seven.
I don't have a chance,
To give life a glance.
I want to live,
I want to give.
I want to love,
I want to fly high above.
I'm trying to be strong
Or am I doing it wrong?
I just have to believe,
I will not be deceived,
Until the day is here
I will not live in fear.

Treasures
Chapter Six

About the Author
Selected biographies
of competitors
and members of the
National Authors Registry.

Angulo, Gerardo L. - Born on June 26, 1972 in Nogales, Sonora, Mexico. I was raised and live in Nogales, Arizona. Graduated from Lourdes Catholic High School in May of 1990. Received associate degrees in General Studies and Social Services. Obtained a Bachelor of Arts degree from Prescott College in September of 1995. My inspirational sources are God and my mother, Mrs. Bertha Maxie Angulo, who passed away in November of 1995. I know in my heart that God has granted her eternal life in His heavenly kingdom. Ever since she left from this world, writing poetry for her has been very therapeutic for me. After all, I find poetry to be medicine for the soul.

Armstrong, Robert F. - I have been a licenses Architect and an instructor in several colleges and universities for over thirty-six years. I am kept very busy working at my profession of Architecture, teaching and now writing. My wife of forty-three years and I are looking forward to retirement and spending more time with our four children and four grandchildren. Retirement is just several years away and not looking forward to the abrupt change in lifestyle, I began writing about two years ago. I currently have two works of fiction in progress, one a sci-fi and the other a murder mystery. The creative atmosphere that is predominant in the field of Architectural Design has made the transition to writing very easy. I am a very emotional and sentimental person and writing poetry has been very rewarding and enabled me to express my true feeling about life and my fellow human beings. The specific poem, "A Father's Thanks," was written for my four children. It was my effort to return the feelings of love which they have extended to me over the years.

Atcheson, B.J. Vienot - Let me introduce me...Barbara, Julia, Catherine, Mary. Born 11/25/24 at Washington Heights, New York City. Daughter of Margaret Vienot, nee McIver, and Walter Vienot. Mother a stay at home mom and dad one of New York's finest. N.Y.P.D. I would turn out to be, not only their only daughter, but their only child. A lot of irish on mother's side and dad's side divided up between a mother from Leipzig, Germany and a father from Alsace-Lorrain. I did most of my early developing in a part of the Bronx called Highbridge. Highbridge was situated between two famous arenas. Yankee Stadium and the Polo Grounds. P.S. 73 was my academic home from kindergarten to the eighth grade. Then on to Walton high School. A school for girls (However, DeWitt Clinton High School for boys was nearby, and the boys, too, rode the same subways as the girls rode). I was sixteen and in my junior year when my mother's illness and death occurred. At eighteen my father died. Major, you might say, earthquake changes (today we would say traumas) in my young life. Marriage followed at age nineteen and I was off on what I thought was to be the adventure of my life...and it was! Twenty years and five children (one daughter, four sons) later, DIVORCE! Followed by sixteen years of trying to mend what could not be mended. Well past mid-life, this displaced home-maker hit the market place. At fifty-three I began recreating my life. I became a full time working woman and I continue to recreate. At seventy-two I am still a full time working woman who (with any luck) will be recreating her life at 100 years+.

Atwell, Samantha - Is a 15 year old who lives in a small town called Tipton, located in the San Joaquin Valley of central California. She loves California and never wishes to leave. She's a sophomore at Tulare Western High School, and hope to attend the Univeristy of San Diego after graduating from high school. She is interested in studying to be a Marine Biologist. She loves animals and her hobbies include swimming, skating, reading/writing, listening to music, hanging out at the mall, playing baseball, and spending time with her boyfriend, Kenneth. She lives with her parents, Donna and Willie Atwell, and her 14 year old brother, Joe. Included in the Atwell family is her black kitten, Cuddles. Her poem "Soul-Mates" was inspired by the friendship and love she receives from her own "soul-mate" and best friend Stacie Gravito.

Bahr, Shersti Lou - I am from Payson, UT and have lived here almost all my life. I am twenty years old. I graduated from Payson High and I am currently attending Utah Valley State College. I will get my Associates of Science degree with an emphasis in English. I plan to transfer to Brigham Young University. I will get a bachelors and Ph.D. in English Communications at BYU. I will then become a college professor and a professional writer. I am mostly interested in being a novelist and a poet, but Journalism is also a favorite of mine. I come from a large family consisting of my mother and father, and seven brothers and six sisters. We are not extremely well-off, but have fun and work hard. Each of us children are dependable and will all be good citizens and honorable people. We have high ideals and goals. I am a sports, outdoors, and music lover. I played soccer in high school on the girls' team. I play basketball and other sports for fun. I love to watch football, basketball and soccer the most, but I enjoy all sports. I love camping, hiking and canoeing, and outdoor things. I love music. I play the violin, piano, and sing. I am teaching myself the guitar and harmonica. I love classical music and Broadway and opera. But I also enjoy Regavé, Alternative, R & B, Jazz, Oldies, Light Sounds, Pop Rock, and almost anything, except most country. I am a member of several different groups worth mentioning: the National Geographic Society, National Children's Cancer Society, and a Donor. I support the Paralyzed Veterans of America as well. I am also a member of the church of Jesus Christ of Latter-Day Saints, with short name of the Mormons.

Bateham, Thomas Allen - I was born 12/26/71. I live in the mid-western United States. I'm the oldest of three boys. I grew up in a middle class family with loving parents who support me in my writing and in life. I have a G.E.D. and have taken some classes at a local community college. I have been writing since I was twelve when I had to write a story for school. My hobbies are reading, writing of all kinds, working out, watching T.V. and movies and playing role playing games. My person quote: Yearn for your dreams, strive to achieve them, and trust in God to succeed. I have poems being published by The National Library of Poetry in *Days Gone By* and *Dawn's Twilight* and another with Sparrowgrass in *Poetic Voices of America* and three more called *Turning Back the Hands of Time*, *Ages & Stages*, and *Sweetheart 1998* along with many others under consideration at this time.

Bero, Mark A. - Born June 29, 1959 in Newark, Ohio to George and Beverly Bero. Married Yvonne Bero on Jul 1, 1979. They have three children, Chad, Tiffany and Jessica. Mark graduated Utica High in 1978 and spent a 10 year enlistment in the Armed Services. His current occupation is Loss Prevention Division. He is an Honorable Mention award winner with Iliad Press. His work appears in a National Library of Poetry anthology and much of his poetry is themed around the military. Personal note: "I write from the heart and soul. The words I share are meaning and true, a poet will live forever."

Bond-Louden, Jenna - (Pen name: André Carson). I am fourteen years of age and I am an upper school sophomore at the Friends School of Baltimore. I enjoy the company of my friends and family, the major influences of my work. I'm a devoted Coca-Cola fan. My home is Baltimore, MD and my family is originally from Maryland. I have adored poetry from the time attended Grace and Saint Peter's School (elementary). I aspire to be a professional poet/writer and cultural anthropologist. I'm currently studying the works of Maya Angelou and Zora Neale Hurston to guide me. I enjoy all of my classes, especially Drama. Song writing, essays, and entertaining are my other attributes. I would like to thank the Iliad Literary Awards Program for this opportunity. Further, I give gratitude to my grandmother, Virginia Bond, who has worked her whole life to see the welfare of all children and adults. She's dedicated to the mentally unique, the invalid, the destitute, her family, her friends, my mother, and her heaviest load—me. I love you! Thank You! To Mom-Mom, Thank you for going above and beyond the mark for my benefit. You have spent your whole life working hard to make the world better for you and me. You have continuously climbed the mountain the strong way and you have brought others with you. I am proud that you have never settled to the situation, but you have risen to beat the situation. From Duke to Executive Director, to reiterate the last lines of Maya Angelou's *And Still I Rise*: "You rise, You rise, You rise." To my father, Thank you for being there. Thanks for teaching me to think. Thanks for teaching me to look for different perspectives. Thank you for teaching me to expand my mind and grow. Thank you for teaching me to be practical and thanks for the spectacular trip to Walt Disney World. Brief thanks to: Mrs. Porter, Mr. Laird Mortimer, my aunts, and my uncles.

Branch, Bryant Jerome - Born: March 13, 1959 in Bonham, Texas. Parents: Jack and Frances Branch. Education: I attended schools in Fort Worth, Texas: Morningside Elementary; Daggett Middle School; graduated from Paschal High School; attended Fort Worth Trade School, major: Automotive Technician. Now I am presently attending Tarrant County Junior College. Major: English - the art of writing. Awards: Eight Editor's Choice Awards from the National Library of Poetry; a Special Award from the International Publications: American Collegiate Poets Contest. Memberships: I was awarded membership into the International Society of Poets. Also, one of my works is currently under contract to go to music, song titled "I Am All That I Am." I started writing in 1995. Now, with twenty publications, record contract, awards and membership, I have truly enjoyed the experience and am looking forward to much more success. Philosophical Statement: Words are the keys that open everyone's heart and eyes to the truth and purpose of life. Words are the tools which bring about change through conviction, pain, and success. Words bring Patience, Love and Gratitude.

Brookins, Naomi A. - a teacher, librarian, college lecturer, public speaker, and author was born Naomi A. Newsome to Carrence and Maggie Newsome in the state of Mississippi. After graduation from Lanier High School in Jackson, Mississippi, she migrated to Chicago, Illinois to attend college. She acquired an AA Degree, BA Degree in Education, MS in Librarianship, MA in U.S. History, and did post graduate work at Norther Illinois University. She married and became the mother of four sons. Brookins taught in the Chicago Public School System for twenty-five years, was director of Illinois Association for Media in Education (Region 3) for three years, taught the Junior & Senior Great Books Discussions groups, worked with the Boards of Christian Education and Missions at her church, was awarded the Superior Public Service Award for outstanding services in the Chicago Metropolitan Area, and for the past five years has been a Docent at the Harold Washington Library Center in Chicago, Illinois. In 1996, she wrote her first book, "Naomi's Story: You Don't Have To Be Broken." It is an autobiographical work written for a multi-cultural audience. it is a powerful message intended to restore hope for those who think it is impossible for them to become positive forces/people in our troubled world. Its message must be heard clearly and loudly as we prepare to exit the 20th century and enter the year 2001. The book may be purchased from your local bookstores, Baker & Taylor, Washington Book, or from the publisher, American Literary Press in Baltimore, Maryland 21236, (800)873-2003. Naomi has also written a literary work titled "Youth Soaring Toward the Year 2001 By Making the right Tough Choices Today. The author resides in the Chatham Community of the Chicago Metropolitan Area.

Brown, Juanita - Lord make me and mold me. For you are the potter and I am the clay. In 1993, I gave my life to the Lord. I accepted Jesus as my Lord and Savior. Since that time my life has truly been changed. I read and study His word with understanding and my relationship with Him has grown closer and closer. I am married to Michael Terry Brown Sr. We have a total of five children, three girls and two boys. We are also grandparents to two girls and a boy. At times our house is very full but I love every minute of it. In July 1994 the Lord revealed to me that I would write. I was sitting in our finished garage when I began to ask the Lord what is my job. What work will I do for you? He gave me one word [write]. I assumed it was to write a book. Well that never took off. Almost two years later in June 1996 my true gift was revealed to me, after praying with my family all night. The following day I wrote my first poem. I have not stopped since. I am constantly inspired by the Lord to write poems. They serve as mini messages for His people. I give God the glory for it is from Him my words flow. I read my poems regularly in church. I have made arrangements to start reading in my job chapel. I also read to my coworkers and patients. I work in an intensive care unit and life threatening illnesses are prevalent. This is when I can really do the Lords' work. My desire is to have my poems published and available to the multitudes. I would like to see them spread out near and far. My poems bring hope, joy, peace, love and comfort to God's people. I also write poems for special occasions, auxiliaries, etc. I have written 116 poems to date. I hope you enjoy my poems and know that I write them with love.

Burleson, Matthew J. - I've been writing off and on ever since I was in grade school and I enjoyed the responses I got to my poems then. People seemed genuinely interested in my work and I knew I had a talent when I was told by my principle that a poem I wrote about the month of December would be the first poem to ever be published in the school newspaper and from that point onward I worked on developing my writing ability as much as I could. Over time it became a great outlet for deeply held emotional feelings and thoughts and observations about the world around me. "A Walk Down Ocean Avenue" was one observation in which I described the scenery on the road through the town's agricultural community to surf beach outside of town and how wonderful it is in summer time. The poem "The Long Night of Mr. Smith" was inspired by the Benny Goodman song "Goodby" and how it made me think of how some construction workers in the past may have felt when they lost some of their friends in the building of the United States' great city bridges and how they may have blamed themselves. I have many more thoughts and observations about my hometown which I've lived in all my life and its surrounding area as well as thoughts about music, literature, art, and some of the more humorous sides of life to write about as well and I do plan on writing about them all in the future. What ever I write about I plan to write it carefully so I can communicate the feelings and thoughts I feel as perfectly as I can to the reader and to further develop my writing talents.

Caudle, Kathy - Born in 1950s East St. Louis, Illinois, Kathy Caudle grew up not knowing her family. Because her mother died when she was small the author missed knowing not only her mother but also her maternal relatives. Not having her mother or her maternal relatives, when she was growing up, bored deep loneliness into Kathy Caudle. To fill the oppressive void Ms. Caudle found a voice in writing. She wrote her first poem when she was eleven. By writing Ms. Caudle found she could express her deepest thoughts, and share her story. But the story of the author worsened when she was a teenager, and Kathy Caudle was removed from the custody of her father and stepmother. Being forced to leaver her home in East St. Louis was devastating for the sixteen year old. After finishing high school then working in the local area for two years, Ms. Caudle permanently left East St. Louis at age twenty. For a few years she traveled. At age twenty-three Ms Caudle married. When she was twenty-four the author gave birth to her only child. Then Ms. Caudle lost her beloved son. The next year, when she was twenty-five, she was divorced. Her spirit unbroken, the author set about rebuilding her life. Though working kept her busy, writing kept her sane. By 1981, Ms. Caudle added writing to her working credits on her resume. Since then the author has gradually increased her body of literary work. In keeping with her humble beginnings, Kathy Caudle seeks to share her experiences with others, writing on subjects of universal interest. Philosophical issues, like home, anyone can identify with. Home is where the author returned to recently. She found not the East St. Louis of her girlhood, but a changed East St. Louis. Though she still loves the place of her roots, the author was compelled to leave again. Back on the road, Ms. Caudle captured her varied experiences in words. Some of her more deeply contemplated thoughts she has put into her most recent essay.

Chapman, Debra Anne - Address: Branson, Missouri. Status: Married. The Ozarks is an inspirational and beautiful land that creates the basis for the poems I am able to write. It is a peaceful setting that I recommend to anyone who enjoys writing poems. Without the creative imaginations of my children, the beautiful scenery of the Ozarks, and my wonderful husband of sixteen years, my poetry would not be the same.

Clark, Tiffany L. - For me, writing is a hobby that I would very much like to turn into a productive career. I love writing poetry, short stories, and other forms of writing such as informative stories and pieces of that nature. I write poetry for my own pleasure and enjoyment and I write about things that I know. Things that I experience, things that I feel, things that I see, and many other personal subjects. I truly write for myself and I never thought anyone besides my close family and friends would ever see any of my work. I am a very shy person and to show a person my work is a very big deal to me. I have to trust them and know that they support me. This is the first time that I've ever entered any of my work into a contest and it has been an enjoyable experience. To know that there are other people out there like me who love poetry just because they love it is a wonderful discovery. People are often surprised when they find out how young I am because I've always been mature and intelligent for my age. I am 19 years old and I was born in Tyler, Texas on may 23, 1978. My parents are John and Donna Clark (whom are now divorced) and I have a brother and sister that are 15 year old twins, Ben and Lindsey. I am currently attending school at Tyler Junior College and am majoring in Political Science and thinking of minoring in English. I once read a quote that I really enjoyed and I keep it hanging on my wall. It says: "Dreams are like stars; you will not succeed in reaching them with your hands. But like the seafaring men on the desert of waters, you choose them as your guides, and following them you will reach your destiny." I truly believe that.

Comas, Julio - I'm a New York born Puerto Rican and I have lived most of my life in the Big Apple. I served this great nation honorably in the United States Marine Corps, which left me with a passion and pride for this country which is frequently reflected in my poetry. I had a complete Catholic school education and started writing when I was a teenager. I am currently employed in the medical field as a Cardio-Vascular and Interventional Technologist. I find great reward in helping and comforting others through their time of pain and suffering. Because of tragedies in my life, writing had been dead in my heart for many years. The passion for writing has been recently rebirthed by the love of a woman, my Maria.

Cook, Todd Tarran, Jr. - *Pen Name*: Legion. *Date of Birth*: January 26, 1979. *Memberships*: International Society of Poets. *Personal Statement*: Human existence is a complex of cycles, each holding its own lesson. We relive a cycle until we overcome it, by learning its lesson, or until we are ground into dust and destroyed. When we overcome a cycle, we grow and change. I capture the essences of these cycles, from the ever changing perspectives of personas transformed.

Crawford, David Allen - I was born in Cuba City, Wisconsin on November 8, 1964. My parents Jim and Arlene are still married. They had four sons and three daughters. I am the youngest son. I have never been married and have no children. All of the men are in the construction business. I have been employed in concrete construction. We were raised in a rural setting in a small town called Dickeyville. I lived most of my life in southwest Wisconsin. I graduated at Cuba City Public High School in May 1983. I earned a B.S. degree in Social Science at the University of Wisconsin, Plateville. I went on their foreign-exchange program for one semester to Ealing College of Higher Education, School of Humanities. While living in England, I enjoyed traveling to Norway, France and Holland.

d'Avignon, Angela Christine - Hi! My name is Angela and I am 12. When I was younger, when I was in 1st or 2nd grade, one of my little friends and I would make a "book." They would write the words and I would draw the pictures. It was then I decided to be an artist. My friends and I never finished a "book." But I did, all by myself. As I got older and more realistic, I realized I would be better off being a writer. I was discouraged by the other students who drew better than me. So, with my new "profession" I tried to accomplish, once more "books." Long books with 100 pages or more. It didn't work out that way. I would be bored with the plot and leave that one unfinished, and went on with a new one. I was getting nowhere. One summer, I took a creative writing class. It was one of the best classes I have been in. Instead of writing long, drawn-out "books," I learned about how to write short stories. So, I wrote short stories. I didn't discover poetry and the art of rhyming until later on in the class. It was there I wrote my first poem. I was very proud of it, even though now, compared to my latest poems, it wasn't very good. But it was pretty good for a ten-year-old. The rest of that summer I wrote only a couple of poems, because this way of expression was new and strange to me. The next year, this one, I took the same class, and I requested that we work on poetry. There, I was inspired to be a poet. The impact the teacher, Ms. Lyons, made on my was so big and wonderful that I have written 33 poems by now. If it wasn't for Ms. Lyons, I wouldn't be the poet I am today. And that is how I got here.

Davis, Clarice Lawson - lives and works in Huntington, West Virginia. Mother of three sons. Ms. Davis has been successful as a freelance writer. Her poems and short stories have been published in numerous newspapers and magazines. She has had one book published (poetry and prose) in 1974, entitled *The Meadows*. Now working on her second book of poetry and short stories. Ms. Davis loves to travel, read, and of course "write." Ms. Davis ancestry dates back to her family, who came to this country from England in the early 1800's, and settled in Patrick County, at Meadows-Of-Dan, Virginia, which has been in the inspiration for most of her poetry. Clarice Lawson Davis was born in Milburn, West Virginia, the daughter of the late Mr. and Mrs. John Lawson. Ms. Davis was graduated from Huntington East High, and studied Journalism at Marshall University. Ms. Davis currently works for the Huntington West Virginia Housing Authority.

Day, Eric - The child you're currently reading about is seventeen. The seventeen year old child couldn't speak English properly until he turned four. The child you're still reading about is still growing. Physically and mentally. But, the writer you're reading about extends beyond the simple boundaries of the child. That child exists as any other boy, so, I'll trim those trite details short. Yet, the writer exists as a bell. Molded and polished into shades and shapes to the creator's likeness. Only when it's struck, or agitated somehow will the full aesthetic-nature be exposed. And yes, going with the banal crowd, I also had a teacher to thank. She was a harsh mallet. Since my teacher agitated me, I've been writing when needed for two years. Some of the first works I've made myself do aren't very well, and to say it simply, suck. I've thought of regressing and rewriting some of those, but it wouldn't be fair to the child who wrote them. He had a dream to become a writer. And when that was passed, he had a fantastic dream to go much further.

RAE - [born] April 26, 1945 in San Francisco, CA. [educ] Woodrow Wilson High School-1964. [military service] cook from '65 to '68. After the military attempted to re-enter school but could not cope with school, dropped out the first year. Later through different doctors - found infliction of Attention Deficit Disorder. In some cases even today, I am the same way due to A.D.D. This is the reason that I can not work. This has caused me to become an introvert. All of my work is done as a form of mediation and I like to keep my animity. I have never been able to really find any niche, until now. Thank you for everything...and the little ego booster to boot! RAE is an honorable mention winner in the Summer 1997 Iliad Literary Awards Program.

English, Christine L. - Poetry does not come easy to most people without some sorrow in their lives. It is an art form that does as much for the soul as prayer. This was the motivation for Christine Louise English at the early age of fourteen. Christine lived her entire life in the suburbs of Chicago with a variety of trips to other states and countries. Family and friends have always been very important to her in everything that she tackled. Socialize is high on her list, even though her need for accomplishment may outweigh some events. A well organized person, who schedules her life in order to do the activities that are important, Christine constantly looks for order in life itself. This is the most frustrating of all inner beliefs: that all things will happen in an orderly fashion. Christine's life has been filled recently with ice skating, gymnastics, yearbook committee, basketball, church confirmation, and her new found love of poetry. Each year brings new adventures which will replace some of the old, but the relationships encountered on these travels will live forever in her total being, as she has expressed in her poetry.

Farmer, Micah - Micah Aaron Farmer (born February 14, 1980) found his love for writing at age eight as a result of drawing characters and making up stories about them with his friends in Baltimore, Maryland where he attended elementary school. As he got older, he continued writing and reading many works by has favorite writer, Edgar Allan Poe (who was also a native of Baltimore). After changing school twice, Micah found a home at Perry Hall Christian School at the age of 13 where he is still currently, as he approaches his junior year in '97-98. He would like to thank his parents, Rodney and Hope for raising him in a Christian home, his younger brother Zachary and his older brother Jeremiah for supporting him, and he especially thanks God for helping him juggle his time with his academics, high school sports (soccer, basketball, and baseball), his job, and writing, of course.

Farris, Candy M. - I was born in Mountain Home, Arkansas on August 20, 1973. My childhood was pretty good. I can't complain anyway. My family and I moved here to Missoula, Montana about ten years ago and have been here ever since. It's really a beautiful place. I have two wonderful children whom I love and care for deeply. My son, Russell E. McMahan, is the age of 5 and was born on June 19, 1992. My daughter, Jimmy-Lynn Thomas, is the age of 7 and was born on July 22, 1990. I gave birth to them both here in Montana. My children are my life and I thank the Lord for blessing me with them everyday. I have another very special person in my life as well, he's not only my best friend, but he is someone I love very much. That person is Brain P. Hartry. Not only do we have a wonderful relationship, he's also a great influence for my children. I thank the Lord for Brian as well, I tell him he's my angel from Heaven. Poetry is something I love writing. My poems are a very special part of me and I love sharing them with others. Not only do they come from my heart, but they are feelings I have as well.

Felmet, Rachelle L. - I have been married twenty-seven years, and blessed with three children, six grandchildren, and one great-granddaughter. It was after a most unique experience that I was inspired to write poetry. Since then I have been richly blessed with many honors, and I am very grateful for every opportunity for growth. This past year has been especially exciting. God and family is my inspiration, and I pray that every word I write will be a blessing to someone. I'm trusting this work will find favor in His sight, for He alone is Holy.

Fesperman, Louise Kilby - I was born Louise Kilby to Mary Elizabeth and John Kilby in the lovely state of North Carolina. My ancestors were Bible translators who came from England to Culpepper, Virginia in the seventeen hundreds. I was the ninth child, having four sisters and four brothers. My father spent many hours telling wonderful stories to me about my ancestors and the love of Jesus Christ, instilling within me the true spirituality of life and the real meaning of love. I married at the age of twenty-two and moved to Nassau Bahamas, later in 1953 we moved to Alaska, driving over the Alcan Highway. Alaska was still a territory and the last Frontier, strangely different from my southern heritage. I discovered a different kind of beauty, the many species of birds and animals that enhance the charm of our state, the awesomeness of the Aurora Borealis, the grandeur of wild flowers and the vastness of mountains and glaciers surrounding our state. I also discovered the horror of the erupting volcano's and the terror of the largest earthquake to ever hit the North American continent. I am a high school graduate, and the mother of twin girls and four wonderful grandchildren. Some of my hobbies are writing, reading, sewing, gardening, traveling, and singing. My special influences and inspirations came from my mother and father growing up on the farm. There I learned the wonder and beauty of God's magnificent creation as I watched the birth of springtime blossom into a beautiful fairyland. Writing poetry is an inspirational gift from the heart to be shared with others. My goal as a writer is to create inspirational poems and books to enhance and uplift the human soul for those who read them.

Fields, Linda M. - Linda was born in Toledo, Ohio to Wilma (Pat) and Harold

White. She graduated Woodward High School in 1965, and Stautzenberger Business College in 1966. Her daughters, Dawn and Erica Fields, were born in Detroit, Michigan where Linda lived while married. She and her daughters moved in with her mother on the shore of Lake Erie in Luna Pier, Michigan in 1976 after the death of Linda's father. It was in this home that Linda started writing in 1978. Her first novel *Demon's Sorrow* is currently being sold over the internet (www.1stbooks.com), and she is currently working on her second novel (Lake of Lost Souls) which should appear through 1st Books before the end of '97. She has written several short horror stories, many of which were inspired by Lake Erie. A collection of these stories will also appear in the 1st Books Library within the next few months. Although Linda no longer lives on Lake Erie the inspiration the lake instilled in her is strong, and she hopes one day she'll once again live on the lake shore. Linda enjoys writing horror because: "Nothing is as scary as reality. If I want to be sad and depressed all I have to do is watch the news, or read the newspaper. Horror, in comparison, is fun because we know that no matter how scared we get it's just make believe."

Fonda, Sheridan - (Pen name of Vincent J. Fondacaro) has a B.S. Degree in American Literature and Creative Writing; an M.A. Degree in American Literature and English Literature, both from Columbia University. He also holds a Diploma in Art (Drawing, Painting, Sculpture and History of Art) from The Leonardo da Vinci Art School which is no longer in existence. He has taught English Literature, American Literature, World Literature, Creative Writing and The Humanities at the high school and community college levels. In addition to his writing, he does pencil and pen-and-ink drawings, watercolor as well as sculpture. He has designed the cover for the opera program for The Treasure Coast Opera Association (1991-92 Opera Season) of Fort Pierce, Florida. He is the author of two small volumes of poetry, *It Was a Narrow Time*, 1992, *Search for ITHAKA*, 1995. "Poetry is word-music," Sheridan Fonda reminds us. "When I conceive a poem, it is in terms of tonality--sounds of distinct pitch, quality and duration, blended intricately with semantic meaning and the wonder of creating images, tone color and tone language."

Gablick, Richard - is a songwriter who founded the musical project NUNDA DEVY. Known for its eclectic and obscure sound, NUNDA DEVY has aired on local radio and television shows in Pittsburgh. Richard Gablick was born in Brackenridge, PA. He studied art and poetry while attending Highlands High School. Mr. Gablick studied voice and jazz dance while attending fine arts classes at Point Park College in Pittsburgh. A self-taught guitar player, Mr. Gablick also took piano lessons which provided the background for his songwriting. Currently, Mr. Gablick is studying recording engineer classes at Audiomation Studios in Pittsburgh. Mr. Gablick is employed by Family Services of Western Pa. He has worked in Residential Services as a program worker for ten years. Mr. Gablick provides direct care services for mentally disabled adults. His credits include music therapy and creative visualization groups while working on the Respite Unit. Outside of his musical project, Mr. Gablick enjoys reading books on psychology, philosophy and metaphysics. Mr. Gablick is a current member of the National Authors Registry and Taxi (A Los Angeles based A&R Company) which provides music to record companies, television networks and the motion picture industry.

Gallagher, Kristin - born on October 15, 1979 in New Brunswick, N.J. She graduated from Old Bridge High School where she was a member of the concert choir, select choir, and piano accompanist. She is listed in the 1995/96 edition of *Who's Who Among American High School Students*. She is also a member of the Laurence Harbor Covenant Community Church where she has taught Sunday School and sung in the choir. Kristin has studied dance for eleven years and piano for eight years. Since elementary school, Kristin has been keeping journals of family trips and special events. As mucic became linked closer and closer with the words forming on the page, it was natural that poetry wold become her favorite means of expressing thoughts and feelings. Poems cover her walls and fill many journals. One poem will be published by the National Library of Poetry. Another, "Her Hope," became the lyrics to a song she wrote and performed with the OBHS concert choir. Kristin is currently a student at Juniata College in Huntingdon, PA where she is studying psychology and music. In addition, Kris continues to blend her love of words and music to create meaningful poetry.

Ghattas, Christine Bonnie - was born on October 19, 1984, in Anderson, South Carolina. She lives in Marietta, Georgia, and attends Pine Mountain Middle School. Christine plays the cello in her school's orchestra. Her hobbies include playing soccer, writing poetry, reading, and sewing.

Gibson, Edwin Wray, Sr. - born in Lubbock, Texas, and grew up in Eastland, Texas. He attended Warner College in Eastland, Texas. Mr. Gibson holds a bachelor of arts degree from Berea College, Berea, Kentucky. He was president of the dramatic club, two years; president of Alpha Iota Chapter of Alpha Psi Omega national dramatic fraternity, one year, and a member of Kappa Sigma. He lettered in basketball and track. While residing in New York, he was engaged in Tool and Die Making and Machine Manufacture. He patented angle positioning devices for use in machine shops, and invented safety devices for the handicapped. He retired June 5, 1971, and moved to Fredericksburg, Texas, where he now lives. Mr. Gibson is a charter member for the United States Horse Cavalry Association, is a member of Rotary International Club, Senior Active, Presently he serves on the executive board of the Fredricksburg Music Club, Inc., and is on the board of directors of the van der Stucken International Music Festival. He wrote columns and articles for several newspapers for a number of years; wrote articles for and was a member of the staff of *Click Magazine*; wrote for other magazines; published *Collected Stories and Essays*, one volume; composed *Fritztown Polka*, words and music, which was recorded, and is gaining popularity both in the U.S.A. and abroad. He is a former member of the Montana Historical Society and of the Fandangle Association of Albany, Texas. Presently he keeps busy writing, composing music, gardening, playing bridge, (not well), working for the Fredericksburg Music Club Inc. and for the van der Stucken International Music Festival. Mr Gibson has traveled extensively in China, Europe, Canada, Mexico and the Caribbean.

Groleau, Anthony Thomas - I was born at St. Francis Memorial Hospital in Escanaba, MI on December 7, 1974. I was raised in Sturgeon Bay, WI my first 15 years. My parents, Carl Thomas Groleau(1952) and Mary Margaret Ritter (1956) divorced when I was four years old. I lived with my mom and one sister, Dawn Marie Groleau (1976). My dad remarried to Patricia McClain and later had two children, Christina Marie Groleau(1983) and Joshua Everett Thomas Groleau(1986). I moved to Norfolk, VA at the age of 15 where I lived for one year. We moved to Charleston, SC where we lived for two months. We moved to Tampa, FL where I was forced to move to St. Jacques, MI where I lived with my dad for the remainder of my sophomore year of high school. I moved back to Tampa, FL with my mom where I graduated from Bloomingdale High School in June 1993. I was sent to Navy Boot Camp on August 23, 1993. I served for three years as an Engineman on board the newly commissioned Aegis Class Destroyer USS Paul Hamilton (DDG-60). We sailed the ship from Bath, ME to Charleston, SC where it was commissioned in May of 1995. We then crossed the Panama Canal and sailed across the Pacific to Pearl Harbor, HI where the ship would be home ported. I received my discharge on July 1, 1996. I now work full time in a warehouse for Storopack Corp. and run a part-time home business. I enjoy playing my guitar, writing poetry and lyrics, bowling and spending time with nature. I have been playing guitar since I was 15 years old and I have been writing poetry and lyrics since I was 14 years old. I had my first poem published in a contest with The National Library of Poetry. The poem titled "Everburning Fire" is featured in their book titled *A Prism of Thoughts* which will be published in November 1997. I hope to some day have all my poems published into one book for all poetry lovers to read.

Guinn, James D. - age 16, is the son of Donnie G. Guinn of Muskogee, Oklahoma, and Marla J. Atkinson of Owasso, Oklahoma. James is a sophomore at Owasso High School. His favorite pass time is writing poetry. His best subject in school is History and he is an expert on the Civil War.

Hardjana, Astrid - is a Canadian student entering grade twelve and a member of her high school's "Literary Anthology Club." She was first encouraged to write poetry and stories when she was younger because of the writing contests organized by her elementary school. Astrid began to express her feelings through composition when she discovered that she had a talent and became more motivated to express her feelings when she was diagnosed as an epileptic. Astrid's outlook of the trials and tribulations as a teenage are represented strongly and epilepsy has given her the strength to reveal her heart's consciousness and passion. Strongly supported by her family, Astrid's aspiration is to become a psychologist for youths. It is her wish to be able to help young adults with similar experiences and share her insight and empathy through her words. Astrid enjoys writing children's stories in her spare time but composing poetry is her first love.

Harmon, Melanie Kim - I was born October 2, 1975 to Earl and Denise Harmon. I am the oldest and only daughter of four children. Having been born into a devote Christian family, I was raised with the knowledge, love, and adoration of the Lord. Although only 21 years of age, I've experienced a lot of trials and tribulations. The type of life that I've lived has given me a special gift to portray my world for the betterment of others. If I could influence one person, or help them better understand that they are not alone, that there is help...my job, no..., my mission is complete. No jail is as harsh as the jail we make for ourselves. My goal is for a better understanding in one's self. The Bible says that the strong will bear the infirmities of the weak. Hopefully, my words of inspiration and motivation will give the weak a strong voice. To go on in spite of the way they're feeling. Currently, I reside in Columbus, Ohio. I'm in the process of obtaining my Associate Degree in Freelance at ICS Correspondence School. I hope to continue in the field of writing for many years to come. Without the various people in my life who cared enough to help, I wouldn't be this far to potentially be able to help someone else. I would like to thank the people at Iliad Press for giving us young writers a chance to have a strong voice. I send much love to my family and friends who believe in me...Thank You God!

Harris, Krystal - daughter of Keith and Rita Harris, was born March 11, 1983 in Pittsburgh, Pennsylvania. There she lives with her mother, father, siblings Keisha (age 19), Keith (age 18) and Kristina (age 10). This 14 years old Honor Roll student attends Schenley high School. There she plays the cello for her school orchestra, which she's been studying for six years. After high school Krystal plans to go on to college and become a music and business major. The winner of the "1998 President's Award for Literary Excellence," Krystal has been writing poetry since age 12. Other hobbies and talents include playing the piano, reading, speaking German (which she's speaking for 9 years), and like any normal teenager shopping and spending time with her friends.

Headrick, Carolyn M. - born Carolyn M. Spurgeon in Kansas City, Kansas. Worked in the art department at Hallmark Cards in Kansas City, Missouri. Married and moved to New York. Raised three sons then went to college. Divorced. Hobby gardening. Earned a Bachelors in Art Studio and a Masters in Elementary Education, both from the State University of New York at Binghamton. Worked as a teacher's aide with emotionally handicapped children, then as a substitute teacher. Became a New York Registered Daycare Provider continuing to the present time. Poems included in anthologies published by JMW Publishing Company, *Visions*; The Poetry Guild, *Dreams of Everyday*; and Sparrowgrass Poetry Forumn, *Treasured Poems of America*.

Higgins, Ms. N. Loy Kuhn - Place of Birth: Louisville, Kentucky, USA. Parents: Arthur Louis Kuhn (deceased) & Nina Waller Kuhn. Spouse: Dr. David Michael Higgins. Memberships: The National Authors Registry and International Society of Poets (Distinguished Member). Awards: 1997 President's Award for Literary Excellence sponsored by NAR; several Honorable Mention Awards in various competitions by Iliad Press and *Verses* Magazine; International Poet of Merit Award and Bronze Medallion, The International Society of Poets 1996 Convention and Symposium; Honorable Mention Awards in poetry competitions throughout the USA; Editor's Choice Awards from The National Library of Poetry. Writing Credits: Poems published by the following: (1) Iliad Press, (2) the Modern Poetry Society of Dunnellon, FL, (3) The National Library of Poetry, (4) The Mile High Poetry Society of Denver, CO, (5) *The Marshall Islands Journal*, and (6) *Verses* Magazine. Articles and stories published in *PACIFIC* Magazine. Writings: Poems, humorous short stories, and lyrics. Writer & publisher of POETRY LINES, Framable Poetic Prints, notecards, and bookmarks. Personal Note or Philosophical Statement: Poets and musicians are the historians of the world who chronicle events through eloquent expression and harmonious sound. Other: Moving from Arizona, have resided in Ajeltake, Majuro Atoll, Marshall Islands with husband, Dr. Dave, and mother, Nina, since March 1996. Hobbies include traveling and living abroad, reading and writing, playing piano, keyboard, and ukulele.

Hoggan, Judith A. - Bar Admissions: Maryland, 1982; District of Columbia, 1983; Virginia, 1989. Education: Georgetown University Law Center (Juris Doctor, 1982). Activities: Associate Editor, *The Tax Lawyer*; Volunteer legal assistant, Montgomery County Crisis Center, Abused Persons Program. University of Maryland, College Park. B.S. Psychology/Personnel Management, 1977, summa cum laude. Honors Societies: Phi Kappa Phi; Alpha Sigma Lambda. Experience: Fourteen years experience in general practice of law with specialties in general litigation, commercial litigation, real estate litigation, bankruptcy (representing creditors), collections, landlord and tenant law and litigation, and family law. Principal in The Law Offices of Judith A. Hoggan, P.C., practicing in Maryland, D.C., and Virginia. Twelve years' experience in business before entering the practice of law. Pro bono litigation and will-drafting assistance for Legal Counsel for the Elderly (1986-1997). Mediator (1987-present). Co-chair, Legislative Subcommittee, Family Division of the District of Columbia Bar Association (1988-1989). Speaker, Career Real Estate Women (CREW) monthly seminar, on negotiation. Bethesda, MD (Feb. 20, 1991). Foster Parent (1992-current). Speaker, American Association of Marriage and Family Therapists, on legal issues in liability of therapist, Chicago, Illinois (Nov. 4, 1994). Pro bono trainer/facilitator, Alternatives to Violence Program (1995). Speaker, panel presentation on children with troubling behavior, Center for the Study of Children with Troubling Behavior, University of Maryland, College Park, Maryland (March 24, 1995). Panel member, Montgomery County Bar Association Fee Arbitration Committee (1995-current). Speaker, Center for Divorcing Families, Montgomery County, Maryland (1996).

Hollister, Maegan Amanda - I was born in eugene, Oregon March 15, 1982. I love to travel, try new things, and be an individual. Right now, I am living in a small historic town in Oregon called Oakland. I am a sophomore at Oakland High School, and my G.P.A. is 3.8. I have received many awards for academics, and have been a Honor Roll student since fourth grade. I am a member of the Who's Who Among American High School students and the All-American Schoolers. My poetry has been published in our school newspaper and other poetry books. My goal is to publish a book of my own. Not only of my poetry, but perhaps essays, quotes, and other thoughts. I strive to write my poetry on subjects that will cause people to meditate. There are so many other things in life that are actually very big, but treated as if they are very small. I hope my writing makes people stop and think about the world today, society, and our role in it. I try to explain people, their thoughts, their actions, nature, and the mysterious things in life. Though, there are some things that have no explanation, at least one that makes sense. One of those things is racism. Racism is purely a mental things. When people read "Sweet Freedom, Turned Sour," I hope they realize that as a society, we have a very narrow mind. Does your individual role in society contribute to the general opinion? The general opinion is that if other humans look or act different, we should treat them different. Consider that society's opinion has cost us real freedom. My dream is to someday travel the world. I want to study and understand the different cultures of this earth. There is a piece of everyone we meet inside of us. So, maybe if we try to understand others first, we will have a better understanding of ourselves. My motto in life: "Treat people the way you wish to be treated."

Iroegbu, Monica T. - I was born May 4, 1959 in Ridgewood, New Jersey. I am married (my husband's name is Aloysius) and have two children (Katrina and Anthony). My parents are Louis and Nancy Brune. I attended Thomas S. Wootoon High School and graduated in 1977. I attended Immaculata College and graduated in 1981 with a Bachelor of Music degree. I am certified to teach music education and piano is my major instrument. My occupation is Computer Training Specialist. Memberships include the following organizations: National Association of Female Executives (NAFE); Washington WordPerfect User Group; National and State Music Teacher's Association; and Montgomery County Music Teacher's Association. Personal comments: I had courses in writing for Children's Literature. I feel more comfortable and natural writing poetry. I've been writing poetry since high school, and regret that I did not submit my poetry earlier.

Iverson, Viola - I am a retired teacher from the St. Paul Department of Education, St. Paul. Minnesota. After a year of normal training following high school graduation, I taught three years in rural schools and three years in town schools before getting my second year at St. Cloud Teacher's College, St. Cloud, Minnesota. Later while teaching in the St. Paul School System, I attended the University of Minnesota getting my Bachelor of Science Degree. Extra curricular work included a workshop at Hemline University, St. Paul, Minnesota and a summer session with a Poet in Residence, Douglas County, Minnesota. I am a member of the Alpha Delta Kappa society, a former president of Theta Chapter. We are altruistic and provide scholarships for young educators. As representative of the Jr. Red Cross, I was in charge of the gift box program in which children filled boxes to send overseas to needy children. I was on several committees for the St.Paul Federation of Teachers. As a retired teacher, I was on the committee for writing up the history of the St. Paul schools. I also contributed articles to the Gopher Historian Magazine for the Minnesota Historical Society. During the summer I belonged to the Brush and Palette Club at Alexandria, Minnesota near my home town of Nelson named after Senator Knute Nelson. I co-chaired the Douglas County Art Displays at the Douglas County Fair. I enjoy traveling and express myself through painting and writing poetry. Memberships in poetry clubs and honors received include: Who's Who for Poetry in 1990, Member Sparrowgrass Poetry Forum, Inc., CSS Publications. I received the Golden Poet Award and Certificate of Poetic Achievement under the World of Poetry.

Joynes, Ben - I was born on December 8, 1981. I have lived in San Francisco, California all my life. I am presently in the ninth grade. I have no specific faiths, save for those of being. I am an improvisational keyboardist. My favorite studies include spacetime structure, personal growth, and fundamental particle physics. Communication with others through expression is truly the most amazing aspect of the experience of life. To be included in any way in such a compilation of others' thoughts and feelings, is as humbling as it is exhilarating. I wish to thank Iliad Press for this, and likewise, those who read this, thereby taking part in the act of creation. Thank you for this experience. All experiences are worthwhile in great ways. This is why life can never be meaningless!

Kabe, Aino - Mrs. Kabe is an artist, author of poetry, novels, and numerous articles, as well as a homemaker and grandmother. She is a member of the Southern California Chapter of the Estonian University Women's Association, the International Society of Poets, the Creative Arts and Writer's Association, and the Estonian Lutheran Church Council. Aino has received several first prize honors for her sculpture, ceramics, and leathercraft. She was awarded the Golden Poet Award for 1991/1992, the Editor's Choice Award for 1993, 1994, 1995 and again in 1996, and was a Poet of the Year nominee in 1996 by the International Society of Poets. In addition to *Observer*, published in 1996 by Noble House, Aino has published two other collections of poetry: *Thoughts from a Windy Land* in Stockholm in 1987, and *Across the Distances* in Estonia in 1992. A collection of seven Estonian-language novels will be published in the near future in Estonia. Aino state: "I write poetry because I have to. Poetry allows my soul to speak. My job as a poet is to observe and tell the truth! It is not so much about writing words, but about discovering the meaning behind the visible, the feelings of the soul."ed in The International Poetry Hall of Fame Museum. The following poems I have written: National Library of Poetry, "What is a Mother's Love," Editor's Choice Award 1996; National Library of Poetry, "Looking Down From the Cross," Editor's Choice Award 1997; Poetry Guild published "Four Season's of Love," 1997; National Library of Poetry, "Time for Me," *Best Poems of 1998*; Boston Firefighter Digest published "Unselfish Sacrifices," October-November issue. Now I am honored to be published in Iliad Press-Spring 1997 *Treasures*, "With You" "Without You," Honorable Mention for "Without You." Also, Iliad Press, Summer 1997 Awards Program, "Some Quiet Time," Honorable Mention, "My Special Place." I want to thank Iliad Press for the recognition.

Ou, Kear - I'm a fifteen year old Cambodian girl from Revere, Massachusetts. I was born in the Philippines but grew up in the United States. I was raised by my young loving and caring mother, Sok Dy. I have a younger sister, Channy and a younger brother, Tira. They look up to me as their role model. They support me in everything I do. I give my mother a lot of credit for raising three kids all by herself. She's worked hard to be there for each and every one of us whenever we need her. I'm the oldest child in my family so I have a lot of responsibilities. I only have a short period of time to myself each day. And for those times, I either watch television or listen to the radio to relax. I hate writing and reading at the moment because I never read or see any books that interest me. One day, my second grade teacher read a poem to me and the rhymes at the end of each line held back my thoughts about writing. I try to write poems whenever I have a chance. Poems that have rhymes. As the years go on, my poems start to develop more details and become more meaningful. Since writing poems isn't that bad for me, I learned to like writing stories too. But whenever I start writing a story, I never finish it. Until the age of ten, I wrote a children's book. I was the author and the illustrator. And in the eighth grade, Mrs. Pedi, my English teacher had the class write a story for the children of their age. I chose the seventh and eighth graders because the story I was planning to write about involved gangs. The book is called "Friends." Again, I was the author and illustrator. Savorn Cheth and Monica Rana were my partners. They had worked hard to put this book together. I'm a freshman at Revere High School was has been nominated for honorary award recognition in the *Who's Who Among American High School Students*, 1996-1997.

Panaggio, Edna - Born on June 4, 1927 to Thomas and Amelia (Caldarone) Falciglia, in Providence, Rhode Island. At a very young age, she began to show signs of talent as an actress. She was married in 1952 and had one son and one daughter. In 1963, the family moved to Baltimore, Maryland. She continued to act in community theater, model, commentate and produce fashion shows. Eventually, she incorporated E & P Productions. With her talented group of performers, they presented cabarets and fashion shows for fundraisers, conventions, private supper and country clubs. When her marriage ended in 1981, she began writing. She became deeply moved by the change that had confronted her. Her spirituality turned to the things of God through scripture in the Holy Bible. To this day she finds great comfort from the Word. In 1987, she returned to Rhode Island when her daughter blessed her with her third grandchild. She continues to live in Cranston, Rhode Island as a loving grandmother; shares her life experiences with students as an instructor of acting and modeling for a nationally known modeling and career school, is a talent scout as R.I. Director of Talent America, an organization which opens doors for aspiring actors and models, and as an AFTRA/SAG actress, has acted in many national and regional commercials, with runway and print modeling to her credits. She recently assisted Dr. Enrico Garzilli, composer/lyricist/playwright, as casting producer, for his world musical premiere of "Rage of the Heart" presented in April, 1997.

Paulsen, Jessie - Born April 30, 1952, at Blackfoot Idaho, to Ralph and Gladys Carrier. The author has won numerous awards and merits for her poetry. She has been inducted into the Honorary Society of International Poets. She has won the "Award of Merit" for the years 1990, 1991, 1992; the "Golden Poet Award" for the years 1991, 1992; the "Editor's Choice Award" for the years 1993, 1994, 1995; six poems have been published worldwide and have won awards for "Outstanding Achievement." Two additional poems published nationwide. The author had a book of poetry published December 1994 entitled *Treasured Collections*, which may be ordered through the Lit "O" Red Hen Co., P.O. Box 5317, Cottonwood CA 96022, phone 916/347/9644. The *Lake California News* has published her work locally in Cottonwood, where the author resides with her husband Terry. She has three beautiful daughters, Angela, Jennifer and Crystal. Crystal is running for Cottonwood Rodeo Queen. One granddaughter, Shyann, featured in *Treasured Collections* won the "Little Miss Doll Face" beauty contest and will go to "Nationals" in July. Shyann will be two, July 17, 1995. The author anxiously awaits the birth of her first grandson, due June 10, 1995. The family will help out in the Lit "O" Red Hen Co. where their talents are used. Jennifer uses her office skills; Crystal helps with the lay out; Angela, the artist, designs and creates beautiful greeting cards. They write advice letters to children, via Lit "O" Red Hen's Chick "O" lets. The family is currently working on a second book, a book of Proverbs.

Payne, Tim S. - I am of Cherokee lineage and proud of it. My great, great grandmother, Elizabeth Woods, and her parents were among a small band of Indians that eluded federal troops who were rounding up the Cherokee Indians for the forced relocation to Oklahoma in 1838. They managed to escape to the Appalachian Mountains of North Carolina. Poetic talent has been in the Payne family since the early 1800's. Recently, I visited our family burial plot at Chandler Cemetery in Gordon County and found poetic verses hand-etched in the marble grave markers. Besides my family, the major influences on my life as a poet were Robert Frost and Dylan Thomas. I was born in Rome, Georgia in the summer of '58. I lived there until I was five years old, at which time my parents separated and later divorced. My mother and I moved to the Techwood Projects, one of the roughest neighborhoods in Atlanta. I was one of many children known as "latch key kids." I wore a key on a string around my neck. When I walked home after school each day, I was supposed to let myself in, lock the door behind me, and not go outside for anything. I can remember many nights going to bed before my mother got off from work at 9:00 p.m. While living in Atlanta, I was an abused and neglected child. At age fifteen I ended the ordeal by returning to Rome to live with my father. I attended Floyd College and North Georgia College in Dahlonega, Georgia. I presently reside in Rome with my wife, Cynthia, and our son, Thomas. My hobbies are collecting native art and researching my family lineage.

Peirce, James W. - has lived and worked in Maryland since 1948. He enlisted in the Navy during the Korean conflict, and became a ship's serviceman and construction driver in an amphibious construction battalion. Jim received his B.A. and M.Ed. from the University of Maryland at College Park and is listed in *Outstanding Educators in America* for the 1970s. He is a life-member of the University of Maryland Alumni Association, the Maryland PTA, and the American Legion. Jim retired after thirty-four years as an American history, civics and geography teacher in the public schools of Prince George's County. His three favorite writings are: Johann Goethe's "Faust," Dante's "Divine Comedy" and "Henry Thoreau's "Walden." Two great influences are his wife and grandfather. Nancy, an elementary teacher is an ever present editor. His grandfather, James Roller, was an engineer on the Baltimore and Ohio Railroad. Both are very influential in the forming of his ideas on the problems facing the middle class working man. Their perception of Maryland's river valleys filled with hard working and energetic people is ever present in his writing. He sees middle class destiny as controlled by the outside forces of politics, economics, fire and flood, and their underlying theme as a commitment to equality and fairness. Jim is presently a historian with the American Legion. His research is wide enough to include the State of Maryland, but is usually restricted to the western shore of the Chesapeake Bay. His monthly column on the American Legion appears in the *Beltsville News*. These recent attempts at poetry serve as a change of pace and a genuine challenge.

Pepple, Alexander - is a software engineer for a major computer firm in the San Francisco Bay area of California, and holds an M.Eng. degree in electrical engineering. Even though he is new to the world of poetry (he started poetry writing as a hobby at the beginning of 1997 inspired by what he amusingly calls "my Ill Year") he has been really encouraged by his output so far. The results have been even more so—his poems have made it to the final judging stages in four national contest including this one. In all four cases, they have been selected for publication in the associated hardbound poetry anthologies. This also includes the National Library of Poetry where besides wining the 2nd prize and hardcopy publication in *Dreaming in Metaphors*, his submission has been selected to feature in their special audio release, *The Sound of Poetry*— an honor accorded to only their ten best entries. He is now polishing up the manuscript for a book of poetry titled *Riding Oceans and Continents in 101 Poems of Love x Life x Lust*, which he fondly calls L^3 poetry, with an engineering voice. Any interested agents/publishers? He may be reached at *alex_pepple@lotus.com* by e-mail.

Pettine, Paul C. - **Pen name**: POE. **Occupation**: cafe bar tender (Junni Moons). **Hobbies**: singing, writing, painting confusing people, saving the world. **Family life**: I live with my parents who have been married for 23 years (wow!). I have four sisters and one brother, plus one dog. **Favorite musicians**: Tori Amos, Ani DiFranco, Bjork, Jewel, lots more... **My hero**: Tori Amos because she has suffered greatly to get where she is and still after all the bad times she still has the strength to write the most beautiful music I have yet to have heard. **What I want to be**: I would really like to be a famous singer. I have a lot of songs written and no one to listen to them. **Famous quote**: "Never stop going. Always fight for who you are. Whatever it takes just be yourself no matter what they say. Be real. Be true. Be you. Till the end."

Reichert, Rebecca - Most of my family and friends call me Becky. I live in a small town in south central Pennsylvania called Abbottstown. I live with my mom and dad. I am a junior in high school in Spring Grove School District. I love animals. I have a two year old Dalmatian named Princess and two cats, Tigger and Eeyore. I have one brother, Randy, and one sister, Missy. After high school, I plan to go to Empire Beauty School to be a beautician. I also plan to write more poetry because it is something I like to do.

Roark, Sheila B. - Born and raised in New York but now lives in Euless, Texas. She is married to an Engineering Consultant, has three adult daughters, and a new granddaughter named Alexandria. Her early life was filled with a career in show business which took up most of her time. Her career kept her so busy that she only went to school two days a week. Sheila started writing poetry twenty years ago at a time when she had three young children and a troubled marriage. She found that writing her thoughts on paper helped ease the pain in her heart. She is still writing today and has expanded her writing to include short stories and articles. Her works have appeared in more than seventy anthologies and forty-five literary magazines. Among the many awards she has received are: first place from Drury's Publishing and second place from DDDD Publishing. "Writing is like any other activity we pursue," says Sheila. "It must be practiced every day if writers are to become proficient in their craft." That's exactly what Sheila does, she writes every day and keeps sending in those submissions. This formula has worked very well for her.

Ross, Kimberly - Born February 17, 1989. Kimberly has a dog named Rusty. She has one sister, Jennifer. She likes to read and color.

Rothbauer, Jan - [b.] January 18, 1942, Augusta, WI; [p.] Dorothy Zank, Alfred Zank (deceased); [m.] Ron Rothbauer, April 22, 1961; [ch.] two girls, one seventeen year old granddaughter raised from infancy; [ed.] High School; [occ.] bookkeeper for my husband's IGA grocery store business of 30 years; [memb.] A member of Messiah Lutheran Church (CLC), Eau Claire, WI; [hon.] My honors and awards are many, but different than most. They are not written on paper nor inscribed in wood or marble, but held in my heart; [pers.] Open heart surgery in 1995 and heart disease has made me appreciate the smallest blessings in life. The world of poetry has forever been an important part of my life. Poetry speaks and touches lives as spoken words cannot. I only write truisms from what I see, know and feel within. My deep love and faith in God is my life's inspiration; [a.] Cadott, WI.

Ruthledge, Kathleen Comstock - I would like to share my story with you, it's a unique story of a woman that had a dream all her life and it took her daughters encouragement to make her dream a reality. My dream started when I was a little girl. I would write plays and act them out with my sisters. The thing I remember the most about my youth, I was 12 when I wrote my first poem. I don't know why I started to write poetry, all I knew is it gave me enjoyment to create a beautiful story. By the time I was 15, I'd written a dozen poems. At 17, I started to write my first book but never finished it. I can't remember why I stopped because it was or would have been a good book and it still stands out in my mind today. I continued to write poetry off and on till I was 27, then I just stopped for 16 years. I guess I felt I needed to be more educated to be the writer of my dreams so I gave up. Then one day two years ago my daughter came to me asking for my help on a school project. It was to write a poem. After we wrote the poem together she said, "Mom, how did you know how to do that so well?" I explained to her all about how I wanted to be a famous poet when I was you. She said, "Mom, you can still have your dream. Will you write me a special poem?". Indeed I did and since that day I've been writing strong. I decided to do it for me because I truly enjoy writing and I truly did miss it. A few months ago my daughter saw an ad in a magazine for a poetry contest. A friend told me once, "I should not deny the world the beauty I produce."

Sarff, Extry Ronald - Born in Minnesota January 25, 1927, Extry was the eighth child of nine born to Rosamond and Marvin Sarff. After education in Agriculture at Sandpoint and Moscow, Idaho, Extry served in the second world war as both a sailor and a soldier. Extry married Lela Doge in 1948 and following the timber falling trade, raised their four daughters in Idaho, Montana, and Oregon. After a serious logging accident, Extry and Lela moved to Wrangell, Alaska in 1975 where he joined the commercial fishing trade. In 1985 oyster farming beckoned and ten years were spent with his family, raising oysters in the wilderness of Prince of Wales Island. Retired in 1995, Extry and Lela await their golden wedding anniversary may 17, 1998 at their home in Whale Pass, Prince of Whales Island. Extry has added writing to his hobbies of fishing, hunting, trapping, and beach combing. All are invited to this happy home for coffee.

Schaefer, Blake E. - Grew up in Southern Indiana and has lived most of his life there. He has also lived in Illinois and the St. Louis area. These settings are the background for most of his writing. He loves animals, especially dogs and cats. Animals play great roles in most of his writing. His profession is a truck parts salesman. He is a writer by hobby and would like to one day write full time. He is currently working on his first novel which happens to be a sci-fi thriller with cats playing a major role in the story.

Shrake, Heather - Age 18. I was born to be different, with my differences I became an artist. I live for my becoming intuition, I live to die remaining an influence, for I deal with life as an experience. I deal with experience to preserve life. I treat joy as I would pain. I treat pain to create art, for it's our likenesses in art, that our differences will come to be. So don't hate me for my beauty. Don't love me for my desire. But take what words I write in depth, and the words left shall inspire.

Smith, Tiffany Michelle - Tiffany's life began early on the morning of September twenty-fourth, nineteen hundred eighty-two. God blessed her with two loving and caring parents, Doug and Teresa Peters-Smith. Her family resided in Van, West Virginia until she was twelve years old. By this time there was a new edition to their family, a younger brother. Joseph, her brother, was born in January of 1987. Her brother attended elementary school with her a Wharton Elementary. While she attended Wharton Elementary, she won many great honors and awards. These included being a member of the math Field Day team, Eastern Coal's Academic Bowl team, and many awards for her individual outstanding scholastic achievements. The principal also chose her out of her class to receive the Principal Award for great leadership, personality, behavior, and good grades. She was also voted president of her sixth grade class. Her poem "Seems Like Yesterday" was then written for her "President's Address" on their graduation day. The Smith Family moved to Foster, West Virginia in November of her sixth grade year. Her mother drove Joseph and her back the thirty miles to Wharton everyday for the remaining time left in that school year. The next fall she began her seventh grade school year at Madison Middle School. While she attended MMS she won many other honors and awards such as being a member of the math Field Day team, winning a Young Writer's Award for a short story she wrote titled "The Magical Birthday Gift," and also winning West Virginia's most prestigious award for young West Virginians "The West Virginia Golden Horseshoe." At this time Tiffany has now moved on to Scott High School. She has not had enough time to win awards or special honors, but her grades are still very high; she hopes to continue to proceed into the twenty-first century by being one outstanding asset to the American population. *Tiffany would like to dedicate this poem to all of her beloved teachers and friends that she left behind at Wharton Elementary School when she moved on.*

Strauss, Catie Tara - Inspired by the many problems in our world, I, Catie Tara Strauss, (age thirteen) wrote "My Dream" and "If Only" as a way to express my feelings of what's going on around me. I was born in Quantico, Virginia, on a military base, where, right away, I was exposed to one fo the world's biggest problems. With our world's problems increasing every year, I began writing stories as well as poems at around the age of seven. Of course in second grade my writings had nothing to do with the world's problems, but with each new year came new stories and poems. As a product of my earlier writings, I wrote these two poems at the age of thirteen about what is going on in my mind, and what I feel the world should be like. I enjoy writing stories and poems a great deal, especially when I get to let others know through writing what I can't say in words. I also enjoy dancing. I have been taking ballet lessons for about seven years now and would like to continue dancing in the years to come, because ballet expresses beauty. When I'm not writing or dancing, I'm either doing school work to maintain my 4.0 grade average, or babysitting. As for my future writing plans, I plan to continue writing stories and poems about the world's problems. I hope to make people more aware and willing to help out to make the world a better place. I now live in Claymount, Delaware in a pleasant neighborhood in the suburbs. I live with my two loving parents, Debra-Sue and Dr. Stanley Strauss, my brother Chad, and two adorable dogs, Jessey and Gizmo. After all, isn't family (and cuddly creatures) what love is all about?

Yip Tong, Mimi - (Pen name: Theresa WONG) was born and lives in Mauritius, so-called "Star and Key of the Indian Ocean" ("Stella Clavisque Maris Indici"). She was educated in the island-State's best Girls' State Secondary School (1967-1974); then went to Reunion Island University and the south of France on Scholarship Awards granted by the French Government and obtained a B.A. (1978) and an M.A. (1979) in French and French Literature. Since 1981, she was Education Officer in the Ministry of Education, Arts & Culture until 1997, teaching at secondary level. After obtaining a Post-graduate Diploma in Translation Studies (English-French) through Distance Education at the University of South Africa, and made a beginning in the translating profession, she has responded to the urge and call of Creating Writing. She is a member of the International Society of Authors and Artists and of the National Authors Registry. Publications: The National Library of Poetry, Creative Arts & Science Enterprises (CASE), Sparrowgrass Poetry Forum, Iliad Press, Starburst Journal, The Armadillo Poetry Press, The Candlight Poetry Journal, Quill Books, Poetry Press, Poetry Unlimited. Mentions & Awards: "Model," (Accomplishment of Merit from CASE); "Death-gates," Fall 1996 Literary Awards Program Honorable Mention/Iliad Press and President's Award for Literary Excellence/Iliad Press & NAR; "To be above earth-level," Fall 1997 Honorable Mention/Iliad Press; Editor's Choice Award/The National Library of Poetry 1997. She is married with two girls of 13 and 8 years old. Besides poetry she enjoys the Arts and the love of Nature.

Turner, Jeffery Wayne - (Pen name, Jeffie Turner). I was born April 23, 1966 in Vernon, AL. My father's name is Thomas Turner and my mother's name is Evelyn Turner. I attended Sulligent High School, Sulligent, Alabama. I'm a member of the Royal Neighbors of America. I wrote many other poems, like President Bill Clinton, Princess Diana, Mother Teresa, my sister and many others. My God and my sister were my reasons to start writing. My number one TV show is the "Bionic Woman" and my number one actress in Lindsay Wagner. I listen to rock, country and gospel music. I thank God for what I've truly got. I have two dear friends, Mrs. Vera Burnette and Mrs. Louise Shackelford. I have one sister named Susie Gann, who I love very much. I have one grandmother named Lola Marler and one aunt named Dorothy Quandt. I think people should be good and love one another because this world doesn't have much of it anymore.

Vanskiver, Colleen D. - I was born in the city of Baltimore, in the great state of Maryland. I am a homemaker and mother. I have always held a full time job outside the home. I attended Eastern High School in Baltimore and I am a graduate of The Institute of Children's Literature. I am also a member of The National Authors Registry and the Poet's Guild. Some of things I am proudest of in my life are: the day I became Mrs. Vanskiver; together with the man I married, and with the help of God. We gave the world five unique individuals (our children). The first poem I ever entered into any kind of competition was "Battle of the Soul"; I am very proud and excited that it has won so many awards. This work has also won best song of the month from Chapel Record Co and is being recorded as a Gospel song. Some of my works are: "And God Know," Poetry Press; "Just a Housewife" and "These Blind Eyes," Iliad Press; "The Poet's Prayer," American Poetry Annual; "The Hiding Place," Iliad Press & North American Open Poetry contest semi-finalist; "Oak Tree," Sparrowgrass Publishing; "A Friend," *Treasure the Moment*, Quill Books. My passion for writing comes from the love of words. To move someone with words is truly what writing is all about. If you can make someone smile, shed a tear, or just stop and think, with words, you have a God-given talent. If I can do that I have accomplished my goal. It took me twenty-five years to write "Battle of the Soul." I just could not find the words. Now that it's done, I just can't stop writing. My dream to touch someone else with words. "Glory" is a poem I did while thinking about my son after he came back from The Desert Storm war. He is just not the same. My hope is for the world to become kinder, so no one's son, daughter, or loved one ever has to "walk into glory" again! This is one dream I hope will come true.

Voss, Jamie E. - I was born in Detroit, Michigan on November 3, 1976 to Kenneth and Suzanne. I have three younger sisters, Jennifer, Jessica and June. I currently live in Madison Heights where I grew up most of my life. I graduated on June 10, 1995 from Lamphere High School. I'm now attending college studying Computer Information Systems and writing in my free time. I've been writing poetry for about ten years and during high school I was involved in the school yearbook and newspaper. In high school I won awards in Exposition and Research, Marketing Co-op, Introduction to Yearbook, Introduction to Newspaper, Yearbook Staff, newspaper Staff, Newspaper Student of the Year, Newspaper Most Outstanding First Year Staff Member, Year's Best News Story and Honorable Mention for By-lined Opinion Article from the Michigan Interscholastic Press Association (MIPA). I am a member of the International Society of Poet's and The International Poetry Hall of Fame. Poetry awards include: The National Author's Registry President's Award for Literary Excellence (1997); 1996 Iliad Literary Awards and two Editor's Choice Awards from The National Library of Poetry. Published Works (poetry): "The Killer," *A Voyage to Remember*, The National Library of Poetry; "The Littlest Things," "L.C.R.," and "Lifelong Friend," *The American Poetry Annual*, The Amherst Society; "Mother Earth," *Interludes*, The Wexford Poetry Society; "The Fight," and "Keep Smilin'," *Meditations*, Iliad Press; "Darkness," and "L.C.R.," *Keepsakes*, Iliad Press; "The Littlest Things," *Best Poems of the 90's*, The National Library of Poetry; and "L.C.R.," *Best Poems of 1997*, The National Library of Poetry. Through my poetry I express what I feel deep inside that I can't express through day to day conversations with friends and family. I hope one day to become a computer programmer and a writer.

Warner, Ruth - **Born:** October 6, 1923 in Toledo, Ohio. **Married:** Neal E. Warner October 27, 1945. **Education:** Attended Woodward High School. **Special Studies:** Stautzenberger Secretarial School. **Occupation:** Housewife (former secretary). **Memberships:** International Society of Poets, International Society of Authors and Artists, National Authors Registry. **Other Published Works:** Poetry "After the Final Out," published in *Treasured Poems of America*, 1997; "Lord, Guide My Steps," published in *Footsteps in the Sand*, 1996; "Hungering for Love" published in *Beginnings*, 1997; "The Number of My Days" published in *Moonlight and Wishes*, 1997. **Honors and Awards:** (2) Editor's Choice Awards 1996, (2) President's Awards for Literary Excellence 1996, Editor's Preference Award of Excellence 1996, (1) Honorable Mention Award 1997, Editor's Preference Award of Excellence 1997.

Wigley, Tasha - I'm 18 years old and my birthday is on July 24, 1979. I was born in Barrie Ontario and now live in Belleville Ontario. I have three older brothers (ages 31, 30, and 29) and one younger sister (16). I love to read books, mostly you'll see me reading a scary book, which I like most of the time. I also love to write stories. I'm deaf, but I had a cochlear implant in my left ear. I've had it since 1995 and it works really well. but I still have to learn to interpret sounds, just like someone learning a new language. I can read lips really well. I'm shy around most kids my age but I'm starting to overcome my shyness now. I really dislike people who take drugs and people that smoke a lot. You can write to me on the internet at: tashasw@blvl.igs.net Special thanks go to Jennifer Kincaid for suggesting me to enter my poem to Iliad Press...and to my parents for always telling me to write something.

Young, Fran - A resident of Lubbock, Texas, Fran was born April 18, 1940 to Earl and Bessie Hudman in High Rolls, New Mexico. On September 14, 1986, she married Leland Young. Together, they have one child, Lee Wallace. Fran graduated in 1958 from Alamogordo High School, Alamogordo, New Mexico. Retired, Fran says, "I have been writing poetry most of my adult life for friends and family and my own enjoyment. In February this year (1997), I began to enter poetry in contests. I have had nine poems accepted for publication to date. Other works: "For Love of Birdie," *Tracing Shadows*, July 1997; "Burning Bridges," *Through the Looking Glass,* October 1997; "Hold Back the Night," *Priceless Treasures*, March 1998; "Keep These Three Things," *Passages of Light*, April 1998; "The Purr," *Echoes of Destiny*, March 1998; "Gossip," *The Promise of Tomorrow*, April 1998; "Star Dreamer," *Best Poems of 1998*, April 1998; "Phantoms in the Night," *Treasured Poems of America 1998*, April 1998. Fran has written one book of poems titled *Simply Me* which is in search of a publisher and she's begun working on her second book.

Treasures Index

Alphabetical Index
of Contributors
Arranged by last name.

Alphabetical Index by Author

A

Aagard, Carol, 185
Aaron, 267
Abbott, S. Elisabeth M., 25
Abejuela, Harmony Raylen, 193
Acker, Geri, 25
Ackerson, Dee Ann, 193
Adams, Audrey, 25
Adams, Sharon S., 25
Addo, Peter E., 193
Aggers, Allen L., 193
Agreda, Cindy Joset, 194
Ahmed, Naveen, 25
Ahrens, Jackson, 194
Aiello, Elizabeth A., 194
Aishman, Samantha Brook, 194
Aker, Debra Beck, 194
Akers, Jennifer, 195
Al-wazzan, Shammara J., 26
Albertson, Jr., Donald P., 4, 195
Alexander, David, 195
Ali, Shazia, 25
Aliff, William L., 195
Allen, Gene R., 26
Allen, Kari E., 195
Allen, Krystal, 195
Allen, Michael W., 195
Allooloo-Laraque, Siku, 26
Alverson, April, 196
Alverson, Kathy, 196
Amber, Alexis, 196
Andang, Aishah, 4
Anderson, Brooke, 196
Anderson, Candice Marie, 27
Anderson, Emily May, 26
Anderson, Jason, 27
Anderson, Jeana Louise, 26
Anderson, Maria, 27
Anderson, Stacey Michelle, 196
Andren, Lauraine A., 27, 196
Andress, Jennifer, 3
Andreyko, Nicole, 197
Andria, Paula, 27
Andrysek, Kathy, 28
Angermeyer, Shanon M., 28
Angulo, Gerardo L., 28, 197, 387
Angus, Aneeka A., 28
Ankney, Crystal Ann, 29
Anonymous, 139
Anselmo, Giovanni, 197
Anthamatten, Katie, 29
Antweiler, Rhia, 197
Apodaca, Maria Elena, 29
Appel, Brenda Lee, 29, 197
Arbing, Amber Joy, 197
Arcolano, Tina, 198
Ardiff, Meggan E., 29
Aristide, Deine, 198
Armstrong, Audrey J., 188
Armstrong, Jenny, 198
Armstrong, Lydia, 198
Armstrong, Robert F., 198, 387
Arnold, Ashley A., 199
Ash, 213
Ashouri, Nazgol, 30
Ashtor, Gila, 199
Atcheson, B.J. Vienot, 387
Attiogbe, Delali, 199
Atwell, K., 199
Atwell, Samantha, 199, 387
Audino, Frank L., 30
Audiss, Vivianne, 30
Augustyniak, Barbara, 30
Austin, Laura A., 31
Autry, Brandi, 200
Aynat, Joanna, 200

B

Bacon, Pamela Jo Francis, 200
Badger, Janna M., 31, 200
Baggott, Allison K., 200
Bahmer, Elissa, 201
Bahr, Shersti, 201, 387
Baird, Christina M., 31
Baker, Mary Melissa, 201
Baker, Matt, 2
Baker, Sharron, 31
Bakker, Vera Ogden, 4
Ballam, Heather, 201
Bank, Richard, 201
Bankole, Adisa Olubayo, 4
Banks, Cindy, 201
Baraghoshi, Alicia, 32
Barberio, Mandy Elena, 202
Barker, Kerry Lynn, 32
Barnes, Chad Michael, 32
Barnes-Bourgillon, Juanita C., 32
Barrios, Crystal, 32
Barry, Amanda, 5
Bateham, Thomas Allen, 202, 387
Bateman, Alexis Helen, 202
Batista, Alba, 202
Bauer, Aimee, 5
Bauers, Joe W., 33
Baumann, Lisa M., 33
Bay, Laura, 203
Beam, Morgan L., 33
Beasley, Joan Ostrom, 33, 203
Bechert, Tiffany, 203
Beck, Kelsey, 33
Bedard, Sahwn W., 34
Behr, Julie, 204
Behrens, Nicole, 204
Beining, Denise, 204
Beland, Jessica, 204
Bell, Linda, 34
Bell-Massey, Jacquelyn, 34
Belyeu, Elizabeth, 204
Benham, Tina, 34
Bennett, Carrie B., 205
Bennett, Emilee A., 205
Benninghoven, Marina, 35
Benson, Jessie, 205
Benson, Lacy, 205
Berger, Rachel, 35
Berkowsky, G.F., 35
Bero, Mark A., 205, 387
Berrios, Diana, 205
Berry, Marcella, 5, 206
Berthiaume, Alyssa, 206
Beshai, Lisa, 35
Betel, Sal, 35
Bethea, Lisa, 206
Bettys, Amy, 36
Bickels, Shannon, 36
Bing, LaCrystal R., 206
Bird, Gina, 206
Birdi, Heena, 36
Black, Robin Janea, 206
Blackburn, Jolene, 206
Blackburn, Sabrina, 36
Blackwell, Lindsey Nicole, 36
Blain, Amanda, 36
Blake, Marcus, 206
Bland, Vanessa, 207
Blankenship, Erin, 207
Blevins, Kristin, 207
Blossom, Willow, 214
Blues, Krystdevon, 37
Blumenfeld, Steven, 37
Bockmiller, Jennifer, 37
Bodle, Rebecca, 37, 207
Bodner, Nika, 37, 208
Boeglin, Juli, 38
Boeling, Casey, 208
Boes, Danielle, 208
Bonari, Angela, 208
Bond-Louden, Jenna, 38, 387
Bonilla, Renee, 209
Borgeson, Bethel, 5
Boronski, Emily, 209
Bowman, Brandy, 38
Box, Maranda Leigh, 38
Boyett, Brittany, 38
Boykin, Tiffany, 38
Boyle, Brighid Bryan, 209
Boyle, Sydney, 39
Braden, Jennifer, 209
Bradley, Tiffany Ann, 209, 210
Brady, Jaime, 210
Brainard, Alicia Aileen, 210
Branch, Bryant Jerome, 39, 387
Brand, Valerie, 39
Branson, Mindy Jo, 210
Braun, Erin, 210
Bray, Caroline M., 211
Breault, Chloe, 39
Breault, Diesssa, 210
Breedlove, Anna Danielle, 211
Breish, Heather, 39
Breitzman-Lacey, Bonnie, 211
Bridges, Jacob Russell, 211
Bridges, Michelle, 40
Brinson, Pamela Denise, 40
Brittain, Janice, 40
Brittain, Tennessee Catherine, 30, 199
Brockwell, Victor Newman, 211
Bronson, Rae, 40
Brookins, Naomi A., 40, 387
Brosman, Jessica R., 211
Brown, Brittney, 211
Brown, Carol, 40
Brown, C. Lawry, 212
Brown, Jenny, 41
Brown, Juanita, 212, 388
Brown, Katie, 212
Brown, Nicole L., 41
Brown, Rebecca, 212
Brown, Sarah Lee, 41
Brownson, Lauren, 41
Broyles, Amy Renee, 42
Buchalter, Shawn, 203
Buchanan, Malisa Ranee, 42
Buck, Lauren, 212
Bucks, Lauren, 42
Budman, Karen, 213
Buller, Michelle, 6
Bultje, Andrea, 42
Burch, Terrie D., 212
Burgeson, Joseph, 2
Burgess, Lance P., 42
Burke, Jamie, 43
Burkhart, Ron, 43
Burleson, Matthew, 43, 213, 388
Burnett, Jamie Elaine, 43
Burris, Rebecca, 44
Burton, Jennifer, 44
Burton, Judy A., 43
Bush, Stacy Denise, 44
Buskey, Kathleen E., 44
Busselman, Nicholas, 214
Butler, Erin, 214
Buxton, Dana E., 44
Buzard, Melanie S., 45
Byrd, Dell, 214
Byrum, Ashlee, 215

C

Caeidhe, Ana W., 215
Cain, Amber, 215
Caldwell, Ryan, 215
Calhoun, K., 342
Calhoun, Merlin Dale, 216
Callahan, Heather, 216
Callen, Ashley, 216
Calvert, Mindy, 216
Calzada, D.J., 217
Camou, Jean, 305
Campbell, Trisha, 45
Campomizzi, Diane, 45, 217
Canett, Neomi Marie, 217
Cannella, John C., 217
Carapella, Lindsay, 47
Carey, Jeffrey D., 217
Carlino, Kristin, 45
Carlo, Lindsey J., 217
Carlotta The III, 326
Carlson, Sandra, 45
Carpenter, Amanda, 46
Carr, Joe, 218
Carrillo, Courtney, 218
Carter, Ashley, 46, 218
Carter, Cheryl S., 218
Carter, Janet, 218
Casey, Maggie, 218
Cashin, Melissa, 219
Cassin, Artilee, 46
Castaneda, Carmalita Alvina, 46
Caudle, Kathy, 219, 388
Cedro, Stefanie M., 46
Cha, Amy, 47
Chaffin, Erin, 219
Chandler, Abby, 47
Chang, Sandra I., 47
Chang Ph.D., Janice M., 47

Chapline, Joseph A., 219
Chapman, Debra Anne, 48, 219, 388
Chapman, Jennifer, 48
Chatham, Barbara Anne, 48
Chatham, Cynthia Lynn, 220
Chavez, Joy, 220
Cheek, Jessica, 48
Cheeki, 178
Chen, Jennifer, 220
Chesney, Alicia B., 48
Chhoun, Phanly, 220
Chieco, Nicole, 49
Childs, Linda, 220
Chiles, Tara, 220
Chism, Lori, 221
Chohan, Sonia, 221
Church, Elan, 49
Churchill, Leslie, 221
Cikalo, Miranda, 221
Cisz, Vanessa A., 6
Clark, Elizabeth, 49
Clark, Jesse D., 221
Clark, Miles, 49
Clark, Shannon, 49
Clark, Tiffany L., 222, 388
Clausen, Alice, 49, 222
Clements, Kiersten, 50
Clierre, Kina, 222
Cochran, Donald, 50
Cody, Jennifer, 222
Coffindaffer, Heather, 222
Coker, Eric Lee, 6
Coleman, Barbra Lee, 223
Coleman. Cara, 50
Coleman, Melissa, 223
Collins, Linda, 223
Collins, V. June, 185
Coln, Stephanie, 223
Comas, Julio, 223, 388
Congdon, Heather, 50
Conkel, Michael R., 50
Conn, Carolann, 224
Conner, Abby, 7
Conrad, Sara, 224
Cook, Cynthia A., 224
Cook, Jamie, 224
Cook, K. Catherine, 224, 225
Cook, Toni, 225
Cook Jr., Todd, 50, 388
Cooke, Tiffany Monique, 224
Cooper, Karla K., 225
Corbitt, D'Ambra, 225
Cord, Justin Patrick, 51
Cordes, Preston Lee, 6
Corey, Kerri Lynn, 225
Cornelius, Petrani Erema, 51
Correla, Christina, 51
Cortez, Joyce, 226
Cottone, Josephine, 51
Cox, Barry, 51
Cox, Diane Draper, 52
Cox, Meagan, 226
Craig, Angela, 226
Craig, Karen, 226
Craig, Tereta Dawn, 226
Crain, Alecia, 52
Crandall, Stephanie, 226
Crawford, David Allen, 227, 388
Crego, Holli, 7
Crisp, Amber, 227
Crisp, Erika, 52
Croce, Paul J., 52
Crosby-Helms, Devon, 7
Crow, Christy, 227

Crow, Lindsay, 7
Crowe, Amber, 227
Cruz, Lillis, 52
Cryer, Wendy, 7
Cuipylo, Melissa, 53
Cumiskey, Ciara, 227
Cummings, Nicole, 228
Curren, Richard, 53, 228
Curry, Erica, 228
Cutler, Shallee, 53

D

d'Avignon, Angela, 54, 231, 389
D'Angelo, Ann Marie, 229
D'Elia, Deborah, 57
D'Alonzo, Kimberly Ann, 54
DaCosta, Trudy, 228
Daeges, Melissa Kay, 53
Dahl, Deanna B., 53
Daigle, Angela E., 228
Dahlgren, Martin, 7
Daily, Matt, 228
Daley, Joseoh Raymond, 229
Dalipe, Roselynn A., 229
Dalton, Tracy, 229
Daniele, Daniel, 229, 230
Daniels, James Robert, 54
Daniels, Michael, 54
Danko, Jason M., 230
Dark, Mi Mi, 54
Dascani, Sam, 230
Datoush, Kim W., 230
Daubert, Megan K., 230
Daugherty, Lee A., 8
Daughtry, Robin, 230
Davidson, Abel, 54
Davis, Andrew, 54
Davis, Catherine Jean, 55
Davis, Clarice Lawson, 231, 389
Davis, Elizabeth A., 55
Davis, Emily, 8
Davis, Julie, 55
Davis, Lacey M., 231
Davis, Margaret L., 55, 231
Davis, Melissa, 55
Davis, Nicholas, 231
Davis, Nicole, 232
Davis, Stephanie M., 232
Day, Eric, 389
DeBlois, Rebeccah A., 55
DeCook, Kathryn L., 56
DeGroot, Malinda, 232
DeHart, Jason, 56
De La Garza, Ana, 232
DeLancey, Michelle, 232
DeMarco, Don Roman, 82
de la Pena, Rosalyn, 56
delaPena, Tanya, 233
de los Santos, Lester J., 8
DeLarre, Linnette, 233
DeLaurentis, John, 56
DeVelbiss, Carrie, 8, 234
Decker, Lindsay, 232
Degenshein, Anya, 56
DeLeo, Kristie M., 56
Denning, Danielle, 57
Dennis, Crystal, 233
Densmore, Cathy C., 57
de Sousa, Sara, 234
Devlin, Erin K., 234
Di Stefano, Rosa, 57
DiBella, Gracey L.A., 234
DiPaola, Alba, 233

Dickey, J. David, 57, 234
Dickinson, Franklyn, 8
Diermier, Jesica, 234
DiGiando, David, 57
Dixon-Sullivan, Sarah, 235
Dlugos, Jennifer, 58
Dodge, Cathy, 235
Doherty, Allison, 58
Donithan, Jesse, 235
Dooley, Siera Kay, 235
Dopheide, Angelica, 235
Dorn, Dawn, 235
Dotzler, Wendy, 235
Doubet, Dorothy, 236
Dowling, Lauren, 58
Down, Annie, 236
Doyker, Deneene Raphael, 58
Doyler, Ed, 9
Dozier, Farrah Sheree, 236
Drake, Alisha, 59
Drake, Kristin A., 236
Drinkwater, Deborah L., 59
DuPont, Melanie, 59
Dufresne, Sarah, 236
Dugan, Kelly P., 236
Dugas, Roxane, 59
Duncan, Tara, 236
Dunphu, Christina, 59
Dupuis, Jennifer, 237
Dupuy, Roy, 60
Durocher, Jessica, 237
Dziedzic, Jeremy N., 237

E

Eades, Lauren, 9
Earlywine, Courtney, 60
Earp, Tricia, 237
Eastcott, Lorna, 237
Ebbecke, Allison, 237
Ebersole, Hayley, 238
Eck, Kimberly R., 238
Edel, Beth, 238
Edelshteyn, Rachel, 238
Edwards, Scott, 238
Edwards, Tasheena, 238
Eggers, Amanda Anne, 239
Eisenberg, Michelle M., 239
Eisenstein, Jana, 60
El Nachef, M.D., M. W., 60, 239
Elkins, Kristan, 239
Ellingson, Rick, 239, 389
Elmer, Holly, 60
Elston, Luretta, 60
Englebright, Stephani, 239
English, Brandie, 240
English, Christine L., 240, 389
Enscoe, Vicki, 60, 240
Erb, Elisha, 240, 241
Erb, Sara, 241
Ercek, Karen LaRene, 241
Ericksen, Amy R., 61
Erickson, Betty, 9
Erickson, Brandis, 241
Erickson, Jennifer, 61
Eskandarian, Selin, 241
Ettel, Kathleen Ann, 61
Evans, Heather, 61
Evans, Jennifer, 242
Evens, Susan, 242
Eyermann, Sarah, 61

F

Faatz, Melinda, 242
Fabian, Tara, 62
Fach, Angela Sue, 242
Fajna, Betty J., 152
Falletta, Jo Ann, 62, 242
Farley, Elizabeth Nicole, 242, 243
Farmer, Micah, 62, 389
Farnen, Larry, 62
Farris, Candy, 243, 389
Faucher, Amanda, 243, 244
Faykes, Jeanna, 62
Fears, Nicole, 63
Feehan, Trisha, 244
Feher, Kristine, 63
Fekete, Clarissa Nicole, 63
Felago, John, 9
Felmet, Rachelle, 63, 186, 244, 389
Felton, Angela, 244
Fenech, Raymond, 186
Fennell, Paul, 245
Ferguson, Michele, 63
Fernandez, Melissa Figueroa, 63
Fesperman, Louise M., 245, 389
Fetters, Mike, 245
Fettig, Brad, 64
Fiehn, Teresa, 245
Fields, Linda M., 245, 389
Fields, Rachel E., 246
Figgeroa, Sarah M., 64
Filipowicz, Jillian, 64
Filippov, Olga, 246
Finch, Ellie, 246
Fiorella, Mary Beth, 246
Fischer, Ashton John, 246
Fish, JoAnna, 247
Fisher, Jeremia N., 247
Fister, Allison, 246
Fitchorn, Amanda, 247
Fitzgerald, Jeanna, 247
Fitzhugh, Nicole, 247
Flack, Lynzy, 248
Flategraff, Zacary, 248
Flaten, Kirsten, 64
Flaum, Erin, 248
Fledderjohann, Jasmine, 64
Fleming, Bonnie E., 10
Flokowitsch, Karla, 248
Florence, Jillian Marie, 248
Flory, Malina, 64
Flynn, Barbara A., 249
Flynn, Rebecca E.M., 65
Fogarty, Mary, 65
Foglia, Lucas, 249
Fonda, Sheridan, 65, 390
Fons, Tammy, 65
Foos, Heather, 249
Forbes, Christina, 249
Ford, Morgan, 249
Formanek, Hedy Wolf, 250
Forner-Greenaway, Michele, 66
Foster, Mary R., 66
Fowler, Steph, 250
Fraley, Sandra, 251
Frame, Alan, 188, 189
Franey, Desiree, 250
Franklin, Allison, 66
Franklin, Peggy E., 250
Frazer, Patrick Michael, 10
Frith, Renee, 251
Fritz, Mary, 66, 251
Fu, Rose, 66

Fujii, Dee L., 251
Fuller, Kathryn, 251
Fuller, Sara, 66
Fulp, SteAnn Lee, 252

G

Gabbard, Candy L., 252
Gable, April, 67
Gablick, Richard, 390
Gaboury, Lelian, 67
Gain, Jaclyn, 67
Gaines, Kristin, 252
Gallagher, Kristin, 252, 390
Galloway, Max, 252
Gariano, Joseph, 252
Garman, Jennifer, 67
Garrett, Hollie, 68
Gass, Karen S., 67, 253
Gates, Jessica, 10
Gatewood, Eileen, 253
Gauthereaux, Earl J., 68
Gavlinski, A., 10
Gay, April, 253
Gee, Ivonne, 68
Geier, Shawna, 68
Gelber, Beth, 68
Gephardt, Sarah, 253
Gerber, Kristin, 253
Ghattas, Christine Bonnie, 253, 390
Giacalone, Joseph J., 10
Gibbons, Erin, 68
Gibson, Edwin, 254, 390
Gibson, Michele E., 69
Gifford, Cheetah C., 69
Gill, Raymond J., 254
Gill, Rebecca Erin, 254
Gillespie, Rene's, 146
Gillette, Wendy M., 69
Gilliatte, Katie, 69
Gillmore, Elizabeth Clare, 70
Gilmour, Jennifer, 70
Glenn, Stacia Angelique, 70, 254
Glentz, Karla, 254
Glick, Sally A., 255
Godfrey, Jenna M., 70
Golden, Heather, 71
Goldshmidt, Anna, 71
Golston, Lynnette, 71
Gomez, Margarita, 71
Gomez, Robyn L., 255
Gomm, Emily Hope, 255
Gonzalez, Dortha J., 72
Gonzalez, Eddie, 255
Goodin, Bryan, 72
Goodrich, Elizabeth Farley, 255
Goodson, Elisha, 256
Goodwin, Joan, 72
Gordon, Erin, 72
Gordon, Patricia, 73
Gosma, Lindsey Nicole, 11
Goss, Daphne, 256
Goulart, Laura, 73
Goulet, Shannon Marie, 73, 256
Gouthier, Jennifer L., 73
Grabiec, Clarissa, 73
Gracey, Amy E., 74
Graham, Rita S., 74
Gray, C.E., 272
Gray, Christina, 256
Gray, Christle L., 74
Gray, Daniel, 74
Gray, Patty, 75
Grayson, Sonya, 257

Gredler, Sara, 74
Greek, Lyn, 11
Green, Amanda, 75
Green, Jason E., 257
Greger, L. S., 75
Gregory, Tiffany Jolyn, 257
Gresham, Valene Jasmine, 257
Grider, Brandy Jean, 257
Griffin, Allison Marie, 75
Griffin, Sarah L., 75
Groleau, Anthony T., 75, 390
Grubb, Mary, 76, 257
Guarino, Alison, 258
Guerin, Emily E., 258
Guerrero, Maria, 258
Guild, Carol Mason, 76
Guilkey, Joyce, 11, 258
Guinn, James D., 258, 390
Guitreau, Kayla, 259
Gulan, Bonnie M., 76
Gulati, Anjuman, 76
Gumber, Roni, 259
Gutana, Julie, 259
Gutto, Kristen, 259
Guy, Dylan, 11
Gwost, Amanda Rose, 259

H

Haddock, Pattie Reynolds, 77
Hadzariga, Alex, 259
Haines, Melissa L., 260
Halbsqut, Lisa R., 260
Hall, Alissa, 260
Hall, Crystal, 77
Hall, Kelly R., 76
Hall, Maria, 260
Hall, Monica, 261
Hall, Robie Glenn, 11
Hall, Sabrina, 77
Hallahan, Erin, 260
Hallberg, Al, 260
Hallim, Tania Rita, 77
Hallock, Lindsay, 77
Halm, Dawn M., 261
Halper, Arianna, 77
Hamberger, Emily, 261
Hamilton, Elizabeth B., 261
Hamilton, Henry L., 12
Hamlett, Savannah Rose, 261
Hammerwold, Stephanie, 78
Hampel, Elizabeth, 12
Hampton, Georgia, 78
Handshoe, Leslie, 262
Haney, Nicole, 262
Hanna, Amber, 78
Hannawacker, Lori Jo, 78
Hansen, Amy, 262
Hansen, Janie K., 78
Hanson, Amber Jude, 262
Hanson, Traci, 262
Harding, Terri, 78
Hardjana, Astrid, 79, 390
Hargis, Tiffany, 79
Hargrave, Caroline, 79
Harman III, Paul A., 263
Harmon, Melanie, 79, 390
Harold, Caitlin, 263
Harper, Lynnann, 79
Harr, Kyra A., 80
Harrell, Christina, 263
Harrell, Virginia L., 263
Harrington, Heather, 263
Harris, Caron, 264

Harris, Edyth V., 188
Harris, Krystal, 264, 391
Harris, Sandra Joy, 79
Harris, Sharon Lee, 80
Harris, Tanya, 264
Harrison, Dony, 264
Hartshorn, Maureen, 80
Harvey, Elisabeth Nicole, 80, 264
Hash, Joy Renee, 80
Haskell, Rashawn, 264
Hatch, Cassie Lynne, 265
Hatcher, Gar, 81
Haughton, Kedesha, 265
Hawkins, Krista, 265
Hawklen, Zeyphyre, 81
Hawks, Brett, 81
Haynes, Kimberly, 81
Headrick, Carolyn M., 81, 265, 391
Heard, Holly M., 82
Heffert, Denise, 265
Henderson, Gladys E., 82
Henry, Kalesha, 266
Heredia, Jennifer, 82
Hernandez, David, 266
Hernandez, Heidi Margarete, 266
Hershberg, Jay, 82
Heslop, Jr., Roger, 266
Hess, Eva, 82
Hess, Holly A., 83
Hett, Morgan, 266
Hickel, Silvia, 266
Hididd, Melissa A., 83
Higgins, N Loy, 83, 188, 391
Highland, Colin, 267
Hill, Jennifer, 83
Hill, Michelle, 267
Hill, Rebecca Elizabeth, 84
Hillyard, Amber Rose, 268
Hitchcock, Evelyn A., 84
Hockenberry, Suzie, 84
Hoffman, Carl, 268
Hoffman, Jeannine, 84
Hofmann, Kris, 84
Hoggan, Judith A., 85, 268, 391
Hollister, Maegan A., 85, 391
Hollmon, Veronica E., 268, 269
Hollock, Lindsay, 269
Holm, Sarah, 269
Holness, Adrienne, 269
Holt, Kimberly, 84
Holt, Shannon, 85
Holton, Stefanie, 270
Holz, Vicki Lyn, 85
Honeyfield, Sabrina, 270
Honkanen, Sarah, 270
Hood, Pamela C., 270
Hopkinson, Jill, 270
Hopper, Amy, 271
Horn, Darle Michelle, 271
Hornung, Shannan Leigh, 271
Howard, Robin L., 85
Hudy, Joanne, 86
Huffman, Cathy, 271
Hulek-Doyle, Michele M., 271
Hull, Jennifer, 272
Hull, Kathryn B., 86
Hultgren, Jenny, 86
Humphrey, Betty Jane, 86
Hunt, James M., 87
Hunt, Joan E., 12
Huntington, Maegan, 272
Hurd, Shirley J., 272
Hurtack, Kevin, 13
Hussey, Lloyd F., 12
Hysell, Lee, 87

I

Iffert, Beth, 272
Indaburu, Martha Adelaida, 87
Ingram, Jennifer, 273
Iolana, Patricia E.S., 87
Irish, Charles K., 273
Iroegbu, Monica, 88, 391
Irving, Ellen, 6
Irving, Robyn Ann, 273
Isaacs, Theresa, 88
Iverson, Viola, 88, 391
Ives, Aeron, 273
Iwanejko, Kim, 273

J

Jackson, G.D., 274
Jackson, Jennifer, 88
Jackson, Jessica, 274
Jackson, Thomas D., 274
Jacob, Christy, 89
Jacob, Chris, 274
Jacobs, Cathy, 274
Jacobs, Janine Crystal, 89
Jacobson, Romy T., 89, 275
Jacoby, Christine, 89
James, Leah, 89, 275
Jamie, 296
Jamison, Lindsey, 274
Jamison, Nicole, 275
Janeksela, Jeremiah S., 275
Janes, Misty Ann, 276
Janssen, Jennifer, 89
Jantz, Andrew, 90
Jardine, Christine, 90
Jayme, Mary, 90
Jeddry, Jennie, 276
Jeffers, Noelene, 90
Jeffers, Robert, 276
Jeffries, Teresa M., 90
Jenkins, Casey, 276
Jenkins, Jennifer, 277
Jensky, Heather, 91
Jesse, Emily, 91
Jody, Shannon, 91
Joelle, 295
Johanson, Tina, 91
Johnen, Casey, 276
Johnson, Aaron, 92
Johnson, Dawn, 277
Johnson, Jesi, 276
Johnson, Jessica, 277
Johnson, Lindsey, 91
Johnson, Mary E., 91
Johnson, Misty, 277
Johnson, Steve, 13
Johnson, Terri L., 92, 277
Johnson, Terry, 92
Johnston, Brooke, 92, 277
Jones, Alice M., 93
Jones, CeCe, 278
Jones, Christie, 278
Jones, Crystal A., 93
Jones, Danny, 278
Jones, Erin, 278
Jones, Hanako, 278
Jones, Nella, 278
Jones, Stacy, 93
Jones, Tawnya Sue, 279
Joost, Emily, 93
Joshi, Vishnu P., 93

Joy, Joy Joy, 279
Joynes, Ben, 94, 392
Juelis, Michele, 94
Juneau, Rebecca, 94

K

KCV, 372
Kabe, Aino, 392
Kadow, Cynthia M., 94
Kahler, Roy, 94
Kai, Cyrus, 108
Kalil, J., 94
Kalinowski, Jamie, 279
Kalkan, Erika, 279
Kane, Paul Michael, 95
Kanumalla, Anju, 279
Karczewski, Briana, 95
Karmol, Stephen N., 95
Katznelson, George, 280
Kaufman, Shayna Jo, 280
Kay, Donna, 185
Keding, Kara, 280
Keihl, Laura, 95
Kelley, Dwight H., 95
Kelley, Kindra, 280
Kellhofer, Jeremy, 280
Kelly, Amber D., 281
Kelly, Sandra, 95
Kelly, Shannon K., 281
Kelly, Stephanie, 281
Kelly, Steve, 281
Kelsey, Heather, 282
Keltonic, Julie, 282
Kennedy, Megan, 282
Kennedy, Natasha Latreena, 96
Kennedy, Peggy Boogaard, 96, 282
Kennon, Carel, 283
Kerfoot, Andrea G., 283
Kerr, Jill, 283
Khwaja, Shanen, 96
Kidder, Patrick S., 283
Kieper, Sarah, 96
Kierstead, Sheldon J., 96
Killough, Kristyn, 96
Kim, Yumi, 13
Kimberly, Jamie, 283
Kimmel, Jessica, 97
Kinderman, Laura, 97
King, Mandy, 284
King, Clif, 284
King, Dennis, 284
King, Lauren, 97
King, Moses, 113
King, Sarah, 284
King, Tiffany, 285
King, Whitney Lee, 97
Kinsella, Jessica, 285
Kintner, Jodi, 285
Kinzeler, Jennifer, 285
Kiper, 280
Kirby, Brianna Marie, 285
Kirkwood, Megan E., 285
Kirouac, Deborah, 97
Kisner, Laurie Marie, 97
Kitt, Eugene, 285
Kiyomi, Robyn, 286
Kleiman, Connie, 286
Klein, Meryl, 286
Klenitsky, Alice, 98
Klier, Arminda L., 286
Kline, Roger A., 98

Klinger, Charles Elias, 286
Klinger, Jessica, 287
Klinkhammer, April P., 287
Knapp, Greta Mae, 98
Knight, E. Luann, 98
Knuckey, Ted, 98
Koblich, Kenneth P., 99
Koch, Amanda, 287, 288
Koch, Kelli, 99
Kochansky, Laura, 288
Koehn, Darcy, 288
Kohn, Sarah, 288
Kokino, Olga, 99, 288
Kokkinos, Erika, 99
Koo, Grant, 13
Kooyman, Sonja A., 289
Kopel, Stephen, 99
Koprencka, Nevila, 100
Korte, Amber, 100, 289
Kouba, Terri M., 100
Krakowitz, Erica, 100, 289
Kraus, Brenna M., 3
Krausz, Loretta, 100, 289
Krazmien, AnnMarie, 289
Kreider, Matthew, 290
Krogman, Jessica, 100
Kroner, Lucille M., 100
Krynytzky, Marta, 290
Kuhlmeier, Keri, 290
Kunderd, Robert A., 101
Kunze, Craig, 291
Kurtz, Dodie, 291
Kuschill, Carol, 291

L

LaBruyere, Nikki Jean, 291
Lacara, Philomene C., 13
Lagace, April, 101
Lake, Amber, 101
Lam, Rebecca, 101
Lambert, Alison Jewell, 291
Lance, Christina, 292
Landis, Cherie, 292
Lane, Jacquelyn, 292
Langford, Ian T., 292
Langosch, Marianna, 101
Lansing, Teal, 292
Lara, John, 292
Largent, Beverly A., 102, 293
Larkin, Sandra, 102
Larsen, Denise, 293
Larson, Bethany, 293
Laskowski, Melissa, 102
Lathia, Julie, 293
Latzer, Bobbie, 102
Laude, Shanna, 102, 294
Lauren, Mia, 20
Lawrence, Meghan, 14
Lawrence, Tanya, 294
Lawson, Jay Lawrence, 103
Layugan, Marie, 294
Le Mier, Curtis, 104
Leach, Amanda, 294
Leaman, Tamara, 295
Lear, Kristian, 295
Leathers, Laura, 295
Ledo, Tricia M., 103
Lee, Heather Lynne, 296
Lee, Melissa Ann, 296
Lee, Talene, 14
Leeming, Amanda, 103
LeFevre, Tricia, 337
Legan, Anne Marie, 103, 188

Leibovitz, Arianna, 104
Lemon, Rosemary, 296
Lennox, Brent, 14
Leonard Jr., Robert Tirrell, 104
Lerdo, Ashley, 296
Lett, Dwaine, 104
Leung, Helen, 104, 297
Lewandowski, Christina R., 104
Lewandowski, Kristen, 297
Lewis, Crystal, 297
Lewis, Donna A., 297
Lewis, Gina A., 105
Lewis, Oatry C., 297
Li Hollo, Loriel, 105
Lias-Hughes, Rhonda M., 105
Libertucci, Ashley, 297
Lichtsinn, Jade, 105
Liivam, Samantha Danielle, 298
Lim, Deliah M., 105
Lin, Audrey, 106
Lin, Mindy, 298
Lindner, Patricia A., 106
Lindstaedt, Samantha J., 106
Linquist, Cherie Nechvatal, 107, 298
Lipe, Carrie, 107
Liptak, Edward A., 107
Litawa, Eleanor Summer, 59
Lively, Becky, 107
Livingston, Angela, 106
Livingston, Sara, 299
Llewellyn, David, 108
Locke, Robynne Anne, 299
Loeffler, Emily, 299
Loera, Cassie Y., 299
Lonette, Kim, 108
Lopez, Jessica Cecilia, 108
Lopez, Yen Marie, 300
Lore, Katy D., 300
Lorenz, Jenny, 300
Loring, Keri, 108
Lotovski, Yakov, 109
Louch, Tessa, 300
Louden, Tiffany, 300
Louis, Kristen Alicia, 300
Lucas, Kim, 300
Luchetta, Jennifer, 301
Luchmun, Saroj, 109
Luciano, Suzanne Carol, 301
Luebbering, Candice, 109
Luebbert, Alyssa, 109
Lunas, Trisha, 301
Lundquist, Jessica, 301
Luper, Betty Mills, 110, 301
Lurie, Rita, 189
Lustig, Nachshon, 14
Lynar, Eleanor A., 110
Lynch, Maura, 110
Lynn, Sherri, 287
Lyon, Meredith, 110, 302
Lyons, Oliver V., 302
Lyulkin, Elizabeth, 110

M

MacGillivray, Rachel Anne, 111
MacLaren, Cindy, 111
Macias, Vania, 111
Mackety, Derek, 302
Macrander, Nicole Marie, 302
Madden, Rebecca Rose, 112
Maddock, Rebecca, 112
Maestas, Jessica Louise, 302
Mahoney, Monica Claire, 112

Maldonado, Rachel, 112
Malloy, Josie, 112
Manheimer, Dione, 302
Manieri, Joanna, 112
Mann, Sandra, 14
Mann, Vicki, 113, 303
Manning, Ronald M., 113
Mansour, Chris, 303
Maquet, Michelle, 113
Marchu, Kristina, 303
Marcinak, Kathryn Anne, 303
Marsh, Jonathan Daniel, 304
Marshall, Sherene Ann, 113
Marshall, Veronica, 303
Martin, Dorothy A., 114
Martin, Melinda L., 114
Martin, Michael, 304
Martin, Roman, 72
Martinez, Breeann, 304
Martinez, Deandra S., 114
Martinez, Jessica C., 114
Martinez, Roger D., 188
Martocchio, Chris, 115
Martos Jr., Santiago, 304
Mashburn, Courtney, 304
Mason, Aaron, 15
Mason, Dena, 304
Mason, Nicole M., 305
Massey, Delores M., 115
Mateo, Kainoa Nichole, 115
Matherly, Jolene, 305
Matherne, Kalani, 115
Matheson, Betsy, 115
Mathews, B.J., 116
Mathews, Lindsay, 116
Mattison, Cynthia Ann, 116
Mauk, Courtney Elizabeth, 116
Mauk, Jenna, 116
Maximillian, Ramona, 117
Mayer, Cora Lee, 305
Mayer, Emily, 117
Mayes, Shawn, 305
McCall, Betsy, 117
McCann, Kay, 305
McCarty, Cristie L., 117, 306
McClain, Avia, 306
McClendon, Eric, 123
McCoskey, Linzie, 306
McCulla, Jessica, 15
McCulloch, Joe, 306
McCullough, Sarah Lynn, 117, 307
McCurdy, Elizabeth C., 307
McDermott, Shane Patrick, 307, 308
McDonald, Carolyn, 118
McDonald, Laurie N., 118
McDonald, Shaley K., 118
McElroy, Kristian E., 308
McEvoy, Jeanne, 308
McFadden, Mary Mac, 118
McGee, Robert, 15
McGinley, Jerry, 15
McGinnis, Dana, 308
McGinnis, Karen, 308
McGowan, Alisandra, 379
McGroarty, Meredith, 119
McKibben, Lauren, 308
McKinney, Kelli R., 309
McKone, Mark, 309
McLean, Anna, 118
McLean, Helen, 118, 309
McMaken, Melissa Anne, 309
McManus, Sherri, 309
McMillen, Marieta L., 188
McMillian, Laura, 119, 310

McNeil, Sheena, 310
McNeill, Lisa Brooke, 119
McParlin, Audrey Ann, 120
McPherson, Jennifer, 120
McTeer, Myra M., 311
McTeer, Tara, 310
McWood, Allison, 120
Meadows Jr., Martin D., 310
Mech, Dolyce, 120
Meinhold, Amber, 311
Melson-Brannon, Debbie, 120
Melton, Jennifer, 121
Melton, Martha Ann, 122
Mendoza, Yolanda, 121
Mercado, Amanda P., 311
Merrill, Chanda, 16
Merrill, Karen, 121
Merritt, Megan Rose, 121
Meska, Megan, 312
Meyer, Gena, 311
Meyer, Josh, 121
Miara, Melissa A., 311
Micarsos, Karlynne P., 312
Michael, Sara, 122
Michels, Matthew D., 122
Mihovich, Jennifer, 312
Milan, Amelia Elizabeth, 122
Miles, Nicci, 122
Milkes, A.R., 123, 186, 188
Miller, Robin R., 313
Miller, Ashley, 312
Miller, Cori R., 312
Miller, Elyss Rani, 123
Miller, James F., 123
Miller, Jessica, 123
Miller, Jolene, 313
Miller, Mandy, 123
Miller, Mindy Lee, 313
Miller, Susan, 124
Miller, Wendy, 124
Miller, II, James F., 123
Millison, Marjorie, 188, 189
Millman, Kristina, 124
Mills, Afrika Afeni, 313
Mills, Priscilla M., 124
Minigan, Jesse, 124
Minor, Jerry D., 125
Minshew, Chris F., 314
Miola, Christine, 313
Mislich, Jennifer, 125
Mitchell, Cherry, 189
Mitchell, Erin L., 313
Mitchell, Kristina Rene', 314
Mitchell, Randy, 16
Mix, Stephania M., 125
Moeller, Wendy, 314
Money, Diane M., 125, 314
Monis, Haroon, 125
Monsees, Dawn, 126
Montgomery, Laura, 126
Montgomery, Sarah K., 126
Montoya, Jessie, 314
Moore, Lisa, 16
Morales, Elizabeth D., 314
Morales, Theresa, 126
Moran, Carlos, 126
Moran, Katherine, 127
Morgan, Juli L., 127
Morgan, Laura J., 127, 315
Moritz, Beth Anne, 127
Morone, Michelle Ann, 315
Morrill, Heather, 315
Morris, Ashley, 315
Morrison, Karen C., 315
Morrison, Nicole, 316

Morrow, Ramona D., 316
Morrow, Zoe, 316
Moscato, Tina, 316
Moyar, Denise, 127, 317
Moyer, Andrew James, 128
Mrock, Anna M., 128
Mulheren, Melissa M., 316
Munden-Dixon, Kate, 128
Munder, Laura, 128
Murdaugh, Andrea N., 317
Murgia, Angela, 128
Murphy, Abby, 128
Murray, Norma Susan, 129
Myers, Diane, 16
Myers, Nicholas, 317

N

Nagle, Rachel, 129
Nail, Joanne, 129
Nancoo, Joseph E., 129
Natera, Melinda, 130
Navarro, Cesar, 317
Neal, Connie, 130, 317
Neff, Rachel, 318
Nelen, Colleen, 130
Nelson, Lori, 318
Nelthrope, Alice G., 130
Nesthus, Michelle, 130
Nettles, David E., 318
Nettles, T. Harold, 131
Newkirk, Rachel Ann, 131
Newman, Lindsay, 318
Newton, Natalie, 131
Nguyen, Quy Ngoc, 131
Nichols, Jessica Lynn, 131
Nielson-Buckholdt, Christian, 318
Nieman, Jennifer, 131
Nieuwsma, Rachel, 132
Noeth, Beth, 318
Nolen, Jennifer, 132
Norby, Amanda, 319
Norman, Louise, 188
Norris, Heather, 2,3
Norris, Stephanie, 319
North, Kristi, 319
Nowak, Kristen, 132
Nuernberg, Evelyn, 17
Numminen, Saana, 319
Nydegger, Joanne Ellison, 132

O

O'Brien, Caitlin, 133, 320
O'Brien, Meagan, 133
O'Dell, Mindy Ann, 133
O'Neal, Lillian M., 134, 322
O'Rourke, James C., 133
O'Rourke, Michael, 17
Oban, Kristin, 319
Obermyer, Tanya, 320
Obikpo, Grace Adaku, 320
Occhiogrosso, Rachel, 320
Odamtten, Yom, 321
Oesterle, Angela, 321
Ohlmeyer, Lindsay, 133
Okapal, Pamela A., 133
Oliver, Nicole Dawn, 321
Ollison, LaDraper, 134
Olney, Nicole, 321
Olson, Heather, 134, 322
Olson, Katherina, 134
Olson, Sarah, 322

Olson, Sherry L., 322
Ontiveros, Rachel Rivera, 134
Orais, Ashley, 322
Orgill, Jennifer Ann, 322
Ori, Shannon, 322
Ormsbee, Nancy Harris, 134
Orsatelli, Athena, 151
Osborn, Candace, 323
Osborne, Jennifer, 323
Ou, Kear, 323, 392
Overton, Kristy, 135
Overton, Misty A., 135
Owen, Stefany, 135
Owens, Jesse, 323
Owens, Tracy, 135, 323
Owl, Kyla, 135

P

Pakan, Nicole, 135
Palmer, LaDonna Lin, 136
Palumbo, Jennifer, 136
Panaggio, Edna, 136, 324, 392
Pappas, Kelly, 324
Pappas, Kimberly, 324
Parker, Carol Ann, 17
Parks, Kylie, 324
Parratt, Nellie Linn, 324
Parrish, Jaclyn E., 324
Paschke, Melissa, 136
Patterson, Christopher, 17
Patzkowski, Amy, 325
Paul, Peggy, 136
Paulsen, Jessie, 392
Pavlik, Anna, 325
Paxton, James H., 18
Payne, Cherron M., 137
Payne, Donnica, 137
Payne, Rebecca, 325
Payne, Tim S., 137, 392
Peak, Natasha, 325
Pearl, Ebony, 137
Peasley, Naomie, 325
Peery, Alana, 326
Pegan, Erinn, 138
Peice, James W., 392
Peller, Kimberly, 138
Peltier, Maggie, 138
Penland, Robert R., 138, 326
Pennino, Natalie, 138
Pepple, Alexander, 139, 393
Perkins, Litisha, 139
Perry, Holly Michele, 326
Peschon, Lisa, 326
Peters, Dawn, 327
Peters, Jamice, 18
Peters, Janna, 327
Peterson, Vanessa, 327
Peterson, III, James, 139
Peterson, RN, Ronnie, 327
Pettine, Paul, 328, 393
Pettinger, Shannan, 140
Petzold, Kate, 140, 328
Peyton, Betsi, 328
Phillips, Christal L., 328
Phoa, Sharon S., 140
Pickell, Amanda, 140
Pieper, Mark A., 18
Pierson, Zachary, 329
Pineiro, Elizabeth, 328
Pingrey, Nicole, 140
Piotrowski, Alicia, 329
Pippin, Misha L., 329
Pirog, Katieann, 140

Plair, Quentin J., 329
Plaskon, Robert R., 329
Ploss, Jim, 19
Plathy, Mandy, 330
Plourde, Lynn, 141
Pneumonia, Phoebe M., 20
Pobre, Carmelita, 18, 330
Poirrier, Annette M., 330
Pool, Jennifer, 330
Popham, Francesca, 330
Porter, Darci, 331
Porter, Tara Lee, 141
Post, Cindy, 331
Power, Suzanne, 19
Pretzer, Randall E., 141
Prevost, Denise, 316
Price, Jelyna, 141
Price, Melissa, 331
Price, Mitchell, 141
Pringle, Mary, 331
Privett, Marjorie Marie, 331
Prtichard, Megan, 331
Prucka, Suzy, 141
Pruitt, Sumie Marie, 332
Pugh, Bobbie J., 142
Puleo, Pam, 332
Punt, Douglas, 332
Pupshis, Nicole, 142, 332
Pursley, Paula M., 142
Pytlak, Allison E., 142

Q

Queener, Kelly, 143, 332
Quilici, Lisa, 332
Quinlan, Leif, 333
Quinones, Karen Janine, 333
Quintana, Melissa, 142
Quintanilla, Joleen Santos, 143, 333

R

Rae, Jesselle, 143, 370
Rager, Dennis E., 19, 143
Ramirez, Dawn Marie, 333
Ramos, Hattie, 333
Rampersaud, Selma, 144
Rangel, Fawn S., 144
Rangel, Griselda M., 207
Rangel, Richard, 334
Ranney, Anne, 144
Rapp, Amy, 334
Rasokas, Tamara, 334
Ratcliffe, Jane J., 144
Ratliff, Hope, 334, 335
Rausch, Amanda, 335
Ravich, Drew, 335
Ray, Charles A., 144
Ray, Lucinda B., 145
Raymer, Bridget, 335
Raymond, Kimberly, 145
Raynor, Wilma, 335
Reardon, Christina Ann, 145
Redfield, Kristie, 145
Redinger, Shannon, 335
Reed, Amber Nykole, 145
Reed, Jessica, 145
Reed, Michelle, 336
Reed, Susan M., 145
Reeves, Emily, 146
Reichert, Rebecca Ann, 146
Reing, Jessica, 336, 393
Renaud, Amanda, 146

Alphabetical Index by Author

Rencher, Alicia, 336
Renner, Richele, 336
Rentschler, Sheryl, 146
Reusser, Jennifer S., 147
Rex, Jerry H., 147
Reynolds, Cerisa R., 147
Reynolds, Dennis S., 147
Rezai, MD, Pei M., 336
Rhodus, Samantha, 336
Rice, Carolyn, 148
Richardi, Erica Marie, 337
Richards, Leslie Anne, 148
Richardson, Jennifer, 148
Richey, Jessica, 337
Richmond, Nicole, 148
Rickman, Crystal Sunshine, 148
Ricks, Charles Douglas, 149
Ridgway, Madeline Johnson, 337
Rieswyk, Jennifer, 149
Rikard, Megan, 149
Rippa, Philip, 337
Ripple, Jolene Raye, 149
Riscoe, Lori, 338
Ristanovic, Sanya, 338
Rittmann, Teri, 338
Rivet, Catherine, 338
Roach, Erin, 150
Roark, Sheila B., 149, 339, 393
Roberts, Kristin Lynn, 339
Roberts, Sara Gaye, 149, 339
Robey, Ashley, 150
Robinson, Adam, 150
Robinson, Sheri, 339
Robinson, Teresa, 339
Robinson, William F., 150
Robles, Maria Luisa, 150
Robles, Rosanna, 339
Rock, Natalie E., 150
Rodgers, Sheena, 151
Rodriguez, Alexander C., 340
Rogers, Dominique Marie, 151
Rollings, Jennifer, 151, 340
Rollins, Sara, 340
Romanko, Karen, 340
Romano, Gena, 151
Rombough, Stacy, 151
Rone, Amanda C., 341
Rose, Angela, 92
Rose, David L., 341
Rose, Norma, 152
Rose, Tyrone, 341
Roseman, Librada E., 341
Rosenbaum, Diane, 152
Rosenberger, Kelly, 152
Rosenzweig, Gregg Evan, 152
Ross, Doris, 153
Ross, Kimberly, 153, 393
Ross, Larry E., 153
Rothbauer, Jan, 153, 342, 393
Rountree, Philip Anderson, 342
Rourke, Patricia G., 153
Rowe, Cicely A., 153
Roy, Lindsay, 154
Rubin, Basha Frost, 342
Ruddick, Sandra, 154
Ruhl, Lauren, 154
Rupp, Jenn, 154
Rush, Jessica Lynn, 154
Russell, Todd, 154
Russell, Valerie Josephs, 342
Russo, Jennifer A., 19
Rutledge, Kathleen, 155, 393
Rutledge, Krista Lyn, 342
Rydalch, Jenn, 155
Rygh, Danielle Maria, 293

S

Saari Jr., E. Donald, 343
Sabocik, Angela, 343
Sabot, Brenda L., 155
Saffioti, Katherine Rose, 343
Sage, Joyce, 343
Sakoda, Stuart, 155
Salazar, Lucia, 156
Saltus, Sheridan, 343
Salvail, Cora, 156
Sammons, Virgie McCoy, 156, 344
Samperi, Daniella, 344
Sanchez, Yaritsa Arenas, 344
Sanders, Crystal, 156
Sanders, Gail, 156
Sandlin, Rita Akin, 345
Sanford, Mark H., 344
Sansom, Sean M., 345
Santoianni, Jenna, 345
Saputo, Elizabeth, 345
Sarff, Extry R., 186, 393
Savage, Stephanie, 345
Savage, Susie, 346
Sayre, Angela K., 156
Sayson, Shannon, 346
Scarborough, Christine L., 157, 346
Scarfe, Angela, 346
Scarpitti, Tina, 157
Schaefer, Blake E., 346, 393
Schafer, Jennifer, 347
Schefkind, Alyson, 157
Schick, Barbara, 20, 347
Schiff, Amber-Dawn M., 157
Schimpf, Laura J., 347
Schlegel, Shannon, 348
Schlossnagle, Cindy, 157
Schmid, Charles W. Raven, 158
Schmidt, Jason, 347, 348
Schmidt, Millicent, 158
Schmier, Alex, 158
Scheider, David, 20
Schnobrich, Jr., Gayln, 348
Scholl, Margaret, 348
Schongalla, Sabrina, 348, 349
Schranz, Peter, 349
Schroeder, Crystal, 349
Schroeder, Kathy, 187
Schultz, Crystal Dawn, 158
Schultz, Stacey, 349
Schwalbe, Heather Rose, 158
Schwalm, Marcie C., 158
Schwartz, Dana Marie, 349
Scott, Linn, 111
Scott, Michelle M., 20
Sears, Patricia R., 159
Sebastian, Sarah, 350
Seely, Kevin L., 350
Selafani, Tara, 349
Serr, Kathi, 159, 350
Servon, Rebecca, 350
Sewright, Mariel, 350
Seymour, Heather, 159, 351
Shalom, 340
Shampine, Melinda, 351
Shank, Tabatha, 159
Sharp, Doris G., 160
Shaw, Ashley, 351
Sheehy, Kelly, 160
Shelton, Joyce E., 160
Shenefelt, Shawn, 351
Shenkenberg, William L., 352
Sherrod, Philip L., 351

Sherwood, Kristin, 161
Shine, Jenny, 243
Shrake, Heather, 161, 352, 393
Siegel, Kate, 352
Silver, Jennifer, 161
Silverman, Sharon A., 352
Simmons, Cheryl, 160
Simon, Jason, 163, 352
Simpson, Cassandra Lynn, 163
Simpson, Jacqueline, 161, 353
Simpson, Vanessa Elizabeth, 353
Sims, Jennifer, 161
Sims-Jones, Rainboe, 353
Sisco, Cleo E., 353
Sivils, Whitney Anne, 353
Sizemore, Dawn, 354
Skaggs, Brandy, 161
Skripochenko, Nicole, 354
Skurich, Nicole, 354
Skwarczek, Marta, 162
Slaven, Heather Lee, 354
Slaymaker, Angela, 162
Smedsrud, Erica Wren, 162
Smilie, Jr., Robert S., 354
Smith, Carissa A., 162
Smith, Christine, 354
Smith, Debra H., 162
Smith, Emily O'Doherty, 162
Smith, Jacquelyn K., 355
Smith, Jamie Lynn, 355
Smith, Jason W., 355
Smith, Kelamenter, 355
Smith, Kelsea, 163
Smith, Michele, 356
Smith, Tiffany M., 163, 393
Smolcich, Rebecca, 356
Snitkowski, Tracey, 163
Snow, Crystal A., 163
Somes, Olivia, 356
Sommers, Regina C., 356
Southerland, Carol E., 185
Souza, Rachael Marie, 163
Spark, Paula J., 357
Sparrow, Sarah L., 164
Speake, Daniel, 164, 357
Speranza, Amanda, 357
Spezza, Kathryn T., 357
Spires, Ashlea, 357
Spreacker, Anita, 164
St.Cooper, Pierre, 1
Stamatious, Kiki, 358
Stambler, Michelle, 358
Stampley, Joanne, 358
Stanek, Amanda, 358
Stanley, Melinda, 358
Stansfield, Katie, 358
Stanton, Melissa, 359
Staton, Lynda, 164
Steele, Renee, 359
Stein, Pamela, 359
Steinmeyer, Robert Charles, 186
Stephens, Alena, 359
Stephens, Curtis W., 21
Stephens, Kiley, 165
Sterling, Sheila, 360
Sternberg, Claudette F., 165
Stessman, Patrick, 21
Stevens, Kelly M., 359
Stewart, Jamie, 165
Stewart, Jaqueline, 165
Stich, Paula, 360
Stidham, Martha, 360
Stiles, Joseph, 360
Stines, Danielle, 360
Strachan, Billy, 360

Stratton, Butch, 21
Strauss, Catie Tara, 165, 361, 394
Stricker, Jennifer Jean, 361
Stroude, Carlena, 361
Stuckert, Janet, 361
Stumbaugh, Nicole, 165, 362
Stuwart, Demetrius, 166
Sullivan, Colleen Martha, 361
Sullivan, Lauren, 362
Summer, Sam, 282
Sura, Linda, 166
Surdam, Tanya L., 362
Suriani, Tricia A., 166
Surowiec, Laura, 362
Susin, Linsey Rose, 363
Svoboda, Bob, 363
Swann, Amanda Michelle, 167
Swann, Jennifer, 166
Swartz, Ann, 363
Swick, Jennifer, 363
Swiggum, Steph, 167
Szoldra, Natalie Anne, 363, 364

T

Taajiogueu, Jacqueline, 364
Talley, Cecile, 364
Tan, Edgar, 364
Tanner, Robert, 167
Tanyu, Lorraine Hazel, 365
Tarman, Shelley, 167
Taylor, Jessica, 21
Taylor, Katrina, 21
Taylor, Mary Ann, 365
Teaster, Kristina, 168
Tees, Sidra, 365
Tejani, Aliya, 365
Telander, C. Chris, 168, 365
Telep, Rebecca, 365
Templin, Meredith, 366
Tench, Amy, 366
Tendler, Bella, 367
Tentis, Sarah, 366
Terrell, Shelby, 367
Thaler, Ashley J., 367
Thierbach, Jennifer, 367
Thomas, Jeremy, 168
Thomas, Lyell, 367
Thomas, Shanna Nerissa, 168, 368
Thomas, Tammy, 168
Thompson, Brooke, 368
Thompson, Cecilia, 169, 368
Thompson, Kara Don, 368
Thompson, Shannon, 169
Thurston, April Sarah, 169
Tillman, Alicia, 369
Tillotson, Brianne, 368
Tingle, Alisha, 169
Tippie, Chris, 369
Tivera, Brandilynn, 369
Tjoeng, Charise, 369
To, Jenette, 169
Tomlinson, Carrie, 170
Tooke, Stephanie Lynn Elizabeth, 370
Topping, Ellen, 170, 369
Torruellas, Brigette, 170
Torruellas, Natasha M., 369
Toxey, Robert C., 170
Transue, JerryMarie, 370
Traynor, James A., 170
Trease, Crysal A., 370
Trew, Darla, 370
Trimble, Joanna Rebeka, 370

Trinh, Anna, 22
Troczynska, Justyna, 371
Trotter, Jessica L., 371
Tuders, Tiffany, 171, 370
Tuinstra, Tresa, 171
Tunison, Katie, 171
Turner, Jeffery Wayne, 191, 394
Turner, Tennille Kristine, 171
Tuter, Shanon, 371
Tuttle, English, 171
Twitchell, Ilene E., 171, 371
Tyree, Danielle, 172
Tyson, Kate, 372

U

Udell, Emilie A., 372
Ugoiji, Chika, 172
Underhill, Robert, 22
Unseld, Heather Renee, 372
Urban, Cheryl, 172
Urling, Kae M., 372

V

Valiukas, Tina Marie, 372
Van Y, Sharon Kay, 172
VanSchoik, Sarah, 373
VandeWouwer, Erica, 373
Vander Velde, Erin, 373
Vanskiver, Colleen, 373, 394
Vedar, Jennifer, 373
Ventrudo, Dena, 374
Veriha, Julie, 374
Verma, Nisha, 374
Viruet, Gezel, 172
Vitale, Stephanie, 374
Vitanzo, Doris E., 374, 375
Vitello, Cheryl, 172
Vittitow, Rhianna, 173
Vo, Doan, 375
Vo, Katherine H., 173
Vogel, Patricia, 173
Vollstedt, Tawnia, 375
Vopnford, Erika, 375
Vosloo, Niki, 173
Voss, Clara M., 173
Voss, Jamie E., 174, 376, 394
Vowell, Dena Sue, 174
Voyles, Heather A., 374

W

W., Donte', 377
Wade, Dellen A., 174
Wadzinski, Bethany, 174
Waechter, Melinda A., 175
Waggoner, Kimberly A., 175
Wagoner, Kelli, 174
Waite, Mary E., 22
Waldron, Erin Elizabeth, 175
Walker, April Jannette, 376
Walker, Jessica, 176
Walkup, Shannon, 376
Wallace, Michelle, 376
Waller, Pamela, 376
Walston, Jennifer R., 376
Wambolt, Mysti Dawn, 175
Wampole, Millie, 176
Warner, Ashlye, 377
Warner, Ruth, 176, 377, 394
Warren, Dean A., 377

Washington, Jennie, 22
Wasserman, Jennifer, 377
Watson, Jessica, 176
Watson, Shawn, 176
Watson, Tyffanie, 377
Waychoff, Tara, 23
Wearden, Bob, 23
Webb, Alison, 176
Webster, Joan, 176, 377
Wedding, Stacey Renea, 378
Weirsky, Michele, 177
Weis, Rob, 177
Weiss, Tiffany, 378
Weixelman, Audra Lea, 378
Welch, Catherine Nancy Grace, 378
Welfley, Jami, 177
Welsch, Melissa, 177, 378
Werner, Melissa, 378
Wessler, Marisa, 378
West, Jennifer R., 379
Westcott, Kassie, 379
Wheeler, Michelle, 177
Whigham, Charlotte D., 379
Whitaker, Katie Lynn, 379
White, Carlena, 177
White, Patricia I., 178
White, Sara L., 380
White, Siobhan, 379
White, Tara Janine, 178
Whittaker, Steed, 178
Wichern II, Daniel Mark, 380
Wick, Tara, 380
Wiegmann, Ariel, 380
Wielgus, Dawn, 380
Wigley, Tasha S., 179, 394
Wilcox, Jessica Lea, 380
Wilde, Shannon, 23
Wilhite, III, John C., 179
Williams, Emily, 381
Williams, Jennifer, 179
Williams, Melanie A., 179
Williams III, Silas H., 180
Willis, Kristi Nicole, 381
Wills, Meaghen, 23
Wilson, Daniel "Church", 180
Wilson, Krista, 381
Wilson-Myles, Ellen L., 180
Winkler, Rachael C., 180
Wishart, Jeniene, 381
Wittman, Kati, 213
Wodtke, Laura, 381
Wojtysiak, Loraine A., 180
Wolfe, Lauren, 382
Wolff, Cassandra Renee, 382
Wolfgang, Carol J., 192
Wolverton, Farrah Renee, 382
Woman, Running Elk, 178
Wood, Alexis C., 382
Woods, Douglas B., 382
Woods, Jo Ann P., 383
Woods, Jr., W.R., 180
Woolery, Nikki J., 383
Workman, Jerome, 23
Wray, Emily, 383
Wright, Bethany Nicole, 181
Wright, Christine A., 24
Wright, Georgia, 383
Wright, Robyn, 181, 384
Wright, Sheri, 384
Wulfekuhl, Tabitha S., 384
Wyan, Heather, 181

X

Xaysena, Oranout, 181
Xiong, Pang, 24

Y

Yahnke, Tisha Lynn, 181
Yamada, Linda, 384
Yamashita, Amy, 384
Yamin, Samantha B., 182
Yang, Fan, 182
Yap, Carolyn J., 385
Yavorsky, Jill, 182
Yeater, Alishia, 182
Yip Tong, Mimi, 394
Yom, Alyssa, 182
Yost, Paula J., 385
Young, Fran, 385, 394
Yu, Emerald, 385

Z

Zawitaj, Devon, 385
Zeien, Emily, 385
Zenga, Calvin D., 183
Zetocha, Miranda D., 179
Zick, Cassandra R., 183, 386
Ziegler, Rose, 24
Zikoski, Robin, 386
Zimmer, Monica, 386
Zimmerman, Jessica, 183
Zyzdryn, Agnes, 183

Alphabetical Index by Author